D1038533

Piedmont
College Library

DEMOREST, GEORGIA

74096

R
CLASS
301.451

BOOK
W 989

Encyclopedic Directory

of

Ethnic Organizations in the United States

Encyclopedic Directory
of
Ethnic Organizations in the United States

Lubomyr R. Wynar

with the assistance of
LOIS BUTTLAR and ANNA T. WYNAR

Libraries Unlimited, Inc. — Littleton, Colo. — 1975

Copyright © 1975 Lubomyr R. Wynar
All Rights Reserved
Printed in the United States of America

LIBRARIES UNLIMITED, INC.
P.O. Box 263
Littleton, Colorado 80120

Library of Congress Cataloging in Publication Data

Wynar, Lubomyr Roman, 1932–
    Encyclopedic directory of ethnic organizations in the
Unit ed States.

    Includes index.
    1. Minorities—United States—Societies, etc.—Direc-
tories. I. Buttlar, Lois, 1934-   joint author.
II. Wynar, Anna T., 1944-   joint author.
III. Title.
E184.A1W94   301.45'1'04206273   75-28150
ISBN 0-87287-120-7

1/8/76 Baker + Tylor 19.50

TABLE OF CONTENTS

PREFACE

This *Encyclopedic Directory of Ethnic Organizations* is the first comprehensive reference guide to major ethnic organizations in this country. The fact that in the United States there exist hundreds of organizations created by various ethnic communities demonstrates the pluralistic character of the American society. The historian, sociologist, political scientist, or any other researcher studying American ethnicity must closely scrutinize the phenomenon of ethnic organized life as it is reflected in the objectives of various ethnic organizations. For the researcher, ethnic organizations serve as "primary sources" since they reflect the social structure of the ethnic group. Ethnic organizations and the ethnic press are the primary indicators of the actual state of life and activities of the individual ethnic groups. Therefore, it is imperative for any serious researcher involved in ethnic studies to become familiar with ethnic associations—their goals, objectives, and numerical strength.

For the reference librarian this *Encyclopedic Directory* will serve as an indispensable tool for providing answers or solving various reference questions pertaining to major ethnic groups in the United States, as well as to significant research institutions involved in the study of ethnicity. This publication has its own "history." In 1972 the *Encyclopedic Directory of Ethnic Newspapers and Periodicals in the United States* (Libraries Unlimited, 1972, 260p.) was published on the basis of a survey that covered major ethnic periodicals and newspapers in the United States. At this time plans were made to conduct an additional survey—to cover major ethnic organizations in the U.S.—and to prepare a companion reference work on ethnic organizations. From 1973 through April 1975 a special survey was conducted, which resulted in the publication of this present reference guide.

The major objective of this *Encyclopedic Directory* is to identify major ethnic organizations in terms of their objectives, publications, and activities. The publication is intended primarily to serve scholars engaged in the study of ethnic groups, as well as reference librarians and libraries that are developing special library programs for individual ethnic groups in this country. Until now, a reference tool covering ethnic organizations in the United States did not exist.

The *Encyclopedic Directory* consists of the following parts:
1. Preface
2. Introduction
3. The nature of ethnic organizations
4. A listing of 1,475 ethnic organizations categorized under 73 headings, each of which represents a separate ethnic group.

5. Appendix, containing a selective list of major multi-ethnic and research organizations.

6. Name index of organizations.

It is hoped that this guide will fill an important gap in library reference literature.

Acknowledgment

A number of persons contributed, either directly or indirectly, to completion of this directory. First of all, I would like to express my gratitude to the many officials of ethnic organizations and editors of ethnic periodicals who cooperated in our survey of ethnic organizations by submitting relevant data on ethnic organizations and by filling out the questionnaires. Special gratitude is also expressed to all foreign embassies that provided some information on ethnic organizations in the United States.

I would especially like to thank my graduate assistants and students at the School of Library Science and the Center for the Study of Ethnic Publications, Kent State University. Those who assisted in this project and were involved in checking the questionnaires are Ruth Patterson, Victoria Thornbury, Jane Faires, Ilona Kovacs, Daina Kojelis, Kevin Rosswurm, Jungnam Kwon, Hwi-Sook Koh, and others. I greatly appreciate the aid of Dr. Roy Hirabayashi, Asian American Studies Program, San Jose University; Dr. William A. Douglass, University of Nevada; Dr. John Epstein, U.S. Office of Education; Ms. Linda Wing, Coordinator of Asian American Studies, Berkeley; and many other persons who provided important information on ethnic organizations.

Lubomyr R. Wynar

INTRODUCTION

Until the publication of this *Encyclopedic Directory of Ethnic Organizations*, there existed a serious gap in library reference publications dealing with ethnic organizations. The comprehensive *Encyclopedia of Associations* (9th ed., Detroit, Gale Research Co., 1974) lists about 450 organizations directly or indirectly related to ethnic communities. Many of the entries for these organizations lack annotations. A regional directory was recently published for Michigan (*Ethnic Directory 1*, Detroit, Southeastern Michigan Regional Ethnic Heritage Studies Center, 1973) and a local Cleveland-area directory (*Greater Cleveland Nationalities Directory 1974*, Cleveland, Sun Newspapers and The Nationalities Services Center, 1974) appeared in 1974. Both of these publications, which are designed for local use, are simply rosters of organizations located within the two regions.

In addition to the above-mentioned publications, which are multi-ethnic in content, a small number of major ethnic groups have published listings of their organizations, which serve as useful tools in studying these particular groups—e.g., Charles L. Sanders and Linda McLean, comps., *Directory of National Black Organizations* (New York: Afram Associates, Inc., 1972); *The Ebony Handbook*, by the editors of Ebony (Chicago: Johnson Publishing Company, Inc., 1974); *American Jewish Year Book 1974* (New York: The American Jewish Committee, 1974); The Cabinet Committee on Opportunity for the Spanish Speaking, *Directory of Spanish Speaking Organizations in the United States* (Washington, D.C.: Government Printing Office, 1970). It was felt, therefore, that a separate reference tool, which covers, on a comparative basis, all major ethnic groups and their associations, would prove to be indispensable to students engaged in ethnic research projects and to librarians providing special reference service to library patrons. It is hoped that this publication will fill the gap that exists in the professional reference literature in the area of ethnic organizations.

Methodology

The data provided in this *Encyclopedic Directory* are based on a comprehensive survey of ethnic organizations in the United States, which was conducted from 1973 through April 1975. For the survey a special questionnaire was designed and distributed to all known major ethnic organizations. The addresses of these organizations were obtained from a special ethnic associations file at the Center for the Study of Ethnic Publications at Kent State University, from the editors of ethnic newspapers and periodicals, from local ethnic directories, and from foreign embassies. Also, many officials of ethnic organizations indicated, in a special section of the questionnaire, the names and addresses of other organizations that they thought should be included in our publication. In all, 2,546 questionnaires were mailed to known addresses of ethnic organizations. Two follow-up letters were mailed to organizations that did not reply. A total of 1,758 questionnaires were returned and analyzed. On the basis of this analysis, 1,250 organizations were included and 508 were excluded—either because they were local or regional branches of a national organization already included in our survey or because they did not meet the criteria of the directory. Some of the returned questionnaires contained only partial answers. The listings for an additional 225 organizations are based on secondary sources, particularly on the ethnic press. In many instances these entries contain only the address of the organization. It was found that, although some ethnic groups responded fully to our survey, other groups proved to be rather elusive. We regret that some organizations failed to participate in our survey and, therefore, in spite of our follow-up attempts, are not listed in the present publication. It is hoped that during the next comprehensive survey we will be able to obtain the cooperation of all major ethnic organizations.

Scope of the Encyclopedic Directory

The *Encyclopedic Directory* includes organizations representing 73 ethnic groups. Many of the national ethnic associations have additional branches on regional and local levels, and these branches were generally omitted because of their large numbers. Although the aim of this publication is to include organizations that are national in scope, in certain cases associations that are regional and local in scope have been incorporated. This is especially the case for those ethnic groups that lack a well-developed organizational system on a national scale, as well as in the case of smaller organizations with special objectives. In some instances ethnic organizations that are international in scope are also listed because of their major influence on the relevant ethnic groups in the United States.

Our survey revealed that the Black-American, Indian-American, Jewish-American, and Spanish speaking-American ethnic groups each have a great number of organizations of various types. Including all of these organizations would have required a separate directory for each group. Since listings of organizations of each of these ethnic groups are already published, we found it best to include only major organizations of each of these ethnic communities on a selective basis, especially in view of the fact that this directory uses a multi-ethnic approach.

The Appendix provides a list of major research-oriented non-ethnic organizations involved in the study of ethnicity. This *Encyclopedic Directory* lists major cultural, religious (lay), fraternal, professional, educational, scholarly, youth, and other ethnic organizations that reflect the organizational structure of a given ethnic community. Excluded are all ethnic parishes, religious orders and seminaries, schools, libraries, museums, banks, credit unions, or similar economic institutions.

Also omitted are those organizations that did not respond to our questionnaire, if we were unable to find information on their existence or activities through secondary sources.

Arrangement

Organizations are arranged in alphabetical order under 73 individual ethnic groups. Each group is listed alphabetically, with necessary cross references and brief editorial introductions. The Egyptian, Iraqi, Lebanese, Palestinian, and Syrian-American organizations are listed with cross references under Arab-American Organizations. Multi-ethnic and research organizations are listed alphabetically in the Appendix.

Complete entries provide information in the following sequences:

1. Name of organization
2. Address
3. Telephone
4. Principal officers
5. Permanent staff
6. Date founded
7. Branches
8. Membership
9. Membership dues
10. Scope
11. Special requirements for membership
12. Nature of organization
13. Publications
14. Affiliations
15. Major conventions/meetings
16. Comments

In some instances entries do not contain complete information, due to the fact that some organizations failed to complete all items on the questionnaire. In these cases NI (no information) was indicated. A sample entry is provided below:

1. Name: ARMENIAN GENERAL ATHLETIC UNION (AGAU)
2. Address: 116 38th St.
                Union City, New Jersey 07087
3. Telephone: (201) 865-0057
4. Principal officers: Jack Takajian, President
5. Permanent staff: 4
6. Date founded: 1921
7. Branches: NI
8. Membership: 500
9. Membership dues: $5.00
10. Scope: national

11. Special requirements for membership: Armenian ancestry
12. Nature of organization: cultural, educational, sport, youth
13. Publications: *AGAU Bulletin*, 1927– . quarterly.
14. Affiliations: NI
15. Major conventions/meetings: annual convention
16. Comments: Although AGAU is primarily oriented toward the development of athletics among Armenians, it also promotes social, cultural and educational activities within Armenian communities. Provides indoor sport and recreational facilities, promotes lectures and debates, sponsors annual tournaments, trophies and medals. Also has established a special scholarship fund.

Name of the Organization

All names of organizations are listed in English. Names in native languages indicated on the questionnaires have been omitted, unless this was the only name submitted for the organization.

Annotation

Each brief descriptive annotation is based on the official statement given in the questionnaire, and in many instances also on the organization's official publication (by-laws, official bulletins, etc.). If no statement of the organization's objectives was available, the descriptive annotation has been omitted.

Index

The index includes names of organizations arranged in alphabetical order, with geographical location indicated in parentheses. The Table of Contents serves as the subject index.

THE NATURE OF ETHNIC ORGANIZATIONS

America is God's Crucible, the great Melting Pot where all the races of Europe are melting and reforming! – Here you stand good folk, think I, when I see you at Ellis Island, here you stand, in fifty groups, with your fifty languages and histories, and your fifty blood hatreds and rivalries. But you won't be long like that brother, for these are the fires of God you come to... German and Frenchman, Irishman and Englishman, Jews and Russians, into the Crucible with you all! God is making the American ... the real American has not yet arrived... He will be the union of all races, perhaps the coming superman.[1]

It has been over six-and-a-half decades since these words were uttered in the play *The Melting Pot: Drama in Four Acts* by Israel Zangwill. And for some time to come, especially prior to World War I, America was viewed as the "Melting Pot," the cauldron within which all immigrant cultures would naturally melt and fuse, and from which the "American" would finally emerge. And with the birth of this "superman" a homogeneous American culture would crystallize, based on social-likeness and cultural solidarity. The emergence of such a mono-cultural system was thought to be the inevitable product of a two-way assimilative process that was once viewed as being a natural, easy, and rapid event. This one-culture concept remained a part of American social thought for some time to come. However, with the passage of time, social scientists began to perceive that no emergence of the anticipated cultural fusion actually took place. Immigrant communities persisted, especially as a result of the tendency of immigrants to concentrate in ethnic colonies within major cities. Hundreds of ethnic organizations flourished, and they published numerous periodicals and newspapers in the various native tongues. The original concept behind the "melting pot" theory, which viewed assimilation as an inevitable, rapid, and natural process, began to be questioned.

As organized ethnic life persisted through the years, new theories emerged regarding assimilation. The "melting pot" theory was, for the most part, rejected by social scientists, although the general lay population continued to view American society as being in a process of continuous fusion. Around the time of World War I the error of the "melting pot" was brought to focus. Assimilation was no longer viewed as being an inevitable rapid, natural, and easy two-way process, but rather, as resulting from organized and deliberate efforts on the part of American agencies to de-nationalize the immigrant by stripping him of his heritage and identity, and then to re-nationalize him in the image dictated by the existing social order. Assimilation was viewed, therefore, as being a one-way process characterized by conformity to and acceptance of the dominant culture. This new theory of assimilation culminated in what is commonly known as Americanization. The Americanization theory and its subsequent "Americanization movement" was actually an outgrowth of the need for national unity during World War I. Its advocates initiated various Americanization programs, which formally and deliberately aimed at making "good citizens" of the "foreigners" by suppressing their heritage, language, and organized life and replacing them with prescribed "virtues" and "requisites." The Americanization theory and movement contained within itself the seeds of a superior (American Anglo-Saxon Protestant) culture versus the inferior non-Anglo-Saxon Protestant cultures. Like the "melting pot" theory preceding it, the Americanization concept also aimed at standardization and conformity. However, whereas the "melting pot" theory foresaw the emergence of a "superior culture" through the fusion and blending of many cultures, the Americanization movement's final homogeneous society was to be achieved by the process of forced rejection of the immigrant heritage and deliberate conformity and adoption of the dominant order.

The Americanization movement brought to ethnic communities and their many organizations their most difficult times. Its view that assimilation was to be a one-way process, which deliberately stamped out all vestiges of the immigrant culture, gave rise to ethnocentricism and further kindled the fires of prejudice. Since ethnic non-Anglo cultures were perceived as being "inferior" to the Anglo cultures, it followed, therefore, that ethnics were "inferior," "unpatriotic," and "un-American." In order to become truly "American," they were compelled to divest themselves of their customs, traditions, language, and values in order to be swallowed up into the "superior" cultural value system of the host society.

When it became evident that forced assimilation for the purpose of rigid standardization was not yielding the expected results, social scientists began to look toward new theories concerning American society and assimilation. The continued existence of ethnic organizations, presses, values, customs, languages, etc., showed the fallacy behind the one-culture concept of both the "melting pot" and the Americanization theories. The view of assimilation as essentially a one-way integrative process into the dominant American culture was also proven a fallacy. The concept of "injection" of the dominant culture, which was the basis of many programs of the Americanization movement, also failed to meet the promised results, but not before it introduced deeply rooted prejudicial sentiments toward ethnic Americans, their institutions, and their cultures. Furthermore, this movement was largely responsible for sowing, in the psyche of many non-Anglo Americans, the seeds of self-doubt, inferiority, and even self-hate. Unfortunately, even today we are still reaping the harvest of Americanization. The idea that anything "ethnic" has an inferior status is still prevalent. Ethnic organizations are somehow not considered to be on a par with establishment organizations; ethnic cultures, traditions, and values are somehow perceived as being "unsophisticated" and even "foreign." According to Andrew Greeley, although present theories point to cultural pluralism, "our behavior insists on as much assimilation as possible as quickly as possible.... We are torn between pride in the heritage of our own group and resentment at being trapped in that heritage. This ambivalence is probably the result of the agonies of the acculturation experience in which an immigrant group alternately felt shame over the fact that it was different and unwanted and a defensive pride about its own excellence, which the rest of society seemed neither to appreciate nor understand."[2]

The negativism behind the "Americanization" concept was gradually replaced by the positivism of cultural pluralism. The concept of cultural pluralism, with its various theoretical variations, developed from a reaction to the harshness of the Americanization movement as well as from the obvious failure of that movement to produce the American Anglo-Saxon civilization. American society was now to be viewed as heterogeneous and pluralistic in nature, and assimilation was viewed basically as a reciprocal process that depended on the immigrant groups' contribution to the entire order. Thus, the cultural pluralism approach differs from the "melting pot" and Americanization theories basically in its acceptance of American society as a mosaic within which the immigrant has the right to retain his cultural heritage. Social scientists today often compare American society to an orchestra within which each ethnic group represents a separate instrument; the interaction of these separate groups forms the harmonious whole.

■ ■ ■

The survival of ethnic communities and an ethnic "life" is largely a result of the continued existence of ethnic organizations, for it is mainly these organizations and their various activities that insure the continuation of the ethnic society. To a very large extent the structural complexity or simplicity of an ethnic group is determined by the types and characteristics of existing organizations. It is often these organizations that provide the ethos and spirit behind an ethnic existence. The various conflicts within ethnic communities are usually fought on the organizational level. In this respect it is the organized life of an ethnic community that provides one of the more reliable indices of not only the structure and nature of a particular ethnic community, but also the degree of its assimilation and acculturation. Only through the study of ethnic organizations, their activities, and their influence on ethnic communities can a total picture of "ethnicity" emerge, for these organizations mirror the realities of an ethnic existence.

Like the ethnic press, ethnic organizations have often been viewed as constituting a "foreign" body within a host society. Undoubtedly, the persistence of this view is partially due to the earlier Americanization policies and programs. Yaroslav Chyz and Read Lewis note that agencies created by English-speaking nationality groups were regarded as "American" by virtue of the fact that immigrants from English-speaking countries formed the majority in the United States and thus had the power to impress their institutions and language on other immigrants. On the other hand, similar institutional developments by the non-Anglo immigrant were classified as "foreign," primarily because non-English languages were used in the organization of these institutions.[3] The use of a non-English language in the initial stages of forming an organization was considered, therefore, as a factor in determining the "Americanism" or "non-Americanism" of an institution, even though in later years most members are unable to communicate in their original native tongues. Since a majority of the ethnic organizations in the United States arose in order to meet the same basic needs and were actually adaptations to existing conditions, they must be accepted as being "American" regardless of the country of origin of the initiating members.

Like all organizations, ethnic voluntary associations also arose in order to meet needs not satisfied by institutions within the existing social order. A large number of the present-day American ethnic organizations began initially as immigrant associations, although today the term "immigrant" is hardly applicable to most of them. Originally, these organizations were established by the newly arrived immigrants either to fulfill the desire of continuing old wants (e.g., preservation of religion, culture, language, etc.) or to meet new needs created as a result of migration. The passage of time transformed these early American "immigrant" organizations into American "ethnic" ones; the membership was now primarily American-born, and the initial goals, activities, and structure were transformed in order to conform to new realities and to meet different needs.

Although a large proportion of the present-day ethnic organizations can trace their roots to immigrant beginnings, a number of the organizations lack this immigrant origin. This group of ethnic associations was formed by second-, third-, or even fourth-generation Americans to meet wants shared by other fellow ethnics but not with members of the larger society. Thus, organizations in this group never experienced the process of transformation from American immigrant status to American ethnic status. Thus, the needs they were designed to meet were not a direct outgrowth of the actual migration.

Another category of ethnic organizations consists of those established not as a response to existing conditions in this country, but rather as an outgrowth and reflection of conditions in the home country. Some of these organizations were directly transplanted by the immigrants themselves. Examples of this transplantation can be found in a number of ideological and cultural associations introduced into the United States by immigrants arriving from the Soviet Union and Eastern Europe following World War II. These organizations were originally formed abroad, then reestablished by arriving immigrants. Another category of organizations that arose in response to conditions in the native land consists of those established by American ethnics. It differs from the former not only as to its place of origin but also in the fact that while the former was established and transplanted by immigrants, the latter was organized by ethnic Americans. In many instances such organizations are often officially affiliated with the parent organizations abroad, although in the course of time they also attain an American character.

As mentioned earlier, ethnic organizations are formed to fulfill group needs not fulfilled by the existing established order. Stanley H. Chapman noted that the ethnic group that "provides a complete way of life for itself has achieved a ghetto; the minority that finds adequate outlet for activity and satisfying organizational benefits in the existing social structure has been assimilated. In the first case, the minority has constructed its own community; in the second, it is absorbed into the existing community. These are the two extremes between which the organization of minority groups takes place."[4] The type and number of organizations established as well as the degree of participation within them is determined by a number of factors. A major element is the amount or degree of disparity that exists between the established host society and the newly arrived immigrant group. The greater the cultural disparity, the more likely is the immigrant group to establish a larger number of organizations, since there are more types of needs unlikely to be fulfilled by the American social order. The language difference alone is an important element in this sense. The various needs are not only based on cultural disparity, but also may be a result of the differences in the socioeconomic standing of immigrants within the same nationality group, the causes behind emigration (e.g., economic, political, religious, voluntary or involuntary, etc.), and the psychological factors (such as desire to assimilate or remain distinct). For example, the post-World War II mass emigration of refugees from the Soviet Union and Eastern Europe brought a high percentage of well-educated, politically aware, and socially active individuals. As a result, many types of educational, academic, professional, political, and cultural organizations were formed, because the needs of these immigrants were more complex and varied than the needs of the uneducated groups of the earlier immigrants. Furthermore, it is not unusual to find that immigrants who arrived in rather large numbers as a result of political conditions, thus making the immigration involuntary in nature, tend to transplant political, ideological, and cultural organizations that existed in their native land, again as in the case of the East Europeans. The cause behind the emigration (economic, political, religious, etc.), the nature of the immigration (voluntary or involuntary), the former and present socioeconomic status of the immigrant (occupation, education, social class, etc.), and the degree of the cultural disparity with the host society are all elements that combine to form the psychological outlook toward assimilation. This psychological factor regarding the degree of assimilation is in itself an important element that determines, in a certain respect, the character and extent of organized life to be developed. Thus, groups that aim to preserve the cultural heritage are more likely to organize schools, youth groups, cultural and academic associations, etc., all designed to promote and preserve the native background.

Another important factor that lies behind the need to establish ethnic organizations is that of exclusion or discrimination. Up to this point we have discussed the needs that are unfulfilled within the established social order mainly because the institutionalized structures are unable to provide an adequate outlet or because a group prefers to maintain some degree of separateness. In the case of exclusion, the provision for satisfaction of needs does lie within the established social order, as does the desire for participation; because of prejudice and discrimination toward certain groups, however, their members are not permitted entry. As a result, organizations are often created to counteract this condition. For example, many Black and Jewish organizations emerged as a result of non-acceptance by the established institutions.

Because there are many types of ethnic organizations, it is difficult to provide a completely satisfactory classification. The broadest classification is provided for by Chyz and Lewis, who group agencies organized by nationality groups into three types: religious (primarily churches, but also church-sponsored organizations); secular organizations; and the foreign-language press and radio.[5] The authors note that this classification is not to be regarded as rigid because overlapping does tend to occur, especially with respect to activities. Robert E. Park and Herbert Miller also introduced a rather broad categorization. They group immigrant institutions under the following headings: first-aid institutions, which are designed to assist newcomers in adjusting (may be charitable or a business enterprise such as banks, steamship ticket offices, boarding houses, employment bureaus, real estate brokerages, etc.); mutual aid and benefit societies formed in order to provide assistance for sickness, death, burial, etc. (e.g., mutual benefit, fraternal insurance society, and associated lodges and orders); nationalistic organizations that focus their attention on the country of origin; and cultural institutions, such as the press, theater, schools, churches, social organizations, athletic societies, academic, etc.[6] This same classification was also adapted by William Carlson Smith in his study on assimilation.[7] A less broad categorization is presented by Stanley Chapman, who classifies minority group organizations into the following groups: benevolent and fraternal; religious; social; economic; political; and action and protest.[8] On the basis of the survey conducted we have found that ethnic organizations fall into the following categories: religious; mutual aid or benefit associations designed to provide aid at critical times (such as unemployment, illness, accident, or death); social welfare or philanthropic associations through which assistance is given to the less successful members; political and ideological organizations, which either focus on the home land or reflect the political situation of the host country; occupational and professional associations; social, recreational, and sport associations; scholarly and research institutes; youth groups; women's organizations; veterans' organizations; special cultural associations such as theater, music, choral, drama groups, etc. In addition, there are ethnic educational institutions, ethnic business institutions (banks, credit unions, etc.), and museums and libraries.

Regarding objectives, functions, and activities of these organizations, it may be said that although some are limited and singular in purpose, many others fulfill a variety of needs; thus, they are not mutually exclusive. For example, the Ukrainian National Association, founded initially as a fraternal and mutual aid organization, also publishes a daily newspaper, organizes various social and cultural functions, maintains an extensive recreational resort, and offers a variety of educational programs and youth activities.

The above classification of organizations is based on a functional approach. The sphere or domain of influence may be yet another variable by which categorization may be accomplished. Using this as the basis, the following types exist: 1) The local organization, which is unique in the sense that it exists only within a local area (usually a city). It focuses on the special needs found within this confined geographic area, and it does not have any branches outside the area, nor is it a branch of a larger organization. 2) The state or regional organizations, which are limited to individual states or geographic regions. These may or may not have branches, may serve as action-coordinating bodies, or may simply exist as a single organization with a larger sphere of influence than the local type. 3) The national organization. In a few areas such organizations are not based on a branch system, but rather draw their membership directly on a national scale. However, it was found that the majority of the national organizations are structured on the basis of an extensive local, state, and regional branch system. In fact, the hundreds of local organizations that exist throughout the country are actually branches of a particular national association. The policies, goals, and activities are set by the national organization and these are followed by the branches, although the branches do have autonomy when strictly local issues need to be resolved. The national-branch organization has a highly structured hierarchical system, which may or may not serve as a basis for social status and power within the ethnic community, depending on the nature and status of the organization itself. The national non-branch associations usually lack this extensive hierarchy. 4) The international organizations. Organizations of this type are either: a) associations that were transplanted by the immigrant to the various host societies; or b) organizations that were initially formed in the United States and later developed either chapters and branches, or the same ethnic membership in other countries. Again, using the Ukrainian-American ethnic community as an illustration, the youth organization "PLAST," which is the Ukrainian counterpart of Boy Scouts and Girl Scouts, has been transplanted to the various nations within the free world to which Ukrainians immigrated in significant numbers. Usually there is broad coordination regarding general goals, but each organization within each country is free to develop activities and policies that allow it to adapt to existing conditions. In time these organizations develop characteristics that reflect those of the host society and thus become more autonomous in character. 5) Coordinating or umbrella organizations. These organizations serve as vehicles that effect the coordination of the activities of various associations. Usually a number of different types of organizations are members of such coordinating bodies; however, they are not subject to their rule. The coordination itself is usually very general in nature and is primarily related to issues affecting the entire ethnic community. In addition, these organizations also have their own activities, policies, and goals. Umbrella associations vary with respect to their sphere of influence—that is, they can be local, regional, national, or, in a few cases, even international. The national is the most prevalent type.

From the above discussion it can be seen that ethnic organizations are formed 1) to meet needs unfulfilled by the established institutions within the social order because of cultural disparity and because of the unique nature of these wants; 2) as a result of a group's desire to maintain some degree of separateness in order to retard assimilation; and 3) as a reaction to exclusion and discrimination. Whatever the factor or combination of factors behind the formation, an ethnic organization, in order to be classified as "ethnic," must 1) be formed by individuals who consciously identify themselves as members of the ethnic group; 2) fulfill needs that are common to persons of that particular ethnic group and not necessarily to members of the greater society; and 3) identify itself as being part of the ethnic community. The concept of "ethnicity" or "ethnic group" as it exists in North America may be defined as people who identify themselves as being members of a particular group, or who are identified by others as belonging to that group, on the basis of common national or geographic origin, race, religion, culture, and language, or a combination of these elements.[9] Ethnic organizations may or may not display the element of exclusion. Whether the organization is strictly limited to persons who are members of the particular ethnic group, or whether it allows within its membership rolls people not part of such a group, depends largely on the degree of separateness it intends to maintain. If the organization welcomes participation by non-ethnics, these members must accept the goals, causes, policies, and ethnic nature of the organization in question. It was found that groups that allow such involvement do so primarily for reasons of cultural exchange, in order to introduce greater understanding between various peoples.

In addition to the various specialized needs for which the organizations are established, ethnic organizations also perform a larger function. These functions may be summarized as follows: 1) Ethnic organizations provide a degree of structure, complexity, stability, and continuity to the ethnic community. 2) They regulate behavior and provide a sense of social responsibility. 3) They provide a sense of identity by maintaining group solidarity. 4) They provide roots to one's historical and cultural past through the preservation of customs, culture, language, etc. In this sense they provide their members with a sense of pride in their heritage. 5) They serve as agencies that ease the process of adjustment. 6) They are important in both promoting and retarding the assimilative process.

It is important to note that, although the ethnic communities and their organizations have survived, they themselves have undergone and are continuing to undergo various evolutionary changes in order to survive in a constantly changing society. The various assimilative forces of the dominant society have a great impact in changing the original character of ethnic organizations. However, these groups have remained identifiably ethnic, even though they have lost their immigrant nature. The "immigrant" community, ghetto, society, or organization has now become the American "ethnic" community. And it is the continued existence of many different ethnic communities that has earned the American society its title of "cultural pluralism." The condition is best described by Nathan Glazer and Daniel Moynihan:

> . . . as the groups were transformed by influences in American society, stripped of their original attributes, they were recreated as something new, but still as identifiable groups. Concretely, persons think of themselves as members of that group, with that name; they are thought of by others as members of that group, with that name; and most significantly, they are linked to other members of the group by new attributes that the original immigrants would never have recognized as identifying their group, but which nevertheless serve to mark them off, by more than simply name and association, in the third generation and even beyond.[10]

Whether cultural pluralism will triumph or whether the "melting pot" concept will eventually return to claim victory remains to be seen. The present realities favor heterogeneity and pluralism. The final outcome lies in the future.

Footnotes

1. Israel Zangwill, *The Melting Pot: Drama in Four Acts* (New York: Macmillan Company, 1909), pp. 37-38.

2. Andrew M. Greeley, *Ethnicity in the United States* (New York: John Wiley & Sons, 1974), p. 17.

3. Yaroslav J. Chyz and Read Lewis, "Agencies Organized by Nationality Groups in the United States," *The Annals of the American Academy of Political and Social Science* 262 (March 1949) : 148.

4. Stanley H. Chapman, "Organizations of Minority Groups," in *One America*, edited by Frances J. Brown and Joseph S. Roucek (Westport, Connecticut: Negro University Press, 1970), p. 416.

5. Chyz and Lewis, "Agencies Organized by Nationality Groups," p. 149.

6. Robert E. Park and Herbert A. Miller, *Old World Traits Transplanted* (New York: Harper & Brothers Publishers, 1921), pp. 121-144.

7. William Carlson Smith, *Americans in the Making* (New York: D. Appleton-Century Co., 1939), pp. 87-108.

8. Chapman, "Organizations of Minority Groups," pp. 416-425.

9. For an analysis of the various definitions see Wsevold W. Isajiw, "Definition of Ethnicity," in *Ethnicity* 1 (1974) : 111-124.

10. Nathan Glazer and Daniel P. Moynihan, *Beyond the Melting Pot* (Cambridge, Massachusetts: MIT Press, 1966), p. 13.

AFRO-AMERICAN ORGANIZATIONS

See Black-American Organizations

ALBANIAN-AMERICAN ORGANIZATIONS

Additional information on Albanians, their organizations, and their religious life may be obtained from officers of the Albanian Orthodox Diocese of America (54 Burroughs Street, Jamaica Plain, Massachusetts 02130). See also *Greater Cleveland Nationalities Directory 1974* (Cleveland: Sun Newspapers and the Nationalities Services Center, 1974) and *Ethnic Directory I* (Detroit: Southeastern Michigan Regional Ethnic Heritage Studies Center, 1973).

THE ALBANIAN AMERICAN CATHOLIC LEAGUE, INC.
4221 Park Avenue   (212) 792-4044/5 or
Bronx, New York 10457   (212) 828-3063
Principal officers: Joseph J. Oroshi, President
Joseph O'Brien, Executive Vice President
Frank Shkreli, Executive Secretary

Permanent staff: 24   Membership: 200
Date founded: 1962   Membership dues: $12.00 (annual)
Branches: none   Scope: NI

Special requirements for membership: "Must be Albanian or of Albanian descent and a practicing Roman Catholic."

Nature of organization: educational, cultural, religious

Publications: *Catholic Albanian Life*, 1966– (quarterly). Also publishes books.

Major conventions/meetings: monthly

Comments: Aids Albanians with schooling, health, and welfare problems. Also offers spiritual and cultural guidance. Maintains both a library and archives.

ALBANIAN AMERICAN ETHNIC COMMUNITY CORPORATION OF NEW YORK
1759 Castle Hill Avenue
Bronx, New York 10462

ALBANIAN AMERICAN ISLAMIC CENTER, INC.
13-25 Alberale Road
Brooklyn, New York 11226

ALBANIAN-AMERICAN MOSLEM SOCIETY
20426 Country Club
Harper Woods, Michigan 48236

ALBANIAN DEMOCRATIC PARTY
1111 Dorchester
Birmingham, Michigan 48010   (313) 646-5109
Principal officers: Eqrem Bardha

Permanent staff: NI   Membership: NI
Date founded: 1939   Membership dues: NI
Branches: NI   Scope: national

Special requirements for membership: Albanian descent

Nature of organization: political

Publications: *Zeri i Ballit*, 1950– (quarterly)

Comments: Major objective of the organization is to oppose communism in Albania.

1

ALBANIAN SOCIAL CLUB
2000 Sagamore Drive
Cleveland, Ohio 44117   (216) 486-5403

Principal officers: Candida P. Rinaldi, President
                     Anthony Bianco, Vice President
                     Cinderella P. Wilk, Secretary

Permanent staff: 4	Membership: 50
Date founded: 1972	Membership dues: $12.00
Branches: none	Scope: local

Special requirements for membership: Albanian descent or related by marriage

Nature of organization: social

Major conventions/meetings: monthly

Comments: Organized primarily to provide social contact for Albanians in the Cleveland area and to promote social activities for Albanian youth.

FIRST ALBANIAN TEKE BEKTASHIAN IN AMERICA
21749 Northline
Taylor, Michigan 48180   (313) 287-3646

Principal officers: E. Baraha, Vice President
                     H. Aliko, Secretary

Permanent staff: 3	Membership: 1,000
Date founded: 1954	Membership dues: donation
Branches: none	Scope: national

Special requirements for membership: Bektashiane faith

Nature of organization: religious

Publications: *The Voice of Bektashiane*, 1959– (semiannual). Also publishes books.

Major conventions/meetings: religious meetings three times a year

Comments: This is a religious order which formed its own "Teqe" (monastery) to spread the Bektashian faith in the United States and to teach, govern, and discipline in accordance with the customs and regulations of Bektashism. The Teqe, its clergy, and members encourage the use of the Albanian language and promote educational, philanthropic, and social activities in accordance with Bektashian practice. The order maintains its own library and archives.

THE FREE ALBANIA COMMITTEE (FAC)
150 Fifth Avenue, Room 1103
New York, New York 10011   (212) 691-9797

Principal officers: Rexhep Krasniqi, President
                     Vasil Germenji, Vice President
                     Michael Dibra, Secretary

Permanent staff: 5	Membership: NI
Date founded: 1956	Membership dues: NI
Branches: 0	Scope: national

Nature of organization: political, cultural

Publications: *The Free Albanian*, 1957– (semiannual). Also publishes books and booklets.

Comments: This organization is concerned primarily with protecting the political rights of Albanians in the free world. Cooperates with other similar national groups originating in East Central Europe. Aids in the immigration of Albanian political refugees to the United States by assisting with the various problems of resettlement. Maintains a small library as well as archival materials.

FREE ALBANIA ORGANIZATION (FAO)
397 B West Broadway
South Boston, Massachusetts 02127   (617) 269-5192

Principal officers: John T. Nasse, President
                     Selam Tosun, Vice President
                     Bill Govnaris, Secretary

FREE ALBANIA ORGANIZATION (FAO) (cont'd)

Permanent staff: 2

Date founded: 1942

Branches: NI

Membership: 1,200

Membership dues: $12.00 (annual)

Scope: national

Special requirements for membership: interest in Albanian-American activity

Nature of organization: cultural

Publications: *Liria*, 1942– (weekly)

Major conventions/meetings: annual

Comments: The purpose of the organization is to promote Albanian traditions and culture in the United States. The major function of the FAO is the publication of the weekly newspaper *Liria*. The newspaper provides news on the social and cultural activities of various Albanian groups, societies, and churches.

PAN ALBANIAN FEDERATION OF AMERICA, "VATRA"
25 Huntington Avenue, Room 412A
Boston, Massachusetts 02116

Principal officers: James Thanas, President

Permanent staff: 2

Date founded: 1912

Branches: 21

Membership: 1,500

Membership dues: NI

Scope: national

Special requirements for membership: Albanians (age 18 or older) living in the United States

Nature of organization: cultural, charitable, educational

Publications: *Dielli* (The Sun), 1909– (weekly). Also publishes books.

Major conventions/meetings: annual (Labor Day weekend in Boston)

Comments: The main purpose of this federation is to sponsor cultural and charitable activities and to publish books on Albanian subjects. The educational foundation of this federation provides scholarships for college students of Albanian extraction.

ROYAL PARTY
Albanian Moslem Bektashi Monastery
c/o Mr. Toptani
21749 Northline
Taylor, Michigan 48180   (313) 825-8066

Nature of organization: political

VILLAGERS' PARTY
c/o Mr. Kol Mehilli
5425 Porter
Detroit, Michigan 48209

Permanent staff: NI

Date founded: NI

Branches: NI

Membership: NI

Membership dues: NI

Scope: national

Nature of organization: political

Comments: This group, which is the major faction of the Balli Kombetar (Albanian Democratic Party), began in Italy in 1948 as the Italian Agrarian Party and then merged with the Democratic Party.

AMERICAN INDIAN ORGANIZATIONS

A survey of American Indian organizations yielded valuable data concerning the organized life of American Indians. It was found that there are many Native American organizations, councils, and centers. To list and describe most of the national, regional, state, or local organizations would require a separate directory of American Indian associations. Because they are too numerous to be included within the scope of this guide, and because such a listing already exists, it was decided to list here, on a highly selective basis, only a few major organizations.

Those interested in obtaining a more extensive list of Native American associations should consult the following source: Barry Klein (ed.), *Reference Encyclopedia of the American Indian*, 2nd ed., Vol. 1 (New York: Todd Publications, 1973). This encyclopedia lists American Indian associations, reservations, tribal councils, committees, schools, and urban Indian centers. Some of the entries are annotated. Addresses are included.

For additional information, contact the Bureau of Indian Affairs, 1951 Constitution Avenue, N.W., Washington, D.C. 20242.

AMERICAN INDIAN DEVELOPMENT, INC. (AID)
408 Zook Building
431 West Colfax
Denver, Colorado 80204   (303) 266-9202

Principal officers: Robert L. Bennett, President

Permanent staff: 3
Date founded: 1957
Branches: none

Membership: not a membership organization
Membership dues: none
Scope: national

Nature of organization: educational

Major conventions/meetings: Workshop of American Indian Affairs Scholars Conference

Comments: The major purpose of the organization is to conduct research and to act as a liaison between other agencies and organizations. It conducts workshops on American Indian affairs, provides a speaker's bureau for organizations, and is involved in community education projects. A 300-volume library and an archival collection are maintained.

THE AMERICAN INDIAN HISTORICAL SOCIETY
1451 Masonic Avenue
San Francisco, California 94117   (415) 626-5236

Principal officers: Rupert Costo, President
Leroy Selam, Vice President
Gwen Shunatona, Treasurer

Permanent staff: NI
Date founded: 1964
Branches: none

Membership: NI
Membership dues: $15.00 (annual)
Scope: national

Special requirements for membership: interest in Indian history

Nature of organization: educational, cultural, scholarly

Publications: *The Indian Historian* (quarterly); *The Weewish Tree* (bimonthly); *Annual Index to Literature on the American Indian* (annual); also publishes textbooks.

Comments: The major objectives of the organization are to preserve and promote the American Indian culture and to advance the education and general welfare of the American Indian while preserving his language, philosophy, and values. It has founded several publications; it produces educational and informational materials, conducts seminars for classroom teachers, and designs programs in curriculum development. It is conducting a water resources inventory survey of the San Juan River Basin to preserve five large reservations from economic extinction because of loss of Indian water rights. It has organized and maintains an outstanding research library and Indian archives.

AMERICAN INDIAN MOVEMENT
553 Aurora Avenue
St. Paul, Minnesota   (612) 227-0651

AMERICAN INDIAN MOVEMENT (cont'd)

Permanent staff: NI   Membership: 2,000
Date founded: 1968   Membership dues: NI
Branches: NI   Scope: national

Special requirements for membership: interest in bettering conditions of the urban Indian

Nature of organization: political, cultural, economic, social, recreational, sports

Publications: *A.I.M. News* (monthly)

Affiliations: Indian Women's League, Indian American Youth Center

Major conventions/meetings: annual

Comments: The objectives of the organization are to unite the Indian people, to keep them informed of community and local affairs, and to encourage participation in community affairs. It also strives to improve the economic status of the American Indian. It was formerly known as the Concerned Indian American Coalition. It sponsors a housing program, youth program, employment assistance, programs in Indian culture, an Indian Patrol, a sewing group, and Amerind Alcoholics Anonymous. AIM is "portrayed as a militant, change-oriented action group."

AMERICANS FOR INDIAN OPPORTUNITY (AIO)

1816 Jefferson Place, N.W.
Washington, D.C. 20036   (202) 466-8420

Principal officers: La Donna Harris, President

Permanent staff: 8   Membership: NI
Date founded: NI   Membership dues: none
Branches: none   Scope: national

Special requirements for membership: none

Nature of organization: political, social, cultural

ASSOCIATION ON AMERICAN INDIAN AFFAIRS, INC.

432 Park Avenue South
New York, New York 10016   (212) 689-8720

Principal officers: Professor Alfonso Ortiz, President
                       Roger C. Ernst, Vice President
                       Mrs. Henry S. Forbes, Secretary

Permanent staff: 15   Membership: 75,000
Date founded: 1923   Membership dues: $15.00
Branches: NI $5.00 for students
                                            Scope: national

Nature of organization: social, educational

Publications: *Indian Affairs* (quarterly); *Indian Family Defense* (quarterly). Also publishes books.

Major conventions/meetings: annual membership meeting

Comments: The association conducts continuing programs in Indian economic and community development; health, education, and welfare; legal defense; public education; the arts and crafts (through the American Indian Arts Center). It helps Indian tribes to mobilize all available resources—federal, state and private—for a coordinated attack on the problems of poverty. The Association has just launched a special G. E. Larky Indian Resources Scholarship for Indian graduate students studying in any fields related to the conservation and development of Indian physical resources. Plans to publish a directory of sources of financial support for American Indian graduate students.

COALITION OF EASTERN NATIVE AMERICANS (CENA)
927 15th Street
Washington, D.C. 20005

Principal officers: W. J. Strickland, Executive Administrative Director

Permanent staff: NI
Date founded: 1972
Branches: in 18 states

Membership: 53 tribes and organizations; 189,981 individuals
Membership dues: NI
Scope: regional

Special requirements for membership: tribal and organizational membership

Nature of organization: economic, cultural, educational, social

Affiliations: member tribes

Comments: The goal of CENA is to assist in the economic, cultural, and social advancement of the Native American people in the eastern half of the United States. CENA serves as a means of communication for all member tribes, provides technical assistance to the Indian communities on matters relating to federal programs, and coordinates the services of state and federal agencies. It represents tribes from the states of Connecticut, Maine, Massachusetts, Rhode Island, New Jersey, New York, Pennsylvania, Delaware, Maryland, Virginia, Alabama, Florida, North Carolina, South Carolina, Michigan, Wisconsin, Louisiana, and Ohio.

INDIAN RIGHTS ASSOCIATION (IRA)
1505 Race Street
Philadelphia, Pennsylvania 19102   (215) 563-8349

Principal officers: Thomas Wistar, President
Jonathan M. Steere, Jr., Executive Vice President
Theodore B. Hetzel, Executive Secretary

Permanent staff: 3
Date founded: 1892
Branches: none

Membership: 2,500
Membership dues: $10.00 (annual)
Scope: national

Special requirements for membership: none

Nature of organization: social

Publications: *Indian Truth*, 1924– (irregular)

Major conventions/meetings: annual

Comments: The objectives of the organization are to protect the civil rights of the Indian and to promote his moral and physical well-being.

NATIONAL CONGRESS OF AMERICAN INDIANS
1765 "P" Street, N.W.
Washington, D.C. 20036

Principal officers: Deloria Vine, Jr., Executive Director

Permanent staff: NI
Date founded: 1944
Branches: NI

Membership: 600 (105 tribes)
Membership dues: NI
Scope: NI

Nature of organization: educational, cultural, economic

Major conventions/meetings: annual convention of tribes

Comments: The objectives of this organization are to provide information and research programs for Indian tribes and the general public on topics of Indian interest—e.g., legislation, history, current problems and movements, education, and economic opportunities.

NATIONAL INDIAN EDUCATION ASSOCIATION (NIEA)
Hubbard Building, Suite 100
2675 University Avenue
St. Paul, Minnesota 55114   (612) 646-6349

NATIONAL INDIAN EDUCATION ASSOCIATION (NIEA) (cont'd)

Principal officers: Dillon Platero, President
Ada Deer, Vice President
Elizabeth Whiteman, Secretary

Permanent staff: 1
Date founded: 1970
Branches: none

Membership: 800
Membership dues: $10 (annual); $100
(annual) for organizations
Scope: national

Special requirements for membership: none

Nature of organization: educational

Publications: *Indian Education* (monthly)

Affiliations: National Council on Indian Opportunity

Major conventions/meetings: annual conference

Comments: The major objectives of the organization are to conduct educational conferences
and workshops, to evaluate and improve state and local educational sources, to assess
and coordinate technical assistance sources, to serve as a clearinghouse on Indian education affairs, and to bring Indian educators together as a united voice. NIEA sponsors
lectures, panel discussions, and seminars for presentation to interested groups.

SURVIVAL OF AMERICAN INDIANS ASSOCIATION
P.O. Box 719
Tacoma, Washington 98401   (206) 456-1375

Principal officers: Don Matheson, President
Maiselle Bridges, Vice President
Suzette Mills, Executive Secretary

Permanent staff: 12
Date founded: NI
Branches: 1 national office; 1 local office

Membership: NI
Membership dues: none
Scope: national

Special requirements for membership: none

Nature of organization: political, educational, cultural, economic

Publications: *The Renegade*, 1967– (annual)

Comments: SAIA was organized to fight for just treaty rights for American Indians, protection of Indian land and natural resources, and recognition as a sovereign nation. It
negotiates and lobbies at the state and federal levels on issues concerning the Indian
economy, education, or court cases. It endeavors to educate foreign governments about
American Indian issues.

TANANA CHIEFS CONFERENCE, INC.
102 Lacey Street
Fairbanks, Alaska 99701   (907) 452-1746

Principal officers: Mitch Demientieff, President
Barbara Haggland, Secretary
Nancy Gray Akpik, Executive Director

Permanent staff: 50
Date founded: 1971
Branches: 4 subregional

Membership: 10,000
Membership dues: none
Scope: regional

Nature of organization: cultural, economic, social, educational

Affiliations: Alaska Federation of Natives, Inc.

Major conventions/meetings: annual meeting; semiannual special meeting

Comments: The purpose of the organization is to organize Alaskan American Indians on
issues and services involving health, education, etc. It sponsors the Tanana Survival
School.

UNITED INDIAN DEVELOPMENT ASSOCIATION
1541 Wilshire Boulevard
Los Angeles, California 90017   (213) 483-1460

Principal officers: A. David Lester, President
                      Edward Sloan, Secretary
                      Robert Concho, Controller

Permanent staff: 14   Membership: NI
Date founded: 1970   Membership dues: NI
Branches: 3   Scope: regional

Nature of organization: economic

Publications: *UIDA Reporter*, 1971– (monthly); *American Indian Business Directory*, 1972– (annual)

Affiliations: none

Major conventions/meetings: quarterly workshops; monthly board meetings

Comments: The purpose of the organization is to assist Indian-owned businesses and profit enterprises. Until 1973 it was known as the Urban Indian Development Association. It provides services in business planning, market study, financial planning, and packaging. A library of 300 volumes and an archival collection of business-related materials are maintained.

ARAB-AMERICAN ORGANIZATIONS

This section on Arab-American organizations in the United States includes organizations representing various Arab nations (e.g., Egyptian, Iraqi, Lebanese, Palestinian, Syrian, and others). For additional information on Arab communities in the United States, see Barbara C. Aswad, (ed.), *Arabic Speaking Communities in American Cities* (New York: Center for Migration Studies & Association of Arab-American University Graduates, 1974). Also, for regional and local organizations, see *Greater Cleveland Nationalities Directory 1974* (Cleveland: Sun Newspapers and the Nationalities Services Center, 1974) and *Ethnic Directory I* (Detroit: Southeastern Michigan Regional Ethnic Heritage Studies Center, 1973).

ACTION COMMITTEE ON AMERICAN-ARAB RELATIONS (ACAAR)
441 Lexington Avenue, Room 1002
New York, New York 10017   (212) 682-1154

Principal officers: Dr. M. T. Mehdi, Secretary-General

Permanent staff: 3   Membership: 30,000
Date founded: 1964   Membership dues: NI
Branches: NI   Scope: national

Special requirements for membership: individuals interested in improving American-Arab relations

Nature of organization: social, political

Publications: *Action*, 1969– (weekly); *ACAAR Yearbook* (annual)

Major conventions/meetings: annual

Comments: A politically moderate organization whose activities include picketing, demonstrating, filing lawsuits, and registering complaints with the Federal Communications Commission about undesirable portrayal of Arabs by the media. It offers aid to American Arabs in the process of becoming naturalized.

AD HOC COMMITTEE FOR A FREE PALESTINE
2418 Pied Piper Lane
Wausau, Wisconsin 54401

AMERICAN AID FOR ARAB REFUGEES, INC. (AAAR)
P.O. Box 67
Brooklyn, New York 11209   (212) 833-8245
Principal officers: Robert W. Thabit, President
                       Olga Jabara, Executive Vice President
                       Mona Johnson, Executive Secretary

Permanent staff: none   Membership: 50-100
Date founded: 1967   Membership dues: $5.00 (annual)
Branches: none   Scope: regional

Special requirements for membership: none

Nature of organization: charitable

Publications: Publishes books.

Affiliations: none

Major conventions/meetings: annual

Comments: Primarily a charitable organization whose major purpose is to provide aid to Arab
    refugees in the Middle East. Funds collected by the organization are distributed accord-
    ing to the instructions of the Board of Directors. Since 1970, needy Arab orphans
    have been awarded scholarships to the University of Cairo, the University of Jordan,
    Damascus University, American University of Beirut, and the Beirut College for Women.

AMERICAN-ARAB ASSOCIATION (AMARA)
1611 Varnum Street, N.W.
Washington, D.C. 20018

Permanent staff: NI   Membership: NI
Date founded: NI   Membership dues: NI
Branches: various regional branches Scope: national

Comments: This organization is interested in promoting the Arab culture in America. It has
    branches in Cincinnati, Boston, and Syracuse, New York.

AMERICAN-ARAB ASSOCIATION FOR COMMERCE AND INDUSTRY, INC.
505 Fifth Avenue, Suite 1701
New York, New York 10017   (212) 986-7229
Principal officers: Jamal A. Sa'd, Executive Director

Permanent staff: NI   Membership: 120
Date founded: NI   Membership dues: NI
Branches: NI   Scope: national

Nature of organization: commercial and economic

Publications: *Bulletin* (10 issues/year)

Major conventions/meetings: annual meeting in New York City

Comments: Principal purpose of the association is to promote and expand trade between
    the United States and the Middle East. It holds industry workshops.

AMERICAN ARAB CONGRESS FOR PALESTINE
P.O. Box 5421
Chicago, Illinois 60680

AMERICAN-ARAB FEDERATION
71 Birckhead Place
Toledo, Ohio 43608

AMERICAN ARAB RELIEF AGENCY (AARA)
2760 East Grand Boulevard
Detroit, Michigan 48211   (313) 874-2959
Principal officers: Thomas Ruffin, Chairman

Permanent staff: 1; board members, 15   Membership: NI
Date founded: 1967   Membership dues: NI
Branches: NI   Scope: national

Special requirements for membership: Arabic-speaking persons

Nature of organization: charitable

Comments: Prime objective of AARA is to raise funds to aid refugees in the Middle East.

AMERICAN-ARAB SOCIETY
500 Jefferson Building
Houston, Texas 77002

AMERICAN ARAB YEMEN BENEVOLENT SOCIETY
10327 Dix
Dearborn, Michigan 48120

AMERICAN FRIENDS OF THE MIDDLE EAST, INC. (AFME)
1717 Massachusetts Avenue, N.W.
Washington, D.C. 20036   (202) 234-7500
Principal officers: Virgil C. Crippen, Executive Vice President

Permanent staff: NI   Membership: NI
Date founded: 1951   Membership dues: NI
Branches: 6 overseas centers   Scope: national

Special requirements for membership: Americans interested in the Middle East

Nature of organization: social, cultural, educational

Publications: *Report* (quarterly); *Study & Research in the Middle East & North Africa* (annual); *Teaching Opportunities in the Middle East & North Africa* (annual). Also publishes books.

Comments: The organization aims to promote Middle East-American relations. It provides educational counseling services and assists in placing Arab students in United States schools, in obtaining scholarships and funds for transportation, etc. It supervises scholarship programs funded by industry and the government.

AMERICAN MIDDLE EAST REHABILITATION, INC. (AMER)
777 United Nations Plaza, Room 7 E
New York, New York 10017   (212) 661-0178
Principal officers: Mary Anne Kolidas, Director

Permanent staff: 1   Membership: NI
Date founded: 1948   Membership dues: NI
Branches: NI   Scope: national

Nature of organizations: social

Affiliations: American Near East Refugee Aid

Comments: The organization assists Palestinian refugees by collecting and distributing medical supplies to the Middle East. It also sponsors scholarships in vocational training through the U.N. Relief and Works Agency Centers.

AMERICAN MOSLEM ASSOCIATION
9945 West Vernor Highway
Dearborn, Michigan 48120

AMERICAN NEAR EAST REFUGEE AID (ANERA)
733 15th Street, N.W.
Washington, D.C. 20005 (202) 347-2558

Principal officers: John P. Richardson, Executive Vice President

Permanent staff: 6	Membership: 600
Date founded: 1968	Membership dues: NI
Branches: NI	Scope: national

Nature of organization: social and economic

Publications: *ANERA Newsletter* (bimonthly); *Newsline* (irregular)

Affiliations: American Aid for Arab Refugees; Musa Alami Foundations; Pal-Aid International; U.S. OMEN

Major conventions/meetings: annual

Comments: The organization attempts to aid Palestinian refugees and other needy Arabs and to acquaint Americans with the Arab refugee problem. It sponsors fund-raising appeals, and it prepares and distributes materials explaining their relief program. In 1971 it absorbed the American Middle East Rehabilitation, which now serves as a division of this organization.

AMERICAN RAMALLAH CLUB OF CLEVELAND (RAMALLAH CLUB)
2779 Carmen Drive
Rocky River, Ohio 44116 (216) 333-8425

Principal officers: Peter Salah, President
Labib Hishmeh, Vice President
Salwa Gazala, Secretary

Permanent staff: 8	Membership: 47
Date founded: 1960	Membership dues: $20.00
Branches: NI	Scope: local

Special requirements for membership: 18 years of age

Nature of organization: social, educational, charitable

Publications: none

Affiliations: American Ramallah Federation; Midwest Federation of American Syrian-Lebanese Clubs

Comments: Socially oriented. Members meet to discuss educational and charitable programs. It supports organizations that promote American-Arab relations as well as those that offer aid to Arabs in the Middle East.

AMERICAN RAMALLAH FEDERATION
P.O. Box 116
Dearborn Heights, Michigan 48127

AMERICAN SYRIAN LEBANESE ASSOCIATION
11203 Nashville
Detroit, Michigan 48205

AMERICAN WOMEN FOR THE MIDDLE EAST (NAJDA)
P.O. Box 6051
Alborny, California 94706

AMVETS AMERICAN SYRIAN LEBANESE POST
13718 Woodward
Highland Park, Michigan 48203

ARAB-AMERICAN ASSOCIATION
439 Warren Avenue
Cincinnati, Ohio 45220   (513) 751-3603

Principal officers: Victor S. Asfour, President
Adib Tabri, Executive Vice President
Leila Habiby, Executive Secretary

Permanent staff: none   Membership: 61
Date founded: 1967   Membership dues: $20 (annual) family;
Branches: none $10 (annual) individual; $5 (annual)
                                                                     student

Special requirements for membership: none

Nature of organization: social, educational, cultural, philanthropic

Publications: *Arab-American Association Newsletter*, 1972– (10 issues per year)

Major conventions/meetings: monthly board conference and monthly activities meeting

Comments: This organization is non-profit, non-political, and non-sectarian in nature. Its
principal objective is to stimulate further understanding between the American and
Arab communities through the sponsoring of educational and social activities. Funds
are raised in order to provide for the educational needs of Arab refugee children. The
organization participates in local civic affairs in Cincinnati, sponsors benefit dances,
and provides speakers to local civic groups and schools.

ARAB AMERICAN UNIVERSITY GRADUATES
Jeffersonian Building
Detroit, Michigan 48214   (313) 345-7985

Principal officers: Subhi Abdel Satar

Permanent staff: NI   Membership: NI
Date founded: NI   Membership dues: NI
Branches: NI   Scope: national

Comments: The purpose of this organization is to provide opportunities for members to meet
and discuss the political and social affairs of the Arab world.

ARAB AMERICAN WOMEN'S FRIENDSHIP ASSOCIATION (AAWFA)
4 Washington Square Village
New York, New York 10012   (212) 777-1793

Principal officers: Aida Malouf, President
Litia Namoura, Executive Vice President
Ruth Berger, Executive Secretary

Permanent staff: NI   Membership: 50
Date founded: 1966   Membership dues: $10.00 (annual)
Branches: NI   Scope: local

Special requirements for membership: none

Nature of organization: social, cultural

Publications: none

Major conventions/meetings: none

Comments: Prime objective is the promotion of friendship between women of the Arab and
American worlds. Activities are centered around social and cultural gatherings such as
teas, luncheons, lectures, and films. Members sponsor orphans in Jerusalem through
Project Ryait in Kokomo, Indiana. Aid is also provided to the needy upon a submitted
request. Membership includes wives of Arab diplomats.

ARAB INFORMATION CENTER
405 Lexington Avenue
New York, New York 10017

Comments: See the annotation for the next entry.

ARAB INFORMATION CENTER–LEAGUE OF ARAB STATES
234 World Trade Center
San Francisco, California 94111   (415) 986-5911

Principal officers: Ibrahim Tawasha, Director

Permanent staff: 2   Membership: all members of League
Date founded: 1955   of Arab States
Branches: 5 in U.S.; 1 in Canada; others in   Membership dues: none
  Europe and South America   Scope: international

Special requirements for membership: none

Nature of organization: cultural, political, educational, informational

Publications: *Palestine Digest*, 1971– (monthly). Also publishes numerous books and
    pamphlets.

Affiliations: various Arab-American organizations

Comments: Although AIC is international in scope, it merits listing because it is affiliated
    with many Arabic-American clubs here in the United States. Furthermore, AIC acts
    as the general information office in the United States with respect to the distribution
    of data concerning the League of Arab States. The organization provides speakers to
    lecture in schools and also makes available films on the Mid-East situation. Maintains
    an extensive library and archives.

ARAB REFUGEE RELIEF FUND OF WESTERN PENNSYLVANIA
P.O. Box 7191
Pittsburgh, Pennsylvania 15213

Permanent staff: NI   Membership: NI
Date founded: NI   Membership dues: NI
Branches: NI   Scope: regional

THE ARAB WOMEN'S UNION
P.O. Box 153
Dearborn Heights, Michigan 48121

Principal officers: Wafa Salah

Nature of organization: charitable, cultural

Comments: The major objective of this organization is to provide activities that promote Arabic
    culture; it also performs charitable acts to families in need.

ARABIC-ISLAMIC COMMUNITY
Hashmie Hall
10401 Dix
Dearborn, Michigan 48120

ASSOCIATION OF ARAB-AMERICAN UNIVERSITY GRADUATES (AAUG)
P.O. Box 85
North Dartmouth, Massachusetts 02747   (617) 994-2235

Principal officers: Hassan Haddad, President
                   Ibrahim Oweiss, Vice President
                   Nazik Kazimi, Secretary

Permanent staff: 2   Membership: 1,000
Date founded: 1967   Membership dues: $25.00/$15.00/
Branches: 2 regional; 7 state; 4 local $5.00, depending on membership
                                           category
                                           Scope: United States and Canada

Special requirements for membership: university graduates of Arab origin

Nature of organization: cultural, educational, professional, scholarly, scientific

Publications: *AAUG Newsletter*, 1968– (bimonthly); *Membership Directory* (annual). Also
    publishes books.

Affiliations: none

ASSOCIATION OF ARAB-AMERICAN UNIVERSITY GRADUATES (AAUG) (cont'd)
Major conventions/meetings: annual
Comments: Promotes activities that serve to strengthen the bonds of understanding between
Arab and American peoples. Encourages the establishment of links among Arab-American
professionals and promotes cooperation in their respective professions. Aims at
disseminating accurate scientific and cultural information about the Arab world. The
organization also assists in the development of the Arab world by providing the pro-
fessional services of its members. It is non-profit, non-political, and non-sectarian.
Sponsors seminars, study groups, and scholarship programs. Awards AAUG Citations.
Maintains AAUG historical archives.

BOSTON SYRIAN WOMEN'S CLUB
287 Commonwealth Avenue
Boston, Massachusetts 12115

CEDARS OF LEBANON BAR ASSOCIATION
Cadillac Tower, 20th Floor
Detroit, Michigan 48226

CHALDEAN IRAQUI ASSOCIATION
20101 Burt Road
Detroit, Michigan 48219

CITIZEN'S CLUB OF UNION CITY
700 79th Street
North Bergen, New Jersey 07047

COMMITTEE TO SUPPORT MIDDLE EAST LIBERATION
P.O. Box 948
New York, New York 10027

FEDERATION OF ISLAMIC ASSOCIATIONS IN AMERICA AND CANADA
1711 Riverside Drive
Dearborn, Michigan 48120
Principal officers: Mr. James Kalil, President

Permanent staff: NI	Membership: NI
Date founded: NI	Membership dues: NI
Branches: NI	Scope: regional

FEDERATION OF ISLAMIC ASSOCIATIONS IN THE U.S. AND CANADA
2551 Massachusetts Avenue, N.W.
Washington, D.C. 20008

Permanent staff: NI	Membership: NI
Date founded: NI	Membership dues: NI
Branches: NI	Scope: national

FORUM FOR ARAB ART AND CULTURE
P.O. Box 354
San Francisco, California 94101

GREATER CLEVELAND ASSOCIATION OF ARAB AMERICANS
c/o Joanne Fedor McKenna
21309 Lake Road
Rocky River, Ohio 44116   (216) 526-1138

HATHIHE RAMALLAH
P.O. Box 116
Dearborn Heights, Michigan 48127
Principal officers: Nadim S. Ajlouny, President
                     William M. Harb, Secretary

Permanent staff: 14   Membership: NI
Date founded: 1952   Membership dues: $10.00 (annual)
Branches: none, but correspondents in major   Scope: national
   cities

Special requirements for membership: descent from the town of Ramallah in Palestine

Nature of organization: cultural, social, educational, youth

Publications: books and other publications

Affiliations: American Ramallah Federation

Major conventions/meetings: annual convention with the American Ramallah Federation

Comments: In 1952 the Ramallah Federation was established by students from Wayne State
   University, Detroit, Michigan. Its purpose was to serve as a communications network
   to allow emigrants from the town of Ramallah, Palestine, to keep in touch with each
   other. The Federation sponsors scholarships, youth activities, and welfare programs.
   Organized as the American Ramallah Federation in 1959.

INTERNATIONAL ARAB FEDERATION
302 East Central Avenue   (419) 729-4539 or
Toledo, Ohio 43608   (419) 729-4400
Principal officers: Joseph Hayeck, President
                     Deib Hady, Vice President
                     Souheil Hamoui, Secretary General
Permanent staff: 15   Membership: NI
Date founded: 1967   Membership dues: $10.00 (annual)
Branches: NI   Scope: international

Special requirements for membership: Arabs, or persons of Arab origin, or those interested
   in the Arab cause

Nature of organization: cultural, political, social, educational

Publications: *Arab Tribune*, 1972– (monthly)

Major conventions/meetings: annual convention

Comments: The purpose of the IAF is to promote the unity of Arab immigrants throughout
   the world. It also defends the legitimate rights of Arab immigrants in their host countries. Encourages the establishment of Arabic schools, participation in community
   affairs, preservation of Arabic heritage, and the strengthening of the economic, cultural,
   social, and touristic relationships between the host countries and the Arab world. Maintains a large library and archival materials on the Arab world.

LEBANESE AMERICAN CULTURAL SOCIETY
126 Chestnut Street
Philadelphia, Pennsylvania 19106

LEBANON AMERICAN SOCIAL SOCIETY
13461 Jos. Campua
Detroit, Michigan 48212   (313) 892-9570

MIDWEST FEDERATION OF AMERICAN SYRIAN-LEBANESE CLUBS
9119 Brookpark Road
Parma, Ohio 44129

THE MUSLIM STUDENTS' ASSOCIATION OF THE UNITED STATES AND CANADA (M.S.A.)
3702 West 11th Avenue
Gary, Indiana 46404 (219) 949-1859

Principal officers: E. A. Abugideiri, President
M. Ataur Rahman, Vice President
Mohammed A. Badr, Secretary

Permanent staff: 10 Membership: 3,000
Date founded: 1963 Membership dues: $5.00
Branches: 8 regional; 130 local Scope: national

Special requirements for membership: Muslims-full membership; non-Muslims-honorary membership

Nature of organization: social, educational, cultural, religious, sports, fraternal, scholarly, youth

Publications: *Alittihad*, 1964– (quarterly); *MSA News*, 1964– (monthly). Also publishes books and pamphlets.

Affiliations: local chapters in various cities

Major conventions/meetings: annual convention

Comments: Primarily religious in nature. Promotes the Islamic traditions among its members and encourages cooperation between Muslims and non-Muslims. Sponsors camps for adults and children. Holds training sessions and workshops.

NATIONAL ASSOCIATION OF ARAB-AMERICANS
1834 "K" Street, N.W.
Washington, D.C. 20006

Permanent staff: NI Membership: NI
Date founded: NI Membership dues: NI
Branches: NI Scope: national

ORGANIZATION OF ARAB STUDENTS IN THE USA & CANADA (OAS)
2929 Broadway, 5th Floor
New York, New York 10025

Principal officers: Nabeel A. Shaarth, President

Permanent staff: 2 Membership: 7,000
Date founded: 1952 Membership dues: NI
Branches: 102 local Scope: national

Special requirements for membership: college student of Arabic descent

Nature of organization: cultural, educational, scholarly

Publications: *News* (bimonthly); *Arab Journal*, 1953– (quarterly); *Yearbook* (annual). Also publishes informational statements and reports.

Major conventions/meetings: annual

Comments: The organization aims to preserve the Arab heritage and to promote Arab interests in the United States and better understanding of the Arab people and situation. It sponsors research on all aspects of life in the Middle East and North Africa.

PALESTINE ARAB DELEGATION
441 Lexington Avenue, Room 509
New York, New York 10017 (212) 682-7353

Principal officers: Issa Nakhleh, Director

Permanent staff: NI Membership: NI
Date founded: 1956 Membership dues: NI
Branches: NI Scope: national

Nature of organization: political

Publications: releases and pamphlets

Comments: The main purpose of this organization is to familiarize the United Nations General Assembly with the problems of the Palestinian Arabs.

PALESTINE LIBERATION ORGANIZATION
101 Park Avenue
New York, New York 10017

RAMALLAH MEN AND WOMEN'S SOCIETY OF DETROIT
29154 Meadowlark
Livonia, Michigan 48237   (313) 425-8489

Principal officers: Issa Ajlouny

Special requirements for membership: must be from Ramallah in Palestine

Nature of organization: social, political

Comments: The major objective of this organization is to provide social activities for members;
some of its programs are political in nature.

THE RAMALLAH YOUTH SOCIETY
31206 Schoolcraft
Livonia, Michigan 48150

SOUTHERN FEDERATION OF SYRIAN-LEBANESE AMERICAN CLUBS
4143 Marlowe
Houston, Texas 77005

Permanent staff: NI   Membership: NI
Date founded: NI   Membership dues: NI
Branches: NI   Scope: regional

SYRIAN-LEBANESE AMERICAN ASSOCIATION
117 Pine Street
Lowell, Massachusetts 01851

SYRIAN-LEBANESE CLUBS
127 Boylston East
Seattle, Washington 98102

SYRIAN-LEBANON SOCIETY OF NEW HAVEN, INC.
449 Central Avenue
New Haven, Connecticut 06515

SYRIAN ORTHODOX YOUTH ORGANIZATION
c/o 358 Mountain Road
Englewood, New Jersey 07631

Principal officers: Most Rev. Metropolitan Archbishop Philip Saliba
Alan Abraham, President
Louis Courey, Vice President
Georgette Nader, Secretary
Priscilla Deban, Treasurer

Permanent staff: NI   Membership: NI
Date founded: ca. 1939   Membership dues: NI
Branches: 6 in Canada and the U.S.   Scope: United States and Canada

Special requirements for membership: any person of the Orthodox faith under the jurisdiction of the Syrian Antiochian Orthodox Archdiocese

Nature of organization: religious, charitable

Publications: *S.O.Y.O. Digest*, 1957– (monthly); regional newsletters

Affiliations: Council of Eastern Orthodox Youth Leaders of the Americas

Major conventions/meetings: annual meeting of the council

Comments: Major goals are to establish formal structures (choirs, Sunday schools, contests,
etc.) that will help the Antiochian Orthodox Christian Archdiocese reach its membership and serve its needs. SOYO conducts regional Parish Life Conferences; regional
organizations award scholarships to members and support charities. The recording
secretary of the Council keeps all records and archives (on a regional basis).

UNITED AMERICAN-ARAB APPEAL
15 Arrowood Road
Cohasset, Massachusetts 02025

UNITED AMERICAN-ARAB CONGRESS (UAAC)
P.O. Box 3337
Los Angeles, California 90028   (213) 467-1314

Principal officers: Spear Sayegh, President
                       Mustafa Siam, Secretary
                       Ali Kalla, Treasurer

Permanent staff: NI   Membership: NI
Date founded: 1967   Membership dues: $12.00 (annual)
Branches: NI   Scope: national

Special requirements for membership: Arabic ancestry and a U.S. citizen

Nature of organization: political, cultural

Publications: publishes periodicals

Affiliations: Federation of American-Arab Organizations

Major conventions/meetings: annual

Comments: The major objective is to organize the Arab-Americans and to promote deeper
     understanding between Arabs and Americans. It provides information on the Middle
     East problems and particularly on the Palestinian problems from an Arab point of view.

UNITED HOLY LAND FUND
503 East Washington Street
Syracuse, New York 13202   (315) 474-4628

Principal officers: George T. Mahshie, President
                       Ibrahim Yashruti, Vice President
                       Osamah Toukan, Secretary

Permanent staff: none   Membership: 22
Date founded: 1967   Membership dues: none
Branches: yes—number not given   Scope: national

Special requirements for membership: none

Nature of organization: philanthropic

Publications: none

Affiliations: Red Crescent Society

Major conventions/meetings: quarterly national and local meetings

Comments: Solicits funds on a monthly basis from members and raises funds by holding
     social events; distributes the money to philanthropic organizations in the Middle East
     such as orphanages and the Red Crescent Society. Also helps needy Arab refugee
     students continue their education.

UNITED NORTH LEBANESE SOCIETY
9917 Berkshire
Detroit, Michigan 48224   (313) 839-4018

Principal officers: Ms. Labbie Assaf

Nature of organizations: charitable, political

Major conventions/meetings: monthly meetings; annual banquet

Comments: The major objective of the organization is to perform benevolent works for
     members and their families and to support Lebanese political candidates for office.

US ORGANIZATION FOR MEDICAL AND EDUCATIONAL NEEDS (US OMEN)
P.O. Box 4581
Sacramento, California 95825   (916) 483-9154

Principal officers: Samira Z. Al-Qazzaz, President
                       Akef Shihabi, Executive Vice President
                       Lillian Herzig, Executive Secretary

Permanent staff: 6   Membership: 39 families
Date founded: 1969   Membership dues: $5.00 (annual)
Branches: 4 (state)   Scope: state

Special requirements for membership: none

Nature of organization: social, educational, cultural, recreational, medical

Publications: *US OMEN Newsletter*, 1972– (monthly)

Affiliations: Anera, Palestinian Red Crescent Society

Major conventions/meetings: semiannual convention

Comments: The principal objective of OMEN is to raise funds in order to provide educational
    and medical aid to Palestinians living in refugee camps.

WORLD LEBANESE CULTURAL UNION
3710 Riviera Street
Marlow Heights, Maryland 20031
Principal officers: Dr. George Hajjar, President

ARGENTINE-AMERICAN ORGANIZATIONS

Additional information on Argentine-American organizations may be
obtained from the office of the Argentinian Embassy (1600 New Hampshire Avenue,
Washington, D.C. 20009).

ARGENTINA ASOCIACION DE LOS ANGELES
5818 West Third
Los Angeles, California 90036

ARGENTINE-AMERICAN CHAMBER OF COMMERCE
11 Broadway
New York, New York 10004   (212) 943-8753

CLUB ARGENTINO
1557 Yorktown
Grosse Point, Michigan 48236

DETROIT ARGENTINE ASSOCIATION (AADD)
P.O. Box 81
Clawson, Michigan 48107   (313) 881-1296

Principal officers: Felix Andrakovich, President
                       C. Iovannitti, Vice President
                       M. Wockenfuss, Secretary

Permanent staff: none   Membership: 100 families
Date founded: 1967   Membership dues: $5.00 (annual)
Branches: none   Scope: state

Special requirements for membership: none

Nature of organization: social, cultural, recreational, sports, fraternal

Publications: *Buletin Informativo de la Asociacion Argentina*, 1967– (quarterly)

DETROIT ARGENTINE ASSOCIATION (AADD)

Affiliations: none

Comments: The Detroit Argentine Association (AADD) strives for close interaction among Argentinians residing in Michigan. It sponsors various cultural, social, and recreational activities. It promotes the retention of Argentinian traditions and customs, and helps newly arrived Argentinians adjust to life in the United States.

ARMENIAN-AMERICAN ORGANIZATIONS

Additional information on Armenian organizations in the United States may be obtained from the National Association for Armenian Studies and Research (175 Mt. Auburn Street, Cambridge, Massachusetts 02138). See also *Diocese of the Armenian Church of America Diary/Directory 1974* (New York: Diocese of the Armenian Church of America, 1974— ; order from: 630 Second Avenue, New York, New York 10016) *Greater Cleveland Nationalities Directory 1974* (Cleveland: Sun Newspapers and the Nationalities Services Center, 1974) and *Ethnic Directory I* (Detroit: Southeastern Michigan Regional Ethnic Heritage Studies Center, 1973).

AMERICAN NATIONAL COMMITTEE TO AID HOMELESS ARMENIANS

240 Stockton Street
San Francisco, California 94108   (415) 362-3903

Principal officers: George M. Mardikian, President

Permanent staff: NI	Membership: NI
Date founded: 1948	Membership dues: NI
Branches: 15 local	Scope: national

Nature of organization: charitable

Comments: The purpose of the organization is to help Armenian refugees and to resettle Iron Curtain escapees in the United States, Canada, South America, and Australia.

ARMENIAN AMERICAN VETERANS' MEMORIAL ASSOCIATION

22050 Southfield Road
Southfield, Michigan 48075   (313) 356-2701

THE ARMENIAN ASSEMBLY CHARITABLE TRUST

522 21st Street, N.W., Suite 120
Washington, D.C. 20006   (202) 833-1367

Principal officers: Robert A. Kaloosdian, First Vice Chairman
Dennis Papazian, Second Vice Chairman
Avedis K. Sanjian, Secretary
Harry Sachaklian, Treasurer

Permanent staff: 3	Membership: 150
Date founded: 1972	Membership dues: not applicable
Branches: 6 regional	Scope: national

Special requirements for membership: invitation from Assembly

Nature of organization: educational, cultural, professional, scholarly, charitable, political

Publications: Publishes books and other materials.

Major conventions/meetings: sexennial assembly of members

THE ARMENIAN ASSEMBLY CHARITABLE TRUST (cont'd)

Comments: Organized in order to provide a common meeting ground for all of the organizations and institutions of the Armenian-American community. A non-profit organization that is charitable and educational in nature. Main objectives are to provide a
forum and national framework for the promotion, cooperation, and coordination
of the Armenian community; to promote awareness and appreciation of the Armenian
cultural and historical identity; to provide a forum through which Armenians can
speak on issues of concern; to encourage research, data collection, and dissemination
of information dealing with Armenians, and with their history, education, culture,
and religious life; and to assist Armenian subjects whose basic civil and human rights
are violated. The organization maintains both a library and archives on Armenian affairs.

ARMENIAN CATHOLIC COMMUNITY
343 West 25th Street
New York, New York 10001   (212) 924-2116

ARMENIAN CHURCH YOUTH ORGANIZATION OF AMERICA (ACYOA)
630 Second Avenue
New York, New York 10016   (212) 686-0710

Principal officers: Hovhannes Kasparian, Executive Secretary

Permanent staff: 2   Membership: 1,000
Date founded: 1946   Membership dues: NI
Branches: 38 local chapters   Scope: national

Special requirements for membership: young people between the ages of 14 and 26 who are
members of the Armenian Church

Nature of organization: religious, educational, cultural, social

Publications: *Armenian Guardian*, 1946– (monthly); *Directory of Chapter Executives* (annual)

Major conventions/meetings: annual convention

Comments: The organization attempts to preserve Armenian culture and heritage in the
United States by providing various social, athletic, recreational, cultural, and religious
activities for Armenian youth. It also sponsors educational programs and provides
scholarship funds for youth of Armenian descent.

ARMENIAN CHURCH YOUTH ORGANIZATION OF CALIFORNIA (ACYO)
1201 North Vine Street
Hollywood, California 90038   (213) 466-5265

Principal officers: Bishop Vatche Housepian, President
                       Laurie Menendian, Chairman
                       Betty Barsamian, Secretary

Permanent staff: none   Membership: 400
Date founded: 1945   Membership dues: decided by local
Branches: 15   chapter; a fixed minimum goes to the
                                               Central Council
                                             Scope: state

Special requirements for membership: at least 12 years of age and baptized in the Armenian
Church

Nature of organization: educational, cultural, religious

Publications: *Central Council News*, 1952– (quarterly); also publishes books

Affiliations: Western Diocese of the Armenian Church of North America

Major conventions/meetings: annual convention

Comments: Primarily concerned with teaching and encouraging the practice of religious
activities in accordance with the doctrines and traditions of the Armenian Church.
Also engages in promoting the study and appreciation of the Armenian cultural
heritage. Maintains archival materials consisting primarily of the Central Council's
records. Sponsors special religious retreats, cultural and educational programs, and

ARMENIAN CHURCH YOUTH ORGANIZATION OF CALIFORNIA (ACYO) (cont'd)

social and sports affairs. All these activities are sponsored locally, as well as state-wide. Offers general and seminarian scholarships to students. Presents an annual Achievement Award.

ARMENIAN CHURCHES SPORTS ASSOCIATION (ACSA)

c/o Commissioner Peter Jelalian
33-31 73rd Street
Jackson Heights, New York 11372

Principal officers: Peter Jelalian, Commissioner

Permanent staff: NI	Membership: 120
Date founded: 1967	Membership dues: none
Branches: 10	Scope: regional

Special requirements for membership: youth who are members of the Armenian churches in the area

Nature of organization: sports, social

Affiliations: with member churches

Major conventions/meetings: annual tournaments in various sports

Comments: The association promotes competitive sports events among the Armenian youth belonging to member churches; sponsors annual tournaments in basketball, track, and bowling.

ARMENIAN CULTURAL ASSOCIATION

P.O. Box 550, Lenox Hill Station
New York, New York 10016   (212) 249-0931

Principal officers: Herand Markarian, President

Permanent staff: NI	Membership: 200
Date founded: 1967	Membership dues: $5.00, $3.00
Branches: NI	students
	Scope: NI

Nature of organization: cultural, social, educational

Publications: *ECHO* newsletter, about four times per year

Comments: The intent is to promote the Armenian heritage and culture in the United States. It sponsors a chorus, classes and performances in Armenian folk dancing, performances of Armenian plays, and lectures. It provides social activities for uniting Armenians in the area. A library is maintained.

ARMENIAN CULTURAL CENTER

22001 Northwestern Highway
Southfield, Michigan 48075

ARMENIAN CULTURAL CENTER OF FOREST HILLS, INC.

71-53 Manse Street
Forest Hills, New York 11375   (212) 268-3111

Principal officers: Archak Sahakian, Secretary

Permanent staff: 9	Membership: 90
Date founded: 1971	Membership dues: $10 (annual); $2.00
Branches: NI	(annual) students
	Scope: regional

Special requirements for membership: Armenian descent

Nature of organization: cultural, social, educational

Comments: The organization provides lectures and social activities for members; a community center building is planned.

ARMENIAN DEMOCRATIC LEAGUE
755 Mt. Auburn Street
Watertown, Massachusetts 02172

ARMENIAN DEMOCRATIC LIBERAL ORGANIZATION
755 Mt. Auburn Street
Watertown, Massachusetts 02172   (617) 924-4420

ARMENIAN-DETROIT CULTURAL ORGANIZATION
17505 Winora
Southfield, Michigan 48075   (313) 356-0457

ARMENIAN EDUCATIONAL FOUNDATION (AEF)
5300 Santa Monica Boulevard
Los Angeles, California 90029   (213) 462-8257
Principal officers: Puzant Granian, Executive Secretary

Permanent staff: NI   Membership: 40
Date founded: 1950   Membership dues: NI
Branches: NI   Scope: NI

Nature of organization: educational, charitable

Major conventions/meetings: annual symposium

Comments: The aim of the organization is to preserve the Armenian culture in the United
     States by providing social, cultural, literary and musical activities for its members. It
     supports Armenian schools in the United States and other countries, and it grants
     scholarships to youth of Armenian descent.

ARMENIAN GENERAL ATHLETIC UNION (AGAU)
116 38th Street
Union City, New Jersey 07087   (201) 865-0057
Principal officers: Jack Takakjian, President
                       Shah Arslan, Secretary
                       M. Megerdichian, Editor-Trustee

Permanent staff: 4   Membership: 500
Date founded: 1921   Membership dues: $5.00
Branches: NI   Scope: national

Special requirements for membership: Armenian ancestry

Nature of organization: cultural, educational, sports, youth

Publications: *AGAU Bulletin*, 1927– (quarterly)

Major conventions/meetings: annaul convention

Comments: Although AGAU is primarily concerned with developing athletics among
     Armenians, it also promotes social, cultural, and educational activities within Armenian
     communities. Provides indoor sports and recreational facilities, promotes lectures and
     debates, sponsors annual tournaments, and awards trophies and medals. Also has
     established a special scholarship fund.

ARMENIAN GENERAL BENEVOLENT UNION OF AMERICA (AGBU of America)
628 Second Avenue
New York, New York 10016   (212) 684-7530
Principal officers: Edward Mardigian, President
                       Lionel Galstaun, Vice President
                       Alice Bashian, Secretary

Permanent staff: 18   Membership: 8,000
Date founded: 1906   Membership dues: $10.00 (annual)
Branches: 101 local   Scope: national

Special requirements for membership: Armenian ancestry

Nature of organization: cultural, educational, youth

ARMENIAN GENERAL BENEVOLENT UNION OF
AMERICA (AGBU of America) (cont'd)

Publications: *The Prompter* (Hoosharar), 1906– (semimonthly); *Ararat*, 1960– (quarterly). The Union has also published other materials.

Affiliations: The World Body of Armenian General Benevolent Unions

Major conventions/meetings: National and District Annual conventions; chapter annual meetings

Comments: The association aids poor and needy Armenians. It promotes the incorporation of Armenian studies in the curriculum of private schools that have a large Armenian student body and strives to create cultural centers in areas of substantial Armenian population. It encourages the dissemination of instructive materials on Armenian culture and heritage to non-Armenian Americans, sponsors two primary schools, a secondary school, two summer camps for children, and special Armenian studies programs in a few universities. Presents Benefactor and Merit Awards to members who make outstanding contributions of funds or service; a library collection of over 1,000 volumes is maintained, plus special historical material.

ARMENIAN LITERARY SOCIETY
114 First Street
Yonkers, New York 10704   (914) 237-5751

Principal officers: Mr. K. N. Magarian, Secretary

Permanent staff: NI   Membership: 400
Date founded: 1956   Membership dues: $5.00 (annual)
Branches: NI   Scope: NI

Special requirements for membership: individuals of Armenian descent interested in Armenian literature

Nature of organization: educational

Publications: *Kir ou Kirk*, 1956– (quarterly)

Major conventions/meetings: biennial

Comments: The primary purpose of this society is to help Armenian authors by promoting and distributing their publications. It conducts lectures about Armenian literature and culture, and it sends books to libraries, schools, and student organizations in the United States and abroad. It has compiled lists of books in print relating to Armenia and Armenians.

ARMENIAN MISSIONARY ASSOCIATION OF AMERICA (AMAA)
140 Forest Avenue
Paramus, New Jersey 07652   (201) 265-2607/8

Principal officers: George Philibosian, President
                       Dr. M. S. Agbabian, Vice President
                       Rev. Dr. G. H. Chopourian, Secretary

Permanent staff: 5   Membership: 4,000
Date founded: 1918   Membership dues: $5.00 or more
Branches: 22 regional   Scope: national

Special requirements for membership: dues

Nature of organization: educational, cultural, religious

Publications: *The Armenian-American Outlook*, 1962– (3 times a year); *Newsletter* (4 times a year). Also publishes books.

Affiliations: The Stephen Philibosian Foundation; Armenian Evangelical Union of North America; Armenian Evangelical Union of France; Union of Armenian Evangelical Churches–Near East.

Major conventions/meetings: annual meeting at the end of each fiscal year

Comments: Formed by the Union of the Armenian Evangelical Churches in the United States in order to provide religious, social, and economic aid to persons whose lives were disrupted as a result of Turkish massacres. Although AMAA was primarily founded as a relief organization, it now serves as an educational institution. In 1956 the

ARMENIAN MISSIONARY ASSOCIATION OF AMERICA (AMAA) (cont'd)
>Association founded a degree-giving college in Beirut, Lebanon, which at the present time has over 650 students. AMAA is active in the Middle East, France, and South America. Sponsors teacher training programs and awards scholarships. Maintains a library and archives, which contain a collection of ancient books on the history of Armenia.

ARMENIAN PROGRESSIVE LEAGUE OF AMERICA (APLA)
>151 West 25th Street
>New York, New York 10001   (212) 929-8335

Publications: *Lraper*, 1937– (semiweekly)

Comments: APLA's aim is to inform Armenians living in America about life in their homeland. This organization also works to restore democracy and peace to Armenia.

ARMENIAN RELIEF SOCIETY, INC. (ARS)
>212 Stuart Street
>Boston, Massachusetts 02116   (617) 542-0528

Principal officers: Seta Terzian, President
>Lisa Dogdigian, Executive Vice President
>Sona Gregian, Executive Secretary

Permanent staff: 2   Membership: 16,000
Date founded: 1910   Membership dues: $10.00 (annual)
Branches: 67 in North America   Scope: national and international

Special requirements for membership: Armenian, age 18 years or older

Nature of organization: educational, cultural, humanitarian relief

Publications: *Armenian Heart*, 1940– (quarterly); also
>publishes books and pamphlets

Affiliations: Armenian Revolutionary Federation; Armenian Cultural Association; Armenian Youth Federation

Major conventions/meetings: annual convention

Comments: During its early stages, this organization was dedicated to the care of the sick and destitute survivors of the Armenian population in Turkey. Later, permanent institutions (clinics, dispensaries, summer camps and schools) were founded. At the present, welfare, social service, educational, and cultural programs are maintained in order to preserve the Armenian ethnic identity. The Society sponsors summer and day camps, teacher training programs, Armenian studies programs, cultural and recreational activities. Offers grants to universities for courses on Armenian language and culture. Awards scholarships to Armenian students. Presents annual honorary awards to members with 25 and 50 years of service. Maintains organizational archives.

ARMENIAN REVOLUTIONARY FEDERATION OF AMERICA (ARFA)
>212 Stuart Street
>Boston, Massachusetts 02116   (617) 542-3650

Principal officers: Minas Toloyan, Executive Secretary

Permanent staff: NI   Membership: NI
Date founded: 1891   Membership dues: NI
Branches: NI   Scope: national

Nature of organization: cultural

Publications: *Hairenik*, 1899– (daily except Sunday and Monday); *Asbarez*, 1908– (semiweekly); *Hairenik* (in Armenian; monthly); *Armenian Review*, 1947– (quarterly)

Major conventions/meetings: annual convention, always in July

Comments: Works to preserve the Armenian heritage and spirit. Celebrates various Armenian holidays. Strongly anti-communist; dedicated to a "free" Armenia.

ARMENIAN SCIENTIFIC ASSOCIATION OF AMERICA
30 Half Moon Lane
Irvington, New York 10533   (914) 591-7454
Principal officers: Dr. V. D. Migrdichian, President
                       Dr. P. Z. Bedoukian, Vice President
                       N. A. Almoian, Secretary

Permanent staff: none   Membership: 50
Date founded: 1928   Membership dues: $5.00 (annual)
Branches: NI   Scope: national

Special requirements for membership: college degree

Nature of organization: educational

Publications: *Bulletin of the Armenian Scientific Association of America*, 1968– (semi-annual)

Comments: The organization aims to bring ethnic Armenian scientists and scholars together for discussion and to establish a cultural exchange with ethnic Armenian professionals in other parts of the world. It aids scholars by providing financial assistance, books, journals, and necessary equipment.

ARMENIAN STUDENTS' ASSOCIATION OF AMERICA, INC. (ASA)
P.O. Box 1557
New York, New York 10001

Principal officers: John Dilsizian, President
                       Elizabeth Hamoian, Vice President
                       Gloria Keleshian, Secretary

Permanent staff: NI   Membership: 1,000+
Date founded: 1910   Membership dues: $5.00 (annual)
Branches: 10 regional   Scope: regional

Special requirements for membership: Armenian descent and high school graduate

Nature of organization: cultural, economic, youth

Publications: *ASA News*, 1948– (quarterly)

Major conventions/meetings: annual national convention

Comments: Primarily educational, cultural, and philanthropic in nature. Sponsors lectures and artistic projects. Awards scholarships and provides loans to students. Presents annual awards in the areas of humanities, science, and citizenship. Maintains archival materials dealing with organizational matters.

ARMENIAN WOMEN'S WELFARE ASSOCIATION
431 Pond Street
Jamaica Plain, Massachusetts 02130   (617) 522-2600

Permanent staff: NI   Membership: 500
Date founded: 1921   Membership dues: NI
Branches: NI   Scope: NI

Special requirements for membership: Armenian women interested in helping with charitable works

Nature of organization: social, charitable

Major conventions/meetings: annual meeting, always held in May, in Boston

Comments: The organization provides social and charitable activities for its members. It supports an Armenian nursing home for the elderly.

ARMENIAN YOUTH FEDERATION OF AMERICA (AYF)
304-A School Street
Watertown, Massachusetts 02172   (617) 926-3860

Permanent staff: 1   Membership: 3,000
Date founded: NI   Membership dues: NI
Branches: 60 local chapters   Scope: national

ARMENIAN YOUTH FEDERATION OF AMERICA (AYF) (cont'd)

Special requirements for membership: North American young people (13-30 years of age) of Armenian parentage.

Publications: *Armenian Weekly*, 1933– (formerly *ARF Tzeghagrons*; weekly)

Affiliations: Armenian Revolutionary Federation

Major conventions/meetings: regional conferences and an annual national olympic

Comments: The objective of the Federation, a youth branch of the Armenian Revolutionary Federation, is to achieve a free Armenia. In addition, it supports youth camp programs in Massachusetts and California and grants financial assistance to Armenian students in various fields.

THE BAIKAR ASSOCIATION
755 Mt. Auburn Street
Watertown, Massachusetts 02172

Publications: *Baikar*, 1922– (daily); *The Armenian Mirror-Spectator*, 1934– (weekly)

EDUCATIONAL ASSOCIATION OF MALATIA, CENTRAL EXECUTIVE BOARD
12813 Gay Avenue
Cleveland, Ohio 44105

Publications: *Pap Oukhti*, 1935– (quarterly)

HAIRENIK ASSOCIATION
212 Stuart Street
Boston, Massachusetts 02116

Publications: *The Armenian Review*, 1947– (quarterly); *The Armenian Weekly*, 1933– (weekly)

HUNCHAKIAN SOCIAL DEMOCRATIC PARTY
P.O. Box 9, Madison Square Station
New York, New York 10010   (212) 675-7138

Publications: *Yeritasard Hayastan*, 1903– (weekly)

KNIGHTS OF VARTAN, INC.
85 Hillside Road
Watertown, Massachusetts 02172

Principal officers: Rev. Dr. Youhanna Mugar, Grand Secretary

Permanent staff: NI   Membership: NI
Date founded: 1948   Membership dues: NI
Branches: NI   Scope: national

Nature of organization: social

Major conventions/meetings: annaul

NATIONAL ASSOCIATION FOR ARMENIAN STUDIES AND RESEARCH (NAASR)
175 Mt. Auburn Street
Cambridge, Massachusetts 02138   (617) 876-7630

Principal officers: Manoog S. Young, Chairman, Board of Directors

Permanent staff: NI   Membership: 2,500
Date founded: 1955   Membership dues: NI
Branches: NI   Scope: national

Nature of organization: educational, scholarly

Publications: *Report of NAASR* (quarterly); *Bulletin for the Advancement of Armenian Studies* (semiannual)

Major conventions/meetings: annual convention

NATIONAL ASSOCIATION FOR ARMENIAN STUDIES AND RESEARCH (NAASR) (cont'd)

Comments: The goal of the organization is to maintain a continuum of scholarly research and interest in Armenian studies in the United States. It has endowed a Chair of Armenian Studies at Harvard University, which supports a learning and research center there. Similar programs are encouraged at other major universities—e.g., University of California at Los Angeles and Columbia University. Emphasis is on Armenian history, culture, and language classes; a 500-volume library is maintained.

THE NEW YAZGAD ASSOCIATION
23600 Evergreen
Southfield, Michigan 48075

ORDER OF AMARANTH (O of A)
164 Mountain Avenue
Westfield, New Jersey 07090

Principal officers: Mrs. Elsie S. Tomasko, Grand Secretary

Permanent staff: NI	Membersnip: 95,231
Date founded: 1873	Membership dues: NI
Branches: NI	Scope: national

Special requirements for membership: wife, mother, daughter, adopted daughter, or grand-daughter of a master mason

Publications: *Roster* (annual)

Major conventions/meetings: annual convention, always in May, always in Atlantic City, New Jersey

Comments: Masonic organization

SOCIETY OF AFKERETSIS
30370 Vernor Drive
Birmingham, Michigan 48010

THE TEKEYAN CULTURAL ASSOCIATION
c/o Mr. A. Poladian
628 Second Avenue
New York, New York 10016

UNION OF MARASH ARMENIANS
36-33 169th Street
Flushing, New York 11358

Publications: *Germanik*, 1930– (quarterly)

UNITED ASSOCIATION OF TOMARZA
c/o St. Mesrob Armenian Apostolic Church Hall
4605 Erie Street
Racine, Wisconsin 53402

Principal officers: Murad Gengozian, President
Helen Kalagian, Vice President
Toros Madaghjian, Secretary

Permanent staff: 7	Membership: 40
Date founded: 1909	Membership dues: $2.00 (annual)
Branches: none	Scope: local

Special requirements for membership: native or descendant of Tomarza (or related by marriage to a native or descendant)

Nature of organization: social, charitable

Publications: none

Affiliations: none

UNITED ASSOCIATION OF TOMARZA (cont'd)

Major conventions/meetings: none

Comments: Social and charitable association which provides aid to refugees from the city of Tomarza. Aims at preserving the name "Tomarza."

WESTERN ARMENIAN ATHLETIC ASSOCIATION (WAAA)
963 87th Avenue
Oakland, California 94621   (415) 569-9225
Permanent staff: none   Membership: NI
Date founded: 1971   Membership dues: none
Branches: none   Scope: national

Special requirements for membership: none

Nature of organization: sports

Publications: annual olympics program books

Comments: Major goal is to unite the various segments within the Armenian community through athletic competition. Awards an annual athletic scholarship. Maintains special archival materials consisting of competition results.

ASIAN-AMERICAN ORGANIZATIONS

See Bangladesh-American, Chinese-American, Filipino-American, Indian-American, Indonesian-American, Japanese-American, Korean-American, Pakistani-American, Thai-American, and Vietnamese-American Organizations

A comprehensive list of national, regional, and local Asian-American organizations is maintained by the Asian-American Studies Program (School of Social Science, San Jose State University, San Jose, California 95192).

ASSYRIAN-AMERICAN ORGANIZATIONS

Additional information on Assyrian-American organizations may be obtained from the Assyrian American Educational Association, Inc. (8100 Fourth Avenue, North Bergen, New Jersey 07047).

ASSYRIAN AMERICAN ASSOCIATION OF PHILADELPHIA
Sommerdale and Pratt Streets
Philadelphia, Pennsylvania 10124

ASSYRIAN AMERICAN EDUCATIONAL ASSOCIATION, INC. (AAEA)
8100 Fourth Avenue
North Bergen, New Jersey 07047
Principal officers: Malak Tannourji, President
                      Adrika Sharou, Vice President
                      Rose B. Dartley, Corresponding Secretary
Permanent staff: 6   Membership: 25
Date founded: 1949   Membership dues: $6.00 (annual)
Branches: none   Scope: regional

Special requirements for membership: Assyrian-American background

Nature of organization: cultural, social, scholarly, educational

Publications: *Assyrian American Educational Association*, 1954– (annual); also publishes Christmas seals and letters.

ASSYRIAN AMERICAN EDUCATIONAL ASSOCIATION, INC. (AAEA) (cont'd)

Affiliations: Assyrian American Federation

Major conventions/meetings: monthly meetings

Comments: The organization supports Assyrian schools teaching the Assyrian (Aramaic) language. Offers financial support for Assyrian publications dealing with Assyrian culture, history, and heritage, as well as present-day social, cultural, and scholarly achievements. Supports Assyrian authors, historians, composers, and scholars in their works dealing with ancient and modern Assyrians. Grants tuition aid to needy Assyrian-American students.

ASSYRIAN AMERICAN FEDERATION

4875 North Ashland Avenue
Chicago, Illinois 60640   (312) 334-0519

Principal officers: Mr. Alex Evans, President

Permanent staff: NI   Membership: NI
Date founded: NI   Membership dues: NI
Branches: NI   Scope: national

Publications: *The Assyrian Star*, 1933– (bimonthly)

Affiliations: Assyrian American Educational Association, Inc. (AAEA)

Major conventions/meetings: annual convention

Comments: The organization attempts to preserve the Assyrian heritage and tradition in the United States. It sponsors trips to the homeland for Assyrian-Americans.

ASSYRIAN WELFARE COUNCIL

4930 North Bernard
Chicago, Illinois 60625

Principal officers: Sargon Yonan, President

AUSTRALIAN-AMERICAN ORGANIZATIONS

Additional information on Australian-American organizations may be obtained from the Office of the Australian Embassy (1601 Massachusetts Avenue, Washington, D.C. 20036).

AMERICAN-AUSTRALIAN ASSOCIATION

P.O. Box 4096
Glendale, California 91202   (213) 243-7770

Principal officers: Gordon Currie, President
                       Alan Chase, Vice President

Permanent staff: none   Membership: 75
Date founded: 1965   Membership dues: $10.00 (annual)
Branches: none   Scope: state

Special requirements for membership: interest in promoting U.S.-Australia relations

Nature of organization: cultural, economic

Publications: publishes books

Affiliations: Australian American Association, Sydney, Australia

Major conventions/meetings: irregular

Comments: Acts as an advisory body in the area of cultural and business affairs. Aids in handling press and personal relations activities of major Australian business and political figures visiting the United States. Offers counseling to corporations planning to expand in the South Pacific region. Offers the Distinguished Visitor Award.

THE AMERICAN-AUSTRALIAN ASSOCIATION
140 Broadway
New York, New York 10005   (212) 269-0197

Principal officers: Peter M. Saint Germain, Secretary

Permanent staff: NI   Membership: 125
Date founded: 1948   Membership dues: NI
Branches: NI   Scope: NI

Comments: See comments for preceding entry.

AMERICAN AUSTRALIAN ASSOCIATION OF HONOLULU
P.O. Box 3468
Honolulu, Hawaii 96801   (808) 946-0771

Principal officers: L. S. Dillingham, President
                     E. R. Champion, Executive Director and Secretary

Permanent staff: none   Membership: 50
Date founded: 1967   Membership dues: NI
Branches: none   Scope: international

Special requirements for membership: none

Nature of organization: cultural, economic, social

Publications: none

Affiliations: Australian-American Associations in Australia; American-Australian
     Associations in the USA

Major conventions/meetings: General Assembly (infrequent)

Comments: Informal association of Hawaii business organizations operating in or interested
     in Australia or New Zealand. Provides a platform for visiting Australian or New
     Zealand statesmen and members of U.S. government concerned with Pacific affairs,
     and provides an opportunity for Australian and New Zealand government officials
     and businessmen to meet Hawaiian civic and business leaders. Serves business and
     community through cultural exchanges.

AUSTRALIA KANGAROO CLUB (A.K.C.)
17991 Mann Street
P.O. Box 4230
Irvine, California 92664   (714) 552-8357

Principal officers: Elaine Y. Bermingham, President
                     Nita Sisk, Vice President
                     Elaine Hiller, Secretary

Permanent staff: 1   Membership: 4,000
Date founded: 1971   Membership dues: $15.00 (annual)
Branches: none   Scope: national

Special requirements for membership: none

Nature of organization: educational

Publications: *AKC Newsletter* (monthly); *AKC Directory* (annual)

Affiliations: none

Major conventions/meetings: every six weeks

Comments: Promotes interest in Australia and New Zealand on an educational, business,
     social, and cultural level. Organization stresses social functions and guest speakers from
     Australia. Also provides special tours to Australia and New Zealand at discount
     prices.

AUSTRALIAN AMERICAN ASSOCIATION
c/o Mr. W. A. Lusse, President
400 California Street
San Francisco, California 94104

Principal officers: Mr. W. A. Lusse, President

AUSTRALIAN CLUB OF SOUTHERN CALIFORNIA
223 St. Joseph Street
Long Beach, California 90803

AUSTRALIAN-NEW ZEALAND SOCIETY OF NEW YORK
c/o Quantas Airways
542 Fifth Avenue
New York, New York 10036   (212) 697-6050

Principal officers: David Thawley, President

Permanent staff: NI   Membership: 200
Date founded: 1939   Membership dues: NI
Branches: NI   Scope: national

Special requirements for membership: interest in Australia and New Zealand and in promoting relations between America and Australia and New Zealand

Nature of organization: cultural, educational

Publications: *Bulletin*

Affiliations: American Field Service

Major conventions/meetings: annual convention

Comments: The aim of the organization is to create closer ties among America, Australia, and New Zealand. It sponsors a student exchange program through American Field Service.

THE DOWN UNDER CLUB
3346 Glen Oaks Avenue
White Bear Lake, Minnesota 55110   (612) 777-9430

Principal officers: Dr. Graham E. Gurr, President
Alex Ashwood, Vice President
Mrs. Marlene Gurr, Secretary
Tom Stack, Treasurer

Permanent staff: none   Membership: NI
Date founded: 1971   Membership dues: $5.00 family; $2.50
Branches: none   per person; $1.00 student
Scope: local

Special requirements for membership: Australian and New Zealand citizens or persons who have resided there; interest in Australia

Nature of organization: social

Publications: occasional newsletter

Major conventions/meetings: annual convention and committee meetings

Comments: Prime objective is to assist persons from Australia and New Zealand in adjusting to their new life in Minnesota. Also disseminates information about Australia and provides social activities for Australians.

SOCIETY OF AUSTRALASIAN SPECIALISTS
1638 19th Street
Cuyahoga Falls, Ohio 44223

Principal officers: Robert L. Cocklin, Secretary-Treasurer

Permanent staff: NI   Membership: 307
Date founded: 1936   Membership dues: NI
Branches: NI   Scope: NI

Special requirements for membership: stamp collectors who specialize in stamps, stationery, and postal history of Australia and New Zealand

Nature of organization: philatelic

Publications: *The Australian Informer* (monthly); *Bylaws and Membership List* (biennial)

Comments: The major objectives of this organization are to operate exchange and sales departments for specialists in stamps, stationery, and postal history. It maintains a library of handbooks, catalogs, etc.

THE SOUTHERN CROSS CLUB
5805 Roosevelt Street
Bethesda, Maryland 20034   (301) 530-8643
Principal officers: Faye M. Abrams, President
                       Patricia Rehrig, Vice President
                       Kay Norton, Secretary

Permanent staff: none   Membership: 265
Date founded: 1946   Membership dues: $6.00 (annual)
Branches: none   Scope: local

Special requirements for membership: Australian/New Zealand ancestry or extended
    contact with either country

Nature of organization: cultural, social, recreational, charitable

Publications: *The Southern Cross Reporter*, 1946– (bimonthly); also publishes club directory.

Affiliations: British Commonwealth Society of North America

Major conventions/meetings: bimonthly meetings

Comments: Founded in Washington by Australian and New Zealand war brides and the
    respective embassies. Major purpose is both social and cultural, with emphasis placed
    on assisting recent arrivals from Australia and New Zealand to adapt to their new
    surroundings in Washington. Also sponsors reduced-fare trips to Australia and New
    Zealand, as well as round-trip fares to the United States for relatives residing in
    New Zealand and Australia.

AUSTRIAN-AMERICAN ORGANIZATIONS

Additional information on Austrian-American organizations may be
obtained from the Office of the Austrian Embassy (2343 Massachusetts Avenue,
Washington, D.C. 20008). See also *Greater Cleveland Nationalities Directory 1974*
(Cleveland: Sun Newspapers and the Nationalities Services Center, 1974), and
Ethnic Directory I (Detroit: Southeastern Michigan Regional Ethnic Heritage
Studies Center, 1973).

AMERICAN AUSTRIAN SOCIETY
1156 15th Street, N.W.
Washington, D.C. 20005
Principal officers: Dr. Alfred Obernberg, President

Permanent staff: NI   Membership: 275
Date founded: 1954   Membership dues: NI
Branches: NI   Scope: NI

Nature of organization: cultural, social

Publications: *Newsletter* (monthly); *American Austrian Society Directory* (annual)

Affiliations: Austro-American Society, Vienna, Austria

Major conventions/meetings: annual, in May, in Washington, D.C.

Comments: The organization attempts to unite Austrians in the United States by providing
    cultural and social activities that help to preserve the Austrian culture in this country.
    Activities sponsored are: films, musical programs, discussion groups, Austrian guest
    lecturers, and other related events.

AMERICAN-AUSTRIAN SOCIETY OF THE MIDWEST
212 South Dwyer
Arlington Heights, Illinois 60005   (312) 259-0024
Principal officers: Joseph F. Schneller, President
                       Gerald Keidel, Vice President
                       Franz Herbstofer, Vice President

AMERICAN-AUSTRIAN SOCIETY OF THE MIDWEST (cont'd)
Hedy Richfield, Secretary
Franz Goranin, Treasurer

Permanent staff: none
Date founded: 1971
Branches: 2

Membership: 215 families
Membership dues: $10.00 per family
Scope: regional

Special requirements for membership: interest in Austrian culture, music, and art

Nature of organization: social, cultural

Publications: none

Major conventions/meetings: monthly meetings

Comments: Promotes and preserves Austrian cultural, musical, and artistic heritage. Social
functions.

AMERICAN FRIENDS OF AUSTRIA
10 South La Salle Street
Chicago, Illinois 60603   (312) 726-6726

Principal officers: William D. Saltiel, President
Carl Kandlbinder, Vice President
Robert Lock, Vice President
Mrs. Roy Levy, Secretary

Permanent staff: NI
Date founded: 1939
Branches: none

Membership: 500
Membership dues: $25.00 (sponsor);
$15.00 (regular)
Scope: regional

Special requirements for membership: American citizenship

Nature of organization: cultural

Publications: none

Affiliations: none

Major conventions/meetings: none

Comments: Encourages closer cultural relations between the United States and Austria.
Holds frequent meetings, lectures, and social functions. Awards scholarships to American students studying political science and music at the University of Vienna. Also
provides subsidy to medical students from Austria serving hospitals in Chicago for
several months.

AMERICAN FRIENDS OF AUSTRIAN LABOR
c/o Professor Ernst Papanek
1 West 64th Street
New York, New York 10023

AUSTRIAN AMERICAN ASSOCIATION
423 E. Rivo Alto Island
Miami Beach, Florida 33139   (305) 538-2912

Principal officers: Dr. Hans Walter Hannau, President
Wilhelm Apfel, Vice President
Marianne Wechsler, Secretary

Permanent staff: none
Date founded: 1954
Branches: none

Membership: approximately 180
Membership dues: none
Scope: regional

Special requirements for membership: interest in Austrian culture

Nature of organization: cultural

Publications: none

Affiliations: none

AUSTRIAN AMERICAN ASSOCIATION (cont'd)

Major conventions/meetings: none

Comments: Promotes interest in Austrian music, literature, and culture. Sponsors meetings, lectures, and social activities.

AUSTRIAN-AMERICAN CLUB
1651 Comstock Avenue
Los Angeles, California 90024

Principal officers: Dr. Robert Mueller, President

AUSTRIAN-AMERICAN FEDERATION, INC.
55 West 42nd Street, Room 842
New York, New York 10036

AUSTRIAN-AMERICAN SOCIETY
c/o Ms. Gertrude M. Warner
3708 Orchard Avenue North
Minneapolis, Minnesota 53422

AUSTRIAN FORUM
c/o Austrian Institute
11 East 52nd Street
New York, New York 10022   (212) 759-5165

Principal officers: Mrs. Irene Harand

Permanent staff: NI   Membership: NI
Date founded: 1942   Membership dues: NI
Branches: NI   Scope: national

Special requirements for membership: none

Nature of organization: educational, cultural

Affiliations: American-Austrian Music Society

Major conventions/meetings: program is from September through May

Comments: The aim is to preserve Austrian culture in the United States and to promote Austrian-American understanding and relations. The organization also arranges lectures and performances in the arts and humanities and exchange programs with other organizations connected with Austrian-American activities.

AUSTRIAN INSTITUTE
c/o Cultural Affairs Section
Austrian Consulate General
11 East 52nd Street
New York, New York 10022   (212) 759-5165

Principal officers: Dr. Richard Sickinger, Director

Comments: An Austrian government agency concerned with cultural and scientific relations between the United States and Austria. Not a membership organization.

AUSTRIAN SOCIETY
31 West Balcon Street
Buffalo, New York 14209

Principal officers: George Walcher, President

AUSTRIAN SOCIETY OF DETROIT
31260 Saratoga
Warren, Michigan 48093

Principal officers: Leo Polleiner

AUSTRIAN SOCIETY OF DETROIT (cont'd)

Permanent staff: NI	Membership: 400
Date founded: NI	Membership dues: NI
Branches: NI	Scope: national

Nature of organization: cultural, social

Affiliations: Parent organization for Austrian Ski Club, Austrian Children's Club

Major conventions/meetings: 4 per year

Comments: The major objectives of the organization are to provide social and cultural activities for those of Austrian descent. It serves as a parent organization for a number of Austrian groups and sponsors four special programs each year: the Austrian Christmas Celebration, the Austrian Folklore Celebration, Evening in Vienna Ball, and Johann Strauss Ball.

AUSTRIAN SOCIETY OF THE PACIFIC NORTHWEST
Generalkonsul Henry Bloch
10007 N.W. 24th Avenue
Portland, Oregon 97210

Permanent staff: NI	Membership: NI
Date founded: NI	Membership dues: NI
Branches: NI	Scope: regional

THE AUSTRIANS' SOCIAL CLUB
6031 North Navarre
Chicago, Illinois 60631   (312) 792-3590

Principal officers: Walter E. Pomper, President
                Anton Donko, Vice President
                Stephanie Pomper, Secretary
                Frank Birkhoffer, Treasurer

Permanent staff: none	Membership: 50
Date founded: 1973	Membership dues: $6.00 (annual)
Branches: none	Scope: local

Special requirements for membership: 18 years of age

Nature of organization: social

Publications: none

Affiliations: none

Major conventions/meetings: monthly

Comments: The purpose of the club is to preserve Austrian customs and traditions. Sponsors social and charitable activities for members and provides aid to needy members.

AUSTRO-AMERICAN ASSOCIATION OF BOSTON (A.A.A.)
88 Marlborough Street
Boston, Massachusetts 02116   (617) 536-7539

Principal officers: Martha Brunner-Orne, M.D., President
                Dr. Otto Hochstadt, Vice President
                Dr. Erica Taxer, Vice President
                Dr. Kurt Toman, Vice President
                Martha Stasa, Secretary

Permanent staff: 4	Membership: 150
Date founded: 1944	Membership dues: $6.00 single; $10.00 couple; $15.00 sponsor; $25.00 patron
Branches: none	Scope: local

Special requirements for membership: none

Nature of organization: cultural, social

Publications: *AAA News* (monthly)

AUSTRO-AMERICAN ASSOCIATION OF BOSTON (A.A.A.) (cont'd)

Affiliations: none

Major conventions/meetings: annual

Comments: Major purpose is to further interest in Austrian culture and to foster Austro-American friendship. The organization sponsors cultural, educational, and social activities. Awards scholarships to students.

AUSTRO-AMERICAN SOCIETY OF PHILADELPHIA
6133 North 8th Street
Philadelphia, Pennsylvania 19120

BUFFALO AUSTRIAN BENEVOLENT SOCIETY, INC.
600 East North Street
Buffalo, New York 14201

BURGENLAND SOCIETY (B. G. Austria)
6766 North Onarga Avenue
Chicago, Illinois 60631   (312) 775-0985

Principal officers: Julius Gmoser, President
                       Joe Baumann, Vice President

Permanent staff: 15   Membership: 5,000 U.S.A.; 1,000
Date founded: 1955   Canada
Branches: 6 regional; 5 state; 1 local   Membership dues: $8.00
                                           Scope: national

Special requirements for membership: to be of Austrian nationality

Nature of organization: social, educational, cultural, youth

Publications: *Burgenland Society*, 1955– (monthly)

Major conventions/meetings: anniversary celebration of members of the Land of Burgenland

Comments: Primarily social in nature. Provides opportunity for meetings, dances, and dinners. Promotes tours to Austria and arranges charter flights from the United States and Canada to Austria.

**BURGENLAENDER-AMERICAN BENEFIT SOCIETY OF PASSAIC
& VICINITY, INC.**
74 Dayton Avenue
Passaic, New Jersey 07055

Permanent staff: NI   Membership: NI
Date founded: NI   Membership dues: NI
Branches: NI   Scope: regional

BURGENLAENDISCHER VEREIN MILWAUKEE
c/o Mr. Kelly Knorr
6766 North Onarga
Chicago, Illinois 60631

FRIENDS OF AUSTRIA
105 Montgomery Street, Room 300
San Francisco, California 94104

MILWAUKEE ZITHER CLUB
c/o Hans Gassner
2952 North 48th Street
Milwaukee, Wisconsin 53210

ROSEGGER-STEIRER CLUB
c/o Mary Kler, Secretary
8137 South Christiana
Chicago, Illinois 60652
Principal officers: Mary Kler, Secretary

STEIRER CLUB VON CHICAGO
c/o Gerhard Sorger
1324 Greenleaf Avenue
Evanston, Illinois 60202

TIROLER BENEFICIAL SOCIETY
4829 Rising Sun Avenue
Philadelphia, Pennsylvania 19120

VEREIN OESTERREICH, INC.
6127 Harwood Avenue
Oakland, California 94618
Principal officers: Louis A. Riinthaler, President

BALTIC-AMERICAN ORGANIZATIONS

*See Estonian-American, Latvian-American, and
Lithuanian-American Organizations*

Information on Baltic-American organizations may be obtained from The
Association for the Advancement of Baltic Studies (c/o Valters Nollendorts,
President, 366 86th Street, Brooklyn, New York 11209).

BANGLADESH-AMERICAN ORGANIZATIONS

See also Indian-American Organizations

Additional information on Bangladesh-American organizations in the United
States may be obtained from the Office of the Bangladesh Embassy (2123 California Street, Washington, D.C. 20008). Some Bengali organizations are included under
Bangladesh-American organizations, while others are listed under Indian-American
organizations.

BANGLADESH ASSOCIATION OF AMERICA
518 Brush
Detroit, Michigan 48226   (313) 963-0617
Permanent staff: NI   Membership: NI
Date founded: NI   Membership dues: NI
Branches: NI   Scope: local
Nature of organization: cultural

BANGLADESH CULTURAL ASSOCIATION
60 Second Avenue
New York, New York 10003   (212) 475-9704
Principal officers: Mohammed Ismail, Secretary
Permanent staff: NI   Membership: 165
Date founded: 1965   Membership dues: NI
Branches: NI   Scope: national
Nature of organization: cultural

BANGLADESH CULTURAL ASSOCIATION (cont'd)

Publications: *Kiran Bengali* (monthly)

Comments: The major purpose of the organization is to preserve the Bangladesh culture in the United States and to promote U.S.-Bangladesh relations through the use of movies, exhibits, literature, art, religious services, and various social activities. Offers instruction in Bangladesh language and religion.

BASQUE-AMERICAN ORGANIZATIONS

Additional information on Basque-American organizations in the United States may be obtained from the Basque Studies Program, The University of Nevada (Reno, Nevada 89507) and from the North American Basque Organization, Inc. (c/o Mrs. Janet Inda, 742 Roberts Street, Reno, Nevada 89502).

BASQUE CLUB, INC.
P.O. Box 27021
San Francisco, California 94116   (415) 661-3543

Permanent staff: 13   Membership: 500
Date founded: 1960   Membership dues: $12.00 (annual)
Branches: 0   Scope: local

Special requirements for membership: Basque descent

Nature of organization: social, cultural

Comments: Attempts to unite Basque-Americans native to the area in social and cultural activities.

CHINO BASQUE CLUB
12707 Oak Street
Chino, California 91710

Permanent staff: NI   Membership: NI
Date founded: NI   Membership dues: NI
Branches: NI   Scope: local

Special requirements for membership: Basque descent

Nature of organization: social, cultural

Comments: Main purpose of the organization is social, but it is also interested in preserving Basque culture and traditions. Annually sponsors Basque exhibits and festivals that feature folk dancing and Basque athletic events such as weightlifting and woodchopping.

ELKO BASQUE CLUB
P.O. Box 1321
Elko, Nevada 89801

Permanent staff: NI
Date founded: NI
Branches: NI

Membership: NI
Membership dues: NI
Scope: local

Special requirements for membership: Basque descent

Nature of organization: social, cultural

Comments: Major purpose is to preserve the Basque traditions in the United States and to unite Basque-Americans for social activities. Participates in annual Basque Festival with demonstrations of Basque weightlifting, woodchopping, and folk dancing.

ELY BASQUE CLUB, INC.
P.O. Box 1014
Ely, Nevada 89301

Permanent staff: NI
Date founded: 1960
Branches: none

Membership: 40
Membership dues: $5.00 (annual)
Scope: local

Special requirements for membership: Basque descent

Nature of organization: social, cultural

Comments: A social and cultural group which also takes part in the annual Basque Festival featuring folk dancing and such traditionally Basque athletic events as weightlifting and woodchopping.

EUZKALDUNAK, INC.
P.O. Box 2613
Boise, Idaho 83701

Permanent staff: NI
Date founded: NI
Branches: NI

Membership: NI
Membership dues: NI
Scope: regional

Special requirements for membership: Basque descent

Nature of organization: cultural, social

Affiliations: North American Basque Organization, Inc.

Comments: The primary purpose of the organization is to preserve the Basque traditions and heritage in the United States. It sponsors a group of young Basque dancers (Oinkari Basque Dancers) who perform Basque folk dancing throughout the West and at fairs (including the world's fairs at Montreal and Spokane).

NORTH AMERICAN BASQUE ORGANIZATIONS, INC.
c/o Mrs. Janet Inda
742 Roberts Street
Reno, Nevada 89502

Principal officers: Mrs. Janet Inda, Executive Secretary

Permanent staff: NI
Date founded: NI
Branches: NI

Membership: NI
Membership dues: NI
Scope: national

Nature of organization: social, cultural

Comments: Acts as a coordinating agency for nine Basque social clubs in the United States. Its purpose is to preserve Basque culture and promote cultural liaisons between the Basques in America and their homeland (e.g., bringing Basque musicians, artists, etc., to perform in the United States).

ZAZPIAK BAT BASQUE CLUB
P.O. Box 7771
Reno, Nevada 89502

Permanent staff: NI
Date founded: NI
Branches: NI

Membership: NI
Membership dues: NI
Scope: local

Special requirements for membership: Basque descent

Nature of organization: social, cultural

Comments: The primary purpose of the organization is to unite local Basque-Americans in social activities.

BELGIAN-AMERICAN ORGANIZATIONS

Additional information on Belgian-American organizations in the United States may be obtained from the Office of the Belgian Embassy (3330 Garfield Street, Washington, D.C. 20008). See also *Ethnic Directory I* (Detroit: Southeastern Michigan Regional Ethnic Heritage Studies Center, 1973).

B. K. CLUB
721 South West Street
Mishawaka, Indiana 46544   (219) 255-0498

Principal officers: Henry J. Nauts, President
Rene DeLoof, Vice President
Kenneth C. Heston, Secretary

Permanent staff: none
Date founded: 1925
Branches: none

Membership: 500 "A"; 500 social
Membership dues: $12.00 "A"; $2.00 social
Scope: local

Special requirements for membership: Belgian, of Belgian descent, or married to a Belgian

Nature of organization: fraternal, social, sport

Publications: none

Affiliations: none

Major conventions/meetings: monthly meetings

Comments: Primarily a sports-oriented organization. Promotes social activities such as card parties and bingo. Sponsors bowling, softball, baseball, and football teams.

BELGIAN-AMERICAN BUSINESS MEN'S ASSOCIATION
20623 Country Club
Harper Woods, Michigan 48236

BELGIAN AMERICAN BUSINESS MEN'S BAND
4145 Concord
Detroit, Michigan 48207   (313) 925-7292

Principal officers: Antoon Huyghe, President
Oscar Vercruysse, Secretary
Joseph Edelmayer, Director

Permanent staff: 8
Date founded: 1931
Branches: none

Membership: 40
Membership dues: none
Scope: local

Special requirements for membership: musician of Belgian descent (or with committee approval), 16 years of age, sponsored by present member

Nature of organization: cultural, recreational, musical

BELGIAN AMERICAN BUSINESS MEN'S BAND (cont'd)

Publications: none

Affiliations: Belgian American Businessmen's Association

Major conventions/meetings: bimonthly rehearsals; concerts

Comments: Primary aim is to develop an interest in Belgian music. Encourages social interaction among members of the Belgian community in Detroit.

BELGIAN AMERICAN CHAMBER OF COMMERCE IN THE UNITED STATES
50 Rockefeller Plaza
New York, New York 10020   (212) 247-7613

Principal officers: Albert Van Oppens, Executive Secretary

Permanent staff: NI   Membership: 600
Date founded: 1925   Membership dues: NI
Branches: NI   Scope: national

Nature of organization: economic

Publications: *Belgian Trade Review* (monthly); *Belgian American Trade Directory* (triennial)

Major conventions/meetings: annual

Comments: The objective is to distribute information about economic enterprises; also acts in
an advisory capacity. Until 1968 it was known as the Belgian Chamber of Commerce in
the United States.

BELGIAN AMERICAN CLUB
2803 East Belleview Place
Milwaukee, Wisconsin 53211

BELGIAN AMERICAN CLUB OF LOS ANGELES
16624 Hamil Street
Van Nuys, California 91406

BELGIAN AMERICAN EDUCATIONAL FOUNDATION
420 Lexington Avenue
New York, New York 10017   (212) 683-1496

Principal officers: L. A. Fraikin, President

Permanent staff: 4   Membership: 120
Date founded: 1920   Membership dues: NI
Branches: NI   Scope: NI

Nature of organization: an educational foundation rather than a membership organization

Major conventions/meetings: annual convention

Comments: Encourages closer relations between the United States and Belgium. Gives fellowships to graduate students in one country for study in the other country.

BELGIAN AMERICAN LADIES CLUB
5539 Lenox
Detroit, Michigan 48213
Principal officers: Alice Van Landeghem

BELGIAN BENEVOLENT SOCIETY
1750 Clay Street
San Francisco, California 94109

BELGIAN BUREAU
502 West 41st Street
New York, New York 10036

BELGIAN MILITARY CIRCLE
22733 Harper Lake Drive
St. Clair Shores, Michigan 48080
Principal officers: Jules Naert

CENTER FOR BELGIAN CULTURE OF WESTERN ILLINOIS (CBC)
1714 7th Street
Moline, Illinois 61265   (309) 762-0167
Principal officers: LaVerne Kastelic, President
                           Florence Acke, Vice President
                           Rev. Francis Engels, Secretary

Permanent staff: none   Membership: 536
Date founded: 1963   Membership dues: $4.00 (annual)
Branches: none   Scope: regional

Special requirements for membership: none

Nature of organization: cultural

Publications: *Center for Belgian Culture Newsletter*, 1965– (monthly); also publishes books.

Major conventions/meetings: biennial membership meetings

Comments: Major objective is the preservation of the Belgian culture and heritage, especially among the younger generation.

FLEMISH AMERICAN CLUB
313 North Burr Boulevard
Kewanee, Illinois 61443

FLEMISH-AMERICAN CLUB OF SOUTHERN CALIFORNIA
5021 West Bolsa Street
Santa Ana, California 92703   (714) 531-9324
Principal officers: Gustaaf de Schryver, President
                           Otto Swiggers, Vice President
                           Mrs. Lee Newman, Secretary
                           Galina de Schryver, Treasurer

Permanent staff: 12   Membership: 130
Date founded: 1940   Membership dues: $8.00 per couple;
Branches: NI $5.00 single
                                           Scope: regional

Special requirements for membership: none

Nature of organization: social

Publications: none

Major conventions/meetings: monthly business meetings

Comments: A non-profit organization, the Flemish-American Club of Southern California provides social activities for its members. It helps individuals with citizenship problems and adjustment. Occasionally awards a scholarship to a deserving student whose parents are members of the club.

ST. CHARLES BENEFICIAL SOCIETY
2604 Princeton
St. Clair Shores, Michigan 48081
Principal officers: Jerome Deneweth

THE UNITED BELGIAN-AMERICAN SOCIETIES
R.R. 2, Goetz Road
Carsonville, Michigan 48419   (313) 622-8662
Principal officers: Morris Opsommrere

THE UNITED BELGIAN-AMERICAN SOCIETIES (cont'd)

Permanent staff: NI   Membership: 4,000
Date founded: NI   Membership dues: NI
Branches: NI   Scope: NI

Comments: The organization coordinates the activities of the 20 Belgian organizations in
the Detroit area. It holds monthly meetings with representatives from each
organization.

UNITED BELGIAN AMERICAN SOCIETIES
1921 West Lunt Avenue
Chicago, Illinois 60626

BLACK-AMERICAN ORGANIZATIONS

There exist approximately 300 major Black national organizations in the
United States. To this number may be added hundreds of organizations that list
themselves as either regional, state, or local. Since their number is too great to be
listed in this directory, and since special guides have already been published, only a
limited number of major organizations are included here. For more complete
reference to organized Black life in the United States, the following sources should
be used: Charles L. Sanders and Linda McLean (comps.), *Directory of National
Black Organizations* (New York: Afram Associates, Inc., 1972). This directory
includes most of the major Black organizations and Black caucuses within
predominantly white organizations. It does not list private and profit-making
organizations.

Also see *The Ebony Handbook* by the editors of *Ebony* (Chicago: Johnson
Publishing Company, Inc., 1974). This reference work provides basic information
on all phases of Black-Americans and their activities, including a highly selective list
of their major organizations.

ALPHA KAPPA ALPHA SORORITY, INC.
5211 South Greenwood Avenue
Chicago, Illinois 60615   (312) 684-1282

Principal officers: Mattelia B. Grays, National President
Carey B. Preston, Executive Secretary

Permanent staff: NI   Membership: over 40,000
Date founded: 1908   Membership dues: NI
Branches: 200 chapters   Scope: national

Special requirements for membership: a woman pursuing a degree or who has received a
degree from a 4-year accredited college with a minimum average of C+

Nature of organization: social, fraternal

Publications: *The Ivy Leaf* (quarterly)

Comments: The aim of the organization is to encourage the ideals of service and high
scholastic standards among college women. It grants travel funds to high school girls
and undergraduates. Through the Cleveland Job Corps Center for Women, cash scholarships are awarded to high school graduates entering college.

ALPHA PHI ALPHA
4432 South Parkway
Chicago, Illinois 60655   (312) 373-1819

ALPHA PHI ALPHA (cont'd)
Principal officers: Judge Ernest Morial, President, Chairman of the Board
                       Lawrence T. Young, Executive Secretary
Permanent staff: NI   Membership: NI
Date founded: NI   Membership dues: NI
Branches: various graduate and undergraduate Scope: national
 chapters
Special requirements for membership: approval by a fraternity chapter
Nature of organization: social, fraternal
Publications: *Sphinx* (monthly)
Comments: This fraternity emphasizes social service.

ASSOCIATION FOR THE STUDY OF AFRO-AMERICAN LIFE AND HISTORY
     1401 14th Street, N.W.
     Washington, D.C. 20005   (202) 667-2822
Principal officers: Willie L. Miles
Permanent staff: 14   Membership: 30,000
Date founded: 1915   Membership dues: NI
Branches: 30 state groups   Scope: national
Special requirements for membership: historians, students, and scholars interested in the study
 of Afro-American life
Nature of organization: scholarly, educational
Publications: *Afro-American History Bulletin* (8 issues per year); *Journal of Afro-American
 History* (quarterly)
Major conventions/meetings: annual
Comments: The objective of this organization is to conduct research on the Black people
 throughout the world with the hope of furthering understanding of the races and
 promoting unity between them. Black contributions are emphasized. The former
 name (until 1973) was the Association for the Study of Negro Life and History.

BLACK ACADEMY OF ARTS AND LETTERS (BAAL)
     475 Riverside Drive
     New York, New York 10027   (212) 663-4740
Principal officers: John O. Killens, President
                       Doris E. Saunders, Secretary
Permanent staff: 2   Membership: 73
Date founded: 1969   Membership dues: NI
Branches: NI   Scope: national
Special requirements for membership: individuals who have made some contribution to the
 arts and letters of Black people
Nature of organization: scholarly
Major conventions/meetings: annual
Comments: Purpose of the organization is to give recognition to scholars, artists, and
 performers making noteworthy contributions to Black culture, and to promote and
 encourage Black arts and letters.

BLACK WORLD FOUNDATION
     P.O. Box 908
     2658 Bridgeway
     Sausalito, California 94965   (415) 332-3131
Principal officers: Nathan Hare, President
Permanent staff: 8   Membership: 10,000
Date founded: 1969   Membership dues: NI
Branches: NI   Scope: national

BLACK WORLD FOUNDATION (cont'd)

Special requirements for membership: open to Blacks interested in developing the Black culture

Nature of organization: cultural, political, youth

Publications: *The Black Scholar* (monthly)

Comments: The intent is to unite Black scholars, to evaluate the future of the Black movement, to promote Black culture, and to promote Black publications in the arts, the social and political sciences, and literature (including children's works). It sponsors a Black Scholar Essay Contest for young adults and the Black Scholar Book Club, distributes Black publications to prisoners, and maintains a speaker's bureau and library.

COALITION OF CONCERNED BLACK AMERICANS
475 Riverside Drive, Room 636
New York, New York 10027   (212) 850-0100

Principal officers: Jewell Handy Gresham, Acting Executive Director
                       Regina Davis, Associate Director

Permanent staff: 5   Membership: 3 national organizations
Date founded: 1971   Membership dues: none
Branches: none   Scope: national

Special requirements for membership: New York-based national organizations (religious, academic, legal, or civic groups) concerned with the negative effects of criminal justice practices with regard to Black Americans

Nature of organization: educational, professional, research

Publications: none

Major conventions/meetings: none

Comments: The purpose of the coalition is to study criminal justice practices with respect to Black Americans. It is concerned with alleviating problems and negative effects of legislation concerning the Black American. It promotes a strong relationship with other organizations within the Black community which deal with welfare problems of Blacks.

CONGRESS OF RACIAL EQUALITY (CORE)
200 West 135th Street
New York, New York 10030   (212) 281-9650

Principal officers: Roy Innis, Director

Permanent staff: 2   Membership: 70,000
Date founded: 1942   Membership dues: NI
Branches: 180 local groups   Scope: national

Special requirements for membership: persons interested in attaining full civil rights of Blacks through non-violent methods

Nature of organization: civil rights, political

Publications: *CORElator* (bimonthly)

Major conventions/meetings: annual

Comments: The goal of the organization is to better race relations in the United States and, particularly, to improve the civil rights and change discriminatory policies toward Blacks. Emphasis is on voting rights in the South and community problems in the North (e.g., better housing, urban renewal, action against police brutality, etc.).

THE CONGRESSIONAL BLACK CAUCUS (CBC)
House of Representatives, Annex Room 306
Washington, D.C. 20515   (202) 225-1691

Principal officers: Louis Stokes, Chairman
                       Parren Mitchell, Vice President
                       Charles Rangel, Secretary

THE CONGRESSIONAL BLACK CAUCUS (CBC) (cont'd)

Permanent staff: 6   Membership: 16
Date founded: 1969   Membership dues: NI
Branches: none   Scope: national

Special requirements for membership: Black Congresspersons

Nature of organization: political

Publications: *Congressional Black Caucus Newsletter*, 1971– (semiannual)

Affiliations: National organizations dedicated to finding solutions to Black and minority problems

Major conventions/meetings: annual

Comments: The Congressional Black Caucus was formed primarily to press for legislative, administrative, and judicial actions that would benefit Black and other similarly situated groups throughout the United States. The issues and concerns of the Caucus are action programs in the areas of economic security and development, political equity, community and urban development, and justice and civil rights. In 1971 the Caucus adopted its present name, having previously been referred to as the Democratic Select Committee. Holds various hearings on Black problems.

COUNCIL OF INDEPENDENT BLACK INSTITUTIONS (C.I.B.I.)

P.O. Box 57
Lefferts Station
Brooklyn, New York 11238   (212) 636-9400

Principal officers: Kasisi Jitu Weusi, Chairman Central Committee

Permanent staff: 3   Membership: 22 organizations
Date founded: 1972   Membership dues: $100.00 (annual)
Branches: 22 local   Scope: national

Special requirements for membership: the organization must be an independent Black educational facility and be in agreement with the objectives of C.I.B.I.

Nature of organization: educational, cultural, professional, scholarly, youth

Publications: *C.I.B.I. Newsletter*, 1972– (quarterly); *Black Educational Annual*, 1973– (annual); also publishes books.

Affiliations: Congress of Afrikan People

Major conventions/meetings: annual convention of the National Black Parent Organization

Comments: The major priority of C.I.B.I. is the erection of an independent national Black educational system. At present the organization is a network of schools in the United States that serve Black children from ages 3 through 18. The principal purpose of C.I.B.I. is to be the "political vehicle through which a qualitatively different people is produced. The Independent Black Institution is charged with the responsibility of developing the moral character of its students and staff, and of providing the clear, sane, and well-reasoned leadership which is imperative to a correct struggle for freedom and internal community development." The schools have developed a curriculum, methodology, and materials that deal specifically with the experiences of the Black people in America. Sponsors teacher training workshops; maintains a library of over 250 books on Black education.

FRONTIERS INTERNATIONAL, INC.

1901 West Girard Avenue
Philadelphia, Pennsylvania 19130   (215) 235-5959

Principal officers: Charles A. Moore, President
                       Malcolm Williams, Vice President
                       Harold L. Pilgrim, Executive Secretary

Permanent staff: 2   Membership: 2,000
Date founded: 1936   Membership dues: $25.00 (annual)
Branches: 24 state groups; 64 local groups   Scope: national

Special requirements for membership: must be male, over 21 years of age, and invited to join by a member

FRONTIERS INTERNATIONAL, INC. (cont'd)

Nature of organization: service, social

Publications: *The Frontiersman*, 1964– (quarterly)

Affiliations: none

Major conventions/meetings: annual

Comments: The purpose of the organization is to serve the needy directly or by making financial contributions to other community service organizations. Until 1961 the name was Frontiers of America. Projects are determined at the local level. The national group sponsors the "Buddy" project, through which members select a boy whose cultural, scholastic, moral and spiritual development they will aid. It also sponsors National Frontiers Vitiligo Foundation, Inc., dedicated to medical research on pigmentation problems.

NATION OF ISLAM (BLACK MUSLIMS)

5335 South Greenwood Avenue
Chicago, Illinois 60615 (312) 236-9850

Principal officers: Elijah Muhammad

Permanent staff: NI	Membership: NI
Date founded: NI	Membership dues: NI
Branches: NI	Scope: national

Special requirements for membership: persons willing to accept the philosophy of Elijah Muhammad

Nature of organization: religious

Publications: *Muhammad Speaks* (weekly)

Comments: The major purpose of the organization is to perpetuate the teachings and philosophies of Elijah Muhammad—i.e., to build a separate nation under Allah. Sponsors various schools, radio programs, and business activities.

NATIONAL ASSOCIATION FOR THE ADVANCEMENT OF COLORED PEOPLE (NAACP)

1790 Broadway
New York, New York 11213 (212) 245-2100

Principal officers: Kivie Kaplan, President
Bishop Stephen G. Spottswood, Chairman, Board of Directors
Roy Wilkins, Executive Director

Permanent staff: 180	Membership: 412,019
Date founded: 1909	Membership dues: $4.00 and up
Branches: 1,600 local	Scope: national

Special requirements for membership: none

Nature of organization: civil rights

Publications: *The Crisis*, 1910– (monthly, except for the combined June/July/August issue); annual report (yearly); also publishes a history of the Association.

Affiliations: Leadership Conference on Civil Rights

Major conventions/meetings: annual convention

Comments: Official goals are to "end all barriers to racial justice and guarantee full equality of opportunity and achievement in the United States." It attempts to eliminate discrimination in housing, employment, education, legislation, sports, etc.; it sponsors the NAACP National Housing Corp., engaging minority firms for construction. Its various branches and divisions are concerned with health, education, youth, housing, labor, fund raising, vocational training. Archival materials are maintained.

NATIONAL ASSOCIATION OF COLORED WOMEN'S CLUBS (NACWC)

5808 16th Street, N.W.
Washington, D.C. 20011 (202) 726-2044

Principal officers: Carole A. Early, Secretary

NATIONAL ASSOCIATION OF COLORED WOMEN'S CLUBS (NACWC) (cont'd)

Permanent staff: 2	Membership: 100,000
Date founded: 1896	Membership dues: NI
Branches: 38 state groups; 2,000 local groups	Scope: national

Special requirements for membership: Black woman's club

Nature of organization: service, educational, political, philanthropic

Publications: *National Notes* (quarterly)

Major conventions/meetings: biennial

Comments: This federation of Black women's clubs was formed by a merger of the National Colored Women's League and National Federation of Afro-American Women. It sponsors activities and programs of community service, of home and child care, and activities for youth.

NATIONAL ASSOCIATION OF NEGRO BUSINESS AND PROFESSIONAL WOMEN'S CLUBS, INC.

2861 Urban Avenue
Columbus, Georgia 31907

Principal officers: Mrs. Rosalie McGuire, President
Mrs. V. Alyce Foster, Secretary

Permanent staff: NI	Membership: ca. 5,000
Date founded: 1935	Membership dues: NI
Branches: NI	Scope: national

Special requirements for membership: a Negro business or professional woman

Nature of organization: social, economic, professional

Publications: *President's Newsletter* (monthly); *Responsibility* (semiannual)

Major conventions/meetings: annual convention

Comments: Promotes the interests of Black business and professional women through scholarships, special training, job opportunities, etc. Sponsors junior workshops.

NATIONAL BAR ASSOCIATION

1314 North 5th Street
Kansas City, Kansas 66101   (913) 281-4583

Principal officers: Archie B. Weston, President
Elmer C. Jackson, Jr., Executive Secretary

Permanent staff: 2	Membership: 1,100
Date founded: 1925	Membership dues: $40.00 (annual)
Branches: 21 state branches	Scope: national

Special requirements for membership: "admission to practice law"

Nature of organization: legal

Publications: *National Bar Bulletin*; also publishes a National Bar Directory.

Affiliations: American Bar Association

Major conventions/meetings: annual convention

Comments: The association primarily serves to promote the field of jurisprudence among Blacks as well as to serve the needs of predominately Black lawyers and judges in the United States. Sponsors seminars and annually presents the C. Francis Stratford Award. Maintains a law library.

NATIONAL BLACK POLITICAL ASSEMBLY

401 Broadway
Gary, Indiana 46402   (219) 944-6501

Principal officers: Congressman Diggs, President
Mayor R. G. Hatcher, Executive Vice President
General Imamu Imri Baraka, Executive Secretary

NATIONAL BLACK POLITICAL ASSEMBLY (cont'd)

Permanent staff: NI
Membership: NI
Date founded: 1972
Membership dues: $25.00 (annual)
Branches: 36 state; 1 local
Scope: national

Special requirements for membership: elected by state caucus

Nature of organization: political

Affiliations: none

Major conventions/meetings: none

Comments: The primary objective of the National Black Political Convention is to procure political power for the advancement and self-determination of Black people, both nationally and internationally. Strives to establish a permanent political movement that addresses itself to the basic control and reshaping of American institutions currently exploiting Black America. Seeks to empower the Black community, not simply its representatives. The primary fields of concentrated endeavor are: economic empowerment; human development; control of educational facilities used primarily by Blacks; influencing international policy toward Third World nations; communications representation; rural development; environmental protection; and the self-determination of persons living in the District of Columbia.

NATIONAL BUSINESS LEAGUE

4324 Georgia Avenue, N.W.
Washington, D.C. 20010   (202) 726-6200

Principal officers: Berkeley Burrell, President
Charles T. Williams, Chairman of the Board
Edward L. Feggans, Secretary

Permanent staff: 20
Membership: 15,000
Date founded: 1900
Membership dues: NI
Branches: 80
Scope: national

Special requirements for membership: minority businessman

Nature of organization: economic

Publications: *Washington Rap* (biweekly); *National Memo* (monthly)

Major conventions/meetings: annual

Comments: The purpose of the organization is to assist minority businessmen by encouraging Black ownership of small businesses and by providing management training programs, technical assistance, and help in attaining financial backing. It grants special awards to minority businessmen.

NATIONAL COUNCIL OF NEGRO WOMEN, INC.

1346 Connecticut Avenue, N.W., Suite 832
Washington, D.C. 20036   (202) 223-2363

Principal officers: Dorothy I. Height, National President
Ruth Sykes, Special Assistant
Sylvia Williams, Director of Development

Permanent staff: 53
Membership: 4,000,000
Date founded: 1935
Membership dues: NI
Branches: 167 local groups
Scope: national

Special requirements for membership: none

Nature of organization: educational, social, welfare, charitable

Publications: newsletters and reports

Affiliations: National Council of Women of the United States; International Council of Women; National Assembly for Social Policy and Development

Major conventions/meetings: biennial

Comments: This organization was originally established to serve as a clearinghouse for the activities of various other organizations. It mainly represents the concerns of women with respect to their social, economic, educational, and other needs.

E. Louise Patten Library
Piedmont College
Demorest, Georgia 30535

NATIONAL DENTAL ASSOCIATION (NDA)
P.O. Box 197
Charlottesville, Virginia 22902   (703) 293-8253
Principal officers: M. W. Rosemond, President
              Charles Williams, Executive Vice President
              Ellard N. Jackson, Executive Director

Permanent staff: 4	Membership: 1,800
Date founded: 1913	Membership dues: $50.00 (annual)
Branches: 25 state	Scope: national

Special requirements for membership: "Graduation from a reputable dental school with a DDS degree . . . "

Nature of organization: professional

Publications: *The Quarterly* (quarterly)

Affiliations: none

Major conventions/meetings: annual convention

Comments: The objectives are to promote the field of dentistry among Blacks and to eliminate social discrimination and segregation from American dental institutions, clinics, and organizations. Other goals include raising the standards of dental education and the profession; stimulating favorable relations between dentists; supporting and sponsoring the enactment of better dental laws and improved public health legislation.

THE NATIONAL MEDICAL ASSOCIATION
1717 Massachusetts Avenue
Washington, D.C. 20036   (202) 338-8266
Principal officers: Dr. Wiley Thurber Armstrong, President

Permanent staff: 8	Membership: 5,000
Date founded: 1895	Membership dues: NI
Branches: 50 state groups; 72 local groups	Scope: national

Special requirements for membership: Black physician

Nature of organization: professional

Publications: *Journal* (bimonthly)

Affiliations: Woman's Auxiliary

Major conventions/meetings: annual

Comments: This professional association of Black physicians is divided into 13 sections based on the areas of specialization of the member physicians.

NATIONAL NEWSPAPER PUBLISHERS' ASSOCIATION
3636 16th Street
Washington, D.C. 20010   (202) 332-7174
Principal officers: Carlton B. Goodlet, President
              Howard B. Woods, Vice President

Permanent staff: NI	Membership: 90
Date founded: 1940	Membership dues: NI
Branches: NI	Scope: national

Special requirements for membership: publisher of daily or weekly newspaper

Nature of organization: professional

Publications: *Publishers' Auxiliary* (semimonthly); *National Directory of Weekly Newspapers* (annual)

Major conventions/meetings: annual

Comments: The objective of the organization is to unite Black publishers and strengthen the interest of the Black press. Until 1956 the organization was known as the National Editorial Association. It presents an annual service award for significant contributions in Black leadership; it operates American Newspaper Representatives, Inc.

NATIONAL URBAN LEAGUE
55 East 52nd Street
New York, New York 10022   (212) 751-0300

Principal officers: Vernon Jordan, Director
                       Donald McGannon, President
                       Helen Mervis, Secretary

Permanent staff: 2,000   Membership: 50,000
Date founded: 1910   Membership dues: NI
Branches: 5 regional; 101 local   Scope: national

Special requirements for membership: none

Nature of organization: non-profit community service agency

Publications: *Urban League Housing News* (monthly); *Urban League News* (monthly); *Black Executive Exchange Program (BEEP) Newsletter* (quarterly); *The Builder* (quarterly)

Major conventions/meetings: annual

Comments: The major goal of the organization is to secure equality in all social areas for minority group members—e.g., housing, employment, education, health and welfare, law, business development. It also has special community service programs to assist in family planning, problems of mental retardation, youth and student agencies, labor, veterans affairs, etc. It was originally the National League on Urban Conditions among Negroes, which then merged with the Committee for Improving the Industrial Conditions of Negroes in New York to become the National Urban League.

NEGRO ACTORS GUILD OF AMERICA, INC. (NAG)
1674 Broadway
New York, New York 10019   (212) 245-4343

Principal officers: Charles Honi Coles, President
                       Anita Bush, Secretary
                       Emory Evans, Treasurer

Permanent staff: 1   Membership: 600
Date founded: 1936   Membership dues: $5.00 (annual)
Branches: NI   active; $10.00 patron
                                               Scope: national

Special requirements for membership: a performing artist or persons interested in the theatre

Nature of organization: professional, welfare

Publications: *Newsletter* (bimonthly)

Comments: Aims to assist those involved in the theatrical profession at times of financial crisis, and to promote the theatre, and to promote understanding between the members of the profession and the public. Services provided include aid to the sick, legal counsel, informational services, social activities, and memorial services for members.

OMEGA PSI PHI FRATERNITY, INC.
2714 Georgia Avenue, N.W.
Washington, D.C. 20001   (202) 667-7158

Principal officers: Marion W. Gamett, President
                       Edward Braynon, Executive Vice President
                       C. D. Henry, Executive Secretary

Permanent staff: 5   Membership: 45,000
Date founded: 1911   Membership dues: NI
Branches: 435 regional   Scope: national

Special requirements for membership: college student or completion of Bachelor's degree

Nature of organization: fraternal

Publications: *Oracle*, 1919– (quarterly); *Omega Bulletin*, 1960– (quarterly); also publishes books.

Affiliations: NAACP; Leadership Conference on Civil Rights

OMEGA PSI PHI FRATERNITY, INC. (cont'd)

Major conventions/meetings: national convention every 18 months

Comments: The purpose of this fraternal organization is to unite college men concerned with social action in the civic and political life of their community and nation. It sponsors various community projects and scholarship programs.

SOUTHERN CHRISTIAN LEADERSHIP CONFERENCE
330 Auburn Avenue, N.E.
Atlanta, Georgia 30303   (404) 522-1420

Principal officers: Dr. Ralph D. Abernathy, President
                       Dr. J. E. Lowery, Chairman of the Board

Permanent staff: 98	Membership: NI
Date founded: 1957	Membership dues: NI
Branches: NI	Scope: national

Special requirements for membership: none

Nature of organization: political, educational, cultural, welfare

Publications: *Newsletter* (monthly)

Major conventions/meetings: annual

Comments: This service agency coordinates the efforts of local organizations striving to attain equality in human rights. It subscribes to a non-violent philosophy of attaining "full citizenship rights, equality, and the integration of the Negro in all aspects of American life." Most activity is carried on in 16 Southern states; assistance is given in political and legal problems, in financial aid for health, handicapped, etc. Educational programs help instruct in problems of reading, income tax forms, Social Security. The organization sponsors lectures and conferences and distributes literature aimed at increasing the Negro vote.

BRAZILIAN-AMERICAN ORGANIZATIONS

Additional information on Brazilian-American organizations in the United States may be obtained from the Office of the Brazilian Embassy (3006 Whitehaven Street, Washington, D.C. 20008), or from the Brazilian American Chamber of Commerce (22 West 48th Street, New York, New York 10036).

BRAZILIAN AMERICAN CHAMBER OF COMMERCE
22 West 48th Street
New York, New York 10036   (212) 246-3950

Principal officers: Mrs. Suzanne Kincaid Barner, Executive Director

Nature of organization: economic

Publications: *News Bulletin* (monthly)

Comments: Objectives of the organization are to promote Brazilian-American business ties. Until 1968 it was known as the American-Brazilian Association. It compiles statistics, provides special mailings, press releases, information, etc. The organization also sponsors discussion groups and socials. It maintains a reference library.

BRAZILIAN AMERICAN CULTURAL INSTITUTE (BACI)
4201 Connecticut Avenue, N.W.
Suite 211
Washington, D.C. 20008   (202) 362-8334

Principal officers: Jose Neistein, Executive Director

Permanent staff: 9	Membership: 700
Date founded: 1964	Membership dues: NI
Branches: NI	Scope: NI

BRAZILIAN AMERICAN CULTURAL INSTITUTE (BACI) (cont'd)

Special requirements for membership: persons interested in U.S.-Brazilian relations and
cultural exchange

Nature of organization: cultural, educational

Publications: *Bulletin* (quarterly)

Major conventions/meetings: annual seminars of Brazilian studies

Comments: The objectives of the Institute are to promote cultural exchange between the
United States and Brazil. It also sponsors courses in Portuguese language and Brazilian
literature, an art gallery of American and Brazilian works, annual seminars of Brazilian
studies, movies, lectures, and concerts. A library of 3,000 volumes (Portuguese and
English titles), photos, slides, records, and tapes is maintained.

BRAZILIAN-AMERICAN SOCIETY (B.A.S.)

57 West 46th Street
New York, New York 10036   (212) 765-6409

Principal officers: Benito C. Romero, President
                        Jamil Degan, Vice President
                        Fred Santos, Secretary

Permanent staff: 5   Membership: 3,600
Date founded: 1969   Membership dues: $15.00 single (annual);
Branches: 1 regional $25.00 couple

Special requirements for membership: none

Nature of organizations: social, cultural, sport, educational, recreational, travel

Publications: *B.A.S. Bulletin*, 1970– (monthly)

Comments: The organization provides its members with the following services: entertainment
within the scope of Brazilian culture; distribution and sale of artifacts, magazines,
newspapers, records and specialties typically Brazilian; arrangement of group flights
to Brazil at great savings; instruction in the Portuguese language; assistance for
Brazilians adjusting to life in the United States.

BRAZILIAN CENTER OF NEW YORK, INC.

30 West 57th Street
New York, New York 10019   (212) 247-1236

Principal officers: Nair de Mesquita, President
                        Stefen H. Robock, Executive Vice President
                        Ademir Nunes Pinheiro, Secretary of Finances

Permanent staff: 4   Membership: 200
Date founded: 1958   Membership dues: $50.00 family
Branches: none   (annual); $36.00 single (annual)

Special requirements for membership: none

Nature of organization: social, educational, cultural, recreational, sport, fraternal, youth

Publications: monthly bulletin, 1958–

Affiliations: none

Major conventions/meetings: none

Comments: Primarily organized to further friendship and cooperation between the American
and Brazilian people. The Center promotes trips to and from Brazil, organizes conferences, concerts, art showings, and Portuguese language classes. Also offers assistance
to Brazilians settling in the United States by aiding in job placement, school enroll-
ment, and housing. Organizes various social activities such as dances, picnics, and sports
events. Maintains a large library collection of over 3,000 volumes, as well as archival
materials.

BRITISH-AMERICAN ORGANIZATIONS

See also Manx-American Organizations, Scottish-American Organizations, and Welsh-American Organizations

Additional information on British-American organizations may be obtained from the Office of the British Embassy (3100 Massachusetts Avenue, Washington, D.C. 20008) and The British-American Chamber of Commerce (10 East 40th Street, New York, New York 10016). For regional and local organizations, see *Greater Cleveland Nationalities Directory 1974* (Cleveland: Sun Newspapers and the Nationalities Services Center, 1974).

ANGLO-AMERICAN ASSOCIATES (AAA)
117 East 35th Street
New York, New York 10016 (212) 684-4528
Principal officers: Ruth Emery, Executive Secretary
Permanent staff: 5 Membership: 250
Date founded: 1964 Membership dues: NI
Branches: NI Scope: NI
Special requirements for membership: scholars in the field of British studies in history, literature, and the fine arts
Nature of organization: educational, cultural
Publications: *British Studies Monitor* (quarterly); *Research in Progress in British Studies* (biennial)
Comments: The purpose of the organization is to strengthen the lines of communication between scholars in Great Britain and America. The organization also arranges lectures for visiting British scholars.

ANGLO-AMERICAN FAMILIES ASSOCIATION
49 West 72nd Street
New York, New York 10023

ANGLO-AMERICAN FRIENDSHIP ASSOCIATION, INC.
5019 Avenue I
Brooklyn, New York 11234

ASSOCIATION OF BRITISH SECRETARIES IN AMERICA, LTD.
Park Royal Hotel, No. 205
23 West 73rd Street
New York, New York 10023

BRITISH-AMERICAN EDUCATIONAL FOUNDATION
426 East 89th Street
New York, New York 10028 (212) 722-3196
Principal officers: Mrs. Frederick V. P. Bryan, Executive Director
Permanent staff: NI Membership: NI
Date founded: NI Membership dues: NI
Branches: NI Scope: international
Nature of organization: educational, cultural
Comments: The purpose of the organization is to promote U.S.-Great Britain relations and to provide opportunities for student exchange programs on the college level.

BRITISH BRIDES CLUB
906 South Grundy Street
Baltimore, Maryland 21205

BRITISH COMMONWEALTH MEDICAL SOCIETY OF NEW YORK
525 East 68th Street
New York, New York 10021

BRITISH SOCIAL AND ATHLETIC CLUB (BSAC)
13429 Tiara Street
Van Nuys, California 91401   (213) 787-9985

Principal officers: Mrs. Thomas A. Selby, President
                      Ernest Jones, Vice President
                      Alan Crump, Secretary
                      Ralph Levy, Treasurer

Permanent staff: 1   Membership: 30,000 families
Date founded: 1966   Membership dues: $5.00 single;
Branches: 10 state $10.00 family
                                      Scope: state plus branches in U.K.,
                                         New Zealand, and Australia

Special requirements for membership: recommendation

Nature of organization: social, recreational, sport

Publications: 10 monthly chapter magazines

Comments: The club emphasizes social activities, such as dances and get-togethers. It is
    active in promoting and teaching cricket and soccer. Sponsors charter flights to Great
    Britain, New Zealand, Australia, and Hong Kong.

BRITONS IN AMERICA CLUB (B.I.A. CLUB)
6167 Randolph Road
Cleveland, Ohio 44121

Principal officers: Bernard Kerwin, President
                      Robert Black, Vice President
                      Bernard Woodward, Secretary

Permanent staff: NI   Membership: 295
Date founded: 1959   Membership dues: $10.00
Branches: none   Scope: local

Special requirements for membership: active: birth in England, Scotland, Wales and Ireland
    and immediate families; associate: recommendation by two members in good standing;
    honorary: by 2/3 affirmative votes of Executive Board

Nature of organization: social

Publications: *Courier*, 1963– (monthly)

Major conventions/meetings: monthly meetings

Comments: Primarily social in nature.

ENGLISH SPEAKING UNION OF THE UNITED STATES (BRITISH)
16 East 69th Street
New York, New York 10021

Principal officers: William G. Gridley, Executive Director

Permanent staff: 32   Membership: 37,000
Date founded: 1920   Membership dues: NI
Branches: 75 local   Scope: NI

Affiliations: English Speaking Union of the Commonwealth (sister society)

Major conventions/meetings: annual

Comments: The objectives of the organization are to promote understanding and fellowship
    among Americans and the British. It administers travel and information programs,
    arranges for speakers and lectures, and grants funds for travel and scholarships.

NATIONAL SOCIETY, DAUGHTERS OF THE BRITISH EMPIRE IN THE UNITED STATES OF AMERICA
4703 Ivanhoe
Houston, Texas 77027   (713) 626-7221

Principal officers: Mrs. Ben T. Withers, National President

Permanent staff: NI   Membership: 5,500
Date founded: 1909   Membership dues: NI
Branches: in various states   Scope: national

Special requirements for membership: women of British birth or descent

Nature of organization: social, charitable

Affiliations: Imperial Order Daughters of the Empire (Canadian)

Major conventions/meetings: annual

Comments: The society maintains homes for the aged of British descent.

PILGRIMS OF THE UNITED STATES
74 Trinity Place
New York, New York 10006   (212) 943-0635

Permanent staff: 1   Membership: 1,000
Date founded: 1903   Membership dues: NI
Branches: NI   Scope: NI

Affiliations: English organization—Pilgrims of Great Britain

Comments: The aim of the organization is to promote Anglo-American relations by inviting speakers to Pilgrim dinners in each country.

ROYAL AIR FORCES ASSOCIATION (RAFA)
c/o British Consulate General
845 Third Avenue
New York, New York 10022

Principal officers: Robert W. Thomson, Secretary

Permanent staff: NI   Membership: 75
Date founded: 1950   Membership dues: NI
Branches: NI   Scope: NI

Special requirements for membership: veterans of the Royal Air Force or Commonwealth air forces (e.g., Canadian, Australian, etc.)

Affiliations: Royal Air Force, London

Major conventions/meetings: annual convention

Comments: The purpose of the organization is "to raise funds to help distressed members."

THE ROYAL NAVAL ASSOCIATION, NEW YORK BRANCH
c/o Mr. Frederick H. Price
248 West 17th Street
New York, New York 10011

Principal officers: F. H. Price, Chairman

Permanent staff: NI   Membership: 24
Date founded: NI   Membership dues: NI
Branches: NI   Scope: NI

Special requirements for membership: past or present member of the British Commonwealth Naval Forces

Comments: This organization provides fraternal and social activities for members. It is particularly active when British ships visit the United States.

ROYAL NAVAL OFFICERS' CLUB OF NEW YORK
P.O. Box 234
37 West 44th Street
New York, New York 10036   (212) 986-7800

Principal officers: Alexander K. Reddin, Secretary

Permanent staff: NI   Membership: 45
Date founded: 1954   Membership dues: NI
Branches: NI   Scope: NI

Special requirements for membership: ex-officers of the (British) Royal navies and
associates

Comments: The objectives of the organization are to unite former British officers and to
provide opportunities for friendship, sailing excursions, and contests.

ROYAL NAVAL VOLUNTEER RESERVE OFFICERS' ASSOCIATION
Mr. Peter D. Buckland
c/o Dominick & Dominick, Inc.
320 Park Avenue
New York, New York 10022

ST. GEORGE'S SOCIETY OF NEW YORK
15 East 26th Street
New York, New York 10010   (212) 532-2816

Principal officers: Hon. John A. Ford, President
                        G. H. P. Robins, Vice President
                        Charles G. Mills, Secretary

Permanent staff: 2   Membership: 850
Date founded: 1770   Membership dues: $15.00 member
Branches: NI   (annual); $100.00 corporate

Special requirements for membership: admits male persons who are natives or descendants of
natives of England, the British Isles, and Commonwealth

Nature of organization: charitable

Publications: annual report (annual)

Major conventions/meetings: business meetings, twice a year

Comments: Major purpose is to provide assistance to needy persons from Great Britain and
the Commonwealth nations who may be faced with illness, poverty, and other such
adversities in the New York area.

TRANSATLANTIC BRIDES AND PARENTS ASSOCIATION—U.S. AND CANADA DIVISION
4719 East 38th Street
Indianapolis, Indiana 46218   (317) 547-1862

Principal officers: Alex White, Chairman
                        Kathleen Holmes, Secretary
                        Vera Redfern, Treasurer

Permanent staff: none   Membership: 12,000
Date founded: 1968 (U.S. division)   Membership dues: approximately $5.00
Branches: 22 regional; 321 branches   Scope: national

Special requirements for membership: British immigrants, their spouses and children,
children's spouses, etc.

Nature of organization: social

Publications: *Together Again* (monthly)

Affiliations: Transatlantic Brides and Parents Association—United Kingdom Division

Major conventions/meetings: biennial convention

TRANSATLANTIC BRIDES AND PARENTS ASSOCIATION—U.S. AND CANADA DIVISION (cont'd)

Comments: As the name implies, this organization, TBPA, was formed for the benefit of the parents and families in the United Kingdom whose daughters married American or Canadian servicemen during World War II. Later, membership was made available to such daughters, their husbands, and children. The Association provides advice to families, fosters Anglo-American and Anglo-Canadian relations, and organizes tours to the United Kingdom. Divisions of this organization exist also in England and Canada.

BULGARIAN-AMERICAN ORGANIZATIONS

Additional information on Bulgarian-American organizations, religion, and life in the United States may be obtained from the diocese of the Bulgarian Eastern Orthodox Church (312 West 101st Street, New York, New York 10025). For regional and local organizations, see *Ethnic Directory I* (Detroit: Southeastern Michigan Regional Ethnic Heritage Studies Center, 1973).

AMERICAN BULGARIAN LEAGUE (ABL)
35 Sutton Place
New York, New York 10022 (212) 755-8480
Principal officers: Dr. George Obreshkow, President

Permanent staff: NI Membership: 600
Date founded: 1944 Membership dues: NI
Branches: NI Scope: national
Special requirements for membership: of Bulgarian descent
Nature of organization: cultural
Publications: *American Bulgarian Review* (irregular)
Major conventions/meetings: annual

BULGARIAN LADIES' BENEVOLENT SOCIETY
St. John's Church
Woodward and Fisher Freeway
Detroit, Michigan 48230 (313) 869-0492
Principal officers: Mrs. Daskalov

Permanent staff: NI Membership: NI
Date founded: NI Membership dues: NI
Branches: NI Scope: regional
Special requirements for membership: Bulgarian descent
Nature of organization: social
Publications: none
Affiliations: International Institute; Bulgarian Macedonian American Cultural Club
Major conventions/meetings: annual
Comments: A social organization for women of Bulgarian descent; it promotes cultural activities and concerts.

BULGARIAN MACEDONIAN AMERICAN CULTURAL CLUB
315 West Nevada
Detroit, Michigan 48203
Principal officers: Peter Paycheff

Permanent staff: NI Membership: NI
Date founded: NI Membership dues: NI
Branches: NI Scope: regional

BULGARIAN MACEDONIAN AMERICAN CULTURAL CLUB (cont'd)

Nature of organization: cultural, social

Publications: none

Affiliations: International Institute

Major conventions/meetings: annual concert

Comments: This club strives to preserve Bulgarian heritage and culture in the United States. It sponsors concerts and cultural activities and raises money for Bulgarian radio programs.

BULGARIAN NATIONAL COMMITTEE

200 West 57th Street
New York, New York 10019

Permanent staff: NI	Membership: NI
Date founded: NI	Membership dues: NI
Branches: NI	Scope: national

Nature of organization: political, educational

Publications: *Free and Independent Bulgaria*, 1949– (bimonthly)

Comments: The purpose of this organization is to promote interest in and support for the cause of independence for Bulgaria.

BULGARIAN NATIONAL FRONT

P.O. Box 1204, Grand Central Station
New York, New York 10017   (212) 362-7266

Principal officers: Dr. Ivan Docheff, President

Permanent staff: NI	Membership: 1,000
Date founded: 1948	Membership dues: NI
Branches: NI	Scope: national

Special requirements for membership: none

Nature of organization: cultural, political

Publications: *Borba* (monthly)

Major conventions/meetings: annual

Comments: The organization attempts to preserve Bulgarian culture in the United States and to promote freedom for communist Bulgaria. It conducts seminars on Bulgarian history and culture.

BULGARIAN SOCIALIST LABOR FEDERATION

5406 Russell Street
Detroit, Michigan 48211

Nature of organization: political, economic, labor education

Publications: *Labor Education*, 1911– (monthly)

Comments: The purpose of the organization is to keep its members informed about events in Bulgaria and news items on Bulgarian-Americans. Emphasis is on providing information and discussions on labor and other political issues.

MACEDONIAN PATRIOTIC ORGANIZATIONS OF THE US AND CANADA (MPO)

542 South Meridian Street
Indianapolis, Indiana 46225   (317) 635-2157

Principal officers: Dimiter N. Popov, National Secretary

Permanent staff: NI	Membership: NI
Date founded: 1922	Membership dues: NI
Branches: NI	Scope: NI

Special requirements for membership: Macedonian origin

Nature of organization: political

Publications: *Macedonian Tribune* (Makedonska Tribina), 1927– (weekly)

**MACEDONIAN PATRIOTIC ORGANIZATIONS OF THE US AND
CANADA (MPO) (cont'd)**

Major conventions/meetings: annual convention

Comments: The objectives of the organization are to preserve the Macedonian heritage
through uniting Macedonian organizations in the United States. It sponsors cultural and
social activities and it promotes political autonomy for Macedonia.

BYELORUSSIAN-AMERICAN ORGANIZATIONS

Additional information on Byelorussian-American organizations may be
obtained from the Byelorussian Congress Committee of America (85-26 125th
Street, Queens, New York 11415). For regional and local organizations, see also
Greater Cleveland Nationalities Directory 1974 (Cleveland: Sun Newspapers and
the Nationalities Services Center, 1974) and *Ethnic Directory I* (Detroit: Southeastern Michigan Regional Ethnic Heritage Studies Center, 1973).

AMERICAN-BYELORUSSIAN CULTURAL RELIEF ASSOCIATION
c/o Arkadjusz Socewicz
4501 Tiedeman Road
Cleveland, Ohio 44109

Principal officers: Nina Abramczyk, Secretary

Permanent staff: NI   Membership: 65
Date founded: 1957   Membership dues: NI
Branches: NI   Scope: NI

Special requirements for membership: Byelorussian birth or descent

Nature of organization: cultural, welfare

Comments: The objectives of the organization are to provide assistance to Byelorussians in
need and to unite Byelorussians in activities that preserve the Byelorussian culture.
Anti-communist activities are also sponsored.

**AMERICAN FRIENDS OF ANTI-BOLSHEVIK BLOC OF NATIONS—BYELORUSSIAN
DIVISION (AF-ABN Byelorussian Division)**
c/o Mr. A. Pleskachevski
314 South 21st Street
Irvington, New Jersey 07111   (201) 374-5881

Principal officers: Anatol Pleskachevski, President
Michael Bachar, Vice President
Michael Senko, Secretary

Permanent staff: 3   Membership: 22
Date founded: 1953   Membership dues: donations
Branches: NI   Scope: national

Special requirements for membership: interest in Byelorussian national liberation and anti-
communist stand

Nature of organization: political

Affiliations: American Friends of ABN

Major conventions/meetings: triennial conventions; also conferences

Comments: Primarily devoted to the cause of liberating Byelorussia from Soviet Russian
domination, as well as the restoration of a democratic non-communist government
in Byelorussia. Maintains archival materials.

AMERICAN FRIENDS OF BYELORUSSIAN CENTRAL COUNCIL
233 Paulison Avenue
Passaic, New Jersey 07055   (201) 471-0008
Principal officers: Emanuel Jasiuk, President
                        Ksenofont Wojciechowski, Vice President
                        Witali Ciarpicki, Secretary

Permanent staff: 5   Membership: 150
Date founded: 1960   Membership dues: $1.00
Branches: NI   Scope: national

Special requirements for membership: proof of nationality

Nature of organization: political

Publications: none

Major conventions/meetings: annual conference

BYELORUSSIAN-AMERICAN ASSOCIATION, INC. (BAZA)
166-34 Gothic Drive
Jamaica, New York 11432   (212) 746-1971
Principal officers: Dr. Roger Horoshko, President
                        Walter Stankievich, Vice President
                        Raisa Stankevic, Secretary

Permanent staff: 12   Membership: 1,800
Date founded: 1949   Membership dues: $12.00 (annual)
Branches: 7 regional; 3 local   Scope: national

Special requirements for membership: none

Nature of organization: social, educational, cultural

Publications: *Bielarus*, 1950– (monthly); *Bulletin of the Byelorussian-American Association*
    (irregular); also publishes books

Major conventions/meetings: biennial conventions

Comments: Major objectives are to coordinate and intensify Byelorussian-American participa-
    tion in U.S. peace efforts and to strengthen and propagate the American way of life; to
    support Byelorussian struggle for freedom and independence; and to demand fair treat-
    ment of Byelorussians in their native land. Promotes lectures of Byelorussian history
    and culture. Organizes commemorations, celebrations, and political meetings. Opposes
    communism. Maintains a library of over 4,000 volumes and extensive archives.

BYELORUSSIAN-AMERICAN COUNCIL OF CHICAGO
c/o Mr. U. Minkevich
1500 North Maplewood Avenue
Chicago, Illinois 60622

BYELORUSSIAN-AMERICAN REPUBLICAN NATIONAL FEDERATION
82-21 164th Place
Jamaica, New York 11432

BYELORUSSIAN-AMERICAN UNION OF NEW YORK
104-29 Atlantic Avenue
Richmond Hill, New York 11419   (212) 441-8053
Principal officers: Constant Mierlak, President
                        Peter Melianovich, Vice President
                        Vasil Scecka, Secretary

Permanent staff: none   Membership: 120
Date founded: 1965   Membership dues: $12.00 (annual)
Branches: NI   Scope: state

Special requirements for membership: none

Nature of organization: cultural

Publications: none

BYELORUSSIAN-AMERICAN UNION OF NEW YORK (cont'd)

Major conventions/meetings: general membership meeting, biennial

Comments: Promotes the American way of life among Byelorussian-Americans and encourages their participation in political elections. Supports the independence and freedom of Byelorussia. Maintains archives on the Byelorussian liberation movement.

BYELORUSSIAN-AMERICAN VETERANS' ASSOCIATION
46 Broadway
Passaic, New Jersey 07055

Principal officers: Andrew Minczuk, Commander
Constant Mierlak, Vice President
Simon Zemojda, Secretary

Permanent staff: 4
Date founded: 1964
Branches: 3 regional

Membership: 150
Membership dues: $1.00
Scope: regional

Special requirements for membership: discharge from U.S. Army

Nature of organization: veterans

Publications: none

Comments: Promotes the welfare of Byelorussian-American veterans. Acts on interests affecting veterans. Holds celebrations of various events.

BYELORUSSIAN-AMERICAN YOUTH ORGANIZATION (BAYO)
166-34 Gothic Drive
Jamaica, New York 11432

Principal officers: Raisa Stankievic, President

Permanent staff: NI
Date founded: 1950
Branches: 7 state

Membership: 600
Membership dues: NI
Scope: national

Special requirements for membership: young people (15-35 years of age) of Byelorussian descent

Nature of organization: cultural, social

Publications: *Byelorussian Youth* (quarterly); also publishes books

Major conventions/meetings: biennial

Comments: The organization attempts to preserve the Byelorussian culture and heritage in the United States. It promotes the Byelorussian language and encourages young people to attain higher education. Until 1967 it was known as the Byelorussian Youth Association of America. The organization provides information on conditions in Byelorussia under Soviet domination; it organizes meetings, clubs, lectures, seminars, and social events. Summer camps are sponsored for teaching Byelorussian language, culture, and history. A library is maintained.

BYELORUSSIAN CENTER
c/o Rev. N. Lapitzki
192 Turnpike Road
South River, New Jersey 08882

BYELORUSSIAN CONGRESS COMMITTEE OF AMERICA
85-26 125th Street
Queens, New York 11415

(212) 847-0719

Principal officers: John Kosiak, President
Michael Bachar, Vice President
Michael Sienko, Secretary

Permanent staff: none
Date founded: 1951
Branches: 8 state; 20 local

Membership: 2,000
Membership dues: $10.00 (annual)
Scope: national

BYELORUSSIAN CONGRESS COMMITTEE OF AMERICA (cont'd)

Special requirements for membership: individuals of Byelorussian birth or descent, or organizations composed of Byelorussian members

Nature of organization: political

Publications: *Byelorussian Thought*, 1959– (semiannual); *Bulletin* (irregular); also publishes books

Affiliations: Byelorussian Veterans Organization; Byelorussian Church Organization; Byelorussian Youth Organization

Major conventions/meetings: annual

Comments: Promotes support in the fight for the liberation of Byelorussia from Soviet communist control. Supports the restoration of an independent Byelorussian state according to the formulation of the First and Second Byelorussian Congresses. Supports the United States government and the United States Constitution. Provides information on the present state of affairs in Byelorussia. Until 1966 the organization was known as the Whiteruthenian (Byelorussian) Congress Committee of America.

BYELORUSSIAN LIBERATION FRONT (BLF)
5610 Luelda Avenue
Cleveland, Ohio 44129

Principal officers: Konstant Matylicki, Secretary

Permanent staff: NI	Membership: 250
Date founded: 1957	Membership dues: NI
Branches: 5	Scope: NI

Nature of organization: political

Publications: *Baracba* (Struggle)

Major conventions/meetings: annual

Comments: The intent of the organization is to unite Byelorussians in America and to promote the struggle for a free Byelorussian government.

BYELORUSSIAN NATIONAL COUNCIL IN CHICAGO
1500 North Maplewood Avenue
Chicago, Illinois 60622

BYELORUSSIAN UNITED METHODIST REPRESENTATION IN DIASPORA
1716 N.E. 7th Terrace
Gainesville, Florida 32601   (904) 378-3951

Principal officers: Rev. Dr. John Piotrowski, President
Alice Piotrowski, Executive Secretary

Permanent staff: 2	Membership: NI
Date founded: 1961	Membership dues: NI
Branches: none	Scope: national

Special requirements for membership: none

Nature of organization: political, educational, cultural, religious

Publications: *The Torch of Christian Teaching*, 1933– (monthly); also publishes books

Affiliations: Byelorussian Congress Committee

Comments: Acts as a central organization for Methodists who left Byelorussia after World War II. Promotes Protestantism. It is also involved in cultural, educational, and political activities. Maintains a library of over 1,000 volumes and archival materials consisting of manuscripts and letters.

BYELORUSSIAN VETERANS' ASSOCIATION IN THE USA
9 River Road
Highland Park, New Jersey 08904

COUNCIL OF BYELORUSSIAN DEMOCRATIC REPUBLIC
166-34 Gothic Drive
Jamaica, New York 11432

THE JOHN AND ALICE PIOTROWSKI BYELORUSSIAN CHARITABLE EDUCATIONAL FUND
1716 N.E. 7th Terrace
Gainesville, Florida 32601   (904) 378-3951

Principal officers: Rev. Dr. John Piotrowski, President
                       Mrs. Alice Piotrowski, Secretary

Permanent staff: none   Membership: NI
Date founded: 1973   Membership dues: contributions
Branches: none   Scope: national

Special requirements for membership: none

Nature of organization: educational

Publications: publishes books

Affiliations: none

Major conventions/meetings: none

Comments: Fund set up for the publication of historical, cultural, and literary works in
    Byelorussian.

KASTUS KALINOWSKI BYELORUSSIAN SOCIETY ASSEMBLY 319 UWA
85-26 125th Street
Kew Gardens, New York 11415   (212) 847-0719

Principal officers: Wladimir Pielesa, Secretary

Permanent staff: none   Membership: 15
Date founded: 1955   Membership dues: none
Branches: none   Scope: NI

Special requirements for membership: none

Nature of organization: economic

Publications: none

UNITED WHITERUTHENIAN AMERICAN RELIEF COMMITTEE
192 Turnpike Road
South River, New Jersey 08882

Principal officers: Very Rev. Nikolaj Lapitzki, Secretary

Permanent staff: NI   Membership: 478
Date founded: 1948   Membership dues: NI
Branches: 3 regional   Scope: national

Special requirements for membership: of Byelorussian descent

Nature of organization: welfare, cultural, fraternal

Publications: publishes books

Affiliations: Byelorussian Congress Committee

Major conventions/meetings: annual

Comments: This welfare organization provides relief and assistance to Byelorussians in need.

WHITERUTHENIAN INSTITUTE OF ARTS AND SCIENCE (BYELORUSSIAN)
3441 Tibbett Avenue
Bronx, New York 10463   (212) 549-5395

Principal officers: Jan Zaprudnik, Secretary

Permanent staff: NI   Membership: 70
Date founded: 1951   Membership dues: NI
Branches: 1   Scope: NI

Publications: *Konadni*, 1955– (in Byelorussian; irregular); *Annals* (in Byelorussian; irregular);
    also publishes books

**WHITERUTHENIAN INSTITUTE OF ARTS AND SCIENCE
(BYELORUSSIAN)** (cont'd)

Major conventions/meetings: biennial, always in November, in New York City

Comments: The organization is concerned with scholarly research, writing, and works of art. Emphasis is on Byelorussia as a country, its history and traditions. Other activities in literature and the fine arts are also sponsored.

CANADIAN-AMERICAN ORGANIZATIONS

Additional information on Canadian-American organizations in the United States may be obtained from the Office of the Canadian Embassy (1746 Massachusetts Avenue, Washington, D.C. 20036), or from the Canada-United States Committee (c/o Chamber of Commerce of the U.S., 1615 "H" Street, N.W., Washington, D.C. 20006).

ASSOCIATION CANADO AMERICAINE (ACA)
52 Concord Street
Manchester, New Hampshire 03101   (603) 625-8577

Principal officers: Gerald Robert, President General
                     Lucille Maihiot, Secretary General

Permanent staff: 80   Membership: 30,359
Date founded: 1896   Membership dues: varies
Branches: 9 state; 72 local   Scope: national

Special requirements for membership: American and Canadian Roman Catholics of French descent

Nature of organization: fraternal insurance, educational

Publications: *Le Canado-Americain* (bimonthly)

Major conventions/meetings: quadrennial, next in 1976

Comments: The major purpose of this organization is to provide life insurance benefits to its members. It also promotes interest in French literature and French immigration in North America. A 25,000-volume library is maintained.

CANADA-UNITED STATES COMMITTEE
c/o Chamber of Commerce of the U.S.
1615 "H" Street, N.W.
Washington, D.C. 20006   (202) 659-6113

Principal officers: Frederick W. Stokeld, Secretary

Permanent staff: NI   Membership: 36
Date founded: 1933   Membership dues: NI
Branches: two sections (for United States and   Scope: national
  Canada)

Nature of organization: economic

Publications: publishes booklets

Affiliations: Chamber of Commerce of the U.S.; Canadian Chamber of Commerce

Major conventions/meetings: semiannual

Comments: This organization is composed of 18 members from each country (United States and Canada). It conducts research in trade and investment problems of both countries, particularly problems that are of mutual concern.

THE CANADIAN AMERICAN ASSOCIATION OF NORTHERN CALIFORNIA
406 Sutter Street, Suite 400
San Francisco, California 94108

Permanent staff: NI
Date founded: NI
Branches: NI

Membership: NI
Membership dues: NI
Scope: regional

CANADIAN-AMERICAN COMMITTEE
c/o National Planning Association
1606 New Hampshire Avenue
Washington, D.C. 20009   (202) 265-7685

Principal officers: John Miller, Secretary

Permanent staff: NI
Date founded: 1957
Branches: NI

Membership: 90
Membership dues: NI
Scope: national

Nature of organization: professional, economic

Major conventions/meetings: semiannual

Comments: This organization of business and professional leaders from Canada and America studies the long-range problems involved in greater exchange and sharing between the United States and Canada of resources, trade, and investment. It is sponsored jointly by the National Planning Association and the C. D. Howe Research Institute.

THE CANADIAN CLUB OF BOSTON
40 Indian Road
Medfield, Massachusetts 02052

Principal officers: Mr. Allan J. Hatfield, Jr., President

CANADIAN CLUB OF CHICAGO
332 South Michigan Avenue, Suite 410
Chicago, Illinois 60604   (312) 782-3760

Principal officers: D. E. Alexander, President
D. R. Henderson, Vice President
J. L. Hopper, Vice President
Miss V. B. Bryant, Secretary

Permanent staff: none
Date founded: 1942
Branches: none

Membership: 240
Membership dues: $10.00 (annual)
Scope: local

Special requirements for membership: Canadian citizenship or former citizenship; or business or fraternal interests in Canada

Nature of organization: fraternal

Publications: none

Major conventions/meetings: six meetings a year

Comments: The club strives to provide Americans with a better understanding of Canada and to give Canadians a realistic interpretation of the American way of life. It also helps the many Canadians settling in Chicago to adjust to the life style of this country. Promotes good citizenship concepts in both countries.

CANADIAN CLUB OF NEW ORLEANS
937 Henry Clay Avenue
New Orleans, Louisiana 70115

Principal officers: Dr. Lindsay Graham, President

CANADIAN CLUB OF NEW YORK (CCNY)
Waldorf-Astoria Hotel
New York, New York 10022   (212) 753-6162

Principal officers: James J. MacDougall, Manager

CANADIAN CLUB OF NEW YORK (CCNY) (cont'd)

Permanent staff: NI

Date founded: 1903

Branches: NI

Membership: 1,673

Membership dues: NI

Scope: regional

Publications: *Maple Leaf* (quarterly)

Comments: A Canadian men's social club.

LE COMITÉ DE VIE FRANCO-AMÉRICAINE

341 4th Street

Fall River, Massachusetts 02721

Principal officers: Dr. Francois J. Martineau, President

ROYAL CANADIAN LEGION

Great Lakes States Command

2394 Goodenough Avenue

Akron, Ohio 44320

Principal officers: Hilda Savage, Commander

Special requirements for membership: male or female veterans of the Canadian armed forces

Nature of organization: social, educational, welfare

Comments: This veterans' organization assists needy veterans and their dependents, provides social activities for members, and sponsors community projects concerned with health and education.

SOCIÉTÉ HISTORIQUE FRANCO-AMÉRICAINE

213 Laurel Street

Manchester, New Hampshire 03103

Principal officers: Msgr. Adrien Verrette, President

Permanent staff: NI

Date founded: NI

Branches: NI

Membership: NI

Membership dues: NI

Scope: national

Nature of organization: historical

WOMEN'S CANADIAN CLUB OF THE SAN FRANCISCO BAY AREA

1370 Washington Street (president's residence)

San Francisco, California 94109

(415) 474-8074

Principal officers: Audrey Chisholm, President

Patricia Mack, Vice President

Beatrice Allen, Secretary

Permanent staff: none

Date founded: 1966

Branches: 2 state; 1 local

Membership: 88

Membership dues: $5.00 (annual)

Scope: national

Special requirements for membership: women who are native-born or naturalized Canadians and wives of native-born or naturalized Canadians

Nature of organization: social, scholarly

Publications: none

Affiliations: British Commonwealth Club

Major conventions/meetings: monthly meetings

Comments: The objective of the club is to promote philanthropy and to provide fellowship and social and intellectual association among women of Canadian birth or ancestry. Sponsors a scholarship in the form of board and room at the International House.

CARPATHO-RUTHENIAN-AMERICAN ORGANIZATIONS

The Carpatho-Ruthenian-American community in the United States asserts itself as constituting a separate ethnic group embracing immigrants from Carpatho-Ukraine and the Lemkian region. Presently "Carpatho-Ruthenia" or "Carpatian Rus" constitutes an integral part of the Soviet Ukraine.

For background information on Carpatho-Ruthenians in the United States, see Walter C. Warzeski, *Byzantine Rite Rusins in Carpatho-Ruthenia and America* (Pittsburgh: Byzantine Seminary Press, 1971) and *Greater Cleveland Nationalities Directory 1974* (Cleveland: Sun Newspapers and the Nationalities Services Center, 1974). *See also* Russian-American Organizations.

AMERICAN CARPATHO-RUSSIAN YOUTH OF THE ORTHODOX GREEK CATHOLIC CHURCH (ACRY)

312 Garfield Street
Johnstown, Pennsylvania 15906 (814) 536-4207
Principal officers: Alex R. Breno, President
Ronald L. Ross, Vice President
Barbara A. Dasher, Secretary

Permanent staff: NI
Date founded: 1937
Branches: 5 district; 30 chapters

Membership: 1,000
Membership dues: $3.00
Scope: National

Special requirements for membership: Orthodox Christian of at least 16 years of age and a members of Carpatho-Russian Orthodox parish

Nature of organization: social, religious, educational, sport, youth

Publications: *ACRY Annual and Church Almanac*, 1949– (annual); the organization has also published other items

Affiliations: American Carpatho-Russian Orthodox Greek Catholic Diocese; Council of Eastern Orthodox Youth Leaders of the Americas

Major conventions/meetings: annual convention

Comments: The objective of the organization is to perpetuate and maintain the Orthodox faith and to promote the social, cultural, and educational development of young Americans of Carpatho-Russian origin. Organizes projects that aid local churches. Sponsors social and recreational activities, summer camps, leadership training courses, and retreats. Awards scholarships to college students each year. Maintains an archival collection.

AMERICAN RUSSIAN CARPATHIAN WELFARE CLUB

298 Clinton Street
Binghamton, New York 13900

CARPATHO-RUSSIAN BENEVOLENT ASSOCIATION LIBERTY

249 Butler Avenue
Johnstown, Pennsylvania 15906

CARPATHO-RUSSIAN LITERARY ASSOCIATION

Hardy Lane
Trumbull, Connecticut 06611 (203) 268-2359
Principal officers: Peter S. Hardy, President
Joseph G. Simko, Secretary

Permanent staff: 3
Date founded: 1970
Branches: none

Membership: 250
Membership dues: none
Scope: national

Special requirements for membership: none

CARPATHO-RUSSIAN LITERARY ASSOCIATION (cont'd)
Nature of organization: educational, cultural, scholarly
Publications: publishes books
Major conventions/meetings: annual conference
Comments: Compiles, edits, and publishes library materials from various original sources.
  Maintains a library of over 1,500 volumes as well as historical archival materials.

FEDERATED RUSSIAN ORTHODOX CLUBS OF AMERICA (FROC)
  84 East Market Street
  Wilkes-Barre, Pennsylvania 18701   (717) 825-3158
Principal officers: Mrs. Helen R. Zionce, Administrative Secretary
Permanent staff: 1   Membership: 5,000
Date founded: 1927   Membership dues: NI
Branches: 13 regional; 170 local   Scope: national
Special requirements for membership: young persons of Russian Orthodox faith
Nature of organization: religious, cultural, social, athletic, youth, charitable
Publications: *The Russian Orthodox Journal*, 1927– (monthly); *F.R.O.C. Directory* (annual)
Affiliations: Council Eastern Orthodox Youth Leaders of the Americas
Major conventions/meetings: annual convention
Comments: The aim of the organization is to provide religious, cultural, charitable, social, and
  athletic programs for young people in the United States of Russian Orthodox faith. It
  maintains a Junior Division for 10 to 17 year-olds; it sponsors oratorical contests and a
  Choir Director's School, and it grants scholarships to members.

GREEK CATHOLIC CARPATHO-RUSSIAN BENEVOLENT ASSOCIATION LIBERTY
  152 Broad Street
  Perth Amboy, New Jersey 08861

GREEK CATHOLIC UNION OF THE USA
  502 East 8th Avenue
  Munhall, Pennsylvania 15120   (412) 682-3465
Principal officers: George Batyko, President
                      John Masic, Secretary
Permanent staff: NI   Membership: 50,000
Date founded: 1892   Membership dues: NI
Branches: 1,093 local lodges   Scope: national
Special requirements for membership: be insurable
Nature of organization: fraternal
Publications: *Viestnik*, 1892– (weekly)
Major conventions/meetings: quadrennial conventions
Comments: The major aim of this organization is to provide life insurance benefits to its
  members. Sponsors religious, cultural, and recreational activities; grants scholarships.

LEMKO ASSOCIATION
  556 Yonkers Avenue
  Yonkers, New York 10704
Principal officers: Joseph Frycki, Secretary-General
Permanent staff: 4   Membership: 1,500
Date founded: NI   Membership dues: NI
Branches: NI   Scope: national
Nature of organization: fraternal, cultural
Publications: *Karpatska Rus*, 1927– (weekly); *Lemko Youth Journal* (bimonthly); *Almanac
  Calendar* (annual)

LEMKO ASSOCIATION (cont'd)
Major conventions/meetings: biennial meetings
Comments: The association is a Carpatho-Russian fraternal and cultural organization.

RUSSIAN BROTHERHOOD ORGANIZATION OF THE USA
    1733 Spring Garden Street
    Philadelphia, Pennsylvania 19130   (215) 563-2537
Principal officers: Peter Smey, Recording Secretary

Permanent staff: 15	Membership: 12,084
Date founded: 1900	Membership dues: NI
Branches: 5 state; 387 local	Scope: national

Special requirements for membership: be of Russian or Slavonic descent
Nature of organization: fraternal
Publications: *The Truth*, 1900– (monthly)
Major conventions/meetings: quadrennial conventions
Comments: The major objective of the organization is to provide insurance benefits to members. It also awards the SS Cyril and Methodius Scholarship.

RUSSIAN ORTHODOX CATHOLIC MUTUAL AID SOCIETY OF USA
    84 East Market Street
    Wilkes-Barre, Pennsylvania 18701   (717) 822-8591
Principal officers: Basil Homick, Secretary

Permanent staff: NI	Membership: 2,222
Date founded: 1895	Membership dues: NI
Branches: 185 lodges	Scope: national

Nature of organization: fraternal, cultural, religious
Publications: *Svit* (The Light), 1897– (semimonthly); also publishes books
Major conventions/meetings: quadrennial conventions
Comments: The major purpose of the organization is to provide insurance benefits to its members. Sponsors cultural and religious activities.

UNITED RUSSIAN ORTHODOX BROTHERHOOD OF AMERICA (URUBA)
    333 Boulevard of Allies
    Pittsburgh, Pennsylvania 15222
Principal Officers: Anna Karas, Recording Secretary-Treasurer

Permanent staff: NI	Membership: 3,300
Date founded: 1915	Membership dues: NI
Branches: 140 local lodges	Scope: national

Nature of organization: fraternal
Publications: *Russian Messenger*, 1916– (bimonthly)
Major conventions/meetings: quadrennial conventions
Comments: The major objective of the organization is to provide life insurance benefits to members.

UNITED SOCIETIES OF THE UNITED STATES OF AMERICA
    613 Sinclair Street
    McKeesport, Pennsylvania 15132   (717) 342-3294
Principal officers: Nicholas M. Kish, President
                George N. Pegula, Vice President
                Rev. Stephen Loya, Supreme Secretary

Permanent staff: NI	Membership: 34,000
Date founded: 1903	Membership dues: NI
Branches: 183 lodges	Scope: national

Special requirements for membership: belong to a Greek Catholic parish

UNITED SOCIETIES OF THE UNITED STATES OF AMERICA (cont'd)
Nature of organization: fraternal, cultural, religious
Publications: *Enlightenment*, 1917– (monthly)
Major conventions/meetings: quadrennial conventions
Comments: Major goal of the organization is to provide life insurance benefits to its members.

CHILEAN-AMERICAN ORGANIZATIONS

See also Spanish-American Organizations

Additional information on Chilean-American organizations in the United States may be obtained from the Office of the Chilean Embassy (1736 Massachusetts Avenue, Washington, D.C. 20036).

CHILEAN CLUB OF MICHIGAN
900 Normandy
Royal Oak, Michigan 48073
Principal officers: Dr. Pedro Medrano, President
Nelson Munoz, Vice President
Juana Booker, Secretary

Permanent staff: NI
Date founded: NI
Branches: none

Membership: 125
Membership dues: $5.00 (annual)
Scope: state

Special requirements for membership: none
Nature of organization: social, cultural, recreational
Publications: *El Condor*, 1973– (quarterly)
Major conventions/meetings: annual
Comments: This is a cultural and social organization that helps Chilean immigrants adjust to American life. At the same time it attempts to preserve and promote Chilean customs and language among the Chileans of Michigan. Disseminates information about Chile and awards a trip to Chile each year.

CLUB CHILEAN
640 Temple
Detroit, Michigan 48201

CHINESE-AMERICAN ORGANIZATIONS

Additional information on Chinese-American organizations in the United States may be obtained from the Office of the Embassy of the Republic of China (2311 Massachusetts Avenue, Washington, D.C. 20008), from *Special Publication of New York Chinese Laundry Social Athletic Club, Inc.* (New York: New York Chinese Laundry Social Athletic Club, Inc., 1974; *see* appendix), or from the Asian Studies Program (School of Social Science, San Jose State University, San Jose, California 95192). Regional and local information and organizations may be found in *Greater Cleveland Nationalities Directory 1974* (Cleveland: Sun Newspapers and the Nationalities Services Center, 1974) and *Ethnic Directory I* (Detroit: Southeastern Michigan Regional Ethnic Heritage Studies Center, 1973).

AMERICAN ASSOCIATION OF TEACHERS OF CHINESE LANGUAGE AND CULTURE
Sun Yat Sen Hall
St. John's University
Jamaica, New York 11439   (212) 969-8000

Principal officers: Paul K. T. Sih, Executive Secretary

Permanent staff: NI   Membership: 357
Date founded: 1958   Membership dues: NI
Branches: NI   Scope: NI

Special requirements for membership: scholars engaged in teaching Chinese language and
    Chinese cultural subjects in American colleges and universities, and persons interested in
    Chinese culture

Publications: *Newsletter* (semiannual); *Directory of Members* (irregular); also publishes
    monographs and teaching aids

Major conventions/meetings: annual conference

Comments: The major function of this organization is to unite teachers of Chinese culture and
    language in the United States; it also compiles statistics and acts as a placement bureau
    for its members. It publishes teaching aids, conducts scholarly research in Chinese
    studies, and compiles statistics.

ARKANSAS CHINESE ASSOCIATION
Lock's Food Center
Hughes, Arkansas 72348

CENTER FOR CHINESE RESEARCH MATERIALS
Association of Research Libraries
1527 New Hampshire Avenue, N.W.
Washington, D.C. 20036   (202) 387-7172

Principal officers: P. K. Yu, Director

Permanent staff: 5   Membership: NI
Date founded: 1967   Membership dues: NI
Branches: NI   Scope: NI

Nature of organization: educational

Publications: *Newsletter* (irregular)

Comments: The purpose of the organization is to compile complete lists of Chinese publications
    and to strengthen the existing Chinese collections of books, periodicals, and newspapers.

CHINA BUDDHIST ASSOCIATION
169 Canal Street
New York, New York 10013

CHINA INSTITUTE IN AMERICA (CIA)
125 East 65th Street
New York, New York 10021   (212) 744-8181

Principal officers: F. Richard Hsu, President

Permanent staff: 25   Membership: 1,000
Date founded: 1926   Membership dues: NI
Branches: NI   Scope: national

Nature of organization: cultural

Publications: *School Catalogue* (annual)

Major conventions/meetings: annual

Comments: The major function of this organization is to preserve the Chinese customs and
    traditions in America, and to aid Chinese-Americans in the process of acculturation.
    Courses in Chinese history, art, literature, language, philosophy, and cookery are
    offered. A 1,000-volume library is maintained.

CHINESE AMATEUR MUSICIAN ASSOCIATION (CAMA)
18715 Martinique Drive
Houston, Texas 77058   (713) 333-2541
Principal officers: Peggy Pei-Kei King, President
                        Stanton Yao, Vice President
                        Mary Yin, Secretary
Permanent staff: 5   Membership: 56
Date founded: 1972   Membership dues: $2.00 (annual)
Branches: none   Scope: local
Special requirements for membership: Chinese with basic music training
Nature of organization: cultural, social, educational, recreational
Publications: none
Comments: Non-profit organization which promotes musical training among young Americans
        of Chinese origin and promotes the preservation of Chinese musical heritage.

CHINESE AMERICAN ASSOCIATION OF MINNESOTA
P.O. Box 1048
Minneapolis, Minnesota 55440

CHINESE AMERICAN CITIZENS' ALLIANCE
1044 Stockton Street
San Francisco, California 94108   (415) 982-4618
Principal officers: Albert Gee, President
                        Nowland C. Hong, Vice President
                        Harold Y. G. Fong, Secretary
Permanent staff: 1   Membership: 2,000
Date founded: 1895   Membership dues: $5.00 (annual)
Branches: 13 local   Scope: national
Special requirements for membership: males of Chinese descent 18 years of age or over
Nature of organization: fraternal
Publications: *The Chinese American*, 1962– (quarterly)
Major conventions/meetings: biennial
Comments: Purpose is to unite American citizens of Chinese ancestry, to insure legal and
        civil rights of members, to secure equal economic and political opportunities of the
        Chinese community, and to encourage political and voting participation within it.

CHINESE AMERICAN CIVIC COUNCIL (CACC)
2249 South Wentworth Street
Chicago, Illinois 60616   (312) 225-0234
Principal officers: Ping Tom, President
                        Jean Eng, Vice President
                        Helen Wong Jean, Secretary
Permanent staff: 1   Membership: 650
Date founded: 1952   Membership dues: $5.00 (annual)
Branches: none   Scope: regional
Special requirements for membership: none
Nature of organization: educational, cultural, charitable, youth
Publications: *Chinese American Progress* (annual)
Affiliations: none
Major conventions/meetings: none
Comments: Non-partisan, non-sectarian, and non-profit in nature. Charitable and educational
        providing aid to the poor, sponsoring community lectures, and combatting community
        deterioration and juvenile delinquency. Aids in the integration of Chinese residents
        into the mainstream of American life. Awards scholarships.

CHINESE-AMERICAN CULTURAL ASSOCIATION, INC. (CACA)
8122 Mayfield
Chesterland, Ohio 44026   (216) 729-9937
Principal officers: Peter Wang, President
                        J. H. Chang, Vice President
                        Rose K. Wang, Secretary

CHINESE-AMERICAN CULTURAL ASSOCIATION, INC. (CACA) (cont'd)

Permanent staff: 7
Date founded: 1964
Branches: NI

Membership: 810
Membership dues: $2.00 (annual)
Scope: national

Nature of organization: cultural

Publications: *Pamir*, 1973– (monthly)

Major conventions/meetings: annual conference

Comments: The primary objective of this organization is to preserve the Chinese culture in America. A library of 2,000 Chinese books is maintained.

CHINESE-AMERICAN EDUCATIONAL FOUNDATION

2237 South Wentworth Avenue
Chicago, Illinois 60616   (312) 225-7683

Principal officers: Tze-Chung Li, President

Permanent staff: NI
Date founded: 1965
Branches: NI

Membership: 100
Membership dues: NI
Scope: NI

Publications: *Letter to Members* (irregular)

Comments: Grants college and seminary scholarships for students in Taiwan. Funds are raised from churches and businesses interested in providing educational opportunities for Chinese youth.

CHINESE-AMERICAN WOMEN'S CLUB

1526 Chicago Boulevard
Detroit, Michigan 48206

CHINESE ANTI-COMMUNIST LEAGUE

923 North Broadway
Los Angeles, California 90012

CHINESE BENEVOLENT ASSOCIATION

3153 Cass
Detroit, Michigan 48201   (313) 832-3344

Principal officers: Mr. Henry Yee

Permanent staff: NI
Date founded: NI
Branches: branches in various large cities

Membership: NI
Membership dues: NI
Scope: national

Comments: The purpose of this organization is to unite the Chinese in America and to provide help to Chinese merchants.

CHINESE BUDDHIST ASSOCIATION OF HAWAII

42 Kawananakoa Place
Honolulu, Hawaii 96817

CHINESE CATHOLIC CLUB OF HONOLULU

1124 7th Avenue
Honolulu, Hawaii 96816

Principal officers: George Holeso, President
Francis Yim, Vice President
Gwendolyn Chu, Secretary

Permanent staff: none
Date founded: 1925
Branches: none

Membership: 141
Membership dues: $2.00-$3.00 (annual)
Scope: local

Special requirements for membership: Chinese ancestry

Nature of organization: educational, religious, charitable

CHINESE CATHOLIC CLUB OF HONOLULU (cont'd)

Publications: *Chinese Catholic Club News*, 1940– (monthly)

Affiliations: none

Comments: Promotes the spiritual development of members as well as fellowship. Organizes various charitable projects to aid the poor and raises funds for displaced refugees of the Far East. Awards yearly scholarship for higher education as well as for religious vocations.

CHINESE CHAMBER OF COMMERCE
42 North King Street
Honolulu, Hawaii 96817

CHINESE CHAMBER OF COMMERCE
3440 North 16th Street
Phoenix, Arizona 85016

CHINESE CHAMBER OF COMMERCE
1633 N.E. 42nd Avenue
Portland, Oregon 97213

CHINESE COMMUNITY SERVICE ORGANIZATION
3049 Beacon Avenue South
Seattle, Washington 98144

CHINESE CONSOLIDATED BENEVOLENT ASSOCIATION
171 Third Avenue
New York, New York 10003   (212) 777-2195

Principal officers: Chung Ping Tom, President

Permanent staff: 11   Membership: 60,000
Date founded: 1880   Membership dues: NI
Branches: NI   Scope: national

Comments: The aim of this organization is to promote cultural understanding through educational, charitable, social, and recreational activities.

CHINESE CULTURAL ASSOCIATION
P.O. Box 1272
Palo Alto, California 94302   (415) 948-2251

Principal officers: Prof. P. F. Tao, Executive Officer

Permanent staff: NI   Membership: 1,055
Date founded: 1966   Membership dues: NI
Branches: NI   Scope: NI

Special requirements for membership: professors, scientists, engineers, artists, and businessmen

Nature of organization: social, cultural, and educational

Publications: *Journal* (2 or 3 times a year)

Comments: The primary purpose of the organization is to promote understanding of the Chinese culture in the United States and to encourage understanding of other cultures by the Chinese. It provides social activities of cultural interest for members—e.g., lectures, concerts, Chinese painting—and also sponsors films, discussions, and seminars.

CHINESE CULTURAL FOUNDATION OF HAWAII
2746 Pali Highway
Honolulu, Hawaii 96817

CHINESE CULTURE CENTER
Holiday Inn, 3rd Floor
Kearny and Washington Street
San Francisco, California 94111
Principal officers: Kim P. Lee

CHINESE CULTURE FOUNDATION OF SAN FRANCISCO
750 Kearny Street
San Francisco, California 94108   (415) 982-7611
Principal officers: W. D. Y. Wu, Executive Director

Permanent staff: NI	Membership: 920
Date founded: 1965	Membership dues: NI
Branches: NI	Scope: national

Nature of Organization: social, cultural, educational

Comments: The major purpose of the organization is to establish a cultural center in San
    Francisco, where a large Chinese population is found. Plans include an exhibition hall
    to present art works, and a performing arts auditorium. A library and lecture halls
    are also proposed. The goal is to preserve the Chinese culture and tradition in the
    United States and to promote intercultural understanding.

CHINESE DEMOCRATIC CONSTITUTIONAL PARTY
1124 Smith Street
Honolulu, Hawaii 96817

CHINESE DEVELOPMENT COUNCIL (CDC)
5 Division Street
New York, New York 10002   (212) 966-6340
Principal officers: David Ho, Executive Director

Permanent staff: 24	Membership: 1,000
Date founded: 1968	Membership dues: NI
Branches: NI	Scope: NI

Special requirements for membership: immigrants and youth groups, including high school
    clubs and youth gangs

Nature of organization: social

Publications: *Chinatown Magazine* (bimonthly)

Comments: The organization aims to provide employment training and opportunities to
    immigrants and youth in New York's Chinatown. Other services provided are instruc-
    tion in sewing and the English language; recreational activities and facilities are
    provided. It sponsors an annual community leadership award. Publications of interest
    to youth are maintained in a library collection. Until 1972 the organization was known
    as The Chinese Youth Council.

CHINESE EDUCATIONAL WELFARE ASSOCIATION
61 Henry Street
New York, New York 10002

CHINESE HISTORICAL SOCIETY OF AMERICA
17 Adler Place
San Francisco, California 94133
Principal officers: Daisy Wong Chinn, President
                        Charles C. Chan, Executive Vice President
                        Pauline Lee, Executive Secretary

Permanent staff: none	Membership: 500
Date founded: 1963	Membership dues: $5.00 (annual)
Branches: none	Scope: national

Special requirements for membership: none

CHINESE HISTORICAL SOCIETY OF AMERICA (cont'd)
Nature of organization: historical
Publications: *Bulletin*, 1966– (monthly); also publishes books
Affiliations: Conference of California Historical Societies
Major conventions/meetings: annual
Comments: Non-profit in nature, the society relies entirely on volunteer staff. One of the
major Chinese historical societies in Western America. Purposes include the maintenance
and operation of scientific, library, and educational structure; the study, recording, and
preserving of all suitable artifacts and cultural items (such as books, manuscripts,
works of art) that have a bearing on the history of the Chinese living in the United
States; issuing papers and reports on the Society's findings; promoting the contributions
of Chinese living in the United States. The organization maintains a museum.

CHINESE INFORMATION SERVICE
159 Lexington Avenue
New York, New York 10016   (212) 725-4950
Principal officers: I-cheng Loh, Director
Te-cheng Chiang, Deputy Director
Mrs. Chu-tsing Huang, Executive Secretary

Permanent staff: 14	Membership: NI
Date founded: 1946	Membership dues: NI
Branches: 2 regional	Scope: regional

Special requirements for membership: none
Nature of organization: information and public relations
Publications: *Free China Weekly* (weekly); *News from China* (daily); *Free China Review*
(monthly); *China Yearbook* (annual)
Major conventions/meetings: none
Comments: Provides printed information, photographs, and documentary films on the
Republic of China to students and schools at all levels as reference material. Maintains
a library of over 5,000 volumes which is open to visitors all year round.

CHINESE INSTITUTE OF ENGINEERS
124 East 65th Street
New York, New York 10021
Principal officers: Roger King, Secretary

Permanent staff: NI	Membership: 400
Date founded: 1953	Membership dues: NI
Branches: NI	Scope: national

Special requirements for membership: professional engineers and scientists
Nature of organization: scientific and educational
Publications: *Newsletter* (quarterly); *Membership Directory* (annual); *Yearbook and Conven-*
tion Journal (annual); *Seminar Transaction* (biennial)
Affiliations: Chinese Institute of Engineers, Republic of China
Major conventions/meetings: annual
Comments: The major objective of this professional organization is to promote scientific and
educational accomplishments of Chinese engineers and scientists as well as the
industrialization of China. It conducts special training sessions in computer technology;
it bestows awards and provides scholarships for Chinese students. A library is
maintained.

CHINESE LANGUAGE TEACHERS ASSOCIATION (CLTA)
Department of Asian Studies
Seton Hall University
South Orange, New Jersey 07079   (201) 762-9000
Principal officers: Dr. Winston L. Y. Yang, Secretary-Treasurer

CHINESE LANGUAGE TEACHERS ASSOCIATION (CLTA) (cont'd)

Permanent staff: 1   Membership: 500
Date founded: 1963   Membership dues: NI
Branches: NI   Scope: national

Special requirements for membership: teachers and scholars of the Chinese language, linguistics, and literature

Publications: *Journal* (3 issues per year); *Directory* (annual; in *Journal*)

Affiliations: Modern Language Association; Association for Asian Studies

Major conventions/meetings: annual

Comments: Promotes the study of Chinese language, linguistics, and literature. One of its important services is to maintain a placement service for Chinese teachers and scholars.

CHINESE MERCHANTS ASSOCIATION

83 Mott Street
New York, New York 10013   (212) 962-3734
Principal officers: Jimmy Eng, Secretary

CHINESE MERCHANTS MUTUAL ASSOCIATION

417 Parkway Avenue
Greenwood, Mississippi 38930

CHINESE MUSICAL AND THEATRICAL ASSOCIATION

181 Canal Street
New York, New York 10013   (212) 226-8744
Principal officers: Standley Chiu, Executive Chairman

Permanent staff: NI   Membership: 150
Date founded: 1934   Membership dues: NI
Branches: NI   Scope: NI

Comments: The prime objective of this organization is to preserve Chinese culture and customs, including music and art in the United States.

CHINESE NATIONAL HERITAGE CULTURE FEDERATION

c/o Chinese American Bank
225 Park Row
New York, New York 10038

CHINESE PROFESSIONAL CLUB OF HOUSTON (CPC)

9019 Jackwood
Houston, Texas 77036   (713) 771-8277
Principal officers: Wann Sheng Huang, President
                      Paul Yee, Vice President
                      Kay Chen, Secretary

Permanent staff: 8   Membership: 200
Date founded: 1953   Membership dues: $6.00 (annual)
Branches: none   Scope: local

Special requirements for membership: college students or graduates of Chinese descent

Nature of organization: social

Publications: *Newsletter*, 1973– (monthly)

Affiliations: none

Major conventions/meetings: none

Comments: Promotes social interaction between its members. Organizes seven or eight social events during each year.

CHINESE PROFESSIONAL SOCIAL CLUB
601 Stacy Court
Towson, Maryland 21204

CHINESE PROFESSIONALS ASSOCIATION (CPA)
c/o Dr. Yau Tin Ching
793 Euclid
Elmhurst, Illinois 60126   (312) 279-8671

Principal officers: Dr. Yau Tin Ching, President
                        Dr. Cheuk-Kin Chau, Vice President
                        In-lan Wang Li, Secretary

Permanent staff: NI   Membership: 100
Date founded: 1973   Membership dues: $10.00
Branches: NI   Scope: national

Special requirements for membership: Chinese professionals

Nature of organization: social, professional

Publications: *Chinese Professionals Association Newsletter*, 1973– (irregular)

Comments: Principle objectives are to promote better communications among Chinese
     professionals in the United States and to serve as a forum for discussion and for the
     exchange of ideas on various topics.

CHINESE WOMEN NEW LIFE MOVEMENT CLUB
923 N. Broadway
Los Angeles, California 90012

CHINESE WOMEN'S ASSOCIATION (CWA)
5432 152nd Street
Flushing, New York 11355   (212) 359-1803

Principal officers: Miss Ruth R. Goodman, Secretary

Permanent staff: 3   Membership: 520
Date founded: 1932   Membership dues: NI
Branches: NI   Scope: national

Nature of organization: cultural

Publications: *Chinese Women* (quarterly)

Major conventions/meetings: triennial

Comments: The Association attempts to preserve the Chinese culture and heritage in the
     United States. It sponsors cultural activities and activities aimed at promoting the
     welfare of free China and the Chinese in the United States. A 3,800-volume library is
     maintained.

CHINESE WOMEN'S BENEVOLENT ASSOCIATION
22 Pell Street
New York, New York 10013   (212) 267-4764

Principal officers: Mrs. Louis F. S. Hong, President

Permanent staff: NI   Membership: NI
Date founded: NI   Membership dues: NI
Branches: NI   Scope: regional

Nature of organization: philanthropic

Comments: This philanthropic association raises funds to aid Chinese students in need as
     well as other Chinese needing assistance. The Association also provides translating
     and interpreting services.

GREATER BOSTON CHINESE CULTURAL ASSOCIATION
c/o 8 Conestoga Road
Lexington, Massachusetts 02173

HAWAII CHINESE EDUCATIONAL ASSOCIATION
c/o Chong Kong Young, President
634-G North Vineyard Boulevard
Honolulu, Hawaii 96817
Principal officers: Chong Kong Young, President

HAWAII CHINESE HISTORY CENTER (HCHC)
89 North King Street, Room 4
Honolulu, Hawaii 96817   (808) 521-5948
Principal officers: Tin Chong Goo, President
                      Toy Len Chang, Vice President
                      Larry C. W. Ing, Secretary

Permanent staff: 2   Membership: over 400
Date founded: 1971   Membership dues: varies from $5.00 to
Branches: none $500.00
                                          Scope: local

Special requirements for membership: none

Nature of organization: educational

Publications: *Hawaii Chinese History Center Newsletter*, 1971– (quarterly)

Major conventions/meetings: annual meeting

Comments: Primarily educational in nature, HCHC promotes active interest and research on
    the Chinese in Hawaii by sponsoring oral history workshops, lectures, and trips to
    neighboring islands in order to gather historical data. In cooperation with the
    University of Hawaii, it published an annotated bibliography on the Chinese in Hawaii.

INSTITUTE OF CHINESE CULTURE
185 Canal Street
New York, New York 10013   (212) 925-7910
Principal officers: Paul Cardinal Yu-Pin, President
                      K. G. Lee, Vice President
                      George Young, Secretary

Permanent staff: 3   Membership: NI
Date founded: 1946   Membership dues: NI
Branches: NI   Scope: regional

Special requirements for membership: nomination by two members and confirmation by the
    Board of Directors

Nature of organization: cultural

Publications: publishes pamphlets on Chinese history and culture

Comments: Founded to further cultural relations between the United States and the
    Republic of China and to promote cultural and educational programs between the
    American and Chinese people. Members consist of both American and Chinese
    scholars and also leaders within the Chinese community. ICC sponsors such activities
    as Chinese forums; classes in Chinese art, culture, and language; art exhibits by Chinese
    artists; lectures; annual awards for scholarly achievements; conferences on Chinese topics.
    Also publishes pamphlets on Chinese history and culture.

THE INTERNATIONAL FOUNDATION (TIF)
P.O. Box 101
Englewood, New Jersey 07207   (201) 567-0248
Principal officers: Mrs. Robert G. McCausland, Executive Secretary

Permanent staff: NI   Membership: 8
Date founded: 1948   Membership dues: NI
Branches: NI   Scope: NI

Comments: The aim of this foundation is to support medical and educational projects; was
    formerly China International Foundation.

MID-WEST CHAPTER OF THE NATIONAL COUNCIL ON CHINESE CULTURE RENAISSANCE

c/o Dr. T. C. Li
211 Elgin Avenue
Forest Park, Illinois 60130   (312) 369-8808

Principal officers: Dr. Tze-chung Li, Chairman
                       Wing Shu Chan, Vice Chairman
                       Peter S. Wang, Executive Secretary

Permanent staff: NI   Membership: 30
Date founded: 1973   Membership dues: none
Branches: NI   Scope: regional

Special requirements for membership: by invitation only to Chinese

Nature of organization: political

Major conventions/meetings: annual conference

Comments: Promotes Chinese culture through books, art exhibits, Chinese language schools, and lectures.

MID-WEST CHINESE AMERICAN LIBRARIANS ASSOCIATION (MCALA)

P.O. Box 444
Oak Park, Illinois 60303

Principal officers: Tze-chung Li, President
                       Peter S. Wang, Secretary

Permanent staff: NI   Membership: 50
Date founded: 1973   Membership dues: NI
Branches: NI   Scope: regional

Special requirements for membership: Chinese librarian

Nature of organization: educational

Publications: "Letter to Members and Friends," 1973– (irregular)

Major conventions/meetings: annual conference

Comments: Purpose is to promote communication among Chinese-American librarians and also to support the development of Chinese librarianship.

SINO-AMERICAN AMITY FUND (SAAF)

86 Riverside Drive
New York, New York 10024   (212) 787-6969

Principal officers: Paul Yu-pin, President

Permanent staff: NI   Membership: 150
Date founded: 1951   Membership dues: NI
Branches: NI   Scope: NI

Comments: The organization attempts to improve the understanding of Chinese culture in the United States and to promote that culture. It sponsors activities to unite Chinese-Americans on a social basis; it also sponsors educational and religious programs. Financial assistance is provided for needy Chinese college students.

SINO-AMERICAN CULTURAL SOCIETY

2000 "P" Street, N.W., Suite 200
Washington, D.C. 20036   (202) 293-3898

Principal officers: Dr. William G. Carr, President

Permanent staff: NI   Membership: 500
Date founded: 1958   Membership dues: NI
Branches: NI   Scope: NI

Nature of organizations: educational, cultural

Comments: The organization offers courses on Chinese history, culture, language, and painting; it also publishes materials on Chinese culture and education.

UNITED CHINESE SOCIETY
42 North King Street
Honolulu, Hawaii 96817   (808) 536-4621
Principal officers: Kam On Lum, President
                        Wallace W. Y. Wong, Vice President
                        Larry C. W. Ing, Secretary

Permanent staff: 2   Membership: approximately 500
Date founded: 1884   Membership dues: $2.00 (annual)
Branches: none   Scope: state

Special requirements for membership: Chinese origin with a Chinese surname

Nature of organization: cultural, fraternal

Publications: anniversary brochure

Major conventions/meetings: annual meeting and banquet

Comments: As the parent organization for 79 Chinese societies in Hawaii, the United Chinese
      Society serves as a liaison agency between the Chinese and other races. It is often
      called upon to entertain visiting dignitaries from the East and West. In the early days
      of its existence it was the governing body for the overseas Chinese. The officers
      interpreted local laws and events, helped secure employment, settled disputes, and
      wrote letters to families and friends in the homeland. It cooperates with other charitable
      groups and welfare agencies in fund drives to aid the Chinese in Hawaii. Awards an
      annual Model Father and Mother of the Year recognition to emphasize the respect that
      the Chinese display toward elders; also awards scholarships for students at Chinese
      schools.

YING ON MERCHANT AND LABOR BENEVOLENT ASSOCIATION
2912 West Mariposa
Phoenix, Arizona 85017

COSSACK-AMERICAN ORGANIZATIONS

Additional information on Cossack-American organizations may be obtained
from Cossack's Library in New York (208 East Ninth Street, New York, New
York 10003).

COSSAC-AMERICAN NATIONAL ALLIANCE, INC.
602 Public Street
Providence, Rhode Island 02907   (401) 461-2948
Principal officers: G. L. Jeremenko, President
                        T. G. Bihday, Executive Vice President
                        Mrs. H. Boychevsky, Executive Secretary

Permanent staff: none   Membership: NI
Date founded: 1952   Membership dues: none
Branches: 3 state   Scope: national

Special requirements for membership: must be of Cossack nationality

Nature of organization: social, cultural

Publications: *Cossacks Life*, 1952– (quarterly); also publishes books

Affiliations: none

Major conventions/meetings: national conference irregularly

Comments: Organized primarily to publish *Cossacks Life* as well as books dealing with
      Cossack history, culture, traditions, language, etc. Provides assistance to members in
      need. Maintains both a library and archives.

COSSACK AMERICAN CITIZENS COMMITTEE
P.O. Box 1095, Grand Central Station
New York, New York 10017   (212) 475-4789

Principal officers: W. G. Glaskow, President
                       T. I. Byckov, First Vice President
                       V. G. Lazareff, General Secretary

Permanent staff: 12   Membership: 10,378
Date founded: 1964   Membership dues: $12.00
Branches: 16 state; 53 local   Scope: national

Special requirements for membership: U.S. citizenship

Nature of organization: cultural, political, educational

Publications: *Cossack American Bulletin*; *Cossack's Newsletters*, 1964– (monthly)

Major conventions/meetings: convention every three years

Comments: Formed in order to represent the interests of Americans of Cossack origin, and
    also to aid in the preservation of the Cossack heritage and culture through various youth
    educational programs.

COSSACK NATIONAL STANITZA
10122 Curran Avenue
Cleveland, Ohio 44111   (216) 961-8782

Principal officers: Feodor Moshowoi, President

COSSACK'S LIBRARY IN NEW YORK
208 East Ninth Street
New York, New York 10003   (212) 475-4789

Principal officers: W. G. Glaskow, President
                       M. A. Markov, Vice President
                       Dm. Kravchenko, Secretary

Permanent staff: 5   Membership: NI
Date founded: 1962   Membership dues: $48.00 (annual)
Branches: none   Scope: local

Special requirements for membership: Cossack descent

Nature of organization: cultural, scholarly, educational

Affiliations: other Cossack organizations

Major conventions/meetings: annual and biennial conferences

Comments: Serves as a cultural, educational, and scholarly institution for both Americans and
    Cossacks living in the New York area. Sponsors panels on Cossack themes. Maintains
    a library of over 7,000 volumes on Cossack culture, history, traditions, economy, etc.
    Also has archival materials that relate to the Cossack liberation movement.

DON COSSACK STANITZA OF NEW YORK
34-27 6th Street
Woodside, Long Island, New York 11377

NEW KUBAN, INC. OF ALL COSSACKS COMMUNITY
Don Cossack Road
New Kuban, Buena, New Jersey 08310   (609) 697-0827

Principal officers: Josef N. Schwedin, President
                       Alexa Duchnay, Vice President
                       B. Dudin, Secretary

Permanent staff: 5   Membership: NI
Date founded: 1973   Membership dues: $60.00
Branches: NI   Scope: national

Special requirements for membership: Cossack descent or friend of Cossacks

Nature of organization: cultural, fraternal, educational

NEW KUBAN, INC. OF ALL COSSACKS COMMUNITY (cont'd)

Publications: none

Affiliations: affiliated with all Cossack organizations

Major conventions/meetings: annual meeting; monthly conferences

Comments: Major objective is the preservation of the Cossack heritage through educational projects. Also engaged in various social, religious, and fraternal activities. Collects materials and artifacts dealing with the history and traditions of Cossacks; these materials are to be housed in a special museum. Maintains a library of 1,700 volumes dealing with Cossack topics. Awards the Cossack Freedom Prize annually.

SUPREME COSSACK REPRESENTATION
206 East Ninth Street
New York, New York 10003 (212) 475-4789

Principal officers: W. G. Glaskow, President
Paul Poljakov, Vice President
Ph. Zuvcenko, Secretary

Permanent staff: 5 Membership: NI
Date founded: 1948 Membership dues: $24.00
Branches: (in U.S.) 17 state; 96 local Scope: international

Special requirements for membership: Cossack descent

Nature of organization: political

Publications: *The Cossack's Herald*, 1941– (monthly); magazine *Cossackia*, 1948– (bimonthly); *The Cossack*, 1952–

Major conventions/meetings: convention, triennial

Comments: Major Cossack organization both here and in the free world. Activities involve maintaining contacts with Cossacks in the U.S.S.R. Purpose is to establish a free and independent nation, Cossackia. Maintains archival materials of a historical nature. Publishes books on Cossack topics.

COSTA RICAN-AMERICAN ORGANIZATIONS

Additional information on Costa Rican-American organizations may be obtained from the Office of the Costa Rican Embassy (2112 "S" Street, Washington, D.C. 20008).

COSTA RICANS SOCIAL CONFRATERNITY OF CLEVELAND
3230 West 111th Street
Cleveland, Ohio 44111 (216) 476-0821

Principal officers: Fernando E. Hernandez, President
Ramon Masis, Vice President
Flor Ivette Banyai, Secretary

Permanent staff: 5 Membership: 40
Date founded: 1972 Membership dues: NI
Branches: none Scope: local

Special requirements for membership: none

Nature of organization: cultural, fraternal, social

Publications: none

Major conventions/meetings: quarterly membership meeting

Comments: Major purposes of this non-profit organization are to maintain the customs and culture of Costa Rica and to promote good citizenship and friendship between the United States and Costa Rica. Sponsors various social, cultural, and civic activities. Archival holdings consist of Costa Rican newspapers.

CROATIAN-AMERICAN ORGANIZATIONS

Additional information on Croatian-American organizations in the United States may be obtained from the Croatian National Congress (280 East 270th Street, Cleveland, Ohio 44132). Regional and local organizations are listed in *Greater Cleveland Nationalities Directory 1974* (Cleveland: Sun Newspapers and the Nationalities Services Center, 1974) and *Ethnic Directory I* (Detroit: Southeastern Michigan Regional Ethnic Heritage Studies Center, 1974).

AMERICAN CROATIAN ACADEMIC CLUB (ACAC)
P.O. Box 18081
Cleveland, Ohio 44118 (212) 361-3037
Principal officers: Joseph T. Bombelles, President
J. V. Bosiljevic, Vice President
Neven S. Lovrekovic, Secretary

Permanent staff: NI   Membership: 75
Date founded: 1959   Membership dues: NI
Branches: NI   Scope: national

Special requirements for membership: persons of Croatian descent who have completed higher education

Nature of organization: educational, scholarly, professional, cultural

Publications: *American Croatian Academic Bulletin*, 1960– (irregular; 4 or 5 issues a year)

Major conventions/meetings: biennial seminar, annual convention

Comments: The goal of the organization is to promote study of Croatia's history and culture as well as its contemporary problems; it conducts lectures and other academic programs. Activities include promoting history and culture of Croatia; supporting issues and activities that encourage social contacts among Croatians; and awarding a partial scholarship on an annual basis. Maintains a small library and archives.

AMERICAN CROATIAN CULTURAL AND EDUCATIONAL SOCIETY, INC.
6045 Hopkins Road
Cleveland, Ohio 44060 (216) 257-2451
Principal officers: Nick Bucar, President
Mile Galic, Secretary

Permanent staff: NI   Membership: NI
Date founded: 1965   Membership dues: NI
Branches: NI   Scope: local

Nature of organization: cultural, educational

Comments: The purpose of the organization is to provide social and cultural activities that will perpetuate the Croatian culture and traditions in the United States and that will unite those of Croatian background.

AMERICAN FRIENDS OF THE CROATIAN NATIONAL RESISTANCE "DRINA"
1068 East 69th Street
Cleveland, Ohio 44103 (216) 391-2475
Principal officers: Michael Maslac, President
Frane Pesut, Secretary

Permanent staff: NI   Membership: NI
Date founded: NI   Membership dues: NI
Branches: NI   Scope: national

Nature of organization: political

Comments: The intent of the organization is to promote support in the fight for an independent Croatia.

AMERICAN SOCIETY FOR CROATIAN MIGRATION, INC.

1062 East 62nd Street   (216) 431-2770 or
Cleveland, Ohio 44103   (216) 391-6484

Principal officers: Joseph V. Bosilievic, President
                 Milan Milkovic, Secretary

Permanent staff: NI   Membership: 5,000
Date founded: 1949   Membership dues: NI
Branches: NI   Scope: national

Nature of organization: charitable

Comments: A Catholic-sponsored organization, the society's main purpose is to help Croatian immigrants adjust to life in the United States.

THE CROATIAN ACADEMY OF AMERICA, INC.

P.O. Box 1767, Grand Central Station
New York, New York 10017

Principal officers: Dusko I. Duisin, President
                 Ivo Vucicevic, Executive Vice President
                 Rudolf M. Baricevic, Executive Secretary

Permanent staff: none   Membership: 210
Date founded: 1953   Membership dues: $15.00 (annual)
Branches: 3 regional   Scope: national

Nature of organization: educational, scholarly

Publications: *Journal of Croatian Studies*, 1960– (annual); *Announcement*, 1953– (quarterly)

Major conventions/meetings: annual general assembly

Comments: The purpose of CAA is to educate its members and the public about Croatian literature, culture, and history through lectures and publications. Raises funds for such purposes. Annually awards $300.00 for original unpublished manuscripts on Croatian history and culture.

CROATIAN AMERICAN REPUBLICAN CLUB OF CLEVELAND, OHIO

c/o Steve Skertic, President
1082 East 68th Street
Cleveland, Ohio 44103

Principal officers: Steve Skertic, President

Permanent staff: NI   Membership: NI
Date founded: NI   Membership dues: NI
Branches: NI   Scope: regional

Nature of organization: political

CROATIAN AMERICAN REPUBLICAN FEDERATION OF OHIO

c/o Joseph V. Bosilievic, President
1073 Addison Road
Cleveland, Ohio 44103   (216) 391-6484

Principal officers: Joseph V. Bosilievic, President
                 Joseph Bombelles, Secretary

Permanent staff: NI   Membership: NI
Date founded: NI   Membership dues: NI
Branches: NI   Scope: regional

Nature of organization: political

CROATION AMERICAN VETERANS' ASSOCIATION

c/o Anthony Pivac, President
880 Lakewood Boulevard
Akron, Ohio 44314   (216) 391-2004

CROATION AMERICAN VETERANS' ASSOCIATION (cont'd)
Principal officers: Anthony Pivac, President
Ivan Dzeba, Secretary

Permanent staff: NI	Membership: NI
Date founded: NI	Membership dues: NI
Branches: NI	Scope: national

CROATIAN BOARD OF TRADE
5021 Trowbridge
Hamtramck, Michigan 48212

Principal officers: Anthony Bunnta
Mrs. Frances Koltonowicz

Permanent staff: NI	Membership: NI
Date founded: NI	Membership dues: NI
Branches: NI	Scope: regional

Special requirements for membership: American-born Croatians

Nature of organization: cultural, philanthropic

Comments: The organization attempts to preserve Croatian culture in the United States; it supports Croatian publications by buying them and distributing them as gifts to public areas in the Detroit area. It sponsors concerts and other fund-raising activities. It has donated proceeds to the Detroit Symphony, and it provides an annual scholarship for a Croation student.

CROATIAN CATHOLIC UNION OF U.S.A.
125 West Fifth Avenue
Gary, Indiana 46402   (219) 885-7325

Principal officers: Joseph Saban, President
William Poje, Vice President
Steve M. Cvetetic, Secretary

Permanent staff: 8	Membership: 11,075
Date founded: 1921	Membership dues: NI
Branches: 7 regional; 7 state; 3 local	Scope: national

Special requirements for membership: must be a practicing Catholic

Nature of organization: fraternal

Publications: *Our Hope*, 1921– (weekly)

Affiliations: National Fraternal Congress of America; Canadian Fraternal Associations

Major conventions/meetings: convention, quadrennial

Comments: Provides life insurance to members. Promotes the "temporal and spiritual welfare" of members. Provides financial aid to seminarians and other students. Supports Catholic institutions and charitable causes. Assumes an active role in civic and patriotic projects. Administers aid in cases of natural disasters.

CROATIAN CENTER ASSOCIATION
4851 Drexel Boulevard
Chicago, Illinois 60615

Permanent staff: NI	Membership: NI
Date founded: NI	Membership dues: NI
Branches: NI	Scope: regional

Nature of organization: cultural, political

Publications: *Danica* (The Morning Star), 1921– (weekly)

Comments: The organization's aim is to promote the cause of Croatian national independence. It also provides cultural and social activities to unite Croatian-Americans in the United States.

CROATIAN FOUNDATION OF AMERICA
P.O. Box 18118
Cleveland, Ohio 44118   (216) 932-9823
Principal officers: Victor Koludrovich, M.D., President
                      Branko Yirka, Secretary

Permanent staff: NI   Membership: NI
Date founded: 1968   Membership dues: NI
Branches: NI   Scope: NI

Nature of organization: cultural

Publications: *Hrvatsko Kolo* (Ethnic News & Views) (monthly)

Comments: The organization is interested in preserving the Croatian culture in the United
      States. It supports activities and programs that promote the Croatian customs,
      language, and traditions.

CROATIAN FRATERNAL UNION JUNIOR CULTURAL FEDERATION
100 Delaney Drive
Pittsburgh, Pennsylvania 15235   (412) 531-3909
Principal officers: William Coleff, President
                      Wayne Odorizzi, First Vice President
                      Steve Namesnik, Jr., Secretary

Permanent staff: NI   Membership: NI
Date founded: 1966   Membership dues: $10.00 (annual)
Branches: 37   Scope: national

Special requirements for membership: approval of membership

Nature of organization: cultural, fraternal

Publications: *Junior Magazine*, 1940– (bimonthly)

Affiliations: Croatian Fraternal Union of America

Major conventions/meetings: annual

Comments: The CFU Jjnior Cultural Federation is an ethnic and cultural organization whose
      objectives are to promote and further the tamburitza culture of the Jugoslav people–
      Croatians. Member tamburitza groups maintain their own autonomy and operational
      guidelines.

CROATIAN FRATERNAL UNION OF AMERICA (CFU)
100 Delaney Drive
Pittsburgh, Pennsylvania 15235   (412) 351-3909
Principal officers: John Badovinac, President
                      Milan Vranes, First Vice President
                      Joseph Bella, National Secretary

Permanent staff: 37   Membership: 112,000
Date founded: 1894   Membership dues: dependent upon
Branches: 800 (in 26 states and Canada)   amount of insurance carried
                                         Scope: international

Special requirements for membership: must be of Slavic descent; medical examinations
      required for applicants over age 50

Nature of organization: fraternal

Publications: *Zajedničar*, 1906– (weekly); *Junior Magazine*, 1940– (bimonthly)

Affiliations: National Fraternal Congress of America and membership in 10 state congresses

Major conventions/meetings: convention, quadrennial

Comments: Major purpose is the provision of "life, endowed, health and accident, surgical
      and hospital insurance protection on the fraternal plan." However, the organization
      also encourages educational programs that promote the history and national heritage of
      Croatians. Also, it maintains a scholarship foundation to assist needy students and an old
      age benefit fund. In 1924 the CFU was formed by merger of the National Croatian
      Society and the Croatian League of Illinois.

CROATIAN NATIONAL CONGRESS (CNC)
280 East 270th Street
Cleveland, Ohio 44132   (216) 261-4622

Principal officers: Ante M. Doshen, President
                        Bozidar T. Abjanic, Secretary

Permanent staff: 18   Membership: unknown
Date founded: 1974   Membership dues: donation
Branches: 5   Scope: international

Special requirements for membership: must favor independence for Croatia

Nature of organization: political

Publications: *Vjesnik-Hnv* (Bulletin of CNC), 1974– (bimonthly)

Major conventions/meetings: annual

Comments: The intent of CNC is to promote an independent state of Croatia. It is a coalition of Croatian political organizations in the free world. It prints documentary materials and sponsors political activities and national radio programs on behalf of Croatia. A 300-volume library and archival collection are maintained.

CROATIAN NATIONAL COUNCIL
P.O. Box 43215
Cleveland, Ohio 44143

CROATION PEASANT PARTY
c/o Blaz Kausic, National President
1541 East 191st Street
Cleveland, Ohio 44117   (216) 481-1784

CROATIAN PHILATELIC SOCIETY (CPS)
1512 Lancelot Road
Borger, Texas 79007   (806) 273-7225

Principal officers: Thomas E. Gaughan, President
                        Jerome Colich, Vice President
                        Ekrem Spahich, Secretary

Permanent staff: 2   Membership: 300
Date founded: 1972   Membership dues: $5.00 (annual)
Branches: NI   Scope: international

Special requirements for membership: interest in stamps

Nature of organization: cultural, philatelic

Publications: *Trubljac*, 1972– (quarterly)

Affiliations: American Philatelic Society

Major conventions/meetings: annual convention

Comments: An international non-profit cultural organization devoted to the study and exchange of information on Croatian and Balkan area postal issues and history. Organizes study groups by area to research Balkan philately—e.g., Jugoslavian, Romanian, Serbian, Montenegrin, Bosnian, Croatian, Hungarian, Slovenian, and Triestean study groups. Permanent committees are the Expertizing Committee and the Translation Committee. A 100-volume library of philatelic literature is held.

CROATIAN SOCIETY FOR THE RELIEF TO CROATIAN REFUGEES
1073 Addison Road
Cleveland, Ohio 44103

Principal officers: Joseph Bosiljevic

Permanent staff: NI   Membership: NI
Date founded: NI   Membership dues: NI
Branches: NI   Scope: national

Nature of organization: welfare

HOME DEFENDERS OF CROATIA IN AMERICA
894 East 75th Street
Cleveland, Ohio 44103

Principal officers: Mile Glamuzin

Permanent staff: NI
Date founded: 1930
Branches: NI

Membership: NI
Membership dues: NI
Scope: national

Nature of organization: political

Publications: *The Croatian Nation*, 1959– (irregular)

Comments: The major functions of this primarily political organization are to fight for
independence of Croatia as a free nation and to promote the Croatian heritage in the
United States.

LEAGUE OF THE CROATIAN CATHOLIC PRIESTS IN THE USA AND CANADA
917 North 49th Street
Milwaukee, Wisconsin 53208

Principal officers: Rev. Castimir Majic, OFM, Secretary

Permanent staff: NI
Date founded: NI
Branches: NI

Membership: NI
Membership dues: NI
Scope: national

Special requirements for membership: Croatian Catholic priest

Nature of organization: religious, social

Comments: The purposes of the League are to unite Croatian priests in the United States and
Canada and to promote the Catholic faith of the Croatian Catholic Church and the
Croatian heritage in America.

MOTHERS' CLUB OF NEST 318
1721 East McNichols
Detroit, Michigan 48203   (313) 896-2626

Permanent staff: NI
Date founded: NI
Branches: NI

Membership: NI
Membership dues: NI
Scope: regional

Special requirements for membership: women from 18 to 50 of Croatian descent

Nature of organization: social

Affiliations: CFU Junior Cultural Federation

Comments: Mothers of members of the CFU Junior Cultural Federation meet for social
activities–e.g., bowling, card games, dances. Nest No. 318 is the largest youth chapter
in the CFU, with over 800 members.

NORTH AMERICAN COUNCIL FOR INDEPENDENCE OF CROATIA .
c/o Theodore Abjanic, President
280 East 270th Street
Cleveland, Ohio 44103

Permanent staff: NI
Date founded: NI
Branches: NI

Membership: NI
Membership dues: NI
Scope: national

SLAVONIC MUTUAL AND BENEVOLENT SOCIETY
60 Onondage Avenue
San Francisco, California 94112

Principal officers: Philip Vulian, President

Permanent staff: NI
Date founded: 1857
Branches: NI

Membership: NI
Membership dues: varies
Scope: national

Nature of organization: fraternal

SLAVONIC MUTUAL AND BENEVOLENT SOCIETY (cont'd)

Comments: The major purpose of this organization is to provide insurance benefits for its members and to sponsor social and cultural activities to unite Americans of Croatian descent.

UNITED AMERICAN CROATS (UAC)
552 West 50th Street
New York, New York 10018   (212) 565-4300
Principal officers: Vinko Kuzina, Secretary

Permanent staff: 12	Membership: 5,000
Date founded: 1946	Membership dues: NI
Branches: 16	Scope: national

Special requirements for membership: U.S. residents and citizens of Croatian descent

Nature of organization: cultural, political

Publications: *Bulletin*, 1960– (bimonthly)

Major conventions/meetings: triennial

Comments: The stated objective of the organization is "to preserve and promote national, historical, and cultural traits of the Croatian people and to assist in the Croatian national struggle for freedom and independence." Cultural activities sponsored are folk dances and exhibitions of folk art. Until 1966 the group was known as the United American Croatians.

UNITED CROATIANS OF AMERICA
68-32 Groton Hills
Long Island, New York 11375
Principal officers: Miro Gal, President

Permanent staff: NI	Membership: NI
Date founded: NI	Membership dues: NI
Branches: NI	Scope: national

CUBAN-AMERICAN ORGANIZATIONS

See also Spanish-American Organizations

Additional information on Cuban-American organizations may be obtained from the Latin Chamber of Commerce (601 N.W. 22nd Avenue, Miami, Florida 33125) and the *Directory of Spanish Speaking Organizations in the United States* (Washington, D.C.: Cabinet Committee on Opportunity for the Spanish Speaking, 1970).

ALPHA 66 ORGANIZACION REVOLUCIONARIA CUBANA
1528 N.W. 36th Street
Miami, Florida 33142

AMERICAN CLUB
Northeast Airlines Building
150 S.E. Second Avenue
Miami, Florida 33132
Principal officers: Juan Acosta, President

Permanent staff: 17	Membership: 709
Date founded: 1965	Membership dues: NI
Branches: NI	Scope: NI

Special requirements for membership: Cuban expatriates

AMERICAN CLUB (cont'd)

Nature of organization: political, social, cultural

Comments: The purpose of the club is to improve relations between the United States and Latin America.

ASOCIACION INTERAMERICANA DE HOMBRES DE EMPRESA
3128 Coral Way
Miami, Florida 33134 (305) 448-8001

Permanent staff: NI
Date founded: 1960
Branches: NI

Membership: NI
Membership dues: NI
Scope: NI

CENTRO MATER
406 S.W. Fourth Street
Miami, Florida 33130 (305) 545-6049

Principal officers: Sister Margarita Miranda, General Coordinator
Mrs. Paquita C. Aldrich, Head, Board of Directors

Nature of organization: charitable, religious

Affiliations: Catholic Service Bureau

Comments: Activities such as music, crafts, dance, swimming classes, sports, and games are provided for low-income Latin-American children. The organization works in conjunction with the Catholic Service Bureau. Also provides field trips and summer camps. Food and a large part of the expenses come from the generosity of Centro Mater's Cuban Fair, known as "Fiesta Guajtra."

CIRCULO CUBAN ASSOCIATION OF CLEVELAND
P.O. Box 6315
Cleveland, Ohio 44101 (216) 234-7111

Principal officers: Frank Gonzalez, President
Eduardo Mont, Secretary

CIRCULO GUINERODE LOS ANGELES
434 South Alvarado Street
Los Angeles, California 90057 (213) 483-9126

Principal officers: Efren Besanilla, President

Permanent staff: NI
Date founded: 1968
Branches: NI

Membership: NI
Membership dues: NI
Scope: local

Nature of organization: cultural, social

Major conventions/meetings: weekly

Comments: The organization's goal is to preserve the Cuban cultural heritage in the United States. Besides sponsoring social and cultural activities and meetings, it provides assistance to members in need.

CLUB CUBANO
3540 28th Street
Detroit, Michigan 48210

COLLEGE OF ARCHITECTS OF CUBA IN EXILE ASSOCIATION
1001 S.W. First Street, Room 205
Miami, Florida 33130 (305) 371-5223

Principal officers: Jose M. Bens, Executive Secretary

Permanent staff: NI
Date founded: 1961
Branches: NI

Membership: 435
Membership dues: NI
Scope: national

COLLEGE OF ARCHITECTS OF CUBA IN EXILE ASSOCIATION (cont'd)
Special requirements for membership: architects exiled from Cuba
Nature of organization: professional
Publications: *Architecture in Exile* (irregular)
Affiliations: Confederacion Profesionales Cubanos
Major conventions/meetings: annual
Comments: This organization consists of members of the Colegio de Arquitectos de Cuba who
reorganized their group in the United States. Their major purpose is to seek liberty
for Cuba and to maintain programs of research in architecture, city planning, social
welfare, etc., in the United States. Former Cubans who have become architects are also
allowed to join; the association sponsors exhibits and awards.

CUBAN CHILDREN'S PROGRAM
1325 West Flagler
Miami, Florida 33135

CUBAN LICEUM OF DETROIT
27802 Woodmont
Roseville, Michigan 48066   (313) 354-4269
Principal officers: Jose I. Mendez, President
                        Phillip Garcia, Vice President
                        Blanca Martinez, Secretary
Permanent staff: 11   Membership: 120 families
Date founded: 1971   Membership dues: $24.00 (annual)
Branches: none   Scope: local
Special requirements for membership: signature of two members and approval of the Board
of Directors
Nature of organization: cultural, social
Publications: *Cuban Liceum Echos* (Ecos del Liceo Cubano), 1973– (monthly)
Affiliations: none
Major conventions/meetings: annual general meeting
Comments: Principle objectives are to promote social and cultural activities of Cubans in
Detroit and surrounding areas. Conducts English language classes for Cuban-Americans.

CUBAN MUNICIPALITIES IN EXILE
1460 West Flagler
Miami, Florida 33134   (305) 643-9174
Principal officers: Nicomedes Hernandez, President
Permanent staff: NI   Membership: NI
Date founded: 1964   Membership dues: NI
Branches: NI   Scope: national
Special requirements for membership: Cuban refugees now living in the United States
Nature of organization: cultural, political, social, welfare
Publications: *La Nacion*
Major conventions/meetings: monthly
Comments: The objectives of this organization are to preserve the Cuban heritage in the
United States, to promote a free Cuba, to fight communism, and to give assistance to
refugees as they arrive in the United States.

CUBAN NURSES ASSOCIATION IN EXILE
802 First Street, N.W.
Miami, Florida 33135   (305) 379-1955
Permanent staff: NI   Membership: NI
Date founded: 1962   Membership dues: NI
Branches: NI   Scope: national

CUBAN NURSES ASSOCIATION IN EXILE (cont'd)

Major conventions/meetings: monthly

Comments: The purpose of the organization is to help Cuban nurses find job opportunities in the United States.

CUBAN REFUGEE ASSISTANCE PROGRAM
127 N.W. Second Street
Miami, Florida 33128

CUBAN REPRESENTATION OF EXILES
1784 West Flagler Street, Room 21
Miami, Florida 33135

Principal officers: Michael Echegoyen, Executive Secretary

Permanent staff: NI   Membership: NI
Date founded: NI   Membership dues: NI
Branches: NI   Scope: national

Special requirements for membership: Cuban exile

Nature of organization: political

Publications: *RECE* (monthly)

Comments: The major purpose of this organization is to promote the liberty of Cuba by raising funds and by disseminating anti-communist materials and materials that describe the Cuban situation.

FREE CUBA PATRIOTIC MOVEMENT
355 East 72nd Street
Apartment 14C
New York, New York 10021

Principal officers: Carlos Marquez Sterling, General Delegate

Permanent staff: NI   Membership: 8,000
Date founded: 1963   Membership dues: NI
Branches: NI   Scope: national

Special requirements for membership: Cuban exiles

Nature of organization: political

Comments: The major purpose of the group is to promote a free Cuba. It disseminates information on the Cuban situation through educational programs. Maintains a library of materials on Latin America and books by Cuban authors.

HOUSTON CUBAN ASSOCIATION
803 West Gray
Houston, Texas 77019   (713) 528-9944

Principal officers: E. Tomas Perez, President

Permanent staff: NI   Membership: NI
Date founded: 1966   Membership dues: NI
Branches: NI   Scope: local

Special requirements for membership: Cuban origin

Nature of organization: social, cultural

Publications: *El Cuban Libre* (bimonthly)

Comments: The major purpose of the organization is the preservation of the Cuban heritage in the United States. It publishes literature on Cuba and sponsors social and cultural activities.

LATIN CHAMBER OF COMMERCE
601 N.W. 22nd Avenue
Miami, Florida 33125 (305) 642-3870

Principal officers: Luis Sabines, President
Benjamin Leon, Vice President
Isidoro Rodriguez, Secretary

Permanent staff: 25 Membership: 1,750
Date founded: 1965 Membership dues: $60.00 (annual)
Branches: none Scope: national

Special requirements for membership: must have an established business; must be approved by the Executive Board

Nature of organization: non-profit economic, professional, educational

Publications: *Industria Y Comercio* (Industry and Commerce), 1968– (monthly); *Supplemento* (Supplement), 1968– (monthly); also publishes directories for businessmen

Affiliations: U.S. Department of Commerce

Comments: To serve area businessmen. The organization includes committees to modify bylaws; to arrange meetings; to promote international relations, press, and public relations; to encourage new members; to educate against drugs and crime; to arrange bilingual programs, etc.

LICEO CUBANO
51 West San Fernando Street
San Jose, California 95113 (408) 294-3413

Principal officers: Gervasio Gutierrez, President

Permanent staff: NI Membership: NI
Date founded: 1968 Membership dues: NI
Branches: NI Scope: regional

Major conventions/meetings: monthly

Comments: Attempts to preserve Cuban customs and culture in the United States. It sponsors social, cultural, and recreational activities.

LITTLE HAVANA ACTIVITIES CENTER
819 S.W. 12th Avenue
Miami, Florida 33135 (305) 643-4484

Principal officers: Angel M. Moreno, President
Luis Gonzalez, Vice President
Fernando Freire, Secretary
Francisco Formentin, Treasurer

Permanent staff: 8 Membership: 1,700
Date founded: 1973 (October) Membership dues: none
Branches: 4 local Scope: local

Special requirements for membership: 60 years of age or over

Nature of organization: charitable

Publications: none

Affiliations: United Fund of Dade County

Major conventions/meetings: none

Comments: This organization primarily serves individuals 60 years of age and over. Services to senior citizens include such programs as counseling, information and referral, transportation, education, recreation, civic, cultural, social, and arts and crafts. A special Geriatric Nutrition Program serves 400 hot meals daily to the elderly at four local community centers.

MIDWEST CUBAN FEDERATION
c/o Dr. Lincoln S. Mendez
42 Buttermilk Park
Ft. Mitchell, Kentucky 41017   (606) 221-8282
Principal officers: Lincoln S. Mendez, Secretary

Permanent staff: NI   Membership: 9 organizations
Date founded: 1967   Membership dues: NI
Branches: NI   Scope: regional

Nature of organization: charitable

Publications: publishes books

Comments: This organization coordinates the various efforts of other Midwestern Cuban
organizations in aiding new rufugees. It also sponsors activities that promote and preserve
the Cuban language and culture in the United States. It publishes books on Cuba and
provides information on the political situation there. A small library is maintained.

RESCATE DEMOCRATICO REVOLUCIONARIO
111 West 42nd Street, Room 302
New York, New York 10036

Principal officers: Dr. Manuel A. De Varona, Secretary

Permanent staff: NI   Membership: 10,000
Date founded: 1960   Membership dues: NI
Branches: NI   Scope: international

Nature of organization: political, educational

Publications: *Rescate Bulletin* (monthly)

Major conventions/meetings: weekly meetings

Comments: The purposes of this organization are to support the struggle for a free Cuba and to
fight communism. It sponsors lectures and other activities that provide information about
Cuba and its political problems.

UNION OF CUBANS IN EXILE
21 S.W. 13th Avenue
Miami, Florida 33135

U.S. CITIZENS COMMITTEE FOR A FREE CUBA
National Press Building, Room 721
Washington, D.C. 20004

Principal officers: Paul D. Bethel, Executive Director

Permanent staff: 4   Membership: 42
Date founded: 1963   Membership dues: NI
Branches: NI   Scope: national

Nature of organization: political, educational

Publications: *Latin America Report* (semimonthly); *Cuba Policy Research Series* (irregular);
Studies (irregular)

Comments: The primary purpose of this organization is to support efforts in behalf of a free
Cuba, to oust communism there, and to provide information on the Cuban political
situation to the press, radio, Congress, and the Administration from its files and records.
Archival records are maintained. Until 1968 the group was known as the Citizens
Committee for a Free Cuba.

WORKERS CUBAN CONFEDERATION IN EXILE
802 First Street, N.W.
Second Floor, Apt. 1
Miami, Florida 33128   (305) 379-1955

Permanent staff: NI   Membership: NI
Date founded: 1961   Membership dues: NI
Branches: NI   Scope: national

WORKERS CUBAN CONFEDERATION IN EXILE (cont'd)
Major conventions/meetings: monthly
Comments: The organization's intent is to help Cubans who want to join the United States
labor force to organize or incorporate themselves into labor unions.

CZECH-AMERICAN ORGANIZATIONS

Additional information on Czech-American organizations in the United States
may be obtained from the Czechoslovak Society of Arts and Sciences in America,
Inc. (Room 2121, 381 Park Avenue South, New York, New York 10016). Regional
and local information may be obtained from *Greater Cleveland Nationalities
Directory 1974* (Cleveland: Sun Newspapers and the Nationalities Services Center,
1974) and *Ethnic Directory I* (Detroit: Southeastern Michigan Regional Ethnic
Heritage Studies Center, 1973).

ALLIANCE OF CZECHOSLOVAK EXILES IN CHICAGO
2619 South Lawndale Avenue
Chicago, Illinois 60623
Publications: *Zpravodaj* (Reporter), 1969– (monthly)

AMERICAN COMMITTEE FOR LIBERATION OF CZECHOSLOVAKIA
12204 Longmead Avenue
Cleveland, Ohio 44135   (216) 252-6052
Principal officers: James P. Kocian, President
                      J. Ingrid Hyncik, Secretary

AMERICAN CZECHOSLOVAK HISTORICAL SOCIETY
700 North Collington Avenue
Baltimore, Maryland 21205

AMERICAN FUND FOR CZECHOSLOVAK REFUGEES (AFCR)
790 Broadway, Room 513
New York, New York 10019   (212) 265-1919
Principal officers: Dr. Jan Papanek, President
Permanent staff: 18   Membership: NI
Date founded: 1948   Membership dues: NI
Branches: field offices in Munich, Vienna, Rome   Scope: international
 and Paris
Nature of organization: social, charitable
Comments: The purpose of the organization is to provide food, clothing, and shelter, on a
         temporary basis, for refugees from Czechoslovakia to the free world. It also helps them
         find employment in the United States.

AMERICAN SOKOL ORGANIZATION (A.S.O.)
6426 West Cermak Road
Berwyn, Illinois 60402   (312) 795-6671
Principal officers: Stanley Barcal, President
                      Betty Prener, Vice President
                      June Pros, Secretary
Permanent staff: 3   Membership: 7,750
Date founded: 1865   Membership dues: NI
Branches: 72 local   Scope: national
Special requirements for membership: Czechoslovak or other Slav extraction; men (18 years
         old), women (17 years old); U.S. citizen or intent to become one

AMERICAN SOKOL ORGANIZATION (A.S.O.) (cont'd)
Nature of organization: educational, cultural, sports (gymnastics), youth
Publications: *American Sokol*, 1879– (monthly); *Sokol Gymnast* (monthly)
Affiliations: AAU, USGF, US Olympic Committee
Major conventions/meetings: convention, every five years
Comments: Principal objective is to instill in young people the true meaning of sportsmanship
through gymnastic and sports competitions. Also promotes cultural heritage through folk
dancing, language classes, displays, singing and discussions. Senior membership numbers
7,750 (ages 17 to 90). Children's classes, for pre-schoolers through teens, number over
9,000 participants. Branches are located in 20 states. Sponsors schools, camps, and
gymnastic festivals. Awards medals, citations, and trophies. Maintains both a library and
archival materials.

BOHEMIAN FREE THINKING SCHOOL SOCIETY
2707 Kenilworth Avenue
Berwyn, Illinois 60402
Principal officers: Bela Kotrsol, Secretary

Permanent staff: 7	Membership: NI
Date founded: 1863	Membership dues: NI
Branches: NI	Scope: national

Nature of organization: cultural, social
Publications: *Svobodna Skola* (Free Thinking School), 1893– (bimonthly)
Comments: The purpose of the organization is to preserve the Czech language and culture in
the United States. It sponsors activities promoting Czech music and culture.

CATHOLIC WOMEN'S FRATERNAL OF TEXAS
P.O. Box 18844
Austin, Texas 78767
Publications: *KJZT News*, 1955– (monthly)

CATHOLIC WORKMAN (CW)
107 North Central Avenue
New Prague, Minnesota 56071   (612) 758-2229
Principal officers: Rudy G. Faimon, President
                       Frank G. Drahozal, Executive Vice President
                       S. F. Wagner, Executive Secretary

Permanent staff: 17	Membership: 18,362
Date founded: 1891	Membership dues: $2.00
Branches: 126 local	Scope: national

Special requirements for membership: must be a practicing Catholic
Nature of organization: fraternal
Publications: *Catholic Workman*, 1909– (monthly)
Affiliations: National Alliance of Czech Catholics
Major conventions/meetings: convention, quadrennial
Comments: Provides life insurance and other benefits. Local branches are expected to promote
activities and services that are religious, educational, social, and patriotic in nature. Also
provides assistance to members in distress. Awards scholarships to needy students.
Maintains archival materials.

CZECH AMERICAN CLUB OF SENIOR CITIZENS
Sokol Center
26550 Woodshire
Dearborn Heights, Michigan 48127
Principal officers: Charles Van Cura

CZECH AMERICAN CLUB OF SENIOR CITIZENS (cont'd)

Permanent staff: NI

Date founded: NI

Branches: NI

Membership: NI

Membership dues: NI

Scope: regional

Nature of organization: cultural, social

Comments: The purpose of the organization is to keep Czech senior citizens socially and physically active in community activities that promote the Czech language and culture.

CZECH AMERICAN NATIONAL ALLIANCE (CANA)

4029 West 25th Place

Chicago, Illinois 60623 (312) 521-0120

Principal officers: Marie Kacer, President

Permanent staff: NI

Date founded: NI

Branches: NI

Membership: NI

Membership dues: NI

Scope: national

Nature of organization: cultural, charitable

Publications: *Svobodne Ceskoslovensko* (Free Czechoslovakia), 1943– (monthly)

Major conventions/meetings: annual

Comments: Attempts to preserve the Czech heritage and traditions in the United States by sponsoring cultural programs, particularly those stressing Czech folklore. It provides assistance to Czech-Americans in need.

CZECH-AMERICAN WORKINGMEN'S SOKOL

24-19 24th Avenue

Astoria, New York 11102

Principal officers: Vaclav Pechar, President

Charles Balek, Executive Vice President

Mildred Matous, Executive Secretary

Permanent staff: none

Date founded: 1892

Branches: 7 regional

Membership: 400

Membership dues: varies

Scope: regional

Special requirements for membership: 18 years of age, U.S. citizen, and recommendation of two members

Nature of organization: cultural, fraternal

Publications: *Besidka*, 1898– (monthly)

Affiliations: American Sokol; Sokol U.S.A.; AAU; FIG

Major conventions/meetings: biennial convention

Comments: Promotes brotherhood between members through various cultural and sports activities. Sponsors special gymnastic and physical education programs.

CZECH CATHOLIC UNION

5349 Dolloff Road

Cleveland, Ohio 44127 (216) 341-0444

Principal officers: Anna M. Veverka, President

Joseph A. Kocab, Vice President

Elsie M. Filous, Secretary

Permanent staff: 5

Date founded: 1879

Branches: NI

Membership: approximately 6,000

Membership dues: NI

Scope: national

Special requirements for membership: Roman Catholic

Nature of organization: fraternal

Publications: *Posel* (quarterly)

Affiliations: National Fraternal Congress

CZECH CATHOLIC UNION (cont'd)
Major conventions/meetings: convention held every 4 years
Comments: Fraternal organization, operating on the lodge system. Holds various civic and
    religious events, sponsors social get-togethers. Funds used for charitable purposes. Awards
    religious scholarships.

CZECH CATHOLIC UNION OF TEXAS
    P.O. Box 158
    Granger, Texas 76530
Permanent staff: NI   Membership: NI
Date founded: NI   Membership dues: NI
Branches: NI   Scope: state
Publications: *Nasinec* (Fellow Countryman), 1914– (weekly)

CZECH DAY COMMITTEE
    Tabor, South Dakota 57063
Principal officers: Bernard Zitka, President
                      Lloyd Aten, Secretary
Permanent staff: none   Membership: approximately 50
Date founded: 1950   Membership dues: $5.00 (annual)
Branches: none   Scope: local
Special requirements for membership: none
Nature of organization: cultural
Publications: publishes books
Affiliations: none
Major conventions/meetings: none
Comments: This committee functions as a sponsoring agent of the "Czech Day" celebration
    in the town of Tabor, South Dakota. The town of Tabor (600 pop.) was founded by
    Czech immigrants in 1872. Since most of its residents are third or fourth generation
    Czech-Americans, the annual "Czech Days" celebration promotes the retention of the
    various aspects of Czech culture.

CZECH KARLIN HALL
    5304 Fleet Avenue
    Cleveland, Ohio 44105   (216) 883-4760
Principal officers: George Tesar, Jr., President
                      Frank Gillette, Vice President
                      Joseph A. Kocab, Secretary
Permanent staff: 11   Membership: 2,500
Date founded: 1936   Membership dues: NI
Branches: none   Scope: local
Special requirements for membership: Czech or Slovak background
Nature of organization: cultural, fraternal, social, religious, educational, recreational, sports
Publications: publishes bulletins
Affiliations: Czech Catholic Union; National Alliance of Czech Catholics
Major conventions/meetings: none

CZECHOSLOVAK BAPTIST CONVENTION OF U.S. AND CANADA
    316 South Park Street
    Westmont, Illinois 60559
Permanent staff: NI   Membership: NI
Date founded: NI   Membership dues: NI
Branches: NI   Scope: national (including Canada)
Nature of organization: religious
Publications: *Pravda a Slavna Nadeje* (Truth and Glorious Hope), 1919– (monthly)

CZECHOSLOVAK NATIONAL COUNCIL OF AMERICA
2137 South Lombard Avenue
Cicero, Illinois 60650

Publications: *Vestnik* (Herald), 1954– (monthly)

CZECHOSLOVAK SOCIETY OF AMERICA (CSA)
2138 South 61st Court
Cicero, Illinois 60650 (312) 242-2224

Principal officers: Frank J. Vodrazka, President
Charles T. Kropik, Vice President
James V. Krakora, Secretary

Permanent staff: 31   Membership: 46,736
Date founded: 1854   Membership dues: NI
Branches: 22 state   Scope: national

Special requirements for membership: membership is by application, medical examination, or
other evidence of insurability

Nature of organization: fraternal

Publications: *C.S.A. Journal*, 1877– (monthly)

Affiliations: Czechoslovak National Council; American Sokol; Czech Free Thinking Schools;
National Fraternal Congress of America

Major conventions/meetings: convention, quadrennial

Comments: Provides term and life insurance, endowment and annuity certificates, disability
payments, and death benefits to its members. It further promotes fraternal and charitable
activities and the perpetuation of Czech and Slovak language and culture. Annually awards
scholarships. Sponsors classes in the Czech and English languages.

CZECHOSLOVAK SOCIETY OF ARTS AND SCIENCES IN AMERICA, INC. (SVU)
381 Park Avenue South, Room 1121
New York, New York 10016 (212) 686-4220

Principal officers: Prof. Francis Schwarzenberg, President
Dr. John G. Lexa, Secretary

Permanent staff: 1   Membership: 1,500
Date founded: 1958   Membership dues: $12.00 (annual)
Branches: 2 regional; 15 local   Scope: international

Special requirements for membership: academic degree or equivalent

Nature of organization: educational, cultural, literary, scholarly

Publications: *Zprávy SVU*, 1959– (10 issues per year) (Bulletin of the CSASA);
Metamorphoses, 1964– (quarterly)

Affiliations: none

Major conventions/meetings: congresses, biennially

Comments: SVU is a cultural non-profit organization whose prime purpose is the advancement
of Czechoslovak studies. The society coordinates the educational, scientific, literary, and
artistic endeavors of the Czech and Slovak intelligentsia in the free world. The society
maintains both archives and a library.

FARMERS MUTUAL PROTECTION ASSOCIATION OF TEXAS
P.O. Box 426
Granger, Texas 76530

Permanent staff: NI   Membership: NI
Date founded: NI   Membership dues: NI
Branches: NI   Scope: state

Publications: *Texasky Rolnik* (Texas Farmer), 1930– (quarterly)

FIRST CZECHOSLOVAK PHILATELIC CLUB OF AMERICA
c/o Masaryk School Building
5701 West 22nd Place
Cicero, Illinois 60650   (312) 447-0459
Principal officers: J. J. Janecka, President

Permanent staff: NI   Membership: 185
Date founded: 1924   Membership dues: NI
Branches: NI   Scope: national

Special requirements for membership: a stamp collector of Czechoslovak descent

Publications: *Bulletin* (3-4 issues per year); also publishes statistics on new stamp issues

Affiliations: Society of Philatelic Americans

Major conventions/meetings: annual; always in March, in Cicero, Illinois

Comments: Stamp collectors in this organization are of Czech descent but collect stamps of
all countries. They sponsor an annual exhibition and also publish statistical information
on new stamps that are issued.

GYMNASTIC SOKOL SOCIETY FUEGNER TYRS
5601 South 21st Street
Omaha, Nebraska 68107   (402) 731-1065
Principal officers: E. J. Pavoucek, President
                     Karel Forman, Executive Vice President
                     Joseph Hermanek, Executive Secretary

Permanent staff: 35   Membership: 450
Date founded: 1888   Membership dues: $7.80 (annual)
Branches: 75 regional   Scope: national

Special requirements for membership: none

Nature of organization: educational, cultural, sports, fraternal, youth

Publications: *American Sokol* (monthly); *South Omaha Sokol*; also publishes other works

Affiliations: American Sokol Organization

Major conventions/meetings: national convention every 5 years

Comments: Like the other Sokol societies, this organization is also "dedicated to the physical,
mental and cultural advancement of members." Major activities center around
gymnastic programs. Also holds educational courses in Czech culture and language.

MASARYK INSTITUTE (Czech)
c/o Harkins
420 West 118th Street
New York, New York 10027   (212) 280-4623
Principal officers: William E. Harkins, President

Permanent staff: NI   Membership: 25
Date founded: 1937   Membership dues: NI
Branches: NI   Scope: NI

Nature of organization: cultural

Major conventions/meetings: annual in New York City

Comments: The prime purpose of this institute is "to honor the memory of Thomas G.
Masaryk. The institute is involved in researching various topics in Czech history, with
a special emphasis on President Masaryk's life and activities. A publication honoring
Masaryk is planned as a celebration of the 125th anniversary of his birthday.

MOVEMENT OF CZECHOSLOVAK CHRISTIAN-DEMOCRATS IN EXILE
1502 Broad Street
Hartford, Connecticut 06106   (203) 524-5741
Principal officers: Rudolph Krempl, U.S. Representative

MOVEMENT OF CZECHOSLOVAK CHRISTIAN-DEMOCRATS IN EXILE (cont'd)

Permanent staff: NI

Date founded: 1957

Branches: 6 regional

Membership: NI

Membership dues: NI

Scope: NI

Special requirements for membership: Czechs living in the U.S. who have left their homeland as political refugees

Nature of organization: political

Publications: *Demokracia v Exilu* (Democracy in Exile); *The Ambassador* (irregular)

Major conventions/meetings: annual

Comments: The organization attempts to promote activities on behalf of a free Czechoslovakia and to aid political refugees. It disseminates information and literature opposing communism and collects materials on Czech culture, history, and literature. A library is maintained.

NATIONAL ALLIANCE OF CZECH CATHOLICS

2636 South Central Park Avenue

Chicago, Illinois 60623 (312) 522-7575

Principal officers: Victoria Voller, President

Fr. W. Michalicka, Executive Vice President

Mrs. A. Marek, Executive Secretary

Permanent staff: 1

Date founded: 1917

Branches: 5 regional

Membership: 2,000

Membership dues: $2.00 (annual)

Scope: national

Special requirements for membership: none

Nature of organization: cultural, religious

Publications: none

Affiliations: none

Major conventions/meetings: meetings annually; convention triennially

Comments: This is basically an ethnic cultural and religious unit supporting Catholic education. It unites all Czech Catholic fraternal organizations under a single leadership. Awards scholarships. Maintains an archival collection pertaining to Czechs in America.

NATIONAL COUNCIL OF WOMEN OF FREE CZECHOSLOVAKIA (NCWFC)

P.O. Box 121

Newark, New Jersey 07101 (201) 484-1591

Principal officers: Mrs. Jan Papanek, President

Permanent staff: 1

Date founded: 1951

Branches: 4 local groups

Membership: 125

Membership dues: NI

Scope: national

Special requirements for membership: women of Czechoslovak origin or background

Publications: *Bulletin* (3 issues per year)

Affiliations: National Council of Women of the U.S.

Major conventions/meetings: annual

Comments: The organization sponsors cultural, educational, and charitable activities that attempt to promote the Czech heritage in the United States and to benefit Czech refugees. It schedules art and handcraft exhibits and other educational activities.

NEBRASKA CZECHS INCORPORATED

321 South Harris Street

Wilber, Nebraska 68465 (402) 821-3567

Principal officers: Rose Storm, President

Anton Novotny, Vice President

Irma Ourecky, Secretary

Permanent staff: none

Date founded: 1962

Branches: 7 regional

Membership: NI

Membership dues: NI

Scope: state

NEBRASKA CZECHS INCORPORATED (cont'd)
Special requirements for membership: none
Nature of organization: cultural
Publications: none
Major conventions/meetings: none
Comments: The group acts as coordinating agent for all activities sponsored by chapters for the annual Czech Festival.

OMAHA CZECH CLUB
    3908 "W" Street
    Omaha, Nebraska 68107   (402) 731-8669
Principal officers: Frank M. Smrz, President
                    Frank T. Tesar, Vice President
                    Miss Vlasta Dostal, Secretary

Permanent staff: 4   Membership: 25
Date founded: 1960   Membership dues: $10.00
Branches: 1 local   Scope: state
Special requirements for membership: none
Nature of organization: cultural
Publications: none
Affiliations: Nebraska Czechs, Inc.
Major conventions/meetings: business meeting annually
Comments: Promotes the preservation of Czech language, traditions, music, and folklore. Sponsors annual public programs of Czech songs and music.

OMAHA CZECH CULTURE CLUB
    Sokol Auditorium
    2234 South 13th Street
    Omaha, Nebraska 68108   (402) 342-9252
Principal officers: Frank J. Smrz, President
                    Frank Tesar, Vice President
                    Miss Vlasta Dostal, Secretary

Permanent staff: 1   Membership: 30
Date founded: 1959   Membership dues: $10.00 (2 sessions)
Branches: none   Scope: state
Special requirements for membership: none
Nature of organization: social, educational, cultural
Publications: publishes books
Affiliations: Nebraska Czechs, Inc.
Major conventions/meetings: none
Comments: The club promotes the Czech language among Czechs throughout Nebraska. It organizes language classes at both beginning and advanced levels in various parts of the state. Maintains a library containing books relating to Czech language, culture, and heritage.

SLAVONIC BENEVOLENT ORDER OF THE STATE OF TEXAS
    P.O. Box 100
    Temple, Texas 76501   (817) 773-1575
Principal officers: Nick A. Morris, President
                    Joe B. Hejny, Vice President
                    Leonard Mikesha, Secretary-Treasurer

Permanent staff: 15   Membership: 46,000+
Date founded: 1897   Membership dues: NI
Branches: 131 local   Scope: state

SLAVONIC BENEVOLENT ORDER OF THE STATE OF TEXAS (cont'd)
Special requirements for membership: "be insurable"
Nature of organization: fraternal life insurance
Publications: *Herald* (Vestnik), 1912– (weekly)
Affiliations: National Fraternal Congress; Texas State Fraternal Congress
Major conventions/meetings: convention quadrennially
Comments: The objectives of this organization are to provide economic and social security to
its members and their families in the event of death. Society is composed of local lodges
in the various counties, communities, and towns throughout Texas. The society promote
the retention of traditions, customs, and language. Sponsors camps and training programs. Awards scholarships. Maintains museum, library, and archives.

SOCIETY FOR CZECHOSLOVAK PHILATELY
c/o Edward Lisy
87 Carmita Avenue
Rutherford, New Jersey 07070
Principal officers: Edward Lisy, Secretary
Permanent staff: NI   Membership: 300
Date founded: 1939   Membership dues: NI
Branches: 2 local groups   Scope: NI
Special requirements for membership: collectors of Czechoslovakian stamps
Nature of organization: philatelic
Publications: *The Czechoslovak Specialist* (monthly)
Comments: The purpose of the organization is to collect Czechoslovakian postage stamps and
to provide an exchange service for philatelic items. It maintains a library of over 80
volumes pertaining to Czechoslovakian stamps.

UNION OF CZECH CATHOLIC WOMEN OF TEXAS
Davilla Street
Granger, Texas 76530
Publications: *Novy Domov* (New Home), 1894– (weekly)

UNITY OF CZECH LADIES AND MEN
6907 West Cermak Road
Berwyn, Illinois 60401
Permanent staff: NI   Membership: 11,500
Date founded: 1880   Membership dues: NI
Branches: 125 local groups   Scope: national
Major conventions/meetings: quadrennial
Comments: Fraternal benefit life insurance society.

UNITY OF THE BRETHREN IN TEXAS
5905 Carleen Drive
Austin, Texas 78731

WESTERN BOHEMIAN FRATERNAL ASSOCIATION
1402 "B" Street
Omaha, Nebraska 68108

WESTERN FRATERNAL LIFE ASSOCIATION (WFLA)
1900 First Avenue, N.E.
Cedar Rapids, Iowa 52402   (515) 363-2653
Principal officers: Charles H. Vyskocil, President
Elmer F. Karasek, Executive Vice President
Jerry P. Drahovzal, Executive Secretary

WESTERN FRATERNAL LIFE ASSOCIATION (WFLA) (cont'd)

Permanent staff: 23
Date founded: 1897
Branches: 280 local
Membership: 60,000
Membership dues: none
Scope: national

Nature of organization: fraternal

Publications: *Fraternal Herald*, 1898– (monthly)

Affiliations: Cedar Rapids Chamber of Commerce; National Fraternal Congress of America

Major conventions/meetings: national convention quadrennially

Comments: Primarily fraternal in nature. Provides a system of insurance for its members. Aids in educational advancement. Offers assistance for disaster victims. Encourages educational lectures, establishment of Czech libraries, and the use of the Czech language among members. Maintains both a library and archives.

DANISH-AMERICAN ORGANIZATIONS

Additional information on Danish-American organizations may be obtained from the Office of the Danish Embassy (3200 Whitehaven Street, Washington, D.C. 20008).

AID SOCIETY DENMARK
562 82nd Street
Brooklyn, New York 11209
Principal officers: Mrs. Mary Groth, President

AMERICAN SOCIETY OF DANISH ENGINEERS (ASDE)
6 Great Hill Road
Darien, Connecticut 06820 (203) 655-8537
Principal officers: Gunner Block-Petersen, Secretary-Treasurer

Permanent staff: NI
Date founded: 1930
Branches: state
Membership: 200
Membership dues: NI
Scope: national

Special requirements for membership: engineers of Danish birth or descent residing in the United States or Canada

Publications: *Newsletter* (3 issues per year)

Affiliations: Society of Danish Engineers (Denmark)

Major conventions/meetings: semiannual

Comments: The purpose of the organization is to unite Danish engineers in the United States. It also awards scholarships.

CHICAGO DANISH CLUB
719 Echo Lane
Chicago, Illinois
Principal officers: Walter G. Andersen, Secretary

DANIA LADIES SOCIETY DANNEBROG OF CALIFORNIA AND NEVADA (DLSD)
6185 North Lafayette
Fresno, California 93705   (209) 439-3697
Principal officers: Agnes Lind, Grand President
                       Anna Bertelsen, Vice President
                       Inger Rasmussen, Secretary

Permanent staff: 10   Membership: 1,551
Date founded: 1915   Membership dues: $1.00
Branches: 17 local   Scope: regional

Special requirements for membership: women over 14 years of age, of Danish descent, or married to a Dane

Nature of organization: social

Publications: *Grand Lodge Dania Newsletter*, 1972– (monthly)

Major conventions/meetings: annual convention

Comments: Principal objective is to bring together Danish women in the states of California and Nevada. The organization works toward the preservation of Danish language, culture, history, and customs. It further provides assistance during times of personal or family distress.

DANIA SOCIETY
5006 Altgeld Avenue
Chicago, Illinois 60639
Principal officers: Viggo Hoyer, Secretary

DANISH AID AND RELIEF SOCIETY
c/o Axel Sorensen
4133 North Leclaire
Chicago, Illinois 60641

DANISH AMERICAN ATHLETIC CLUB
4624 North Pulaski Road
Chicago, Illinois 60630

DANISH AMERICAN CLUB
73 A Kensington Road
Bronxville, New York 10708
Principal officers: Richard K. Pedersen, President

DANISH-AMERICAN SOCIETY, INC.
Four Roses Distillers Co.
375 Park Avenue
New York, New York 10002
Principal officers: John E. Heilmann, President

DANISH AMERICAN TRADE COUNCIL, INC. (DATCO)
979 Third Avenue, Suite 1605
New York, New York 10022
Principal officers: Knud Sorensen, President
                       Erik Norup, Secretary

DANISH AMERICAN TRADE COUNCIL, INC. (DATCO) (cont'd)

Permanent staff: none
Date founded: 1964
Branches: none

Membership: 100
Membership dues: $100.00 corporations;
 $50.00 individuals
Scope: national

Special requirements for membership: none

Nature of organization: professional

Publications: newsletter

Affiliations: none

Major conventions/meetings: none

Comments: DATCO is primarily involved in fostering the development of trade and economic relations between the United States and Denmark.

DANISH BROTHERHOOD IN AMERICA (DB)

3717 Harney Street
Omaha, Nebraska 68131   (402) 341-5049

Principal officers: Einar Danielsen, President
                         Kristen Jorgensen, Vice President
                         George Jacobsen, Secretary

Permanent staff: 8
Date founded: 1882
Branches: 150 local

Membership: 10,000
Membership dues: varies with lodge
Scope: national

Special requirements for membership: must be Danish, of Danish origin, married to a Dane, or related to member of Danish Brotherhood

Nature of organization: fraternal

Publications: none

Affiliations: none

Major conventions/meetings: none

Comments: Provides assistance to members during unemployment, illness, or death. Also promotes the retention of Danish culture and traditions. Each lodge sponsors various social, cultural, and recreational activities. Besides insurance protection, the Brotherhood also awards, on an annual basis, four-year college scholarships. Recipients are free to use such scholarships at any accredited college and for any field of study.

DANISH CLUB OF DETROIT, INC.

22711 Grand River
Detroit, Michigan 48219   (313) 332-2790

Permanent staff: NI
Date founded: NI
Branches: NI

Membership: NI
Membership dues: NI
Scope: local

Nature of organization: cultural, social

Comments: The organization is interested in preserving the Danish heritage in the United States. It sponsors lectures, tours and trips, and social activities for its members.

THE DANISH CLUB OF WASHINGTON, D.C., INC.

2400 41st Street, N.W.
Apartment 110
Washington, D.C. 20007   (202) 337-7643

Principal officers: Børge Christensen, President
                         Ib I. Andersen and Miss Helle Starcke, Vice Presidents
                         Mrs. Bodil McD. Creamer, Treasurer

Permanent staff: NI
Date founded: 1931
Branches: NI

Membership: NI
Membership dues: $8.00 single; $15.00
 couple; $4.00 members under 21 years
 of age
Scope: local

THE DANISH CLUB OF WASHINGTON, D.C., INC. (cont'd)

Special requirements for membership: Danish heritage or interest in Denmark and Danish culture

Nature of organization: charitable, cultural, educational, fraternal

Affiliations: Scandinavian Joint Planning Council of Washington, D.C.

Major conventions/meetings: annual business meeting

Comments: Objectives of the club are as follows: preservation of Danish traditions, culture, heritage, and language; promotion of fellowship among persons of Danish ancestry and others interested in Danish culture; educational; aid to recently arrived Danes; promotion of cultural exchange between Denmark and the United States; fund-raising activities and charitable, civic, philanthropic, and social works.

DANISH INTEREST CONFERENCE, LUTHERAN CHURCH IN AMERICA (DIC)
Grand View College (Secretary's address)
1200 Grandview Avenue (515) 265-2726 or
Des Moines, Iowa 50316 (515) 262-5274 (home number)

Principal officers: Enok Mortensen, President
Pastor Thorvald Hansen, Secretary
Folmer U. Hansen, Treasurer

Permanent staff: none Membership: no official membership—
Date founded: 1962 about 500 to 1,000 adherents
Branches: none Membership dues: none
Scope: national

Special requirements for membership: none

Nature of organization: cultural, religious

Publications: *Kirke og Folk*, 1952– (20 issues per year); also publishes books

Affiliations: Lutheran Church in America

Major conventions/meetings: biennial convention

Comments: Informal organization whose primary purpose is the preservation and perpetuation of the Danish culture. Maintains an archival collection of Danish newspapers, letters, books, and memorabilia.

DANISH OLD SETTLERS
2950 Logan Boulevard
Chicago, Illinois 60647 (312) 486-6278

Principal officers: Johannes Nielsen, President
Adolf Nieman, Vice President
Signe Bang, Secretary

Permanent staff: 8 Membership: 125
Date founded: 1933 Membership dues: $4.00 (annual)
Branches: none Scope: local, but membership is
national

Special requirements for membership: "Must have been born in Denmark and have lived in U.S. 25 years."

Nature of organization: social

Publications: none

Affiliations: none

Major conventions/meetings: none

Comments: The society is primarily social in nature. It promotes fellowship among old-time Danish citizens. Although it is located in Chicago, it welcomes members from anywhere in the United States as long as membership requirements are met.

DANISH ROYAL GUARD ASSOCIATION
300 Knickerbocker Road
Gresskill, New Jersey 07626
Principal officers: Holger Nissen, President

DANISH SAILORS' AND FIREMEN'S UNION
38 Pearl Street
New York, New York 10004   (202) 943-2340
Principal officers: Soren Hansen, Representative

Permanent staff: NI   Membership: NI
Date founded: 1897   Membership dues: NI
Branches: NI   Scope: NI

Special requirements for membership: sailors and firemen employed on Danish vessels

Publications: *Ny Tid and Falken* (monthly)

Comments: Members of this union are from two independent Danish unions.

DANISH SEAMAN'S CHURCH, NEW YORK, INC.
102 Willow Street
Brooklyn, New York 11201   (212) 875-0042
Principal officers: Consul General E. Krog-Meyer, President
                       Pastor Ronald Petersen, Vice President and Secretary
                       Per U. Vranum, Treasurer

Permanent staff: 3   Membership: NI
Date founded: 1880   Membership dues: none
Branches: none   Scope: local

Special requirements for membership: any Dane living in New York and any Danish seaman in
the New York harbor who is not a member of another church is automatically a member

Nature of organization: religious, cultural, social

Publications: none

Affiliations: none

Major conventions/meetings: none

Comments: The organization serves Danish seamen during the time their ships are in New York
harbor. Provides church service and recreational and social activities. Maintains a library
of books and newspapers in Danish.

INDEPENDENT ORDER OF ODD FELLOWS, BERTHEL THORVALDSEN LODGE
NO. 530, I.O.O.F.
220 East 15th Street
New York, New York 10003   (212) 539-9769
Principal officers: Kaj Mogensen, Grand Noble
                       Joseph Gentile, Vice President
                       Svend A. Hansen, Secretary
                       Arne Vranum, Treasurer

Permanent staff: 5   Membership: 96
Date founded: 1885   Membership dues: $15.00 (annual)
Branches: 1 state   Scope: international (headquarters in
                                          Maryland)

Special requirements for membership: belief in God

Nature of organization: fraternal, charitable

Publications: *Danish Odd Fellow Bulletin* (every two months)

Comments: Provides aid to the sick and those in distress; educates the orphaned; maintains an
eye bank and heart fund. Sponsors a children's camp, and sponsors visits to the U.N. for
young people from the entire country. Donates to medical research.

ODIN DANISH RELIEF SOCIETY, INC.
220 East 15th Street
New York, New York 10003

SOCIETY DANIA
562 82nd Street
Brooklyn, New York 11209
Principal officers: Charles Groth, President

SUPREME LODGE OF THE DANISH SISTERHOOD OF AMERICA (DSA)
3438 North Opal
Chicago, Illinois 60634   (312) 625-9031
Principal officers: Virginia A. Christensen, National Secretary

Permanent staff: 7   Membership: 5,000
Date founded: 1883   Membership dues: NI
Branches: 120 local groups   Scope: NI

Special requirements for membership: women of Danish birth, descent, or heritage, or
    married to a man of Danish descent

Publications: *Danish Sisterhood News*, 1947– (monthly)

Major conventions/meetings: sexennial

DUTCH-AMERICAN ORGANIZATIONS

Additional information on Dutch-American organizations may be obtained
from the Office of the Netherlands Embassy (4200 Linnean Avenue, Washington,
D.C. 20008).

DUTCH-AMERICAN HISTORICAL COMMISSION
Netherlands Museum
8 East 12th Street
Holland, Michigan 49423   (616) 392-3129
Principal officers: Donald Bruggink, President

Permanent staff: NI   Membership: NI
Date founded: NI   Membership dues: NI
Branches: NI   Scope: regional

Special requirements for membership: limited to representatives of two colleges, two
    seminaries, and the Netherlands Museum in Western Michigan

Publications: publishes guidebooks

Comments: The commission attempts to collect materials on the Dutch in Western Michigan
    and make them available to scholars studying the Dutch in the United States.

DUTCH IMMIGRANT SOCIETY (D.I.S.)
P.O. Box 6462
Grand Rapids, Michigan 49506   (616) 949-8338
Principal officers: William Turkenburg, President
                      Cornelis DeRuiter, Vice President
                      John Witte, Secretary
                      Clarence Visser, General Adjunct

Permanent staff: 8   Membership: 10,500 families; 1,000
Date founded: 1950   single people
Branches: branch in Netherlands and committee   Membership dues: $3.00 (annual)
  in Chicago   Scope: national

Special requirements for membership: none

DUTCH IMMIGRANT SOCIETY (D.I.S.) (cont'd)
Nature of organization: social, cultural, religious
Publications: *D.I.S.*, 1970– (quarterly); newsletters (irregular); *Introducing You to D.I.S.*
Comments: Primarily a socio-cultural organization. Sponsors charter flights and tours, cultural
    events, and religious, social, and recreational activities. Awards scholarships to various
    colleges.

HOLLAND SOCIETY OF NEW YORK
        122 East 58th Street
        New York, New York 10028   (212) 758-1675
Principal officers: Julian K. Roosevelt, President
                       Gerrit W. Van Schaick, Secretary
                       John A. Pruyn, Treasurer
Permanent staff: 1   Membership: 950
Date founded: 1885   Membership dues: $30.00 (annual)
Branches: 12 regional   Scope: national
Special requirements for membership: 18 years of age and the descendant of a Dutchman in the
    direct male line
Nature of organization: historical
Publications: *The Half Moon*, 1926– (quarterly)
Affiliations: none
Major conventions/meetings: annual meeting
Comments: Major objectives include collecting and preserving data dealing with the early
    settlement and history of the Dutch in New York City and state; perpetuating of Dutch
    traditions; organizing a library of books relating to the Dutch experience in America;
    publishing materials on the Dutch in the United States; and contributing to literary,
    educational, religious, artistic, and philanthropic activities. Maintains a library of over
    3,800 volumes.

THE NETHERLAND-AMERICA FOUNDATION
        1 Rockefeller Plaza
        New York, New York 10020   (212) 246-0200
Principal officers: H. Y. de Schepper, President
Permanent staff: NI   Membership: NI
Date founded: 1921   Membership dues: NI
Branches: none   Scope: national
Nature of organization: educational
Comments: Non-profit organization founded in order to develop the educational, literary,
    artistic, scientific, historical, and cultural relations between the Netherlands and the
    United States. Presently, the main activity is the Trainee Program, which arranges
    traineeship in the United States of young citizens from the Netherlands. The Founda-
    tion has also sponsored grants or loans to young Americans for study in the
    Netherlands.

NETHERLAND BENEVOLENT SOCIETY OF NEW YORK, INC.
        1 Rockefeller Plaza, 11th Floor
        New York, New York 10020   (212) 265-6649
Principal officers: H. Y. de Schepper, President
                       Elizabeth Kayton, Administrator
                       Hans Van Den Houten, Secretary
Permanent staff: 1   Membership: 350
Date founded: 1908   Membership dues: $5.00 member;
Branches: none $10.00 patron; $25.00 donor (annual)
                                              Scope: national
Special requirements for membership: none

NETHERLAND BENEVOLENT SOCIETY OF NEW YORK, INC. (cont'd)

Nature of organization: charitable

Publications: *Annual Report*

Major conventions/meetings: annual meeting

Comments: Major objectives are to assist financially, and any other way, persons of Dutch birth or ancestry.

NETHERLAND CLUB OF NEW YORK
10 Rockefeller Plaza
New York, New York 10020   (212) 265-9500

Principal officers: H. L. A. Vanden Wall Bake, Manager

Permanent staff: NI	Membership: 700
Date founded: 1903	Membership dues: NI
Branches: NI	Scope: NI

Special requirements for membership: persons of Dutch birth or ancestry

Nature of organization: cultural

NETHERLANDS-AMERICA SOCIETY
New York Life Insurance Company
17000 West 8 Mile Road
Southfield, Michigan 48075

Principal officers: Paul Van Den Muysenberg

NETHERLANDS AND COLONIAL PHILATELY
45 Quincy Lane
Bergenfield, New Jersey 07621

Principal officers: Johannes De Kruyf, Editor

Permanent staff: NI	Membership: 250
Date founded: 1934	Membership dues: NI
Branches: NI	Scope: international

Nature of organization: educational

Publications: *Netherlands and Colonial Philately* (quarterly)

Major conventions/meetings: monthly meetings, always in New York City

Comments: Members collect stamps issued in the Netherlands and its colonies. It sponsors postage stamp sales and exchanges.

NETHERLANDS CHAMBER OF COMMERCE IN THE UNITED STATES
1 Rockefeller Plaza
New York, New York 10020   (212) 265-6460

Principal officers: J. M. Bakels, Executive Secretary

Permanent staff: NI	Membership: 1,000
Date founded: 1920	Membership dues: NI
Branches: 1	Scope: international

Nature of organization: commercial

Publications: *Netherlands North America Trade* (11 issues per year)

NETHERLANDS INTERNATIONAL SERVICE CENTER
City Hall
Holland, Michigan 49423

THE NETHERLANDS MUSEUM
8 East 12th Street
Holland, Michigan 49423   (616) 392-9084

THE NETHERLANDS MUSEUM (cont'd)
Principal officers: Willard C. Wichers, President
John Donnelly, Executive Vice President
Vernon Ten Cate, Executive Secretary

Permanent staff: 2   Membership: NI
Date founded: 1937   Membership dues: NI
Branches: NI   Scope: local

Special requirements for membership: none

Nature of organization: educational, cultural

Publications: none

Affiliations: none

Major conventions/meetings: none

Comments: Dedicated to perpetuating the memory of the founders of the Dutch "Kolonie" of Western Michigan. Exhibits show the history of the settlements and Dutch heritage. Maintains archival collection.

SOCIETY OF DAUGHTERS OF HOLLAND DAMES
570 Park Avenue
New York, New York 10021

Principal officers: Anne H. Joyce, Director

Permanent staff: NI   Membership: 150
Date founded: 1895   Membership dues: NI
Branches: NI   Scope: national

Special requirements for membership: a female descendant of the founders of New Netherlands (New York) prior to 1674

Nature of organization: social, genealogical, historical

Major conventions/meetings: monthly

Comments: The society attempts to preserve the Dutch tradition and heritage in America. It collects and preserves records of the Dutch settlers.

ECUADOREAN-AMERICAN ORGANIZATIONS

Additional information on Ecuadorean-American organizations in the United States may be obtained from the Ecuadorean Embassy (2535 15th Street, Washington, D.C. 20009).

ECUADOREAN AMERICAN ASSOCIATION (EAA)
55 Liberty Street
New York, New York 10005   (212) 233-7776

Principal officers: Paul E. Calvert, Secretary

Permanent staff: NI   Membership: 100
Date founded: 1932   Membership dues: NI
Branches: NI   Scope: national

Nature of organization: economic, cultural

Publications: *Bulletin* (monthly)

Comments: Major purpose of the organization is to promote cultural and economic relations between the United States and Ecuador through trade and travel, etc.

EGYPTIAN-AMERICAN ORGANIZATIONS

See Arab-American Organizations

ENGLISH-AMERICAN ORGANIZATIONS

See British-American Organizations

ESKIMO-AMERICAN ORGANIZATIONS

See American-Indian Organizations

ESTONIAN-AMERICAN ORGANIZATIONS

Additional information on Estonian-American organizations in the United States may be obtained from the Office of the Estonian Consulate General (9 Rockefeller Plaza, New York, New York 10020), the Association for the Advancement of Baltic Studies (c/o Valters Nollendorts, President, 366 86th Street, Brooklyn, New York 11209), and *Kalendar 1974* (New York: Nordic Press, 1974).

AMERICANS FOR CONGRESSIONAL ACTION TO FREE THE BALTIC STATES
41 Morristown Road
Bernardsville, New Jersey 07924

THE BALTIC-AMERICAN SOCIETY OF NEW ENGLAND
287 Commonwealth Avenue
Boston, Massachusetts 02116

BALTIC WOMEN'S COUNCIL (BWC)
24 Central Avenue
Ridgefield Park, New Jersey 07660   (201) 440-1563
Principal officers: Mrs. Mall Jurma, President

Permanent staff: NI	Membership: NI
Date founded: 1947	Membership dues: NI
Branches: NI	Scope: NI

Special requirements for membership: must be an Estonian, Latvian, or Lithuanian women's club

Affiliations: General Federation of Women's Clubs

Major conventions/meetings: annual

Comments: The organization attempts to preserve the native culture of the Baltic countries by providing cultural activities in the fields of literature, art, and music. It provides financial assistance to refugee activities in Germany, Austria, and the Baltic nations, and it also assists and supports action taken to restore political freedom to these nations.

THE BOSTON ESTONIAN SOCIETY
c/o International Institute
287 Commonwealth Avenue
Boston, Massachusetts 02115
Principal officers: Oskar Lukk, President
                    Raoul Pettai, Vice President
                    Tõnu Hansman, Secretary

Permanent staff: none	Membership: 79
Date founded: 1937	Membership dues: $5.00 (annual)
Branches: none	Scope: regional

Special requirements for membership: Estonian birth or parentage. Supporting members may be of any nationality, but they cannot vote.

THE BOSTON ESTONIAN SOCIETY (cont'd)

Nature of organization: social, cultural, recreational

Publications: none

Affiliations: The International Institute of Boston

Major conventions/meetings: none

Comments: The purpose is to maintain and propogate Estonian cultural life. Organizes lectures and films on Estonia or by Estonians. Sponsors concerts for Estonian musicians and singers as well as exhibitions for artists. Holds social get-togethers for the purpose of Estonian interaction. Maintains an archival collection.

CENTER FOR ESTONIAN SCHOOLS IN THE UNITED STATES
c/o Mr. Gaston O. Randvee
220 Mansfield Avenue
Willimantic, Connecticut 06226   (203) 423-2937

Principal officers: Gaston O. Randvee, President
                        Eduard Karner, Vice President
                        Lilliam Esop, Secretary

Permanent staff: 9   Membership: none (14 schools)
Date founded: 1970   Membership dues: none
Branches: none   Scope: national

Nature of organization: educational

Publications: biannual newsletter; mimeographed lectures of Estonian Teacher's summer seminars; a handbook

Affiliations: Estonian American National Council

Major conventions/meetings: biennial conference

Comments: The center provides assistance and academic consultation to the 14 Estonian language schools in the United States, with respect to books and teaching aids. It also gathers annual reports of the teachers, students, and school activities. Promotes teaching of Estonian language, history, geography, literature, and music. Maintains archival materials on Estonian schools. Sponsors summer seminars for Estonian teachers.

THE CONNECTICUT ESTONIAN SOCIETY, INC.
200 Maple Street
Manchester, Connecticut 06040   (203) 649-3997

Principal officers: Vaike Lugus, President
                        Erich Siismets, Vice President
                        August Hinnov, Secretary
                        Hilja Sulev, Treasurer

Permanent staff: none   Membership: 185
Date founded: NI   Membership dues: $5.00
Branches: none   Scope: state

Special requirements for membership: Estonian descent

Nature of organization: cultural, educational, charitable

Publications: *Events Bulletin* (as needed)

Affiliations: Estonian-American National Council

Major conventions/meetings: annual convention

Comments: Promotes the preservation of the Estonian cultural and historical heritage. Sponsors concerts, holds classes in language, culture, and history; organizes social and recreational activities. Assists destitute Estonian Americans.

COUNCIL OF ESTONIAN SCOUTING IN USA
c/o M. Koiva
Route 66
Columbia, Connecticut 06237   (203) 228-3731
Principal officers: Mati Koiva, President
               G. O. Randvee, Vice President
               Endel Reinpold, Secretary

Permanent staff: none   Membership: 350
Date founded: 1949   Membership dues: $2.00 boys; $3.00
Branches: 3 regional; 11 local   adults
                                    Scope: national

Special requirements for membership: Estonian descent

Nature of organization: youth

Publications: *Bulletin* (Ringkiri), 1949– (irregular)

Affiliations: Congress of Estonian-American Organizations

Major conventions/meetings: annual conference

Comments: Organizes scouting units of Estonian-Americans in cooperation with the Boy Scouts of America. Provides such units with supplemental training materials on the Estonian culture. Organizes camps and tours for members. Every three years there is a worldwide encampment of Estonian scouts. Awards honors and merits annually. Maintains archives.

ESTONIAN AID
P.O. Box 357
41 Union Square West
New York, New York 10003   (212) 675-0825
Principal officers: Walter Brunberg, President
               Aleksander Hinno, Vice President
               Erich Park, Secretary

Permanent staff: 2   Membership: varies
Date founded: 1950   Membership dues: $10.00
Branches: none   Scope: national

Special requirements for membership: none

Nature of organization: cultural, service

Publications: irregular bulletins

Major conventions/meetings: annual

Comments: This service organization assists refugees and immigrants of Estonian origin, providing financial aid in resettlement. It also supports overseas relief work, sponsors summer camps, and grants financial aid to Estonian youth organizations and college scholarships for students of Estonian descent. A library collection is maintained.

ESTONIAN AMERICAN CULTURAL CLUB OF MIAMI
111 West 29th Street
Hialeah, Florida 33012   (305) 887-0887
Principal officers: Anna Seeberg, President
               Meeta Sepp, Vice President
               Hermi Vooder, Secretary

Permanent staff: 7   Membership: 250
Date founded: 1949   Membership dues: $5.00 (annual)
Branches: none   Scope: state

Special requirements for membership: natives of Estonia, without criminal records, not communists; non-Estonians accepted as amity members

Nature of organization: cultural

Publications: none

Affiliations: none

ESTONIAN AMERICAN CULTURAL CLUB OF MIAMI (cont'd)

Comments: Promotes the retention of Estonian language, culture, history, art, music, etc. Arranges numerous concerts, theatrical performances, art expositions, etc., every year. Maintains a library collection consisting primarily of fiction in the Estonian language.

ESTONIAN AMERICAN NATIONAL COUNCIL
243 East 34th Street
New York, New York 10016   (212) 685-0776

Principal officers: Ilmar Pleer, President
                      Vaike Lugus, Harry Must, Vice Presidents
                      Eduard Vallaste, Secretary

Permanent staff: 2   Membership: 10,000
Date founded: 1952   Membership dues: donations
Branches: 4 regional; 10 state   Scope: national

Special requirements for membership: American citizen of Estonian descent

Nature of organization: cultural, political

Publications: publishes books

Affiliations: Estonian World Council; Baltic World Conference

Major conventions/meetings: annual meeting of 50 representatives—National Assembly

Comments: This is the supreme organization representing all Americans of Estonian descent. In 1971 it adopted its present official name. The national representative body consists of 50 persons secretly and directly elected by all Estonians in the United States. President and officers are elected from these 50 representatives. Term of office for all is three years. Objectives are political, cultural, organizational, and financial. Coordinates all political and cultural activities of other Estonian organizations. Encourages the retention of the Estonian language, culture, and heritage. Supports Estonian language schools, youth, organizations, camps. Provides research grants for the study of Estonian subjects. Maintains a 600-volume collection of Estonian titles. Also has an archival collection pertaining to Estonian-American life.

THE ESTONIAN-AMERICAN REPUBLICAN CLUB OF MICHIGAN
10831 West 11 Mile Road
Huntington Woods, Michigan 48070   (313) 546-4232

Principal officers: Edgar Erm, President
                      Harry Kord, Vice President
                      Arda Kord, Secretary
                      Maimu Looke, Treasurer

Permanent staff: none   Membership: 31
Date founded: 1963   Membership dues: $2.50 (annual)
Branches: none   Scope: state

Special requirements for membership: U.S. citizenship, 18 years of age

Nature of organization: political

Publications: none

Affiliations: Estonian-American Republican National Committee; Republican State Nationalities Council of Michigan

Comments: Objectives of this organization are to represent citizens of Estonian descent in the Republican State Nationality Council; to organize Estonian-Americans sympathetic to the principles of the Republican Party; to encourage citizen participation at all levels of political life; and to promote a deeper understanding of Estonian consciousness.

ESTONIAN ASSOCIATION AT SEABROOK
P.O. Box 116
Seabrook, New Jersey 08302

Principal officers: Albert Vilms, President
                      H. Truumees, Vice President
                      Mai Ollino, Secretary

ESTONIAN ASSOCIATION AT SEABROOK (cont'd)

Permanent staff: 13
Date founded: 1949
Branches: none

Membership: 140
Membership dues: $2.00
Scope: local

Special requirements for membership: none

Nature of organization: social, cultural

Publications: none

Major conventions/meetings: monthly conference

Comments: Attempts to promote Estonian culture, literature, and music by sponsoring cultural and social events and activities for its members. Organizes archives and promotes independence for Estonia.

ESTONIAN ASSOCIATION OF CLEVELAND

6607 Barton Road
North Olmstead, Ohio 44070

Principal officers: Agnes Pampe, President
Andy Mannis, Vice President
Tolvo Merrik, Secretary

Permanent staff: 7
Date founded: 1948
Branches: none

Membership: 175
Membership dues: $2.00
Scope: local

Special requirements for membership: Estonian descent

Nature of organization: social, cultural

Publications: *Sonumied*, 1950– (monthly)

Affiliations: Estonian National Committee

Major conventions/meetings: quarterly conference

Comments: The objective of the organization is to preserve the Estonian culture, language, and heritage in the United States, particularly in Cleveland and the Western Reserve. It sponsors cultural and social activities for members. Archival records are maintained.

ESTONIAN EDUCATIONAL SOCIETY, INC.

243 East 34th Street
New York, New York 10016   (212) 684-0336

Principal officers: Linold Milles, President
Voldemar Vaher, Vice President
Endel Reinpold, Secretary

Permanent staff: 8
Date founded: 1929
Branches: none

Membership: 868
Membership dues: $15.00 (annual)
Scope: national and local

Special requirements for membership: must be of Estonian origin

Nature of organization: social, educational, cultural, sports, youth

Publications: none

Affiliations: none

Major conventions/meetings: none

Comments: Provides a place for various cultural, social, and educational activities of Estonian organizations and people in New York. Also allows the use of its facilities to individual members. Sponsors Estonian language schools, Boy Scouts, Girl Scouts, chorus, and folk dancing. Administers a children's summer camp on Long Island. Maintains a collection of 1,500 volumes on Estonian subjects.

ESTONIAN EDUCATIONAL SOCIETY OF DETROIT (D.E.H. KODU)

P.O. Box 344
Trenton, Michigan 48183   (313) 676-8783

ESTONIAN EDUCATIONAL SOCIETY OF DETROIT (D.E.H. KODU) (cont'd)

Principal officers: Thomas Ruben, President
Hilda Kansman, Vice President
Peeter Einpaul, Secretary

Permanent staff: 6
Date founded: 1926
Branches: none

Membership: 50
Membership dues: $5.00 (annual)
Scope: local

Special requirements for membership: 18 years of age

Nature of organization: cultural, educational

Publications: none

Affiliations: The Estonian-American National Council

Major conventions/meetings: annual membership meeting

Comments: Objectives are to perpetuate the Estonian language, culture, and tradition; to encourage Estonian-speaking persons in Michigan to participate in activities; and to provide assistance to Estonians in need. Holds lectures, concerts, and summer camps. All activities are conducted in the Estonian language. Maintains a library collection of over 3,000 volumes.

ESTONIAN EVANGELICAL LUTHERAN CONGREGATION

10711 West Outer Drive (church)
Detroit, Michigan 48223   (313) 625-2933
or
6103 Middle Lake Road
Clarkston, Michigan 48016

Principal officers: Toivo Somer, President
Raimond Suurna, Vice President
Otto Veervald, Secretary

Permanent staff: 1
Date founded: 1951
Branches: none

Membership: 120
Membership dues: $25.00 (annual)
Scope: local

Special requirements for membership: Estonian Lutheran

Nature of organization: religious

Publications: *Congregation News*, 1955– (4-5 times a year)

Major conventions/meetings: yearly congregational meeting

Comments: Sponsors Sunday school for the youth; maintains both library and archives.

ESTONIAN GIRL SCOUTS

c/o Mrs. Ella Karner
1047 Huntsbridge Road
Yonkers, New York 10704

ESTONIAN HOUSE, INC.

1932 Belair Road
Baltimore, Maryland 21213   (301) 327-7634

Principal officers: Voldemar Liiv, President
Juhan Raidma, Vice President
Jaan Sulg, Secretary

Permanent staff: none
Date founded: 1964
Branches: none

Membership: 300
Membership dues: none
Scope: local

Special requirements for membership: "To obtain at least a full share in the Estonian House, Inc."

Nature of organization: social, educational, cultural

Publications: none

ESTONIAN HOUSE, INC. (cont'd)

Affiliations: none

Major conventions/meetings: membership general meeting annually

Comments: Objective is to provide a meeting place for Estonian schools, choruses, youth organizations, and special cultural exhibits and activities.

ESTONIAN HOUSE, INC.
243 East 34th Street
New York, New York 10016 (212) 684-0336
Principal officers: Jaan Ulesoo, President
Veeliks Ling, Treasurer
Eduard Rubel, Secretary

Permanent staff: none Membership: 200
Date founded: 1943 Membership dues: none
Branches: none Scope: national

Special requirements for membership: American of Estonian ancestry

Nature of organization: cultural, educational, recreational

Affiliations: Estonian Educational Society, Inc.

Major conventions/meetings: annual convention

Comments: Primarily this organization sells stock to members for the purpose of accumulating necessary capital to purchase a house or real estate.

ESTONIAN LEARNED SOCIETY IN AMERICA
Estonian House
243 East 34th Street
New York, New York 10016
Principal officers: Viktor Koressaar, President
Tonu Parming, Secretary
Villi Kangro, Treasurer

Permanent staff: none Membership: 200
Date founded: 1950 Membership dues: $10.00 (annual)
Branches: none Scope: national

Special requirements for membership: Master's or doctoral degree and Estonian descent

Nature of organization: scholarly

Publications: *Yearbook of the Estonian Learned Society in America*, 1954– (published every 3-4 years); also publishes other books

Affiliations: none

Major conventions/meetings: none

Comments: The purpose of the organization is to support "Estonian studies," with an emphasis on English-language publications. The society has also supported financially the publication of an Italian-language anthology of Estonian poetry in Italy and the translation of Estonian poetry into English. In 1974 the society sponsored research for a volume on Estonian-American history.

ESTONIAN MUSIC CENTER (EHK)
243 East 34th Street
New York, New York 10016 (212) 684-0336
Principal officers: Juta Kurman, President
Meta Noorkukk, Executive Vice President
Meeme Mälgi, Executive Secretary

Permanent staff: 10 Membership: 100
Date founded: 1956 Membership dues: $3.00 (annual)
Branches: 1 local Scope: national

ESTONIAN MUSIC CENTER (EHK) (cont'd)
Special requirements for membership: must be of Estonian origin
Nature of organization: educational, cultural, recreational, professional, scholarly
Publications: publishes sheet music
Affiliations: none
Major conventions/meetings: convention quadrennially
Comments: The center is primarily devoted to the promotion and publication of Estonian music. Organizes concerts in order to promote Estonian musicians. Grants scholarships to Estonian students of music. Participates in Estonian worldwide festivals, as well as American musical events.

ESTONIAN MUSIC FUND
243 East 34th Street
New York, New York 10016
Principal officers: Endel Kalam, President
                       Juta Kurman, Executive Vice President
                       Velli Kerjan, Executive Secretary

Permanent staff: none	Membership: NI
Date founded: 1957	Membership dues: NI
Branches: none	Scope: national

Special requirements for membership: none
Nature of organization: cultural
Publications: publishes music
Affiliations: none
Major conventions/meetings: none
Comments: Estonian Music Fund was established in memory of Ludvig Juht, Estonian-born former member of the Boston Symphony Orchestra, in order to promote Estonian musical life in exile. EMF consists of representatives of the Estonian Music Students Fraternity, Estonian Male Chorus, Estonian Music Center, and the World Association of Estonians. The fund has commissioned works by eight Estonian composers and has published three volumes of piano music. Sponsors a music scholarship fund. Has given concerts in New York and sponsored radio programs.

ESTONIAN PROGRESSIVE SOCIETY "KIR"
150 East 121st Street
New York, New York 10035

ESTONIAN RELIEF COMMITTEE, INC. (ERC)
243 East 34th Street
New York, New York 10016   (212) 685-7467
Principal officers: Alfred J. Anderson, Secretary-General

Permanent staff: NI	Membership: 1,000
Date founded: 1941	Membership dues: NI
Branches: NI	Scope: national

Nature of organization: charitable
Major conventions/meetings: annual, in New York City in May
Comments: The purposes of the organization are to aid Estonians through relief funds, to provide assistance on matters of immigration, and to help Estonians in the United States to find employment and to obtain their civil rights. It also supports the Estonian Boy and Girl Scout organizations.

ESTONIAN SOCIETY, INC.
4150 North Elston Avenue
Chicago, Illinois 60618

ESTONIAN SOCIETY OF SAN FRANCISCO (SFES)
537 Brannan Street
San Francisco, California 94107   (415) 797-7892

Principal officers: August Kollom, President
                              Leo Keerberg, Vice President
                              Ilse-Elfriede Gruener, Secretary

Permanent staff: none   Membership: 196
Date founded: 1949   Membership dues: $6.00 (annual)
Branches: none   Scope: local

Special requirements for membership: must be of Estonian descent for voting membership; supporting membership has no restrictions

Nature of organization: cultural

Publications: *Announcements* (approximately 6 times a year)

Affiliations: Estonian League of the West Coast

Major conventions/meetings: general membership meeting annually

Comments: Major objectives are the preservation and perpetuation of scientific and artistic presentations, as well as numerous social gatherings. Provides aid to Estonians in need. Sponsors the Estonian Boy Scout Troop, Estonian School of San Francisco, and Estonian Dancers of San Francisco. Maintains a library of 500 volumes and a reading room.

ESTONIAN STUDENTS ASSOCIATION IN USA
243 East 34th Street
New York, New York 10016

Principal officers: Ers Andrus, President
                              Urmas Karner, Vice President
                              Victor V. Vinkman, Secretary

Permanent staff: varies from 3 to 5   Membership: 300
Date founded: 1949   Membership dues: $2.00 (annual)
Branches: none   Scope: national

Special requirements for membership: speaking ability in Estonian; student in accredited university or college

Nature of organization: cultural, social, scholarly, educational

Publications: *Sonumitooja* (Newsletter), 1961– (2-4 annually)

Affiliations: Estonian Students Fund

Major conventions/meetings: semiannual conventions

Comments: Promotes the preservation of the Estonian cultural heritage. Provides a rallying point for students interested in Estonian folklore, language, etc. Scholarships are granted via the Estonian Students Fund for studies in Finland as well as for research papers and publications. Sponsors Estonian language courses, as well as a week-long camp for the purpose of studying history, language, and literature.

FEDERATED ESTONIAN WOMEN'S CLUBS (FEWC)
243 East 34th Street
New York, New York 10016

Principal officers: Juta Kurman, President
                              Aino Suuberg, Executive Vice President
                              Helmi Martin, Executive Secretary

FEDERATED ESTONIAN WOMEN'S CLUBS (FEWC) (cont'd)

Permanent staff: 10   Membership: over 1,000
Date founded: 1966   Membership dues: $5.00 (annual)
Branches: 25 international   Scope: international

Special requirements for membership: none

Nature of organization: political, social, cultural, educational

Publications: none

Affiliations: General Federation of Women's Clubs, Washington, D.C.

Major conventions/meetings: convention annually

Comments: Promotes worldwide contacts among Estonian women's organizations. Preserves
    ancient and modern Estonian folk art. Provides financial assistance for educational
    purposes (scholarships and publications). Promotes the restoration of a free and inde-
    pendent Estonia. Sponsors camps, language courses, and handicraft classes. Maintains
    organizational archives.

THE LEGION OF ESTONIAN LIBERATION, CONNECTICUT POST, INC.
(LEL, INC. or EVUCONN)
        200 Maple Street
        Manchester, Connecticut 06040

Principal officers: E. Kool, President
                       Y. Anson, Vice President
                       V. Parson, Secretary

Permanent staff: none   Membership: 52
Date founded: 1953   Membership dues: $5.00 (annual)
Branches: state branches   Scope: national

Special requirements for membership: Estonian descent

Nature of organization: fraternal, veterans

Publications: a newsletter, 1954– (monthly)

Affiliations: Legion of Estonian Liberation, Inc.

Major conventions/meetings: monthly meetings

Comments: Objectives are to organize Estonian veterans of all wars; to carry out non-partisan
    political activity in order to enlighten the public about conditions in Estonia; to conduct
    educational and social meetings; and to support any activity aimed at the restoration of
    self-determination and liberty in Estonia and other East European nations. Maintains
    archives.

WASHINGTON ESTONIAN SOCIETY
        c/o Mr. M. Valge
        9810 Cherry Tree Lane
        Silver Spring, Maryland 20901

WORLD ASSOCIATION OF ESTONIANS
        243 East 34th Street
        New York, New York 10016   (212) 684-9281

Principal officers: Harald Raudsepp, Secretary

Permanent staff: NI   Membership: 500
Date founded: NI   Membership dues: NI
Branches: NI   Scope: NI

Special requirements for membership: Americans of Estonian descent and Estonians in other
    countries of the Free World

Publications: *Meie Tee* (monthly)

Comments: The association's aims are: to spread culture and friendship between the United
    States and Estonia, and to gather information about communist atrocities in occupied
    Estonia and use the data in the fight against communism.

FILIPINO-AMERICAN ORGANIZATIONS

See also Asian-American Organizations

Additional information on Filipino-American organizations in the United States may be obtained from the Office of the Filipino Embassy (1617 Massachusetts Avenue, Washington, D.C. 20036).

ASSOCIATION OF PHILIPPINE-AMERICAN WOMEN (APAW)
1718 21st Street, N.W.
Washington, D.C. 20009 (202) 332-9800
Principal officers: Beatriz Bartolome, Secretary

Permanent staff: NI   Membership: NI
Date founded: 1947   Membership dues: NI
Branches: NI   Scope: NI

Special requirements for membership: women interested in promoting Philippine-American relations

Nature of organization: social, charitable

Publications: *News-Bulletin* (monthly)

Affiliations: General Federation of Women's Clubs

Major conventions/meetings: annual

Comments: The purpose of the organization is to provide social and cultural activities that promote Philippine-American relations. The majority of the members are wives of ambassadors or officials who have served in the Philippines. They sponsor charitable programs and provide scholarships.

CLUB FILIPINO
2734 Barry Avenue
Los Angeles, California 90064 (213) 477-1650
Principal officers: Jess I. Trompeta, President
                    Linesto Macahilig, Vice President
                    Penny Pardee, Secretary

Permanent staff: 12   Membership: 200
Date founded: 1969   Membership dues: $12.00
Branches: NI   Scope: state

Special requirements for membership: professionals of Filipino descent

Nature of organization: cultural, social, professional, civic

Publications: *Club Filipino Newsletter*, 1969– (monthly)

Affiliations: Filipino American Council of California and Southern California

Major conventions/meetings: annual conference

Comments: The club's aim is to protect the Filipino cultural heritage. It arranges charitable and civic activities and provides scholarships to students of Filipino origin.

FEDERATION OF FILIPINOS OF MICHIGAN
11713 Ashbury Park
Detroit, Michigan 48227 (313) 835-0173
Principal officers: Faustino Gorospe

Comments: This organization, mainly comprised of pre-World War II immigrants, is the oldest Filipino group in Michigan.

FILIPINO-AMERICAN CIVIC LEAGUE
P.O. Box 5022
Alisal Branch
Salinas, California 93901

FILIPINO AMERICAN COMMUNITY OF COACHELLA VALLEY
91-448 5th Street
Mecca, California 92254   (714) 396-2422
Principal officers: Emilio Camaddo, President
                       Sammy Bumagat, Vice President
                       Mildred Bumagat, Secretary

Permanent staff: 10   Membership: 61
Date founded: 1973   Membership dues: $5.00 (entrance fee);
Branches: NI $12.00 membership fee
                                                 Scope: local

Special requirements for membership: residents of Coachella Valley of Filipino descent or
    related by marriage

Nature of organization: cultural, social, youth

Publications: none

Affiliations: none

Major conventions/meetings: monthly meetings

Comments: Promotes the preservation and appreciation of the Filipino cultural heritage.
    Organizes youth and social activities.

FILIPINO AMERICAN COUNCIL OF CALIFORNIA
2045 Lawton Street
San Francisco, California 94122
Principal officers: Alex Esclamado, President

FILIPINO-AMERICAN COUNCIL OF SO. CALIFORNIA
c/o Mabuhay Travel Agency
3250 Wilshire Boulevard, Suite 1009
Los Angeles, California 90005
Principal officers: Ben Manibog, President

FILIPINO AMERICAN POLITICAL ASSOCIATION (FAPA)
c/o T. A. Mendoza
3156 Wilshire Boulevard, Suite 20
Los Angeles, California 90010   (213) 380-0620
Principal officers: T. A. Mendoza, National President

Permanent staff: NI   Membership: 280
Date founded: 1965   Membership dues: NI
Branches: NI   Scope: NI

Special requirements for membership: persons of Filipino ancestry or whose wives or
    husbands are of Filipino ancestry

Publications: *Fil-Am Express* (monthly)

Major conventions/meetings: annual

Comments: Seeks to raise the economic, political, and social conditions of the Filipino Ameri-
    can through non-violent political action, using such means as the right of public
    assembly, petition to the government, and the right of public protest and political
    involvement through the government. Serves as a congressional and legislative lobby for
    Filipino-Americans. Sponsors programs on housing, economic research, education,
    voter registration, and immigration assistance. Conducts semiannual leadership training
    for younger Filipino-Americans; holds seminars on political leadership.

FILIPINO CATHOLIC ASSOCIATION
12813 Jingle Lane
Silver Spring, Maryland 20906

FILIPINO MEDICAL ASSOCIATION
35021 Balmoral Drive
Livonia, Michigan 48151

FILIPINO WOMEN'S CLUB
7601 Fielding
Detroit, Michigan 48228
Principal officers: Mrs. Home Sheppard
Permanent staff: NI   Membership: NI
Date founded: NI   Membership dues: NI
Branches: NI   Scope: local
Nature of organization: social, cultural
Comments: This organization is very active, sponsoring cultural and social activities for
    members at the International Institute.

GRAN ORIENTE FILIPINO
    158 East Jackson Street   (408) 295-2200 or
    San Jose, California 95112   (408) 297-9878
Principal officers: Severino E. Ruste, Grand Master
                       J. Reyes, Senior Warden
                       Jhon Ricafort, Secretary
Permanent staff: 13   Membership: 500
Date founded: 1923   Membership dues: $40.00 (annual)
Branches: none   Scope: national and state
Special requirements for membership: "Must be 21-55 years old and male."
Nature of organization: fraternal
Publications: *Cable Masonico*, 1942– (biannual)
Affiliations: none
Major conventions/meetings: annual meeting
Comments: This Masonic organization sponsors children's activities.

KATIPUNAN ASSOCIATION
    911 1A Belgian Avenue
    Baltimore, Maryland 21218

KNIGHTS OF RIZAL
    2217 "Q" Street, N.W.
    Washington, D.C. 20008

LEGIONARIOS DEL TRABAJO IN AMERICA, INC.
    2154 South San Joaquin Street
    Stockton, California 95206   (209) 463-6516
Principal officers: Antonio T. Santos, Grand Master
Nature of organization: fraternal
Publications: *Bulletin* (monthly)
Major conventions/meetings: triennial

PANGASINAN-ILOCANO ASSOCIATION
    5901 Nassau Street
    District Heights, Maryland 20028

PHILIPPINE-AMERICAN CHAMBER OF COMMERCE
565 Fifth Avenue
New York, New York 10017   (212) 972-9326
Principal officers: Lucie Toehl, Executive-Secretary

Permanent staff: NI   Membership: 135
Date founded: 1920   Membership dues: NI
Branches: NI   Scope: NI

PHILIPPINE ASSOCIATION (PA)
501 Madison Avenue
New York, New York 10022   (212) 688-2755
Principal officers: George Peabody, U.S. Director

Permanent staff: 34   Membership: 110
Date founded: 1950   Membership dues: NI
Branches: NI   Scope: NI

Publications: *Legislative Reports on Philippine Congress* (weekly when in session); *Philippine Weekly Economic Review* (weekly); *Philippine Mining Reports* (monthly)

Major conventions/meetings: annual

Comments: Mainly comprised of Filipino business firms promoting the economic interests of the Philippines. The association conducts research and publishes reports on the development of the Philippine economy and maintains a research library of materials on Philippine economics and law.

PHILIPPINE CHAMBER OF COMMERCE OF AMERICA
24 California Street
San Francisco, California 94111   (415) 781-6342
Principal officers: Rufino Ancheta, Secretary-Treasurer

PHILIPPINE CULTURAL CENTER FOUNDATION OF SANTA CLARA COUNTY, INC.
588 North Central Avenue   (408) 374-4407 or
Campbell, California 95008   (408) 378-9004
Principal officers: Alice E. Balahadia, President
                       Jacinto Siquig, Vice President
                       Reppie Bautista, Secretary

Permanent staff: 25   Membership: NI
Date founded: 1973   Membership dues: NI
Branches: none   Scope: county

Nature of organization: cultural, educational, charitable

Publications: *PCCF Newsletter*, 1973– (biannual)

Major conventions/meetings: bimonthly Board of Director's conference

Comments: Formed exclusively as educational and charitable organization for the purpose of furthering cultural, educational, and historical interests. Sponsors activities in support of the above objectives. Encourages research into the culture and history of the Philippines. Organizes various social gatherings, concerts, lectures, and folk art exhibits. Maintains a library collection. The members of the Board of Directors represent eight cities within Santa Clara County.

PHILIPPINE MEDICAL ASSOCIATION IN MICHIGAN (PMAM)
P.O. Box 5292, Mack Avenue
Grosse Pointe Farms, Michigan 48236
Principal officers: Dr. Renato S. Roxas, President
                       Dr. Eulogio Caoili, Vice President
                       Dr. Rebecca Aguino, Secretary

PHILIPPINE MEDICAL ASSOCIATION IN MICHIGAN (PMAM) (cont'd)

Permanent staff: none
Date founded: 1963
Branches: 4 state

Membership: 300
Membership dues: $10.00
Scope: state

Special requirements for membership: Filipino physician

Nature of organization: professional

Publications: *PMAM Newsletter*, 1965– (twice a month)

Affiliations: Philippine Medical Association in America

Comments: PMAM helps physicians of Filipino origin to meet residency requirements, set up private practice, and finish training programs.

PHILIPPINE MEDICAL ASSOCIATION OF METROPOLITAN WASHINGTON (PMAMW)

5317 16th Street, N.W.
Washington, D.C. 20011   (202) 723-2079

Principal officers: Nestor F. de Venecia, President
Florentino Palmon, Vice President
Lydia Barot, Secretary

Permanent staff: NI
Date founded: 1968
Branches: NI

Membership: 120
Membership dues: $30.00 (annual)
Scope: local

Special requirements for membership: medical doctor–practicing or house staff

Nature of organization: professional

Publications: *PMAMW Newsletter* (monthly)

Major conventions/meetings: general meeting, quarterly

Comments: This non-profit organization promotes the art and science of medicine among Filipino-Americans. Medical knowledge is used to advance the practice of medicine in the Philippines. Sponsors scholarships at the University of the Philippines. Holds social and recreational activities.

PHILIPPINE SOCIETY

c/o Dr. R. C. Rodriguez
1045 Dongton Circle
Towson, Maryland 21204

PHILIPPINE SOCIETY OF WASHINGTON

8016 Piney Branch Road
Silver Spring, Maryland 20910

SAMAHANG-FILIPINO

1927 Pembridge Plaza
Detroit, Michigan

UNITED FILIPINO AMERICAN ASSOCIATION

200 St. Andrews Drive
Oxon Hill, Maryland 20021

FINNISH-AMERICAN ORGANIZATIONS

See also Scandinavian-American Organizations

Additional information on Finnish-American organizations in the United States may be obtained from the Office of the Finnish Embassy (1900 24th Street, Washington, D.C. 20008) or the Finnish American Chamber of Commerce (540 Madison Avenue, New York, New York 10022).

FINLANDIA FOUNDATION, NATIONAL CAPITAL CHAPTER, INC.
6312 Yellowstone Drive
Alexandria, Virginia 22312   (703) 256-3943
Principal officers: Col. Arthur E. Stanat, President
                       Mrs. Oiva Juusela, Vice President
                       Mrs. Elvi Stevens, Secretary
                       Mrs. Marianna Parssinen, Treasurer

Permanent staff: NI   Membership: NI
Date founded: 1959   Membership dues: NI
Branches: NI   Scope: Washington, D.C. area

Special requirements for membership: none

Nature of organization: cultural

Affiliations: The Finlandia Foundation, Inc.; Scandinavian Joint Planning Council of Washington, D.C.

Comments: The purpose of the Finlandia Foundation is to cultivate and strengthen the cultural relations between the United States and Finland and to preserve and cultivate the heritage and cultural interests of both Americans and Finns.

THE FINLANDIA FOUNDATION, NATIONAL HEADQUARTERS
1433 San Vicente Boulevard
Santa Monica, California 10402
Principal officers: V. A. Hoover, President

Permanent staff: NI   Membership: 1,600
Date founded: 1953   Membership dues: NI
Branches: 23 local groups   Scope: NI

Publications: *Newsletter* (quarterly)

Comments: The major purpose of the organization is "to further cultural exchange between the United States and Finland."

FINNISH AMERICAN CHAMBER OF COMMERCE
540 Madison Avenue
New York, New York 10022   (212) 832-2588
Principal officers: E. Korpivaara, Executive-Secretary

Permanent staff: NI   Membership: 190
Date founded: 1958   Membership dues: NI
Branches: NI   Scope: NI

FINNISH-AMERICAN HISTORICAL ARCHIVES
Suomi College
Hancock, Michigan 49930
Principal officers: Armas K. E. Holmio, Archivist

Permanent staff: 2   Membership: NI
Date founded: 1932   Membership dues: NI
Branches: NI   Scope: NI

Comments: Conducts research and collects materials on the history and immigration of Finns to America; promotes the preservation of the Finnish culture in the United States.

FINNISH AMERICAN HISTORICAL SOCIETY OF MICHIGAN
19885 Melrose
Southfield, Michigan 48075

Principal officers: Whitney Smith, Director

Permanent staff: NI
Date founded: 1945
Branches: NI

Membership: 100
Membership dues: NI
Scope: NI

Major conventions/meetings: annual

Comments: The organization was established to conduct research on Finnish studies in the Michigan area. It attempts to preserve the Finnish culture and writings in the United States. A 200-volume library of Finnish-language materials is maintained.

THE FINNISH AMERICAN HISTORICAL SOCIETY OF THE WEST
P.O. Box 3515
Portland, Oregon 97208   (503) 227-4205

Principal officers: Walter Mattila, President
                       Carlo Poutala, Executive Vice President
                       Ida Nevala, Executive Secretary

Permanent staff: none
Date founded: 1960
Branches: none

Membership: 550
Membership dues: $1.50 (annual)
Scope: regional

Special requirements for membership: none

Nature of organization: cultural

Publications: publishes books

Affiliations: Oregon Historical Society; Suomi Seura; Literary Society of Finland

Major conventions/meetings: annual Board conference

Comments: The society's primary activities have been in researching and publishing material on Finnish pioneers in the Pacific Northwest, with some notice of their life before coming to this country. It is also active in the preservation of Finnish culture; it sponsors monuments, tape recordings, lectures, Finnish language classes, and trips to Finland. Has established a Finnish book collection at Portland State University and at the Oregon Historical Museum.

FINNISH AMERICAN LEAGUE FOR DEMOCRACY (FALD)
811 Main Street
Fitchburg, Massachusetts 01420   (617) 343-3822

Principal officers: Lauri Rein, President
                       Savele Syrjala, Executive Secretary

Permanent staff: 1
Date founded: 1904
Branches: NI

Membership: 500
Membership dues: $1.00 (annual)
Scope: national

Special requirements for membership: none

Nature of organization: political, social, cultural, educational

Publications: *Pioneer*, 1905– (semiweekly)

Major conventions/meetings: annual convention

Comments: The league was originally organized as the Finnish Socialist Federation and was affiliated with the Socialist Party until it severed its connection in 1940. Since then the league has followed the lines of the Social Democratic Party in Finland, working within the democratic structure to improve the lot of the average man in society. Sponsors cultural events such as theater, bands, lectures, choruses, and discussion groups.

FINNISH CENTER ASSOCIATION
32449 Hearthstone
Farmington, Michigan 48024   (313) 476-0259
Principal officers: Dr. Arvid Jacobson

Comments: Many Finnish social and cultural activities are sponsored through this parent
organization. It sponsors concerts and exhibitions by Finnish performers in the fine arts,
Finnish-language classes, and a summer camp, and it grants scholarships for students of
Finnish background.

FINNISH WAR VETERANS IN AMERICA (FWVA)
4923 8th Avenue
Brooklyn, New York 11220
Principal officers: Toivo M. Saastamoinen, President

Permanent staff: NI   Membership: 370
Date founded: 1934   Membership dues: NI
Branches: NI   Scope: NI

Special requirements for membership: Finnish veterans of the wars of 1918, 1939-40,
1941-44

Publications: *Aseveli* (Brother in Arms) (irregular)

Comments: Assists Finnish veterans in Finland and America.

ST. ANDREW'S SOCIETY OF THE MIDDLE SOUTH
17 Ridge Drive
Birmingham, Alabama 35213

SUOMI COLLEGE ALUMNAE ASSOCIATION
19 Fairwood
Pleasant Ridge, Michigan 48069   (313) 542-3942
Principal officers: Edward Happa

Special requirements for membership: Suomi College alumnus

Major conventions/meetings: annual reunions

Comments: The purpose of the organization is to promote and raise funds for Suomi College,
a Finnish school in Hancock, Michigan. Social activities (such as class reunions) are
also held.

SUOMI FREE CONFERENCE OF THE LUTHERAN CHURCH IN AMERICA
122 West Franklin Avenue
Minneapolis, Minnesota 55404   (612) 871-8565
Principal officers: Raymond W. Wargelin, President
Eugene J. Kunos, Executive Vice President
Rudolph Kemppainen, Executive Secretary

Permanent staff: none   Membership: NI
Date founded: 1962   Membership dues: none
Branches: 8 regional   Scope: international

Special requirements for membership: "Finnish speaking members (lay and clergy) of the
Lutheran Church in America."

Nature of organization: cultural, religious

Publications: *Faith of the Fathers* (monthly); *Churchly Calendar*, 1902– (annually); also
publishes books

Major conventions/meetings: annual conference

Comments: This organization provides fellowship for Finnish-speaking members of the Lutheran
Church in America. Its activities (such as Bible camps, publications, programs, lecture
tours, and religious services) are aimed at Finnish Americans. Presents a Church of Finland Scholarship for clergy and students of theology.

TYOMIES SOCIETY
601-3 Tower Avenue
Superior, Wisconsin 54880

FRENCH-AMERICAN ORGANIZATIONS

Additional information on French-American organizations in the United States may be obtained from the Office of the French Embassy (2535 Belmont, Washington, D.C. 20008) or the French Chamber of Commerce in the United States (1350 Avenue of the Americas, New York, New York 10019). Information on local and regional organizations may be obtained from *Greater Cleveland Nationalities Directory 1974* (Cleveland: Sun Newspapers and the Nationalities Services Center, 1974) or *Ethnic Directory I* (Detroit: Southeastern Michigan Regional Ethnic Heritage Studies Center, 1973).

ALLIANCE FRANÇAISE
15 Charlotte Place
Baltimore, Maryland 21218

AMERICAN ORDER OF THE FRENCH CROIX DE GUERRE
4 West 43rd Street
New York, New York 10036

Principal officers: Lt. Col. Steven F. Kovach, President

Permanent staff: NI	Membership: 200
Date founded: 1954	Membership dues: NI
Branches: NI	Scope: national

Special requirements for membership: American or French veterans holding the Croix de Guerre medal

Nature of organization: fraternal

Comments: The purpose of the organization is to unite veterans and holders of the French Croix de Guerre medal; it provides social and cultural activities and promotes French-American relations.

AMERICAN SOCIETY OF THE FRENCH LEGION OF HONOR
22 East 60th Street
New York, New York 10022

Principal officers: Grayson Kirk, President

Permanent staff: NI	Membership: 480
Date founded: 1922	Membership dues: NI
Branches: NI	Scope: national

Nature of organization: fraternal, social, cultural

Publications: *ASLH Magazine*, 1930– (quarterly)

Major conventions/meetings: annual

Comments: The purpose of the organization is to promote and preserve the French culture and traditions in the United States and good relations between the United States and France. It provides social activities to unite members of the French Order of the Legion of Honor living in the United States.

ASSOCIATION CANADO-AMÉRICAINE (ACA)
52 Concord Street
Manchester, New Hampshire 03101   (603) 625-8577

ASSOCIATION CANADO-AMÉRICAINE (ACA) (cont'd)

Principal officers: Gerald Robert, President
        Edouard J. Lampron, Vice President
        Lucille Mailhiot, Secretary

Permanent staff: 25   Membership: 30,589
Date founded: 1896   Membership dues: life insurance rates
Branches: 65 regional   Scope: regional

Special requirements for membership: "To become an adult beneficiary member, must be of French ancestry or affinity or be considered as such and profess the Roman Catholic faith."

Nature of organization: fraternal

Publications: *Le Canado-Americain*, 1900– (quarterly); also publishes books

Affiliations: National Fraternal Congress of America; New England Fraternal Congress; Canadian Fraternal Association

Major conventions/meetings: quadrennial convention

Comments: The purpose of the organization is to unite "Catholics of French ancestry or affinity in America" and to promote "their religious, civic, economic progress." The association provides insurance policies, maintains a scholarship fund, publishes a cultural journal, and organizes social gatherings. It maintains a library of around 40,000 volumes; its archival holdings consist of manuscripts as well as materials dealing with the French in North America.

ASSOCIATION DES PROFESSEURS FRANCO-AMÉRICAINS (APFA)

    341 4th Street
    Fall River, Massachusetts 02721   (617) 672-0408

Principal officers: Francis J. Martineau, Executive Secretary

Permanent staff: NI   Membership: 250
Date founded: 1964   Membership dues: NI
Branches: NI   Scope: NI

Comments: Goals of the organization are to improve teaching of the French language and to provide a placement service for French teachers. It provides workshops and a small library.

ASSOCIATION OF THE FREE FRENCH IN THE U.S.

    40 Park Avenue
    New York, New York 10007   (212) 679-8192

Principal officers: A. Tchenkell-Thamys, President

Permanent staff: NI   Membership: 400
Date founded: 1945   Membership dues: NI
Branches: NI   Scope: NI

Special requirements for membership: must be a former member of the Free French Forces, France Forever, or the American Field Service under de Gaulle or during World War II

Nature of organization: fraternal

Publications: *Bulletin* (monthly)

Affiliations: Association des Français Libres (Paris)

Comments: The function of the association is to unite former members of the Free French Forces, France Forever, or the American Field Service who were involved in World War II and who now reside in the United States.

COMMITTEE OF FRENCH AMERICAN WIVES

    22 East 60th Street
    New York, New York 10022   (212) 688-4949

Permanent staff: NI   Membership: 100
Date founded: 1939   Membership dues: NI
Branches: NI   Scope: NI

COMMITTEE OF FRENCH AMERICAN WIVES (cont'd)

Comments: The purpose of the organization is to provide relief and assistance to French children in need. It also supports other charitable organizations.

COMMITTEE OF FRENCH SPEAKING SOCIETIES
11 West 42nd Street
New York, New York 10036

Principal officers: Georges Ittel, Executive Officer

Permanent staff: NI
Date founded: 1927
Branches: NI

Membership: 2,500
Membership dues: NI
Scope: national

Major conventions/meetings: quarterly

Comments: The organization is a federation of French and French-speaking groups in the United States. It sponsors cultural activities and celebrations of French holidays.

FEDERATION OF FRENCH ALLIANCES IN THE UNITED STATES (FFAUS)
22 East 60th Street
New York, New York 10022   (212) 753-7948

Principal officers: George I. Duca, Executive Director

Permanent staff: NI
Date founded: 1902
Branches: NI

Membership: 250 clubs; 19,000
   individuals
Membership dues: NI
Scope: national

Special requirements for membership: a French language or culture group

Nature of organization: cultural

Publications: *Annual Report*

Major conventions/meetings: annual

Comments: This alliance represents social and cultural groups, French-language groups and schools, and French clubs at universities. It helps individual clubs sponsor programs in French-language instruction and grants annual awards to French students.

FEDERATION OF FRENCH AMERICAN WOMEN
57 Main Street
Suncook, New Hampshire 03275   (603) 485-3151

Principal officers: Mrs. Jean L. LeBlanc, President
                      Miss C. Poirier, Vice President
                      Mrs. Lucien Jean, Secretary
                      Miss Marguerite Perron, Treasurer

Permanent staff: 22 executives; 55 directors
Date founded: 1961
Branches: 89 societies

Membership: 14,000
Membership dues: $5.00
Scope: regional

Special requirements for membership: membership in a Franco-American organization in New England

Nature of organization: cultural, educational

Publications: *Le Bulletin*, 1961– (newsletter)

Major conventions/meetings: biennial convention

Comments: Promotes the retention of the French cultural heritage. Organizes worldwide travel tours. Holds courses in French language, culture, history, etc. Sponsors a scholarship. Maintains a library and archives.

FEDERATION OF FRENCH WAR VETERANS
11 West 42nd Street
New York, New York 10036   (212) 524-0755
Principal officers: Dr. Jules Pierre, President

Permanent staff: NI   Membership: 500
Date founded: 1919   Membership dues: NI
Branches: NI   Scope: NI

Special requirements for membership: veterans of World War I and World War II who are of French descent

Nature of organization: fraternal

Comments: The purpose of the organization is to unite war veterans of French descent in the United States.

FRANCE-AMERICA SOCIETY, INC.
c/o Council of French-American Societies in New York
630 Fifth Avenue
New York, New York 10020

FRANCO-AMERICAN TEACHERS' ASSOCIATION (APFA)
103 Oak Street
Manchester, New Hampshire 03104   (603) 622-9351
Principal officers: Elphège E. Roy, President
                      Francia Terrault, Executive Vice President
                      François J. Martineau, Secretary-Treasurer

Permanent staff: 6 directors plus officers   Membership: 250
Date founded: 1963   Membership dues: $3.00 (annual)
Branches: none   Scope: regional

Special requirements for membership: must be Franco-American (French-Canadian or French) and be a teacher of French

Nature of organization: educational

Publications: publishes books

Major conventions/meetings: general meeting biennially

Comments: Originally organized to help teaching nuns in the Franco-American parochial schools modernize their methods of teaching the French language. Organizes institutes for French language teachers as well as workshops and training sessions. Has two scholarship funds for Franco-American teachers. Maintains archival materials. Receives grants from the French government as well as from the Quebec government.

FRENCH-AMERICAN ATLANTIQUE ASSOCIATION
809 UN Plaza
New York, New York 10017   (212) 867-0400
Principal officers: Richard B. Myer, Secretary

Permanent staff: NI   Membership: 15
Date founded: 1947   Membership dues: NI
Branches: NI   Scope: NI

Nature of organization: educational

Comments: The major purpose of the association is to sponsor an exchange program between the United States and France for graduate students and scholars in social welfare, rehabilitation of the handicapped, arts, engineering, and related fields.

FRENCH CHAMBER OF COMMERCE IN THE UNITED STATES
1350 Avenue of the Americas
New York, New York 10019   (212) 581-4554
Principal officers: Jacques Douguet, General Manager

FRENCH CHAMBER OF COMMERCE IN THE UNITED STATES (cont'd)

Permanent staff: NI
Date founded: 1896
Branches: NI

Membership: 1,500
Membership dues: NI
Scope: NI

Nature of organization: economic

Publications: *French American Commerce* (bimonthly)

Comments: The purpose of this business and economic organization is to promote trade between the United States and France.

FRENCH ENGINEERS IN THE UNITED STATES

P.O. Box 734, Stuyvesant Station
New York, New York 10009   (516) 575-9186

Principal officers: Marcel Piry, President

Permanent staff: 5
Date founded: 1944
Branches: 2

Membership: 220
Membership dues: NI
Scope: national

Special requirements for membership: professional engineers

Nature of organization: professional

Publications: *Newsletter* (monthly)

Affiliations: Société des Ingénieurs Civils de France

Major conventions/meetings: annual

Comments: The purpose of the society is to unite engineers of French descent in the United States and to promote relations between French and American engineers. Prominent engineers are sponsored at monthly lectures in New York City.

FRENCH FOLKLORE SOCIETY

56-52 203rd Street
Bayside, Long Island, New York 11364   (212) 225-4453

Principal officers: Pierre Courtines, President

Permanent staff: NI
Date founded: 1936
Branches: NI

Membership: 100
Membership dues: NI
Scope: regional

Special requirements for membership: interest in French folklore and history

Nature of organization: historical, cultural

Publications: *Bulletin of French Folklore Society* (annual)

Comments: Also known as Société Historique et Folklorique Française, the organization attempts to promote historical studies and cultural activities concerning French topics. It commemorates Franco-American events and national figures.

FRENCH INSTITUTE–ALLIANCE FRANÇAISE DE NEW YORK

22 East 60th Street
New York, New York 10022   (212) 759-4747

Principal officers: Jean Vallier, Executive Director

Permanent staff: 26
Date founded: 1971
Branches: NI

Membership: 6,000
Membership dues: NI
Scope: national

Nature of organization: cultural, scholarly

Publications: *French XX Bibliography* (annual)

Comments: The organization seeks to promote not only the French culture in the United States but also study of French language and history. It sponsors language courses, films, lectures, and concerts, and it grants special graduate scholarships to French students in the United States and American students studying in France. Maintains a library of 35,000 volumes of French writings. In 1971 the Alliance Française de New York (founded 1898) and the French Institute in the United States (founded 1911) merged to form this new national organization.

FRENCH WOMEN'S BENEVOLENT CLUB
12445 Abington
Detroit, Michigan 48227

FRIENDS OF A. D. I. R., INC.
875 Park Avenue
New York, New York 10021   (212) 861-2244
Principal officers: Caroline Ferriday, Chairman
                       Colette Combemale, Vice Chairman
                       Zelina Brunschwig, Vice Chairman

Permanent staff: none   Membership: NI
Date founded: 1950   Membership dues: none
Branches: none   Scope: NI

Special requirements for membership: none

Nature of organization: relief purposes

Publications: *Voix et Visages* (bimonthly)

Affiliations: none

Major conventions/meetings: none

Comments: Originally organized by a small group of French Americans in order to help
    French déportées (deported by Germans for resistance activities) adjust to society.
    Today the organization aids women who are too old to be employed.

HERITAGE FRANCO-AMERICAN
c/o Dr. Paul J. Fortier
111 Webster Street
Lewiston, Maine 04240

HUGUENOT HISTORICAL SOCIETY
14 Forest Glen Road
New Paltz, New York 12561   (914) 255-1669
Principal officers: Kenneth E. Hasbrouck, President

Permanent staff: 8   Membership: 3,500
Date founded: 1894   Membership dues: NI
Branches: 11   Scope: national

Special requirements for membership: none

Nature of organization: historical, cultural

Publications: publishes books and reports

Major conventions/meetings: annual

Comments: The society attempts to preserve historic sites, buildings, and relics that illuminate
    the French Huguenot life style in America. It has rebuilt a 1717 French church and small
    village. Maintains a library of 4,000 volumes and historical archives.

NATIONAL HUGUENOT SOCIETY
40 High Street
Goffstown, New Hampshire 03045   (603) 497-2313
Principal officers: David V. Prugh, President General

Permanent staff: NI   Membership: 4,600
Date founded: NI   Membership dues: NI
Branches: 37 state   Scope: national

Special requirements for membership: Huguenot descendant and Protestant

Nature of organization: cultural, educational, historical, religious

Publications: *Cross of Languedoc* (quarterly); *Proceedings* (biennial)

Major conventions/meetings: annual

Comments: The organization attempts to preserve the history and artifacts of the French
    Huguenot life and traditions in the United States. It sponsors social, patriotic, religious,
    educational, and charitable projects.

PARIS AMERICAN CLUB
c/o Council of French-American Societies in New York
630 Fifth Avenue
New York, New York 10020

SALON LITTÉRAIRE, ARTISTIQUE ET DIPLOMATIQUE (SLAD)
40 East 64th Street
New York, New York 10021

SOCIÉTÉ DES PROFESSEURS FRANÇAIS EN AMÉRIQUE
Department of Romance Languages
Princeton University
Princeton, New Jersey 08540   (609) 452-4498

Principal officers: André Marman, President

Permanent staff: NI   Membership: 975
Date founded: 1904   Membership dues: NI
Branches: NI   Scope: national

Special requirements for membership: French persons teaching the French language in the
    United States

Nature of organization: professional

Publications: *Bulletin de la Société des Professeurs Français en Amérique* (annual)

Major conventions/meetings: quarterly

Comments: This organization of French teachers in the United States sponsors annual high
    school contests in French language and supports research and Ph.D. dissertations in
    French. It also grants scholarships for study of French in France or in French Canada;
    it provides a placement service for French persons teaching in the United States.

SOCIÉTÉ HISTORIQUE FRANCO-AMÉRICAINE
52 Concord Street
Manchester, New Hampshire 03101

Principal officers: Adrien Verrette, President
                       Gerald Robert, Vice President
                       Richard Santerre, Secretary

Permanent staff: NI   Membership: 340
Date founded: 1899   Membership dues: $5.00 (annual)
Branches: none   Scope: national

Nature of organization: cultural

Publications: *Bulletin de la Société Historique Franco-Américaine*, 1903– (annual)

Major conventions/meetings: annual

Comments: The major purpose of the society is to preserve the Franco-American heritage in
    the United States and to promote French history and culture. An annual "Medaille
    Grand Prix" is awarded. A library of 15,000 volumes and an archival collection are
    maintained.

SOCIETY FOR FRENCH-AMERICAN AFFAIRS (SFAA)
P.O. Box 551, Cathedral Station
New York, New York 10025   (212) 749-3843

Principal officers: Benjamin Protter, Secretary-General

Permanent staff: NI   Membership: NI
Date founded: 1952   Membership dues: $15.00 (annual)
Branches: none   Scope: national and international

Special requirements for membership: none

Nature of organization: political, educational, cultural, scholarly

Publications: *Today in France*, 1961– (bimonthly)

Affiliations: none

SOCIETY FOR FRENCH-AMERICAN AFFAIRS (SFAA) (cont'd)

Comments: Disseminates information on French and American political affairs. Encourages cooperation between the two nations. Accepts institutional memberships, especially universities. Distributes publications on French matters to libraries.

SOCIETY FOR FRENCH AMERICAN CULTURAL SERVICES AND EDUCATIONAL AID (FACSEA)
972 Fifth Avenue
New York, New York 10021

Principal officers: Miss Yvette Mallet, Executive Director

Permanent staff: NI   Membership: NI
Date founded: 1955   Membership dues: NI
Branches: NI   Scope: national

Comments: The purpose of the society is to prepare materials for educational institutions that may be used in French language, history, art, and culture courses. Multi-media materials are loaned for a fee.

SOCIETY FOR FRENCH HISTORICAL STUDIES (SFHS)
c/o Mr. Charles K. Warner
Department of History
University of Kansas
Lawrence, Kansas 66044   (913) 864-4363

Principal officers: Charles K. Warner, Secretary

Permanent staff: 1   Membership: 450
Date founded: 1955   Membership dues: NI
Branches: NI   Scope: NI

Special requirements for membership: interest in French history

Nature of organization: professional, scholarly, historical

Publications: *French Historical Studies* (semiannual)

Affiliations: Société d'Histoire Moderne, Paris, France

Major conventions/meetings: annual

Comments: The goal of the organization is to further the study of French history and culture in the United States and Canada.

UNION SAINT-JEAN BAPTISTE (USJB)
One Social Street
Woonsocket, Rhode Island 02895   (401) 769-0520

Principal officers: J. Henri Goguen, President
                       Philippe LeBlond, First Vice President
                       Louise Courcy, Executive Secretary

Permanent staff: 40   Membership: 49,000
Date founded: 1900   Membership dues: depending on
Branches: none   contract
                                            Scope: regional

Special requirements for membership: "be a practicing Catholic; be of French origin, or married to a person of French origin, or dedicated to French culture and civilization"

Nature of organization: fraternal

Publications: *L'Union*, 1902– (quarterly)

Affiliations: National Fraternal Congress; New England Fraternal Congress; Franco-American Historical Society

Major conventions/meetings: convention biennially

UNION SAINT-JEAN BAPTISTE (USJB) (cont'd)

Comments: Non-profit mutual benefit society founded for the purpose of organizing French-American Catholics into one organization. Promotes preservation of French cultural heritage. Provides financial and charitable assistance. Sponsors scholarships and awards grants to French departments at institutions of higher learning. Awards honors to those who promote the French culture. Maintains a library of 5,000 volumes and archival materials relating to the French experience in the United States.

GERMAN-AMERICAN ORGANIZATIONS

Additional information on German-American organizations in the United States may be obtained from the Office of the German Embassy (4645 Reservoir Road, Washington, D.C. 20007) or the German American National Congress (4740 North Western Avenue, Chicago, Illinois 60625). For local and regional organizations see *Greater Cleveland Nationalities Directory 1974* (Cleveland: Sun Newspapers and the Nationalities Services Center, 1974) and *Ethnic Directory I* (Detroit: Southeastern Michigan Regional Ethnic Heritage Studies Center, 1973).

THE ALLIANCE OF TRANSYLVANIAN SAXONS
303 Leader Building
Cleveland, Ohio 44114   (216) 621-8627

Principal officers: John E. Hallner, Secretary

Permanent staff: 4   Membership: 9,871
Date founded: 1902   Membership dues: NI
Branches: 43   Scope: NI

Nature of organization: fraternal; insurance

Publications: *Volksblatt* (weekly)

Major conventions/meetings: annual

Comments: A fraternal life insurance society for Americans of Translvanian Saxon descent.

AMERICAN COUNCIL ON GERMANY (ACG)
99 Park Avenue, 18th Floor
New York, New York 10021   (212) 744-2816

Principal officers: Sara Ann Fagan, Secretary

Permanent staff: 3   Membership: NI
Date founded: 1951   Membership dues: NI
Branches: NI   Scope: national

Nature of organization: educational

Publications: *Meet Germany* (annual)

Major conventions/meetings: biennial

Comments: Promotes the understanding of Germany and German enterprises in the United States. Sponsors lecture meetings and tours of important Germans throughout the United States. Also sponsors conferences and publishes materials on the problems and issues facing Germany.

AMERICAN GOETHE SOCIETY OF WASHINGTON, D.C.
5309 Westpath Way
Washington, D.C. 20016   (301) 229-1282

Principal officers: Dr. Hugo J. Mueller, President
                    Prof. Obernberger, Vice President
                    Ms. Inge Wekerle, Secretary

AMERICAN GOETHE SOCIETY OF WASHINGTON, D.C. (cont'd)

Permanent staff: 5
Date founded: 1931
Branches: none

Membership: 200
Membership dues: $5.00 single; $8.00
couple; $2.00 student
Scope: local

Special requirements for membership: a working knowledge of the German language

Nature of organization: cultural

Publications: none

Major conventions/meetings: monthly meetings

Comments: Arranges lectures and discussions specifically dealing with German literature. The society serves as a forum for German intellectual life in Washington, D.C.

AMERICAN ST. BONIFACE SOCIETY

1050 East 233rd Street
Bronx, New York 10466   (212) 882-7209

Principal officers: Rev. John Thenen, President
Dr. Hans Hafner, Vice President
Mr. Albert Sattler, Secretary
Rev. Hans Peter Gross, Executive Director

Permanent staff: NI
Date founded: 1920
Branches: none

Membership: NI
Membership dues: NI
Scope: national

Nature of organization: religious

Affiliations: none

Major conventions/meetings: none

Comments: This organization is a religious mission society.

AMERICAN SUDETEN ASSOCIATION

77-22 86th Street
Brooklyn, New York 11227

AMERIKANISCHER TURNERBUND

1550 Clinton Avenue
North Rochester, New York 14621

ASSOCIATION OF GERMAN-AMERICAN SOCIETIES IN WASHINGTON

6306 Roanoke Avenue
Riverdale, Maryland 20840

Principal officers: Elisabeth Schmid, Secretary

ASSOCIATION OF GERMAN-AMERICAN TECHNOLOGISTS

252 Westfield Avenue
Elizabeth, New Jersey 07200

ASSOCIATION OF GERMAN BROADCASTERS

1 East 57th Street
New York, New York 10022

Principal officers: David Berger, Executive Officer

Permanent staff: 6
Date founded: 1955
Branches: NI

Membership: 9
Membership dues: NI
Scope: national

Special requirements for membership: non-commercial radio and TV networks from the
Federal Republic of Germany that wish to distribute German programs throughout
the United States

Nature of organization: professional

ASSOCIATION OF GERMAN BROADCASTERS (cont'd)

Comments: The purpose of the organization is to distribute radio and TV programs of German origin throughout the United States, in order to promote better relations and an understanding of the German culture and trends in German music.

BAVARIAN FESTIVAL SOCIETY, INC.
RD 2
Kempton, Pennsylvania 19529   (215) 756-3000

Principal officers: Kermit Dietrich, President
Donald Conover, Vice President
Reba Conover, Secretary
Alta Dietrich, Treasurer

Permanent staff: 4   Membership: NI
Date founded: 1968   Membership dues: none
Branches: NI   Scope: national

Special requirements for membership: none

Nature of organization: social, entertainment, cultural

Major conventions/meetings: annual convention

Comments: Non-profit organization based solely on membership. Objectives involve the promotion of and assistance for the annual "Bavarian Summer Festival." The society also encourages the retention of the German language, culture, and traditions. Sponsors chartered flights to Germany. Offers summer courses in German language, folk art, dancing, literature, etc.

BAYERISCHER VOLKSFESTVEREIN
9940 Haldeman Avenue
Philadelphia, Pennsylvania 19115

BERLINER CLUB, DETROIT, INC.
P.O. Box 231
St. Clair Shores, Michigan 48083   (313) 778-1574

Principal officers: Klaus Krumme, President
Ferdinand Werner, Vice President
Dagmar Beckton, Secretary

Permanent staff: 9   Membership: 280
Date founded: 1967   Membership dues: $15.00 per couple
Branches: none   Scope: local

Special requirements for membership: recommendations

Nature of organization: social

Publications: none

Affiliations: German American Cultural Center

Comments: Promotes solidarity among its members as well as the cultivation of native customs, practices, and language. Aids newly arrived German immigrants. Offers assistance to members in need.

BERLINER VEREIN VON NEW YORK
2 D Patton Drive
Bloomfield, New Jersey 07003

Principal officers: Johannes Abicht, President

BURGENLANDER AMERICAN BENEFIT SOCIETY
115 President Street
Passaic, New Jersey 07055

CANNSTATTER VOLKSFESTVEREIN, NEW YORK, INC.
73 King Avenue
Weehawken, New Jersey 07087

CARPATHIA CLUB, INC.
7592 Republic
Warren, Michigan 48091   (313) 755-6464
Principal officers: Peter Rausch, President
                       Johann Klimach, Vice President
                       Josef Hinz, Secretary

Permanent staff: 15   Membership: 1,400
Date founded: 1913   Membership dues: $6.00
Branches: none   Scope: local

Special requirements for membership: German descent

Nature of organization: cultural, social, scholarly, educational, sport, youth

Publications: none

Affiliations: German American Cultural Center

Major conventions/meetings: quarterly conference

Comments: Promotes the retention of all aspects of German culture. The club consists of
    eight groups—choir, soccer team, girls circle, youth group, German school, ladies
    group, brass band, and hunting group.

CATHOLIC KOLPING SOCIETY OF AMERICA
581 Waikiki Drive
Des Plaines, Illinois 60016   (312) 824-8768
Principal officers: William B. Mahrenholz, National Secretary

Permanent staff: 10   Membership: 2,000
Date founded: 1928   Membership dues: NI
Branches: 11   Scope: national

Special requirements for membership: none

Nature of organization: social, recreational, philanthropic, religious

Publications: *Kolping Banner* (monthly)

Major conventions/meetings: biennial

Comments: This organization was founded by Father Kolping in Germany. It is a religious
    society that provides Catholic instruction and that sponsors centers for youth and
    senior citizens, boarding facilities for Catholic young men, Boy Scout troops and dens,
    and other community programs. It presents biennial awards.

CATHOLIC WOMEN'S UNION
St. Elizabeth House
421 East 148th Street
Bronx, New York 10400

CHRISTIAN UNITY PRESS
2211 Lincoln Avenue
York, Nebraska 68467   (402) 362-5133
Principal officers: Fritz Friedrich, President
                       Otto Sommerfeld, Executive Vice President
                       Oscar Berzins, Executive Secretary

Permanent staff: 3   Membership: NI
Date founded: 1895   Membership dues: none
Branches: none   Scope: national and international

Special requirements for membership: none

Nature of organization: religious

Publications: *Gospel Trumpet*, 1895– (semimonthly); *International Bible Lessons*, 1922–
    (every three months)

CHRISTIAN UNITY PRESS (cont'd)
Affiliations: Church of God, Anderson, Indiana
Major conventions/meetings: none
Comments: A non-profit organization promoting Christian ideals.

CONCORDIA SINGING SOCIETY, INC.
c/o German American Cultural Center
5251 East Outer Drive
Detroit, Michigan 48234   (313) 884-9320
Principal officers: Kurt F. Hartlieb, President
Carl Keckhut, Vice President
Fred Rahmann, Secretary
Permanent staff: 7   Membership: 30
Date founded: 1865   Membership dues: $10.00
Branches: none   Scope: local
Special requirements for membership: ability to sing; knowledge of German helps
Nature of organization: cultural
Publications: none
Affiliations: North American Singers Union and Michigan Singers District
Comments: Founded in 1865 by eight Civil War veterans of German descent. The society has
preserved the German musical heritage in the Detroit area.

CONNECTICUT SÄNGERBUND (CS-B)
24 Acre Drive
Danbury, Connecticut 06810   (203) 743-9363
Principal officers: Richard Karthaus, President
Albert Wüstefeld, Vice President
George Herrmann, Secretary
Permanent staff: 5   Membership: between 1,000 and 1,200
Date founded: 1882   Membership dues: varies
Branches: 26   Scope: regional
Special requirements for membership: membership in a Bundesvereine
Nature of organization: cultural
Publications: publishes programs for annual songfest
Comments: The aim of the Sängerbund is to unite all singing societies of the New England
states. Promotes the preservation of German songs.

DEUTSCH-AMERIKANISCHER SCHULVEREIN
207 East 84th Street
New York, New York 10028

DEUTSCHER KULTURKREIS
823 Monroe
Dearborn, Michigan 48124
Principal officers: Ellen M. Joost, Secretary

EDELWEISS CLUB, INC.
3009 West Belvedere Avenue
Baltimore, Maryland 21215   (301) 542-1414
Principal officers: Paul Ludtke, President
William K. Klein, Vice President
Theo. Stegmueller, Secretary
E. Koehler, Treasurer

EDELWEISS CLUB, INC. (cont'd)

Permanent staff: 5
Date founded: 1968
Branches: none

Membership: 1,200
Membership dues: $3.00 single; $5.00
  couple
Scope: regional

Nature of organization: social, cultural, travel

Major conventions/meetings: conference (bimonthly); annual membership meeting

Comments: Promotes the study of German language, history, culture, and traditions.
  Organizes social gatherings and trips. Sponsors scholarships.

**THE FEDERATION OF AMERICAN CITIZENS OF GERMAN DESCENT
IN THE U.S.A., INC. (FACGD)**
  460 Chapman Street
  Irvington, New Jersey 07111   (201) 375-1632

Principal officers: Robert Brueckner, President
                      Al Bayersdorfer, Executive Vice President
                      Edmund F. Eckhardt, Executive Secretary

Permanent staff: NI
Date founded: 1945
Branches: 17

Membership: 3,850
Membership dues: $8.00 single (annual);
  $10.00 couple (annual)
Scope: national

Special requirements for membership: "Must be of German descent."

Nature of organization: cultural

Publications: *Voice of the Federation* (10 issues per year)

Affiliations: none

Major conventions/meetings: annual convention; monthly branch meetings

Comments: The FACGD promotes the unity of German Americans for the purpose of fostering
  the German language and cultural heritage, combating the defamation of the German
  character and people, and bettering the understanding between the German and American people. The organization further supports a free and united Germany, as well as free
  elections for all countries behind the Iron Curtain. Encourages active participation in
  American civic, social, and political institutions.

FEDERATION OF GERMAN AMERICAN SOCIETIES, INC.
  580 St. Paul Street
  Rochester, New York 14580

Principal officers: Harold W. Tausch, President
                      Frances Gradl, Vice President
                      Gary Munger, Treasurer
                      Judith Tausch, Secretary

Permanent staff: NI
Date founded: 1920
Branches: none

Membership: NI
Membership dues: NI
Scope: local

Special requirements for membership: membership in one of the German-American societies
  in Rochester

Nature of organization: social, educational, cultural, sport, youth

Publications: none

Comments: Supports the learning of the German language and preservation of the German
  cultural heritage. The federation organizes various social events and recreational
  activities. It supports 15 affiliated German-American societies in the Rochester area
  and also provides financial assistance for German language classes.

FEDERATION OF WORKERS' SINGING SOCIETIES OF AMERICA
1832 Hillsdale Avenue
Dayton, Ohio 45414   (513) 275-5460
Principal officers: J. Mark Winters, President
Nature of organization: musical
Publications: *Saenger-Zeitung*, 1924– (monthly)
Major conventions/meetings: quadrennial
Comments: The organization is a union of German-American choral groups.

FIRST GERMAN SPORT CLUB PHOENIX (Phoenix S.C.)
301 Bristol Road
Feasterville, Pennsylvania 19047   (215) 357-9913
Principal officers: Kurt Jasch, President
                    Camill Stroh, Vice President
                    Fred Knaak, Secretary
                    Klaus Gessat Steward, Chairman

Permanent staff: 1   Membership: 245
Date founded: 1926   Membership dues: $10.00-$12.00
Branches: none   Scope: local
Special requirements for membership: 2 years passive membership
Nature of organization: sport, youth
Publications: *Calendar of Coming Events*, 1959– (quarterly)
Affiliations: none
Major conventions/meetings: monthly active membership meetings
Comments: The Phoenix Sport Club is, as its name indicates, primarily a sports organization. Its principle purpose is to further the popularity of soccer as well as other sporting games and activities. The club has ten junior and three senior soccer teams, four fistball teams and a swimming club with 300 members.

GERMAN ACADEMIC EXCHANGE SERVICE
1 Fifth Avenue
New York, New York 10003   (212) 260-2216
Principal officers: Roland Mohrmann, Director
Permanent staff: NI   Membership: NI
Date founded: NI   Membership dues: NI
Branches: NI   Scope: national
Nature of organization: educational
Comments: The function of the exchange service is to provide information on German studies and the availability of German government grants for research in Germany.

GERMAN AID SOCIETY OF CHICAGO
221 West Ohio Street
Chicago, Illinois 60600

GERMAN AMERICAN CHAMBER OF COMMERCE
666 Fifth Avenue
New York, New York 10019   (212) 582-7788
Principal officers: Christoph Ledermann, General Manager
Permanent staff: NI   Membership: 975
Date founded: 1947   Membership dues: NI
Branches: NI   Scope: national
Nature of organization: economic
Publications: *German Business Weekly* (weekly); *German American Trade News*, 1946– (monthly); *The German Market* (monthly)

GERMAN AMERICAN CITIZENS ASSOCIATION
Eichenkranz Restaurant
611 South Fagley Street
Baltimore, Maryland 21200

GERMAN AMERICAN CLUB
4165 Lakeside Drive
Jacksonville, Florida 32200

GERMAN AMERICAN CULTURAL CENTER
5251 East Outer Drive
Detroit, Michigan 48200

GERMAN-AMERICAN FOOTBALL ASSOCIATION, INC. (GASL)
P.O. Box 1117
Secaucus, New Jersey 07094   (201) 863-3132
Principal officers: Herbert Heilpern, President
                        Heinz Laut, Vice President
                        Fritz L. Marth, Secretary
Permanent staff: NI   Membership: 30,000
Date founded: 1923   Membership dues: $500.00 per club
Branches: 41 clubs   Scope: regional
Special requirements for membership: soccer club in good standing with National Soccer
    Association
Nature of organization: sport
Publications: *GASL News* (weekly)
Affiliations: United States Soccer Football Association
Major conventions/meetings: convention annually
Comments: The objective of this association is to promote soccer among its members. It has
    both senior and junior teams and awards annual trophies to all division winners.

GERMAN AMERICAN LEAGUE, INC.
9417 Hidden Valley Place
Beverly Hills, California 90210

GERMAN AMERICAN MARKSMANSHIP CLUB (D.A.S.V.)
2650 Auburn Road
Pontiac, Michigan 48057   (313) 852-2140
Principal officers: Werner Fischer, President
                        Joseph Eckardt, Vice President
                        George Kuhn, Treasurer
                        Günter Ohlendorf, Secretary
Permanent staff: none   Membership: 135
Date founded: 1939   Membership dues: $12.00
Branches: none   Scope: local
Special requirements for membership: German or German with American citizenship and
    persons with knowledge of German
Nature of organization: social, sport, conservation
Publications: none
Affiliations: German American Cultural Center; Michigan United Conservation Clubs
Comments: As the name implies, the club is sports oriented. The main purpose is to develop
    good sportsmanship as well as good marksmanship.

GERMAN-AMERICAN NATIONAL CONGRESS, INC.
4740 North Western Avenue
Chicago, Illinois 60625   (312) 561-2488

Principal officers: John Hebling, President
                      Ralph Scott, Vice President
                      Erika Voss, Secretary

Permanent staff: 3   Membership: 22,000
Date founded: 1959   Membership dues: $7.00 single; $10.00
Branches: 7 regional; 45 local   couple
                                  Scope: national

Special requirements for membership: German descent

Nature of organization: cultural, political, social, educational, recreational, sport, youth

Publications: *Der Deutsch-Amerikaner* (The German-American), 1960– (monthly)

Affiliations: Federation of American Citizens of German Descent

Major conventions/meetings: biennial convention

Comments: The German-American National Congress (D.A.N.K.) aims to unite all German-Americans, to maintain German culture and customs, to educate members in American citizenship and non-partisan politics, and to foster friendship between the United States and Germany. The local branches have many sport clubs and youth groups as well as German language and culture classes for children from kindergarten through high school age.

GERMAN AMERICAN SOCIAL CLUB
940 Main Street
Peekskill, New York 10566

GERMAN AMERICAN SOCIAL CLUB OF GREATER MIAMI
c/o Knights of Columbus
270 Catalonia Avenue
Coral Gables, Florida 33134

GERMAN AMERICAN SOCIETIES OF WESTCHESTER COUNTY, N.Y.
3 North Tenth Avenue
Mount Vernon, New York 10500

GERMAN AMERICAN SOCIETY
381 Orange Lane
Casselberry, Florida 32707

Permanent staff: NI   Membership: NI
Date founded: NI   Membership dues: NI
Branches: NI   Scope: local

GERMAN AMERICAN WELFARE SOCIETY (GAWS)
625 Polk Street
San Francisco, California 94102   (415) 885-6264

Principal officers: Adolf Schaumloeffel, President
                      Horst Mey, Vice President
                      Ms. Carol Jean Browne, Secretary

Permanent staff: 3   Membership: 100
Date founded: 1954   Membership dues: $10.00
Branches: 1 local   Scope: local

Nature of organization: social, social concern

Publications: none

Comments: The primary aim of GAWS is to help German immigrants adjust to life in the United States. It provides job counseling and housing assistance.

GERMAN BALTIC ASSOCIATION
35 LaVeta Place
Nyack, New York 10960
Principal officers: Nikolai Taupmann, President

GERMAN CULTURAL SOCIETY, INC.
1154 Washington Avenue
Westwood, New Jersey 07675

GERMAN EDUCATIONAL SOCIETY
Schutzenpark
3167 Kennedy Boulevard
North Bergen, New Jersey 07047

GERMAN FAMILY SOCIETY OF AKRON, INC. (G.F.S.A.)
1133 Virginia Avenue
Akron, Ohio 44306   (216) 724-0575
Principal officers: Joseph Rickert, President
                      Fritz Meindl, Vice President
                      Joseph Horn, Secretary
                      Dieter Dambrowsky, Chairman

Permanent staff: NI   Membership: 280
Date founded: 1973   Membership dues: $24.00 (annual)
Branches: none   Scope: local

Special requirements for membership: German heritage

Nature of organization: social, educational, cultural, recreational, sport, youth

Publications: none

Affiliations: National Association of Danube Swabians

Major conventions/meetings: annual meeting

Comments: Primarily social in nature, the society provides cultural, recreational, youth, sport, and educational activities for its members. Also sponsors the German Weekend School for the purpose of teaching the language, culture, customs, and history of the Germans.

GERMAN INTEREST CONFERENCE OF THE LUTHERAN CHURCH IN AMERICA
231 Madison Avenue
New York, New York 10016

GERMAN MASONIC CORPORATION
82-48 156th Street
Jamaica, New York 11482
Principal officers: Jobst Ahrens, Secretary

GERMAN ORDER OF HARUGARI
114-40 122nd Street
South Ozone Park, New York 11420   (212) 848-2744
Principal officers: William Bernd, Grand Secretary

Permanent staff: 2   Membership: 974
Date founded: 1847   Membership dues: NI
Branches: 6 state Grand Lodges; 70 Subordinate   Scope: NI
  Lodges

Nature of organization: fraternal benefit insurance society

Publications: *Der Harugari* (bimonthly)

Major conventions/meetings: biennial

Comments: The purpose of the organization is to provide life insurance benefits to its members.

GERMAN SATURDAY SCHOOL ASSOCIATION
29 Crestview Road
Manchester, New Hampshire 03104

THE GERMAN SOCIETY OF MARYLAND
231 St. Paul Place
Baltimore, Maryland 21202   (301) 685-0450

Principal officers: Vernon H. Wiesand, President
                   Henry P. Thau, First Vice President
                   Morgan H. Pritchett, Second Vice President and Secretary

Permanent staff: 7 officers; 21 directors   Membership: 240
Date founded: 1783   Membership dues: $6.00 (annual)
Branches: none   Scope: state

Special requirements for membership: " . . . application card must be approved by executive committee and voted for"

Nature of organization: benevolent organization

Publications: publishes books

Affiliations: none

Major conventions/meetings: none

Comments: Provides financial and other aid to people of German descent who may be in need. Also distributes scholarships each year to students of German ancestry who study at four-year Maryland colleges and universities.

GERMAN SOCIETY OF PENNSYLVANIA
c/o H. C. Palm
771 East Shawmont Avenue
Philadelphia, Pennsylvania 19128

Permanent staff: 3   Membership: 750
Date founded: 1764   Membership dues: $12.00 active; $6.00
Branches: none   library
                                     Scope: regional and state

Special requirements for membership: none

Nature of organization: cultural, educational

Publications: has published a book

Affiliations: none

Major conventions/meetings: none

Comments: The German Society of Pennsylvania is considered to be one of the oldest German societies in the United States. The society was originally organized to assist distressed German immigrants. Today the society is also involved in cultural and educational activities. The Joseph Horner Memorial Library, maintained by the society, has a collection of over 50,000 books on German literature and culture and on the history of Germans in the United States. The library also maintains German newspapers and periodicals as well as extensive archival holdings on German-Americans.

GERMAN SOCIETY OF THE CITY OF NEW YORK
150 Fifth Avenue
New York, New York 10011

Principal officers: Horst H. Schuchart, Executive Director

Permanent staff: 4   Membership: 350
Date founded: 1784   Membership dues: NI
Branches: NI   Scope: local

Special requirements for membership: interest in assisting German immigrants

Nature of organization: professional, welfare

Publications: *Annual Report*

Major conventions/meetings: annual

GERMAN SOCIETY OF THE CITY OF NEW YORK (cont'd)
Comments: This organization provides assistance to German immigrants and German Americans in the form of professional counseling, medical and welfare services, job opportunities, etc.

GERMAN SPEAKING DAMEN KLUB
c/o American Legion Post No. 2
820 Wingfield Road
Petersburg, Virginia 23803
Principal officers: Brigitte Duncan, Secretary

GOETHE HOUSE
1014 Fifth Avenue
New York, New York 10028   (212) 744-8310

Nature of organization: cultural

Affiliations: Is a branch of the Goethe Institute, Munich, Germany, which also has two other branches in the United States (German Culture Center in Boston and San Francisco).

Comments: Seeks to promote cultural understanding between the United States and Germany. Sponsors lectures, exhibits and concerts. The organization is a branch of the Goethe Institute in Munich; other U.S. branches are the German Cultural Center in Boston and German Cultural Center in San Francisco. A library of 13,000 books by German authors is maintained.

LIEDERKRANZ FOUNDATION
6 East 87th Street
New York, New York 10028   (212) 534-0880

Principal officers: K. Kast, Manager

Permanent staff: NI   Membership: NI
Date founded: 1947   Membership dues: NI
Branches: NI   Scope: national

Nature of organization: cultural, musical

Comments: This foundation attempts to help German musicians in America; it also sponsors the Liederkranz, a German-American musical society that performs in concerts and musical events.

LITERARY SOCIETY FOUNDATION, INC.
P.O. Box 373, Grand Central Station
229 East 85th Street
New York, New York 10028

Principal officers: Max W. Schroeder, President

Permanent staff: NI   Membership: 30
Date founded: 1940   Membership dues: NI
Branches: NI   Scope: NI

Nature of organization: educational

Major conventions/meetings: annual, always in March

Comments: Sponsors lectures in order to create appreciation for German literature, art, science, and language.

NATIONAL CATHOLIC WOMEN'S UNION
3835 Westminister Place
St. Louis, Missouri 63108

Principal officers: H. J. Johnson, Director

Permanent staff: NI   Membership: 16,000
Date founded: 1916   Membership dues: NI
Branches: 10 state groups; 251 local groups Scope: national

Nature of organization: social, religious, charitable

NATIONAL CATHOLIC WOMEN'S UNION (cont'd)
Major conventions/meetings: annual
Comments: A Catholic social action group devoted to charity and good works.

NORDOSTLICHER SÄNDERBUND VON AMERIKA, INC.
220 Somerset Street
North Plainfield, New Jersey 07060

PENNSYLVANIA DUTCH FOLK CULTURE SOCIETY, INC.
Lenhartsville, Pennsylvania 19534   (215) 562-4803 or
                                           (215) 562-8701

Principal officers: Florence Baver, President
                       Ferba Krause, Vice President
                       Thelma Bailey, Secretary

Permanent staff: NI   Membership: 350
Date founded: 1965   Membership dues: $5.00
Branches: NI   Scope: regional

Special requirements for membership: none

Nature of organization: educational, historical

Publications: *Pa. Dutch News and Views*, 1969– (quarterly)

Comments: Although the name of the organization would indicate that it is Dutch in its ethnic origins, it has identified its ethnicity as being "Pennsylvania German." Objectives state that the society shall "foster the preservation of the homelife folk culture, dialect and ancestry of the Pennsylvania Germans." The society has restored some buildings of historical value.

PENNSYLVANIA GERMAN SOCIETY
RD 1, Box 469
Breinigsville, Pennsylvania 18031

Principal officers: Mahlon Hellerich, President
                       Russell Gilbert, Vice President
                       Larry Neff, Secretary to the Board

Permanent staff: NI   Membership: 1,350
Date founded: 1891   Membership dues: $12.50
Branches: NI   Scope: international

Special requirements for membership: none

Nature of organization: cultural

Publications: *Der Das Reggeboge* (The Rainbow), 1967– (quarterly); and other publications

Major conventions/meetings: annual meeting in May

Comments: Promotes the study, research, and preservation of the Pennsylvania Germans. Offers tours to adjoining German settlements known commonly as "Pennsylvania Dutch." Restores historical buildings and preserves materials dealing with the German experience in the United States, particularly in Pennsylvania.

PLATTDEUTSCHER VOLKSFESTVEREIN VON NEW YORK
1542 East 96th Street
Brooklyn, New York 11236

Principal officers: Karl Bottjes, President

SCHLARAFFIA NORD-AMERIKA (GERMAN)
771 East Shawmont Avenue
Philadelphia, Pennsylvania 19128

Principal officers: H. C. Palm, National Secretary

Permanent staff: NI   Membership: 750
Date founded: 1859   Membership dues: NI
Branches: 26   Scope: national

SCHLARAFFIA NORD-AMERIKA (GERMAN) (cont'd)
Special requirements for membership: German-American professional and business men
Publications: *Membership Roster* (annual)
Major conventions/meetings: quinquennial
Comments: The objectives are to unite German-American professional and business men in the United States and to preserve the German tradition and heritage through social and cultural activities.

SCHWABEN INTERNATIONAL, INC.
One World Trade Center Street 2413
New York, New York 10048

SIEBENBURGEN SACHSEN UNTERSTUTZUNGSVEREIN
512 East La Salle
Royal Oak, Michigan 48073
Principal officers: Mari Emrich, Secretary

SOCIETY FOR GERMAN-AMERICAN STUDIES
7204 Langenford Drive
Parma, Ohio 44129

SOCIETY FOR THE HISTORY OF THE GERMAN IN MARYLAND
231 St. Paul Place
Baltimore, Maryland 21202
Principal officers: Dr. Morgan H. Pritchett, Secretary

Permanent staff: 1	Membership: 100
Date founded: 1886	Membership dues: NI
Branches: NI	Scope: NI

Publications: *Report* (triennial)
Major conventions/meetings: annual
Comments: Interested in German-American relations and the preservation and publication of historical material concerning Americans of German descent in Maryland and other states.

SOCIETY OF DANUBE SWABIANS
4219 North Lincoln Avenue
Chicago, Illinois 60618
Principal officers: Nick Schneider, President

Permanent staff: NI	Membership: 3,050
Date founded: 1953	Membership dues: NI
Branches: NI	Scope: NI

Nature of organization: social, civic, cultural
Publications: *Nachrichten* (quarterly)
Major conventions/meetings: annual
Comments: Membership consists of persons who migrated to the United States from the Danube River regions of Yugoslavia, Rumania, and Hungary. Assists in their adjustment to American life and conducts classes in the German language.

STEUBEN SOCIETY OF AMERICA
369 Lexington Avenue, Suite 2003
New York, New York 10017
Principal officers: Robert H. Diedolf, National Secretary

Permanent staff: 3	Membership: NI
Date founded: 1919	Membership dues: NI
Branches: NI	Scope: NI

STEUBEN SOCIETY OF AMERICA (cont'd)
Special requirements for membership: German descent
Publications: *Steuben News*, 1929– (monthly)

TIDEWATER GERMAN-AMERICAN SOCIETY, INC.
P.O. Box 2313
Newport News, Virginia 23602

TIROLER BENEFICIAL SOCIETY
2008 Beyer Avenue
Philadelphia, Pennsylvania 19115
Principal officers: Frank Buzolits

TRANSYLVANIA SAXON SICK BENEFICIAL SOCIETY
17500 East Nine Mile Road
East Detroit, Michigan 48201

TRANSYLVANIA-SAXONS BENEFICIAL SOCIETY
30021 Smith Drive
Warren, Michigan 48000

TYROLEAN AND VABARIAN ZITHER CLUB
5701 South Western Avenue
Los Angeles, California 90037   (213) 291-6776
Principal officers: Frank R. Resta, President
Permanent staff: NI   Membership: 65
Date founded: 1923   Membership dues: NI
Branches: NI   Scope: NI
Nature of organization: cultural
Comments: Interested in promoting and preserving German, particularly Bavarian, customs
in the United States.

UNITED CHORAL CONDUCTORS' CLUB OF AMERICA (GERMAN)
87-23 85th Street
Woodhaven, New York 11421
            or
Mozart Halle
328 East 86th Street
New York, New York 10028
Principal officers: Heinrich Geiger, Secretary

VEREIN DER OSTDEUTSCHEN
Mozart Halle
328 East 86th Street
New York, New York 10028

VEREIN DER PLATTDEUTSCHEN, INC.
29612 Roan Road
Warren, Michigan 48093

VEREIN DER SCHLESIER, INC.
Liederkranz Club
6 East 87th Street
New York, New York 10028

VEREIN ESSENER FREUNDS
24371 Tamarack Circle
Southfield, Michigan 48075
Principal officers: Herbert Friebe, Secretary

VEREINIGUNG DER DONAUSCHWABEN IN CHICAGO, ILL.
4219 North Lincoln Avenue
Chicago, Illinois 60618

Permanent staff: NI
Date founded: NI
Branches: NI

Membership: NI
Membership dues: NI
Scope: local

WANDERER ASSOCIATION
Schultes Waldheim
Kezar Falls, Maine 04047

WARDENS ASSOCIATION
184-31 Hovenden Road
Jamaica, New York 11432
Principal officers: John Westerfeld, Secretary

WOMEN'S AUXILIARY OF THE GERMAN SOCIETY OF MARYLAND
3005 Putty Hill Road
Baltimore, Maryland 21234
Principal officers: Mrs. G. Grofebert

WORKMEN'S BENEFIT FUND OF THE U.S.A.
714 Seneca Avenue
Ridgewood, New York 11227

GREEK-AMERICAN ORGANIZATIONS

Additional information on Greek-American organizations may be obtained from the Order of AHEPA (1422 "K" Street, N.W., Washington, D.C. 20005) and in Michael N. Cutsumbis, *A Bibliographic Guide to Materials on Greeks in the United States, 1890-1968* (Staten Island, N.Y.: Center for Migration Studies, 1970). Regional and local organizations may be found listed in *Greater Cleveland Nationalities Directory 1974* (Cleveland: Sun Newspapers and the Nationalities Services Center, 1974) and *Ethnic Directory I* (Detroit: Southeastern Michigan Regional Ethnic Heritage Studies Center, 1973).

AETOLOAKARAANON SOCIETY
69-40 Exeter Street
Forest Hills, New York 11375
Principal officers: Dr. Aristidis Varsos, President

AMERICAN COMMITTEE FOR DEMOCRACY AND FREEDOM IN GREECE
303 West 42nd Street
New York, New York 10018   (212) 247-4397
Principal officers: Nicholas D. Noulas, Secretary

Permanent staff: 1
Date founded: 1967
Branches: NI

Membership: NI
Membership dues: NI
Scope: national

Special requirements for membership: none

AMERICAN COMMITTEE FOR DEMOCRACY AND FREEDOM IN GREECE (cont'd)

Nature of organization: political

Affiliations: Inter-American Federation for Democracy and Freedom in Greece

Major conventions/meetings: monthly

Comments: The goals of the organization are to unite Greek-Americans in the United States who are interested in opposing the military dictatorship in Greece, to preserve the Greek language and culture in the United States, to keep Americans aware of the situation in Greece, and to promote good relations between Greeks and Americans.

AMERICAN HELLENIC CONGRESS
4200 Cathedral Avenue, N.W.
Washington, D.C. 20016

Principal officers: Peter Chumbris, Secretary

Permanent staff: NI	Membership: NI
Date founded: 1960	Membership dues: NI
Branches: 2,500	Scope: national

Special requirements for membership: must be a national Hellenic organization

Nature of organization: political, philanthropic

Comments: This is a federation of all national Greek organizations in the United States. It appears before Congress as a representative voice for Greek-Americans. It also sponsors philanthropic and civic programs.

AMERICAN SOCIETY FOR NEO-HELLENIC STUDIES
2754 Claflin Avenue
Bronx, New York 10468   (212) 884-2320

Principal officers: Constantine N. Tsirpanlis, Executive Vice President

Permanent staff: NI	Membership: 75
Date founded: 1967	Membership dues: NI
Branches: NI	Scope: NI

Special requirements for membership: professor, author, or student contributing to Greek studies

Nature of organization: scholarly

Publications: *Newsletter* (quarterly)

Major conventions/meetings: annual

Comments: The purpose of the organization is to promote knowledge in and of Greek historical and cultural studies as well as study of the Greek language. Included also are Greek folklore, philosophy and theology, and arts and sciences. Sponsors a monthly lecture on contemporary Greek immigration to the United States.

ANDROS SOCIETY, INC.
11 Jordan Road
Hastings-on-Hudson
New York, New York 10706

Principal officers: Mr. George Loukrezis, President

BYZANTINE FELLOWSHIP
Third and Bedford Streets
Stamford, Connecticut 06905   (203) 348-2108

Principal officers: George Poulos, Executive Officer

Permanent staff: 1	Membership: 10,000
Date founded: 1958	Membership dues: NI
Branches: NI	Scope: national

Special requirements for membership: of Greek Orthodox faith

Nature of organization: religious

BYZANTINE FELLOWSHIP (cont'd)

Publications: *Byzantium* (quarterly)

Comments: Primarily a religious fellowship, but the organization also sponsors educational, travel, and social activities. It plans pilgrimages to Greece and to the Patriarchate at Istanbul, Turkey.

CENTER FOR NEO-HELLENIC STUDIES (CNHS)
1010 West 22nd Street
Austin, Texas 78705   (512) 477-5526

Principal officers: George G. Arnakis, Director

Permanent staff: NI   Membership: 150
Date founded: 1965   Membership dues: NI
Branches: NI   Scope: NI

Nature of organization: scholarly

Publications: *Bulletin* (annual); *Neo-Hellenika* (annual); also publishes books

Comments: Greek historians, scholars, and writers attempt to preserve and promote Greek tradition, language, and culture in the United States by bringing to light Greek studies and contributions. The organization presents the Max Manus Award for Greek literature in the United States and Canada, and the Arthur Sockler Prize for Byzantine and Modern Greek studies.

CEPHALONIAN ASSOCIATION "AENOS"
401 East 74th Street
New York, New York 10021

Principal officers: Takis Metaxas, President

CRETANS' ASSOCIATION OMONOIA
263 West 30th Street
New York, New York 10001   (212) 565-8622

Principal officers: Emmanuel Vernadakis, President

DAUGHTERS OF EVRYTANIA
P.O. Box 394
Charlotte, North Carolina 28201   (704) 375-4112

Principal officers: Mrs. D. N. Polyzos, Secretary

Permanent staff: NI   Membership: 200
Date founded: 1948   Membership dues: NI
Branches: NI   Scope: national

Special requirements for membership: none

Nature of organization: charitable

Affiliations: Evrytanian Association of America

Major conventions/meetings: annual

Comments: The major purpose of the organization is to provide aid to the province of Evrytania in Greece in the form of medical and educational services and equipment.

DAUGHTERS OF PENELOPE
1422 "K" Street, N.W.
Washington, D.C. 20005   (202) 737-7638

Principal officers: Elizabeth Athanasakos, Grand President

Permanent staff: NI   Membership: 13,000
Date founded: 1929   Membership dues: NI
Branches: NI   Scope: national

Special requirements for membership: women of Greek descent

Nature of organization: fraternal

Affiliations: Order of Ahepa

DAUGHTERS OF PENELOPE (cont'd)
Major conventions/meetings: annual
Comments: The purpose of the organization is to unite women of Greek descent in the
    United States. It awards the Helen Karagiannis Scholarship to girls of Greek extraction.

EPIROTAS SOCIETY "ANNAGENESSIA"
25-14 Broadway (Astoria)
Long Island City, New York 11106
Principal officers: Demetrios Vasas, President

EVRYTANIAN ASSOCIATION OF AMERICA "VELOUCHI"
P.O. Box 394
Charlotte, North Carolina 28201   (704) 375-4112
Principal officers: Andrew Kampiziones, President
                George Retsios, Vice President
                D. N. Polyzos, Secretary
Permanent staff: 9 Board members   Membership: 650
Date founded: 1945   Membership dues: $15.00
Branches: 3 (District of Columbia, New Jersey,   Scope: national
  New York, major cities in North Carolina)
Special requirements for membership: must be from the province of Evrytania
Nature of organization: educational, fraternal
Publications: *The Velouchi Bulletin*, 1947– (quarterly); also publishes journals
Affiliations: annual convention
Comments: Main objective is to raise funds in order to build a hospital in Karpenisi, Greece,
    as well as to establish scholarships for underprivileged students in the United States
    and Greece. Supports needy individuals. Organizes social activities for the purpose of
    uniting Greeks from Evrytania. Maintains a 500-volume library.

FEDERATION OF HELLENIC AMERICAN SOCIETIES OF GREATER NEW YORK
203 East 76th Street
New York, New York 10021   (212) 737-0012
Principal officers: Pericles J. Lantzounis, President
Permanent staff: NI   Membership: NI
Date founded: NI   Membership dues: NI
Branches: NI   Scope: state
Special requirements for membership: Greek descent
Major conventions/meetings: annual
Comments: The federation unites all Greek clubs and organizations in the New York City
    area.

THE FEDERATION OF UNITED GREEK SOCIETIES
548 Monroe
Detroit, Michigan 48200   (313) 963-4490
Principal officers: Bazil Lukas
Permanent staff: NI   Membership: 52 organizations
Date founded: NI   Membership dues: NI
Branches: NI   Scope: local
Special requirements for membership: a representative from a Greek organization in Detroit
    area
Nature of organization: cultural, philanthropic
Comments: Representatives from 52 Greek clubs and organizations in the Detroit area meet
    regularly to plan fund-raising activities and social and cultural events for member
    organizations. The federation sponsors Greek schools, helps support Greek churches.

GREEK AMERICAN PROGRESSIVE ASSOCIATION (GAPA)
3600 Fifth Avenue
Pittsburgh, Pennsylvania 15213   (412) 621-4676

Principal officers: Stavros Kalaras, Secretary

Permanent staff: 3   Membership: 10,000
Date founded: 1923   Membership dues: NI
Branches: 150   Scope: national

Nature of organization: social, cultural

Publications: *Tribune of GAPA* (5 issues per year)

Major conventions/meetings: biennial

Comments: Stresses preservation of Greek culture and values and attempts to unite Greek-Americans in the United States.

GREEK ORTHODOX YOUTH OF AMERICA (GOYA)
8 East 79th Street
New York, New York 10021   (212) 628-2500

Principal officers: Nicholas Sakellariov, President
                       Lolia Pappas, Secretary
                       Alexander Karlavtsos, Youth Director

Permanent staff: 5   Membership: 200,000
Date founded: 1951   Membership dues: $2.00 (annual)
Branches: NI   Scope: local

Special requirements for membership: Greek Orthodox youth

Nature of organization: youth, religious, social, cultural, recreational, educational

Publications: *Challenge*, 1965– (monthly); *Be Ye Advised*, 1970– (monthly)

Affiliations: CEOYLA and Syndismos

Comments: The major purpose of the organization is to provide activities that develop the Greek Orthodox faith, promote the Greek heritage in the United States, and allow social and athletic development among the Greek youth.

HELLENIC-AMERICAN CHAMBER OF COMMERCE
25 Broadway
New York, New York 10004

Permanent staff: NI   Membership: NI
Date founded: NI   Membership dues: NI
Branches: NI   Scope: national

Nature of organization: economic

Publications: *Newsletter* (bimonthly); *Journal* (annual)

HYDRAS SOCIETY
601 West 189th Street
New York, New York 10040

Principal officers: Stamatios Kalafatis, President

LACEDOMONIANS ASSOCIATION
149 Bay 44
Brooklyn, New York 11214

Principal officers: Eleftherios Vouyouklis, President

MACEDONIAN PATRIOTIC ORGANIZATION OF U.S. AND CANADA
542 South Meridian Street
Indianapolis, Indiana 46225   (317) 635-2157

Principal officers: Dimiter N. Popov, National Secretary

Permanent staff: NI   Membership: NI
Date founded: 1922   Membership dues: NI
Branches: NI   Scope: national

MACEDONIAN PATRIOTIC ORGANIZATION OF U.S. AND CANADA (cont'd)

Special requirements for membership: of Macedonian origin

Nature of organization: political, cultural, social

Publications: *Makedonska Tribuna* (Macedonian Tribune) (weekly)

Comments: The purpose of the organization is to preserve the Macedonian culture and heritage in the United States and to unite members in social and cultural activities. It also supports political independence for Macedonia. Until 1952 it was known as the Union of Macedonian Political Organizations.

MAIDS OF ATHENS

c/o Daughters of Penelope
1422 "K" Street, N.W.
Washington, D.C. 20005 (202) 237-7638

Principal officers: Cleopatra Notarides, Grand President

Permanent staff: NI
Date founded: 1936
Branches: 155

Membership: 1,300
Membership dues: NI
Scope: national

Special requirements for membership: females of Greek descent

Nature of organization: fraternal

Affiliations: Daughters of Penelope; Order of Ahepa (American Hellenic Educational Progressive Association)

Major conventions/meetings: annual

Comments: A fraternal organization which attempts to preserve Greek traditions and values in the United States.

THE MODERN GREEK STUDIES ASSOCIATION (MGSA)

185 Nassau Street
Princeton, New Jersey 08540

Principal officers: John Petropulos, President
Lily Macrakis, Vice President
Julia Loomis, Secretary
Niki Stavrolakes, Treasurer

Permanent staff: NI
Date founded: 1968
Branches: none

Membership: 425
Membership dues: $15.00 (annual)
Scope: international, national

Special requirements for membership: interest in modern Greek studies

Nature of organization: scholarly

Publications: *The Modern Greek Studies Association Bulletin*

Affiliations: MLA, ACTFL

Major conventions/meetings: annual business meeting; annual seminar MLA

Comments: MGSA is a non-profit, tax-exempt organization of scholars, students, and others interested in promoting modern Greek studies in the United States and Canadian institutions. It sponsors meetings and lectures devoted to modern Greek subjects, and supports scholarly publications. It serves as a center of information on courses, programs, activities, and opportunities in the field of Byzantine and modern Greek. Language plans include the establishment of a chair in the field of modern Greek language, literature, and history.

MONEMVASIOTON SOCIETY

23-62 35th Street
Astoria, Long Island, New York 11105

Principal officers: Vasilios Broutzas, President

NEW YORK GREEK SOCIETY VRYSEON "ANAVRYTIS"
c/o Chelsea Chop House
248 8th Avenue
New York, New York 10011 (212) 924-1467

Principal officers: Paniotis Bayiokos, President
T. Skopas, Secretary
P. Chrisomalis, Vice President
G. Morfogen, Treasurer

Permanent staff: 15 | Membership: 150
Date founded: 1901 | Membership dues: $18.00
Branches: none | Scope: international, national

Special requirements for membership: member or parents born in village of Anavritis

Nature of organization: social, cultural, economic

Publications: none

Affiliations: Hellenic Societies of N.Y.C.

Major conventions/meetings: monthly meetings

ORDER OF AHEPA (AMERICAN HELLENIC EDUCATIONAL PROGRESSIVE ASSOCIATION)
1422 "K" Street, N.W.
Washington, D.C. 20005 (202) 628-4974

Principal officers: Dr. M. N. Spirtos, President
George J. Leber, Executive Secretary
William P. Tsaffaras, Vice President

Permanent staff: 5 | Membership: 49,000
Date founded: 1922 | Membership dues: varies with local chapters
Branches: 440 local chapters with 500 auxiliaries for women and children | Scope: national

Special requirements for membership: none

Nature of organization: social, cultural, fraternal

Publications: *The Ahepan*, 1927– (bimonthly)

Affiliations: American Immigration and Citizenship Conference

Major conventions/meetings: annual national convention: 24 district conventions each year

Comments: Helps newly arrived Greeks adjust to a new way of life. Encourages the dissemination of Hellenic ideas and culture. Provides financial assistance to various charitable causes. Encourages the study of Greek language, culture, and classics. Has helped in the construction of hospitals and health centers in Greece. Sponsors tour to Greece. Grants college scholarships at chapter, district, and national levels. Maintains an archival collection.

PAN-AMERICAN FEDERATION OF AMERICA
2604 Greenway
Royal Oak, Michigan 48073

Principal officers: Thomas J. Pantoleon

PANCRETAN ASSOCIATION OF AMERICA
851 Burlway Road
Burlingame, California 94010

Principal officers: Nick Delis, President

Permanent staff: 4 | Membership: 3,000
Date founded: 1929 | Membership dues: NI
Branches: NI | Scope: NI

Special requirements for membership: Greek descent

Nature of organization: fraternal

Publications: *Crete*, 1928– (monthly)

PANHELLENIC SEAMEN'S FEDERATION (PNO)
Livanos Building
Akti Miaouli 47-49
Piraeus, Greece

or

New York headquarters:
688 8th Avenue
New York, New York 10036   (212) 452-3587

Permanent staff: NI
Date founded: NI
Branches: New York

Membership: NI
Membership dues: NI
Scope: international, national

Special requirements for membership: Greek seamen

Nature of organization: welfare

Comments: Although the headquarters are in Greece, this federation does maintain offices in New York in order to look after the interests of its members—i.e., Greek seamen while they are in the United States.

PAN-MACEDONIAN ASSOCIATION
Kastorians Building
246 Eighth Avenue
New York, New York 10011

Principal officers: V. T. Daniels, Supreme Secretary

Permanent staff: NI
Date founded: 1947
Branches: NI

Membership: 6,000
Membership dues: NI
Scope: NI

Special requirements for membership: persons in U.S. and Canada who emigrated from Macedonia, and their descendants

Nature of organization: cultural, educational, social

Publications: *Macedonia* (Greek and English), 1953– (bimonthly); *Convention Journal* (annual)

Comments: The major objectives of the organization are to promote Greek-American relations, to improve social, educational, and public health conditions in Macedonia, and to collect and distribute information on Macedonia through publications, lectures, and exhibits.

PAN-RHODIAN SOCIETY OF AMERICA "APOLLON" INC.
401 South Garfield Street
Arlington, Virginia 22204   (703) 892-2424

Principal officers: E. S. Athanas, President
           K. Klimenton, Executive Vice President
           A. Anastasiadis, Executive Secretary

Permanent staff: 2
Date founded: 1929
Branches: 25 local

Membership: over 1,000
Membership dues: $60.00 (annual)
Scope: national

Special requirements for membership: "Must be of Greek descent and preferably hailing from Rhodes."

Nature of organization: educational, cultural

Publications: *Apollon*, 1930– (monthly); also publishes books

Affiliations: none

Major conventions/meetings: annual convention

Comments: The society is primarily for those Greeks or their descendants who are from the Rhodes area. The preservation of the Greek Orthodox religion as well as of customs and traditions peculiar to Rhodes are the prime objectives of the society. The society aids in various educational and philanthropic causes. Has established a college scholarship fund for children of members. Maintains societal archives.

PAN-THESSALONIAN UNION
142 East Oakridge
Ferndale, Michigan 48220
Principal officers: Christos Papageorgiou

PIRAIKOS BENEVOLENT ASSOCIATION
350 East 67th Street
New York, New York 10021
Principal officers: Constantine Kotleakos, President

RHODIAN SOCIETY "KOLOSSOS"
13530 Sorrento
Detroit, Michigan 48200

SOCIETY OF KASTORIANS "OMONOIA," INC.
246 8th Avenue
New York, New York 10011
Principal officers: Nicholas Moustakas, President
George Kaitey, Vice President
Mrs. G. Hadjisparashevas, Executive Secretary

Permanent staff: 5	Membership: 700
Date founded: 1910	Membership dues: $10.00
Branches: 3 regional	Scope: regional

Special requirements for membership: family lineage from Kastoria, Greece

Nature of organization: fraternal

Publications: *Kastoriana Nea* (Kastorian News) (quarterly)

Major conventions/meetings: biennial

Comments: This organization aims at uniting Greeks from Kastoria and encouraging the preservation of Kastoria's traditions. It has an established scholarship fund for children of members. Maintains a library of around 200 volumes on Greece.

SPETSIOTON ASSOCIATION "SPETAI"
62011 37th Avenue
Woodside, Long Island, New York 11377
Principal officers: John Thymios, President

STEREA HELLAS ASSOCIATION
c/o Mr. L. Lois
44-08 47th Avenue
Woodside, New York 11377
Principal officers: Theodasio Kioutas, President

THESSALONIKIAN SOCIETY
363 75th Avenue
Room 1405
New York, New York 10001
Principal officers: Sotirios Proios, President

THEVON SOCIETY "EPAMINONDAS"
240 Montgomery Street
Jersey City, New Jersey 07302
Principal officers: Demetrios Stamatelos, President

UNITED STATES COMMITTEE FOR DEMOCRACY IN GREECE
33 West 14th Street
New York, New York 10011   (212) 691-1895
Principal officers: Rep. Don Edwards, Chairman

UNITED STATES COMMITTEE FOR DEMOCRACY IN GREECE (cont'd)

Permanent staff: NI
Date founded: 1968
Branches: NI

Membership: 19 directors and officers
Membership dues: NI
Scope: NI

Nature of organization: political

Publications: *News of Greece* (bimonthly)

Major conventions/meetings: The committee is dedicated to non-partisan support of the cause of reestablishing democracy in Greece. It keeps records of developments in Greece, assists leaders exiled from Greece, and analyzes and distributes information on Greek political and economic situation. Sponsors lectures and speakers in the United States.

VRYSEON "ANAVRYTIS"
c/o George Morfogen(is)
435 Catherine Street
Fort Lee, New Jersey 07024
Principal officers: Pan Bayiakos, President

ZAKINTHION BROTHERHOOD
505 83rd Street
Brooklyn, New York 11209
Principal officers: Danny Pappas, President

HUNGARIAN-AMERICAN ORGANIZATIONS

Additional information on Hungarian-American organizations may be obtained from the American Hungarian Library and Historical Society (215 East 82nd Street, New York, New York 10028). Local and regional organizations are listed in *Greater Cleveland Nationalities Directory 1974* (Cleveland: Sun Newspapers and the Nationalities Services Center, 1974) and *Ethnic Directory I* (Detroit: Southeastern Michigan Regional Ethnic Heritage Studies Center, 1973).

AMERICAN HUNGARIAN CATHOLIC SOCIETY
2889 East 116th Street
Cleveland, Ohio 44120   (216) 231-6663
Principal officers: Stephen Eszterhas, Secretary

Permanent staff: NI
Date founded: 1894
Branches: 30

Membership: 3,300
Membership dues: varies with policy
Scope: NI

Nature of organization: fraternal

Comments: The objective of the organization is to provide life insurance benefits to its members.

AMERICAN HUNGARIAN FEDERATION (AHF)
3216 New Mexico Avenue, N.W.
Washington, D.C. 20016   (202) 966-0502
Principal officers: Hon. Albert A. Fiok, President
                       Rt. Rev. Dr. Zoltan Beky, Chairman of the Board
                       Dr. John Nadas, Chairman, Executive Committee
                       Dr. T. Michael Szaz, Secretary, International Relations

Permanent staff: 2
Date founded: 1906
Branches: 16 state; 49 local

Membership: 120,000
Membership dues: $60.00 (annual);
    $150.00 (annual) corporation
Scope: national

AMERICAN HUNGARIAN FEDERATION (AHF) (cont'd)

Special requirements for membership: an American-Hungarian organization which subscribes to the by-laws of the AHF

Nature of organization: political, cultural

Publications: publishes books

Affiliations: Hungarian Reformed Federation of America; William Penn Fraternal Insurance Company; Hungarian Boy Scout Association of America

Major conventions/meetings: triennial convention

Comments: Serves as the coordinating agency for Hungarian fraternal, religious, social, cultural, youth, and other organizations that are members. Represents the interests of American Hungarians in Congress and government agencies. Coordinates major events and remembrances nationwide. Sponsors various social, cultural, and educational programs through its local branches. Maintains a library collection.

AMERICAN HUNGARIAN LADIES' AND MEN'S AID
1526 Crenshaw Boulevard
Los Angeles, California 90000

AMERICAN HUNGARIAN LIBRARY AND HISTORICAL SOCIETY
215 East 82nd Street
New York, New York 10028   (212) 744-5298

Principal officers: Alexander St.-Ivanyi, President

Permanent staff: NI	Membership: 450
Date founded: 1955	Membership dues: NI
Branches: NI	Scope: national

Major conventions/meetings: annual

Comments: The purpose of the organization is to conduct and promote research and study of Hungarian history and culture as well as of Hungarian contributions to the arts and sciences in the United States. A 3,000-volume library is maintained.

AMERICAN HUNGARIAN LITERARY GUILD
Route 1, Box 59
Astor, Florida 32002   (904) 759-2255

Principal officers: Albert Wass de Czege, President
                      Géza Kovács, Executive Vice President
                      Elizabeth Wass de Czege, Executive Secretary

Permanent staff: 3	Membership: 738
Date founded: 1963	Membership dues: $10.00 (annual)
Branches: none	Scope: national

Special requirements for membership: none

Nature of organization: cultural

Publications: publishes books

Affiliations: none

Major conventions/meetings: none

Comments: Promotes the publication and distribution of Hungarian literary works. Encourages young Hungarian authors and promotes the translation into English of Hungarian classics and other major works.

AMERICAN HUNGARIAN MEDICAL ASSOCIATION
133 East 73rd Street
New York, New York 10021

Principal officers: Dr. Tibor de Cholnoky

Permanent staff: NI	Membership: 200
Date founded: 1924	Membership dues: NI
Branches: NI	Scope: national

AMERICAN HUNGARIAN MEDICAL ASSOCIATION (cont'd)

Special requirements for membership: physicians born or trained in Hungary now living in the United States

Publications: publishes proceedings

Major conventions/meetings: monthly

Comments: Provides scholarships to medical students in the United States of Hungarian origin; sponsors scientific activities and programs.

AMERICAN HUNGARIAN MOVEMENT OF THE CROSS AND THE SWORD
256 Dayton Avenue
Clifton, New Jersey 07011

AMERICAN HUNGARIAN SOCIAL SERVICE
10444½ Magnolia Boulevard
North Hollywood, California 91601   (213) 762-1819
Principal officers: Gizella L. Allen, President
Emita Armi, Vice President
Helen H. Curnow, Secretary

Permanent staff: NI   Membership: 75
Date founded: 1964   Membership dues: $6.00
Branches: none   Scope: local

Special requirements for membership: none

Nature of organization: charitable

Publications: *A Magyar Segítö-Szolgálat Hírei* (Newsletter), 1968–

Affiliations: none

Comments: This organization provides a home for the elderly; helps refugees and newly arrived Hungarians establish themselves in the country; and provides guidance and counseling in religious and moral matters. Offers monthly entertainment.

AMERICAN HUNGARIAN STUDIES FOUNDATION (AHSF)
177 Somerset Street
New Brunswick, New Jersey 08903   (201) 846-5777
Principal officers: August J. Molnar, Executive Director

Permanent staff: NI   Membership: NI
Date founded: 1954   Membership dues: NI
Branches: NI   Scope: national

Nature of organization: historical, cultural, educational

Publications: *Hungarian Studies* newsletter (3 issues per year); *Bulletin*

Major conventions/meetings: annual awards dinner

Comments: The intent of the organization is to aid persons and organizations of Hungarian background; it supports research and publication of Hungarian topics and studies in secondary and college level schools and universities. It presents awards to those aiding Hungarians and to Hungarians achieving success in the United States. Plans to construct a Hungarian Center and Hungarian Research Center. Maintains a library of 33,000 volumes, plus paintings and rare books.

BUCKEYE NEIGHBORHOOD NATIONALITIES CIVIC ASSOCIATION, INC. (BNNCA)
2910 East Boulevard
Cleveland, Ohio 44104   (216) 421-7774
Principal officers: J. Chelenko, President
J. Palasics, Executive Vice President
Anne Comoa, Executive Secretary

Permanent staff: none   Membership: NI
Date founded: 1960   Membership dues: $1.00 (annual)
Branches: none   Scope: local

BUCKEYE NEIGHBORHOOD NATIONALITIES CIVIC ASSOCIATION, INC. (BNNCA) (cont'd)

Special requirements for membership: none

Nature of organization: civic

Publications: *BNNCA Newsletter*

Affiliations: none

Major conventions/meetings: biennial general meeting

Comments: Originally consisted of Hungarians, but now also includes Slovaks. The purpose of the organization is to provide a medium for these and other nationality groups of the community to work toward the retention of the ethnic nature of the geographic area. Encourages the perpetuation of folk festivals and provides a community forum that serves as a voice for elderly and non-English-speaking community residents.

CALIFORNIA HUNGARIAN AMERICAN CULTURAL FOUNDATION, INC.
9727 Corbin Avenue
Northridge, California 91324   (213) 349-8933

Principal officers: George Ashley, President
                        Joseph S. Toth, Executive Vice President
                        Gyula Czudar, Executive Secretary

Permanent staff: 5   Membership: 120
Date founded: 1969   Membership dues: $25.00 (annual)
Branches: none   Scope: national

Special requirements for membership: Hungarian ancestry

Nature of organization: cultural

Publications: none

Affiliations: none

Major conventions/meetings: annual general assembly

Comments: Foundation maintains a private library, organizes cultural and musical presentations, and provides information on Hungarian culture throughout the world. Encourages the retention of the Hungarian cultural heritage. Also provides assistance to scientists, artists, and authors of Hungarian ancestry in the publication of their works in any language. Organizes charter flights all over the world. Offers citizenship courses. Maintains a library of over 5,000 volumes.

CALIFORNIA HUNGARIANS
648 North Western Avenue
Los Angeles, California 90004

CLEVELAND MAGYAR ATHLETIC CLUB
4125 Lorain Road
Cleveland, Ohio 44113   (216) 651-6083

Principal officers: Dezsö L. Frigyes, President
                        Kálmán Elek, Vice President
                        Tibor Lovagi, Secretary

Permanent staff: 21   Membership: 585
Date founded: 1957   Membership dues: $10.00 (annual)
Branches: none   Scope: local

Special requirements for membership: none

Nature of organization: sports

Affiliations: United Hungarian Societies

Major conventions/meetings: annual

CLEVELAND MAGYAR ATHLETIC CLUB (cont'd)

Comments: This Cleveland facility, owned and operated by Hungarian Americans, also houses several other organizations. It provides facilities and equipment for sports events and sponsors internationally known Hungarian athletes as guest visitors. Included is a gym, a rifle range, club rooms, chess teams, fencing, boxing, volleyball, and soccer. It sponsors an annual Athletic Ball and gives a Sportsman of the Year award to a young man and woman at this event.

COORDINATING COMMITTEE OF HUNGARIAN CHURCHES AND ORGANIZATIONS OF METROPOLITAN DETROIT
Holy Cross Church
8423 South Street
Detroit, Michigan 48200

DETROIT'S FIRST SZEKELY MAGYAR ASSOCIATION
855 Manistique
Detroit, Michigan 48200

FEDERATION OF HUNGARIAN FORMER POLITICAL PRISONERS
45 East End Avenue
New York, New York 10028

Permanent staff: NI
Date founded: 1951
Branches: NI

Membership: 15,000
Membership dues: NI
Scope: national

Comments: The federation is comprised of former political prisoners in Hungary, either during World War II in Nazi or Soviet concentration camps, or as part of the 1956 Freedom Fighters revolt. It seeks to promote release of imprisoned Hungarians and publishes and distributes literature on the subject.

FIRST HUNGARIAN LITERARY SOCIETY (FHLS)
30 East 30th Street
New York, New York 10021   (212) 734-9163

Principal officers: Rose Weiss, Recording Secretary

Permanent staff: 25
Date founded: NI
Branches: 6

Membership: 600
Membership dues: NI
Scope: NI

Nature of organization: social, cultural, fraternal

Publications: *Literary Herald*, 1955– (monthly)

Comments: A social and benevolent organization for persons of Hungarian descent.

HUNGARIA FREEDOM FIGHTER MOVEMENT (HFM)
41 Wilson Avenue
Clarion, Pennsylvania 16214   (814) 226-6952

Principal officers: Andor S. Jobb de Papos, President
Elemer Papay, Vice President and Secretary
Tibor Major, Propoganda

Permanent staff: 25
Date founded: 1960 (U.S.A.)
Branches: NI

Membership: NI
Membership dues: varies locally
Scope: international

Special requirements for membership: must be of Hungarian origin

Nature of organization: political, social, educational, cultural, religious, economic, professional, fraternal, scholarly, youth

Publications: *Scytha-Call*, 1960– (monthly)

Affiliations: Cross and Sword Movement; Turul Society

Major conventions/meetings: quarterly leadership meetings; annual convention

HUNGARIA FREEDOM FIGHTER MOVEMENT (HFM) (cont'd)

Comments: A non-profit organization, HFM (or HSZM) is a grassroots movement that exists
to fight for the objectives of the October 23rd, 1956, Hungarian Freedom Fight. These
objectives include an end of foreign domination of Hungary, withdrawal of Soviet
armies, neutrality of Hungary, the establishment of a freely elected government by the
Hungarian people, and restoration of the Hungarian borders that existed prior to 1920.
Organizes lectures, exhibits, and seminars. Maintains a large archival collection.

HUNGARIAN ALUMNI ASSOCIATION
P.O. Box 174
New Brunswick, New Jersey 08903

Principal officers: István Hamza, President
Gyula Oroszváry, Vice President
Judit Antal, Secretary

Permanent staff: NI   Membership: 45
Date founded: 1960   Membership dues: none
Branches: none   Scope: regional

Special requirements for membership: acceptance by membership

Nature of organization: educational, cultural

Publications: none

Affiliations: none

Major conventions/meetings: bimonthly meetings

Comments: The organization attempts to preserve Hungarian art, language, and culture in the
United States by sponsoring a Hungarian school, exhibits, literary and musical programs,
conferences, lectures, etc. College scholarships are granted to students of Hungarian
descent.

HUNGARIAN ARTS CLUB
8683 Dearborn Avenue
Detroit, Michigan 48200   (313) 841-6758

Principal officers: Louis F. Almassy

Permanent staff: NI   Membership: NI
Date founded: NI   Membership dues: NI
Branches: NI   Scope: local

Nature of organization: cultural

Major conventions/meetings: annual

Comments: The organization's goal is to preserve Hungarian traditions and culture in the
United States. It sponsors fund-raising activities to support a scholarship for a Hungarian
student.

HUNGARIAN BAPTIST UNION OF AMERICA
748 Fordham Road
Palm Bay, Florida 32901

Publications: *Evangeliumi Hirnok*, 1908– (semimonthly)

HUNGARIAN CATHOLIC LEAGUE OF AMERICA
30 East 30th Street
New York, New York 10016

Principal officers: Msgr. John S. Sabo, President

Permanent staff: NI   Membership: NI
Date founded: 1943   Membership dues: NI
Branches: 15 state groups   Scope: national

Special requirements for membership: a Catholic of Hungarian descent

Nature of organization: religious, cultural, charitable

Publications: *Catholic Hungarian Sunday* (weekly)

HUNGARIAN CATHOLIC LEAGUE OF AMERICA (cont'd)

Comments: Attempts to aid Hungarian refugees and preserve the Hungarian culture by serving as financial sponsor for Hungarian schools and institutions in Western Europe.

HUNGARIAN CENTRAL COMMITTEE FOR BOOKS AND EDUCATION
16403 Southland Avenue
Cleveland, Ohio 44111 (216) 671-0669

Principal officers: Dr. Gabor Papp, President

Permanent staff: NI	Membership: NI
Date founded: 1958	Membership dues: NI
Branches: NI	Scope: NI

Special requirements for membership: Hungarian descent

Nature of organization: philanthropic

Affiliations: Hungarian School Care Club

Comments: Raises funds for scholarships for Hungarian students in the United States through cultural programs such as concerts, patriotic programs, etc.

HUNGARIAN COMMITTEE
225 East 72nd Street
New York, New York 10021   (212) 744-8210

Principal officers: Msgr. Bela Varga, Chairman

Permanent staff: 3	Membership: NI
Date founded: 1948	Membership dues: NI
Branches: NI	Scope: national

Special requirements for membership: Hungarians who have left Hungary since World War II as political refugees

Nature of organization: political

Publications: publishes books

Affiliations: Assembly of Captive European Nations

Major conventions/meetings: monthly

Comments: The purpose of the organization is to help achieve the restoration of a free Hungarian government. It was formed by merger of the Hungarian National Council and the National Representation of Free Hungary.

HUNGARIAN CULTURAL FOUNDATION, INC. (HCF)
P.O. Box 364
Stone Mountain, Georgia 30083

Principal officers: Joseph M. Ertavy-Barath, President
Steven B. Vardy, Executive Vice President
Katalin Ertavy-Barath, Executive Secretary

Permanent staff: none	Membership: 49
Date founded: 1966	Membership dues: $10.00 (annual)
Branches: NI	Scope: national

Special requirements for membership: "Must have the recommendation of 2 members"

Nature of organization: cultural

Publications: publishes books

Affiliations: none

Major conventions/meetings: annual conference

Comments: Promotes cultural activities and publishes Hungarian literary works. Also has a scholarship fund. Maintains both a library and archives.

HUNGARIAN ETHNIC STUDIES
P.O. Box 45143
Los Angeles, California 90045

HUNGARIAN FREEDOM FIGHTERS FEDERATION, INC. (HFFF)

P.O. Box 214, Union City Station (201) 567-8156 or
Union City, New Jersey 07087 (201) 762-3674

Principal officers: András Pogány, President
Ist ván Gereben, Executive Vice President
George Lovas, Secretary-General

Permanent staff: none
Date founded: 1957
Branches: 29 local

Membership: NI
Membership dues: $10.00 (annual)
Scope: national

Special requirements for membership: none

Nature of organization: educational, cultural, fraternal

Publications: *The Hungarian Freedom Fighter*, 1961— (irregular); *Message*, 1967— (irregular); also publishes books

Affiliations: World Federation of Hungarian Freedom Fighters

Major conventions/meetings: triennial convention

Comments: Principal objectives are the implementation of the ideals of the 1956 Hungarian Fight for Freedom and the dissemination of political information about Hungary to the American public. Promotes educational, cultural, and political activities among Hungarian-Americans. Provides assistance to Hungarian refugees arriving in the United States. The state and local chapters organize their own programs and activities, youth camps, Sunday Schools, Boy Scout units, and social and cultural events. They also publish their own state and local newsletters. HFFF coordinates all branch activities. Also presents an annual Freedom Award. Maintains a library collection of over 650 volumes as well as archival materials such as correspondence, manuscripts, etc.

HUNGARIAN LADIES' SODALITY

3705 Woodlawn Avenue
Los Angeles, California 90011 (213) 234-9246

Principal officers: Theresa Racz, President
Theresa Kerekes, Vice President
Margaret Tasnady, Secretary

Permanent staff: 12
Date founded: 1928
Branches: none

Membership: 80
Membership dues: $2.00 (annual)
Scope: local

Special requirements for membership: Hungarian descent

Nature of organization: religious, cultural, social

Publications: *St. Stephen's Letter* (St. István Körlevél), 1959— (monthly)

Affiliations: Parish Church; Los Angeles Hungarian Diocese

Major conventions/meetings: monthly meeting

Comments: Sponsors social and spiritual gatherings. Promotes the retention of the Hungarian culture, traditions, and language. Maintains a library collection of 1,000 volumes.

HUNGARIAN LIBRARY ASSOCIATION OF AMERICA

810 Loxford Terrace
Silver Spring, Maryland 20901

HUNGARIAN LITERARY SOCIETY

323 East 79th Street
New York, New York 10021

THE HUNGARIAN REFORMED FEDERATION OF AMERICA
3216 New Mexico Avenue, N.W.
Washington, D.C. 20016   (202) 244-7555
Principal officers: Zoltan Beky, President
                        Stephen Szabo, Executive Vice President
                        Arpad George, Executive Secretary

Permanent staff: 18   Membership: 35,000
Date founded: 1896   Membership dues: insurance premium
Branches: 194 regional, state, and local   dues
                                             Scope: national

Special requirements for membership: insurance—life
Nature of organization: fraternal, benefit insurance
Publications: *Fraternity*, 1898— (quarterly); also publishes books
Affiliations: none
Major conventions/meetings: quadrennial convention
Comments: Fraternal organization providing various types of insurances to its members. Also
    organizes a summer school on Hungarian culture, language, and traditions. Maintains
    a scholarship fund. Supports a children's and old-age home in Pennsylvania.

HUNGARIAN SCOUTS ASSOCIATION
P.O. Box 68
Garfield, New Jersey 07626   (201) 772-8810
Principal officers: Gabor Bodnár, President
                        Stephen Gerencser, Executive Vice President
                        Elza Pal, Executive Secretary

Permanent staff: 3   Membership: 5,000
Date founded: 1958 (U.S.A.); 1910 Hungary   Membership dues: $2.00 (annual)
Branches: 80 units (state and local)   Scope: national, international

Special requirements for membership: none
Nature of organization: educational, youth
Publications: *Hungarian Scout Magazine*, 1948— (monthly); *Leaders Magazine*, 1952—
    (monthly); also publishes pocket books and instruction manuals
Affiliations: church and fraternal societies
Major conventions/meetings: annual Leaders Conference; biannual convention
Comments: Provides the usual Scouting activities with accepted world Scouting standards.
    Also teaches Hungarian culture, literature, history, and folklore. Holds camps for both
    boys and girls from ages 8 to 18. Organizes summer schools for leadership training.
    Maintains a library of 2,000 volumes and also archives.

HUNGARIAN WORLD FEDERATION OF THE DEFENSE OF NATION
P.O. Box 38031
Hollywood, California 90038
Publications: *Nemzetvedelmi Tajekoztato* (Information about Defense of Nation), 1967—
    (monthly)

KOSSUTH FOUNDATION (KF)
c/o Butler University
Indianapolis, Indiana 46208   (317) 923-3451
Principal officers: Dr. Janos Horvath, President

Permanent staff: 3   Membership: NI
Date founded: 1957   Membership dues: NI
Branches: NI   Scope: national

Special requirements for membership: none
Nature of organization: cultural, philanthropic
Publications: *The Kossuth Foundation Bulletin* (monthly)

KOSSUTH FOUNDATION (KF) (cont'd)

Comments: Aids Hungarian students in the United States; supports scholarly studies concerning Hungarian history and culture, promotes Hungarian and United States relations. Maintains a 3,000-volume Hungarian research library.

M.H.B.K. HUNGARIAN VETERANS

19772 Goulburn
Detroit, Michigan 48200   (313) 839-2747

Principal officers: Ethel Palfi

Permanent staff: NI   Membership: NI
Date founded: NI   Membership dues: NI
Branches: NI   Scope: local

Nature of organization: social

Comments: A social group which meets at the various local Hungarian churches.

MAGYAR COMMUNION OF FRIENDS

P.O. Box 112
Ada, Ohio 45810   (419) 634-2056

Principal officers: Louis J. Elteto, Editor
                       Andrew Ludányi, Office Manager

Permanent staff: 4   Membership: 600
Date founded: 1967   Membership dues: voluntary contribu-
Branches: none   tions (average $15.00 per year)
                                        Scope: international

Special requirements for membership: none

Nature of organization: cultural, religious

Publications: *Itt-Ott*, 1967– (bimonthly)

Affiliations: Hungarian Cultural and Educational House, Chicago

Major conventions/meetings: annual seminar

Comments: A non-denominational religious and cultural society which promotes Hungarian culture and traditions in the United States.

PATRIA

P.O. Box 2727
Cleveland, Ohio 44111   (216) 521-2005

Principal officers: Dennis Frigyes, President
                       Richard Örley, Vice President
                       Susan Papp, Secretary

Permanent staff: 12   Membership: 116
Date founded: 1973   Membership dues: $10.00 (annual)
Branches: NI   Scope: local

Special requirements for membership: must be between 18-30 years of age and be sponsored by two members

Nature of organization: professional, fraternal, youth

Publications: *Patria–The Newspaper of Young Hungarians*, 1974– (quarterly)

Major conventions/meetings: semiannual

Comments: The purpose of the organization is to provide leaders within the Hungarian community as teachers in the Hungarian schools, leaders in Hungarian Scout groups and in the local sport clubs. Besides publishing a bilingual newspaper, the group sponsors frequent radio programs and serves as the voice of the Hungarian community. Maintains a small library.

ST. STEPHEN'S HUNGARIAN CATHOLIC SOCIETY

3705 Woodlawn Avenue
Los Angeles, California 90011

SOUTHERN CALIFORNIA AMERICAN HUNGARIAN CLUB
992 West San Bernardino Avenue
Bloomington, California 92316   (714) 875-9273
Principal officers: William Somsak, President
                   Agnes Loerincze, Secretary

Permanent staff: 6   Membership: 182
Date founded: 1952   Membership dues: $6.00 (annual)
Branches: none   Scope: local
Special requirements for membership: recommendation
Nature of organization: social, cultural, charitable
Publications: none
Affiliations: none
Major conventions/meetings: monthly

Comments: The purpose of the organization is to unite Hungarians in the United States and to provide social and cultural activities that help preserve the Hungarian heritage in America. Also supports various philanthropic works.

SZENT ISTVÁN MAGYAR R.K. EGYESÜLET (Saint Stephen Roman Catholic Association)
2595 Las Lunas Avenue
Pasadena, California 91107
Principal officers: Romváry Ernö, Elnok (President)

UNITED HUNGARIAN FUND, INC.
P.O. Box 10171
Cleveland, Ohio 44110

THE "VIRRASZTO" RESEARCH COMMITTEE
45-54 41st Street
Apartment 6E
Long Island City, New York 11104
Publications: *Virrasztó* (Watcher), 1970–

WILLIAM PENN ASSOCIATION (WPA)
429 Forbes Avenue
Pittsburgh, Pennsylvania 12500   (412) 281-8950
Principal officers: A. J. Stelkovics, Secretary

Permanent staff: NI   Membership: 66,839
Date founded: 1886   Membership dues: varies with policy
Branches: 84   Scope: national
Nature of organization: fraternal
Publications: *William Penn Life*, 1965– (monthly)
Major conventions/meetings: quadrennial (Pittsburgh)

Comments: The major purpose of the organization is to provide life insurance benefits to its members.

WISCONSIN HUNGARIANS
609 North Plankinto Avenue, Room 508
Milwaukee, Wisconsin 53203

WORLD FEDERATION OF HUNGARIAN ARTISTS
416 East 85th Street
New York, New York 10028   (212) 988-4221
Principal officers: Ernest Gyimesy Kasas, President
                   Joseph Mör, Executive Vice President
                   Maria Ilona Györik, Executive Secretary

WORLD FEDERATION OF HUNGARIAN ARTISTS (cont'd)

Permanent staff: 8
Date founded: 1957
Branches: 3 regional in the U.S.A.

Membership: 400 (in exile)
Membership dues: $12.00 (annual)
Scope: national, international

Special requirements for membership: "must be a professional artist"

Nature of organization: cultural, professional

Publications: *Professional Hungarian Artists*, 1961– (3 issues per year); *Newsletter*, 1961– (irregular); also publishes books

Affiliations: various Hungarian cultural and social organizations

Major conventions/meetings: annual or periodic conventions

Comments: Organizes exhibits of Hungarian artists. Maintains an art library and archives.

ICELANDIC-AMERICAN ORGANIZATIONS

See also Scandinavian-American Organizations

Additional information on Icelandic-American organizations may be obtained from the Office of the Icelandic Embassy (2022 Connecticut Avenue, Washington, D.C. 20008).

THE HEKLA CLUB
c/o Mildred E. Olson
2101 East River Terrace
Minneapolis, Minnesota 55414

Principal officers: Mildred E. Olson, President
Herdis Sigtrygsson, Vice President
Vera Younger, Secretary
Gail Magnusson, Treasurer

Permanent staff: none
Date founded: NI
Branches: none

Membership: 66
Membership dues: $2.00
Scope: local

Special requirements for membership: any woman who is of Icelandic ancestry or the wife of an Icelander

Nature of organization: social, cultural, fraternal

Publications: none

Major conventions/meetings: nine meetings a year

Comments: Promotes a sense of fellowship among individuals of Icelandic descent. Provides assistance to the sick, aged, and needy. Also encourages the retention of Icelandic culture and traditions.

ICELAND VETERANS
2101 Walnut Street
Philadelphia, Pennsylvania 19103   (215) 568-1234

Principal officers: Dave Zinkoff, Caretaker

Permanent staff: NI
Date founded: 1950
Branches: NI

Membership: 1,500
Membership dues: NI
Scope: NI

Special requirements for membership: persons who served in the armed forces or Red Cross during or after World War II

Nature of organization: social

ICELAND VETERANS (cont'd)

Publications: *White Falcon, Jr.* (annual)

Major conventions/meetings: annual

Comments: The major purpose of the organization is to unite Icelandic veterans in the United States. It is also known as "Forgotten Boys of Iceland."

ICELANDIC-AMERICAN CLUB
> c/o Mrs. Olafur Backmann
> P.O. Box 618
> Los Alamitos, California 90720

ICELANDIC-AMERICAN SOCIETY OF NEW YORK
> 630 Fifth Avenue, Room 620
> New York, New York 10020   (212) 974-3867

Principal officers: Sigurdur Helgason, President
                       Stefan Wathne, Vice President
                       Hans Indridason, Secretary

Permanent staff: none   Membership: 600
Date founded: 1942   Membership dues: none
Branches: none   Scope: regional

Special requirements for membership: none

Nature of organization: cultural, social

Publications: none

Affiliations: none

Major conventions/meetings: biannual

Comments: Encourages the preservation of contacts between Icelanders living on the Eastern Coast, especially in New York. Organizes various social and cultural events to promote fellowship.

ICELANDIC ASSOCIATION OF CHICAGO
> 820 Warwick Road
> Deerfield, Illinois 60015

Principal officers: Valur Egilsson, D.D.S., President

THE ICELANDIC ASSOCIATION OF WASHINGTON, D.C.
> 2022 Connecticut Avenue, N.W.
> Washington, D.C. 20008   (202) 234-2929

Principal officers: Sigrun Rockmaker, President
                       Asgeir Petursson, Vice President
                       Svava Vernhards, Secretary
                       Margret Alfonsson, Treasurer

Permanent staff: NI   Membership: NI
Date founded: 1968   Membership dues: $5.00 per family;
Branches: NI $3.00 single
                                        Scope: local

Special requirements for membership: Icelandic heritage or interest in Iceland

Nature of organization: cultural, social

Affiliations: Scandinavian Joint Planning Council of Washington, D.C.

Major conventions/meetings: annual meeting

Comments: The purpose of the association is to provide persons of Icelandic descent with a sense of sociability and fellowship. The organization encourages the preservation of ties with Iceland and Icelandic traditions. The group sponsors various luncheon meetings and dinner-dances.

THE ICELANDIC CLUB OF GREATER SEATTLE
7342 11th Street, N.E.
Seattle, Washington 98115
Principal officers: Vigfus Jakobsson

INDIAN-AMERICAN ORGANIZATIONS

See also Asian-American Organizations

Additional information on Indian-American organizations may be obtained from the Office of the Indian Embassy (2107 Massachusetts Avenue, Washington, D.C. 20008), the Indian Chamber of Commerce of America (501 Fifth Avenue, Suite 1809, New York, New York 10017), and *India Guide* (New York: The Literary Guild of India, Ltd., 1974).

ASSOCIATION OF INDIANS IN AMERICA
663 Fifth Avenue
New York, New York 10022
Principal officers: Dr. Manoranjan Dutta, President
                        Dr. B. Subramanian, Vice President
                        Dr. M. Subramanian, Vice President
                        Sandra Saxena, Secretary
                        Dr. N. K. Chaudhuri, Treasurer

Permanent staff: none   Membership: NI
Date founded: 1967   Membership dues: $5.00 per person;
Branches: 10 $10.00 per family
                                           Scope: national

Special requirements for membership: of Asian-Indian background
Nature of organization: social, educational, cultural, religious, economic
Publications: *From the National Headquarters: AIA*, 1972– (quarterly)
Affiliations: none
Comments: The main purpose of the organization is to preserve Indian culture in the United States and to unite Indian-Americans in social, recreational, religious, economic, educational, and cultural programs and activities. It sponsors dinners, lectures, family camps, and voluntary community services such as fire protection. It promotes research on Indian immigrants to America, and provides assistance to these immigrants. An annual Association of Indians in America award is made to Indian-Americans who have made outstanding contributions to U.S. society in the arts or sciences. Also sponsors special councils for professional groups–e.g., medical affairs, engineering, economics, etc.

BENGAL RELIEF GROUP
Case Western Reserve University
Cleveland, Ohio 44106   (216) 283-0650
Principal officers: Pranab Chatterji, President
                        Ranan Banerji, Vice President
                        M. Datta, Executive Secretary and Treasurer

Permanent staff: 5   Membership: 50
Date founded: 1971   Membership dues: $5.00 (annual)
Branches: none   Scope: NI

Special requirements for membership: none
Nature of organization: political, cultural
Publications: none

BENGAL RELIEF GROUP (cont'd)

Affiliations: none

Major conventions/meetings: none

Comments: The principal objective of the organization is to raise funds for the refugees in India, as well as in Bangladesh. The group also sponsors a cultural program during which Indian music is played.

BHARATHI CULTURAL SOCIETY OF OHIO
11639 Stormes Drive
Cleveland, Ohio 44130   (216) 581-1791

Principal officers: Dr. Dev. Suresh, President
                       M. R. Surrendran, Secretary

Permanent staff: NI   Membership: NI
Date founded: NI   Membership dues: NI
Branches: NI   Scope: state

Nature of organization: cultural, social

BHARATHI SOCIETY OF AMERICA
97-05/4K, Horace Harding Expressway
New York, New York 11368   (212) 592-8039

Principal officers: V. R. Mallikarjuneswara, President
                       R. N. Prabhakar, Executive Secretary
                       S. Ramakrishnan, Secretary

Permanent staff: none   Membership: 250
Date founded: 1967   Membership dues: $5.00 (annual)
Branches: none   Scope: national

Special requirements for membership: none

Nature of organization: cultural

Publications: *Bharathi Society Newsletter*, 1967– (irregular); also publishes program brochures

Affiliations: Joint Committee of Indian Organizations, New York

Major conventions/meetings: none

Comments: The society organizes monthly cultural events on classical Indian music, dance, and drama. In addition it encourages the celebration of major Indian festivals. It sponsors a number of social get-togethers.

BHARATHI SOCIETY OF MINNESOTA
2024 Commonwealth, No. A21
St. Paul, Minnesota 55108

CULTURAL ASSOCIATION OF BENGAL
1322 44th Street, Apartment A8   (212) 871-0661 or
Brooklyn, New York 11219   (212) 475-4613

Principal officers: Ranajit Kumar Datta, President
                       M. K. Datta, Vice President
                       Prabir Kumar Roy, Secretary

Permanent staff: none   Membership: 150
Date founded: 1971   Membership dues: $10.00 (annual)
Branches: none   Scope: national

Special requirements for membership: none

Nature of organization: social, educational, cultural, recreational

Publications: *Sangbad Bichitra*, 1971– (monthly news bulletin)

Affiliations: none

CULTURAL ASSOCIATION OF BENGAL (cont'd)

Major conventions/meetings: none

Comments: A non-profit, non-political, and non-sectarian organization. The association's aim is to foster the cultural and social heritage of Bengal, to popularize the Bengali language and literature in the United States, and to promote cultural exchange between the United States and India and Bangladesh. In order to achieve these objectives, the association is establishing libraries containing books and journals (four such libraries are already in operation), organizing cultural, social and recreational programs, and establishing classes on Bengali language, culture, and history for Bengali children. Many children's classes are already in progress.

FEDERATION OF INDIA ASSOCIATIONS OF THE UNITED STATES AND CANADA

P.O. Box 295
Ann Arbor, Michigan 48107

Principal officers: M. B. Suryanarayana, Secretary

Permanent staff: NI
Date founded: 1969
Branches: NI

Membership: 3,050
Membership dues: NI
Scope: national

Nature of organization: cultural

Publications: *India Digest* (semiannual); *India Federation News* (semiannual)

Major conventions/meetings: annual

Comments: The purpose of the organization is to serve as a nucleus and coordinating agency for various Indian organizations in the United States and Canada. It organizes cultural and educational programs, trips, and activities, and it provides relief funds to Indian students. Sponsors school contests and awards for scholarship and outstanding contributions to American society. In 1970 it absorbed the Federation of India Student Associations of the United States of America, and in 1971 the Indo-American Sports Association.

FRIENDS OF INDIA COMMITTEE

910 17th Street, N.W.
Washington, D.C. 20006   (202) 296-4415

Principal officers: Norman D. Palmer, Chairman

Permanent staff: NI
Date founded: 1961
Branches: NI

Membership: NI
Membership dues: NI
Scope: national

Nature of organization: cultural

Comments: Seeks to promote India-U.S. relations and an exchange of cultural knowledge and understanding. Presently inactive.

HIMALAYA CULTURAL SOCIETY

1646 First Avenue
New York, New York 10028

HINDU CENTER

Des Raj Puri
38-17 Parsons Boulevard
Flushing, New York 11357

Principal officers: Des Raj Puri, President

THE HINDU TEMPLE SOCIETY OF NORTH AMERICA

84-39 Kendrick Place
Jamaica, New York 11432   (212) 657-8731

Principal officers: E. C. Grigg, President
                       A. Alagappan, Secretary

THE HINDU TEMPLE SOCIETY OF NORTH AMERICA (cont'd)

Permanent staff: none   Membership: 250
Date founded: 1970   Membership dues: none
Branches: 1 regional   Scope: national, local

Special requirements for membership: none

Nature of organization: cultural, religious

Publications: none

Affiliations: Balaji Temple at Tirupati, India; Endowments Department, Government of
     Andmra Pradesh, India

Major conventions/meetings: none

Comments: The purpose of this society is to provide a nucleus around which persons of
     Indian origin may develop a wide spectrum of religious, cultural, and social activities.
     Plans are in operation to build a temple in the Hindu style, to establish a gallery contain-
     ing Indian sculpture, and to build a library and auditorium.

INDIA ASSOCIATION OF CLEVELAND (IAC)

18658 Parkland Drive   (216) 831-9373 or
Shaker Heights, Ohio 44122   (216) 751-2432

Principal officers: L. N. Sampath, President
                 S. K. Usman, Executive Vice President
                 N. Chawla, Executive Secretary

Permanent staff: none   Membership: 500
Date founded: 1964   Membership dues: $5.00 family (annual);
Branches: none $3.00 single (annual)
       Scope: local

Special requirements for membership: must be Indian citizen; associate members can be
     non-Indians

Nature of organization: social, cultural

Publications: none

Affiliations: none

Major conventions/meetings: none

Comments: The objectives are to provide the people of Cleveland, Ohio, with a picture of
     Indian traditions, customs, and recent Indian developments. The association arranges the
     celebration of Indian national holidays, encourages closer ties among the Indians of
     Cleveland, and promotes friendship and cultural exchanges with similar ethnic or non-
     ethnic organizations.

INDIA CHAMBER OF COMMERCE OF AMERICA

501 Fifth Avenue, Suite 1809
New York, New York 10017   (212) 986-1885

Principal officers: Fergus M. Sloan, Executive Secretary

Permanent staff: NI   Membership: 80
Date founded: 1938   Membership dues: NI
Branches: NI   Scope: NI

Nature of organization: economic

INDIA CLUB OF COLUMBIA UNIVERSITY (ICCU)

Foreign Student Center
Columbia University
New York, New York 10027   (212) 280-4857

Principal officers: Kiran Seth, President
                 S. Dasgupta, Vice President
                 Renu Verma, Secretary

Permanent staff: none   Membership: 110
Date founded: 1963   Membership dues: $1.00 (annual)
Branches: none   Scope: local

INDIA CLUB OF COLUMBIA UNIVERSITY (ICCU) (cont'd)

Special requirements for membership: students and alumni of Columbia University

Nature of organization: social, cultural

Publications: *Bharat Darshan* (irregular news periodical)

Affiliations: none

Major conventions/meetings: none

Comments: The club is essentially a student and alumni organization of Columbia University. The objective of the club is to promote better understanding among Indian, American, and other students at the university. The club has organized periodic social and cultural functions such as celebration of Indian festivals, music, and dance concerts, visiting local Indian artists, and the screening of Indian films. The club also sponsors a two-hour weekly program of Indian music. The club has established a trust for the promotion of education in India. It has also donated funds for Bangladesh refugees as well as for agricultural, educational, and technological programs in India.

INDIA FRIENDSHIP ASSOCIATION (IFA)

P.O. Box 731
Flushing, New York 11352   (212) 961-3497

Principal officers: M. Bajaj, President
                       V. Malhotra, Executive Vice President
                       A. Sharma, Executive Secretary

Permanent staff: none   Membership: 300
Date founded: 1970   Membership dues: $5.00 (annual)
Branches: none   Scope: national

Special requirements for membership: none

Nature of organization: social, educational, cultural, religious

Publications: *Jyoti*, 1970– (quarterly)

Affiliations: AIA; Hindu Center; ICLANA

Major conventions/meetings: biennial conference

Comments: The association organizes various events of a social, cultural, and religious nature. Also promotes teaching of Indian culture and heritage.

JOINT COMMITTEE OF INDIAN ASSOCIATIONS

c/o Mr. Thomas Puspamanpla
Department of Biology
New York University
Washington Square
New York, New York 10012

LITERARY GUILD OF INDIA, LTD.

P.O. Box 309, Times Plaza Station
Brooklyn, New York 11217   (212) 624-0561

Principal officers: Lalita Rananaware, Executive Director

Permanent staff: NI   Membership: NI
Date founded: NI   Membership dues: NI
Branches: NI   Scope: national

Nature of organization: cultural, professional, scholarly

Publications: *India Guide*

Comments: The major purpose of the organization is to sponsor cultural activities for Indians in the United States–e.g., folk dances, art, etc.–and to publish materials on India. It sponsors India Day at the American Museum of Natural History in New York.

MAHARASHTRA MANDAL

120 West 97th Street
New York, New York 10025

Principal officers: Savita Gokhale, President

SIKH CULTURAL SOCIETY
2239 Forestdale Avenue
Cleveland, Ohio 44109
Principal officers: Ajit Brar, President
Derry Juneja, Secretary

TAGORE SOCIETY OF NEW YORK
50 Kenilworth Place, 3J
Brooklyn, New York 10038
Principal officers: Ambuj Mukherji, President

TAMIL CULTURAL ASSOCIATION OF PENNSYLVANIA
Wakefield Road
Harrisburgh, Pennsylvania 17109

TAMIL SANGAM OF NEW YORK, INC.
166 Logan Avenue
Staten Island, New York 10301   (212) 273-8885
Principal officers: P. Kumaresan, President
Sekhar J. Hendry, Executive Secretary
S. G. Shanmugasundaram, Treasurer

Permanent staff: 9	Membership: 200
Date founded: 1970	Membership dues: $5.00 (annual)
Branches: none	Scope: state

Special requirements for membership: none

Nature of organization: social, educational, cultural, recreational, professional, sport, fraternal, scholarly, youth

Publications: *Home News*, 1971– (monthly)

Affiliations: none

Major conventions/meetings: none

Comments: A non-profit organization that promotes the exchange of ideas and understanding between Tamil and other cultures, the retaining of the Tamil language and culture, and the organization of cultural and social functions.

TELUGU LITERARY AND CULTURAL ASSOCIATION
47-37 45th Street, 5J
Woodside, New York 11377

INDONESIAN-AMERICAN ORGANIZATIONS

See also Asian-American Organizations

Additional information on Indonesian-American organizations in the United States may be obtained from the Office of the Indonesian Embassy (2020 Massachusetts Avenue, Washington, D.C. 20036).

AMERICAN INDONESIAN CHAMBER OF COMMERCE
120 Wall Street
New York, New York 10005   (212) 944-4065
Principal officers: Ladd I. Johnson, Secretary

Permanent staff: NI	Membership: 100
Date founded: 1949	Membership dues: NI
Branches: NI	Scope: national

AMERICAN INDONESIAN CHAMBER OF COMMERCE (cont'd)
Nature of organization: economic
Publications: publishes information bulletins

HAWAII-INDONESIA ASSOCIATION (HIA)
    c/o Soenjono Dardjowidjojo
    Department of Indo-Pacific Languages
    University of Hawaii
    Honolulu, Hawaii 96872   (808) 948-8521
Principal officers: Soenjono Dardjowidjojo, President
                Gunther Schmidt, Vice President
                Garret Solyom, Secretary

Permanent staff: none   Membership: 90
Date founded: 1970   Membership dues: $12.00 per family
Branches: none   (annual)
                                Scope: state

Special requirements for membership: none
Nature of organization: social, educational, cultural, recreational
Publications: *Warta Hawaii-Indonesia*, 1970– (bimonthly)
Comments: This organization was formed in order to promote closer cooperation and under-
    standing between the residents of Hawaii and Indonesia. The association encourages
    cultural and educational exchange between the United States and Indonesia. It also
    sponsors social and cultural events for persons who share an interest in Indonesia.

INDONESIA-AMERICAN SOCIETY OF THE UNITED STATES
    c/o John R. Jeffries
    2522 Heading Street
    San Jose, California 95128

INDONESIAN COMMUNITY ASSOCIATION, INC.
    13509 Rockway Drive
    Baldwin Park, California 91706
Special requirements for membership: former resident of Indonesia

INDONESIAN STUDENTS' ASSOCIATION IN THE UNITED STATES
    P.O. Box 2527
    San Francisco, California 94126

Permanent staff: NI   Membership: 600
Date founded: 1961   Membership dues: NI
Branches: 42   Scope: national
Nature of organization: cultural, educational, scholarly
Publications: *Arena PERMIAS* (also known as *Persatuan Mahasiswa Indonesia di Amerika
    Serikat*) (monthly)
Major conventions/meetings: annual convention; also holds semiannual symposiums

SOCIETY FOR AMERICAN-INDONESIAN FRIENDSHIP, INC.
    P.O. Box 1124
    Newark, Delaware 19711

IRANIAN-AMERICAN ORGANIZATIONS

Additional information on Iranian-American organizations in the United States may be obtained from the Office of the Iranian Embassy (3005 Massachusetts Avenue, Washington, D.C. 20008).

IRAN AMERICAN CHAMBER OF COMMERCE (IACC)
Overhill Building
Scarsdale, New York 10583   (914) 723-5229
Principal officers: Ahmad Saidi, Executive Secretary

Permanent staff: NI   Membership: 75
Date founded: 1945   Membership dues: NI
Branches: NI   Scope: national

Nature of organization: economic

Publications: *Iran American Newsletter* (monthly); *Iran American Review* (annual)

Major conventions/meetings: annual

THE IRAN FOUNDATION, INC.
350 Fifth Avenue
New York, New York 10001   (212) 655-5920
Principal officers: A. Torab Mehra, President
                       Bettina Warburg, Executive Vice President and Secretary
                       Nasroollah Khosroshahi, Treasurer

Permanent staff: 1   Membership: 28
Date founded: 1948   Membership dues: NI
Branches: NI   Scope: U.S. and Iran

Special requirements for membership: none

Nature of organization: educational, cultural, professional

Publications: brochures

Affiliations: none

Major conventions/meetings: annual meeting of the Board of Directors and the Medical Council

Comments: Promotes cultural and educational cooperation between the United States and Iran. Also provides transportation assistance for visiting lecturers and professional consultants going to Iran.

IRANIAN-AMERICAN SOCIETY OF THE U.S., INC.
1503 Amshire Road
Lutherville, Maryland 21093

IRANIAN STUDENTS' ASSOCIATION IN THE UNITED STATES (ISAUS)
P.O. Box 16366
San Francisco, California 94116

IRAQI-AMERICAN ORGANIZATIONS

See Arab-American Organizations

IRISH-AMERICAN ORGANIZATIONS

Additional information on Irish-American organizations in the United States may be obtained from the Office of the Irish Embassy (2234 Massachusetts Avenue, Washington, D.C. 20008). Regional and local organizations may be found in *Greater Cleveland Nationalities Directory 1974* (Cleveland: Sun Newspapers and the Nationalities Services Center, 1974) and *Ethnic Directory I* (Detroit: Southeastern Michigan Regional Ethnic Heritage Studies Center, 1973).

AMERICAN COMMITTEE FOR IRISH STUDIES
English Department
University of Wisconsin
Milwaukee, Wisconsin 53201   (414) 963-4508

Principal officers: John R. Moore, President
L. J. McCaffrey, Vice President
Janet E. Dunleavy, Secretary

Permanent staff: none   Membership: 400
Date founded: 1962   Membership dues: $6.00
Branches: NI   Scope: national

Special requirements for membership: academic interest in Irish studies

Nature of organization: professional, scholarly

Publications: a quarterly newsletter

Affiliations: International Association for the Study of Anglo-Irish Literature (ISAIL); Canadian Association for Irish Studies (CAIS); American Irish Historical Studies (AIHS)

Major conventions/meetings: annual conference

Comments: This is a scholarly interdisciplinary organization whose members are faculty and graduate students in the fields of literature, history, political science, sociology, art, music, and language. Members regularly plan and present section meetings and seminars for the programs of the national Modern Language Association and the American Historical Association. Throughout the year they plan and present symposia in Irish studies at their own universities and for the annual meeting of ACIS. The organization maintains an archival collection.

AMERICAN COMMITTEE FOR ULSTER JUSTICE
353 West 57th Street, Room 333
New York, New York 10019   (212) 581-5578

Principal officers: Dermot Foley, Chairman

Permanent staff: NI   Membership: 600
Date founded: 1971   Membership dues: NI
Branches: 21   Scope: NI

Nature of organization: political

Publications: *Newsletter* (monthly)

Comments: This political organization attempts to disseminate information on and to protest the British occupation of Ireland. It sponsors speakers, films, and lobbying before Congress. A library is maintained.

AMERICAN IRISH HISTORICAL SOCIETY (AIHS)
991 Fifth Avenue
New York, New York 10028   (212) 288-2263

Principal officers: Joseph T. P. Sullivan, President-General
William Griffin, Secretary-General

AMERICAN IRISH HISTORICAL SOCIETY (AIHS) (cont'd)

Permanent staff: 1   Membership: NI

Date founded: 1897   Membership dues: $50.00 over 35

Branches: none   (annual); $25.00 under 35 (annual)

       Scope: national

Special requirements for membership: none

Nature of organization: educational

Publications: *The Recorder of the American Irish Historical Society*, 1901– (annual); *The Bulletin of the American Irish Historical Society*, 1973– (semiannual)

Affiliations: none

Major conventions/meetings: none

Comments: The major objective of the society is to preserve the Irish heritage in America. Maintains a library of 25,000 volumes and an archival collection. A medal is presented annually to a person of Irish descent for outstanding contributions to American society.

ANCIENT ORDER OF HIBERNIANS IN AMERICA (AOH)
27 Mada Avenue
Staten Island, New York 10310

Principal officers: William J. Barnett, Jr., National Secretary

Permanent staff: 12   Membership: 191,000

Date founded: 1836   Membership dues: NI

Branches: 736 local groups   Scope: NI

Special requirements for membership: of Irish-Catholic background

Publications: *National Hibernian Digest* (bimonthly)

Major conventions/meetings: biennial

Comments: The major purpose of the organization is to provide life insurance benefits to members.

BANSHEES (IRISH LITERARY SOCIETIES)
c/o Mr. Joseph B. Foley, President
2915 Cathedral Avenue, N.W.
Washington, D.C. 20008

Principal officers: Joseph B. Foley, President

CHICAGO GAELIC SOCIETY
6004 South Fairfield
Chicago, Illinois 60629   (312) 476-5682

Principal officers: Patrick Brankin, President
                   John McCullough, Treasurer

Permanent staff: none   Membership: 78

Date founded: 1973   Membership dues: $3.00 (annual)

Branches: none   Scope: local

Special requirements for membership: desire to preserve and extend the use of the Gaelic language

Nature of organization: social, educational, cultural

Publications: *An Mheitheal*, Jan. 1975– (monthly)

Affiliations: Conradh na Gaeilge, Dublin, Ireland

Major conventions/meetings: annual

Comments: The purpose of the organization is to preserve the Irish customs and language in the United States. Weekly language classes are sponsored at various levels of instruction in Gaelic. A monthly Mass is held in Gaelic. Annually provides a scholarship to a Gaelic-speaking school.

COUNCIL OF GAELIC SOCIETIES, INC.
P.O. Box 3366, Grand Central Station
New York, New York 10017

Principal officers: Thomas F. Mason, President
John Bergin, Vice President
Cathy Norton, Secretary

Permanent staff: none   Membership: 6 societies
Date founded: 1946   Membership dues: $10.00 (annual)
Branches: 5 regional   Scope: regional, international

Special requirements for membership: member organizations must teach the Irish language and cultural subjects for at least one year

Nature of organization: social, cultural, scholarly

Publications: *An Feinsic*, 1968– (annual)

Major conventions/meetings: annual meeting

Comments: The major objective of the organization is to promote the teaching of the Irish language and history, as well as the traditional dance, music, and culture.

EMERALD ISLE CLUB
110 Bosley Avenue
Cockeysville, Maryland 21030

FRIENDLY SONS OF ST. PATRICK
8269 8 Mile Road   (313) 757-9875 or
Warren, Michigan 48089   (313) 773-1276

Principal officers: James Cassidy

Permanent staff: NI   Membership: 700
Date founded: NI   Membership dues: NI
Branches: various state groups   Scope: regional

Special requirements for membership: Irish descent

Nature of organization: social, charitable

Comments: The major purpose of the organization is to unite those of Irish descent in the United States. It sponsors social and charitable activities for members, nearly all of whom are Irish immigrants.

FRIENDLY SONS OF ST. PATRICK
c/o Mr. John Cullen, Secretary
824 Investment Building
Washington, D.C. 20005

Principal officers: John Cullen, Secretary

GAELIC ATHLETIC ASSOCIATION
4000 Corbor Avenue
Bronx, New York 10463

Permanent staff: NI   Membership: NI
Date founded: NI   Membership dues: NI
Branches: various state groups   Scope: NI

GAELIC LEAGUE
2062 Michigan Avenue
Detroit, Michigan 48216

Permanent staff: NI   Membership: NI
Date founded: NI   Membership dues: NI
Branches: NI   Scope: local

Special requirements for membership: Irish descent

Nature of organization: social, cultural

GAELIC LEAGUE (cont'd)

Comments: The membership of the organization is comprised mainly of first-generation Irish. It sponsors social and cultural activities to unite the Irish in the area, including nightly entertainment at the Gaelic League Hall by performers from Ireland.

HIBERNIAN SOCIETY OF BALTIMORE

c/o John O. Montgomery
P.O. Box 987
Maryland National Bank
Baltimore, Maryland 21203   (301) 962-5442

Principal officers: John O. Montgomery, President
                        Frank J. Fischer, First Vice President
                        Joseph M. Knott, Executive Secretary

Permanent staff: none   Membership: 500
Date founded: 1803   Membership dues: $10.00 (annual)
Branches: none   Scope: national

Special requirements for membership: Irish ancestry

Nature of organization: philanthropic, social, fraternal

Publications: none

Affiliations: none

Major conventions/meetings: none

Comments: Primarily professional in nature, this organization provides all types of assistance to persons of Irish ancestry. The society also sponsors the Oliver Hibernian Free School for Irish children, provides medical care for the needy, and is involved in extensive charitable works.

IRISH AMERICAN CLUB

2068 Michigan
Detroit, Michigan 48216

Principal officers: Chris Murray

Permanent staff: NI   Membership: NI
Date founded: NI   Membership dues: NI
Branches: NI   Scope: local

Nature of organization: cultural

Comments: The organization attempts to promote Irish culture, tradition, and products in the United States.

THE IRISH AMERICAN CLUB OF WASHINGTON, D.C.

3108 Upshur Street
Mt. Rainier, Maryland 20822   (301) 277-3959

Principal officers: Kevin Finnie, President
                        Bernadette O'Reilly, Vice President
                        Ellen Rafferty, Secretary
                        Teresa Maguire, Treasurer

Permanent staff: 12   Membership: 300
Date founded: 1948   Membership dues: $8.00 single; $13.00
Branches: none   married couple
                                               Scope: local

Special requirements for membership: Irish background

Nature of organization: social, cultural, charitable

Publications: *The Amergaei* (monthly)

Comments: The purpose of the club is to promote all aspects of Irish culture, to aid Catholic missionary and charitable works, and to promote loyalty to the United States.

IRISH AMERICAN CULTURAL INSTITUTE (IACI)
683 Osceola Avenue
St. Paul, Minnesota 55105   (612) 647-5678

Principal officers: Eoin McKiernan, President
                        Alfred Muellerleile, Executive Vice President
                        Perry M. Wilson, Jr., Executive Secretary

Permanent staff: 3   Membership: 18,000
Date founded: 1962   Membership dues: $10.00 minimum
Branches: 4 regional   Scope: national

Special requirements for membership: none

Nature of organization: educational, cultural, scholarly

Publications: *Eire-Ireland*, 1965– (quarterly); *Duchas*, 1971– (monthly)

Affiliations: none

Major conventions/meetings: none

Comments: The institute promotes the research and study of all aspects of Irish civilization and
    of Irish-American culture. The institute sponsors the annual Irish Fortnight programs of
    visiting specialists, as well as summer school both in the United States and in Ireland.
    Presents annual artist and literary awards.

IRISH CULTURE SOCIETY
106 Little Falls Street
Falls Church, Virginia 22046   (703) 532-1770

Principal officers: John A. K. Donovan, President

Permanent staff: none   Membership: 40
Date founded: 1966   Membership dues: $12.00 (annual)
Branches: none   Scope: local

Special requirements for membership: none

Nature of organization: cultural

Publications: none

Major conventions/meetings: monthly meetings

Comments: Promotes the knowledge of Irish history, music, art, dance, literature, traditions,
    and culture.

IRISH INSTITUTE (II)
326 West 48th Street
New York, New York 10036   (212) 265-3305

Principal officers: Martin Kileen, President

Permanent staff: 2   Membership: 2,000
Date founded: 1950   Membership dues: NI
Branches: NI   Scope: NI

Special requirements for membership: U.S. citizen of Irish descent

Comments: The function of the organization is to preserve the Irish customs, arts, and culture
    in the United States. It also aids families of political prisoners in Ireland and England.
    It sponsors music, drama, and art competitions. Until 1955 the organization was known
    as the Irish Feis Institute.

IRISH NORTHERN AID COMMITTEE
273 East 194th Street
Bronx, New York 10458

NATIONAL ASSOCIATION FOR IRISH FREEDOM
799 Broadway, Room 422
New York, New York 10003   (212) 254-1757

Principal officers: Seamas Naughton, National Coordinator

NATIONAL ASSOCIATION FOR IRISH FREEDOM (cont'd)

Permanent staff: NI
Date founded: 1971
Branches: NI

Membership: NI
Membership dues: NI
Scope: NI

Special requirements for membership: Irish descent

Nature of organization: fraternal, political, cultural

Affiliations: Northern Ireland Civil Rights Association

Major conventions/meetings: annual

Comments: The major purpose of the organization is to promote the Irish heritage in the United States and to support the goals of the Northern Ireland Civil Rights Association and a free Irish nation. It disseminates information on Irish history and the civil rights struggle in Northern Ireland; it supports political refugees.

SOCIETY FOR THE PRESERVATION OF IRISH MUSIC IN AMERICA
1520 South Huntington Drive
Bloomington, Indiana 47401   (812) 332-3267

Principal officers: Miles A. Krassen, President
Barry A. Kern, Vice President
L. E. McCullough, Secretary

Permanent staff: 4
Date founded: 1974
Branches: 3 regional

Membership: 56
Membership dues: none
Scope: regional

Special requirements for membership: none

Nature of organization: cultural

Publications: none

Major conventions/meetings: annual

SOCIETY OF THE FRIENDLY SONS OF ST. PATRICK IN THE CITY OF NEW YORK
80 Wall Street, Room 1112
New York, New York 10005   (212) 269-1770

Principal officers: Philip J. Curry, Secretary

Permanent staff: NI
Date founded: 1784
Branches: NI

Membership: 1,500
Membership dues: NI
Scope: local

Special requirements for membership: men of Irish descent

Major conventions/meetings: quarterly

Comments: The purpose of the organization is to preserve the Irish heritage in the United States. It sponsors social and charitable activities for its members.

ULSTER-IRISH SOCIETY
342 Madison Avenue, Room 1520
New York, New York 10017

Principal officers: William Simpson, President

Permanent staff: NI
Date founded: 1927
Branches: NI

Membership: 250
Membership dues: NI
Scope: NI

Special requirements for membership: of Northern-Irish descent

Nature of organization; cultural, economic

Comments: The purpose of the society is to promote the Irish culture in the United States and to promote the well-being and economic development of Northern Ireland.

UNITED IRISH COUNTIES ASSOCIATION OF NEW YORK
326 West 48th Street
New York, New York 10036   (212) 265-4226
Principal officers: Maureen Mulcany, Executive Secretary

Permanent staff: 1	Membership: 375
Date founded: 1904	Membership dues: NI
Branches: 32 county associations	Scope: state

Nature of organization: cultural, economic

Major conventions/meetings: monthly meeting, annual Irish Feis, concert, and ball

Comments: The purpose of the organization is to act as a coordinator and federation of smaller, local organizations. Each group is represented by 11 delegates. It sponsors cultural events and maintains a placement bureau.

ITALIAN-AMERICAN ORGANIZATIONS

Additional information on Italian-American organizations in the United States may be obtained from the Office of the Italian Embassy (1601 Fuller Street, Washington, D.C. 20009), the American Italian Congress (111 Columbia Heights, Brooklyn, New York 11201), and the American-Italian Organization (AMERITO) (8516 Warde Terrace, Potomac, Maryland 20854). For regional and local organizations, see *Greater Cleveland Nationalities Directory 1974* (Cleveland: Sun Newspapers and the Nationalities Services Center, 1974) and *Ethnic Directory I* (Detroit: Southeastern Michigan Regional Ethnic Heritage Studies Center, 1973).

AMERICA-ITALY SOCIETY
22 East 60th Street
New York, New York 10022   (212) 838-1560
Principal officers: Hedy Giusti Lanham, Executive Director

Permanent staff: 2	Membership: 1,400
Date founded: 1949	Membership dues: NI
Branches: NI	Scope: national

Special requirements for membership: none

Nature of organization: cultural, educational

Publications: *Newsletter* (quarterly)

Major conventions/meetings: annual

Comments: The main purpose of the organization is to preserve the Italian culture in the United States and to promote Italian-American relations by sponsoring concerts and art exhibits, providing contacts in Italy, and by promoting lectures and the dissemination of literature on Italian-American cultural exchanges.

AMERICAN ASSOCIATION OF TEACHERS OF ITALIAN (AATI)
Department of Italian
Rutgers College
New Brunswick, New Jersey 08903   (201) 247-1766, Extension 6731
Principal officers: Bruno Arcudi, President
                       Michelina Rizzo, Executive Vice President
                       Joseph E. Laggini, Secretary-Treasurer

Permanent staff: none	Membership: 1,950
Date founded: 1924	Membership dues: $8.00 (annual)
Branches: 8 regional	Scope: national

Special requirements for membership: none

AMERICAN ASSOCIATION OF TEACHERS OF ITALIAN (AATI) (cont'd)

Nature of organization: educational, professional, scholarly

Publications: *Italica*, 1924– (quarterly)

Affiliations: none

Major conventions/meetings: annual convention

Comments: Formed primarily to promote the study of the Italian language. Sponsors annual language contests and also awards scholarships.

AMERICAN COMMITTEE ON ITALIAN MIGRATION (ACIM)

9 East 35th Street
New York, New York 10016   (212) 679-4650

Principal officers: Edward E. Swanstrom, President
Joseph A. Cogo, Executive Secretary
Ross J. Di Lorenzo, Secretary

Permanent staff: 6   Membership: 30,000
Date founded: 1952   Membership dues: NI
Branches: 30 local   Scope: national

Special requirements for membership: none

Nature of organization: social

Publications: *ACIM Dispatch*, 1953– (biannual); *ACIM Newsletter*, 1969– (5 issues per year); *The New Way*, 1972– (monthly); *International Migration Review*, 1967– (quarterly)

Affiliations: National Catholic Resettlement Council

Major conventions/meetings: biennial conference

Comments: When ACIM was originally founded in 1952, its major objective was to alter the discriminatory Walter-McCarran immigration law based on national origin. Once the law was abolished in 1965, the purpose of ACIM has become one of assuring the retention of fair immigration policies. ACIM also provides assistance to newly arrived immigrants from Italy in their resettlement and assimilation; it sponsors a radio program and also maintains an archival collection.

AMERICAN ITALIAN CONGRESS

111 Columbia Heights
Brooklyn, New York 11201   (212) 852-2929

Principal officers: John N. La Corte, General Director

Permanent staff: NI   Membership: 700
Date founded: 1949   Membership dues: NI
Branches: NI   Scope: national

Nature of organization: cultural, philanthropic

Publications: *Italian-American Review* (annual); *Brooklyn Review Magazine*

Major conventions/meetings: semiannual

Comments: This organization is a federation of Italian-American groups. It sponsors awards and scholarships to Italian students as well as many cultural and civic activities. It maintains a library of Italian history, literature, and biography.

AMERICAN ITALIAN HISTORICAL ASSOCIATION

209 Flagg Place
Staten Island, New York 10304

Principal officers: Salvatore LaGumina, President
Luciano Iorizzo, Executive Vice President
Patrick Gallo, Executive Secretary

Permanent staff: 1 part-time secretary   Membership: 350
Date founded: 1966   Membership dues: $10.00 (annual)
Branches: none   Scope: national

Special requirements for membership: none

AMERICAN ITALIAN HISTORICAL ASSOCIATION (cont'd)

Nature of organization: educational, scholarly

Publications: *A.I.H.A. Newsletter*, 1966– (quarterly); also publishes books

Affiliations: none

Major conventions/meetings: annual conference

Comments: The association encourages research on the Italian contribution to and role in
American life. It seeks to collect, preserve, publish, and popularize materials that docu-
ment the experience of Italian immigrants and their descendants. Several programs
initiated by the organization include the following: sponsorship of conferences and
seminars devoted to various topics in Italian-American history; publication of a
Newsletter and a journal of Italian American studies; the awarding of graduate fellowships in Italian American studies; awarding of prizes for distinguished work in Italian-
American studies; and the collection and preservation of historical documents and
materials (newspapers, organizational records, pamphlets, books, papers, etc.). The
association maintains a large archival collection.

AMERICAN-ITALIAN ORGANIZATION (AMERITO)

8516 Warde Terrace
Potomac, Maryland 20854   (301) 365-2013

Principal officers: Antonio M. Marinelli, President
Louis Figliozzi, Vice President
Edmund Sabatini, Secretary

Permanent staff: none   Membership: 12 member organizations;
Date founded: 1971   over 1,000 individuals
Branches: none   Membership dues: $25.00 organization
(annual)
Scope: regional

Special requirements for membership: "must be a duly recognized American-Italian
organization"

Nature of organization: social, cultural, religious, professional, fraternal

Affiliations: 12 Italian-American organizations in Washington, D.C., and Maryland area

Comments: AMERITO is an umbrella organization whose purpose is to coordinate the
activities of its 12 member organizations. It maintains close liaison with the Italian
Embassy in Washington, D.C. Among its functions is the organizing of the national
Columbus Day activities in the nation's capitol.

THE AMERICAN-ITALIAN PROFESSIONAL AND BUSINESS WOMEN'S CLUB (AMIT)

31730 Acton
Warren, Michigan 48092   (313) 264-1808

Principal officers: Mrs. Edward M. Baker, President
Mrs. Nino Uberti, Vice President
Mrs. Andrew Falbo, Secretary

Permanent staff: 16   Membership: 90
Date founded: 1956   Membership dues: $5.00
Branches: none   Scope: state

Special requirements for membership: Italian descent or spouse of Italian descent;
professional or executive position; by invitation only

Nature of organization: cultural, charitable

Publications: newsletter (frequency varies)

Affiliations: none

Major conventions/meetings: monthly meetings

Comments: AMIT's objectives are to further cultural, charitable, and social functions,
emphasizing Italian culture whenever the opportunity arises. AMIT has contributed to
Italian relief and various charitable organizations, and has provided scholarships to
local colleges and universities.

AMERICAN SOCIETY OF THE ITALIAN LEGIONS OF MERIT
225 Broadway
New York, New York 10007   (212) 571-0136
Principal officers: Col. Hugo E. Rogers, President

Permanent staff: NI   Membership: 200
Date founded: 1965   Membership dues: NI
Branches: NI   Scope: national

Special requirements for membership: persons knighted by Italy

Nature of organization: philanthropic, educational, fraternal

Comments: The major purpose of the organization is to unite members of the society in the
    United States and to provide funds for selected educational and philanthropic projects.

AMERICANS OF ITALIAN DESCENT (AID)
299 Broadway
New York, New York 10007   (212) 349-0210
Principal officers: Alfred E. Santangelo, President
                       Joseph Calio, Vice President
                       Joseph Valletutti, Secretary

Permanent staff: 2   Membership: 25,000
Date founded: 1967   Membership dues: $10.00 (annual)
Branches: 6   Scope: national

Special requirements for membership: none

Nature of organization: cultural, anti-defamation

Publications: publishes books

Major conventions/meetings: annual conference

Comments: AID seeks to preserve, protect, and perpetuate the record of the contribution of
    Italians to the American culture; to combat the defamation and discrimination against
    Italian-Americans; and to eradicate through education the biased and unfavorable image
    of the Italian-American portrayed by movies, television, radio, and other mass communi-
    cation media. AID is also involved in protecting the civil rights of Italian Americans.

AMITA
P.O. Box 140
Whitestone, New York 11357
Principal officers: Lucile DeGeorge, President

Permanent staff: NI   Membership: 200
Date founded: 1956   Membership dues: NI
Branches: NI   Scope: national

Special requirements for membership: American-Italian women awarded for success in
    business, the arts, or a profession

Nature of organization: fraternal, philanthropic

Publications: *AMITA Gold Book* (annual)

Major conventions/meetings: annual

Comments: AMITA stands for American-Italian Women of Achievement. The major goal of
    the organization is to recognize the contributions to American society and the
    achievements of women of Italian descent. It grants annual achievement awards and
    also sponsors scholarship grants to students of any nationality or background.

ASSOCIATION OF EVANGELICALS FOR ITALIAN MISSIONS
314 Richfield Road
Upper Darby, Pennsylvania 19082   (215) 352-2396
Principal officers: Dr. Anthony F. Vasquez, Editor

Permanent staff: NI   Membership: NI
Date founded: 1968   Membership dues: NI
Branches: NI   Scope: national

ASSOCIATION OF EVANGELICALS FOR ITALIAN MISSIONS (cont'd)

Special requirements for membership: Italian Baptists and members of Evangelical churches

Nature of organization: religious

Publications: *New Aurora*, 1903– (monthly)

Major conventions/meetings: annual

Comments: This religious organization is active in evangelistic programs and activities in Italian Baptist churches. It raises funds to support evangelism in Italy and awards an annual citation to an outstanding layman or minister. The organization was formed by a merger of the Italian Baptist Association of America, which was originated in 1898, and the American Federation of Italian Evangelicals.

ASSOCIATION OF YOUNG ITALIANS, ST. JOSEPH
185 Suydam Street
Brooklyn, New York   (212) 386-0175

Principal officers: Pino Aiosa, President
                       Maria Amorelli, Vice President
                       Lucia Crifasi, Secretary

Permanent staff: none   Membership: 100 to 150
Date founded: 1969   Membership dues: $6.00 (annual)
Branches: none   Scope: local

Special requirements for membership: none

Nature of organization: cultural, fraternal, social, religious, scholarly, educational, recreational, sport, youth

Publications: none

Affiliations: none

Major conventions/meetings: none

Comments: The association's major objective is to help newly arrived Italians adjust to life in the United States. The organization aids in such areas as language, customs, work, housing, and education. Offers various social and religious activities.

ASSOCIATION OF STUDENTS AND PROFESSIONAL ITALIAN-AMERICANS
P.O. Box 3672, Grand Central Station
New York, New York 10017

BOY'S TOWNS OF ITALY
24 West 57th Street
New York, New York 10019   (212) 581-7380

Principal officers: Janet T. Garry, Executive Director

Permanent staff: 5   Membership: NI
Date founded: 1945   Membership dues: NI
Branches: NI   Scope: national

Nature of organization: charitable, welfare

Publications: *News* (monthly)

Comments: Originally established as an organization to provide financial assistance to a shelter in Italy for World War II homeless boys, the work now assists all child-care and rehabilitation centers for children in Italy.

CENTRAL COUNCIL OF THE ITALIAN CATHOLIC FEDERATION
678 Green Street
San Francisco, California 94130

DANTE ALIGHIERI SOCIETY OF SOUTHERN CALIFORNIA
1950 Mandeville Canyon Road
Los Angeles, California 90049

Principal officers: Dr. W. Thomas Marrocco, President

Permanent staff: NI	Membership: 75
Date founded: 1957	Membership dues: NI
Branches: independent branches worldwide	Scope: regional

Nature of organization: cultural

Comments: The organization, named in honor of the famous Italian poet, aims to promote Italian literature, history, arts, music, and other aspects of Italian culture in the United States. Sponsors lectures, exhibits, poetry readings, and other cultural presentations and activities.

FEDERATION OF ITALIAN AMERICAN ORGANIZATIONS
1088 Central Avenue
Scarsdale, New York 10583   (914) 723-9156

Principal officers: Raphael G. Riverso, President

Permanent staff: 1	Membership: 40 organizations
Date founded: 1970	Membership dues: none
Branches: NI	Scope: regional

Special requirements for membership: none

Nature of organization: educational, cultural

Publications: *Avanti*, 1973– (weekly)

Affiliations: Westchester Columbus Committee; Italian Charities of America; Italian Chamber of Commerce; 40 member organizations

Major conventions/meetings: monthly meetings; annual convention

Comments: The federation seeks to promote the retention of Italian values, culture, and language; to demand more representation of Italian Americans in management, education, and other professional fields; to encourage greater Italian-American participation in the political process; to promote programs that are beneficial to the community; and to encourage greater cooperation with other ethnic communities. The organization offers scholarships and maintains a library and archives.

GRAND COUNCIL OF COLUMBIA ASSOCIATION IN CIVIL SERVICES, INC.
299 Broadway
New York, New York 10007   (212) 962-5757

Principal officers: Alphonse F. D'Andrea, Executive Secretary

Permanent staff: NI	Membership: 80,000
Date founded: 1938	Membership dues: NI
Branches: 53	Scope: regional

Special requirements for membership: civil service employees of Italian descent in the New York area

Nature of organization: social, charitable, anti-defamation

Publications: *Columbian Voice* (monthly)

Major conventions/meetings: annual

Comments: The purpose of the organization is to project the best possible image of the Italians in America in textbooks and the media. It also provides social and educational programs for members to unite Italians employed in Civil Service positions in the United States. It sponsors charitable projects and grants scholarships.

ITALIAN-AMERICAN CIVIL RIGHTS LEAGUE
635 Madison Avenue
New York, New York 10021   (212) 486-9415

Principal officers: Nat Marcone, Executive Director

ITALIAN-AMERICAN CIVIL RIGHTS LEAGUE (cont'd)

Permanent staff: NI   Membership: NI
Date founded: NI   Membership dues: NI
Branches: NI   Scope: national

Nature of organization: anti-defamation

Comments: Opposes discrimination or portrayal of Italian-Americans in a negative light.

ITALIAN-AMERICAN COALITION OF THE CITY OF NEW YORK
104 East 40th Street
New York, New York 10016

ITALIAN AMERICAN WAR VETERANS OF THE UNITED STATES (ITAM VETS)
369 South Leonard
Waterbury, Connecticut 06705   (205) 753-9840

Permanent staff: NI   Membership: 8,500
Date founded: 1932   Membership dues: NI
Branches: 10 state; 110 local   Scope: national

Special requirements for membership: persons of Italian descent who served in the U.S. Armed Forces

Nature of organization: political, cultural

Publications: *The Torch* (quarterly); *National Directory* (annual)

Major conventions/meetings: annual

Comments: The major purpose of the organization is to recognize Italian-American contributions to U.S. society, to oppose communism and fascism, and to preserve the Italian culture, history, and traditions in America.

ITALIAN CATHOLIC FEDERATION CENTRAL COUNCIL (ICF)
678 Green Street, Suite 201
San Francisco, California 94133   (415) 421-7993

Principal officers: Felix F. Chialvo, Administrative Director

Permanent staff: NI   Membership: 21,000
Date founded: 1924   Membership dues: NI
Branches: NI   Scope: national

Special requirements for membership: Catholics of Italian descent

Nature of organization: religious, social, cultural, charitable

Publications: *Il Boletino* (monthly)

Major conventions/meetings: annual

Comments: The purpose of the organization is to unite Catholics of Italian descent, to conduct religious activities that perpetuate the Catholic faith, and to sponsor charitable activities and those that help strengthen and preserve the Italian heritage in the United States.

ITALIAN CHAMBER OF COMMERCE
327 South La Salle Street
Chicago, Illinois 60604   (312) 427-3014

Principal officers: Yole Salom, Secretary

Permanent staff: NI   Membership: 500
Date founded: 1907   Membership dues: NI
Branches: NI   Scope: national

Nature of organization: economic

Publications: *Bulletin* (bimonthly)

ITALIAN CHARITIES OF AMERICA (ICA)
83-20 Queens Boulevard
Elmhurst, New York 11373   (212) 639-3047

Principal officers: Joachim Titolo, Executive Director

Permanent staff: 4	Membership: 1,200
Date founded: 1936	Membership dues: NI
Branches: NI	Scope: national

Special requirements for membership: persons of Italian birth or descent

Nature of organization: charitable

Publications: *Bulletin* (monthly)

Comments: This charitable organization unites Italian-Americans in civic and community services, such as camps for underprivileged children, scholarships, and emergency welfare and counseling services. Until 1951 the organization was known as the Italian Charity and Welfare Center.

ITALIAN CIVIC ASSOCIATION (ICA)
208 North Fifth Avenue
Mount Vernon, New York 10550   (914) 667-9063

Principal officers: Emilio Vettorino, President
         Jack Lanetoni, Vice President
         Anthony De Bellis, Secretary

Permanent staff: none	Membership: 550
Date founded: 1916	Membership dues: $20.00 (annual)
Branches: 1	Scope: state

Special requirements for membership: one parent must be Italian

Nature of organization: social, cultural, recreational, scholarly

Publications: *ICA Bulletin* (monthly)

Affiliations: none

Comments: The association attempts to further the position of Italian-Americans in the United States. It encourages the retention of the Italian cultural heritage; organizes various civic, social, cultural, educational, and recreational activities; offers college scholarships, and maintains a library and archives.

ITALIAN CULTURAL INSTITUTE
686 Park Avenue
New York, New York 10021   (212) 879-4242

Principal officers: Giuseppe Cardillo, Director

Permanent staff: 26	Membership: NI
Date founded: NI	Membership dues: NI
Branches: NI	Scope: national

Nature of organization: cultural

Publications: *Newsletter* (with a bibliographical supplement) (bimonthly)

Comments: An agency of the Italian Ministry of Foreign Affairs, the organization promotes Italian culture in the United States and disseminates information on history and conditions in Italy. The organization is also known as Istituto Italiano di Cultura; it maintains a 25,000-volume library as well as a periodical and audiovisual collection.

ITALIAN CULTURE COUNCIL, INC.
1140 Edgewood Parkway
Union, New Jersey 07083   (201) 355-6025

Principal officers: Vincent Visceglia, President Honorary
         Giulio de Petra, Director
         Ella Eckstadt, Secretary-Treasurer

ITALIAN CULTURE COUNCIL, INC. (cont'd)

Permanent staff: 1

Date founded: 1963

Branches: none

Membership: 250

Membership dues: $5.00 individual;
$10.00 universities; $25.00 patrons of
the Council (all above annual)

Scope: national

Special requirements for membership: none

Nature of organization: educational, cultural, scholarly

Publications: *Bulletin* (annual); also publishes books

Affiliations: none

Major conventions/meetings: none

Comments: ICC is a non-profit, tax-exempt educational organization which serves as a clearinghouse and coordinating body diffusing information on all aspects of Italian culture. The *Bulletin* lists the institutions teaching courses on Italian subjects as well as the contributions of Italian academicians. Maintains an archival collection.

ITALIAN EXECUTIVES OF AMERICA

P.O. Box 25

Kensington, Maryland 20795   (301) 933-4447

Principal officers: Elio E. Grandi, President

Edmund Sabatini, Vice President

Ralph G. Urciolo, Secretary

Permanent staff: none

Date founded: 1964

Branches: none

Membership: NI

Membership dues: $35.00 (annual)

Scope: national

Special requirements for membership: active membership: professionals of Italian origin; associate membership: professionals of any national origin

Nature of organization: cultural, professional

Publications: none

Affiliations: none

Major conventions/meetings: annual meeting

Comments: The organization was organized in order to carry out various civic, social, welfare, cultural, and educational activities. It promotes the retention of the Italian culture and language and encourages tourism and exchange programs with Italy. Aids Italian-American candidates for political office. Grants awards or special recognition to Italians in Italy and America who have made significant contributions to the advancement of democracy, education, science, etc. The organization also provides scholarships to students of Italian descent.

ITALIAN HISTORICAL SOCIETY OF AMERICA (IHS)

111 Columbia Heights

Brooklyn, New York 11201   (212) 852-2929

Principal officers: John LaCorte, Director

Permanent staff: NI

Date founded: 1949

Branches: NI

Membership: 700

Membership dues: NI

Scope: national

Special requirements for membership: none

Nature of organization: cultural, historical

Publications: *Italian-American Review*, 1951– (quarterly); *Italian American Newsletter* (irregular)

ITALIAN HISTORICAL SOCIETY OF AMERICA (IHS) (cont'd)
Major conventions/meetings: annual

Comments: The purpose of the organization is to preserve the Italian heritage, customs, and traditions in the United States. It also sponsors cultural activities, such as the First Italian Heritage Cultural Festival in New York (1972). It also encourages research and study in Italian history and culture and presents a triennial award to students.

ITALIAN SOCIETY OF AUTHORS, COMPOSERS AND PUBLISHERS
220 East 42nd Street
New York, New York 10017   (212) 986-0669

Principal officers: Mario Vinciguerra, President

Permanent staff: NI   Membership: NI
Date founded: NI   Membership dues: NI
Branches: NI   Scope: national

Comments: Seeks to promote and advance the welfare of Italian writers, publishers, and composers in the United States.

ITALIAN SOCIETY OF WASHINGTON
4218 Wicomico Avenue
Beltsville, Maryland 20705

Principal officers: Romeo Sabatini, President

ITALIAN WAR VETERANS
1447 Nova Avenue
Coral Hills, Maryland 20027

Principal officers: Dominic Firmani, Commander

ITALIAN WELFARE LEAGUE
250 West 57th Street
New York, New York 10019

Principal officers: Angela M. Rossi, Executive Secretary

Permanent staff: 2   Membership: 600
Date founded: 1920   Membership dues: NI
Branches: NI   Scope: national

Special requirements for membership: Italian descent

Nature of organization: charitable, welfare

Major conventions/meetings: annual

Comments: The purpose is to provide financial assistance to Italians in need, particularly immigrants and graduate students of Italian descent studying at Columbia University School of Social Work.

ITALO AMERICAN NATIONAL UNION
4801 West Peterson Avenue
Chicago, Illinois 60645   (312) 286-1441

ITALO AMERICAN NATIONAL UNION (cont'd)

Principal officers: Anthony J. Paterno, President
Joseph Tolitano, Vice President
Louis Salvino, Vice President
Anthony Sorrentino, Secretary
Joseph Pope, Treasurer

Permanent staff: NI
Date founded: 1895
Branches: 35

Membership: 7,500
Membership dues: varies with policy
Scope: NI

Special requirements for membership: persons of Italian descent or married to an Italian

Nature of organization: fraternal, charitable

Publications: *I.A.N.U. Bulletin* (bimonthly)

Comments: The major purposes of the organization are to provide life insurance benefits to members of Italian descent and to encourage social and cultural activities that promote the Italian heritage. It also sponsors charitable programs such as aid to handicapped children, scholarship programs, etc.

ITALY-AMERICA CHAMBER OF COMMERCE

350 Fifth Avenue
New York, New York 10001   (212) 279-5520

Principal officers: Arthur A. DeSantis, Executive Secretary

Permanent staff: NI
Date founded: 1887
Branches: NI

Membership: 1,150
Membership dues: NI
Scope: NI

Nature of organization: economic

LEONARDO DA VINCI SOCIETY

P.O. Box 25
Fort Lee, New Jersey 07024

Principal officers: Edward F. Ten Broeke, President

Permanent staff: NI
Date founded: 1962
Branches: NI

Membership: 160
Membership dues: NI
Scope: local

Nature of organization: cultural, educational, social

Publications: *Scriptores* (semiannual)

Major conventions/meetings: annual symposium

Comments: This cultural society attempts to promote the Italian arts, literature, and language in the Bergen County, New Jersey, area. It provides opportunities for education in the Italian language, travel, and financial assistance to Italian-American college students.

NATIONAL FEDERATION OF ITALIAN-AMERICAN SOCIETIES, INC.

7502 15th Avenue   (212) 259-4700 or
Brooklyn, New York 11228   (212) 232-9319

Principal officers: Arnaldo A. Ferraro, President
Anthony Colletti, Secretary

Permanent staff: none
Date founded: 1967
Branches: none

Membership: 300
Membership dues: $10.00 men; $5.00
  women (annual)
Scope: presently local, but plans to
  expand into national

Special requirements for membership: Italian-American origin, minimum age of 18 years

Nature of organization: cultural, social, educational, recreational, sport, youth

Publications: *Our News* (monthly)

Affiliations: none

NATIONAL FEDERATION OF ITALIAN-AMERICAN SOCIETIES, INC. (cont'd)

Major conventions/meetings: annual membership meeting

Comments: The purpose of this non-profit organization is to advance the social, cultural, recreational, and civic interests of persons of Italian origin. The federation promotes the preservation of the Italian cultural heritage, encourages cooperation among Italian clubs in the New York area, disseminates information on various Italian activities, and arranges special holiday activities. Offers free English-language courses, arts and crafts classes, and karate lessons. Maintains archival collections.

NORTHEAST COMMUNITY CENTER
544 Wabash Avenue
Kansas City, Missouri 64124   (816) 241-7738

Principal officers: J. B. Bisceglia, Executive Director
Mrs. M. Tamborello, Secretary
Mrs. H. LaMountain, Head Teacher

Permanent staff: 7   Membership: serves several thousand
Date founded: 1908   Membership dues: varies
Branches: none   Scope: local

Special requirements for membership: "moral requirements"

Nature of organization: social, educational, religious, recreational

Publications: *The Messenger*, 1924– (monthly)

Affiliations: none

Major conventions/meetings: none

Comments: Offers major services to Italian families such as a pre-school, pediatric clinic, children's recreational activities, crafts classes, summer camps, adult English language classes, counseling services, aid to needy, and activities for the elderly.

ST. JOSEPH SOCIETY OF BROOKLYN, NEW YORK
1080 Willoughby Avenue
Brooklyn, New York 11237   (212) 287-6604

Principal officers: Pasquale Mastrandrea, President
Michael Bryno, Vice President
Richard E. Riccardelli, Secretary

Permanent staff: NI   Membership: 110
Date founded: 1920   Membership dues: $24.00 (annual)
Branches: none   Scope: local

Special requirements for membership: native or descendant, or married to an Italian from Palo del Colle, Bari, Italy

Nature of organization: fraternal

Publications: none

Affiliations: none

Comments: The society aids newly arrived immigrants from Palo del Colle, Bari, Italy, in their adjustment and settlement in the New York area. Also promotes cooperation and togetherness among its members. Sponsors various social activities.

SOCIETY FOR ITALIAN HISTORICAL STUDIES (SIHS)
University of Connecticut
Storrs, Connecticut 06268   (203) 486-4225

Principal officers: Norman Kogan, Executive Secretary-Treasurer

Permanent staff: NI   Membership: 184
Date founded: NI   Membership dues: NI
Branches: NI   Scope: NI

Special requirements for membership: college and university professors and graduate students who are studying and teaching Italian history

SOCIETY FOR ITALIAN HISTORICAL STUDIES (SIHS) (cont'd)

Nature of organization: scholarly

Publications: *Newsletter* (annual); also publishes membership list

Major conventions/meetings: annual

Comments: The purpose of the organization is to further study and research of Italian history and American-Italian relations. It awards grants and prizes for contributions to the field and gives lectures and conferences.

SONS OF ITALY SUPREME LODGE
1200 South Broad Street
Philadelphia, Pennsylvania 19146   (215) 336-2818

Principal officers: Vincent D. Galzerano, Supreme Financial Secretary

Permanent staff: NI   Membership: NI
Date founded: NI   Membership dues: NI
Branches: various state branches   Scope: national

Special requirements for membership: Italian descent

Nature of organization: fraternal

Major conventions/meetings: biennial

Comments: A fraternal life insurance organization that provides policies and benefits for members who are of Italian descent. The Women's Division sponsors social, recreational, and cultural activities.

UNICO NATIONAL
72 Burroughs Place
Bloomfield, New Jersey 07003   (201) 748-9144

Principal officers: Anthony J. Fornelli, Esq., President
                       Mario Albi, Executive Vice President
                       Paul Alongi, First Vice President
                       Joseph Coccia, Second Vice President
                       A. A. Miele, Secretary

Permanent staff: 3   Membership: 5,000
Date founded: 1922   Membership dues: $12.00
Branches: 25 regional; 117 local chapters   Scope: national

Special requirements for membership: males of Italian descent

Nature of organization: social, civic

Publications: *UNICO National Magazine* (10 issues annually)

Affiliations: none

Major conventions/meetings: annual convention in August

Comments: The non-profit organization is similar to the Lions, Kiwanis, and Rotary. UNICO National works on various national projects as well as community activities that serve to uplift the prestige and image of Italian Americans. Sponsors the National Project in Mental Health Research as well as a scholarship program.

UNIONE VENETA DANIELE MANIN DI MUTUO SOCCORSO, INC.
(UVDM di MS, Inc.)
c/o 4134 Hill Avenue
Bronx, New York 10466   (212) 324-9115

Principal officers: Secondo Mincin, President
                       Peter Martin, Vice President
                       Arrigo Mincin, Secretary
                       Aldo Fabbro, Treasurer

Permanent staff: none   Membership: 19
Date founded: 1899   Membership dues: $15.00 (annual)
Branches: none   Scope: local

UNIONE VENETA DANIELE MANIN DI BUTUO SOCCORSO, INC.
(UVDM di MS, Inc.) (cont'd)

Special requirements for membership: Italians from the eight provinces of Venice, including Trento and Trieste

Nature of organization: social, mutual aid

Publications: none

Affiliations: none

Major conventions/meetings: four meetings a year

Comments: This organization reached the peak of membership in the 1920s and 1930s. It provided financial assistance to its members as well as various forms of cultural activity. During the last 20 years its membership has declined. Most of its present membership is over 75 years of age.

UNITED ITALIAN AMERICAN LABOR COUNCIL (UIALC)
218 West 40th Street
New York, New York 10018

Permanent staff: NI
Date founded: 1941
Branches: NI

Membership: NI
Membership dues: NI
Scope: national

Special requirements for membership: representative of a labor union comprised of Italian-Americans

Nature of organization: economic

Major conventions/meetings: annual

UNITED ITALIAN AMERICAN LEAGUE (UIAL)
233 Broadway
New York, New York 10007   (212) 964-8866

Principal officers: Paul P. Rao, Jr., National President

Nature of organization: political

Comments: The organization is a federation of Italian-American organizations, most of which are political or community oriented.

WESTCHESTER COLUMBUS COMMITTEE
1088 Central Avenue
Scarsdale, New York 10583

Principal officers: Raphael Riverso, President
Nick Saldi, Vice President
Nadia Riverso, Secretary

Permanent staff: 1
Date founded: 1970
Branches: none

Membership: 35,000
Membership dues: contributions
Scope: regional

Special requirements for membership: none

Nature of organization: educational, cultural

Publications: *Avanti* (irregularly)

Affiliations: Federation of Italian American Organizations

Comments: Promotes the preservation of the Italian cultural heritage. Sponsors various cultural and educational activities. Organizes major festivals.

JAPANESE-AMERICAN ORGANIZATIONS

Additional information on the Japanese-American organizations in the United States may be obtained from the Office of the Embassy of Japan (2520 Massachusetts Avenue, Washington, D.C. 20008), the Japanese American Citizen's League (22 Peace Plaza, Suite 203, San Francisco, California 94115), and the Asian-American Studies Program (San Jose State University, School of Social Science, San Jose, California 95192). Regional and local organizations are listed in *Greater Cleveland Nationalities Directory 1974* (Cleveland: Sun Newspapers and the Nationalities Services Center, 1974).

AMERICAN COMMITTEE FOR KEEP
343 South Dearborn Street
Chicago, Illinois 60604   (312) 939-4324
Principal officers: Mrs. Marshall E. Seifert, Administrative Secretary

Permanent staff: 3	Membership: 6,000
Date founded: 1950	Membership dues: NI
Branches: NI	Scope: national

Nature of organization: educational, religious, philanthropic

Publications: annual brochure and directory of members

Major conventions/meetings: annual

Comments: The intent of the organization is to provide assistance to the Zaidan Hojin KEEP in Japan through the Kiyosato Educational Experiment Program, which promotes agriculture, health, and religious training in Japan. A library is maintained.

ASIA FOUNDATION
P.O. Box 3223
San Francisco, California 94119   (415) 982-4640
Principal officers: Haydn Williams, President

Permanent staff: 225	Membership: NI
Date founded: 1954	Membership dues: NI
Branches: NI	Scope: national

Nature of organization: educational, cultural

Publications: *The Asian Student* (biweekly); *Program Quarterly* (quarterly); *Asian Student Orientation Handbook* (annual); *President's Review* (annual)

Major conventions/meetings: quarterly

Comments: The main purpose of the organization is to send assistance to Asian organizations and institutions of educational, cultural, or community-service nature. Sponsors Books for Asians project, which distributes books and journals to institutions in Asian countries. Supports professional exchanges in areas of human resources and development.

ASIAN AMERICANS FOR ACTION
43 West 28th Street
New York, New York 10001

ASSOCIATION OF TEACHERS OF JAPANESE
Department of Far Eastern Languages and Literatures
University of Michigan
Ann Arbor, Michigan 48104
Principal officers: Robert H. Brower, Chairman

ASSOCIATION OF TEACHERS OF JAPANESE (cont'd)

Permanent staff: 3   Membership: 300
Date founded: 1962   Membership dues: NI
Branches: NI   Scope: national

Special requirements for membership: teachers of Japanese language

Nature of organization: scholarly

Publications: *Journal* (3 times per year)

Major conventions/meetings: annual

Comments: Publishes materials on instruction in the Japanese language; sponsors panel discussions and research in Japanese language at the annual Modern Language Association program, and maintains a small library of Japanese language examinations and literature.

HONOLULU JAPANESE CHAMBER OF COMMERCE

2454 South Beretania Street
Honolulu, Hawaii 96814   (808) 949-5531

Principal officers: Ronald H. Nagano, Executive Vice President

Permanent staff: NI   Membership: 550
Date founded: 1900   Membership dues: NI
Branches: NI   Scope: national

Nature of organization: economic

Publications: *Shoko Newsletter* (monthly)

JAPAN-AMERICA INSTITUTE

Hotel Commodore
Park Avenue at 42nd Street
New York, New York 10017   (212) 889-1562

Principal officers: James Kelley, Executive Director

Permanent staff: 6   Membership: NI
Date founded: 1961   Membership dues: NI
Branches: NI   Scope: national

Nature of organization: educational, cultural

Comments: The official title of this organization is the Institute of Japanese-American Cultural Research, Inc. It is a non-profit organization that assists students, scholars, and businessmen from Japan through various counseling services and English language instruction; it is authorized by the government to enroll non-immigrant alien students. It also provides cultural programs and Japanese-language instruction for groups and clubs.

JAPAN AMERICA SOCIETY OF SOUTHERN CALIFORNIA (JASSC)

125 Weller Street
Los Angeles, California 90012   (213) 629-1247

Permanent staff: NI   Membership: 500
Date founded: 1909   Membership dues: NI
Branches: NI   Scope: regional

Nature of organization: cultural, economic, philanthropic

Major conventions/meetings: annual

Comments: The purpose of the organization is to preserve the Japanese heritage in the United States, to promote knowledge and understanding of Japanese culture in the United States and friendly relations between the Japanese and Americans. It also sponsors various philanthropic and cultural programs of a broader nature, such as the Japanese Philharmonic Society of Los Angeles; it provides scholarships in the greater Los Angeles area and presents awards to persons contributing to the Japanese-U.S. cultural exchange.

JAPAN-AMERICA SOCIETY OF WASHINGTON, INC.
1755 Massachusetts Avenue, N.W., Suite 308
Washington, D.C. 20036   (202) 265-0777
Principal officers: Albert H. Zinkand, President
                       Arthur Z. Gardiner, Executive Vice President
                       H. William Tanaka, Executive Secretary

Permanent staff: 2   Membership: 1,100
Date founded: 1957   Membership dues: Annual $10.00
Branches: none   regular; $4.00 student; $100.00
                                         corporate; $100.00 patron; $35.00
                                         sustaining
                                         Scope: local

Special requirements for membership: none

Nature of organization: educational, cultural

Publications: *Bulletin*, 1957– (monthly)

Major conventions/meetings: none

Comments: Non-profit and non-political in nature, the society is an association of Americans and Japanese working together for better understanding and cooperation. Provides a forum for exchange of ideas between Japanese visitors and members. Sponsors lectures, courses, exhibitions, and films, and provides teaching materials on Japan. Maintains a Japanese language school. Sponsors three English-language teachers to Japan to teach English to Japanese teachers. Offers scholarships, loans, and grants to students. Maintains a library of books and periodicals on Japan. Sponsors various exchange programs. Traditionally, the Ambassador of Japan serves as honorary president.

JAPAN INTERNATIONAL CHRISTIAN UNIVERSITY FOUNDATION (JICUF)
475 Riverside Drive, Room 1220
New York, New York 10027   (212) 749-6734
Principal officers: Ruth L. Miller, Executive Director

Permanent staff: NI   Membership: 60
Date founded: 1949   Membership dues: NI
Branches: NI   Scope: national

Special requirements for membership: representatives of cooperating denominations

Nature of organization: religious

Publications: *Newsletter* (semiannual)

Major conventions/meetings: annual

Comments: The purpose of the organization is to unite Japanese Protestant organizations in the United States interested in supporting the International Christian University in Tokyo. Finances are raised to help maintain this graduate school, which is attended by 1,400 Christian students.

JAPAN NORTH AMERICAN COMMISSION ON COOPERATIVE MISSION
475 Riverside Drive, Room 618
New York, New York 10027   (212) 870-2021
Principal officers: Dr. Robert W. Northup, Secretary-Treasurer

Permanent staff: NI   Membership: 10 church boards or
Date founded: 1947   agencies
Branches: NI   Membership dues: NI
                                         Scope: national

Nature of organization: religious

Publications: *Bulletin*; *Missionary Directory*

Major conventions/meetings: annual

Comments: The function of the organization is to promote mission work in Japan and North America and to promote the Christian faith among the Japanese.

JAPAN SCHOLARSHIP FOUNDATION (JSF)
932 Carleton Road
Westfield, New Jersey 07090
Principal officers: Malcolm F. Reed, Executive Director

Permanent staff: NI	Membership: NI
Date founded: 1950	Membership dues: NI
Branches: NI	Scope: national

Nature of organization: philanthropic

Comments: The purpose of the organization is to provide scholarships for students of Japanese extraction.

JAPAN SOCIETY, INC.
333 East 47th Street
New York, New York 10017   (212) 832-1155
Principal officers: Isaac Shapiro, Esq., President
Edgar B. Young, Vice President
Charles R. Stevens, Secretary
Tristan E. Beplat, Treasurer

Permanent staff: 24   Membership: 1,300 individual; 232
Date founded: 1907   corporate
Branches: none   Membership dues: $375-$500 corporate;
$10-$40 individual
Scope: regional, state

Special requirements for membership: interest

Nature of organization: social, educational, cultural

Publications: *Annual Report*; *Japan House Newsletter* (monthly); *Calendar of Activities* (monthly); also publishes books

Comments: A bi-national center where Americans and Japanese from all walks of life meet and work to broaden cooperation and understanding between the two nations. The society serves as a medium for presenting the arts and culture of Japan to the American people. Organizes exchange programs. Headquarters are in the Japan House, a four-story building containing an auditorium, library, conference rooms, gallery, and Japanese gardens. Offers discounts on travel and publications. Sponsors cultural and language courses. Maintains a library of over 4,500 volumes, as well as extensive archival materials.

JAPANESE-AMERICAN ASSOCIATION OF CHICAGO
3744 North Clark Street
Chicago, Illinois 60600

THE JAPANESE AMERICAN ASSOCIATION OF NEW YORK
125 West 72nd Street
New York, New York 10023

JAPANESE AMERICAN CITIZENS' LEAGUE (JACL)
22 Peace Plaza, Suite 203
San Francisco, California 94115   (415) 563-3202
Principal officers: Shigeki Sugiyama, President

Permanent staff: 17   Membership: 30,000
Date founded: 1930   Membership dues: $12.00
Branches: 7 regional offices; 95 chapters Scope: national

Special requirements for membership: American citizenship

Nature of organization: educational, human rights

Publications: *Pacific Citizen*, 1930– (weekly)

Major conventions/meetings: biennial convention

JAPANESE AMERICAN CITIZENS' LEAGUE (JACL) (cont'd)
Comments: JACL is a national human rights and educational organization dedicated to obtaining equal rights for Japanese Americans as well as all other Americans regardless of race, creed, or national origin. Sponsors history workshop, group travel, youth training programs, scholarships. Has a credit union and offers insurance. Maintains a library of over 200 volumes. Presents various awards for distinguished service.

JAPANESE-AMERICAN CULTURAL SOCIETY
368 East First Street
Los Angeles, California 90000

JAPANESE AMERICAN PHILATELIC SOCIETY (JAPS)
P.O. Box 2730
Santa Clara, California 95051
Principal officers: William H. McConnell, Editor

Permanent staff: NI	Membership: 400
Date founded: 1939	Membership dues: NI
Branches: NI	Scope: national

Nature of organization: philatelic

Publications: *Postal Bell* (bimonthly)

Major conventions/meetings: monthly

Comments: The organization is comprised mainly of members in the San Francisco area who are interested in collecting and researching stamps issued by Japan. A stamp library is maintained with philatelic materials.

JAPANESE-AMERICAN SERVICE COMMITTEE OF CHICAGO
3257 North Sheffield Avenue
Chicago, Illinois 60600

THE JAPANESE CHAMBER OF COMMERCE OF CHICAGO
232 North Michigan Avenue
Chicago, Illinois 60600

JAPANESE CHAMBER OF COMMERCE OF NORTHERN CALIFORNIA (JCC/NC)
World Trade Center, Room 137
Ferry Building
San Francisco, California 94121   (415) 986-6140
Principal officers: Masahiko Shima, President
                       Goro Nakagawa, First Vice President
                       Yukio Kumamoto, Secretary

Permanent staff: 2	Membership: 190
Date founded: 1951	Membership dues: $50.00-$500.00
Branches: none	Scope: regional

Special requirements for membership: none

Nature of organization: professional (businessmen's association)

Publications: *California Gaikan* (California Economic Survey), 1972– (biennial); occasional bulletins

Affiliations: none

Comments: Serves as a business and information center for the Japanese community. Arranges business meetings between United States and Japanese businessmen. Aids in translating and interpreting documents. Maintains a business library.

JAPANESE COMMUNITY SERVICES
1624 Post Street
San Francisco, California 94115   (415) 929-7567
Principal officers: Issei Yokota

JAPANESE MUTUAL AID SOCIETY
4410 North Malden Street
Chicago, Illinois 60600

KOYU KAI
2022 "R" Street, N.W.
Washington, D.C. 20009   (202) 387-3291
Principal officers: Paul Ishimoto, President
           Kikuo Endo, Vice President
           Yoshimi Ichino, Secretary

Permanent staff: 6   Membership: 1,400 families
Date founded: 1968   Membership dues: $5.00 plus $10.00
Branches: 3 state   admission fee
                                  Scope: regional

Special requirements for membership: none

Nature of organization: social, educational, cultural, recreational

Publications: *Koyu Kai News*, 1968– (bimonthly)

Major conventions/meetings: quarterly

Comments: The major purpose of the organization is to promote U.S.-Japanese relations and to promote the Japanese culture in the United States. It sponsors trips to Japan and social activities to unite the Japanese in the United States. Also provides cultural and educational programs.

NICHIBEI FUJINKAI
c/o Japan Society
333 East 47th Street
New York, New York 10017
Principal officers: Mrs. Harry P. Koumas, President

Permanent staff: NI   Membership: 300
Date founded: 1948   Membership dues: NI
Branches: NI   Scope: national

Nature of organization: cultural, social, educational

Major conventions/meetings: annual

Comments: The purpose of the organization is to provide social and cultural activities for Japanese women in the United States. It sponsors the English in Action program to help women gain skill in the English language. The membership is not restricted to the New York area but is mainly concentrated there.

NIPPON CLUB
145 West 57th Street
New York, New York 10019   (212) 581-2223
Principal officers: Shichiro Kono, Executive Secretary

Permanent staff: 55   Membership: NI
Date founded: NI   Membership dues: NI
Branches: NI   Scope: NI

Nature of organization: social, cultural

Comments: Provides social, recreational, and cultural activities for members. The organization is concerned with maintaining the Japanese heritage and promoting Japan-U.S. relations.

JEWISH-AMERICAN ORGANIZATIONS

At the present time there exist over 300 national Jewish organizations in the United States. There are also countless state and local societies, councils, and federations. The major organizations perform diverse functions and are, in general, concerned with one or more of the following: religion, education, welfare, culture, social activities, mutual aid, politics, or Zionism. Others may be categorized as being professional, youth, and student associations. It is impossible to list and describe all the national and regional Jewish organizations in this guide; such an undertaking would require a separate directory. Therefore, it was decided to include only very major Jewish organizations in this *Encyclopedia*. For other Jewish organizations, see the comprehensive annotated listing in *American Jewish Year Book, 1974* (New York: The American Jewish Committee, 1974). This publication also serves as a fundamental reference guide to Jewish life in the United States and the world.

AMERICAN ASSOCIATION FOR JEWISH EDUCATION (AAJE)
114 Fifth Avenue
New York, New York 10011   (212) 675-5656
Principal officers: Isaac Toubin, Executive Vice President

Permanent staff: 21   Membership: 1,061
Date founded: 1939   Membership dues: NI
Branches: NI   Scope: national

Nature of organization: scholarly, educational

Publications: *Jewish Education* (quarterly); *Pedagogic Report* (quarterly); *Jewish Audio-Visual Review* (annual); *Jewish Educational Directory* (triennial)

Major conventions/meetings: quinquennial

Comments: This organization acts as a coordinating agency for research and studies involving Jewish education in the United States. Emphasis is on methods and history of education. It sponsors the National Curriculum Research Institute. A 4,000-volume library is maintained.

THE AMERICAN JEWISH COMMITTEE (AJC)
165 East 56th Street
New York, New York 10022   (212) 751-4000
Principal officers: Elmer L. Winter, President
                       Bertram H. Gold, Executive Vice President

Permanent staff: 350   Membership: 42,000
Date founded: 1906   Membership dues: $25.00 (annual)
Branches: 23 chapter offices   Scope: national

Special requirements for membership: none

Nature of organization: community relations

Publications: *What's Doing at the Committee*, 1971– (monthly); *Commentary Magazine*, 1945– (monthly); *American Jewish Year Book*, 1899– (annual); *Present Tense*, 1973– (quarterly); has also published numerous other materials

Affiliations: International League for the Rights of Man; American Conference on Soviet Jewry; National Jewish Community Relations Advisory Committee

Major conventions/meetings: annual meeting

Comments: The purpose of this organization is to promote the interests and rights of Jews in the United States and in Israel, as well as to improve human relations of all mankind. It sponsors social action to improve human and urban relations, housing, and employment opportunities, and it sponsors programs to help maintain the Jewish identity and culture in the United States. A library and archival collection are maintained.

AMERICAN JEWISH CONGRESS (AJC)
15 East 84th Street
New York, New York 10028   (212) 879-4500

Principal officers: Naomi Levine, Executive Director

Permanent staff: 100	Membership: 300 local groups
Date founded: 1918	Membership dues: NI
Branches: NI	Scope: national

Nature of organization: cultural, political

Publications: *Congress*, 1933– (biweekly); *Judaism*, 1952– (quarterly)

Major conventions/meetings: biennial

Comments: The purpose of the organization is to unite Jews in America and to assist Israel. It opposes racism and promotes Jewish cultural activities and programs.

AMERICAN JEWISH HISTORICAL SOCIETY (AJHS)
2 Thornton Road
Waltham, Massachusetts 02154   (617) 891-8110

Principal officers: Olrahan J. Kark, President
                        David Kirschenbaum, Executive Secretary
                        Maurice Vacobs, Chairman–Executive Council

Permanent staff: 7	Membership: 3,000
Date founded: 1892	Membership dues: $15.00 (annual)
Branches: 2 local	Scope: national

Special requirements for membership: none

Nature of organization: educational

Publications: *American Jewish Historical Quarterly*, 1893– (quarterly); *Newsletter*, 1967– (irregular); also publishes books

Affiliations: American Historical Association; National Trust for Historical Preservation; American Association in State and Local History

Major conventions/meetings: annual convention

Comments: The purpose of this historical society is to preserve and promote the Jewish heritage in the United States and to conduct research in Jewish history, immigration, and life in the United States. It sponsors lectures, exhibitions, publications, and an in-service teacher's course. It grants awards and scholarships. A 46,500-volume library is maintained.

AMERICAN ZIONIST FEDERATION (AZF)
515 Park Avenue
New York, New York 10022   (212) 371-7750

Principal officers: Harry A. Steinberg, Executive Director

Permanent staff: 11	Membership: 13 organizations
Date founded: 1939	Membership dues: NI
Branches: 400 local groups	Scope: national

Special requirements for membership: must be a national Zionist organization

Nature of organization: religious

Major conventions/meetings: biennial

Comments: This organization is the coordinating agency for the 13 national Zionist organizations in the United States. It sponsors educational and cultural programs and promotes the Zionist movement in the United States. Member organizations are: AACA; American Jewish League for Israel; Americans for Progressive Israel; B'nai Zion; Hadassah; Labor Zionist Alliance; Mizrachi Women's Organization; Pioneer Women; Religious Zionists of America; United Zionists Revisionists of America.

AMERICAN ZIONIST YOUTH FOUNDATION, INC. (AZYF)
515 Park Avenue
New York, New York 10022   (212) 751-6070

Principal officers: Arnulf M. Pins, Chairman
                     Mrs. Evrett Kalb, Treasurer
                     Mrs. Burt Siris, Executive Secretary

Permanent staff: 35   Membership: not a member organization
Date founded: 1963   Membership dues: none
Branches: 4 regional; 105 field workers (state)   Scope: U.S. and Canada

Special requirements for membership: none

Nature of organization: educational

Publications: publishes books, pamphlets, program guides, leaflets, etc.

Affiliations: World Zionist Organization

Major conventions/meetings: annual fieldworker conference

Comments: Serves as a consultant and resource institution to numerous Jewish youth organizations. It provides educational programs and services that define Jewish history and heritage and seeks to encourage a greater identification of Jewish-American youth with Israel and Jews. Sponsors a summer program for American youth in Israel, workshops, and the Institute for Leaders from Abroad.

ANTI-DEFAMATION LEAGUE OF B'NAI B'RITH (ADL)
315 Lexington Avenue
New York, New York 10016   (212) 689-7400

Principal officers: Seymour Graubard, National Chairman
                     Benjamin R. Epstein, National Director

Permanent staff: 300   Membership: not a membership
Date founded: 1913   organization
Branches: 28 regional   Membership dues: none
                                     Scope: national, regional

Special requirements for membership: none

Nature of organization: educational, human relations

Comments: The major objective of the organization is to combat anti-Semitism and promote the rights and interests of Jewish-Americans. It sponsors programs involved with education, community action, and the communications media.

ASSOCIATION OF JEWISH CENTER WORKERS (AJCW)
15 East 26th Street
New York, New York 10010   (212) 532-4949

Principal officers: Harry R. Rosen, President
                     Myron Berezin, Executive Vice President
                     Louis Kraft, Executive Secretary

Permanent staff: 2   Membership: 945
Date founded: 1918   Membership dues: $5.00-$65.00 depend-
Branches: 10 regional   ing on annual salary
                                     Scope: national, including Canada

Special requirements for membership: "professional workers in Jewish Community Center field"

Nature of organization: professional

Publications: *Viewpoints*, 1965– (semiannual); *Conference Papers*, 1962– (annual); also publishes books

Affiliations: none

Major conventions/meetings: annual conference

Comments: Attempts to advance the Jewish Community Center (YM-YWHA) and provide services to Jewish-Americans through it in areas of recreation, education, and social welfare. Its purpose is to unite the workers in such programs for further training, improvement of working conditions, and to strengthen collective study and action in

ASSOCIATION OF JEWISH CENTER WORKERS (AJCW) (cont'd)

the fields of recreation, education, health, and welfare. Until 1970 the association was known as the National Association of Jewish Center Workers.

ASSOCIATION OF JEWISH LIBRARIES (AJL)

139 Winton Road, South
Rochester, New York 14610 (716) 473-1770

Principal officers: Mrs. Nelson Kirshenbaum, President
Leonard Gold, Vice President
Rose Miskin, Vice President
Irene Levin, Corresponding Secretary

Permanent staff: none
Date founded: 1965
Branches: none

Membership: 300
Membership dues: $12.50 (annual institution membership)
Scope: national

Special requirements for membership: none

Nature of organization: educational, professional

Publications: proceedings of annual conventions, 1965– ; *AJL Bulletin*, 1965– (1 to 2 per year); also publishes bibliographies, books, etc.

Affiliations: none

Major conventions/meetings: annual convention

Comments: The major functions of the association are to improve and benefit libraries of Judaica by providing guidance, information services, and professional workshops, and to unite Jewish librarians in the United States. It grants an annual $100 scholarship to a library student preparing to work in a Jewish library, and grants the annual Kravetz Children's Book Award.

B'NAI B'RITH (BB)

1640 Rhode Island Avenue, N.W.
Washington, D.C. 20036 (202) 393-5284

Principal officers: Rabbi Benjamin M. Kahn, Executive Vice President

Permanent staff: 500
Date founded: 1843
Branches: 75 regional groups; 3,500 local

Membership: 500,000
Membership dues: NI
Scope: national

Special requirements for membership: of Jewish descent

Nature of organization: cultural, philanthropic, fraternal

Publications: *National Jewish Monthly*, 1886– (monthly); *Jewish Heritage*, 1957– (quarterly)

Major conventions/meetings: triennial

Comments: The purpose of the organization is to unite Jews in the United States, to carry on community and civic projects to benefit Jewish-Americans, and to promote the Jewish-American image. It maintains a 15,000-volume library on Judaica.

B'NAI B'RITH HILLEL FOUNDATION, INC.

1640 Rhode Island Avenue, N.W.
Washington, D.C. 20036

Principal officers: Marver Bernstein, Chairman
Alfred Jospe, International Director

Permanent staff: NI
Date founded: 1923
Branches: NI

Membership: 280 chapters
Membership dues: NI
Scope: international

Nature of organization: cultural, religious, educational, social, youth

Publications: *Clearing House*; *Campus*; also publishes books

Comments: Coordinates and sponsors religious, social, educational, cultural, and counseling programs for Jewish students on 280 college and university campus Hillel chapters in the United States and abroad.

B'NAI B'RITH YOUTH ORGANIZATION (BBYO)
1640 Rhode Island Avenue, N.W.
Washington, D.C. 20036　　　　　　　(203) 393-5284
Principal officers:　Max F. Bear, National Director

Permanent staff: 175　　　　　　　　Membership: 41,000
Date founded: 1924　　　　　　　　　Membership dues: NI
Branches: 1,450 local groups　　　　　Scope: national

Special requirements for membership: youth of Jewish background

Nature of organization: educational, social, cultural

Publications: *The Shofar*, 1924– (7 issues per year)

Affiliations: B'nai B'rith

Major conventions/meetings: annual

Comments: A youth organization designed to unite Jewish youth from all backgrounds–
conservative, orthodox, and reform. It sponsors various training programs in social work
or of an educational nature; maintains a small library at Camp B'nai B'rith in Starlight,
Pennsylvania.

B'NAI ZION
136 East 39th Street
New York, New York 10016　　　　　　(212) 725-1211
Principal officers:　Harold Bernstein, President
　　　　　　　　　　Justice Abraham J. Multer, Vice President
　　　　　　　　　　Herman Z. Quittman, Secretary

Permanent staff: 18　　　　　　　　　Membership: 28,000
Date founded: 1906　　　　　　　　　Membership dues: $12.00
Branches: 8 regional; 8 state; 124 local　Scope: national

Special requirements for membership: men and women of Jewish faith

Nature of organization: fraternal

Publications: *B'nai Zion Voice*, 1918– (bimonthly)

Affiliations: Conference of Presidents of Major American Jewish Organizations; American
Zionist Federation

Major conventions/meetings: convention of delegates elected by local chapters, annually

Comments: This fraternal Zionist organization promotes preservation of the Hebrew culture in
the United States and provides insurance benefits to members. It also sponsors youth
centers, medical clinics, and a home for retarded children in Israel. It grants scholarships to students of Hebrew and annual awards for outstanding contributions in promoting equal human rights. It sponsors the American-Israel Friendship League. A small
library is maintained.

CONFERENCE OF PRESIDENTS OF MAJOR AMERICAN JEWISH ORGANIZATIONS
515 Park Avenue
New York, New York 10022　　　　　　(212) 752-1616
Principal officers:　Yehuda Hellman, Executive Director

Permanent staff: 4　　　　　　　　　Membership: 30
Date founded: 1954　　　　　　　　　Membership dues: NI
Branches: NI　　　　　　　　　　　　Scope: national

Nature of organization: cultural, political

Comments: The conference is comprised of most major American Jewish organizations. Its
role is to keep member groups informed about international issues of interest to Jews;
it sponsors lectures and discussion groups.

COORDINATING BOARD OF JEWISH ORGANIZATIONS (CBJO)
1640 Rhode Island Avenue, N.W.
Washington, D.C. 20036　　　　　　　(202) 393-5284
Principal officers:　Herman Edelsberg, Executive Secretary

COORDINATING BOARD OF JEWISH ORGANIZATIONS (CBJO) (cont'd)

Permanent staff: 10

Date founded: 1947

Branches: NI

Membership: NI

Membership dues: NI

Scope: national

Nature of organization: scholarly, political, educational

Comments: This organization coordinates the activities of several Jewish-American groups (including B'nai B'rith), as well as international groups. It acts as a consultant to the United Nations.

COUNCIL OF JEWISH FEDERATION AND WELFARE FUNDS (JFWF)

315 Park Avenue, South

New York, New York 10010　　　　　　　　(212) 673-8200

Principal officers:　　Irving Blum, President

　　　　　　　　　　Philip Bernstein, Executive Vice President

Permanent staff: 50

Date founded: 1932

Branches: none

Membership: 235 associated Jewish community organizations in the U.S.

Membership dues: none

Scope: U.S. and Canada

Special requirements for membership: "Limited to Jewish federations, welfare funds, community councils, etc. which plan and/or finance Jewish social work and meet Jewish communal needs."

Nature of organization: Jewish communal welfare

Publications: *Yearbook of Jewish Social Services* (annual); *Directory of Jewish Federations, Welfare Funds and Community Councils* (annual); *Jewish Communal Services; Programs and Finances* (annual)

Affiliations: none

Major conventions/meetings: annual general assembly

Comments: This organization coordinates the activities of Jewish community groups and acts as a central clearinghouse and headquarters for fund-raising projects. It provides information on health and welfare planning, provides conferences for national leaders to exchange ideas and problems, and organizes welfare work. It grants awards and maintains a library and archival collection.

THE FREE SONS OF ISRAEL

932 Broadway Avenue

New York, New York 10010　　　　　　　　(212) 260-4222

Principal officers:　　Louis Norris, Grand Master

　　　　　　　　　　Murray Birnback, Grand Secretary

Permanent staff: 6

Date founded: 1849

Branches: 50

Membership: 10,000

Membership dues: differs in each branch

Scope: national

Special requirements for membership: Hebrew faith

Nature of organization: fraternal

Publications: *Free Son Reporter* (quarterly); each lodge publishes a monthly bulletin

Affiliations: National Conference of Soviet Jewry

Major conventions/meetings: conventions every three years

Comments: The purpose of the organization is to unite the Jews in the United States and to provide life insurance benefits for members. It also provides assistance to Jews in need and protection from oppression at home and in Europe. It sponsors camps, scholarships, and annual awards. An archival collection of records and minutes is maintained.

HADASSAH, THE WOMEN'S ZIONIST ORGANIZATION OF AMERICA, INC.
62 East 52nd Street
New York, New York 10022   (212) 355-7900

Principal officers: Rose E. Matzkin, President
                      Aline Kaplan, Executive Director

Permanent staff: 125   Membership: 325,000
Date founded: 1912   Membership dues: $10.00 (annual);
Branches: 1,400 chapters and groups in all 50 $150.00 (life membership)
  states and Puerto Rico   Scope: national, local, regional

Special requirements for membership: "must be female"

Nature of organization: educational, medical, social rehabilitation

Publications: *Hadassah Magazine* (10 issues per year); *Headlines* (8 issues per year); also
    publishes booklets and study guides on Jewish history, literature, etc.

Affiliations: National Citizens Committee; World Health Organization; American Zionist
    Federation

Major conventions/meetings: annual convention

Comments: Primarily a women's welfare organization, Hadassah supports and sponsors various
    educational, public health, youth, land reclamation, and medical projects, including the
    Hadassah Hebrew University Medical Center. It grants an annual service award, sponsors
    cultural summer camp programs in the United States and Israel and exchange programs
    with Israeli Scouts. A multimedia library is maintained.

JEWISH ACADEMY OF ARTS AND SCIENCES
Dropsie University
Broad and York Streets
Philadelphia, Pennsylvania 19132

Principal officers: Leo Jung, President
                      Abraham I. Katsh, Board Chairman
                      Hirsch L. Silverman, Executive Secretary

Permanent staff: 5   Membership: 75
Date founded: 1925   Membership dues: honorary
Branches: none   Scope: national

Special requirements for membership: "Distinction in the arts and sciences. Election by
    Fellows of The Academy."

Nature of organization: educational, cultural, religious, scholarly

Publications: *Annals of the Jewish Academy of Arts and Sciences*, 1925– (biannual)

Affiliations: none

Major conventions/meetings: annual convention

Comments: Attempts to recognize scholars making contributions in education, science, arts,
    religion, and culture. It conducts seminars, lectures, and institutes in New York City
    and Philadelphia. An archival collection is maintained.

JEWISH TEACHERS ASSOCIATION (JTA)
11 West 42nd Street
New York, New York 10036

Principal officers: Michael Leinwand, President
                      Jerome Greenblatt, Executive Vice President
                      Dorothy Posner, Executive Secretary

Permanent staff: 5   Membership: 30,000
Date founded: 1927   Membership dues: $5.00 (annual)
Branches: 1,700 regional   Scope: national

Special requirements for membership: Jewish faith and a teacher in public or private schools

Nature of organization: social, educational, cultural, religious, recreational, professional,
    fraternal, scholarly

Publications: *Jewish Teachers Association Newsletter*, 1927– (3 issues per year)

JEWISH TEACHERS ASSOCIATION (JTA) (cont'd)

Affiliations: Council of Jewish Organizations in Civil Services

Major conventions/meetings: annual convention

Comments: The primary goals of JTA are to "promote the religious, social, and moral welfare" of children and teachers. It supports a special scholarship fund program and grants annual awards for service.

NATIONAL COUNCIL OF JEWISH WOMEN (NCJW)
1 West 47th Street
New York, New York 10036   (212) 246-3175

Principal officers: Eleanor Marvin, President
                       Hannah Stein, Executive Director

Permanent staff: none   Membership: 100,000
Date founded: 1893   Membership dues: NI
Branches: 5 district; 200 local   Scope: NI

Special requirements for membership: must be Jewish

Nature of organization: community service, social action, education

Publications: *Council Woman* (5 issues per year); *Hotline* (bimonthly); *Washington Newsletter*; also publishes books

Affiliations: WICS (Women in Community Service); ICJW (International Council of Jewish Women)

Major conventions/meetings: national convention biennially

Comments: This Jewish women's service organization sponsors various social action and welfare projects, particularly for children, youth, the disadvantaged, and the aged. It sponsors various fund-raising programs and grants annual service awards.

NATIONAL FOUNDATION FOR JEWISH CULTURE (NFJC)
122 East 42nd Street
New York, New York 10017   (212) 490-2280

Principal officers: Daniel Jeremy Silver, President
                       Harry I. Barron, Executive Director and Executive Secretary
                       G. M. Zeltzer, Executive Vice President
                       E. Morse, Executive Vice President
                       J. Freeman, Executive Vice President

Permanent staff: 6   Membership: NI
Date founded: 1960   Membership dues: NI
Branches: none   Scope: national

Special requirements for membership: none

Nature of organization: cultural

Publications: *NFJC Reporter*, 1969– (quarterly)

Affiliations: none

Major conventions/meetings: none

Comments: The organization is primarily a cultural agent, advising, supporting, and sponsoring programs for Jewish communities and other smaller organizations. It provides grants and scholarships for scholars in Jewish studies and administers the Joint Cultural Appeal.

NATIONAL JEWISH COMMUNITY RELATIONS ADVISORY COUNCIL
55 West 42nd Street, Room 1530
New York, New York 10036   (212) 564-3450

Principal officers: Isaiah M. Minkoff, Executive Vice Chairman

Permanent staff: 11   Membership: 101 (9 organizations; 92
Date founded: 1944   community councils)
Branches: NI   Membership dues: NI
                                            Scope: national

NATIONAL JEWISH COMMUNITY RELATIONS ADVISORY COUNCIL (cont'd)

Nature of organization: religious, political, cultural

Publications: *Directory of Constituent Organizations* (annual); *Report of Plenary Session* (annual)

Major conventions/meetings: annual

Comments: The organizations comprising this council are involved in political and social issues involving the Jewish community and American society at large. Emphasis is on civil rights, equal rights, and inter-group relations.

NATIONAL JEWISH WELFARE BOARD (JWB)

15 East 26th Street
New York, New York 10010   (212) 532-4949

Principal officers: Morton L. Mandel, President
                       Herbert Millman, Executive Vice President

Permanent staff: 48   Membership: 1,000,000
Date founded: 1917   Membership dues: NI
Branches: 400 local   Scope: national

Special requirements for membership: none

Nature of organization: social, educational, cultural, recreational

Publications: *JWB Circle*, 1946– (7 times per year)

Affiliations: none

Major conventions/meetings: national convention biennially

Comments: Serves the Jewish Community Centers, YM-YWHA's, and Jewish camps by conducting research and by providing consultation services, building guidance, personnel, etc. Also serves the recreational and welfare needs of Jewish military personnel and veterans and their families. It promotes Jewish culture in the United States and relations between Jewish-Americans and Israel.

PIONEER WOMEN (PW), THE WOMAN'S LABOR ZIONIST ORGANIZATION OF AMERICA, INC.

315 Fifth Avenue
New York, New York 10016   (212) 725-8010

Principal officers: Charlotte Stein, President
                       Lilian Hantman, Vice President
                       Frieda Leemon, Vice President
                       Sylvia Snyder, Secretary
                       Faye Laeger, Secretary
                       Zelda Lemberger, Treasurer

Permanent staff: 30   Membership: 50,000
Date founded: 1926   Membership dues: $10.00 (annual)
Branches: 400 clubs   Scope: national

Special requirements for membership: Jewish women

Nature of organization: educational, cultural, philanthropic

Publications: *Pioneer Woman Journal* (8 times per year)

Affiliations: American Zionist Federation; Labor Zionist Alliance; Conference of Presidents of Major Jewish Organizations; Conference on Soviet Jewry

Major conventions/meetings: national convention biennially; area seminars annually

Comments: This women's organization promotes Jewish education and culture in the United States. It sponsors fund-raising activities for various charitable projects. Cooperating with its Israeli counterpart organization, it provides more than 50 percent of the social services available. It grants scholarships for women training as nurses, dental technicians, cosmetologists. A small archival collection of historical documents is maintained.

RABBINICAL ALLIANCE OF AMERICA (RAA)
156 Fifth Avenue
New York, New York 10010   (212) 242-6420
Principal officers: Rabbi Abraham Gross, President
                      Rabbi David B. Hollander, Executive Vice President
                      Rabbi Borich Leibwitz, Executive Secretary

Permanent staff: 2	Membership: 500
Date founded: 1940	Membership dues: NI
Branches: none	Scope: national

Special requirements for membership: "Rabbi and ministering in an orthodox synagogue according to prescribed laws."

Nature of organization: professional

Publications: *Prospective*, 1959– (annual); *RA Newsletter*, 1956– (monthly); also publishes books

Affiliations: none

Major conventions/meetings: annual convention

Comments: The organization's purpose is to unite rabbis and Jewish Day School principals, to "strengthen the ties of orthodoxy," and to serve as a voice on issues affecting the Jewish world. A small library (200 volumes) is maintained.

SYNAGOGUE COUNCIL OF AMERICA
432 Park Avenue South
New York, New York 10016

Principal officers: Irving Lehrman, President
                      Henry Siegman, Executive Vice President

Permanent staff: NI	Membership: NI
Date founded: 1924	Membership dues: NI
Branches: NI	Scope: national

Nature of organization: religious

Publications: *Action Memo*; *Newsletter*; *Analysis*

Comments: This organization represents Orthodox, Conservative, and Reform Judaism in the United States. Its main function is to promote Judaism and the interests of Jewish-Americans.

UNION OF AMERICAN HEBREW CONGREGATIONS (JAHC)
838 Fifth Avenue
New York, New York 10021

Principal officers: Rabbi Maurice N. Eisendrath, President

Permanent staff: 195	Membership: 210,000
Date founded: 1873	Membership dues: NI
Branches: 16 regional	Scope: national

Nature of organization: religious, educational, cultural

Publications: *Keeping Posted*, 1955– (biweekly); *Synagogue Services Bulletin* (bimonthly); *RJA Voice* (quarterly)

Major conventions/meetings: biennial

Comments: A major representative of Reform Judaism in the United States, this organization provides religious, cultural, and educational services to various temples in the United States of like faith.

UNION OF ORTHODOX JEWISH CONGREGATIONS OF AMERICA (UOJCA)
116 East 27th Street
New York, New York 10016   (212) 725-3400

Principal officers: Berel Wein, Executive Vice President

Permanent staff: 50	Membership: 3,100
Date founded: 1898	Membership dues: NI
Branches: 12 regional groups	Scope: NI

UNION OF ORTHODOX JEWISH CONGREGATIONS OF AMERICA
(UOJCA) (cont'd)

Publications: *Keeping Posted*, 1955– (monthly); *Jewish Action* (bimonthly); *Jewish Life*, 1946– (bimonthly)

Major conventions/meetings: biennial

Comments: The congregations represented in this union represent Orthodox Judaism in America. The union acts as a coordinating agency for 3,100 temples; it provides educational, cultural, recreational, social, and religious programs for member groups, including activities of men's clubs and youth groups. It also conducts the national U Kashruth certification service.

UNION OF SEPHARDIC CONGREGATIONS
8 West 70th Street
New York, New York 10023   (212) 873-0300

Principal officers: Victor Tarry, Secretary

Permanent staff: NI   Membership: 63
Date founded: 1929   Membership dues: NI
Branches: NI   Scope: national

Nature of organization: religious

Comments: The major purpose of the organization is to promote and perpetuate the interests of the Sephardic Jews in the United States. It supplies religious leaders to congregations in need of them, and it prepares and distributes religious materials and prayer books in English and in Hebrew.

UNITED ISRAEL APPEAL (UIA)
515 Park Avenue
New York, New York 10022   (212) 755-7400

Principal officers: Gottlieb Hammer, Executive Vice President

Permanent staff: NI   Membership: NI
Date founded: 1927   Membership dues: NI
Branches: NI   Scope: national

Nature of organization: social service

Comments: The purpose of the organization is to raise funds for the Jewish resettlement and immigrant program in Israel, and to help expand the resources of that nation. Assistance is given in job attainment; special programs funded are in health, education, agriculture, housing, etc. In 1966 the organization absorbed the Jewish Agency for Israel.

UNITED JEWISH APPEAL (UJA)
1290 Avenue of the Americas
New York, New York 10019

Principal officers: Irving Bernstein, Executive Vice Chairman

Permanent staff: 200   Membership: NI
Date founded: 1939   Membership dues: NI
Branches: NI   Scope: national

Nature of organization: fund raising

Major conventions/meetings: annual

Comments: The major purpose of this fund-raising organization is to support various efforts on behalf of needy Jews in Europe and Jewish immigrants to Israel and the United States.

UNITED SYNAGOGUE OF AMERICA (USA)
432 Park Avenue, South
New York, New York 10016   (212) 749-8000

Principal officers: Bernard Segal, Executive Vice President

UNITED SYNAGOGUE OF AMERICA (USA) (cont'd)

Permanent staff: NI
Date founded: 1913
Branches: NI

Membership: 835 congregations;
1,750,000 individuals
Membership dues: NI
Scope: national

Special requirements for membership: Jew of Conservative Judaism faith

Nature of organization: religious

Publications: *Our Age–Dorenu* (biweekly); *Kol Atid* (monthly); *Adult Jewish Education*
(quarterly); *Achshav* (quarterly); *Advisors Newsletter* (quarterly); *Conservative
Judaism*, 1943– (quarterly); *Outlook* (quarterly); *Synagogue School*, 1942– (quarterly);
Torch, 1941– (quarterly); *United Synagogue Review*, 1957– (quarterly); *Your Child*,
1968– (quarterly); *Report to the Convention* (biennial)

Affiliations: National Federation of Jewish Men's Club

Major conventions/meetings: biennial

Comments: This organization promotes Conservative Judaism in the United States. It
supports the Conservative faith, including the Torah, Sabbath observance, and
dietary laws. It promotes the Hebrew language and maintains 12 departments and 10
regional offices to help assist the various congregations in cultural and religious training
programs.

THE WORKMEN'S CIRCLE
45 East 33rd Street
New York, New York 10016

Principal officers: Harold Ostroff, President
Vladka Meed, Executive Vice President
William Stern, Executive Secretary

Permanent staff: 50
Date founded: 1900
Branches: 9 regional; 28 state; 350 local

Membership: 52,500
Membership dues: $12.00 women
(annual); $6.00 youth (annual)
Scope: national

Special requirements for membership: none

Nature of organization: social, educational, cultural, fraternal

Publications: *The Workmen's Circle CALL*, 1927– (monthly); *Culture and Life*, 1918–
(bimonthly)

Affiliations: Jewish Labor Committee; American Labor ORT; United HIAS Service

Major conventions/meetings: biennial convention

Comments: The major role of the organization is to provide life insurance benefits to members.
It also promotes the Jewish heritage in the United States by providing social and
cultural activities and programs. It is identified with the labor movement and affiliated
with national labor organizations. A library and archival collection are maintained.

KOREAN-AMERICAN ORGANIZATIONS

Additional information on Korean-American organizations in the United
States may be obtained from the Office of the Korean Embassy (2320
Massachusetts Avenue, Washington, D.C. 20008) and from the Christian Youth
Association of California (4038 South Western, Los Angeles, California 90062).

AMERICAN-KOREAN FOUNDATION (AKF)
345 East 46th Street
New York, New York 10017   (212) 697-1960

AMERICAN-KOREAN FOUNDATION (AKF) (cont'd)

Permanent staff: NI
Date founded: 1952
Branches: NI

Membership: 52 board members
Membership dues: NI
Scope: national

Nature of organization: charitable, educational

Publications: *Newsletter* (semiannual); *Annual Report* (annual)

Major conventions/meetings: semiannual

Comments: Furnishes medical and other assistance to people in Korea and Southeast Asia. Also establishes schools, sponsors educational programs, and grants scholarships in the United States and Korea. Provides advising services to Korean students in the United States and an employment service for Koreans in the New York City area.

AMERICAN-KOREAN FRIENDSHIP AND INFORMATION CENTER

160 Fifth Avenue
New York, New York 10010   (212) 242-0240

Principal officers: Joseph Brandt, Executive Director

Permanent staff: NI
Date founded: 1971
Branches: NI

Membership: NI
Membership dues: NI
Scope: national

Nature of organization: educational, informational

Publications: *Korea Focus* (quarterly)

Comments: Works to promote American-Korean relations. Disseminates information on Korea, conducts lectures and discussions, and sponsors films and slide presentations.

CHRISTIAN YOUTH ASSOCIATION OF CALIFORNIA

4038 South Western
Los Angeles, California 90062   (213) 296-3230

Principal officers: Myung Kyun Kim, President

Permanent staff: 3
Date founded: 1969
Branches: NI

Membership: 3,000
Membership dues: NI
Scope: national

KOREAN AFFAIRS INSTITUTE (KAI)

3900 Watson Place, N.W.
Washington, D.C. 20016   (202) 337-0941

Principal officers: Youngjeung Kim, President

Permanent staff: NI
Date founded: 1943
Branches: NI

Membership: NI
Membership dues: NI
Scope: national

Nature of organization: cultural, political, economic

Comments: The purpose of the organization is to promote research into Korean political and economic history, culture, and other areas of Korean studies.

KOREAN-AMERICAN CHAMBER OF COMMERCE (KACC)

P.O. Box 2801
Washington, D.C. 20013

Principal officers: C. H. Yim, Acting Executive Secretary

Permanent staff: NI
Date founded: 1964
Branches: NI

Membership: 200
Membership dues: NI
Scope: NI

Nature of organization: economic

Publications: *Newsletter* (semimonthly); *Korean-American Journal of Commerce* (monthly); *Korean-American Trade Directory* (annual)

Affiliations: Association of Asian-American Chambers of Commerce

Major conventions/meetings: annual

KOREAN-AMERICAN COMMUNITY SERVICES (KACS)
3435 North Sheffield
Chicago, Illinois 60657 (312) 348-2202

Principal officers: Dr. Paul Chung, President
Jung Ock Lee, Vice President

Permanent staff: 6 Membership: 500
Date founded: 1972 Membership dues: $10.00
Branches: NI Scope: regional

Nature of organization: social, educational

Affiliations: United Christian Community Services

Major conventions/meetings: annual business meeting; monthly Board meeting

Comments: Purpose of KACS is to provide diversified human welfare services to Korean
Americans and others in need in the metropolitan Chicago area through intensive
programs: information and referral services, job placement services, counseling
services, and translation and interpreting services.

KOREAN AMERICAN WIVES' CLUB (KAWC)
1430 Fleming Drive North, Apt. E
Arlington Heights, Illinois 60004 (312) 392-3738

Principal officers: Mrs. Bong Hee Stephens, President
Alvera Chung, Vice President

Permanent staff: 7 Membership: 96
Date founded: 1970 Membership dues: $10.00
Branches: none Scope: local

Special requirements for membership: Korean women married to Americans and American
women married to Koreans

Nature of organization: cultural, social

Publications: *Korean American Wives' Club Newsletter*, 1970– (monthly)

Major conventions/meetings: monthly meeting

Comments: This social and cultural organization promotes cultural exchange between
Koreans and Americans. The club also helps orphanages in Korea. Activities include
an annual picnic and a Christmas party.

KOREAN ARTIST'S ASSOCIATION OF SOUTHERN CALIFORNIA (KAASC)
12030 Califa Street
North Hollywood, California 91607 (213) 762-1663

Principal officers: Bong Tae Kim, President
Yeon Bahk, Vice President

Permanent staff: none Membership: 50
Date founded: 1964 Membership dues: $20.00
Branches: NI Scope: local

Special requirements for membership: graduates of fine arts colleges or working artists
recommended by more than three members

Nature of organization: cultural

Publications: none

Affiliations: none

Comments: This organization has an annual membership exhibition and an annual children's
art competition. Members of the organization teach a Saturday artists' group and help
with other cultural events related to the fine arts.

THE KOREAN ASSOCIATION OF GREATER CLEVELAND (KAGC)
19518 Royalton Road
Strongsville, Ohio 44136 (216) 238-8474

Principal officers: Jung K. Lee, President
Tack J. Whang, Vice President

THE KOREAN ASSOCIATION OF GREATER CLEVELAND (KAGC) (cont'd)

Permanent staff: 2   Membership: 2,000
Date founded: 1960   Membership dues: NI
Branches: NI   Scope: regional

Special requirements for membership: native Korean

Nature of organization: cultural, economic, social, religious, educational, and recreational

Publications: none

Major conventions/meetings: annual meeting

Comments: The purposes of this non-profit organization are social education, vocational upgrading, and approximate adjustment of Koreans. The activities of this organization include lectures, commemoration ceremonies, picnics, and banquets. The association sponsors Korean-language instruction and grants an annual award to an outstanding individual.

KOREAN ASSOCIATION OF GREATER WASHINGTON

1729 21st Street, N.W.   (202) 387-2210 or
Washington, D.C. 20009   (202) 387-2200

Principal officers: Do Young Lee

Permanent staff: NI   Membership: 1,857
Date founded: 1961   Membership dues: NI
Branches: NI   Scope: NI

THE KOREAN ASSOCIATION OF PROFESSIONALS IN CENTRAL ILLINOIS

2719 East California Street
Urbana, Illinois 61801   (217) 367-7508

Principal officers: Keun Suck Park, President
     Kwang Chul Ha, Vice President

Permanent staff: 4   Membership: 80
Date founded: 1970   Membership dues: $5.00
Branches: none   Scope: local

Special requirements for membership: Korean professionals living permanently in the Central Illinois area

Nature of organization: cultural, social, professional, recreational

Publications: *KAP Newsletter*, 1970– (biannual); *KAP Directory*, 1974– (annual)

Affiliations: none

Major conventions/meetings: biannual convention

Comments: The objective of this association is to promote mutual benefits for Korean professionals living in Central Illinois with respect to cultural, recreational, social, and professional interests.

KOREAN ASSOCIATION OF SOUTHERN CALIFORNIA

2559 West Olympic Boulevard
Los Angeles, California 90006   (213) 380-8578

Principal officers: Chong Shik Kim, President

Permanent staff: 3   Membership: 800
Date founded: 1962   Membership dues: NI
Branches: NI   Scope: regional

THE KOREAN ASSOCIATION OF SOUTHWESTERN MICHIGAN

2030 Aberdeen Drive
Kalamazoo, Michigan 49008   (517) 344-2130

Principal officers: Dae Y. Cha, President
     Hee Sung Park, Vice President

THE KOREAN ASSOCIATION OF SOUTHWESTERN MICHIGAN (cont'd)

Permanent staff: NI   Membership: 54 families
Date founded: 1973   Membership dues: $2.00
Branches: 3 local   Scope: local

Special requirements for membership: Koreans and Americans married to Koreans

Nature of organization: social

Publications: none

Affiliations: none

Major conventions/meetings: biannual convention

Comments: The purpose of this association is to promote friendship and cooperation among
Koreans residing in this area, and to enhance mutual understanding between Koreans
and Americans through social and cultural activities.

KOREAN BUSINESSMEN'S ASSOCIATION OF CHICAGO (KBAC)

5106 North Cicero Avenue
Chicago, Illinois 60630   (312) 286-7811

Principal officers: Y. C. Shin, President
                      Hi Kahng, Vice President

Permanent staff: NI   Membership: 48
Date founded: 1974   Membership dues: $50.00
Branches: none   Scope: regional

Special requirements for membership: originally native of Korea or of Korean extraction

Nature of organization: cultural, economic, social, professional

Major conventions/meetings: general membership meeting, once or twice a year

Comments: The prime objective of this organization is to maintain or strengthen the friendship among Korean businessmen in social and economic affairs.

KOREAN COMMUNITY FOUNDATION, INC.

170 West 72nd Street
New York, New York 10023   (212) 787-3277

Principal officers: John Ilhack Kim, President
                      Peter B. Kim, Vice President

Permanent staff: 20   Membership: 150
Date founded: 1968   Membership dues: $20.00
Branches: none   Scope: statewide

Special requirements for membership: minimum age of 25

Nature of organization: cultural, social

Publications: The K.C.F. Bulletin (irregular)

Affiliations: none

Major conventions/meetings: annual conference

Comments: The main objective of this organization is to promote friendship and understanding among different peoples. The foundation aids underprivileged youth in Korea and
also raises funds to grant scholarships for Korean students. Sponsors an annual seminar.
An archival collection is maintained.

KOREAN NATIONAL ASSOCIATION

1368 West Jefferson Boulevard
Los Angeles, California 90007   (213) 735-0424

Principal officers: P. K. Lee, General Manager

Permanent staff: NI   Membership: NI
Date founded: NI   Membership dues: NI
Branches: NI   Scope: national

Nature of organization: educational

Publications: New Korea (weekly)

KOREAN NATIONAL ASSOCIATION (cont'd)

Major conventions/meetings: annual

Comments: The major purpose of the school is to conduct a Korean language school for children and youths and to maintain the Korean heritage and culture in the United States.

THE KOREAN SOCIETY OF GREATER BALTIMORE
33 West North Avenue
Baltimore, Maryland 21201   (301) 323-8976

Principal officers: Chang Ho Kim, President
                Zong Wook Huh, Vice President

Permanent staff: 34   Membership: 5,000
Date founded: 1972   Membership dues: $3.00 per household
Branches: none   Scope: local

Special requirements for membership: Korean Americans, including permanent residents

Nature of organization: cultural, social, educational

Publications: *Baltimore Korean Newsletter*, 1973– (2 times per year)

Major conventions/meetings: annual convention

Comments: The purpose of this organization is to promote cooperation among Koreans in this region and to help them manage their lives in the United States.

KOREAN SOCIETY OF METROPOLITAN DETROIT
9517 West Seven Mile Road
Detroit, Michigan 48219

Principal officers: Ty K. Shin, President
                Byung Soo Park, Vice President
                Mary Joh, Secretary

Permanent staff: none   Membership: NI
Date founded: 1971   Membership dues: $3.00 (annual)
Branches: none   Scope: local

Special requirements for membership: none

Nature of organization: cultural, fraternal, political, social, educational, recreational

Publications: Newsletter from the Detroit Korean Society, 1972– (quarterly)

Major conventions/meetings: annual meeting

Comments: The major goal of the organization is to preserve the cultural heritage of Korea in the United States and to provide social and recreational activities to unite Koreans in the Detroit area. Also sponsors Korean language classes.

KOREAN STUDENT ASSOCIATION OF CALIFORNIA
3660 Wilshire Boulevard
Los Angeles, California 90010   (213) 384-9151

Principal officers: Han Kyu Kim, President

Permanent staff: 3   Membership: 1,200
Date founded: 1957   Membership dues: NI
Branches: NI   Scope: regional

KOREAN WOMEN'S ASSOCIATION OF SOUTHERN CALIFORNIA
821 South Norton Avenue
Los Angeles, California 90005   (213) 939-1781

Principal officers: Ki Soon Kim, President

Permanent staff: 2   Membership: 500
Date founded: 1972   Membership dues: NI
Branches: NI   Scope: regional

THE OVERSEAS KOREAN ASSOCIATION
5 East 57th Street
New York, New York 10022　　　　　　(212) 688-7243
Principal officers:　　Pang Ky Kim, President

Permanent staff: NI　　　　　　　　　Membership: NI
Date founded: 1971　　　　　　　　　Membership dues: none
Branches: NI　　　　　　　　　　　　Scope: national

Nature of organization: cultural, social
Publications: *The Overseas Korean Association News* (3 times per year)
Major conventions/meetings: triennial convention

U.S.-KOREAN ECONOMIC COUNCIL
88 Morningside Drive, Suite 2L
New York, New York 10027　　　　　　(212) 749-4200
Principal officers:　　William Henderson, Executive Director

Permanent staff: 2　　　　　　　　　Membership: 100 organizations
Date founded: 1960　　　　　　　　　Membership dues: NI
Branches: NI　　　　　　　　　　　　Scope: national

Nature of organization: economic
Comments: Promotes U.S.-Korean economic relations that are beneficial to both nations.

LATVIAN-AMERICAN ORGANIZATIONS

Additional information on Latvian-American organizations in the United States may be obtained from the Latvian Consul, Office of the Legation (4325 Seventeenth Street, Washington, D.C. 20008) and from Maruta Karklis, *et al.*, eds., *The Latvians in America 1640-1973* (Dobbs Ferry, New York: Oceana Publications, 1974). For regional and local information, see *Greater Cleveland Nationalities Directory 1974* (Cleveland: Sun Newspapers and the Nationalities Services Center, 1974) and *Ethnic Directory I* (Detroit: Southeastern Michigan Regional Ethnic Heritage Studies Center, 1973).

ACADEMIC FRATERNITY "AUSTRUMS"
13 Revere Street
Jamaica Plain, Massachusetts 02130
Principal officers:　　Juris Veidins, President
　　　　　　　　　　Zigurds Kaktins, Vice President
　　　　　　　　　　Valters Grinbus, Secretary

Permanent staff: NI　　　　　　　　　Membership: 200 international; 70
Date founded: 1883　　　　　　　　　　national
Branches: 1 state; 1 local　　　　　　Membership dues: $11.00
　　　　　　　　　　　　　　　　　　Scope: international, national

Special requirements for membership: Latvian descent, presently attending a university or college, or a college graduate
Nature of organization: cultural, fraternal
Publications: *Austruma Vestis* (Austrums Newsletter), 1968– (semiannual)
Major conventions/meetings: conferences every 6 weeks; national convention every 5 years
Comments: The purpose of the organization is to encourage the retention of the Latvian cultural heritage. Members are encouraged to assume an active role in Latvian churches, choral groups, Boy Scouts, and other similar endeavors. The fraternity maintains a library and archival materials.

AMERICAN LATVIAN ASSOCIATION IN THE UNITED STATES, INC. (ALA)

400 Hurley Avenue
P.O. Box 432
Rockville, Maryland 20850   (202) 347-8064

Principal officers: Ilgvars Spilners, President
                     Adolfs Lejins, Executive Vice President
                     Arvids Blodnieks, Executive Secretary

Permanent staff: 3   Membership: 7,000
Date founded: 1951   Membership dues: $5.00 (annual)
Branches: none   Scope: national

Special requirements for membership: Latvian origin or affiliation

Nature of organization: educational, cultural

Publications: *ALA's Journal*, 1970– (3 issues per year); *ALA Vestis* (quarterly); also publishes books for Latvian schools

Major conventions/meetings: annual convention

Comments: ALA is an educationally oriented non-profit organization which promotes cultural cooperation between Latvian-Americans and other Americans. It sponsors the preparation of textbooks and other educational materials suitable for use in "weekend schools" attended by over 2,000 Latvian children. It encourages the promotion of Latvian folk dances and songs, festivals, arts and crafts activities, concerts featuring Latvian composers and performers, and athletic contests. ALA further supports research on the effects of the present Soviet occupation of Latvia and disseminates information to the American public concerning the Russification policies practiced by the Soviet regime.

ASSOCIATION OF ACADEMIC UNITS IN BOSTON, MASS.

44 Cypress Street
Brookline, Massachusetts 02146   (617) 566-4045

Principal officers: Dr. Bernard P. Skulte, President
                     Gaida Kalnajs, Vice President
                     Mara Efferts, Secretary

Permanent staff: none   Membership: 50
Date founded: 1952   Membership dues: $5.00
Branches: NI   Scope: NI

Special requirements for membership: graduate students

Nature of organization: fraternal

Publications: *Academic Life* (annual)

Major conventions/meetings: meetings of members three to four times per year

Comments: The organization was initially founded in Riga, Latvia. However, since it is prohibited in Soviet Latvia, it was established in the United States in 1952.

CLEVELAND LATVIAN YOUTH GROUP

United Latvian Ev. Church of Cleveland
1385 Andrews Avenue
Cleveland, Ohio 44107   (216) 521-9785

Principal officers: Lauma Lagzdins, President
                     Karlis Ceceris, Vice President
                     Ilze Subers, Secretary

Permanent staff: 11   Membership: 40
Date founded: NI   Membership dues: NI
Branches: NI   Scope: local

Special requirements for membership: willingness to "speak Latvian and learn about God and Latvia in the Latvian language"

Nature of organization: cultural, religious, youth

Affiliations: United Lutheran Latvian Church

Major conventions/meetings: once a month

CLEVELAND LATVIAN YOUTH GROUP (cont'd)

Comments: Church-affiliated organization. Promotes various religious, social, and cultural activities. Raises funds for Latvian summer camps. Affiliated with United Lutheran Latvian Church and the Latvian Evangelical Lutheran Church.

COMMITTEE FOR A FREE LATVIA (ČFL)

12 Ainsworth Avenue
East Brunswick, New Jersey 08816   (201) 247-4623

Principal officers: Villis A. Hazners, President
                        Alfreds Bērziņš, Treasurer and Secretary

Permanent staff: none   Membership: NI
Date founded: 1951   Membership dues: none
Branches: none   Scope: national

Special requirements for membership: none

Nature of organization: political

Publications: *For a Free Latvia*, 1951– (3-4 issues per year); also publishes articles in magazines and newsletters

Affiliations: Assembly of Captive European Nations, Inc.

Major conventions/meetings: none

Comments: A major objective of CFL is to educate and inform the public of the nature of communism in Latvia and the effects of Soviet occupation of Latvia. Promotes the restoration of an independent and democratic Latvian nation. Maintains a library of over 2,000 volumes as well as an archival collection.

FEDERATION OF LATVIAN EVANGELICAL LUTHERAN CHURCHES IN AMERICA, INC. (LELDAA)

c/o Rev. Alexander Veinbergs
2941 Northampton Street, N.W.
Washington, D.C. 20015   (202) 966-9216

Principal officers: Rev. Alexander Veinbergs, President
                        Dr. Armins Rūsis, Vice President
                        Vev. V. Vārsborgs, Vice President
                        Rev. A. Voitkus, Secretary

Permanent staff: none   Membership: approximately 25,000
Date founded: 1957   individuals
Branches: 4 regional; 80 congregations and churches   Membership dues: $2.00-$5.00 per
                                           person
                                         Scope: national (U.S. and Canada)

Special requirements for membership: none

Nature of organization: religious, social, educational, youth

Publications: *Companion*, 1956– (monthly); *Path of the Youth* (quarterly); *Bulletin*, 1950– (quarterly); also publishes devotional, educational, and other religious books in the Latvian language

Major conventions/meetings: regional conferences once a year; general conference every three years

Comments: The federation represents all Latvian Evangelical churches in the United States, whether incorporated or unincorporated. It not only promotes spiritual and religious activities, but is also involved in organizing cultural, social, educational, and recreational events. Sponsors local summer camps and also awards scholarships for theological studies.

LATVIAN ACADEMIC SOCIETY, MINNEAPOLIS

1 Vincent Avenue South
Minneapolis, Minnesota 55405   (612) 374-3009

Principal officers: Pauls Kupčs, President
                        Jānis Dimants, Jr., Vice President
                        Fricis Dravnieks, Secretary

LATVIAN ACADEMIC SOCIETY, MINNEAPOLIS (cont'd)

Permanent staff: NI
Date founded: 1957
Branches: none

Membership: 60
Membership dues: $6.00
Scope: local

Special requirements for membership: student or graduate of college or university

Nature of organization: cultural

Publications: none

Major conventions/meetings: monthly meetings; periodic conferences

Comments: The society promotes the retention of the Latvian language and cultural heritage. Sponsors various lectures and discussions. Offers yearly scholarships to the Latvian High School in West Germany.

LATVIAN-AMERICAN REPUBLICAN NATIONAL FEDERATION

12 Ainsworth Avenue
East Brunswick, New Jersey 08816   (201) 247-4623

Principal officers: Prof. Daumants Hazners, President
                        John Bungs, Jr., Vice President
                        Ivars Berzins, Secretary

Permanent staff: none
Date founded: 1968
Branches: 21 state

Membership: 1,000
Membership dues: $1.00
Scope: national

Nature of organization: political

Major conventions/meetings: annual

Comments: The main goal of the organization is to support and promote the Republican Party on local, state, and national levels. It disseminates information to Latvian-Americans and encourages their participation in the federation; also conducts political seminars and workshops.

LATVIAN ASSOCIATION IN COLUMBUS, OHIO

3093 Mountview Road
Columbus, Ohio 43221   (614) 488-3844

Principal officers: Roland Vilums, President
                        Visvald Dzelzitis, Vice President
                        Maija Berzins, Secretary

Permanent staff: 7
Date founded: 1950
Branches: NI

Membership: approximately 70
Membership dues: $5.00
Scope: local

Special requirements for membership: Latvian origin

Nature of organization: cultural

Publications: none

Affiliations: American Latvian Association

Comments: Supports the development of the Latvian traditions and culture, the teaching of the Latvian language and history, and cooperation with other national organizations. It also promotes attempts to regain independence for Latvia. Offers scholarships to students enrolled in Latvian language courses and to those attending summer camps.

LATVIAN ASSOCIATION IN DETROIT (LAD)

18480 Fenmore Street
Detroit, Michigan 48235   (313) 537-7426

Principal officers: Dainis Rudzitis, President
                        Vilis Ceplevics, Vice President
                        Paulis Baumanis, Secretary

Permanent staff: none
Date founded: 1950
Branches: none

Membership: 220
Membership dues: $10.00 for men (annual); $5.00 for women (annual)
Scope: local

LATVIAN ASSOCIATION IN DETROIT (LAD) (cont'd)

Special requirements for membership: Latvian extraction

Nature of organization: educational, cultural, recreational

Publications: *Vestis*, 1951– (monthly)

Affiliations: American Latvian Association

Major conventions/meetings: annual membership meeting

Comments: Provides various social, cultural, and charitable activities to Latvians in metropolitan Detroit. It also sponsors and supports all Latvian Sunday Schools in the Detroit
area, as well as the Latvian Boy Scouts and Girl Scouts. It also maintains a scholarship
fund for Latvian high school students.

LATVIAN ASSOCIATION OF CLEVELAND (KLB)
1356 Warren Road
Lakewood, Ohio 44107   (216) 226-5581

Principal officers: Aloysius Piterans, President
                   Eriks Ievins, Vice President
                   Indrikis Salme, Secretary
                   Karlis Karnitis, Treasurer

Permanent staff: 9   Membership: 336

Date founded: 1950   Membership dues: $4.00

Branches: NI   Scope: regional

Special requirements for membership: open

Nature of organization: social welfare

Publications: *Latvian Information Bulletins*, 1951– (every three months or as required); also
publishes books

Affiliations: American Latvian Association in the United States, Inc.

Major conventions/meetings: annual membership meeting

Comments: The objectives of the association are to unite Latvians in their struggle for a free
Latvia; to preserve Latvian traditions, culture, and language; to support the activities
of broader Latvian organizations; to represent Latvians in the greater Cleveland area at
official functions; to support Latvian Boy and Girl Scout units; and to provide financial
support to Latvian schools and summer camps. The association maintains a Latvian
library of approximately 1,100 volumes and finances a Latvian radio program.

LATVIAN BOY SCOUTS IN EXILE
1206 West Boulevard
Berkley, Michigan 48072   (313) 547-4395

Principal officers: Alfreds Gaujenieks, Chairman of the Plenipotentiar Committee
                   Fricis Sipols, Chief Scout

Permanent staff: NI   Membership: 813

Date founded: 1917   Membership dues: $5.00 adults; $1.00

Branches: 4 areas are divided into districts,   boys
  then into local units   Scope: international, national

Special requirements for membership: males of ages 8 to 25 with a knowledge of Latvian

Nature of organization: youth

Publications: *Letter to Latvian Scouts*, 1945– (3-4 times per year); *Letter to Latvian Guides
and Scouters*, 1952– (2 times per year); *Latvian Scout and Guide Magazine in Exile*
(discont'd); also publishes books and miscellaneous booklets covering Scout skills and
methods

Affiliations: World Scouting (a Latvian Girl Guide movement); local Boy Scout organizations

Major conventions/meetings: annual leaders' conferences in areas; worldwide camp every
5 years

Comments: Goals include the moral, physical, and intellectual development of youth through
the utilization of the scouting educational method. Activities center around indoor
gatherings, outdoor events, camps, festivals, language courses, sports, jamborees, and
cultural affairs.

LATVIAN CENTER "GAREZERS"
Route 3, Box 363
Three Rivers, Michigan 49093   (616) 244-5441
Principal officers: Nikolajs Riekstins, President
                       Janis Meija, Chairman of the Board
                       Oskars Cakars, Secretary
                       Ansis Berzkalns, Treasurer

Permanent staff: 3   Membership: 144 organizations
Date founded: 1965   Membership dues: donations
Branches: NI   Scope: regional

Special requirements for membership: non-profit organizations

Nature of organization: educational, recreational

Publications: *Garezers Zinas* (quarterly)

Major conventions/meetings: annual membership meeting

Comments: The center offers activities that are educational, religious, cultural, charitable, and
    social in nature. It also maintains a library of approximately 2,000 volumes.

THE LATVIAN CHOIR ASSOCIATION OF U.S., INC.
2175 West 59th Street
Cleveland, Ohio 44102   (216) 961-1655
Principal officers: Ernests Brusubardis, President
                       Jekabs Udris, Vice President
                       Karlis Vanags, Secretary

Permanent staff: 11   Membership: 29 choirs (1,100 singers)
Date founded: 1958   Membership dues: $10.00
Branches: none   Scope: national

Special requirements for membership: ability to sing in the Latvian language

Nature of organization: cultural, educational

Publications: *Latvian Music*, 1969– (twice a year); also publishes collections of songs

Affiliations: none

Major conventions/meetings: convention every five years

Comments: The association collects and publishes Latvian sheet music specifically meant for
    choirs. It also publishes a Latvian music journal, which provides information about
    Latvian composers, their works, and the activities of Latvian choirs in the United States.
    Aids in organizing Latvian song festivals.

LATVIAN CONCERT ASSOCIATION OF CLEVELAND
1385 Andrews Avenue
Lakewood, Ohio 44107
Principal officers: Mrs. Juris A. Kelers, President
                       K. Avens, Vice President
                       A. Pirktins, Secretary

Permanent staff: 7-9   Membership: 200
Date founded: in 1950s   Membership dues: $7.50
Branches: 20   Scope: national

Special requirements for membership: none

Nature of organization: cultural

Publications: *LKA Pasinojums* (LKA Bulletin) (irregular)

Major conventions/meetings: 3 concerts per season

Comments: Coordinates the works of about 20 Latvian concert associations located in the
    United States. It also presents concerts in Cleveland featuring Latvian-American
    artists.

LATVIAN CREDIT UNION
64 Sigourney Street
Jamaica Plains
Boston, Massachusetts 02130   (617) 524-9726
Principal officers: Edgar Brenc, President
                       Janis Klucis, Vice President-Secretary

Permanent staff: 11   Membership: 350
Date founded: 1962   Membership dues: none
Branches: none   Scope: local

Special requirements for membership: Latvian descent

Nature of organization: economic

Publications: publishes annual calendar

Affiliations: Massachusetts Cuna Association

Major conventions/meetings: annual membership meeting

Comments: This credit union allows membership only for individuals who are of Latvian
    origin or married to a Latvian.

LATVIAN DAUGAVAS VANAGI, INC. (DV ASV)
1918 West Hood Avenue
Chicago, Illinois 60660   (312) 973-6383
Principal officers: Joseph Utinans, President
                       Voldemars Aparjods, Vice President
                       Janis Pogenbergs, Secretary
                       Paulis Rudzitis, Treasurer

Permanent staff: none   Membership: 2,995
Date founded: 1950   Membership dues: $6.00
Branches: 25 regional   Scope: national

Special requirements for membership: 18 years of age

Nature of organization: social, educational, cultural, recreational, sport

Publications: *DV Ménešraksts* (6 times per year); *National Committees Newsletter*
    (approximately monthly); branches newsletters (3-4 times per year)

Affiliations: Latvian Daugavas associations in other countries

Major conventions/meetings: annual convention

Comments: The major purpose is to organize and unite persons of Latvian origin, especially
    veterans of various wars and their children. The organization also promotes the preserva-
    tion of the Latvian cultural heritage and language. It maintains a large library collection
    as well as organizational archives.

LATVIAN FOUNDATION
c/o Dr. V. Muiznieks
2330 Gull Road
Kalamazoo, Michigan 49001   (616) 345-4211
Principal officers: Dr. V. Muiznieks, President
                       B. Rubess, Vice President
                       V. Rutenbergs, Jr., Secretary

Permanent staff: none   Membership: 530
Date founded: 1970   Membership dues: $10.00 (monthly)
Branches: none   Scope: international

Special requirements for membership: none

Nature of organizations: educational, cultural

Publications: *Latvian Foundation Bulletin*

Affiliations: none

Major conventions/meetings: annual

LATVIAN FOUNDATION (cont'd)

Comments: The purpose of the organization is to preserve the Latvian culture and language in America and to promote and recognize contributions by Latvians and Latvian-Americans. It sponsors the "Spotlight on Latvia" radio program and maintains an archival collection of program tapes and scripts.

LATVIAN FUND
Dr. V. Rutenbergs
50 Severance Circle
Cleveland Heights, Ohio 44118

LATVIAN GIRL GUIDE MOVEMENT
c/o Mrs. Z. Gaujeniers
3400 Wayne Avenue
Bronx, New York 10467

THE LATVIAN HERITAGE FOUNDATION
c/o Sylvester P. Lambergs
67 Randolph Street
Canton, Massachusetts 02021   (617) 828-4428
Principal officers: Dr. Ingrida Gutbergs-Johansons, President
                       Valentina Lambergs, Vice President
                       Olgerts Kutcers, Secretary

Permanent staff: none   Membership: 150
Date founded: 1969   Membership dues: $60.00 donation
Branches: none   Scope: national
Special requirements for membership: none
Nature of organization: educational, cultural
Publications: none
Affiliations: none
Major conventions/meetings: annual

LATVIAN HOUSE, INC.
2337 Central Avenue, N.E.
Minneapolis, Minnesota 55418   (612) 724-0408
Principal officers: Henry R. Kiperts, President
                       Janis Bergs, Vice President
                       Toms Geistauts, Secretary

Permanent staff: 10   Membership: 400
Date founded: 1964   Membership dues: none
Branches: none   Scope: state
Special requirements for membership: volunteer work
Nature of organization: cultural, social, educational, sport, youth
Publications: none
Major conventions/meetings: monthly meetings
Comments: Serves as a Latvian community house for various activities and purposes.

LATVIAN SOCIETY IN IOWA, INC.
1372 East 12th Street
Des Moines, Iowa 50316   (515) 265-4634
Principal officers: John Z. Dimza, President
                       Albert Smits, Vice President
                       Arturs Arsts, Secretary

Permanent staff: 7   Membership: 160
Date founded: 1958   Membership dues: $3.00
Branches: none   Scope: state

LATVIAN SOCIETY IN IOWA, INC. (cont'd)

Special requirements for membership: none

Nature of organization: cultural, social, scholarly, educational, recreational, youth

Publications: none

Comments: Supports Latvian language schools, youth organizations, concerts, exhibitions, and song festivals. It also provides financial assistance to Latvian-Americans. Maintains a library of over 500 volumes.

LATVIAN SOCIETY OF MINNESOTA, INC. (L.A.M.)

2330 Insbruck Parkway
Minneapolis, Minnesota 55421   (612) 788-2825

Principal officers: Janis Dimants, Jr., President
A. Dombrovskis, Vice President
Dr. B. Zile, Secretary

Permanent staff: 7   Membership: 75
Date founded: 1951   Membership dues: $6.00
Branches: none   Scope: state

Special requirements for membership: persons of American-Latvian descent 18 years of age

Nature of organization: fraternal

Publications: *News*, 1951– (once or twice a year)

Affiliations: American Latvian Association, Inc.

Major conventions/meetings: general annual meeting once a year

Comments: The main purpose of this non-profit and non-political organization is to unite all Latvians in Minnesota for the purpose of preserving the culture and language.

LATVIAN SOCIETY OF PITTSBURGH AND VICINITY

c/o I. Stravinski
700 Penn Center Boulevard, Apt. 712
Pittsburgh, Pennsylvania 15235   (412) 823-1658

Principal officers: Ingrid Stravinski, President
Dr. Ernests Dravnieks, Vice President
Valentins Zervins, Secretary

Permanent staff: none   Membership: 50
Date founded: 1950   Membership dues: $2.00
Branches: NI   Scope: local

Special requirements for membership: persons of Latvian descent who have reached age 18

Nature of organization: social, cultural

Publications: *Bulletin*, 1972– (yearly)

Affiliations: American Latvian Association in the U.S., Inc.

Major conventions/meetings: 5 to 6 meetings per year

Comments: Promotes the preservation of the Latvian culture, traditions, and language. Serves as an information forum on the conditions in Latvia and the Russification of Latvia by the Russian government. Awards scholarships to Latvian summer camps and schools.

LATVIAN WELFARE ASSOCIATION OF CLEVELAND

20615 Clare Avenue
Maple Heights, Ohio 44137   (216) 475-5632

Principal officers: Viktors Zemesarajs, President
Zigurds Reineks, Vice President
Klavs Silis, Secretary

Permanent staff: 10   Membership: 212
Date founded: 1951   Membership dues: $6.00
Branches: 26 regional   Scope: national

Special requirements for membership: 16 years or older and of Latvian descent

LATVIAN WELFARE ASSOCIATION OF CLEVELAND (cont'd)
Nature of organization: cultural
Publications: *Newsletter*; *Bulletin*
Affiliations: Latvian Welfare Association, Inc. USA
Comments: Provides assistance to Latvians who are in need. Promotes the retention of the
Latvian cultural heritage. Also offers scholarships to Latvian summer camps.

LATVIAN WELFARE SOCIETY, DAUGAVAS VANAGI
c/o R. Liepins
14 Orchard Street
Jamaica Plain, Massachusetts 02130

WORLD FEDERATION OF FREE LATVIANS
Shoreman Building, Room 913
806 15th Street, N.W.
Washington, D.C. 20005

LEBANESE-AMERICAN ORGANIZATIONS

See Arab-American Organizations

LITHUANIAN-AMERICAN ORGANIZATIONS

Additional information on Lithuanian-American organizations in the United
States may be obtained from the Lithuanian Consul, Office of the Legation (2622
Sixteenth Street, Washington, D.C. 20009) and from the Lithuanian American
Community of U.S., Inc. (1004 Robinson Building, 42 South 15th Street,
Philadelphia, Pennsylvania 19102). Regional and local information may be
obtained from *Greater Cleveland Nationalities Directory 1974* (Cleveland: Sun
Newspapers and the Nationalities Services Center, 1974) and *Ethnic Directory I*
(Detroit: Southeastern Michigan Regional Ethnic Heritage Studies Center, 1973).

AMERICAN LITHUANIAN ART ASSOCIATION
112 Charlton Avenue
Willow Springs, Illinois 60480   (312) 839-5299
Principal officers: Vladas Vaitekunas, President
                       Mikas Sileikis, Executive Vice President
                       A. Valis-Labokas, Secretary
Permanent staff: none   Membership: 63
Date founded: 1956   Membership dues: $2.00
Branches: none   Scope: U.S. and Canada
Special requirements for membership: professional Lithuanian artists
Nature of organization: cultural
Publications: none
Affiliations: none
Major conventions/meetings: none
Comments: The purpose of the association is to provide a meeting ground for artists of all
generations and to encourage their professional work. It has established the Ciurlionis
Art Gallery in Chicago, which frequently holds exhibits of Lithuanian artists. The gallery
is to serve as a repository of Lithuanian art until Lithuania becomes an independent
nation.

AMERICAN LITHUANIAN CATHOLIC FEDERATION ATEITIS
17689 Goldwin
Southfield, Michigan 48075   (313) 557-5847
Principal officers: Dr. Leonas Bajorunas, General Manager

Permanent staff: 1   Membership: 3,200
Date founded: 1910   Membership dues: NI
Branches: 31   Scope: national

Special requirements for membership: Catholics of Lithuanian descent

Nature of organization: educational, religious, cultural

Publications: *Ateitis* (monthly); *Gaudeamus* (bimonthly)

Major conventions/meetings: quinquennial

Comments: The organization strives to counteract anti-religious philosophies in academic life and sponsors religious activities and annual youth camps for students at all levels.

AMERICAN LITHUANIAN ENGINEERS' AND ARCHITECTS' ASSOCIATION
19 Mellen Street
Dorchester, Massachusetts 02124
Principal officers: Bronius Galinis, Secretary

Permanent staff: NI   Membership: 400
Date founded: 1950   Membership dues: NI
Branches: 9   Scope: national

Special requirements for membership: engineer or architect of Lithuanian descent

Nature of organization: professional

Publications: *Technikos Zodis* (The Engineering Word) (bimonthly)

Major conventions/meetings: biennial

Comments: Unites Lithuanian professionals in the fields of architecture and engineering.

AMERICAN LITHUANIAN PRESS AND RADIO ASSOCIATION–VILTIS
6907 Superior Avenue
Cleveland, Ohio 44103   (216) 431-6344
Principal officers: Aleksas Laikunas, Executive Officer

Permanent staff: NI   Membership: 779
Date founded: 1952   Membership dues: NI
Branches: NI   Scope: national

Nature of organization: professional

Publications: *Dirva* (semiweekly); also publishes books

Major conventions/meetings: biennial

Comments: The purpose of the association is to promote Lithuanian heritage and language in the United States. It provides an annual Short Story Award for Lithuanian literature.

AMERICAN LITHUANIAN ROMAN CATHOLIC WOMEN'S ALLIANCE (ALRK WOMEN'S ALLIANCE)
9428 South Harding Avenue
Evergreen Park, Illinois 60642
Principal officers: Antonia M. Wackell, President
                        Augusta Satkus, Vice President
                        Marie Panavas, Secretary

Permanent staff: none   Membership: approximately 2,000
Date founded: 1914   Membership dues: varies with policy
Branches: 75 in United States   Scope: national

Special requirements for membership: Catholic women of Lithuanian descent or married to a Lithuanian

Nature of organization: fraternal, cultural, social, religious, educational

Publications: *Moteru dirva* (Women's Field), 1914– (bimonthly)

AMERICAN LITHUANIAN ROMAN CATHOLIC WOMEN'S ALLIANCE (ALRK WOMEN'S ALLIANCE) (cont'd)

Major conventions/meetings: biennial convention

Comments: The Alliance was established as a fraternal benefit society for Catholic women of Lithuanian descent. Services and activities vary from chapter to chapter but are of a social, religious, educational, and patriotic nature. Two scholarships are awarded annually to children of members. The organization also aids Lithuanian refugee families in other countries. Maintains organizational archives.

AMERICAN LITHUANIAN SOCIAL DEMOCRATIC FEDERATION

87-81 96th Street
Woodhaven, New York 11421   (212) 441-9139

Principal officers: Jonas Pakalka, President
                       Juozas Skorubskas, Vice President
                       Jonas Vilkaitis, Secretary

Permanent staff: none   Membership: NI
Date founded: 1908   Membership dues: NI
Branches: NI   Scope: national

Special requirements for membership: none

Nature of organization: political, educational

Publications: *Keleivis*, 1905– (weekly)

Affiliations: none

Major conventions/meetings: none

Comments: The objective is to work with various Lithuanian organizations toward achieving the independence of Lithuania. Maintains a library fund for publications that deal primarily with Lithuanian independence.

ASSOCIATION OF LITHUANIAN FORESTERS IN EXILE

2740 West 43rd Street
Chicago, Illinois 60632

Principal officers: Joseph Skeivys, Executive Secretary

Permanent staff: NI   Membership: 68
Date founded: 1949   Membership dues: NI
Branches: NI   Scope: national

Special requirements for membership: former foresters in Lithuania

Nature of organization: professional

Publications: *Gerios Aidas* (Echo of the Forest) (biennial)

Major conventions/meetings: triennial

Comments: Unites foresters in the United States who were formerly working in Lithuania.

ASSOCIATION OF LITHUANIAN JOURNALISTS

2345 West 56th Street
Chicago, Illinois 60636   (312) 737-8400

Principal officers: Joseph Vaisnys, President
                       Vytautas Kasniunas, Executive Vice President
                       Algirdas Puzauskas, Executive Secretary

Permanent staff: 5   Membership: 260
Date founded: 1922   Membership dues: $2.00 (annual)
Branches: none   Scope: national

Special requirements for membership: must be a professional journalist

Nature of organization: professional, cultural

Publications: *The Lithuanian Journalist*, 1971– (3 times per year)

Affiliations: none

Major conventions/meetings: none

ASSOCIATION OF LITHUANIAN JOURNALISTS (cont'd)

Comments: The association is the professional journalism society of Lithuanians in the United States. Members are persons who have proved themselves in the Lithuanian press as being of high caliber. Among its activities, it holds annual journalism camps, especially for young Lithuanians; occasionally it sponsors summer scholarships to deserving students for summer courses in journalism.

ASSOCIATION OF LITHUANIAN WORKERS
104-07 102nd Street
Ozone Park, New York 11417   (212) 641-6699
Principal officers: Richard Janulis, President
                       Helen Esker, Executive Vice President
                       Anne Yakstis, Executive Secretary

Permanent staff: 3   Membership: 3,000
Date founded: 1930   Membership dues: varies with premium
Branches: 100 regional   Scope: national

Special requirements for membership: persons of Lithuanian descent from birth to 60 years of age

Nature of organization: fraternal

Publications: *Truth*, 1930– (monthly); also publishes booklets

Affiliations: none

Major conventions/meetings: biennial

Comments: The purpose of the organization is primarily to provide health and life insurance benefits. It also awards three annual scholarships. Maintains archives.

ATEITIS ASSOCIATION OF LITHUANIAN CATHOLIC INTELLECTUALS
7235 South Sacramento
Chicago, Illinois 60629
Principal officers: Juozas Polikaitis, Executive Secretary

Permanent staff: NI   Membership: 1,100
Date founded: 1920   Membership dues: NI
Branches: 22   Scope: national

Special requirements for membership: college graduate of Roman Catholic and Lithuanian background

Nature of organization: educational, religious, cultural

Affiliations: Pax Romana (Fribourg, Switzerland); American Lithuanian Catholic Federation Ateitis

Major conventions/meetings: biennial

Comments: The purpose of the organization is to support and establish leadership among communities of Lithuanians in exile. It also attempts to preserve the Lithuanian culture through music, art, and literary programs. It endorses political and religious freedom in Lithuania. This autonomous association of the American Lithuanian Catholic Federation Ateitis supports other student Ateitis organizations and summer seminars.

COMMITTEE FOR A FREE LITHUANIA
29 West 57th Street
New York, New York 10019   (212) 753-6628
Principal officers: Vaclovas Sidzikauskas, President
                       Vytautas Vaitiekūnas, Executive Secretary
                       Pranas Vainauskas, Executive Vice President and Treasurer

Permanent staff: 1   Membership: 7
Date founded: 1951   Membership dues: none
Branches: none   Scope: national

Special requirements for membership: Lithuanian citizenship

Nature of organization: political, research

COMMITTEE FOR A FREE LITHUANIA (cont'd)

Affiliations: Assembly of Captive European Nations

Comments: The purpose of the committee is to work for the liberation of Lithuania from Soviet occupation and for the preservation of national identity in the free world. Maintains archival holdings. Until 1952 the organization was known as the Lithuanian Consultative Panel.

DAUGHTERS OF LITHUANIA, INC.
2735 West 71st Street
Chicago, Illinois 60629   (312) 925-3211
Principal officers: Emily Kiela, President
                       Prane Masilionis, Secretary
                       Rev. Felix Gureckas, Executive Director

Permanent staff: 14   Membership: 750
Date founded: 1959   Membership dues: $3.00
Branches: 3 regional; 2 state; 40 local   Scope: national

Special requirements for membership: Lithuanian women 14 years of age and over

Nature of organization: social, charitable

Publications: *Lietuvos Dukteru Draugijos Biuletenis* (Bulletin of Daughters of Lithuania), 1960– (semimonthly); also publishes membership directory

Comments: A non-sectarian, non-profit corporation, the Daughters of Lithuania, Inc., stresses working with needy Lithuanians. They operate the Simas Kudirka Home for elderly and homeless Lithuanians in Chicago. They also grant occasional scholarships to students and offer legal and medical assistance.

DETROIT LITHUANIAN ORGANIZATIONS CENTER
2002 Ferdinand
Detroit, Michigan 48209   (313) 726-5678
Principal officers: Antanas Sukauskas, President
                       E. Paurazas, Vice President
                       S. Brizgis, Secretary

Permanent staff: 7   Membership: 8,000
Date founded: 1943   Membership dues: $1.00
Branches: none   Scope: local

Nature of organization: cultural, political

Publications: none

Affiliations: none

Comments: This political organization is composed of various local Lithuanian groups. The major objective is to continue efforts that will result in the ultimate freedom of Lithuania from Soviet occupation. The organization maintains archives on Lithuanian-American political activities.

FEDERATION OF LITHUANIAN WOMEN'S CLUBS
29 West 57th Street, 12th Floor
New York, New York 10019   (212) 753-6628
Principal officers: Irena Banaitis, President
                       Maria Kregžde, Vice President
                       Malvina Klevečka, Secretary

Permanent staff: none   Membership: 700
Date founded: 1947   Membership dues: $2.00-$4.00
Branches: 25   Scope: international, national

Special requirements for membership: Lithuanian descent

Nature of organization: cultural, political

Publications: irregular pamphlets

Affiliations: General Federation of Women's Clubs; Baltic Women's Council; Council of European Women in Exile

FEDERATION OF LITHUANIAN WOMEN'S CLUBS (cont'd)

Major conventions/meetings: triennial convention

Comments: Originally founded in Europe, the FLWC's goals are to unite women of Lithuanian descent, to further the cause of restoring independence and freedom to Lithuania, to preserve the Lithuanian cultural heritage among the younger generation, and to aid the needy, especially those behind the Iron Curtain. Until 1963 it was known as Lietuviᶙ Moterᶙ Atstovybe (Council of Lithuanian Women). The federation holds folklore and painting exhibitions.

THE FRIENDS OF LITHUANIAN FRONT (LFB)

c/o Dr. K. Ambrozaitis
35 Crest Drive
Dune Acres
Chesterton, Indiana 46304   (219) 787-9220

Principal officers: Dr. P. Kisielius, Chairman of Council
                      Dr. K. Ambrozaitis, Vice President
                      P. Narutis, Secretary

Permanent staff: none	Membership: 1,100
Date founded: 1948	Membership dues: $5.00
Branches: 11 local	Scope: national

Special requirements for membership: Lithuanian descent

Nature of organization: political

Publications: *Towards Freedom*, 1953– (quarterly); also publishes books

Affiliations: Supreme Committee for Lithuanian Liberation; Committee for Free Lithuania

Major conventions/meetings: annual

Comments: This organization promotes the union of Americans of Lithuanian descent in combating communism and in working for the liberation of Lithuania; it strives to re-establish the human rights and fundamental freedoms of the Lithuanian people. The national organization sponsors annually a week-long seminar on Lithuanian subjects in Europe and in North America. In addition, local chapters often sponsor lectures, weekend seminars, etc.

THE INSTITUTE OF LITHUANIAN STUDIES, INC.

c/o Dr. Jurgis Gimbutas, President
119 Woodside Lane
Arlington, Massachusetts 02174   (617) 646-6759

Principal officers: Jurgis Gimbutas, President
                      Simas Sužiedelis, Vice President
                      Vladas Kulbokas, Secretary

Permanent staff: none	Membership: 87
Date founded: 1951	Membership dues: $10.00 (annual)
Branches: none	Scope: national

Special requirements for membership: college or university degree

Nature of organization: scholarly

Publications: *Lituanistikos Darbai* (Lithuanian Studies), 1966– (triennially); *Lituanistikos Instituto Suvažiavimo Darbai* (Proceedings of the Institute of Lithuanian Studies), 1971– (triennially); has also published a book on biographies and bibliographies prior to 1865

Affiliations: none

Major conventions/meetings: triennial convention

Comments: Prime objective of this organization is to gather, classify, and study all documents and scientific data on Lithuanian language, folklore, geography, and history and all other scholarly materials pertaining to Lithuania. It studies and publicizes the history of Lithuanians in the United States. The institute maintains archives of its activities and data about members. Membership in the institute is by invitation of the Board of Directors.

KNIGHTS OF LITHUANIA (K of L)
34 Arthur Street
Brockton, Massachusetts 02402   (617) 586-9325

Principal officers: Susan K. Boroskas, President
          Marion Skobeikis, Vice President
          Irene Adomaitis, Secretary

Permanent staff: none   Membership: 2,000
Date founded: 1913   Membership dues: $6.00
Branches: 46 regional   Scope: national

Special requirements for membership: Catholics of Lithuanian descent or spouse of a Catholic of Lithuanian descent

Nature of organization: political, social, educational, cultural, religious, fraternal, youth

Publications: *Vytis* (The Knight), 1915– (monthly)

Affiliations: none

Major conventions/meetings: annual national convention

Comments: K of L promotes the preservation of the Lithuanian culture and language as well as the independence of Lithuania. It organizes various cultural, political, social, and educational activities that further the achievement of its goals. Also, the organization offers national and regional scholarships. An archival collection of documents is maintained.

LITHUANIAN ALLIANCE OF AMERICA (LAA)
307 West 30th Street
New York, New York 10001   (212) 524-5529

Principal officers: Paul P. Dargis, President
          Alexander Chaplikas, Executive Vice President
          Algirdas Budreckis, Executive Secretary

Permanent staff: 7   Membership: 10,000
Date founded: 1886   Membership dues: depends on size of
Branches: 7 regional; 270 local   life insurance
          Scope: national

Special requirements for membership: none

Nature of organization: social, cultural, economic, fraternal, youth

Publications: *The Fatherland*, 1899– (biweekly); *Convention Work Book*, 1932– (biennial)

Affiliations: Lithuanian American Council (ALT)

Major conventions/meetings: biennial convention

Comments: Major objectives are to unite Lithuanians in the United States with respect to their common goals, to promote educational and intellectual endeavors, and to provide assistance to sick, needy, and orphaned members. The organization pays death benefits and offers scholarships. Maintains a library of over 3,000 volumes as well as archives.

THE LITHUANIAN AMERICAN COMMUNITY OF U.S., INC. (JAV LB)
1004 Robinson Building
42 South 15th Street
Philadelphia, Pennsylvania 19102   (215) 568-1587

Principal officers: Joseph Gaila, President
          Stanley A. Gecys, Vice President
          Antanas Gailiušis, Secretary

Permanent staff: 5   Membership: 250,000
Date founded: 1952   Membership dues: $5.00 employed;
Branches: 7 regional; 77 local $1.00 unemployed
          Scope: national

Special requirements for membership: of Lithuanian ancestry or married to person of Lithuanian descent

Nature of organization: educational, cultural

THE LITHUANIAN AMERICAN COMMUNITY OF U.S., INC. (JAV LB) (cont'd)

Publications: *The World Lithuanian*, 1953– (10 issues per year); *The Lithuanian Quarterly*, 1954– (quarterly); *Yearbook of the Lithuanian Press*, 1952– (annual); also publishes books

Affiliations: World Lithuanian Community, Inc.

Major conventions/meetings: semiannual meeting of Board of Directors

Comments: The purposes of the organization are to provide various benefits to people of Lithuanian descent, to organize the Lithuanian community in various activities and tours, to perpetuate Lithuanian customs, to aid in the re-establishment of independence of Lithuania, and to encourage Lithuanian participation in American cultural life. The organization sponsors national and regional folk song and dance festivals. Scholarships and grants are offered to writers, artists, and journalists who deal with Lithuanian themes. A library and archives are maintained.

LITHUANIAN AMERICAN COUNCIL, INC.

2606 West 63rd Street
Chicago, Illinois 60629   (312) 778-6900

Principal officers: Kazys Bobelis, President
Teodoras Blinstrubas, Vice President
Vladas Simaitis, Secretary

Permanent staff: 14 officers; 29 Board members
Date founded: 1940
Branches: 62 national; 2 state; 1 local

Membership: undetermined–memberships of 9 separate organizations
Membership dues: varies from chapter to chapter
Scope: national

Special requirements for membership: affiliation with member organization

Nature of organization: political

Publications: *Voice of the Lithuanian American Council*

Affiliations: Lithuanian National League of America; Knights of Lithuania; Lithuanian Student Association of North America; Lithuanian National Society of America; Lithuanian Roman Catholic Federation of America; Lithuanian Alliance of America; Lithuanian Roman Catholic Alliance of America; Lithuanian Social Democratic Federation of America; Lithuanian Roman Catholic Women's Alliance of America

Major conventions/meetings: annual convention; congress every 5 years

Comments: Nine organizations comprise the Lithuanian American Council (see affiliations). The principal purpose is to unite all members of these organizations in the common goal of restoring Lithuanian independence, as well as to provide assistance to refugees from Lithuania. The council provides information to the public on conditions in Lithuania.

LITHUANIAN AMERICAN ROMAN CATHOLIC FEDERATION (LARCF)

c/o Lithuanian Chamber of Commerce
13500 South Western Avenue
Blue Island, Illinois 60406

Principal officers: Anthony J. Rudis, President

Permanent staff: NI
Date founded: 1906
Branches: NI

Membership: 140
Membership dues: NI
Scope: national

Comments: This federation of Roman Catholic Lithuanian organizations attempts to promote the Catholic faith and Lithuanian culture in the United States. It provides various social activities to unite Lithuanians in the United States.

LITHUANIAN CATHOLIC "ATEITIS" ALUMNI ASSOCIATION (ASS)

9610 Singleton Drive
Bethesda, Maryland 20034

LITHUANIAN CATHOLIC "ATEITIS" ALUMNI ASSOCIATION (ASS) (cont'd)

Principal officers: Joseph B. Laucka, President
                     Pranas Baltakis, Vice President
                     Jonas Vaitkus, Secretary
                     Mrs. Gene Vasaitas, Treasurer

Permanent staff: NI   Membership: 1,200
Date founded: 1910   Membership dues: $5.00
Branches: 20 local   Scope: national

Special requirements for membership: Catholic faith; completion of higher education; Lithuanian ancestry or interest

Nature or organization: educational, cultural, religious, professional, scholarly

Affiliations: Lithuanian Roman Catholic Federation of America

Major conventions/meetings: convention every three years

Comments: The association is cultural in nature; its goals and activities are based on the Catholic outlook and Lithuanian traditions. It was originally founded in Lithuania in 1910, when the country was under Russian occupation, in order to unite secondary school and university students in a fight for religious and national freedom. In 1940, when the Red Army occupied Lithuania, the organization was banned. Following World War II, the association was re-established in the United States by refugees. The organization's work is along educational, scholarly, cultural, political, and religious lines. It sponsors annual summer camps, study workshops, concerts, and religious retreats, and it offers literary awards.

LITHUANIAN CATHOLIC PRESS SOCIETY
4545 West 63rd Street
Chicago, Illinois 60629   (312) 585-9500

Principal officers: J. Stankevicius, President
                     Anthony Rudis, Executive Vice President
                     Peter P. Cinikas, Executive Secretary

Permanent staff: NI   Membership: NI
Date founded: 1941   Membership dues: NI
Branches: none   Scope: national

Special requirements for membership: by invitation

Nature of organization: educational, cultural, religious

Publications: *Lithuanian Daily Friend*, 1909– (daily except Sunday)

Affiliations: Marian Fathers

Major conventions/meetings: none

Comments: Purpose is to promote religious, cultural, and educational activities through the press.

LITHUANIAN CATHOLIC STUDENT ORGANIZATION ATEITIS
c/o Lithuanian Youth Center
5620 South Claremont Avenue
Chicago, Illinois 60636

Principal officers: Linas Sidrys, President
                     Jonas Lieponis, Vice President
                     Loreta Radvilas, Secretary

Permanent staff: 9   Membership: 300
Date founded: 1910   Membership dues: $5.00
Branches: 10 regional   Scope: international

Special requirements for membership: Lithuanian descent, speaking knowledge of Lithuanian language, Catholic faith

Nature of organization: cultural, religious, educational, youth

Publications: *Gaudeamus* (annual); *Aplinkraslis* (Newsletter) (semiannual)

Affiliations: Pax Romana

LITHUANIAN CATHOLIC STUDENT ORGANIZATION ATEITIS (cont'd)

Major conventions/meetings: annual conference

Comments: Aims at developing a stronger commitment to the Christian religion and to the values of the Catholic faith. It also attempts to preserve the Lithuanian culture and language in the United States. Offers spring courses and summer camps; serves primarily as a youth organization.

LITHUANIAN CATHOLIC YOUTH ASSOCIATION ATEITIS

5725 South Artesian Avenue
Chicago, Illinois 60629

Principal officers: John A. Rackauskas, Chairman Central Committee

Permanent staff: NI	Membership: 1,200
Date founded: 1910	Membership dues: NI
Branches: 36	Scope: national

Special requirements for membership: Catholic student between grades 1-12

Nature of organization: religious, educational

Publications: *Ateitis*, 1911– (monthly)

Affiliations: International Catholic Youth Federation

Major conventions/meetings: biennial

Comments: This autonomous youth association of the American Lithuanian Catholic Federation Ateitis sponsors summer camps, as well as year-round educational, religious, social, educational, recreational, and cultural programs for elementary and secondary school children.

LITHUANIAN CHRISTIAN DEMOCRATIC UNION (LCDU)

894 East 223rd Street
Euclid, Ohio 44123   (216) 261-4994

Principal officers: Algirdas J. Kasulaitis, President
                       Pranas Razgaitis, Executive Vice President
                       Ant. Tamulionis, Executive Secretary

Permanent staff: none	Membership: 500
Date founded: 1945	Membership dues: $6.00 (annual)
Branches: 8 regional	Scope: national

Special requirements for membership: 18 years of age or over

Nature of organization: political

Publications: *Guardian of Homeland*, 1896– (semiannual); also publishes bulletins

Affiliations: none

Major conventions/meetings: triennial convention

Comments: The union is a continuation of the Lithuanian Christian Democratic Party organized in 1918. Its purposes are "to foster Christian democratic ideals, and to aid in the fight for Lithuania's independence." Maintains an archival collection.

LITHUANIAN FEDERATION ATEITIS

17689 Goldwin Drive
Detroit, Michigan 48075   (313) 557-5847

Principal officers: Justinas Pikunas, President
                       Leonas Bajorunas, General Manager

Permanent staff: 1	Membership: 3,200
Date founded: 1910	Membership dues: $5.00, $4.00, and
Branches: 5 regional; 16 state; 80 local	$2.00 (depending on school status)

Special requirements for membership: passing of comprehensive examinations at high school and college level on Lithuanian culture, Catholic faith and ideology

Nature of organization: cultural, religious, scholarly, educational, youth

Publications: *Ateitis*, 1911– (monthly); also publishes 7 to 10 books annually

LITHUANIAN FEDERATION ATEITIS (cont'd)

Major conventions/meetings: congress every five years

Comments: This organization seeks to develop among its members a deeper commitment to the Catholic faith as well as to develop a sense of identity with Lithuanian national and cultural values. The federation sponsors lectures, workshops, concerts, and summer camps. Maintains a collection of over 2,000 volumes.

LITHUANIAN PHILATELIC SOCIETY OF NEW YORK (LPSNY)

c/o Mr. Walter E. Norton
2647 Eddington Street
Philadelphia, Pennsylvania 19137   (215) 744-1312

Principal officers: Walter E. Norton, President and Editor

Permanent staff: NI   Membership: 160
Date founded: 1954   Membership dues: NI
Branches: NI   Scope: national

Special requirements for membership: Lithuanian philatelists and collectors of Lithuanian stamps

Nature of organization: philatelic

Publications: *Bulletin* (5 issues per year); *Directory* (annual)

Major conventions/meetings: semiannual

Comments: The purpose of the organization is to unite Lithuanian stamp collectors and others interested in Lithuanian philately and history. It sponsors exhibitions and maintains catalogs of Lithuanian postage issued.

LITHUANIAN REGENERATION ASSOCIATION

6823 Bayliss Avenue
Cleveland, Ohio 44103   (216) 361-8165

Principal officers: Leonas Virbickas, President
                       M. Blynas, President
                       S. Jakubickas, Executive Vice President
                       Z. Peckus, Executive Secretary

Permanent staff: none   Membership: NI
Date founded: 1948   Membership dues: $5.00 (annual)
Branches: 6 state   Scope: international, national

Special requirements for membership: must be Lithuanian or of Lithuanian origin

Nature of organization: political, cultural

Publications: *Free Lithuania*, 1946– (biweekly); also publishes books

Affiliations: none

Major conventions/meetings: triennial convention; annual or biennial conference

Comments: The goals of the association are to restore the independence of Lithuania and to promote unity among Lithuania, Latvia, and Estonia. It is also involved in political and cultural affairs. Offers literary and art awards. Maintains both archives and a library.

LITHUANIAN ROMAN CATHOLIC ALLIANCE OF AMERICA (LRCA)

71-73 South Washington Street   (717) 823-8876 or
Wilkes-Barre, Pennsylvania 18703   (717) 823-8877

Principal officers: Thomas E. Mack, President
                       Mrs. Alvera Balanda, Vice President
                       John F. Boll, Mrgr., Executive Director
                       Frank J. Katilus, Secretary

Permanent staff: 6-7   Membership: 7,900
Date founded: 1886   Membership dues: NI
Branches: 177 regional; 52 state; 18 local   Scope: national

Special requirements for membership: Roman Catholic faith

Nature of organization: religious, fraternal

LITHUANIAN ROMAN CATHOLIC ALLIANCE OF AMERICA (LRCA) (cont'd)

Publications: *Garsas* (Echo), 1917– (monthly)

Major conventions/meetings: triennial convention

Comments: Originally organized by early Lithuanian settlers in the United States, the alliance serves as a mutual aid society whose main goal is the preservation of the Catholic faith and of the national and cultural heritage of Lithuania. Its objectives are to provide death and disability benefits and to encourage intellectual and scholarly development by publishing and financing research. Also aids charitable causes and institutions.

LITHUANIAN ROMAN CATHOLIC FEDERATION OF AMERICA (ALRK FED.)

6720 South Campbell Avenue
Chicago, Illinois 60629   (312) 737-2212

Principal officers: Joseph B. Jerome, President
                       Zenonas Danilevicius, Vice President
                       Pranas Povilaitis, Secretary

Permanent staff: 10   Membership: various organizations
Date founded: 1906   Membership dues: $10.00 (annual)
Branches: 3 regional   Scope: national

Special requirements for membership: Catholic organizations

Nature of organization: cultural, religious

Publications: a newsletter (irregular); also publishes various other material

Affiliations: National Catholic Welfare Conference

Major conventions/meetings: biennial convention

Comments: This is a federation of all Lithuanian Roman Catholic parishes, newspapers, and lay organizations. Sponsors camps and maintains a library collection.

LITHUANIAN SCOUTS ASSOCIATION, COLLEGIATE DIVISION

168 Morningstar Court
Williamsville, New York 14221   (716) 632-7221

Principal officers: Luitas L. Grinius, President

Permanent staff: 14   Membership: 770
Date founded: 1924   Membership dues: NI
Branches: 28   Scope: national

Special requirements for membership: Boy Scouts or Girl Scouts of Lithuanian descent who attend or graduated from college

Nature of organization: fraternal

Publications: *Musu Vytis* (Our Knight) (quarterly); *Ad Meliorem* (3-4 issues per year); *Directory* (biennial)

Major conventions/meetings: annual

Comments: The association is active in various scouting programs and activities. It maintains a scholarship fund for Lithuanian students and it sponsors camps and training courses for Scout leaders.

LITHUANIAN VETERANS' ASSOCIATION RAMOVE

6616 South Washtenaw Avenue
Chicago, Illinois 60629

Principal officers: Stasys Dirmantas, Chairman

Publications: *Karys* (The Warrior), 1950– (monthly)

LITHUANIAN WORLD COMMUNITY, INC. (PLB)

6804 Maplewood Avenue
Chicago, Illinois 60629   (312) 776-4028

Principal officers: Bronius Nainys, President
Rev. Jonsa Borevičius, Vice President
Juozas Slajus, Secretary
Kostas Dočkus, Treasurer

Permanent staff: 7   Membership: 500,000
Date founded: 1949   Membership dues: $3.00 per person
Branches: 23 state communities   Scope: international, national

Special requirements for membership: of Lithuanian extraction or married to person of
Lithuanian extraction

Nature of organization: educational, sport, youth

Publications: *The World Lithuanian*, 1963– (monthly); also about 200 newspapers, bulletins, and
books are published by the various committees

Major conventions/meetings: Lithuanian World Community Convention every five years

Comments: Chief goals are to preserve Lithuanian culture, language, literature, and history
and to assist schools, youth organizations, newspapers, churches, publishers, etc. Also
supports the fight for Lithuanian independence. The organization assists in maintaining
22 grade schools, 13 high schools, two special schools, and five teachers' colleges in the
United States. It maintains a large library and an extensive archival collection.

LITHUANIAN WRITER'S ASSOCIATION

361 Highland Boulevard
Brooklyn, New York 11207   (212) 827-9865

Principal officers: Rev. Leonardas Andriekus, President
Algirdas Landsbergis, Vice President
Leonardas Žitkevičius, Secretary

Permanent staff: 11   Membership: 90
Date founded: 1920 (in Lithuania)   Membership dues: $5.00 (annual)
Branches: none   Scope: national

Special requirements for membership: publication of at least one book: novel, poetry, drama, or
scientific research in the field of literature

Nature of organization: cultural, literary

Publications: *Lietuvių Rašytojų Draugijos Biuletenis* (The Bulletin of the Lithuanian Writer's
Association) (annual)

Major conventions/meetings: annual convention

Comments: The scope of the association includes assistance to Lithuanian writers, offering
literary awards, and promoting Lithuanian independence.

LITUANUS FOUNDATION, INC.

P.O. Box 9318
Chicago, Illinois 60690

Principal officers: Vytenis Damušis, President
Aldona Zailskas, Secretary

Permanent staff: none   Membership: NI
Date founded: 1954   Membership dues: NI
Branches: none   Scope: national

Nature of organization: educational, scholarly

Publications: *Lituanus*, 1954– (quarterly)

Affiliations: Lithuanian American Community

Major conventions/meetings: none

Comments: The purpose of this foundation is to organize, sponsor, and publish information
pertaining to the Baltic area.

LOS ANGELES LITHUANIAN DRAMA THEATER GROUP
4563 Ambrose Avenue
Los Angeles, California 90027   (213) 665-2619
Principal officers: Juozas Kaributas-Režisorius, President

Permanent staff: 36   Membership: 85
Date founded: NI   Membership dues: none
Branches: none   Scope: national
Special requirements for membership: none
Nature of organization: cultural
Publications: none
Affiliations: none
Major conventions/meetings: none
Comments: The function of the organization is to preserve the Lithuanian culture by producing and performing Lithuanian plays.

NATIONAL LITHUANIAN SOCIETY OF AMERICA
87-80 96th Street
Woodhaven, New York 11421   (212) 441-4172
Principal officers: Mrs. Emilija Cekiene, President

Permanent staff: NI   Membership: 1,250
Date founded: 1949   Membership dues: NI
Branches: 21   Scope: national
Special requirements for membership: of Lithuanian descent
Nature of organization: cultural, educational
Publications: *Dirva*, 1915– (semiweekly)
Major conventions/meetings: annual
Comments: The major goal is to unite Lithuanians and to preserve the Lithuanian arts and traditions in the United States. Sponsors various cultural and educational activities and promotes independence for the nation of Lithuania.

THE NATIONAL NAVAL GUARD OF LITHUANIA IN EXILE, INC.
4525 South Fairfield Avenue
Chicago, Illinois 60632   (312) 254-2665
Principal officers: Mike P. Maksvytis, President
                     Balys Aniulis, Vice President
                     Juozas Ulevičius, Secretary
                     Jonas Klimas, Treasurer

Permanent staff: 8-12   Membership: approximately 450
Date founded: 1963   Membership dues: $3.00
Branches: 4 state   Scope: national
Special requirements for membership: Lithuanian descent
Nature of organization: educational, cultural, recreational, sport
Publications: *Bulletin* (irregular)
Affiliations: The National Guard of Lithuania in Exile; Lithuanian Sea Scouts Association
Major conventions/meetings: annual meeting of all members
Comments: Objectives are "to continue the maritime tradition and activity of the former National Naval Guard of Lithuania." Activities include patriotic education and various water activities.

SANTARA–SVIESA
9432 South Longwood Drive
Chicago, Illinois 60620   (312) 233-0345
Principal officers: Vytautas Vepštas, President
                     Maryte Černius, Secretary

SANTARA–SVIESA (cont'd)

Permanent staff: none
Date founded: 1953
Branches: 3 regional

Membership: 300
Membership dues: none
Scope: national

Special requirements for membership: none

Nature of organization: political, cultural

Publications: *Patterns* (twice a year); also publishes books

Major conventions/meetings: annual convention and biennial conferences

Comments: The organization concentrates on propagating and supporting Lithuanian culture of the more "avant-garde" type. Organizes art exhibits, commissions musical compositions, presents concerts, and publishes various historical and other events. Offers $1,500 award for manuscripts.

SUPREME COMMITTEE FOR LIBERATION OF LITHUANIA (VLIKAS)
29 West 57th Street, 12th Floor
New York, New York 10019   (212) 752-0099
Principal officers: J. K. Valiunas, President
Juozas Audenas, Vice President
Vytautas B. Radzivanas, Secretary

Permanent staff: 7
Date founded: 1943 (1955 in U.S.A.)
Branches: 10

Membership: NI
Membership dues: $100.00 organization
Scope: international, national

Special requirements for membership: none

Nature of organization: political

Publications: *ELTA Information Service*, 1949– (monthly); also publishes various bulletins

Major conventions/meetings: annual convention

Comments: As its name indicates, the organization's principal purpose is a free and democratic Lithuania. Originally organized in 1943 in Lithuania, it consisted of all major underground political parties and organizations, and acted as the voice of the Lithuanian nation. Its main objective was to resist and fight the Nazi's and later the Soviets.

UNITED LITHUANIAN RELIEF FUND OF AMERICA (ULRA)
2606 West 63rd Street
Chicago, Illinois 60629   (312) 776-7582
Principal officers: Mary P. Rudis, National President

Permanent staff: 3
Date founded: 1944
Branches: 6 main; 60 local

Membership: 2,000
Membership dues: NI
Scope: national

Special requirements for membership: none

Nature of organization: welfare

Affiliations: Advisory Committee on Foreign Aid

Major conventions/meetings: biennial

Comments: The organization exists to assist Lithuanian exiles and refugees and those in need under Soviet occupation.

WORLD LITHUANIAN CATHOLIC CONFEDERATION
6027 South Austin Avenue
Chicago, Illinois 60638   (312) 735-4731
Principal officers: Rev. Vincentas Brizgys, President
Kazys Kleiva, Vice President
Birute Miniatas, Secretary

Permanent staff: none
Date founded: 1970
Branches: in many countries around the world

Membership: NI
Membership dues: donations
Scope: international

WORLD LITHUANIAN CATHOLIC CONFEDERATION (cont'd)
Special requirements for membership: Lithuanian Catholic
Nature of organization: religious
Publications: *World Lithuanian Catholic Confederation Bulletin* (irregular)
Affiliations: all central Lithuanian Catholic organizations existing in various countries through-
out the world
Major conventions/meetings: quadriennial
Comments: Coordinates Lithuanian civic and social activities and serves as center for informa-
tion exchange.

LUXEMBOURG-AMERICAN ORGANIZATIONS

Additional information on Luxembourg-American Organizations may be obtained from the Office of the Luxembourg Embassy (2210 Massachusetts Avenue, Washington, D.C. 20008).

BENELUX CLUB
720 Bunker Road
West Palm Beach, Florida 33405
Principal officers: Fred A. Grillo, President
Ted Vonk, Executive Vice President
Sherry Giessen, Executive Secretary

Permanent staff: 12	Membership: 220
Date founded: 1965	Membership dues: $6.00 (annual)
Branches: none	Scope: local

Special requirements for membership: none
Nature of organization: social
Publications: none
Affiliations: none
Major conventions/meetings: none
Comments: This club attempts to promote understanding between the people from the
Benelux countries and Americans, and to help preserve the traditions and heritage
of Belgium, Holland, and Luxembourg in the United States.

LUXEMBOURG AMERICAN SOCIAL CLUB
5085 West Balmoral Avenue
Chicago, Illinois 60630

LUXEMBOURG BROTHERHOOD OF AMERICA
c/o Luxembourg Consulate
111 West Washington Street
Chicago, Illinois 60602

LUXEMBOURG PHILATELIC STUDY CLUB (LPSC)
c/o Greeley and Hansen
5206 Markel Road
Richmond, Virginia 23230   (703) 285-9009
Principal officers: Warren W. Sadler, Secretary-Treasurer

Permanent staff: NI	Membership: 58
Date founded: 1950	Membership dues: NI
Branches: NI	Scope: national

Special requirements for membership: philatelists specializing in Luxembourg stamps
Nature of organization: philatelic

LUXEMBOURG PHILATELIC STUDY CLUB (LPSC) (cont'd)
Publications: *Luxembourg Philatelist* (monthly)
Affiliations: Fédération des Sociétés Philateliques du Grand-Duché de Luxembourg
Comments: Studies the postal history of Luxembourg and special stamps issued by the
　　Ministry of Postal Services of the Grand Duchy of Luxembourg.

LUXEMBOURGERS OF AMERICA, INC.
　　806 South Na-wa-ta Avenue
　　Mount Prospect, Illinois 60056　　　　　　(312) 394-8252
Principal officers:　　Jack Keefer, President
　　　　　　　　　　　Nicholas Colling, Vice President
　　　　　　　　　　　Don Johanek, Secretary
　　　　　　　　　　　Victor Jacoby, Editor
Permanent staff: 11　　　　　　　　　　Membership: 700
Date founded: 1940　　　　　　　　　　Membership dues: $5.00 (annual)
Branches: none　　　　　　　　　　　　Scope: national
Special requirements for membership: subscription to *Luxembourg News of America*
Nature of organization: social
Publications: *Luxembourg News of America*, 1966– (monthly)
Affiliations: none
Comments: This social organization edits and prints a 10-page monthly tabloid for all of its
　　members. The newspaper is entitled *Luxembourg News of America*. The organization
　　also maintains an archive of newspapers.

MACEDONIAN-AMERICAN ORGANIZATIONS

See Bulgarian-American Organizations

MALTESE-AMERICAN ORGANIZATIONS

Additional information on Maltese-American organizations in the United
States may be obtained from the Office of the Maltese Embassy (2017 Connecticut
Avenue, Washington, D.C. 20008).

ANCIENT AND ILLUSTRIOUS ORDER OF KNIGHTS OF MALTA
　　151 Sage Drive
　　Lancaster, Pennsylvania 17602　　　　　(717) 397-9922
Principal officers:　　Loyd J. Rhoads, Supreme Recorder
Permanent staff: NI　　　　　　　　　　Membership: 2,000
Date founded: 1842　　　　　　　　　　Membership dues: NI
Branches: 56　　　　　　　　　　　　　Scope: national
Special requirements for membership: Protestant males·
Nature of organization: fraternal
Publications: *Malta Bulletin* (monthly)
Major conventions/meetings: annual
Comments: The purpose of the organization is to provide life insurance benefits to members.

DAMES OF MALTA (D of M)
4127 Brownsville Road
Pittsburgh, Pennsylvania 15227   (412) 881-1242
Principal officers: Marjorie Barr, Executive Officer

Permanent staff: 3	Membership: 6,558
Date founded: 1896	Membership dues: NI
Branches: NI	Scope: national

Special requirements for membership: women

Nature of organization: fraternal, charitable

Publications: *Malta Chat* (3 issues per year); *Proceedings of Convention* (annual)

Major conventions/meetings: annual

Comments: Sponsors charitable programs and activities; basically a women's Christian fraternal association.

MALTESE-AMERICAN BENEVOLENT SOCIETY (MABS)
1832 Michigan Avenue
Detroit, Michigan 48216   (313) 961-8393
Principal officers: Larry Zahra, President

Permanent staff: NI	Membership: NI
Date founded: NI	Membership dues: NI
Branches: NI ˉ	Scope: national

Nature of organization: social, cultural, educational

Major conventions/meetings: annual

Comments: Primarily a social and cultural organization, this society also assists new immigrants from Malta, sponsors educational and cultural programs, hosts visiting dignitaries from Malta, and grants awards and scholarships for Maltese-Americans. Maintains a small library.

MALTESE UNION CLUB
246 Eighth Avenue
New York, New York 10011   (212) 243-9774
Principal officers: Peter J. Copperstone, Secretary

Permanent staff: NI	Membership: NI
Date founded: 1931	Membership dues: NI
Branches: NI	Scope: national

Special requirements for membership: of Maltese descent

Nature of organization: social, cultural

Major conventions/meetings: bimonthly

Comments: Attempts to unite persons born on the Isle of Malta or of Maltese descent; provides social and cultural activities and programs. A small library of 300 volumes is maintained.

SONS AND DAUGHTERS OF MALTA
9570 Westwood Street
Detroit, Michigan 48228
Principal officers: Alfred Buttigieg, Secretary

Permanent staff: NI	Membership: 246
Date founded: 1946	Membership dues: NI
Branches: NI	Scope: national

Special requirements for membership: Catholic Maltese-Americans

Nature of organization: cultural, charitable

Major conventions/meetings: semiannual

Comments: The major purpose of the organization is to preserve the Maltese heritage in America, to study Maltese history and culture, and to assist Maltese immigrants to the United States. Supports philanthropic projects among the orphanages in Malta.

WESTERN U.S.A. ASSOCIATION OF THE SOVEREIGN MILITARY ORDER OF MALTA
2628 Brooks Avenue
El Cerrito, California 94530

Principal officers: John E. Freed, K.M., President

Permanent staff: NI	Membership: 36
Date founded: 1953	Membership dues: NI
Branches: NI	Scope: national

Nature of organization: religious, charitable

Publications: *International Review* (quarterly)

Affiliations: Order of Malta (Italy)

Major conventions/meetings: 3 per year

Comments: This association is a Roman Catholic charitable and religious service group, composed of laymen and chaplains.

MANX-AMERICAN ORGANIZATIONS

See note provided for British-American organizations.

BISBEE MANX SOCIETY
c/o Mrs. Ivy Dillon
207 Hazzard Street
Bisbee, Arizona 85603

Principal officers: Ivy Dillon

Permanent staff: NI	Membership: NI
Date founded: NI	Membership dues: NI
Branches: NI	Scope: regional

Special requirements for membership: of Manx descent

Nature of organization: cultural

Affiliations: North American Manx Society

Major conventions/meetings: annual

CHICAGO MANX SOCIETY
6858 North Osceola Avenue
Chicago, Illinois 60631

Principal officers: Robert Kelly

Permanent staff: NI	Membership: NI
Date founded: NI	Membership dues: NI
Branches: NI	Scope: regional

Special requirements for membership: of Manx descent

Nature of organization: cultural

Affiliations: North American Manx Society

Major conventions/meetings: annual

GALVA MANX SOCIETY
Rural Route 2
Box 154
Galva, Illinois 61434

Principal officers: Mrs. Clyde Collinson

Permanent staff: NI	Membership: NI
Date founded: NI	Membership dues: NI
Branches: NI	Scope: local

Special requirements for membership: of Manx descent

GALVA MANX SOCIETY (cont'd)
Nature of organization: cultural
Affiliations: North American Manx Society
Major conventions/meetings: annual

MONA'S RELIEF SOCIETY
1223 West Melrose Avenue
Westlake, Ohio 44145   (216) 331-3732
Principal officers: Mrs. Robert S. Cowin, President
                       Mrs. Floyd McClure, Vice President
                       Miss Florence Lyon, Secretary

Permanent staff: none	Membership: 187
Date founded: 1852	Membership dues: $1.00 (annual)
Branches: none	Scope: local

Special requirements for membership: native of Isle of Man, descendant of native, or spouse
      of native

Nature of organization: cultural, economic, fraternal, social

Publications: none

Affiliations: North American Manx Association

Major conventions/meetings: biennial convention

Comments: The purpose of this society is to provide mutual benefit and social welfare to Manx
      people in the Cleveland area. Funds are available from an established endowment fund
      to help needy Manxmen in many ways—from temporary financial aid to burial in a plot
      owned by the Cleveland Manx Society. Meetings are held 10 times per year for fellow-
      ship, slide presentations, news and talks about the Isle of Man, and special programs to
      raise funds for the society (e.g., card parties, bake sales, etc.).

NORTH AMERICAN MANX ASSOCIATION
6858 North Osceola Avenue
Chicago, Illinois 60631
Principal officers: Robert Kelly, President

SOUTHERN CALIFORNIA MANX SOCIETY
c/o Mrs. T. Donald Bain
132 Bonito Avenue
Long Beach, California 90802
Principal officers: Mrs. T. Donald Bain

Permanent staff: NI	Membership: NI
Date founded: NI	Membership dues: NI
Branches: NI	Scope: regional

Special requirements for membership: of Manx descent

Nature of organization: cultural

Affiliations: North American Manx Society

Major conventions/meetings: annual

MEXICAN-AMERICAN ORGANIZATIONS

See also Spanish-American Organizations

Because of the vast number of Spanish-speaking organizations existing in the United States, it was decided to list here only the national and larger regional organizations that are concerned entirely, or primarily, with Mexican-Americans. Other major organizations, more inclusive in their coverage of ethnic groups, may be found in the section on Spanish-American organizations, which includes various Spanish-speaking groups.

For other Mexican-American organizations, see the comprehensive, annotated listings in the following publications: Lois B. Jordan, *Mexican Americans* (Littleton, Colorado: Libraries Unlimited, Inc., 1973) and *Directory of Spanish Speaking Community Organizations in the United States* (Washington, D.C.: Cabinet Committee on Opportunity for the Spanish Speaking, 1970).

AMERICAN G.I. FORUM AUXILIARY
621 Gabaldon Road, N.W.
Albuquerque, New Mexico 87104   (505) 877-6645
Principal officers: Ezequiel Duran, National Secretary-Treasurer

Permanent staff: NI   Membership: 6,000
Date founded: 1948   Membership dues: NI
Branches: NI   Scope: national

Special requirements for membership: wives of members of American G.I. Forum

Nature of organization: social, cultural, political

Affiliations: American G.I. Forum of the U.S.

Major conventions/meetings: annual

Comments: These Mexican-American women meet to assist in projects of the American G.I. Forum of the U.S.; their purpose is to obtain equal civil rights for Mexican-Americans, and to be united in social and cultural activities.

AMERICAN G.I. FORUM OF THE U.S.
621 Gabaldon Road, N.W.
Albuquerque, New Mexico 87104   (505) 877-6645
Principal officers: Dr. Hector P. Garcia, National Chairman
                       Dr. Leo Lopez, National Vice Chairman
                       Ezequiel Duran, National Executive Secretary

Permanent staff: NI   Membership: 20,000
Date founded: 1948   Membership dues: NI
Branches: 23 state; 500 local   Scope: national

Special requirements for membership: U.S. veterans of Mexican descent

Nature of organization: social, educational, political

Publications: *Bulletin* (monthly)

Major conventions/meetings: annual

Comments: Endorses political and religious freedom and the principles of democracy. Seeks to help veterans to secure special rights and privileges and is active in combating juvenile delinquency. Aids needy and disabled Mexican-American veterans. Awards scholarships to needy students.

CHICANO CULTURAL CENTER
P.O. Box 291 (Highway 99E)
Woodburn, Oregon 97071   (503) 792-3616
Principal officers: David Aguilar, Director
                      Kathy Romero, Secretary
                      Jesus Capetillo, Coordinator of Communications

Permanent staff: 3-4	Membership: 12,000 (8,000 Chicanos)
Date founded: 1969	Membership dues: contribution
Branches: NI	Scope: regional

Special requirements for membership: none

Nature of organization: political, social, educational, cultural, economic, professional

Publications: *El Calendario* (The Calendar), 1971– (monthly); *Entre Vecinos* (Among Neighbors), 1973– (bimonthly)

Affiliations: Valley Migrant League; Legal Aid (Marion/Polk Co.); Colegio Cesar Chavez; Oregon State Chicano Concilio

Major conventions/meetings: annual Fiesta del Sol, annual Board of Directors election meeting

Comments: Basic goals are to maintain "a vehicle which fosters the realization of a pluralistic community for Chicanos in the economic, educational and social sectors." The organization also strives to enhance Chicano identity and intercultural exchanges. Activities include publication of a monthly newspaper, arts and crafts groups, in-service training, art and cultural exhibits, annual Fiesta del Sol each summer, TV and radio programs, and fund-raising activities. An intercultural library is provided.

CHICANO PRESS ASSOCIATION
P.O. Box 31004
Los Angeles, California 90031   (213) 261-0128

Permanent staff: NI	Membership: 50 Chicano publishers
Date founded: 1968	Membership dues: NI
Branches: NI	Scope: national

Special requirements for membership: Chicano publisher

Nature of organization: professional

Comments: Supports the La Raza movement for unification and self-determination of Mexican-Americans. Also fights against discrimination of Chicanos in employment, housing, etc.

CHICANO TRAINING CENTER
3520 Montrose, Suite 216
Houston, Texas 77006   (713) 524-0595
Principal officers: Federico Souflee, Jr., Executive Director

Permanent staff: 6	Membership: NI
Date founded: 1971	Membership dues: NI
Branches: NI	Scope: national

Nature of organization: educational

Publications: *Mano a Mano* (bimonthly)

Comments: Acts as a consulting agency to institutions, organizations, and agencies that serve the Mexican-American community. It trains individuals to develop understanding of the Mexican culture and to promote understanding of Chicano values and mental health perspectives. Seminars, workshops, and conferences are conducted for individuals and group representatives.

CHICANOS POR LA CAUSA
116 East Buckeye Road
Phoenix, Arizona 85004   (602) 252-7191
Principal officers: Danny Valenzuela, President-Chairman
                       Edward L. Pastor, Vice President
                       Terri Cruz, Secretary

CHICANOS POR LA CAUSA (cont'd)

Permanent staff: 15   Membership: NI
Date founded: 1969   Membership dues: NI
Branches: NI   Scope: national

Nature of organization: social, cultural, economic, educational

Affiliations: National Council of La Raza

Major conventions/meetings: annual

Comments: Major efforts are along five lines: housing development, community services, economic development, education, and health services in the Mexican-American community. Partially funded by the Ford Foundation.

CLUB SEMBRADORES DE AMISTAD DE HOUSTON

P.O. Box 1786   (713) 729-9614 or
Houston, Texas 77001   (713) 225-1895

Principal officers: Jose Adan Trevino, President

Permanent staff: NI   Membership: NI
Date founded: 1964   Membership dues: NI
Branches: NI   Scope: international, national

Nature of organization: cultural, civil, social, economic

Major conventions/meetings: bimonthly

Comments: Mexican-American professionals who are members help Mexican-American students obtain scholarships. The organization also sponsors various social, civic, and cultural activities and programs.

COMMUNITY AND HUMAN RESOURCES AGENCY (CHRA)

751 South Figueroa Street
Los Angeles, California 90017   (213) 627-6274

Principal officers: James E. Baiz, Chairman

Permanent staff: NI   Membership: NI
Date founded: 1967   Membership dues: NI
Branches: 1 in Long Island, N.Y.   Scope: national

Nature of organization: philanthropic, educational

Comments: This non-profit organization is funded by industry and foundation grants to help the Mexican-American community develop leaders and obtain social and economic opportunities. It implements manpower training programs for employment opportunities for Mexican-American workers, and it sponsors various educational and informational programs.

COMMUNITY SERVICE ORGANIZATION, INC. (CSO)

714 California Avenue
Venice, California 90291   (213) 396-8742

Principal officers: Alberto Pinon, President

Permanent staff: NI   Membership: NI
Date founded: 1947   Membership dues: NI
Branches: NI   Scope: national

Nature of organization: political

Major conventions/meetings: weekly

Comments: The organization attempts to provide political representation for Mexican-Americans, to help them obtain credit unions and legal counseling, and to help with problems of education and employment. It is also a death benefit society, and it provides immigration, health, and welfare service and assistance. Has OEO funding for special programs such as buyers' cooperatives and housing programs.

EL CONGRESO NACIONAL DE ASUNTOS COLEGIALES
One Dupont Circle, N.W.
Washington, D.C. 20036 (202) 293-7050

Principal officers: Pepe Barron, Executive Secretary

Permanent staff: 3 — Membership: 750
Date founded: 1971 — Membership dues: NI
Branches: NI — Scope: national

Special requirements for membership: Mexican-American educators and those involved with community colleges

Nature of organization: professional, educational

Publications: *Boletin* (monthly)

Major conventions/meetings: annual

Comments: This organization is composed primarily of Mexican-American educators who attempt to advance the social, economic, and educational opportunities of Mexican-Americans. It conducts research and assists other Spanish-speaking organizations with similar goals.

EDUCATIONAL LABORATORY FOR INTER-AMERICAN STUDIES (ELIAS)
18111 Nordhoff, Box 96
Northridge, California 91324

Permanent staff: NI — Membership: NI
Date founded: 1967 — Membership dues: NI
Branches: NI — Scope: international, national

Special requirements for membership: school districts serving Mexican-American students

Nature of organization: educational

Comments: The purpose of the organization is to help obtain quality education for Mexican-American school children. Gives assistance in administrative and curriculum areas and provides educational materials for schools serving Mexican-American children.

LEAGUE OF UNITED LATIN AMERICAN CITIZENS (LULAC)
2918 South Birch Street
Santa Ana, California 92707 (714) 545-2816

Principal officers: Hector Godinez, National President

Permanent staff: 2 — Membership: 120,000
Date founded: 1929 — Membership dues: NI
Branches: various state branches — Scope: national

Special requirements for membership: of Mexican descent

Nature of organization: educational, welfare, political

Publications: *LULAC News* (monthly)

Major conventions/meetings: annual

Comments: Originally founded in Harlingen, Texas, this organization is one of the oldest and best-known Mexican-American associations. It assists needy Mexican-Americans and has established various educational and community programs. It also protests against discrimination, but it is non-partisan in political programs.

THE MEXICAN-AMERICAN DOCUMENTATION AND EDUCATIONAL RESEARCH INSTITUTE
1229 East Cypress Street
Anaheim, California 92805 (714) 772-2428

Principal officers: Dr. Daniel J. Gomez, President

Permanent staff: NI — Membership: NI
Date founded: 1969 — Membership dues: contributions
Branches: none — Scope: international, national

Nature of organization: educational, cultural

Comments: The primary purpose of the organization is to promote Mexican-American relations and to assist financially in the education of Mexican-American students.

MEXICAN AMERICAN LEGAL DEFENSE AND EDUCATIONAL FUND
145 Ninth Street
San Francisco, California 94103

Permanent staff: NI	Membership: NI
Date founded: 1968	Membership dues: NI
Branches: NI	Scope: national

Special requirements for membership: Mexican-American background

Nature of organization: professional, educational

Comments: Purpose is to protect the legal rights of Mexican-Americans by providing legal counsel and defense. It also aids young Americans of Mexican descent who are studying to become lawyers and conducts seminars for them. A 2,000-volume library is maintained.

MEXICAN AMERICAN UNITY COUNCIL (MAUC)
712 South Flores Street
San Antonio, Texas 78204   (515) 225-4241

Permanent staff: 75	Membership: 2,500
Date founded: 1967	Membership dues: none
Branches: 3 local	Scope: regional

Special requirements for membership: none

Nature of organization: urban development, cultural, economic, youth

Publications: none

Affiliations: none

Comments: The main objective of this community development corporation is to improve the social conditions of the Chicano community. It has a human service division, which provides family health services, and an economic or urban development division (i.e., housing programs, business, real estate development).

MEXICAN AMERICAN YOUTH ORGANIZATIONS (MAYO)
959 38th Street, S.W.
San Antonio, Texas 77018   (512) 435-1574

Principal officers: Mario Compean, National Chairman

Permanent staff: NI	Membership: NI
Date founded: 1967	Membership dues: NI
Branches: NI	Scope: national

Special requirements for membership: youth of Mexican-American descent

Nature of organization: youth, educational, political

Comments: The purpose of the organization is to assist youth in economic and political areas in Texas. The organization disseminates information.

MEXICAN CHAMBER OF COMMERCE OF THE UNITED STATES
60 Wall Street
New York, New York 10005

Permanent staff: NI	Membership: 600
Date founded: 1921	Membership dues: NI
Branches: NI	Scope: national

Nature of organization: economic

Publications: *Digest* (semimonthly); membership directory

Major conventions/meetings: annual

NATIONAL COUNCIL OF LA RAZA
1025 15th Street, N.W., 4th Floor
Washington, D.C. 20012   (202) 659-1251

NATIONAL COUNCIL OF LA RAZA (cont'd)

Principal officers: Maclovio Barraza, Chairman of the Board
Marta Sotomayor, First Vice President
Ruben Valdez, Second Vice President
Ed Gutierrez, Secretary

Permanent staff: 15
Date founded: 1968
Branches: 18 local

Membership: 18 affiliates
Membership dues: $100.00 lifetime
membership
Scope: national

Nature of organization: civil rights

Publications: *Agenda*, 1970– ; monthly newsletter and quarterly magazine

Major conventions/meetings: semiannual

Comments: This civil rights organization is non-profit, non-partisan, and dedicated to the betterment of life for Mexican-Americans. It supports other barrio organizations in providing information on economic development, education, and housing, and it sponsors a Housing Management Training Program. Until 1973 the organization was known as the Southwest Council of La Raza. It is partially funded by the Ford Foundation.

NATIONAL MEXICAN AMERICAN ANTI-DEFAMATION COMMITTEE
4312 Birchlake Court
Alexandria, Virginia 22306   (703) 780-0396

Principal officers: Domingo Nick Reyes, Executive Director

Permanent staff: 4
Date founded: 1968
Branches: NI

Membership: NI
Membership dues: NI
Scope: national

Nature of organization: anti-defamation

Publications: *Intercom* (monthly); *Annual Directory* (annual; in Spanish)

Major conventions/meetings: annual, in Washington, D.C.

Comments: This committee is composed of various individuals, religious groups, foundations, businesses, industries, non-profit organizations, and other groups seeking to promote the image of the Mexican-American and to oppose a negative or discriminatory image projected by the communications media. It sponsors consultations, seminars, opinion polls, and broadcasting enterprises. Cooperates with Mexican American educational institutions on research projects. Awards an annual prize for an outstanding media contribution to the Mexican-American community.

PADRES ASOCIADOS PARA DERECHOS, RELIGIOSOS, EDUCATIVOS Y SOCIALES
2518 West Commerce Street
San Antonio, Texas 78207   (512) 225-4225

Principal officers: Rev. Juan Romero, Executive Director

Permanent staff: NI
Date founded: 1969
Branches: NI

Membership: 800
Membership dues: NI
Scope: national

Special requirements for membership: Mexican American priests

Nature of organization: religious, educational, social

Publications: *Newsletter* (monthly); also publishes books

Major conventions/meetings: annual

Comments: This organization of priests promotes the religious, educational, and social welfare development of the Mexican-Americans in the United States. It conducts workshops and disseminates information to instruct and train Mexican-Americans in their objectives.

LA RAZA NATIONAL LAWYERS' ASSOCIATION (LRNLA)
145 9th Street
San Francisco, California 94103   (415) 626-6196

LA RAZA NATIONAL LAWYERS' ASSOCIATION (LRNLA) (cont'd)

Principal officers: Mario Obledo, President
                     Cesar A. Perales, Executive Vice President
                     Alfonso Gonzales, Executive Secretary

Permanent staff: 1	Membership: 75
Date founded: 1972	Membership dues: $12.50-$25.00 depend-
Branches: 9 regional	ing upon number of years as a lawyer
	Scope: national

Special requirements for membership: "membership in any state bar"

Nature of organization: professional

Publications: none

Affiliations: none

Major conventions/meetings: annual convention

TEXAS INSTITUTE FOR EDUCATIONAL DEVELOPMENT
      124 West Edwards
      Crystal City, Texas 78879   (512) 374-2298

Principal officers: Jose Angel Gutierrez

Permanent staff: NI	Membership: NI
Date founded: 1969	Membership dues: NI
Branches: NI	Scope: national

Nature of organization: educational

Comments: Sponsors various programs in leadership training and community development as well as educational programs.

TRICOLOR GROUP
      103 Marshall Place
      Longmont, Colorado 80501   (303) 722-0126

Principal officers: Jesus Pinela, President

Permanent staff: NI	Membership: NI
Date founded: 1969	Membership dues: NI
Branches: none	Scope: national

Nature of organization: welfare, cultural

Major conventions/meetings: monthly

Comments: The organization's purpose is to develop a better understanding of the Mexican culture among Anglo-Americans and to promote Mexican and Anglo relations. It also helps Mexican-American families in need and assists in job placement and housing. Sponsors various fund-raising activities and Mexican fiestas.

UNITED CITIZENS
      126 West Crockett Street
      Crystal City, Texas 78839

Principal officers: Julian Salas, President
                     Eduardo Irevino, Vice President
                     Rudolfo Palomo, Secretary

Permanent staff: NI	Membership: 350
Date founded: 1969	Membership dues: $6.00 (annual)
Branches: NI	Scope: regional

Nature of organization: political, social, cultural, economic, fraternal, scholarly

NEGRO-AMERICAN ORGANIZATIONS
See Black-American Organizations

NORWEGIAN-AMERICAN ORGANIZATIONS

See also Scandinavian-American Organizations

Additional information on Norwegian-American organizations in the United States may be obtained from the Norwegian Embassy Information Service (3401 Massachusetts Avenue, Washington, D.C. 20007). Regional and local organizations may be obtained from *Ethnic Directory I* (Detroit: Southeastern Michigan Regional Ethnic Heritage Studies Center, 1973).

BONDEUNGDOMSLAGET
Oslo Drive
Lake Telemark
Rockaway, New Jersey 08866

Principal officers: Harry Haakonsen, President
                   Kjell Skayness, Vice President
                   Anders Karlsen, Secretary

Permanent staff: none   Membership: 70
Date founded: 1925   Membership dues: $12.00
Branches: NI   Scope: local

Special requirements for membership: Norwegian birth or descent

Nature of organization: cultural, social

Major conventions/meetings: annual

Comments: The purpose of the Bondeungdomslaget is to unite persons of Norwegian ancestry in the United States and to preserve the Norwegian language, customs, and traditions. It also sponsors a folk dance group which performs at many social functions and folk dance festivals.

EBENEZER HOME SOCIETY
2545 Portland Avenue
Minneapolis, Minnesota 55404

Permanent staff: NI   Membership: NI
Date founded: 1934   Membership dues: NI
Branches: NI   Scope: regional

Nature of organization: charitable

Publications: *Ebenezer*, 1934– (quarterly)

JOINT COUNCIL OF BYGDELAGS, INC.
4700 11th Avenue South
Minneapolis, Minnesota 55407   (612) 822-9823

Principal officers: O. I. Hertsgaard, President
                   Eivind Horvik, Vice President
                   Thor Ohme, Secretary

Permanent staff: none   Membership: 15 affiliated branches
Date founded: 1916   Membership dues: $5.00
Branches: NI   Scope: national

Special requirements for membership: must be of Norwegian extraction or affiliation

Nature of organization: cultural, social

Publications: district council yearbooks

Major conventions/meetings: annual convention

Comments: Coordinates efforts to promote the work of Bygdelags (district councils) throughout the United States in spreading and preserving the Norwegian culture. The organization has sponsored centennial festivals in Minneapolis celebrating events in Norwegian and Norwegian-American history.

LEIF ERICSON SOCIETY
P.O. Box 1112   (312) 761-1888 or
Evanston, Illinois 60204   (312) 427-8090
Principal officers: W. R. Anderson, President
                 Ivar Christensen, Executive Vice President
                 Gerd T. Anderson, Executive Secretary

Permanent staff: 4	Membership: 550
Date founded: 1963	Membership dues: $5.00
Branches: 2 regional; 2 state	Scope: international

Special requirements for membership: none

Nature of organization: educational, cultural, scholarly

Publications: *Viking News*, 1966– (annual); also publishes bulletins

Affiliations: Norwegian-American Historical Association; Sons of Norway

Major conventions/meetings: convention (no regular frequency)

Comments: The society's primary concern is to further research into Norse Viking exploration and colonization in the Americas. Another objective is to locate artifacts and relics that would illustrate and help preserve the Norse culture. It makes an annual "Miss Viking America" award and an award for the best Norse news item.

LUTHERAN MISSION SOCIETIES, INC. (The Alaska Mission)
1134 South 8th Street
Minneapolis, Minnesota 55404   (612) 332-7635
Principal officers: Oscar Mosby, President
                 Ingolf Marthinussen, Vice President
                 Harald Bjurbeck, Secretary

Permanent staff: 2	Membership: 1,800
Date founded: 1921	Membership dues: none
Branches: 6 local	Scope: international

Special requirements for membership: none

Nature of organization: religious

Publications: *Norwegian Young People*, 1913– (monthly); *Call of the North* (bimonthly)

Affiliations: none

Major conventions/meetings: annual convention

Comments: To perpetuate and spread Lutheran beliefs, especially in Alaska, is the goal of this religious society. It was formerly known as the Federated Norwegian Lutheran Young Peoples Society in America (1921-1961). An archival File of Norsk Ungdom is maintained.

THE NOREGS SINGERS
15120 Burgess
Detroit, Michigan 48223   (313) 531-4198
Principal officers: Peder Rossen

Permanent staff: NI	Membership: NI
Date founded: NI	Membership dues: NI
Branches: NI	Scope: local

Nature of organization: cultural

NORSE CIVIC ASSOCIATION
14007 Longacre
Detroit, Michigan 48227

NORSEMAN'S FEDERATION
19500 St. Mary's
Detroit, Michigan 48235   (313) 838-2655

NORSEMAN'S FEDERATION (cont'd)

Permanent staff: NI

Date founded: NI

Branches: NI

Membership: NI

Membership dues: NI

Scope: national

Special requirements for membership: of Norwegian descent

Nature of organization: cultural, social, genealogical

Publications: English/Norse magazine

Comments: Through its English-Norwegian publication it serves Norwegian communities throughout the world. It offers travel services, shopping information and service, and genealogical service. It also assists in uniting Norwegian families in the United States.

NORTH NORWEGIAN ASSOCIATION

7389 Memory Lane, N.E.

Fridley, Minnesota 55432

(612) 786-2427

Principal officers: Christian K. Skjervold, President
Howard Nordley, Vice President
Jordis Lorentzen, Secretary

Permanent staff: none

Date founded: 1909

Branches: 1 regional; 6 local

Membership: 500

Membership dues: $2.00

Scope: national

Special requirements for membership: North Norwegian by birth or descent

Nature of organization: social, cultural

Publications: *North Norway*, 1909– (quarterly)

Major conventions/meetings: annual

Comments: The purpose is to unite persons of Norwegian ancestry through local meetings and annual conventions, and to preserve the culture and heritage of Norway, and particularly of North Norway.

NORWEGIAN-AMERICAN HISTORICAL ASSOCIATION (NAHA)

St. Olaf College

Northfield, Minnesota 55057

(507) 645-9311

Principal officers: Kenneth O. Bjork, President
Roy Thorshoy, Executive Vice President
Lloyd Hustvedt, Executive Secretary

Permanent staff: none

Date founded: 1925

Branches: none

Membership: 1,100

Membership dues: $7.00 association;
$12.00 sustaining; $25.00 patron;
$100.00 life (all the above annual)

Scope: national

Special requirements for membership: none

Nature of organization: scholarly

Publications: *Newsletter* (irregular); publishes the *Norwegian American Studies* series

Affiliations: none

Major conventions/meetings: triennial convention

Comments: The purpose of the association is to publish and preserve materials on Norwegian-American immigration in the following categories: studies; description and travel; topical studies. Over 50 volumes have been published to date. Maintains a library of 10,000 volumes and archival holdings of documents, papers, books, periodicals, and newspapers pertaining to the Norwegians in America.

THE NORWEGIAN CHURCH SERVICE IN WASHINGTON

c/o Mr. Roy R. Peterson

Route 2, Box 235

Sterling, Virginia 22170

THE NORWEGIAN CHURCH SERVICE IN WASHINGTON (cont'd)

Principal officers: Brit Aabakken Peterson, Chairman of Church Committee
Erna Paulsbo, Secretary

Permanent staff: 3	Membership: 150
Date founded: 1947	Membership dues: none
Branches: none	Scope: local (Washington, D.C., area)

Nature of organization: cultural, religious

Major conventions/meetings: 10 per year

Comments: The major objective is to provide a Norwegian-language church service the second Sunday of the month (September through June); the service is followed by a program of cultural interest designed to preserve the Norwegian heritage. Social activities and dinners are also planned.

NORWEGIAN CLUB
80 Broad Street, Room 2109
New York, New York 10004

Principal officers: Edv. J. Jorgensen, President

Permanent staff: NI	Membership: 100
Date founded: 1904	Membership dues: NI
Branches: NI	Scope: national

Special requirements for membership: Norwegian descent

Nature of organization: cultural

Comments: The purpose of the organization is to preserve the Norwegian traditions, culture, and language in the United States. Also attempts to foster good Norwegian-American relations.

NORWEGIAN CLUB OF DETROIT
Danish Hall
22711 Grand River
Detroit, Michigan 48219

Permanent staff: NI	Membership: NI
Date founded: NI	Membership dues: NI
Branches: 2 local	Scope: regional

Special requirements for membership: males of Norwegian descent

Nature of organization: social, cultural

Major conventions/meetings: monthly

Comments: Maintains the Norwegian culture in the United States by sponsoring Norwegian participation in ethnic festivals; unites Norwegians in the area through various social activities.

NORWEGIAN EMBASSY INFORMATION SERVICE
3401 Massachusetts Avenue
Washington, D.C. 20007

NORWEGIAN FOLKDANCE SOCIETY
740 40th Street
Brooklyn, New York 11232

Principal officers: Bjarne W. Olsen, President
Arne Pedersen, Vice President
Theresa Thorstensen, Secretary

Permanent staff: NI	Membership: 40
Date founded: 1938	Membership dues: $7.50 (annual)
Branches: none	Scope: local

Special requirements for membership: ability to dance

Nature of organization: cultural

NORWEGIAN FOLKDANCE SOCIETY (cont'd)

Publications: none

Comments: The major goal is to preserve Norwegian folk dancing. Members practice the traditional dances and perform in authentic regional costumes.

NORWEGIAN GOVERNMENT SEAMAN'S SERVICE

1401 Reynolds Street
Baltimore, Maryland 21230

NORWEGIAN LADIES AID

3700 Thornapple Street
Chevy Chase, Maryland 20015

NORWEGIAN LUNCHEON CLUB

700 National Building
Minneapolis, Minnesota 55402   (612) 339-7671

Principal officers: R. N. Thorshov, President
                        John L. Werness, Secretary
                        James A. Halls, Treasurer

Permanent staff: none   Membership: 170
Date founded: 1933   Membership dues: $21.00
Branches: NI   Scope: local

Special requirements for membership: part Norwegian ancestry (except for honorary members)

Nature of organization: social, cultural

Affiliations: none

Major conventions/meetings: monthly luncheon with speaker (October through May)

Comments: The club's purpose is to promote interest in Norwegian culture and Norwegian-American relationships. It provides financial support to graduate students from Norway for study at the University of Minnesota; these annual scholarships are intended to contribute to the rebuilding of science, technology, and education in Norway. Maintains archival materials with respect to the club's history and membership.

NORWEGIAN NATIONAL LEAGUE OF DETROIT

16706 Ridge
Detroit, Michigan 48219   (313) 532-6051

Principal officers: Ingvald Orheim

Permanent staff: NI   Membership: NI
Date founded: NI   Membership dues: NI
Branches: NI   Scope: local

Special requirements for membership: Norwegian descent

Nature of organization: cultural

Comments: Members learn and perform traditional Norwegian music and dance; social and cultural activities unite Norwegian-Americans in the area.

NORWEGIAN SEAMAN'S ASSOCIATION

38 Pearl Street
New York, New York 10004   (212) 944-3360

Principal officers: Gunnar Dybdahl, Manager

Permanent staff: NI   Membership: NI
Date founded: NI   Membership dues: NI
Branches: NI   Scope: national

Special requirements for membership: Norwegian seaman

Nature of organization: cultural, fraternal

Major conventions/meetings: quadrennial (in Oslo, Norway)

NORWEGIAN SINGERS ASSOCIATION OF AMERICA

3316 Xenwood Avenue, South
Minneapolis, Minnesota 55416   (612) 925-4658

Principal officers: Erling Stone, Executive Vice President

Permanent staff: NI   Membership: NI
Date founded: NI   Membership dues: NI
Branches: NI   Scope: national

Special requirements for membership: male vocalist of Norwegian descent

Nature of organization: cultural

Publications: *Sanger-Hilson* (Singers Greeting) (bimonthly)

Major conventions/meetings: biennial

Comments: Attempts to preserve Scandinavian and Norwegian music in the United States as one of the Norwegian contributions to American culture and society.

THE NORWEGIAN SOCIETY OF WASHINGTON, D.C.

2305 Whitetail Court
Reston, Virginia 22091   (703) 860-0054

Principal officers: Clifford Paulson, President
                       Grethe Twiford, Secretary
                       Einar Wulfsberg, Treasurer

Permanent staff: 7   Membership: approximately 150
Date founded: 1902   Membership dues: $5.00 couple; $3.00
Branches: none   individual
                            Scope: local (Washington, D.C., area)

Special requirements for membership: Norwegian birth or descent, or interest in Norway and its culture

Nature of organization: social, cultural

Publications: *Norwegian Society Newsletter*, 1972– (monthly)

Affiliations: Scandinavian Joint Planning Council of Washington, D.C.

Major conventions/meetings: annual business meeting

Comments: The aim of the society is to promote friendship among persons of Norwegian birth or descent, to preserve Norwegian culture and history, and to promote knowledge and understanding of Norway today. Records and club meetings and programs are kept in an archival collection.

NORWEGIAN TORSK CLUB

1350 Portland Avenue
St. Paul, Minnesota 55104   (612) 644-0626

Principal officers: Conrad A. Hoff, President
                       Leif Berget, Vice President
                       Robert L. Loughrey, Secretary

Permanent staff: none   Membership: 190
Date founded: 1966   Membership dues: $10.00 (annual)
Branches: none   Scope: local

Special requirements for membership: men of Norse birth or descent; upon unanimous decision of the Board of Directors men of other national origins may be accepted

Nature of organization: cultural, social

Publications: none

Affiliations: none

Major conventions/meetings: monthly, September through April

Comments: The purpose of the club is to provide recreational and social opportunities for members to meet other men of Norwegian descent, and to sponsor projects promoting the Norse culture and heritage. Donations are given for Norwegian language camp scholarships in Norway.

SETESDALSTLAGET OF AMERICA
c/o Mrs. Selma Johnson
Route 2
Trail, Minnesota 56684

Permanent staff: NI
Date founded: 1909
Branches: 0

Membership: NI
Membership dues: none
Scope: national

Principal officers: Oliver Lien, President

Nature of organization: cultural, social

SONS OF NORWAY (SN)
1455 West Lake Street
Minneapolis, Minnesota 55408   (612) 827-3611

Principal officers: Roy C. Eide, President
Harry Ludwigsen, Executive Vice President
Egil Olsen, Executive Secretary

Permanent staff: 50
Date founded: 1895
Branches: 310 regional

Membership: 82,000
Membership dues: $10.00 (annual)
Scope: international

Special requirements for membership: "open for Americans and Canadians of Norse birth, descent, and/or affiliation"

Nature of organization: social, educational, cultural, recreational, economic, sport, fraternal, youth

Publications: *The Viking Magazine*, 1903– (monthly); also publishes books

Affiliations: Fraternal Congress of America

Major conventions/meetings: biennial convention

Comments: The objective of this organization is to promote Norwegian culture, arts and crafts, and language. It sponsors programs in cultural, educational, humanitarian, and fraternal fields and grants scholarships to all age levels including teachers. Also grants scholarships to students in the United States and in Norway, and sponsors Norwegian language classes, camps, and folk art classes. Awards plaques, trophies, and certificates for professional achievement. Maintains a library of 1,000 volumes and archival materials.

VALDRES SAMBAND
RFD 3
Granite Falls, Minnesota 56241   (612) 564-3408

Principal officers: Carl T. Narvestad, President
Joseph Haugen, Vice President
Emma Lerohl, Secretary
Olaf R. Strand, Treasurer

Permanent staff: 3
Date founded: 1899
Branches: 2 local

Membership: 1,000 households
Membership dues: $1.00
Scope: international

Special requirements for membership: born in Valdres, Norway, or of Valdres descent; associate membership for others

Nature of organization: cultural

Publications: *Valdris Helsing*, 1903– (quarterly); *Samband*, 1910– (monthly); *Valdres Samband Newsletter*, 1962– (semiannual); also publishes books

Affiliations: Bygdelagenes Fellersraad

Major conventions/meetings: annual convention

Comments: The organization strives to preserve Norwegian culture and to collect and publish materials on the history of Norwegians in Norway and America; it compiles Norwegian family genealogies. Maintains archival materials of family histories and periodicals.

VIKING CLUB (USDA)
c/o Mr. Orville I. Overboe
1821 North Ohio Street
Arlington, Virginia 22205   (703) 447-4417
Principal officers: Pauline H. Cica, President
Robert L. Nelson, Vice President
Orville I. Overboe, Secretary

Permanent staff: NI   Membership: 200
Date founded: 1938   Membership dues: none
Branches: none   Scope: local

Special requirements for membership: open

Nature of organization: cultural, social

Publications: meeting notices

Affiliations: Scandinavian Joint Planning Council of Washington, D.C.

Comments: The club attempts to promote fellowship among persons of Scandinavian ancestry and to preserve their traditions and history. Sponsors a luncheon where speakers discuss subjects of interest to Scandinavians.

PAKISTANI-AMERICAN ORGANIZATIONS

Additional information on Pakistani-American organizations in the United States may be obtained from the Office of the Pakistan Embassy (2315 Massachusetts Avenue, Washington, D.C. 20008).

PAKISTANI ASSOCIATION OF AMERICA
12524 Broadstreet
Detroit, Michigan 48204

Permanent staff: NI   Membership: NI
Date founded: NI   Membership dues: NI
Branches: NI   Scope: national

Nature of organization: cultural

PALESTINIAN-AMERICAN ORGANIZATIONS

See Arab-American Organizations

PERUVIAN-AMERICAN ORGANIZATIONS

Additional information on Peruvian-American organizations in the United States may be obtained from the Office of the Peruvian Embassy (1700 Massachusetts Avenue, Washington, D.C. 20036).

PERUVIAN AMERICAN ASSOCIATION
c/o Mr. P. E. Sibilia
11 Broadway
New York, New York 10004   (212) 943-8753
Principal officers: P. E. Sibilia, Secretary

PERUVIAN-AMERICAN MEDICAL SOCIETY
540 East Canfield
Detroit, Michigan 48201   (313) 224-0744
Principal officers: Agustin Arbulu, President
Hugo Sanchez Moreno, Vice President
Rudolfo Byrne, Secretary

PERUVIAN-AMERICAN MEDICAL SOCIETY (cont'd)

Permanent staff: NI	Membership: NI
Date founded: 1973	Membership dues: $35.00
Branches: none	Scope: national

Special requirements for membership: registered physicians residing or practicing in the United States

Nature of organization: professional

Publications: none

Affiliations: none

Major conventions/meetings: annual convention

Comments: Objectives of the organization are to improve medical, educational, and cultural relations between Peru and the United States.

PERUVIAN CLUB OF MICHIGAN
P.O. Box 5742
Detroit, Michigan 48239

Principal officers: Agustin Arbulu, President
Arturo Paz, Vice President
Rose B. Feria, Secretary

Permanent staff: 5	Membership: 50
Date founded: 1960	Membership dues: $5.00
Branches: none	Scope: state

Special requirements for membership: Peruvian descent (for active member); others can be honorary members

Nature of organization: cultural

Publications: none

Comments: Objectives of the organization are to provide assistance to those of Peruvian descent and to unite them in social and recreational activities or programs that perpetuate the Peruvian culture in the United States.

POLISH-AMERICAN ORGANIZATIONS

Additional information on Polish-American organizations in the United States may be obtained from the Polish American Congress (220 West Division Street, Chicago, Illinois 60610) and from the Orchard Lake Center for Polish Studies and Culture (c/o St. Mary's College, Orchard Lake, Michigan 48034). Regional and local organizations may be found in *Greater Cleveland Nationalities Directory 1974* (Cleveland: Sun Newspapers and the Nationalities Services Center, 1974) and *Ethnic Directory I* (Detroit: Southeastern Michigan Regional Ethnic Heritage Studies Center, 1973).

ALLIANCE OF POLES OF AMERICA
6966 Broadway Avenue
Cleveland, Ohio 44105   (216) 883-3131

Principal officers: B. A. Michalski, President
Andrew Baracz, Vice President
Genevieve Sandej, Vice President
Stella T. Majsterek, Secretary

Permanent staff: 3	Membership: 17,000
Date founded: 1895	Membership dues: NI
Branches: 83 in three states	Scope: regional (Ohio, Michigan, Pennsylvania)

ALLIANCE OF POLES OF AMERICA (cont'd)

Special requirements for membership: must be of Polish or Slavic extraction

Nature of organization: fraternal

Publications: *Zwiazkowiec* (Alliancer) (twice a month)

Major conventions/meetings: quadrennial convention

Comments: The objectives of the organization are to unite Poles or persons of Polish descent in America, to provide life insurance to members, and to preserve the Polish culture by cooperating with other Polish organizations in national, civic, cultural, and social activities. Until 1916 the name of the organization was Alliance of Poles in State of Ohio. It also sponsors clubs for Polish youth and provides scholarship funds. A library of over 10,000 volumes is maintained.

ALLIANCE OF POLISH KLUBS (ZKM)

1401 West Superior Street
Chicago, Illinois 60622   (312) 421-5897

Permanent staff: caretaker, other volunteers   Membership: various clubs
Date founded: 1927   Membership dues: NI
Branches: NI   Scope: national

Special requirements for membership: Polish origin and interest

Nature of organization: cultural, economic, fraternal

Major conventions/meetings: triennial convention

Comments: Major purpose of this organization is to provide financial aid to the villages or areas in Poland from which the members of the various clubs originated. Helps build schools and churches in these villages, and also sends clothing to Poland. Maintains a small library and archival collection.

AMERICAN COUNCIL OF POLISH CULTURAL CLUBS

6300 Lakeview Drive
Falls Church, Virginia 22041

Principal officers: John A. Wojciechowicz, President
                       Rose Polski Anderson, Vice President
                       Florence L. Serafin, Secretary

Permanent staff: 28   Membership: 1,200
Date founded: 1948   Membership dues: $2.00
Branches: 21   Scope: national

Special requirements for membership: none

Nature of organization: cultural

Publications: *Quarterly Review*, 1948– (quarterly)

Affiliations: none

Major conventions/meetings: annual convention

Comments: The purposes of the council are to preserve and transmit the Polish culture by promoting program artists and materials, acting as a clearinghouse for exchange of information and ideas, giving assistance in forming new clubs and cooperating with other Polish organizations in America. An archival collection of organizational records is maintained.

THE AMERICAN INSTITUTE OF POLISH CULTURE

1000 Brickell Avenue
Miami, Florida 33131   (305) 373-9008

Principal officers: Mrs. Lewis S. Rosenstiel, President
                       George Riabov, Vice President
                       Ewa Szumanska, Secretary
                       Penny Magloire, Public Relations

Permanent staff: 3   Membership: 140
Date founded: 1972   Membership dues: $10.00 or $25.00
Branches: NI   (annual)
                                                     Scope: regional

THE AMERICAN INSTITUTE OF POLISH CULTURE (cont'd)

Special requirements for membership: interest in Polish culture

Nature of organization: cultural

Publications: *Good News* (monthly)

Affiliations: American Council for Polish Cultural Clubs

Major conventions/meetings: biennial

Comments: The major objectives are to preserve the Polish culture in the United States by providing educational facilities and resources for bringing together the latest research and artistic contributions of Polish Americans. The former name of the organization was the Polish-American Cultural Institute. The institute assists scholars at all levels in their studies of Polish culture. It sponsors a Polish language course, a Polish literature course at the University of Miami, radio and TV programs by or about Polish artists and culture, art exhibits, and concerts. It maintains a 300-volume library.

AMERICAN RELIEF FOR POLAND

1200 North Ashland Avenue
Chicago, Illinois 60622   (312) 276-3700

Principal officers: Francis X. Swietik, President

Permanent staff: NI   Membership: NI
Date founded: 1939   Membership dues: NI
Branches: NI   Scope: national

Major conventions/meetings: annual

Comments: Aids the needy in Poland by providing medical supplies and equipment. United States surplus foods are provided for school children in Poland.

ASSOCIATION OF MARIAN HELPERS

The Marian Fathers
Eden Hill
Stockbridge, Massachusetts 01262

Permanent staff: NI   Membership: NI
Date founded: 1944   Membership dues: NI
Branches: NI   Scope: national

Nature of organization: religious

Publications: *Roze Maryi* (Roses of Mary), 1944– (monthly)

ASSOCIATION OF POLISH WOMEN OF THE US

7526 Broadway
Cleveland, Ohio 44105   (216) 641-4900

Principal officers: Angeline C. Pletta, General Secretary

Permanent staff: NI   Membership: NI
Date founded: NI   Membership dues: NI
Branches: NI   Scope: national

Nature of organization: social, cultural

Publications: *Jednosc Polek* (Unity of Polish Women), 1924– (semimonthly)

Major conventions/meetings: quadrennial

Comments: Primarily a social and cultural organization, the purpose of this group is to unite Polish women in the area and to preserve the Polish heritage, language, and traditions through social and cultural programs and charitable activities.

ASSOCIATION OF THE SONS OF POLAND

665 Newark Avenue
Jersey City, New Jersey 07306   (201) 653-1163

Principal officers: Alexander Sudnik, Secretary-Treasurer

Permanent staff: NI   Membership: 18,000
Date founded: 1903   Membership dues: varies with insurance
Branches: 120   policy
                                    Scope: national

ASSOCIATION OF THE SONS OF POLAND (cont'd)

Special requirements for membership: Polish birth or descent

Nature of organization: fraternal

Major conventions/meetings: quadrennial

Comments: The primary purpose of the organization is to provide life insurance benefits to members. It also conducts various social, cultural, and philanthropic activities, and it sponsors scholarships for students of Polish descent.

COPERNICUS FOUNDATION
2952 Milwaukee Avenue
Chicago, Illinois 60618

GENERAL PULASKI HERITAGE FOUNDATION
165 West 46th Street
New York, New York 10036   (212) 765-1662

Principal officers: Dr. J. Maxwell Kucharski, Executive Vice President

Permanent staff: NI   Membership: 2,600
Date founded: 1959   Membership dues: NI
Branches: NI   Scope: national

Nature of organization: cultural, philanthropic

Publications: *Pulaski Bulletin* (quarterly); *Pulaski News Letter* (irregular)

Major conventions/meetings: annual

Comments: Preserves the memory of General Pulaski, a Polish nobleman and hero in the American Revolutionary War. Also sponsors various philanthropic activities, as well as the construction of a museum, research center, clinic, and library of Polish works.

GRAND COUNCIL OF PULASKI ASSOCIATION
61-60 56th Street
Flushing, New York 11378

HENRYK SIENKIEWICZ EDUCATIONAL SOCIETY
263 Prospect Avenue
Brooklyn, New York 11215

JOSEF PILSUDSKI INSTITUTE OF AMERICA
381 Park Avenue South
New York, New York 10016   (212) 683-4342

Principal officers: Jan Fryling, President
                     W. Jedrzejewicz, Vice President
                     Michael Budny, Executive Director

Permanent staff: 6   Membership: 380
Date founded: 1943   Membership dues: $12.00 individual
Branches: NI   (annual); $25.00 organization (annual)
                                    Scope: NI

Nature of organization: educational

Publications: *Biuletyn* (The Bulletin), 1943– (annual); *Independence*, 1944– (irregular)

Affiliations: none

Major conventions/meetings: annual

Comments: The organization's purpose is to conduct research on the modern history of Poland by helping scholars and students to prepare papers, theses, lectures, books, and other publications, and by collecting and preserving books, documents, films, photographs, and memorabilia. Three awards of $500 each have been awarded. A library and an archival collection are maintained.

THE KOSCIUSZKO FOUNDATION
15 East 65th Street
New York, New York 10021   (212) 734-2130

Principal officers: Eugene Kusielewicz, President
                       Charles Nosal, Vice President
                       Edmund I. Zawacki, Secretary

Permanent staff: 7   Membership: 3,500
Date founded: 1925   Membership dues: $10.00 (annual)
Branches: none   Scope: national

Special requirements for membership: none

Nature of organization: cultural

Publications: *The Kosciuszko Foundation Monthly Newsletter*, 1946– (monthly); also
    publishes books

Affiliations: none

Major conventions/meetings: none

Comments: The goal of this charitable organization is to provide scholarships to Polish-
    Americans for graduate study or to persons of any ethnic background for graduate work
    in Polish studies. The foundation attempts to broaden Polish and American cultural
    relationships through the exchange of scholars, artists, and writers. It sponsors summer
    sessions in Poland for Americans, to expose them to Polish culture, history, and tradi-
    tion. It gives an annual Doctoral Dissertation Award. A 4,000-volume library and an
    archival collection of historical documents are maintained.

LEAGUE OF AMERICAN POLES
P.O. Box 737, Athenia Street
Clifton, New Jersey 07013

MASSACHUSETTS FEDERATION OF POLISH WOMEN'S CLUBS, INC.
29 Hemlock Street
South Braintree, Massachusetts 02185   (617) 848-2704

Principal officers: Beatrice Melody, President
                       Genevieve Janosz, Vice President
                       Julia Gelowtsky, Secretary

Permanent staff: 4   Membership: 1,500
Date founded: 1931   Membership dues: $2.00
Branches: 5 regional; 1 state; 19 local   Scope: state

Special requirements for membership: Polish descent

Nature of organization: cultural, social, educational, youth

Publications: *The Massachusetts Federation of Polish Women's Clubs Newsletter*, 1953–
    (biannually); *Federation Annual Reports*, 1961– (annual)

Affiliations: The Kosciuszko Foundation, New York; Polish American Congress, Chicago;
    Boston Public Library–Associate Members

Major conventions/meetings: annual

Comments: The purpose of the federation is to unite women's clubs in Massachusetts whose
    members are of Polish descent, for civic, educational, and cultural programs. It sponsors
    annual scholarship awards, annual essay contests, educational programs, lectures, and
    films. It endowed the Dr. Maria E. Zakrzewska scholarship of $25,000 at the
    Kosciuszko Foundation in New York. Also sponsors a Woman of the Year Award and
    citations to outstanding Poles. Maintains a library of about 200 volumes and archival
    materials of federation records and awards.

MUTUAL AID ASSOCIATION OF THE NEW POLISH IMMIGRATION
1514 North Milwaukee Avenue
Chicago, Illinois 60622   (312) 489-2250

Principal officers: Kazimierz Lukomski, President

MUTUAL AID ASSOCIATION OF THE NEW POLISH IMMIGRATION (cont'd)

Permanent staff: NI   Membership: 750
Date founded: 1903   Membership dues: NI
Branches: NI   Scope: national

Special requirements for membership: Polish immigrants since World War II

Nature of organization: cultural, welfare

Comments: The major purpose of the organization is to assist Polish immigrants, both financially and in their adjustment to life in the United States. It also sponsors various cultural and social programs and activities and conducts a Polish-language school for children.

NATIONAL ADVOCATES SOCIETY
     c/o Mr. Richard Bogusz
     11 South La Salle Street
     Chicago, Illinois 60603   (312) 726-4408

Principal officers: Richard Bogusz, Executive Committee Chairman

Permanent staff: NI   Membership: 1,000
Date founded: NI   Membership dues: NI
Branches: NI   Scope: national

Special requirements for membership: lawyers of Polish descent

Nature of organization: professional

Publications: *Bulletin* (monthly); *Directory* (triennial)

Major conventions/meetings: annual

NATIONAL ASSOCIATION OF POLISH AMERICANS
     3829 W Street, S.E.
     Washington, D.C. 20020

NATIONAL MEDICAL AND DENTAL ASSOCIATION
     15120 Michigan Avenue
     Dearborn, Michigan 48126

Principal officers: Edward S. Wikiera, Executive Secretary

Permanent staff: 2   Membership: 1,000
Date founded: 1900   Membership dues: NI
Branches: NI   Scope: national

Special requirements for membership: physicians and dentists of Polish descent

Nature of organization: professional

NEW JERSEY STATE CONFERENCE OF AMERICAN POLONIANS (NJSCAP)
     622 Bloomfield Avenue
     Bloomfield, New Jersey 07003   (201) 743-9614

Principal officers: Chester Grabowski, Chairman
                    Richard Otherski, Vice Chairman
                    James Lewandowski, General Secretary

Permanent staff: 1   Membership: 200
Date founded: 1972   Membership dues: $100.00
Branches: none   Scope: state

Special requirements for membership: males of Polish heritage, born in the United States, living in the state of New Jersey

Nature of organization: civic

Publications: none

Affiliations: none

Major conventions/meetings: none

Comments: Objectives are to serve as an advisory, information, and grievance board, as an anti-discrimination center, a placement center, a screening board, and a clearinghouse for all activities of Polonians throughout the state of New Jersey.

ORCHARD LAKE CENTER FOR POLISH STUDIES AND CULTURE
St. Mary's College
Orchard Lake, Michigan 48034   (313) 682-1885
Principal officers: T. Polzin, Director

Permanent staff: NI   Membership: NI
Date founded: NI   Membership dues: NI
Branches: NI   Scope: regional

Nature of organization: educational, cultural, scholarly

Publications: publishes books

Affiliations: St. Mary's College; SS. Cyril and Methodius Seminary; St. Mary's Preparatory; Center for Pastoral Studies; Polish American Liturgical Center

Comments: The center publishes monographs on Polish-American topics resulting from research conducted by scholars and historians; also publishes a directory of Polish-American archives.

POLISH ACTIVITIES LEAGUE
3314 Junction
Detroit, Michigan 48210   (313) 825-5330

POLISH ALMA MATER OF AMERICA
4842 West Fullerton
Chicago, Illinois 60639   (312) 622-0132
Principal officers: Theodore L. Skweres, General Secretary

Permanent staff: NI   Membership: 5,300
Date founded: 1897   Membership dues: varies with insurance
Branches: 81   policy
                                Scope: national

Nature of organization: fraternal

Major conventions/meetings: quadrennial

Comments: Provides life insurance benefits to members.

POLISH AMERICAN ACADEMIC ASSOCIATION
9535 Jos. Campau
Hamtramck, Michigan 48212   (313) 873-0285
Principal officers: Elizabeth Stajniak, President
                     Henry Gumul, Vice President
                     Jessie Gumul, Secretary

Permanent staff: 1   Membership: 50
Date founded: 1956   Membership dues: $10.00
Branches: none   Scope: state

Special requirements for membership: Polish descent and either a student at or a graduate of a university

Nature of organization: cultural, scholarly

Publications: *Na Pieterku*, 1960– (monthly)

Major conventions/meetings: annual convention

Comments: The association aims to promote Polish culture by sponsoring lectures, book fairs, and concerts. It also sponsors dances and social functions so that those of Polish descent can become acquainted. It provides financial aid in the form of scholarships for its members. A library of 200 volumes is maintained.

POLISH-AMERICAN COMMERCIAL CLUB
138 Custer Avenue
Evanston, Illinois 60202   (312) 869-3166
Principal officers: Stanley Olech, President
                     Henry S. Bogacki, First Vice President
                     Juliusz Szygowski, Secretary

POLISH-AMERICAN COMMERCIAL CLUB (cont'd)

Permanent staff: 20   Membership: 150
Date founded: 1933   Membership dues: $25.00
Branches: none   Scope: local

Special requirements for membership: citizens of Polish descent in industry, commerce, or the professions

Nature of organization: professional

Publications: none

Major conventions/meetings: monthly meetings

Comments: Objectives of the organization are to encourage development of Polish-American cultural and economic interests and solidarity among the members for better business protection and propagation. It purchases books valuable to Polish culture and history, then donates them to university and public libraries; awards monetary prizes in the Polish Literary Youth Contest.

POLISH AMERICAN CONGRESS (PAC)
1200 North Ashland
Chicago, Illinois 60610

Principal officers: Aloysius Mazewsky, President

Permanent staff: NI   Membership: NI
Date founded: 1944   Membership dues: NI
Branches: NI   Scope: national

Special requirements for membership: Polish descent

Nature of organization: political, cultural, social

Publications: *Polish American Congress Newsletter*, 1959– (quarterly)

Major conventions/meetings: annual

Comments: The major purpose of the organization is to promote the Polish culture and image in the United States, to support freedom and independence for the people of Poland, and to sponsor social and cultural activities within the various branches of the Congress that will unite Polish-Americans in the United States.

POLISH-AMERICAN GUARDIAN SOCIETY (PAGS)
6200 West 64th Street
Chicago, Illinois 60638   (312) 586-4734

Principal officers: Leonard Jarzab, President
                       Edmund Reczek, Vice President
                       Emily Garbacz, Secretary

Permanent staff: 4   Membership: 750
Date founded: 1962   Membership dues: $5.00 (annual)
Branches: none   Scope: national

Special requirements for membership: Polish extraction

Nature of organization: political

Publications: none

Affiliations: none

Major conventions/meetings: biennial conference

Comments: The aim of the society is to guard against derogatory or negative stereotypes of the Polish people in the United States, particularly through the media. It presents an annual "Guardian Award." Maintains a library of 150 volumes and an archival collection.

POLISH AMERICAN HISTORICAL ASSOCIATION (PAHA)
984 Milwaukee Avenue
Chicago, Illinois 60622   (312) 278-3210

Principal officers: Bernadine Pietraszek, President
                       George Lerski, Executive Vice President
                       Donald Bilinski, Executive Secretary

POLISH AMERICAN HISTORICAL ASSOCIATION (PAHA) (cont'd)

Permanent staff: 1

Date founded: 1942

Branches: none

Membership: 450

Membership dues: $10.00 (annual)

Scope: national

Special requirements for membership: none

Nature of organization: scholarly

Publications: *Polish American Studies*, 1942– (semiannual); *PAHA Bulletin*, 1946– (quarterly)

Affiliations: none

Major conventions/meetings: annual convention

Comments: PAHA aims to promote studies of Polish American history and to further research and scholarly publications. Until 1949 it was known as the Polish American Historical Commission. Plans of the association are to award prizes for theses, dissertations, and articles. Maintains archival materials.

POLISH AMERICAN IMMIGRATION AND RELIEF COMMITTEE

17 Irving Place

New York, New York 10003   (212) 254-2240

Principal officers: Hieronim Wyszynski, Executive Director and Secretary

Permanent staff: NI

Date founded: 1947

Branches: NI

Membership: NI

Membership dues: NI

Scope: national

Nature of organization: relief

Major conventions/meetings: annual

Comments: Major goal is to provide assistance in immigration in any way possible. It also helps displaced persons to become reunited with friends and families. Until 1957 the organization was known as the American Commission for Relief of Polish Immigrants.

POLISH AMERICAN INFORMATION BUREAU

55 West 42nd Street

New York, New York 10036

POLISH AMERICAN NUMISMATIC ASSOCIATION

P.O. Box 1873

Chicago, Illinois 60690

POLISH AMERICAN POLICE ASSOCIATION OF ILLINOIS (PAPA)

5755 South Menard Avenue

Chicago, Illinois 60638   (312) 284-0979

Principal officers: Martin J. Bilecki, President

Eugene F. Kosiek, Vice President

Paul S. Jankowski, Secretary

Permanent staff: 19

Date founded: 1964

Branches: in Illinois and in adjoining regions of
 Indiana and Wisconsin

Membership: 1,000

Membership dues: $5.00 active; $10.00
 associate

Scope: state

Special requirements for membership: active: law enforcement officer of Polish or Slavic origin; associate: sponsorship by active member and approval of Board

Nature of organization: professional, fraternal

Publications: a bimonthly newsletter

Affiliations: Polish American Congress; Chicago Patrolman's Association; Polish Roman Catholic Union; Copernicus Foundation

Major conventions/meetings: yearly awards dinner-dance; bimonthly meetings

POLISH AMERICAN POLICE ASSOCIATION OF ILLINOIS (PAPA) (cont'd)

Comments: The organization's purposes are to provide a better understanding of police problems and a medium for exchange of knowledge in the law enforcement field. It provides financial assistance to members in need, and it sponsors social activities for members and families. It gives awards to policemen for acts of heroism and bravery. The group presents gifts to Polish orphans and provides charitable programs for inner-city children.

POLISH ARMY VETERANS ASSOCIATION OF AMERICA
17 Irving Place
New York, New York 10003   (212) 475-5585

Principal officers: John Dec, National Commander
                        Richard Rudnicki, Vice Commander
                        Zbigniew A. Konikowski, Adjutant General

Permanent staff: 2   Membership: 8,100
Date founded: 1921   Membership dues: $7.20 (annual)
Branches: 115 regional; 12 district   Scope: national

Special requirements for membership: Polish veterans who served in the armed forces of the United States, Great Britain, or France, and who were honorably discharged

Nature of organization: military

Publications: *Veteran*, 1921– (monthly); also publishes books

Affiliations: none

Major conventions/meetings: triennial convention

Comments: The association's purpose is to organize all Polish Army veterans of World War I and World War II to assist and provide relief for members and families. It provides scholarships for children of Polish veterans.

POLISH ARTS AND CULTURE FOUNDATION (PACF)
50 Oak Street
San Francisco, California 94102   (415) 861-5926

Principal officers: Wanda Tomczykowska, President
                        Sylvia Janks, Vice President and Secretary
                        John Black, Treasurer

Permanent staff: none   Membership: 100
Date founded: 1966   Membership dues: $25.00 minimum
Branches: NI   Scope: national

Special requirements for membership: by invitation

Nature of organization: educational, cultural

Publications: *Polish Arts and Culture Foundation Monthly Bulletin*, 1966– (monthly); also publishes books

Affiliations: Kosciuszko Foundation in New York City

Comments: The foundation attempts to promote and preserve Polish cultural achievements, arts, and history. It presents exhibitions and programs and loans Polish costumes, arts, crafts, and paintings for use at conferences or in classrooms. It sponsors TV programs and radio programs on Polish music, dance, and language classes, exhibits and film festivals. It grants an award in the annual Copernicus Art Competition. Maintains a library of over 1,000 documents, as well as archives.

POLISH ASSISTANCE, INC.
36 West 56th Street
New York, New York 10019   (212) 245-2087

Principal officers: Marja Dembinski, President

Permanent staff: NI   Membership: NI
Date founded: 1956   Membership dues: NI
Branches: NI   Scope: national

Nature of organization: charitable

POLISH ASSISTANCE, INC. (cont'd)

Publications: *Bulletin* (semiannual); *Annual Report* (annual)

Comments: Sponsors various charitable activities for Poles in the United States. Primarily works with Polish victims of World War II, but also maintains a home for the elderly, disabled, and needy. The organization was formerly known as the Polish Mutual Assistance.

POLISH ASSOCIATION OF AMERICA
1202 West Oklahoma Avenue
Milwaukee, Wisconsin 53215   (414) 645-4076

Principal officers: Louis J. Kielich, Secretary-Treasurer

Permanent staff: NI
Date founded: 1895
Branches: NI

Membership: 6,543
Membership dues: varies with insurance policy
Scope: national

Nature of organization: fraternal

Publications: *Bulletin* (quarterly)

Comments: Provides life insurance benefits to members and financial aid to students. Sponsors recreational and sport activities for youth.

POLISH ASSOCIATION OF FORMER POLITICAL PRISONERS
P.O. Box 2495, Grand Central Station
New York, New York 10017   (212) 849-5841

Principal officers: Michael Preisler, President

Permanent staff: NI
Date founded: 1952
Branches: 7 regional

Membership: 900
Membership dues: NI
Scope: national

Special requirements for membership: former Polish political prisoners

Nature of organization: political, charitable

Publications: *Nasze Drogi* (Our Roads) (quarterly); *Bulletin* (irregular)

Major conventions/meetings: biennial

Comments: Assists former political prisoners and their families. Maintains small library of materials about prison camps.

POLISH BENEFICIAL ASSOCIATION
2595 Orthodox
Philadelphia, Pennsylvania 19137   (215) 753-9856

Principal officers: Julian Zbytniewski, Secretary

Permanent staff: 9
Date founded: 1900
Branches: 132

Membership: 24,654
Membership dues: NI
Scope: national

Special requirements for membership: of Slavic or Polish descent and of the Greek Orthodox or Roman Catholic faith

Nature of organization: fraternal

Publications: *Jednosc*

Major conventions/meetings: quadrennial

Comments: Provides life insurance benefits to members. Also assists needy students and sponsors youth programs of cultural and civic interest (e.g., choral groups, dancing school, etc.).

POLISH COMMUNITY SERVICE CENTER
767 Market Street
San Francisco, California 94103

Publications: *Polonian*, 1969– (bimonthly)

POLISH CULTURAL FOUNDATION, INC.

851 18th Avenue
Irvington, New Jersey 07111   (201) 373-3384

Principal officers: Caesar T. Gaza, President
William Matysek, Vice President
Stephen Stripp, Sr., Secretary

Permanent staff: none   Membership: 250
Date founded: 1972   Membership dues: $10-$1,000
Branches: none   Scope: state

Special requirements for membership: none

Nature of organization: cultural, professional, scholarly, educational, youth

Publications: in planning stage

Affiliations: none

Major conventions/meetings: annual Board of Directors meeting

Comments: The foundation's goal is to create and operate a Polish Cultural Center consisting of a performing arts theatre, classrooms, library archives, gymnasium, and pool. The center will be used to encourage Polish studies and achievements of persons of Polish descent.

POLISH CULTURAL FOUNDATION, INC. (PCF)

777 Fillmore Avenue
Buffalo, New York 14212   (716) 896-4210

Principal officers: John M. Frysiak, President
Walter M. Drzewieniecki, Executive Vice President
Zofia A. Drzewieniecki, Executive Secretary

Permanent staff: none   Membership: 35
Date founded: 1965   Membership dues: $10.00 (and up;
Branches: none   annual)
                                     Scope: state

Special requirements for membership: none

Nature of organization: educational, cultural

Publications: publishes books

Affiliations: none

Major conventions/meetings: semiannual conferences

Comments: The organization's objectives are to preserve the Polish heritage, language, and culture; to promote a positive image of Polish Americans; to provide financial aid to Polish-American university students studying Polish history, institutions, culture, and language; and to publish Polish cultural and historical materials. Until 1971 the organization was known as the Polish-American Council on Cultural Affairs, Inc. It provides scholarships for students in the Polish Program at Buffalo State College. Archives are maintained.

POLISH FALCONS OF AMERICA

97 South 18th Street
Pittsburgh, Pennsylvania 15203   (412) 431-0305

Principal officers: Walter J. Laska, President
Bernard Rogalski, Secretary

Permanent staff: 14   Membership: 28,100
Date founded: 1887   Membership dues: varies with insurance
Branches: NI   policy
                                     Scope: national

Nature of organization: fraternal, cultural

Publications: *Sokol Polski*, 1896– (semimonthly)

Major conventions/meetings: quadrennial

POLISH FALCONS OF AMERICA (cont'd)

Comments: Major purpose is to provide life insurance benefits to members. Also sponsors
various social and cultural activities, such as summer camps, folklore, gymnastics,
sports events. Provides scholarships for students of Polish descent.

POLISH HERITAGE SOCIETY
30 West Washington Street, Suite 928
Chicago, Illinois 60602

**POLISH HISTORICAL COMMISSION OF CENTRAL COUNCIL OF
POLISH ORGANIZATIONS**
4291 Stanton Avenue
Pittsburgh, Pennsylvania 15201   (412) 782-2166

Principal officers: Joseph A. Borkowski, Director
                       Anthony J. Studnicki, President
                       Hedwig Siwicki, Secretary

Permanent staff: 7   Membership: 76
Date founded: 1946   Membership dues: $2.00
Branches: none   Scope: local

Special requirements for membership: none

Nature of organization: cultural, historical

Publications: *Jedniodniuwka*, 1935– (annual)

Affiliations: Pennsylvania Federation of Historical Societies

Major conventions/meetings: quarterly meetings

Comments: The organization supports research on Polish history and culture in Western
Pennsylvania. It acts as a source of historical materials for authors, editors, and students.
Maintains a library and an archival collection.

POLISH INSTITUTE OF ARTS AND SCIENCES IN AMERICA, INC. (PIAS)
59 East 66th Street
New York, New York 10021   (212) 988-4338

Principal officers: Eugene Kleban, Executive Director
                       Thaddeus V. Gromada, Secretary-General

Permanent staff: 7   Membership: 700
Date founded: 1942   Membership dues: $15.00 (annual)
Branches: 2 regional   Scope: Western Hemisphere

Special requirements for membership: "Ph.D. degree or equivalent scholarly achievement"

Nature of organization: educational, cultural, scholarly

Publications: *The Polish Review*, 1956– (quarterly); *Information Bulletin*, 1942– (quarterly)

Affiliations: none

Major conventions/meetings: none

Comments: Objectives of the institute are to publish materials devoted to the study of Polish
culture, arts, and sciences; to promote international programs connected with Polish-
American relations; to offer facilities for research; to organize public lectures, conferences, and exhibitions; and to cooperate with other American and Polish research
institutions. Maintains a library of 13,500 volumes.

POLISH LEGION OF AMERICAN VETERANS, U.S.A.
3024 North Laramie Avenue
Chicago, Illinois 60641   (312) 283-9161

Principal officers: Richard L. Gralinski, National Commander

Permanent staff: NI   Membership: 15,000
Date founded: 1931   Membership dues: NI
Branches: 13 state, 114 local   Scope: national

Special requirements for membership: Americans of Polish descent who served in U.S.
Armed Forces

POLISH LEGION OF AMERICAN VETERANS, U.S.A. (cont'd)

Nature of organization: fraternal

Publications: *National PLAV News* (quarterly)

Affiliations: Ladies Auxiliary; Polish American Congress

Major conventions/meetings: biennial

Comments: The purpose of the group is to unite Polish veterans in the United States. The organization was formed by merger of the Alliance of American Veterans and the Polish Legion of the American Army. It aims to preserve a spirit of patriotism and to combat communist propaganda or other anti-democratic influences. It provides scholarships, training camps, and youth programs for youth of Polish descent. An archival collection is maintained.

POLISH MEDICAL ALLIANCE
2424 North Kedzie Boulevard
Chicago, Illinois 60647   (312) 486-7740

Principal officers: Alexander Rytel, President
         W. Cebulski, Vice President
         Barbara Surmaczynski, Secretary

Permanent staff: NI   Membership: 197
Date founded: 1948   Membership dues: $48.00 practicing
Branches: NI   physicians; $24.00 non-practicing
                     physicians
                     Scope: national

Special requirements for membership: medical degree

Nature of organization: professional, social, cultural

Publications: *Bulletin of Polish Medical History and Science*, 1956– (quarterly)

Major conventions/meetings: biennial

Comments: The alliance serves to promote growth of medical knowledge and achievements by Polish physicians throughout the world. Maintains archives.

POLISH MILITARY HISTORY SOCIETY OF AMERICA
984 North Milwaukee Avenue
Chicago, Illinois 60618

Permanent staff: NI   Membership: NI
Date founded: NI   Membership dues: NI
Branches: NI   Scope: national

POLISH NATIONAL ALLIANCE OF BROOKLYN, U.S.A. (PNA)
155 Noble Street
Brooklyn, New York 11222   (212) 389-4704

Principal officers: Edward A. Kurmel, President
         Leopold S. Malinowski, Executive Vice President
         Józef A. Glowacki, Secretary-General

Permanent staff: 10   Membership: 15,430
Date founded: 1903   Membership dues: none, except for the
Branches: 155 national   payment of life insurance premiums
                     Scope: national

Special requirements for membership: must be of Polish or Slavic descent and 65 years of age or younger

Nature of organization: fraternal life insurance

Publications: *The Polish Weekly Times*, 1905– (weekly)

Affiliations: New York Fraternal Congress; New Jersey Fraternal Congress; Polish Museum of America

Major conventions/meetings: quadrennial convention

POLISH NATIONAL ALLIANCE OF BROOKLYN, U.S.A. (PNA) (cont'd)

Comments: The organization provides life insurance at nominal fees and provides assistance
to needy families of members. It aids community youth programs and educational and
charitable institutions; it also grants scholarships to members who are junior and senior
college students.

POLISH NATIONAL ALLIANCE OF U.S. OF N.A. (PNA)
1520 West Division Street
Chicago, Illinois 60622   (312) 276-0700
Principal officers: Aloysius A. Mazewski, President
                  Helen M. Szymanowicz, Vice President
                  Adolf K. Pachucki, Secretary

Permanent staff: 15   Membership: 317,352
Date founded: 1880   Membership dues: $2.50 plus individual
Branches: 1,350 lodges in 36 states   insurance rates
                                      Scope: national

Special requirements for membership: none

Nature of organization: fraternal

Publications: *Zgoda*, 1881– (bimonthly); *Polish Daily Zgoda*, 1908– (daily); *Alliance Calendar* (almanac)

Major conventions/meetings: national convention every four years

Comments: The objectives of the alliance are to unite Polish Americans; to transmit Polish
culture, traditions, and language; and to restore and preserve Polish independence in
Europe. It owns and operates Alliance College in Cambridge Springs, Pennsylvania;
and it offers scholarships to members to attend it or provides financial loans to attend
other institutions. It sponsors various dance groups and bands, sports programs,
children's Christmas parties, and a Debutante Ball. A library of 10,000 volumes and
historical archives are maintained.

POLISH NATIONAL UNION OF AMERICA
1002 Pittston Avenue
Scranton, Pennsylvania 18505   (717) 344-1513
Principal officers: Joseph H. Kochan, Secretary-General

Permanent staff: 20   Membership: 32,550
Date founded: 1908   Membership dues: vary with insurance
Branches: 231   policy
                                      Scope: national

Nature of organization: fraternal

Publications: *Polish Weekly Straz*, 1897– (weekly); *Branch Directory* (annual)

Major conventions/meetings: quadrennial

Comments: Functions primarily as a life insurance benefit society. It also is active in charitable
works, such as the Spojnia Farm Home for the Aged and Disabled, and the organization
grants scholarships to students of Polish descent. A 2,500-volume library is maintained.

POLISH NOBILITY ASSOCIATION
Villa "Anneslie"
529 Dunkirk Road
Anneslie, Maryland 21212   (301) 377-4352
Principal officers: Rogier Chylinski-Polubinski, Secretary

Permanent staff: NI   Membership: NI
Date founded: 1950   Membership dues: NI
Branches: NI   Scope: national

Special requirements for membership: persons in Poland's *Nobility Archives*

Nature of organization: cultural, genealogical

Publications: *White Eagle* (quarterly); also publishes pamphlets

POLISH NOBILITY ASSOCIATION (cont'd)

Comments: Traces genealogies of titled noblemen and aristocrats and presents an annual Knighthood award for outstanding contributions by persons of Polish descent. Maintains a genealogical reference library.

POLISH PROGRESSIVE ALLIANCE
128 South Patterson Park Avenue
Baltimore, Maryland 21231 (301) 732-1769

Principal officers: Ludwik Chudy-Williams, President
Paul Mazurek, Vice President
Nancy Wisniowiecka, Secretary-Treasurer

Permanent staff: 7 Membership: 150
Date founded: 1969 Membership dues: $15.00
Branches: 3 state Scope: state

Special requirements for membership: membership by invitation only; politicians are excluded

Nature of organization: cultural, fraternal, educational, scholarly, youth

Publications: none

Affiliations: Polish American Congress; Polish National Alliance; All Nations Foundation

Major conventions/meetings: monthly conference; annual convention

Comments: The organization seeks to promote interest in Polish language and history, and in the achievements and contributions of Polish Americans. It sponsors students at Alliance College, and it promotes exhibitions, festivals, and charitable benefits such as children's hospitals in Warsaw. It founded the Krakowiaki Dance Group and coordinated the Kopernik Festival of Baltimore. Grants annual youth awards and maintains a 7,000-volume library and an archival collection.

POLISH ROMAN CATHOLIC UNION OF AMERICA
984 Milwaukee Avenue
Chicago, Illinois 60622 (312) 278-3210

Principal officers: Nicholas J. Nowicki, Secretary-General
Joseph L. Osajda, President

Permanent staff: NI Membership: 129,525
Date founded: 1873 Membership dues: varies with insurance
Branches: state groups in 25 states policy
Scope: national

Nature of organization: fraternal, cultural, recreational, sport

Publications: *Narod Polski*, 1887– (bimonthly)

Major conventions/meetings: quadrennial

Comments: The union's major purpose is to supply life insurance benefits, but it also provides various cultural, social, and recreational activities, particularly for young people (e.g., dancing schools, choral groups, Polish language classes). Sponsors both educational and religious tours to Canada and Europe. Gives financial assistance to students, aids elderly and disabled members. Sports activities include bowling, basketball, softball, golf, and duckpin tournaments.

POLISH ROMAN CATHOLIC UNION, SACRED HEART SOCIETY
St. Michael's Parish
2987 West Flagler Street
Miami, Florida 35135 (305) 649-1811

Principal officers: Pelagia Lukaszewska, President
Elizabeth Bittel, Vice President
Edmund Chwastyk, Secretary

Permanent staff: 5 Membership: NI
Date founded: 1873 Membership dues: varies
Branches: 40 Scope: national

POLISH ROMAN CATHOLIC UNION, SACRED HEART SOCIETY (cont'd)

Special requirements for membership: Roman Catholic religion

Nature of organization: fraternal

Publications: *Narod*, 1875– (twice monthly)

Affiliations: Polish American Congress

Major conventions/meetings: quadrennial convention

Comments: Prime purpose is to preserve the Polish culture in the United States. Particularly interested in perpetuating and preserving Polish folklore; supports the Polish Museum, which is part of the Polish Roman Catholic Union.

POLISH SINGERS ALLIANCE OF AMERICA, INC. (PSAA)

180 Second Avenue

New York, New York 10003

Principal officers: Joseph F. Czechlewski, President

                T. Maksymowicz, Executive Vice President

                Walter Falencki, General Secretary

Permanent staff: none   Membership: 2,000

Date founded: 1889   Membership dues: NI

Branches: 100 regional; 25 state; 15 local   Scope: national

Special requirements for membership: none

Nature of organization: choral singing

Publications: *Singers Mirror*, 1947– (10 issues per year)

Affiliations: none

Major conventions/meetings: national convention triennially

Comments: The alliance proposes to promote Polish culture and the music of Polish composers in America by encouraging participation in choruses, competitions, and concerts. Keeps a musical library of 1,000 Polish songs and archives of song sheets, operas, and orchestrations.

POLISH UNION OF AMERICA, INC.

761 Fillmore Avenue

Buffalo, New York 14212   (716) 893-1365

Principal officers: Daniel J. Kij, President

                Clara G. Weber, General Secretary

Permanent staff: NI   Membership: 12,768

Date founded: 1917   Membership dues: varies with policy

Branches: chapters in 8 states   Scope: national

Nature of organization: fraternal, cultural, social, relief

Publications: *Parade* (monthly)

Major conventions/meetings: quadrennial

Comments: Provides life insurance benefits for members. Also sponsors a daily 15-minute cable-TV program, "PUA News with a Polish Flavor." Sponsors summer youth camps, assists the elderly financially, sponsors housing projects for the elderly, and provides scholarships to students of Polish descent.

POLISH UNION OF THE UNITED STATES OF NORTH AMERICA (P.U. of the U.S. of N.A.)

53-59 North Main Street

Wilkes-Barre, Pennsylvania 18701   (717) 823-1611

Principal officers: Sidney Grabowski, President

                Henry J. Dende, Executive Vice President

                Peter S. Fabian, Executive Secretary

Permanent staff: none   Membership: 15,000

Date founded: 1890   Membership dues: NI

Branches: none   Scope: national

POLISH UNION OF THE UNITED STATES OF NORTH AMERICA
(P.U. of the U.S. of N.A.) (cont'd)

Nature of organization: fraternal

Publications: *Polish American Journal*, 1911– (monthly)

Affiliations: Polish American Congress; National Fraternal Congress; Illinois Fraternal Congress

Major conventions/meetings: quadrennial convention

Comments: The purpose of the organization is to provide life insurance for its members. It also offers college-level scholarship-loans to members.

THE POLISH WHITE EAGLE ASSOCIATION
1302 Second Street, N.E.
Minneapolis, Minnesota 55413

POLISH WOMEN'S ALLIANCE OF AMERICA (PWA)
1309-15 North Ashland Avenue
Chicago, Illinois 60622   (312) 278-2524

Principal officers: Helen Zielinska, President
Helen Wojcik, Vice President
Julia Stroup, Secretary

Permanent staff: 40	Membership: 90,000
Date founded: 1898	Membership dues: insurance premium
Branches: 600 adult groups; 550	plus group dues
juvenile garlands	Scope: national

Special requirements for membership: must be insurable; women and children of Polish birth, descent, or conviction are eligible

Nature of organization: fraternal

Publications: *Polish Women's Voice*, 1910– (bimonthly); also publishes books

Affiliations: Polish American Congress; Illinois Fraternal Congress; National Fraternal Congress

Major conventions/meetings: quadrennial convention

Comments: The alliance was founded to unite women of Polish descent in national and social work, to provide life insurance for members, and to cultivate Polish history, literature, language, and dance programs in the United States. It offers scholarships, old age assistance, classes in folk dancing and language, youth conferences, and essay and art contests. Maintains a library of 10,000 volumes, a museum, and archival records.

POLONUS PHILATELIC SOCIETY
St. James Clubroom
2424 North Mango
Chicago, Illinois 60639

PULASKI ASSOCIATION OF BUSINESS AND PROFESSIONAL MEN, INC.
263 Prospect Avenue
Brooklyn, New York 11215

Principal officers: Stanley J. Nasewicz, President
Raymond S. Dziejma, First Vice President
Gregory Czuchlewski, Secretary

Permanent staff: none	Membership: 127
Date founded: 1958	Membership dues: $25.00
Branches: NI	Scope: local

Special requirements for membership: Polish extraction, employed as a professional or as sole proprietor of a business

Nature of organization: fraternal, professional

Publications: none

Affiliations: Polish American Congress; Kosciuskzo Foundation

PULASKI ASSOCIATION OF BUSINESS AND PROFESSIONAL MEN, INC. (cont'd)

Major conventions/meetings: annual testimonial dinner

Comments: Objectives of the association are to honor a Polish American annually for outstanding achievement, and to promote patriotism and the welfare and image of all Polonia. A $1,000 graduate student scholarship (administered by the Kosciuszko Foundation) is granted and 500 essay contest awards are presented to elementary school graduates. A Man of the Year Award is also granted. Financial support is given to all five Polish Supplementary Schools in New York.

THE PULASKI ASSOCIATION OF THE POLICE DEPARTMENT OF THE CITY OF NEW YORK

New National Hall
61-60 56th Road
Flushing, New York 11378   (914) 738-5513

Principal officers: Peter C. Bartoszek, President
                       Adam Cieslik, First Vice President
                       Raymond Miesiak, Secretary

Permanent staff: 21   Membership: 2,000
Date founded: 1957   Membership dues: $7.00
Branches: none   Scope: local

Special requirements for membership: active or retired police officer of the New York City Police Department

Nature of organization: fraternal, social, religious

Publications: *Pulaskian*, 1958– (monthly)

Affiliations: Grand Council of Pulaski Associations

Major conventions/meetings: general meetings twice a month

Comments: Objectives of the association are to unite members, to provide contributions to charities, to establish a Welfare Fund (for scholarships for the heirs of members), to provide trial counsel in police departmental trials, and to offer legal aid to relatives of a deceased member. Keeps historical archival materials.

SEA LEAGUE OF AMERICA

1082 Milwaukee Avenue
Chicago, Illinois 60622

Permanent staff: NI   Membership: NI
Date founded: NI   Membership dues: NI
Branches: NI   Scope: national

Publications: *Morze* (The Sea), 1940– (monthly)

UNION OF POLES IN AMERICA (UPA)

6501 Lansing Avenue
Cleveland, Ohio 44105   (216) 341-2103

Principal officers: Richard Jablonski, President
                       Frank Franks, Executive Vice President
                       Robert Jess, Executive Secretary

Permanent staff: 3   Membership: NI
Date founded: 1894   Membership dues: varies
Branches: none   Scope: national

Special requirements for membership: Catholic of Polish descent

Nature of organization: fraternal, social, recreational

Publications: *Courier of the Union* (semimonthly)

Affiliations: Polish American Congress; Ohio Fraternal Congress

Major conventions/meetings: quadrennial

Comments: The purpose of the organization is to provide life insurance and mortgage loans to members. Until 1939 it was known as the Polish Roman Catholic Union. It sponsors bowling tournaments and various social activities.

UNION OF POLISH WOMEN IN AMERICA
2636-38 East Allegheny Avenue
Philadelphia, Pennsylvania 19134   (215) 425-3807
Principal officers: Helena Janoska, President
                      Pearl Karpowicz, Vice President
                      Helen J. Bagdzinski, Secretary

Permanent staff: 3   Membership: 9,379
Date founded: 1920   Membership dues: NI
Branches: 3 regional; 74 local   Scope: national

Special requirements for membership: children under the age of 15½ and women are
    eligible

Nature of organization: fraternal, cultural, educational, social

Publications: *Polish Star*, 1902– (weekly)

Affiliations: Polish American Congress; National Fraternal Congress; Pennsylvania, New
    Jersey and Philadelphia Fraternals

Major conventions/meetings: quadrennial convention

Comments: Purpose of the union is to provide life insurance to its members and their children,
    and to maintain cultural, educational, and social programs. It provides instruction in
    Polish folk dance, baton, and glee club. It grants educational scholarships and loans,
    and it participates in ethnic programs of Folk Fair Programs.

UNITED POLISH AMERICAN COUNCIL (UNIPAC)
1194 Manchester Road
Akron, Ohio 44307   (216) 535-3673
Principal officers: Stan Tatko, President
                      Tom Wyzynski, Executive Vice President
                      Rudy Piekarski, Executive Secretary

Permanent staff: 5   Membership: 43 delegates representing
Date founded: 1971   9 organizations
Branches: 1 local   Membership dues: none
                                      Scope: NI

Special requirements for membership: delegates elected from nine Polish organizations

Nature of organization: social, educational, cultural, recreational, sport, fraternal, scholarly,
    youth

Publications: none

Affiliations: none

Major conventions/meetings: none

Comments: The council's main purpose is to be a clearinghouse for all Polish ethnic groups and
    to help advertise and finance Polish events. The national organization sponsors camps,
    colleges, and museums.

UNITED WOMEN'S SOCIETIES OF THE MOST BLESSED SACRAMENT
529 East Locust Street
Scranton, Pennsylvania 18505
Publications: *Polka* (Polish Woman), 1935– (quarterly)

YOUNG POLISH AMERICANS' CLUB
808 Dorchester Avenue
Boston, Massachusetts 02125
Principal officers: Leon Dzygala, President
                      Mark Pisarski, Chairman, Board of Directors

Permanent staff: NI   Membership: NI
Date founded: NI   Membership dues: NI
Branches: NI   Scope: regional

Nature of organization: youth, social

YOUNG POLISH AMERICANS' CLUB (cont'd)
Affiliations: P.N.A. Gr. 398

Comments: The purpose is to provide social events and coffee houses for Polish American youths within the Polish-American community.

PORTUGUESE-AMERICAN ORGANIZATIONS

Additional information on Portuguese-American organizations in the United States may be obtained from the Office of the Portuguese Embassy (2125 Kalorama Road, Washington, D.C. 20008) and the Luso-American Fraternal Federation (230 California Street, San Francisco, California 94111).

AMERICAN PORTUGUESE CULTURAL SOCIETY
29 Broadway
New York, New York 10006

Permanent staff: 1	Membership: 70
Date founded: 1958	Membership dues: NI
Branches: NI	Scope: national

Special requirements for membership: of Portuguese descent

Nature of organization: cultural, educational

Publications: *Bulletin* (quarterly)

Comments: Attempts to help the people of the United States develop an understanding of the Portuguese heritage. Sponsors displays and exhibits by Portuguese artists, as well as lectures and scholarships. Coordinates exchange of Portuguese and U.S. performing artists, and prepares teaching materials about Portuguese history and studies.

CAPE VERDIAN LEAGUE ASSOCIATION
23 West 124th Street
New York, New York 10027   (212) 289-1950

Principal officers: Amando Perry, President

Permanent staff: NI	Membership: 85
Date founded: NI	Membership dues: NI
Branches: NI	Scope: national

Special requirements for membership: Portuguese descent

Nature of organization: fraternal

Comments: The major purpose of the organization is to provide life insurance benefits to those of Portuguese descent in the United States. Membership is concentrated in the New York area.

INTERNATIONAL SOCIETY FOR PORTUGUESE PHILATELY
43 Dundee Road
Stamford, Connecticut 06903

Principal officers: Nancy Gaylord, Secretary

Permanent staff: NI	Membership: NI
Date founded: 1961	Membership dues: NI
Branches: NI	Scope: national

Nature of organization: philatelic

Publications: *Portu-Info* (quarterly)

LUSO-AMERICAN EDUCATION FOUNDATION
230 California Street
San Francisco, California 94111   (415) 392-4903

Principal officers: Barbara Angeja, Secretary

LUSO-AMERICAN EDUCATION FOUNDATION (cont'd)

Permanent staff: NI
Date founded: NI
Branches: NI

Membership: NI
Membership dues: NI
Scope: national

Nature of organization: educational, cultural

Publications: *Friends of the Foundation* (quarterly)

Major conventions/meetings: annual

Comments: Major purpose is to preserve the Portuguese heritage and culture in the United States. Plans high school and college courses in Portuguese language and history. Provides scholarships. Until 1963 the organization was known as the Luso-American Fraternal Federation Scholarship Committee.

LUSO-AMERICAN FRATERNAL FEDERATION
230 California Street
San Francisco, California 94111   (415) 392-5338

Principal officers: Jack Costa, Secretary-Treasurer

Permanent staff: NI
Date founded: 1957
Branches: 8 regional; 93 local

Membership: 13,000
Membership dues: NI
Scope: national

Special requirements for membership: of Portuguese descent

Nature of organization: fraternal

Affiliations: United National Life Insurance; Luso-American Education Foundation

Major conventions/meetings: annual

Comments: Major purpose is to provide life insurance benefits for persons of Portuguese background. The organization also sponsors the Luso-American Education Foundation and a State Youth Council.

PORTUGUESE AMERICAN PROGRESSIVE CLUB OF NEW YORK
179 Varick Street
New York, New York 10014   (212) 924-9864

Principal officers: Antonio R. Alves, Secretary

Permanent staff: NI
Date founded: NI
Branches: NI

Membership: NI
Membership dues: NI
Scope: national

Special requirements for membership: of Portuguese descent

Nature of organization: social, recreational

Major conventions/meetings: annual

PORTUGUESE CONTINENTAL UNION OF THE UNITED STATES OF AMERICA
899 Boylston Street
Boston, Massachusetts 02115   (617) 536-2916

Principal officers: Francisco J. Mendonca, Supreme Secretary

Permanent staff: 5
Date founded: 1925
Branches: NI

Membership: 9,315
Membership dues: varies
Scope: national

Special requirements for membership: Portuguese birth or descent

Nature of organization: fraternal

Major conventions/meetings: annual

Comments: Major purpose is to provide life insurance benefits to Portuguese in the United States. Also sponsors cultural activities, maintains a scholarship program, and contributes to charitable institutions. Awards are made for outstanding contributions by Portuguese Americans. Maintains a 4,000-volume library of Portuguese authors.

PORTUGUESE CULTURAL ASSOCIATION OF RHODE ISLAND
P.O. Box 4295
East Providence, Rhode Island 02914   (401) 246-1693

Principal officers: Myron J. Francis, President
Roy De Mello, Vice President
Linda Costa, Secretary

Permanent staff: none   Membership: 205
Date founded: 1959   Membership dues: $5.00
Branches: NI   Scope: state

Special requirements for membership: Portuguese descent or relation by marriage

Nature of organization: cultural

Publications: none

Affiliations: Portuguese American Federation

Major conventions/meetings: annual

PORTUGUESE SOCIETY QUEEN ST. ISABEL
3031 Telegraph Avenue
Oakland, California 94609

Principal officers: Florence Wentworth, President
Mary C. Trindade, Vice President
Marie I. Wilson, Secretary

Permanent staff: 3   Membership: 13,000
Date founded: 1898   Membership dues: varies
Branches: 122 councils; 14 junior units   Scope: national

Special requirements for membership: of Portuguese descent

Nature of organization: fraternal

Publications: *Boletim da SPRSI*, 1899– (monthly)

Major conventions/meetings: annual

Comments: The organization's major purpose is to provide life insurance benefits to members.
It also assists needy Portuguese and disaster victims, has youth programs and junior
units, and grants scholarships.

PORTUGUESE UNION OF THE STATE OF CALIFORNIA (U.P.E.C.)
1120 East 14th Street
San Leandro, California 94577   (415) 483-7676

Principal officers: Tony Xavier, President
Manuel Simas, Vice President
Carlos Almeida, Secretary

Permanent staff: 6   Membership: 11,550
Date founded: 1880   Membership dues: varies
Branches: 77   Scope: national

Special requirements for membership: none

Nature of organization: social, cultural, fraternal

Publications: *UPEC Life Magazine*, 1898– (quarterly)

Affiliations: California Fraternal Congress

Major conventions/meetings: annual convention

Comments: The major goal is to provide Portuguese-Americans with life and medical insurance
benefits. The organization also promotes the study and preservation of the Portuguese
language and culture in the United States by conducting social and cultural activities
and a cultural center. It supports youth programs and scholarship programs. Maintains
a library of Portuguese authors and sponsors Portuguese and Portuguese-English
publications.

SOCIETY FOR SPANISH AND PORTUGUESE HISTORICAL STUDIES
Department of History
Rutgers University
New Brunswick, New Jersey 08903

Principal officers: David R. Ringrose, General Secretary

Permanent staff: NI	Membership: 120
Date founded: 1969	Membership dues: NI
Branches: NI	Scope: national

Nature of organization: scholarly

Publications: *Newsletter* (quarterly)

Comments: Faculty, graduate students, libraries, and institutions concerned with Portuguese history or research are organized to coordinate and exchange knowledge.

SUPREME COUNCIL OF THE PORTUGUESE SOCIETY QUEEN ST. ISABEL. *See*
PORTUGUESE SOCIETY QUEEN ST. ISABEL (p. 296).

UNITED NATIONAL LIFE INSURANCE SOCIETY
230 California Street
San Francisco, California 94111

Principal officers: Jack Costa, Vice President and Secretary-Treasurer

Permanent staff: 18	Membership: 15,000
Date founded: 1957	Membership dues: varies
Branches: 98	Scope: national

Special requirements for membership: Portuguese birth or descent

Nature of organization: fraternal

Major conventions/meetings: biennial

Comments: Provides life insurance benefits to members and sponsors the Luso-American Education Foundation. The organization was formed by merger of the Benevolent Society of California and the Uniao Portuguese Continental Do Estado Da California.

PUERTO RICAN-AMERICAN ORGANIZATIONS

See also Spanish-American Organizations

Because organizations serving the Puerto Rican community are so numerous, particularly in areas such as New York City where the Puerto Rican population is heavily concentrated, it is impossible to list and describe all these organizations within the scope of this guide. Therefore, it was decided to include only national and major regional organizations. Additional local and regional organizations may be located in *Directory of Spanish Speaking Community Organizations* (Washington, D.C.: Cabinet Committee on Opportunity for the Spanish Speaking, 1970).

AMERICAN PUERTO RICAN ACTION LEAGUE

75 East 110th Street
New York, New York 10029   (212) 369-0102
Principal officers: David Roderiguez, Director

Permanent staff: NI   Membership: 1,200
Date founded: 1960   Membership dues: donations
Branches: NI   Scope: national

Special requirements for membership: Puerto Rican descent

Nature of organization: family service, educational, cultural, recreational

Comments: Provides services to the Puerto Rican community, such as assisting the needy, sponsoring Little League teams, educational and cultural programs for youth and adults, housing programs, and operation of a Family Service Bureau.

ASPIRA OF NEW YORK, INC.

296 Fifth Avenue
New York, New York 11355   (212) 244-1110
Principal officers: Mario A. Anglada, Executive Director
                              Oscar Garcia-Rivera, Chairman of the Board
                              Ramon Raimundi, Secretary

Permanent staff: 80   Membership: over 700
Date founded: 1961   Membership dues: NI
Branches: 5 state; 1 national   Scope: national

Special requirements for membership: none

Nature of organization: educational, youth

Affiliations: Aspira of America

Comments: An educational guidance counseling agency that assists in placing students in college, finds them financial aid, provides remedial studies if necessary for admission. Also provides cultural and social activities for students of Hispanic descent.

ASSOCIATION FOR PUERTO RICAN-HISPANIC CULTURE, INC.

c/o Peter Bloch
83 Park Terrace West
New York, New York 10034   (212) 942-2338
Principal officers: Peter Bloch, President
                              Renée Lana Diener, Secretary

Permanent staff: NI   Membership: 50
Date founded: 1965   Membership dues: $10.00 (annual)
Branches: none   Scope: regional

Special requirements for membership: none

Nature of organization: cultural

Publications: none

Affiliations: none

Major conventions/meetings: annual general meeting

Comments: The association attempts to promote and preserve the Spanish culture in the United States by providing cultural programs and activities and supporting outstanding Hispanic artists and speakers. It also sponsors a Puerto Rican Library and Museum to which it provides guided tours; sponsors exhibits and programs in the Museum of the City of New York and in local schools and institutions.

CONGRESS OF ORGANIZATIONS AND PUERTO RICAN HOMETOWNS
254 West 72nd Street, Room 1A
New York, New York 10023   (212) 799-5266

Principal officers: Gilberto Gerena Valentin, President

Permanent staff:. 12   Membership: 57 organizations
Date founded: 1958   Membership dues: NI
Branches: NI   Scope: national

Special requirements for membership: Puerto Rican organization

Nature of organization: cultural, political, educational

Major conventions/meetings: 3 per year

Comments: Serves as a liaison agency between Puerto Rican organizations and state and municipal authorities. Also provides special educational classes and sponsors summer camps for Puerto Rican children. Until 1964 the group was known as the Congress of Puerto Rican Municipalities.

COUNCIL OF ORGANIZATIONS PRO-ACTIVITIES OF PUERTO RICAN AFFAIRS, INC.
P.O. Box 2747
San Francisco, California 94126   (415) 648-3660

Principal officers: Fobio Ortiz De La Torres, President

Permanent staff: NI   Membership: NI
Date founded: 1966   Membership dues: NI
Branches: NI   Scope: state

Nature of organization: economic, educational

Major conventions/meetings: monthly

Comments: The purpose of the organization is to raise the social and economic living conditions of Puerto Ricans and other Spanish-speaking groups in the United States.

THE COUNCIL OF PUERTO RICAN & HISPANIC ORGANIZATIONS OF THE LOWER EAST SIDE
20-A Clinton Street   (212) 254-0170 or
New York, New York 10002   (212) 254-0193

Principal officers: Roberto Napoleon, President
                 Israel Cruz, Executive Vice President
                 Margarita Cosme, Executive Secretary

Permanent staff: 6   Membership: 25 groups
Date founded: 1962   Membership dues: $5.00 (annual)
Branches: 38   Scope: local

Nature of organization: educational, cultural, economic, community action program

Publications: *Voice of the Puerto Rican Council*, 1965– (annual)

Affiliations: none

Major conventions/meetings: biennial conference

Comments: The organization is involved in community action, consumer action, and economic development programs. It is comprised of 38 affiliated agencies which serve the Puerto Rican community with health, educational, recreational, housing, youth, and counseling services. Conducts summer work programs for the unemployed.

INSTITUTE OF PUERTO RICAN UNITY, INC. (IPRU)
3512 East First Street
Los Angeles, California 90063   (213) 385-0209

Principal officers: David Santiago, President
                 A. Echevarria, Executive Vice President
                 Ellie Coheh, Executive Secretary

INSTITUTE OF PUERTO RICAN UNITY, INC. (IPRU) (cont'd)

Permanent staff: 2
Date founded: 1971
Branches: 1 regional

Membership: 200
Membership dues: $24.00 (annual)
Scope: regional

Special requirements for membership: none

Nature of organization: social, cultural, educational, recreational, economic

Publications: *IPRU Newsletter,* 1973–

Affiliations: Western Council of Puerto Rican Organizations

Major conventions/meetings: none

Comments: Attempts to raise the socioeconomic status of Puerto Ricans in California by providing services in job placement, housing, education, mental health, etc. Maintains a scholarship program and archives of historical records and data.

LADIES COMMITTEE FOR PUERTO RICAN CULTURE, INC.

1712 Pitkin Avenue
Brooklyn, New York 11212   (212) 498-9880

Principal officers: Felicia Arroyo

Permanent staff: NI
Date founded: NI
Branches: NI

Membership: NI
Membership dues: NI
Scope: state

Special requirements for membership: Puerto Rican descent

Nature of organization: cultural

Comments: Major purpose is to preserve the Puerto Rican traditions in the United States and to develop programs of educational and cultural activities. Sponsors seminars and workshops on Puerto Rican history and   culture, and programs by performing artists.

NATIONAL ASSOCIATION FOR PUERTO RICAN CIVIL RIGHTS

175 East 116th Street
New York, New York 10029   (212) 348-3973

Principal officers: Robert Munoz, President

Permanent staff: NI
Date founded: 1963
Branches: NI

Membership: 20,000 individuals; 100 organizations
Membership dues: NI
Scope: national

Special requirements for membership: Puerto Rican individuals or organizations serving the Puerto Rican community

Nature of organization: civil rights

Publications: *Journal* (annual)

Affiliations: Leadership Conference on Civil Rights

Major conventions/meetings: annual

Comments: Attempts to advance and protect the civil rights of the Puerto Rican community in legislative, housing, social, employment, and labor concerns. Sponsors meetings with government and police officials; provides services to Puerto Ricans needing legal advice.

NATIONAL CONFERENCE OF PUERTO RICAN WOMEN

P.O. Box 4804, Cleveland Park Station
Washington, D.C. 20037

Principal officers: Mrs. Paquita Vivo, President

Permanent staff: NI
Date founded: 1972
Branches: 4 local

Membership: NI
Membership dues: NI
Scope: national

Special requirements for membership: women of Puerto Rican descent

Nature of organization: civil rights

Publications: *Newsletter* (irregular)

NATIONAL CONFERENCE OF PUERTO RICAN WOMEN (cont'd)

Major conventions/meetings: annual

Comments: Seeks the attainment of equal rights for Puerto Rican women in social, economic, and political endeavors.

NATIONAL COUNCIL OF PUERTO RICAN VOLUNTEERS
541 South Sixth Avenue
Mount Vernon, New York 10550   (914) 664-2392

Principal officers: Mrs. Petra G. Valdes, Executive Director

Permanent staff: NI   Membership: NI
Date founded: 1964   Membership dues: NI
Branches: NI   Scope: national

Special requirements for membership: Puerto Rican descent and ability to speak English and Spanish

Nature of organization: educational

Affiliations: National Council of Negro Women

Comments: Provides bilingual volunteers to service agencies working with the Puerto Rican community in order that Puerto Rican-Americans might understand the facilities and opportunities available to them.

NATIONAL PUERTO RICAN FORUM, INC.
214 Mercer Street
New York, New York 10012   (212) 533-0100

Principal officers: Hector I. Vasquez, Executive Director

Permanent staff: NI   Membership: NI
Date founded: 1957   Membership dues: NI
Branches: NI   Scope: national

Special requirements for membership: professionals of Puerto Rican descent

Nature of organization: service

Major conventions/meetings: annual

Comments: Attempts to help Puerto Ricans find suitable employment by offering services in business development, job and career training, and community education, primarily in the New York area. Federal, municipal, Ford Foundation, and New York Foundation monies fund this project. The organization offers job skills training, counseling and placement services, and remedial educational programs. Founded ASPIRA agency, which works with Puerto Rican youth; conducts research on conditions in the Puerto Rican community.

PUERTO RICAN BAR ASSOCIATION, INC.
250 West 57th Street, Suite 2002
New York, New York 10019   (212) 247-3108

Principal officers: Demostenes Santiago Roque, President

Permanent staff: NI   Membership: NI
Date founded: 1957   Membership dues: NI
Branches: NI   Scope: national

Special requirements for membership: lawyers of Puerto Rican descent

Nature of organization: professional

Major conventions/meetings: monthly

Comments: Members are Puerto Rican lawyers who propose to advance justice in the United States Puerto Rican communities.

PUERTO RICAN CONGRESS OF CHICAGO
2315 West North Avenue
Chicago, Illinois 60647   (312) 744-4067

Principal officers: Carlos Caribe Ruiz, Executive Director

Permanent staff: NI   Membership: NI
Date founded: 1954   Membership dues: NI
Branches: 11   Scope: regional

Nature of organization: educational, economic, social, cultural, political

Affiliations: Latin American Press and Radio Association; Association of Puerto Rican
Organizations; Puerto Rican Community Center; Board of Coordinators of Puerto
Rican Affairs

Comments: The organization attempts to develop programs of cultural awareness, educational
improvement, and civic, educational, and political development. Sponsors fund-raising
activities and events to unite Puerto Ricans of the area socially.

PUERTO RICAN-HISPANIC YOUTH COALITION, INC.
168 West 100th Street   (212) 666-4463 or
New York, New York 10025   (212) 666-4464

Principal officers: Ralph Santiago, Executive Director
Omar Bordatto, Chairman
Nelson Apunti, Secretary

Permanent staff: 15   Membership: 2,500
Date founded: 1968   Membership dues: none
Branches: NI   Scope: regional

Nature of organization: cultural, economic, social, professional, educational, recreational,
youth

Comments: Serves the Puerto Rican community in problems of economic origin. Attempts to
find employment for youth from the Spanish-speaking community.

PUERTO RICAN INDEPENDENCE
P.O. Box 195, University Station
Seattle, Washington 98105

Principal officers: William H. Davis, Secretary

Permanent staff: 2   Membership: NI
Date founded: 1974   Membership dues: NI
Branches: NI   Scope: national

Nature of organization: research, political

Publications: *For Puerto Rican Independence* (quarterly)

Comments: Main purpose is to help Puerto Rico gain independence; also coordinates informational materials and statistics. An archival collection is maintained.

PUERTO RICAN RESEARCH AND RESOURCES CENTER, INC.
1519 Connecticut Avenue, N.W.
Washington, D.C. 20036

Principal officers: Antonia Pantoja, Executive Director

Permanent staff: NI   Membership: NI
Date founded: NI   Membership dues: NI
Branches: NI   Scope: national

Nature of organization: scholarly, educational

Publications: publishes books

Comments: Goals of the organization are to research problems of the Puerto Rican community,
to help find solutions or resources, and to develop a system of communication among
Puerto Ricans. The center develops curricula on bilingual-bicultural education and helps
Puerto Ricans extend their professional and occupational opportunities.

RAMOS ANTONINI DEVELOPMENTAL CENTER
1707 Mount Vernon Street
Philadelphia, Pennsylvania 19130   (215) 763-9800
Principal officers: Herman S. Delgado, President
                 G. Garcia, Executive Secretary

Permanent staff: 12   Membership: 50
Date founded: 1966   Membership dues: none
Branches: none   Scope: NI
Special requirements for membership: none
Nature of organization: educational
Publications: none
Affiliations: none
Major conventions/meetings: none
Comments: Attempts to better conditions and life of the Spanish-speaking community. Provides job training skills, placement services, and counseling.

SOCIETY OF FRIENDS OF PUERTO RICO
432 Third Avenue
New York, New York 10016   (212) 684-0390
Principal officers: Mariano Guerrero, President

Permanent staff: NI   Membership: 260
Date founded: 1956   Membership dues: NI
Branches: NI   Scope: state
Nature of organization: cultural
Publications: *Newsletter* (quarterly); also publishes books
Affiliations: Art Councils of America
Major conventions/meetings: weekly meetings
Comments: Major purpose of the organization is to promote understanding of the history and culture of Puerto Rico in the United States. Sponsors exhibits of folk arts and crafts and the Center for Puerto Rican Cultural Relations. Until 1962 it was known as the American Friends of Puerto Rico.

ROMANIAN-AMERICAN ORGANIZATIONS

Additional information on Romanian-American organizations in the United States may be obtained from the Romanian Orthodox Episcopate of America (2522 Grey Tower Road, Jackson, Michigan 49201) or from its publication, *Calendarul Solia* (Detroit: The Romanian Orthodox Episcopate, 1974). Regional and local organizations are listed in *Greater Cleveland Nationalities Directory 1974* (Cleveland: Sun Newspapers and the Nationalities Services Center, 1974) and *Ethnic Directory I* (Detroit: Southeastern Michigan Regional Ethnic Heritage Studies Center, 1973).

AMERICAN ROMANIAN ORTHODOX YOUTH (AROY)
2522 Grey Tower Road
Jackson, Michigan 49201   (517) 522-4800
Principal officers: Robert L. Cipu, President
                 George M. Sandru, Executive Vice President
                 Mary J. Buta, Executive Secretary

Permanent staff: none   Membership: 800
Date founded: 1950   Membership dues: $10.00 over 21
Branches: 31 local   (annual); $5.00 under 21 (annual)
                                 Scope: international, national

AMERICAN ROMANIAN ORTHODOX YOUTH (AROY) (cont'd)

Special requirements for membership: must be an Eastern Orthodox Christian

Nature of organization: religious

Publications: *A.R.O.Y. Newsletter*, 1972– (monthly); *The Herald*, 1935– (monthly)

Affiliations: Council of Eastern Orthodox Youth Leaders of America

Major conventions/meetings: annual international convention

Comments: The purpose of the group is to practice and promote the Romanian Orthodox Christian faith and to provide fellowship and programs for the youth. It sponsors Camp Batra for boys and girls and grants the William Stanitz scholarship. Maintains archival materials.

ASSOCIATION OF ROMANIAN CATHOLICS OF AMERICA
4309 Olcott Avenue
East Chicago, Indiana 46312

Principal officers: George T. Strola, President

Permanent staff: NI

Date founded: 1948

Branches: 17

Membership: 4,000

Membership dues: NI

Scope: national

Special requirements for membership: Catholics of the Romanian Byzantine Rite

Nature of organization: religious

Publications: *Unirea* (The Union), 1950– (monthly); *Roman Catholic Church Almanac* (annual)

Major conventions/meetings: annual

Comments: Serves as a coordinating agency between the various Romanian Catholic churches that are members; goals are to preserve and perpetuate the Romanian Catholic faith. Maintains archival materials.

ASSOCIATION OF ROMANIAN ORTHODOX LADIES' AUXILLARIES
2522 Grey Tower Road
Jackson, Michigan 49201   (517) 522-4800

Principal officers: Leona Barbu, President
                       Virginia Calin, Secretary

Permanent staff: NI

Date founded: NI

Branches: NI

Membership: NI

Membership dues: NI

Scope: national

Special requirements for membership: women of Romanian Orthodox background

Nature of organization: religious, cultural, social, charitable

Affiliations: The Romanian Orthodox Episcopate of America

Major conventions/meetings: annual

IULIU MANIU AMERICAN ROMANIAN RELIEF FOUNDATION, INC.
55 West 42nd Street, No. 462
New York, New York 10036   (212) 244-8266

Principal officers: John M. Metes, President
                       Mrs. Ervin Popa, Executive Vice President
                       Elizabeth Vasilescu, Executive Secretary

Permanent staff: none

Date founded: 1952

Branches: none

Membership: 300

Membership dues: $20.00 voting member (annual); $10.00 contributing member (annual)

Scope: national

Special requirements for membership: recommendation by two members of the foundation, who serve as sponsors

Nature of organization: social, educational, cultural, welfare

IULIU MANIU AMERICAN ROMANIAN RELIEF FOUNDATION, INC. (cont'd)

Publications: *Annual Report*, 1953– ; also publishes pamphlets

Affiliations: American Immigration and Citizenship Conference

Major conventions/meetings: annual convention

Comments: Major objectives of the foundation are to provide immigration and naturalization advisory services and to preserve the Romanian culture through lectures and social programs. Financial aid for English language courses is provided. Maintains a folk art collection and a reference library of materials on Romania and on the history of the Romanian-American community.

THE ROMAN CATHOLIC RELIEF COMMITTEE
238 Adeline Street
Trenton, New Jersey 08611   (609) 695-6093

Principal officers: none—there is only an administrator elected by the Romanian priests for a certain period of time (Gabriel Ivascu, administrator)

Permanent staff: none	Membership: none
Date founded: 1946	Membership dues: none
Branches: none	Scope: national

Special requirements for membership: none

Nature of organization: fraternal and beneficial

Publications: none

Affiliations: Catholic Relief Services in New York City

Major conventions/meetings: semiannual conference

Comments: The organization's goal is to provide relief for exiles from the Iron Curtain countries, particularly Romania.

ROMANIAN AMERICAN CULTURAL ASSOCIATION
1105 Hippodrome Building
Cleveland, Ohio 44115   (216) 781-6676

Principal officers: Nick Bucur, Jr., President

Nature of organization: cultural

ROMANIAN BAPTIST ASSOCIATION OF UNITED STATES
c/o Rev. Danila Pascu
9410 Clifton Boulevard
Cleveland, Ohio 44102   (216) 961-5013

Permanent staff: NI	Membership: NI
Date founded: 1916	Membership dues: NI
Branches: NI	Scope: national

Nature of organization: religious

Publications: *Luminatorul*, 1926– (monthly)

Major conventions/meetings: annual

THE ROMANIAN ORTHODOX EPISCOPATE OF AMERICA
2522 Grey Tower Road
Jackson, Michigan 49201   (517) 522-4800

Principal officers: The Most Rev. Archbishop Valerian
                Rev. Fr. John N. Toconita, Secretary to the Bishop
                Rev. Fr. Eugene Lazar, Secretary

Permanent staff: none	Membership: 50,000
Date founded: 1929	Membership dues: NI
Branches: 47 Romanian Orthodox parishes	Scope: national

Special requirements for membership: must be baptized in the Orthodox faith

Nature of organization: religious

THE ROMANIAN ORTHODOX EPISCOPATE OF AMERICA (cont'd)

Publications: *The Herald*, 1936– (monthly)

Affiliations: under the canonical jurisdiction of the Orthodox Church in America

Major conventions/meetings: annual church congress

Comments: The purpose of this group is to preserve and propagate the Eastern Orthodox faith. The organization sponsors summer camps for children and young adults in the United States and Canada, and it maintains a library and archives.

ROMANIAN SOCIETY "FLORIDA"

2223 Madison Street
Hollywood, Florida 33020

Principal officers: Clemente Jacoban, President
George Micsa, Executive Vice President
George Duma, Executive Secretary

Permanent staff: 10   Membership: 31
Date founded: 1960   Membership dues: $1.20 (annual)
Branches: none   Scope: national

Special requirements for membership: must be of Romanian heritage and must purchase an insurance policy from the Union and League of Romanian Societies of America

Nature of organization: parent organization, fraternal

Publications: *America Romanian News*, 1918– (bimonthly)

Affiliations: none

Major conventions/meetings: biannual convention of the parent organization

Comments: The society's goal is to provide insurance policies for members and to preserve the Romanian language, culture, traditions, and religion in the United States.

ROMANIAN STUDIES GROUP

c/o Professor James E. Augerot
Institute for Comparative and Foreign Area Studies
University of Washington
Seattle, Washington 98195   (206) 929-8195

Permanent staff: NI   Membership: NI
Date founded: 1974   Membership dues: NI
Branches: NI   Scope: NI
Nature of organization: scholarly

Publications: *Romanian Studies Group*, 1973– (semiannual)

Comments: To promote interest in Romanian Studies in the United States.

ROMANIAN WELFARE, INC.

93 Groton Street
Forest Hills, New York 11375   (212) 263-6481

Principal officers: G. Duca, Secretary

Permanent staff: NI   Membership: 100
Date founded: 1948   Membership dues: NI
Branches: NI   Scope: national

Special requirements for membership: none

Nature of organization: relief, welfare

Major conventions/meetings: annual

Comments: Assists Romanian refugees as they resettle; also helps other displaced persons. Grants scholarships to Romanian refugees in the United States.

RUMANIAN NATIONAL COMMITTEE

157 West 57th Street
New York, New York 10019

RUMANIAN NATIONAL COMMITTEE (cont'd)

Permanent staff: NI
Date founded: NI
Branches: NI
Publications: *Romania*, 1956– (bimonthly)

Membership: NI
Membership dues: NI
Scope: national

SOCIETY DOINA
1051 Foothill Boulevard
La Canada, California 91011

Principal officers: George Marhao, President
                       Stefan Muciu, Vice President
                       Letitia Codeus, Secretary
                       Joseph Brezean, Treasurer

Permanent staff: 5
Date founded: 1953
Branches: none

Membership: 32
Membership dues: premium varies
Scope: NI

Special requirements for membership: Romanian-American

Nature of organization: cultural, fraternal

Publications: *Doina Bulletin* (annual)

Affiliations: Union and League of Romanian Societies of America

Major conventions/meetings: annual national convention

Comments: Goals of the society are to provide insurance benefits to members, to make
        charitable donations and gifts, and to sponsor social activities for fellowship among
        Romanian-Americans. It grants scholarships to Romanian-American students and main-
        tains a library of approximately 500 volumes.

SOCIETY "VIITORUL ROMAN"
3315 Verdugo Road
Los Angeles, California 90065   (213) 255-8583

Principal officers: Miron Bonca, President
                       Nick Stefan, Executive Vice President
                       George Baln, Executive Secretary

Permanent staff: 6
Date founded: 1926
Branches: none

Membership: 145
Membership dues: $6.00 (annual)
Scope: NI

Special requirements for membership: "at least one parent must be of Romanian origin"

Nature of organization: educational, cultural, fraternal

Publications: none

Affiliations: Union and League of Romanian Societies of America

Major conventions/meetings: none

Comments: Major objective is to provide insurance benefits for members and to preserve the
        Romanian culture and language through music, dances, and cultural programs. Maintains
        archival records.

TRAIAN SI IULIU MANIU
Romanian Orthodox Church Hall
144 30th Street, N.W.
Canton, Ohio 44709   (216) 454-5436

Principal officers: George Caprita, President
                       Don Tonchina, Executive Vice President
                       Helen D. Waltner, Corresponding Secretary

Permanent staff: none
Date founded: 1907-1908
Branches: none

Membership: NI
Membership dues: NI
Scope: national

Special requirements for membership: "must purchase insurance policy"

TRAIAN SI IULIU MANIU (cont'd)

Publications: publishes articles in the *America Romanian News* and yearly almanacs

Affiliations: none

Major conventions/meetings: annual convention

Comments: The organization's main purpose is to provide insurance benefits to members. It also promotes Romanian culture and provides sport and social activities. Scholarships are granted through the national headquarters.

UNION AND LEAGUE OF ROMANIAN SOCIETIES OF AMERICA
2121 West 117th Street
Cleveland, Ohio 44111   (216) 961-3696

Principal officers: John W. Popescu, President
                      Silvia V. Filip, Secretary-Treasurer

Permanent staff: 3   Membership: 4,992 individuals;
Date founded: 1906   62 affiliates
Branches: in 9 states   Membership dues: vary
                                          Scope: national

Special requirements for membership: American of Romanian descent

Nature of organization: fraternal

Publications: *America*, 1906– (biweekly); *America Romanian News*, 1906– (weekly)

Major conventions/meetings: annual

Comments: Major purpose is to provide life insurance benefits to members. Also grants scholarships to Romanian youth and sponsors youth activities, awards, and programs. The organization attempts to unite Romanians in the United States and to preserve the national culture, heritage, and identity.

UNITED ROMANIANS OF TRANSYLVANIA
735 Ash Street
Alliance, Ohio 44601

Principal officers: John Gorun, President
                      John Copacia, Executive Vice President
                      George P. Murarescu, Executive Secretary

Permanent staff: 18   Membership: 260
Date founded: 1903   Membership dues: varies depending on
Branches: none   the insurance policy
                                          Scope: NI

Special requirements for membership: must be from one month to 50 years of age and in good health

Nature of organization: social, cultural, fraternal

Publications: none

Affiliations: Union and League of Romanian Societies of America

Major conventions/meetings: biennial national convention

Comments: The purpose of the organization is to provide insurance to members and to preserve Romanian culture in America through special cultural programs and activities. Maintains archival materials.

RUSSIAN-AMERICAN ORGANIZATIONS

Some Carpatho-Ruthenian organizations designate themselves as Russian and are therefore placed in the Russian-American section.

Additional information on Russian-American organizations may be obtained from the Congress of Russian-Americans, Inc. (322 West 108th Street, New York, New York 10025). Regional and local organizations may be obtained from *Greater Cleveland Nationalities Directory 1974* (Cleveland: Sun Newspapers and the Nationalities Services Center, 1974) and *Ethnic Directory I* (Detroit: Southeastern Michigan Regional Ethnic Heritage Studies Center, 1973).

ALL RUSSIAN MONARCHIST FRONT
520 West 163rd Street
New York, New York 10032
Principal officers: Alexander P. Wolkoff, President

Permanent staff: NI	Membership: NI
Date founded: 1958	Membership dues: NI
Branches: NI	Scope: national

Nature of organization: political

Publications: *Nasha Strana* (Our Country) (weekly); *Znamia Rossii* (The Banner of Russia)

Major conventions/meetings: biennial

Comments: The goals of the organizations that comprise this front are to oppose communism and to restore Russia to its imperial state. It is also known as Obshcherossiiskii Monarkhicheskii Front.

AMERICAN RUSSIAN AID ASSOCIATION (ARAA)
349 West 86th Street
New York, New York 10024   (212) 787-0206
Principal officers: Serge Belosselsky, President

Permanent staff: 10	Membership: 350
Date founded: 1945	Membership dues: NI
Branches: NI	Scope: national

Nature of organization: relief

Publications: *Russian Cause*, 1958– (monthly)

Comments: Aims to assist in resettlement of Russian refugees in the free world; sponsors aid for the aged. It also endeavors to unite Russians in the United States.

ASSOCIATION OF RUSSIAN-AMERICAN SCHOLARS IN U.S.A.
85-20 114th Street
Richmond Hill, New York 11418   (212) 846-6410
Principal officers: Prof. N. S. Arseniev, President
C. G. Belousow, Vice President
A. P. Obolensky, Vice President
A. P. Scherbatow, Secretary

Permanent staff: none	Membership: 166
Date founded: 1947	Membership dues: $5.00
Branches: none	Scope: national

Special requirements for membership: interest in scholarly research

Nature of organization: scholarly

Publications: *Transactions of the Association of Russian-American Scholars in U.S.A.* (annual); also publishes books

Major conventions/meetings: irregular conferences

ASSOCIATION OF RUSSIAN-AMERICAN SCHOLARS IN U.S.A. (cont'd)

Comments: Unites Russian scholars in the United States or those studying some area of Russian culture. The organization also publishes a bilingual journal and organizes and sponsors lectures and symposia.

ASSOCIATION OF RUSSIAN IMPERIAL NAVAL OFFICERS IN AMERICA
349 West 86th Street
New York, New York 10024

Principal officers: Nicholas C. Glad, President

Permanent staff: NI
Date founded: 1923
Branches: NI

Membership: 150
Membership dues: NI
Scope: national

Special requirements for membership: former officers of the Imperial Russian Navy and their descendants

Nature of organization: historical, charitable

Publications: *Bulletin*, 1934– (3 issues per year)

Major conventions/meetings: annual

Comments: The association studies the history of the Imperial Russian Navy and collects materials pertaining to it. It provides aid to members in need and to destitute families abroad. Until 1953 it was known as the Association of Former Russian Naval Officers in America. Maintains a library of 1,000 volumes.

ASSOCIATION OF RUSSIAN WAR INVALIDS OF FIRST WORLD WAR
634 West 135th Street
New York, New York 10031

Principal officers: Alexander Amilakhvary, President

Permanent staff: NI
Date founded: 1954
Branches: NI

Membership: 118
Membership dues: NI
Scope: national

Special requirements for membership: Russian war veterans who have been invalids since World War I

CHRISTIAN EVANGELICAL PENTECOSTAL FAITH
P.O. Box 206
Garfield, New Jersey 07026

Nature of organization: religious

Publications: *Strannik* (Pilgrim), 1945– (quarterly)

CONGRESS OF RUSSIAN AMERICANS, INC.
322 West 108th Street
New York, New York 10025   (212) 666-1711

Principal officers: Professor Alexandroff, Director

Permanent staff: NI
Date founded: NI
Branches: NI

Membership: various Russian-American organizations
Membership dues: NI
Scope: national

Nature of organization: cultural

Comments: Coordinates the activities of various Russian-American organizations in the United States. Promotes preservation of the Russian heritage and culture.

FUND FOR THE RELIEF OF RUSSIAN WRITERS AND SCIENTISTS IN EXILE
243 West 56th Street
New York, New York 10019   (212) 265-5500

Principal officers: Mark Weinbaum, President

FUND FOR THE RELIEF OF RUSSIAN WRITERS AND SCIENTISTS IN EXILE (cont'd)

Permanent staff: NI
Date founded: 1918
Branches: 3

Membership: 274
Membership dues: NI
Scope: national

Special requirements for membership: Americans of Russian descent

Nature of organization: cultural, relief

Major conventions/meetings: annual

Comments: The purpose of the organization is to assist exiled writers and scientists of Russian background, and to promote Russian literature, culture, and achievements in the United States. It sponsors lectures, conferences, and various fund-raising programs.

PACIFIC COAST SLAVIC BAPTIST ASSOCIATION
4540 Marion Court
Sacramento, California 95822

Nature of organization: religious

Publications: *Nashi Dni* (Our Days), 1967– (weekly)

PATRIARCHAL PARISHES OF THE MOSCOW PATRIARCHATE IN AMERICA
St. Nicholas Cathedral
15 East 97th Street
New York, New York 10029   (212) 831-6294

Principal officers: Bishop Makary, President
                       Archpriest Feodor Kovalchuk, Executive Secretary

Permanent staff: 15
Date founded: NI
Branches: 54 regional

Membership: 150,000
Membership dues: NI
Scope: national

Special requirements for membership: member of Orthodox Catholic Church

Nature of organization: religious

Publications: *One Church*, 1948– (bimonthly); *Journal of the Moscow Patriarchate*, 1931– (monthly); *Annual Calendar of the Moscow Patriarchate*, 1945– (annual)

Affiliations: Patriarchate of Moscow; Russian Orthodox Church USSR

Major conventions/meetings: triennial

Comments: The organization aims to unite Russian Orthodox Churches in America and to perpetuate the Orthodox Catholic religious teachings. Its secondary interest is in preserving the Russian culture in America. Until 1970 the organization went under the name of the Exarchate of the Russian Orthodox Church in America. It sponsors St. Seraphim of Sarov Theological Seminary in East Lansing, Michigan. A 20,500 volume library and an archival collection are maintained.

RUSSIAN-AMERICAN SOCIETY "OTRADA" INC.
Rockland Lake Park
Valley Cottage, New York 10989   (914) 268-3782

Principal officers: Oleg M. Rodzianko, President
                       Peter N. Budzivovich, Vice President
                       Olgerd Yasinski, Secretary

Permanent staff: none
Date founded: 1968
Branches: none

Membership: 68 families
Membership dues: $25.00 per family
Scope: national

Special requirements for membership: none

Nature of organization: cultural, recreational, youth

Publications: none

Affiliations: none

Major conventions/meetings: annual convention

RUSSIAN-AMERICAN SOCIETY "OTRADA" INC. (cont'd)

Comments: Objectives of the organization are to sponsor cultural, educational, athletic, and charitable activities for persons of Russian descent. Russian traditions and the beliefs and practices of the Russian Orthodox Church are perpetuated through concerts, theatrical performances, conventions, and recreational and social programs. It sponsors a yearly summer camp and a seminar for youth.

RUSSIAN CHILDREN'S WELFARE SOCIETY, INC.

59 East 2nd Street
New York, New York 10003   (212) 777-9110

Principal officers: Serge C. Bouteneff, President
                       Catherine Nebolsine, Executive Vice President
                       Nathalie Lapteff, Executive Secretary

Permanent staff: 3   Membership: 250
Date founded: 1926   Membership dues: $3.00 (annual)
Branches: 6   Scope: international, national

Special requirements for membership: none

Nature of organization: charitable

Publications: annual report; also publishes articles and appeals in newspapers

Affiliations: none

Major conventions/meetings: none

Comments: The society provides financial aid to sick and destitute children of Russian descent outside of the Soviet Union. It has a Foster Children's Plan and sponsors children at camps. Records and data are kept in Columbia University Archival Collection.

RUSSIAN IMMIGRANTS REPRESENTATIVE ASSOCIATION IN AMERICA, INC.

349 West 86th Street
New York, New York 10024

Publications: *Russkoye Delo* (The Russian Cause), 1958– (monthly)

RUSSIAN INDEPENDENT MUTUAL AID SOCIETY (RIMAS)

917 North Wood Street
Chicago, Illinois 60622   (312) 421-2272

Principal officers: Steve Miskovetz, President
                       John A. Lovda, Secretary

Permanent staff: NI   Membership: 1,471
Date founded: 1931   Membership dues: vary
Branches: in 3 states   Scope: national

Nature of organization: fraternal

Major conventions/meetings: biennial

Comments: Provides life insurance benefits to members.

RUSSIAN NOBILITY ASSOCIATION IN AMERICA, INC.

971 First Avenue
New York, New York 10022   (212) 755-7528

Principal officers: Alexis Scherbatow, President
                       Dimitry Galitzine, Vice President
                       Nicolas Djounkovsky, Secretary

Permanent staff: NI   Membership: 100
Date founded: 1938   Membership dues: $6.00
Branches: NI   Scope: national

Special requirements for membership: persons listed in the nobility archives of the former Russian Imperial Senate (or their descendants)

Nature of organization: historical, genealogical, welfare

RUSSIAN NOBILITY ASSOCIATION IN AMERICA, INC. (cont'd)

Major conventions/meetings: annual

Comments: Provides genealogical services and compiles records of the immigration of former Russian nobles to the United States. Aids members in need and also other Russian-Americans in distress. Maintains a 1,000-volume library and an archival collection.

RUSSIAN ORTHODOX CATHOLIC WOMEN'S MUTUAL AID SOCIETY

1074 Greentree Road
Pittsburgh, Pennsylvania 15220   (412) 343-8933

Principal officers: Mary Maren, President
                        Martha Lomakin, Secretary

Permanent staff: NI   Membership: 20,000
Date founded: 1895   Membership dues: NI
Branches: 55 local groups   Scope: national

Nature of organization: fraternal

Major conventions/meetings: quadrennial; also holds an annual meeting in Pittsburgh

Comments: Major purpose is to provide life insurance benefits to members, but the society also supports two seminaries, a monastery, and various churches. Gives aid to disaster victims and grants scholarships to youth of Russian descent.

RUSSIAN ORTHODOX FRATERNITY LUBOV

212 Bacon Street
Jermyn, Pennsylvania 18433   (717) 876-0525

Principal officers: Stephen Shust, Financial Secretary

Permanent staff: NI   Membership: 1,080
Date founded: 1912   Membership dues: NI
Branches: 73 local groups   Scope: national

Nature of organization: fraternal

Major conventions/meetings: quadrennial

Comments: Major purpose is to provide life insurance benefits to members.

RUSSIAN PEOPLE'S CENTER (RPC)

529 West 138th Street
New York, New York 10031   (212) 283-0865

Principal officers: F. Kossovich, President

Permanent staff: 1   Membership: 500
Date founded: 1929   Membership dues: NI
Branches: NI   Scope: national

Nature of organization: welfare

Major conventions/meetings: annual (in March) in New York City

Comments: A relief organization to help needy Russian-Americans in time of sickness, death, unemployment, etc.

RUSSIAN STUDENT FUND

845 Third Avenue
New York, New York 10022   (212) 421-3740

Permanent staff: NI   Membership: NI
Date founded: 1921   Membership dues: NI
Branches: NI   Scope: national

Special requirements for membership: must be an American student of Russian descent (non-communist)

Nature of organization: student aid

Affiliations: Division of United Student Aid Funds

Comments: Lends money to non-communist students of Russian descent studying in American colleges and universities.

ST. GEORGE'S PATHFINDERS, INC.
116-38 230th Street
Cambria Heights, New York 11411   (212) 527-0050
Principal officers: Andrew V. Ilyinsky, President
                       Alex Zacharin, Executive Vice President
                       Anna Janushevich, Executive Secretary

Permanent staff: NI   Membership: 200
Date founded: 1947   Membership dues: $36.00
Branches: 11 local   adults (annual); $12.00 children
                                                     (annual)
                                                 Scope: regional

Special requirements for membership: Russian ethnic origin

Nature of organization: youth

Publications: *The Campfire of Tsarskoye Selo*, 1952– (quarterly); *The Spark*, 1958–
     (quarterly); *Aid to the Leaders*, 1963– (quarterly); also publishes books

Affiliations: Russian-American Congress; OTRADA

Major conventions/meetings: annual conference

Comments: A scout program for boys and girls, this organization emphasizes the study and
     preservation of the Russian national heritage and Russian Orthodox religious heritage.
     Until 1950 it was known as the Russian Scouts Association in Exile. It sponsors
     summer and winter camps and training courses for patrol leaders and scout masters;
     special achievement awards are granted.

TOLSTOY FOUNDATION (TF)
250 West 57th Street, Room 1004
New York, New York 10019   (212) 247-2922
Principal officers: Alexandra Tolstoy, President
                       Mrs. Tatiana Schaufuss, Executive Vice President
                       John L. Bates, Executive Secretary

Permanent staff: 42   Membership: 7,000
Date founded: 1939   Membership dues: $5.00 and up
Branches: 12 regional   (annual)
                                                 Scope: national

Nature of organization: service, relief, cultural

Publications: *Annual Report*; *TF News* (irregular)

Affiliations: American Council of Voluntary Agencies for Foreign Service; Cooperative for
     American Relief Everywhere; International Council of Voluntary Agencies

Major conventions/meetings: annual (first Thursday in October), in New York City

Comments: Assists refugees from Russia and other communist countries in various ways:
     provides financial assistance, job procurement, immigration help and adjustment;
     helps to locate relatives; provides access to educational programs and information,
     etc. The organization also sponsors cultural programs that promote Russian arts and
     traditions. It maintains homes for the aged, nursing home facilities, and a pavilion for
     the mentally disabled.

SCANDINAVIAN-AMERICAN ORGANIZATIONS

See also Danish-American, Finnish-American, Icelandic-American,
Norwegian-American, and Swedish-American Organizations

Additional information on Scandinavian-American organizations in the
United States may be obtained from the American-Scandinavian Foundation
(127 East 73rd Street, New York, New York 10021).

In a few instances these major Scandinavian organizations include Finland and Iceland in addition to the ethnic groups of Denmark, Norway, and Sweden, which is why we have provided reference to Finnish-American and Icelandic-American organizations.

AMERICAN-SCANDINAVIAN FOUNDATION

127 East 73rd Street
New York, New York 10021   (212) 879-9779

Principal officers: Gene G. Gage, Director

Permanent staff: 15   Membership: 5,500
Date founded: 1910   Membership dues: NI
Branches: 27 local   Scope: national

Special requirements for membership: Americans of Scandinavian descent

Nature of organization: cultural, educational

Publications: *Scan* (8 issues per year); *American Scandinavian Review* (quarterly); *Annual Report* (annual)

Major conventions/meetings: annual

Comments: The purpose of the organization is to promote cultural understanding in America of the Scandinavian way of life and to unite Scandinavians in the United States. Also provides informational and educational programs and activities and presents awards and grants for Scandinavian research studies. The former name of the organization was The Scandinavian Society.

INDEPENDENT ORDER OF SVITHIOD

5520 West Lawrence Avenue
Chicago, Illinois 60630   (312) 736-1191

Principal officers: Harold Wennersten, Secretary-Treasurer
                      Harold G. Ekman, Grand President

Permanent staff: 4   Membership: 8,000
Date founded: 1880   Membership dues: vary
Branches: 52   Scope: national

Special requirements for membership: of Scandinavian descent (or married to someone of Scandinavian descent)

Nature of organization: fraternal

Publications: *The Svithiod Journal* (monthly)

Major conventions/meetings: annual

Comments: Major purpose is to provide life insurance benefits to members. Also maintains the Svithiod Home Fund and a scholarship program.

INDEPENDENT ORDER OF VIKINGS

200 East Ontario Street
Chicago, Illinois 60611

Principal officers: Ted N. Mortivedt, Grand Chief
                      Paul F. Swanson, Vice Grand Chief
                      Wm. A. Johnson, Grand Secretary

Permanent staff: NI   Membership: NI
Date founded: 1890   Membership dues: NI
Branches: NI   Scope: national

Special requirements for membership: Scandinavian birth or descent

Nature of organization: fraternal

Publications: *Vikingen* (monthly)

Comments: Major purpose is to provide life insurance benefits to members. Also awards scholarships to youth who are members or children of members.

ST. ANSGAR'S SCANDINAVIAN CATHOLIC LEAGUE
40 West 13th Street
New York, New York 10011   (212) 675-0400
Principal officers: John T. Dwight, Secretary

Permanent staff: NI   Membership: 700
Date founded: NI   Membership dues: NI
Branches: 7   Scope: national

Nature of organization: religious, social, charitable

Publications: *St. Ansgar's Bulletin* (annual)

Comments: The goal of this religious organization is to unite Catholic Scandinavians in the United States, to provide social and morally uplifting activities, and to aid in supporting the Catholic Church in the Scandinavian countries.

SCANDINAVIAN FRATERNITY OF AMERICA
1350 North Howard Street
Akron, Ohio 44310   (216) 923-0718
Principal officers: Grace I. LeMaster, Supreme Secretary

Permanent staff: NI   Membership: 10,000
Date founded: 1915   Membership dues: vary
Branches: 100   Scope: national

Special requirements for membership: persons of Scandinavian descent

Nature of organization: fraternal

Publications: *Monitor* (monthly)

Major conventions/meetings: triennial

Comments: Formed by merger of the Scandinavian Brotherhood of America, Scandinavian Brotherhood of Montana, and Scandinavian Aid and Fellowship Society.

SCANDINAVIAN SEMINAR
100 East 85th Street
New York, New York 10028   (212) 734-8340
Principal officers: Mrs. Gunnel Wrede, Executive Secretary

Permanent staff: 7   Membership: 1,400 alumni
Date founded: 1949   Membership dues: NI
Branches: NI   Scope: national

Nature of organization: educational

Publications: *Annual Review*; *Bulletin*

Comments: Sponsors American students who undertake programs of study in Scandinavian countries for a year. Some apprenticeships are arranged upon completion of the seminar. Over 1,400 U.S. students have participated in the educational seminar.

SOCIETY FOR THE ADVANCEMENT OF SCANDINAVIAN STUDY
c/o James E. Cathey
Germanic Languages
University of Massachusetts
Amherst, Massachusetts 01002   (413) 545-0314
Principal officers: James E. Cathey

Permanent staff: NI   Membership: 650
Date founded: 1911   Membership dues: $10.00 and up
Branches: NI   (annual)
                              Scope: national

Nature of organization: educational

Publications: *Scandinavian Studies* (quarterly); *American Scandinavian Bibliography* (annual)

Major conventions/meetings: annual

Comments: Promotes research and teaching in Scandinavian studies, language, literature, and culture. Cultures of Denmark, Finland, Iceland, Norway, and Sweden are included.

THANKS TO SCANDINAVIA
527 Madison Avenue, Suite 905
New York, New York 10022   (212) 755-2393
Principal officers: Muriel Bloomberg, Executive Director
                       Victor Borge, National Chairman

Permanent staff: NI	Membership: NI
Date founded: 1965	Membership dues: NI
Branches: NI	Scope: national

Nature of organization: cultural, scholarship fund

Publications: *Newsletter* (annual)

Major conventions/meetings: annual

Comments: Administers a fund commemorating Scandinavian heroes of World War II which awards scholarships to Scandinavian students. Sponsors Scandinavian teachers visiting the United States and promotes concerts and other cultural programs and benefits. Participates in the annual Institute of American Studies at Luther College in Decorah, Iowa.

SCOTCH-IRISH-AMERICAN ORGANIZATIONS

See also Irish-American Organizations

The term Scotch-Irish is used to designate a group of Scots who migrated to Ulster, or the northern province of Ireland, and remained there for several generations before emmigrating from Ireland. Most retained their Presbyterian religion, but they took on the culture and many of the customs of the Irish, and they intermarried with them. A more complete description of the Scotch-Irish may be found in Appendix I of James G. Leyburn's *The Scotch-Irish* (Chapel Hill: The University of North Carolina Press, 1962).

SCOTCH-IRISH SOCIETY OF THE UNITED STATES OF AMERICA
c/o John C. Tuten, Jr., Secretary
3 Parkway, 20th Floor
Philadelphia, Pennsylvania 19102   (215) 563-0650
Principal officers: James H. Stewart, Jr., President
                       Marion D. Patterson, Vice President
                       John C. Tuten, Jr., Secretary

Permanent staff: none	Membership: 360
Date founded: 1949	Membership dues: $5.00 (annual)
Branches: none	Scope: national

Special requirements for membership: descended from Scotch-Irish pioneers

Nature of organization: genealogical

Publications: *Scotch-Irish Proceedings*

Major conventions/meetings: annual meeting

Comments: The purpose of this organization is to trace genealogies of its Scotch-Irish members. A 500-volume library on Scotch-Irish pioneers and their descendants is maintained.

SCOTTISH-AMERICAN ORGANIZATIONS

Additional information on Scottish-American organizations in the United States may be obtained from British Information Services (845 Third Avenue, New York, New York 10022) or from American Scottish Foundation (P.O. Box 537, Lenox Hill Station, New York, New York 10021). Regional and local information may be obtained from *Greater Cleveland Nationalities Directory 1974* (Cleveland: Sun Newspapers and the Nationalities Services Center, 1974) and *Ethnic Directory I* (Detroit: Southeastern Michigan Regional Ethnic Heritage Studies Center, 1973).

AMERICAN SCOTTISH FOUNDATION
P.O. Box 537, Lenox Hill Station
New York, New York 10021

Principal officers: Lady Malcolm Doughlas-Hamilton, President

Permanent staff: NI   Membership: 6,000
Date founded: 1956   Membership dues: NI
Branches: NI   Scope: national

Publications: *The Scotia News* (monthly)

Major conventions/meetings: annual

Comments: Major purpose is to preserve the Scottish heritage and culture in the United States, and to unite those of Scottish descent throughout the nation. The organization plans to establish a center of Scottish culture, information, history, and information called Scotland House in New York City. Sponsors an annual Scotland Week and Annual Conference of Scottish Youth Leaders in the United States. Also provides speakers for cultural and social programs.

BURNS SOCIETY OF THE CITY OF NEW YORK
c/o St. Andrews Society
281 Park Avenue, South
New York, New York 10010   (212) 473-6912

Principal officers: S. Thomas Aitken, Secretary

Permanent staff: NI   Membership: 200
Date founded: 1871   Membership dues: NI
Branches: in most major cities   Scope: international, national

Special requirements for membership: none

Nature of organization: cultural

Publications: *Robert Burns Chronicle* (annual)

Affiliations: The Burns Federation, Kilmarnack, Scotland

Major conventions/meetings: annual

Comments: The organization is composed mainly of persons of Scottish descent who are interested in commemorating the Scottish poet Robert Burns and in promoting his works.

CLAN GRANT NO. 17, ORDER OF SCOTTISH CLANS (I.O.F.)
7441 Hi-View Drive
North Royalton, Ohio 44133   (216) 237-6400

Principal officers: John Noble, Chief
                                Don Skinner, Tanist
                                Alex W. Campbell, Secretary

Permanent staff: 1   Membership: 135
Date founded: 1885   Membership dues: $15.00
Branches: NI   Scope: national

CLAN GRANT NO. 17, ORDER OF SCOTTISH CLANS (I.O.F.) (cont'd)

Special requirements for membership: Scottish descent or related by marriage

Nature of organization: social, fraternal, cultural

Publications: *The Forester*

Major conventions/meetings: semimonthly meetings

Comments: The objectives of the organization are to perpetuate Scottish traditions and ideals; to preserve Scottish music, history, and culture in the United States; and to provide social activities for members.

DAUGHTERS OF SCOTIA
32-67 38th Street
Astoria, New York 11106

Principal officers: Elizabeth Foy, Grand Chief Daughter

Permanent staff: NI

Date founded: 1899

Branches: NI

Membership: 17,000

Membership dues: NI

Scope: national

Special requirements for membership: women of Scottish descent

Nature of organization: cultural, social

Major conventions/meetings: annual

HIGHLAND SOCIETY OF ARIZONA (HSA)
c/o 1901 East Ellis Drive
Tempe, Arizona 85282   (602) 838-1132

Principal officers: Joseph M. Leonard, President
Barbara Johnstone, Vice President
Carol Thompson, Secretary

Permanent staff: none

Date founded: 1971

Branches: none

Membership: 80

Membership dues: none

Scope: state

Special requirements for membership: none

Nature of organization: social, cultural

Publications: *Tartan Times*

Comments: The primary objectives of this society are to provide social activities for members and to conduct and organize the Arizona Highland Games, in which the Scottish tradition is perpetuated through highland dancing, drumming, piping, shot put, and other typical Scottish competitions.

ROYAL ORDER OF SCOTLAND (ROS)
864 National Press Building
Washington, D.C. 20004   (202) 347-2059

Principal officers: Samuel W. McIntosh, Grand Secretary

Permanent staff: NI

Date founded: NI

Branches: NI

Membership: 3,200

Membership dues: NI

Scope: national

Special requirements for membership: Scottish descent

Nature of organization: fraternal, charitable, Masonic

Publications: *Annual Proceedings*

Major conventions/meetings: annual

ST. ANDREW'S SOCIETY OF THE STATE OF NEW YORK
281 Park Avenue South
New York, New York 10010   (212) 473-6912

Principal officers: Walter P. Marshall, Recording Secretary

ST. ANDREW'S SOCIETY OF THE STATE OF NEW YORK (cont'd)

Permanent staff: 2	Membership: 1,200
Date founded: 1756	Membership dues: NI
Branches: NI	Scope: national

Special requirements for membership: Scottish descent

Nature of organization: cultural

Publications: *The Pibroch* (semiannual)

Major conventions/meetings: annual

Comments: Major goal is to unite persons of Scottish birth or ancestry in the United States in cultural and other activities. Sponsors a graduate student program providing scholarships for study in Scotland.

SCOTTISH-AMERICAN ASSOCIATION, INC.

6809 Fourth Avenue
Brooklyn, New York 11220   (212) 748-3222

Principal officers: The Hon. Francis J. Folan

Permanent staff: NI	Membership: NI
Date founded: NI	Membership dues: NI
Branches: NI	Scope: regional

SCOTTISH HISTORIC AND RESEARCH SOCIETY OF THE DELAWARE VALLEY, INC.

2137 MacLarie Lane
Broomall, Pennsylvania 19008   (215) 446-1242

Principal officers: Blair C. Stonier, President
Hugh J. Young, Vice President
Mrs. Stuart Morrison, Secretary

Permanent staff: none	Membership: 350
Date founded: 1964	Membership dues: $15.00 family;
Branches: NI	$10.00 single; $5.00 associate member (all the above annual dues)
	Scope: national

Special requirements for membership: none

Nature of organization: cultural, educational

Publications: *The Rampant Lion*, 1964– (monthly)

Major conventions/meetings: monthly

Comments: The major purpose of the organization is to conduct research in educational projects on Scottish history, literature, or tradition, and to keep members informed of such studies. It also presents lectures or special programs on Scotland or Scottish customs to schools and other organizations. Maintains a 300-volume library and genealogical archives.

THE SCOTTISH SOCIETY OF TEXAS (SST)

408 Brady Lane
Austin, Texas 78746   (512) 327-0875

Principal officers: John Nicol Macdonald, President
Claude Gunn, Jr., Vice President
Mrs. Wayne Edward Heath, Secretary

Permanent staff: none	Membership: 114
Date founded: 1963	Membership dues: $10.00 (annual)
Branches: none	Scope: regional

Special requirements for membership: Scottish lineage

Nature of organization: social, educational, cultural

Publications: *Heather Notes*, 1963– (3 issues per year)

Affiliations: Scottish Society of San Antonio; Scots of Austin

THE SCOTTISH SOCIETY OF TEXAS (SST) (cont'd)

Major conventions/meetings: annual Clan Gathering and Texas Highland Games

Comments: The major purpose of the organization is to preserve the Scottish culture, including customs, dress, and traditions, in the United States. It also unites those of Scottish descent in social and recreational activities. It sponsors the Texas Highland Games and an annual clan gathering at McLennan Community College in Waco, Texas. Also sponsors scholarships to Scottish-American students at this institution.

UNITED SCOTTISH CLANS OF NEW YORK AND NEW JERSEY
32-67 38th Street
Astoria, New York 11103   (212) 626-7466
Principal officers: J. B. Foy, Corresponding Secretary

SERBIAN-AMERICAN ORGANIZATIONS

Additional information on Serbian-American organizations in the United States may be obtained from The Serbian National Committee (3909 West North Avenue, Chicago, Illinois 60647). Regional and local organizations may be obtained from *Greater Cleveland Nationalities Directory 1974* (Cleveland: Sun Newspapers and the Nationalities Services Center, 1974) and *Ethnic Directory I* (Detroit: Southeastern Michigan Regional Ethnic Heritage Studies Center, 1973).

AMERICAN ASSOCIATION OF WAR VETERANS OF THE KINGDOM OF YUGOSLAVIA
5141 West Fullerton Avenue
Chicago, Illinois 60639

           (216) 651-0444

Principal officers: Dragoljub Militich, President
Permanent staff: NI   Membership: NI
Date founded: 1957   Membership dues: $6.00 (annual)
Branches: chapters in main cities   Scope: national

Special requirements for membership: Serbian descent

Nature of organization: veterans

Affiliations: American Association of War Veterans of the Kingdom of Yugoslavia (National Headquarters, Chicago)

Comments: Attempts to unite Serbian veterans residing in the United States, and to provide social and cultural activities that promote and preserve the Serbian heritage. The organization also supports efforts to restore a Serbian monarchy; it assists Serbian veterans and their members in sickness or other need.

BROTHERHOOD OF SERBIAN ORTHODOX CLERGY IN THE U.S.A. AND CANADA
5701 North Redwood Drive
Chicago, Illinois 60631
Principal officers: V. Rev. Mitan Brieich, President
Permanent staff: NI   Membership: NI
Date founded: NI   Membership dues: NI
Branches: NI   Scope: national
Nature of organization: religious

COUNCIL OF SERBIAN ORGANIZATIONS OF GREATER CLEVELAND
c/o Milutin Ristich, President
478 East 222nd Street
Euclid, Ohio 44123
Principal officers: Milutin Ristich, President
Permanent staff: NI   Membership: 11 organizations
Date founded: NI   Membership dues: NI
Branches: NI   Scope: NI

COUNCIL OF SERBIAN ORGANIZATIONS OF GREATER CLEVELAND (cont'd)
Special requirements for membership: Serbian-American organization

Nature of organization: cultural, political, social, recreational

Comments: Coordinates the activities of cultural and other Serbian-American organizations in the Cleveland area.

RAVANICA MOTHER'S CLUB
4575 East Outer Drive
Detroit, Michigan 48234

Special requirements for membership: mothers of children attending St. Lazarus Serbian Orthodox Cathedral Ravanica

Nature of organization: religious, charitable

Affiliations: St. Lazarus Serbian Orthodox Cathedral Ravanica

Comments: This women's group supports the Sunday School of a major Serbian Orthodox Church, St. Lazarus of Detroit. It provides teaching materials and sponsors children at the church summer camp. Plans various social and fund-raising activities.

ST. SAVA SERBIAN CULTURAL CLUB
Cleveland Chapter
4410 Grantwood Drive
Parma, Ohio 33134

Principal officers: Dr. M. Draskovic, President

Permanent staff: NI	Membership: NI
Date founded: 1951	Membership dues: NI
Branches: NI	Scope: national

Special requirements for membership: Serbian descent

Nature of organization: cultural

Publications: *Srpska Borba* (Serbian Struggle) (weekly)

Affiliations: St. Sava Serbian Cultural Club (National Headquarters, Chicago)

Comments: The major purpose of the organization is to preserve the Serbian culture, tradition, and heritage in the United States. It is opposed to communism and supports a free democracy for Serbia.

SERB NATIONAL FEDERATION
3414 Fifth Avenue
Pittsburgh, Pennsylvania 15213   (412) 621-6600

Principal officers: Robert Rade Stone, President
D. J. Ljubenko, First Vice President
Nick Borkovich, Second Vice President
Mitch Trivanovich, Secretary

Permanent staff: 6	Membership: 20,000
Date founded: 1901	Membership dues: vary depending on
Branches: 300 local	life insurance policy
	Scope: national

Special requirements for membership: must be of Serbian or Slav descent, up to age 60

Nature of organization: fraternal

Publications: *American Srbobran*, 1924– (3 per week)

Affiliations: none

Major conventions/meetings: quadrennial convention

Comments: The major goals of this fraternal organization are to provide insurance benefits to members and to preserve the Serbian culture in America.

SERBIAN BROTHER'S HELP, INC.
1911 West Evergreen
Chicago, Illinois 60622

Permanent staff: NI
Date founded: approx. 1953
Branches: NI

Membership: NI
Membership dues: NI
Scope: international, national

Special requirements for membership: Serbian descent

Nature of organization: fraternal

Major conventions/meetings: annual

Comments: Major purpose is to provide life and health benefits to members. The organization sponsors relief and aid to immigrants, refugees, and other needy Serbs (e.g., unemployed, handicapped, aged). Maintains a camp and a home for the aged in Pennsylvania.

SERBIAN CHETNIKS
9663 Maple Avenue
Gary, Indiana 46403

Principal officers: Tomica Ivancevic, President

Permanent staff: NI
Date founded: NI
Branches: NI

Membership: NI
Membership dues: NI
Scope: national

Special requirements for membership: war veterans

Nature of organization: political, veterans, relief

Publications: *Voice of Serbian Freedom Fighters*, 1960– (bimonthly)

SERBIAN HISTORICAL & CULTURAL ASSOCIATION "NJEGOS"
3909 West North Avenue
Chicago, Illinois 60647   (312) 772-7878

Principal officers: Dr. Uros Seferovic, President

Permanent staff: NI
Date founded: 1949
Branches: various state branches

Membership: NI
Membership dues: NI
Scope: national

Special requirements for membership: Serbian descent

Nature of organization: cultural

Publications: *Sloboda* (Liberty), 1952– (weekly)

Affiliations: Serbian National Defense Council

Major conventions/meetings: annual

Comments: Major purpose of the organization is to preserve and perpetuate the Serbian culture and heritage in the United States. The group maintains an orchestra, a church-affiliated choir, and a dance group which performs for social, cultural, and religious programs.

SERBIAN LITERARY ASSOCIATION
448 Barry Avenue
Chicago, Illinois 60657   (312) 549-6111

Permanent staff: NI
Date founded: 1946
Branches: several

Membership: NI
Membership dues: NI
Scope: national

Principal officers: Dr. M. Draskovic, President

Nature of organization: cultural

Publications: *Serbian Struggle*, 1946–

Comments: Major goals are to preserve the Serbian literature, language, and culture in the United States. The organization also strives to strengthen a spirit of freedom among all Serbs. Articles in their publication cover historical, political, social, literary, and theatrical aspects, as well as other topics.

SERBIAN NATIONAL COMMITTEE
3909 West North
Chicago, Illinois 60647   (312) 772-7878
Principal officers: Dr. Uros Seferovic, President

Permanent staff: 1   Membership: NI
Date founded: 1968   Membership dues: NI
Branches: NI   Scope: national

Special requirements for membership: Serbian organizations

Nature of organization: political

Publications: *Democratic Forum*

Comments: Coordinates activities of Serbian organizations. Works to obtain a free and
democratic Serbian people and nation in their homeland. Sponsors activities that
promote and preserve the Serbian heritage in the United States.

SERBIAN NATIONAL DEFENSE COUNCIL (SNDC)
3909 West North
Chicago, Illinois 60647   (312) 772-7878
Principal officers: Dr. Uros Seferovic, President

Permanent staff: NI   Membership: 30,000
Date founded: NI   Membership dues: NI
Branches: NI   Scope: international, national

Special requirements for membership: Serbian descent

Nature of organization: political, relief, cultural

Publications: *Sloboda*, 1952– (weekly)

Major conventions/meetings: annual

Comments: Attempts to preserve the Serbian language and culture in the United States. The
organization also assists Serbian immigrants and refugees and strives to obtain a free
and democratic Serbian homeland.

SERBIAN ORTHODOX TEACHER'S AND YOUTH ASSOCIATION
5701 North Redwood Drive
Chicago, Illinois 60631

Permanent staff: NI   Membership: NI
Date founded: NI   Membership dues: NI
Branches: NI   Scope: national

Special requirements for membership: Serbian descent

Nature of organization: professional, cultural, educational, youth

Comments: Major objectives of the association are to promote education among Serbian youth
in the United States, to unite teachers, and to promote the instruction of Serbian youth
in the Serbian culture.

SERBIAN SINGING FEDERATION OF AMERICA
839 North Dearborn
Chicago, Illinois 60605   (312) 337-7131
Nature of organization: cultural

SLOVAK-AMERICAN ORGANIZATIONS

Additional information on Slovak-American organizations in the United
States may be obtained from The Slovak League of America (313 Ridge Avenue,
Middletown, Pennsylvania 17057). Regional and local organizations are listed in
Greater Cleveland Nationalities Directory 1974 (Cleveland: Sun Newspapers and
the Nationalities Services Center, 1974) and *Ethnic Directory I* (Detroit: South-
eastern Michigan Regional Ethnic Heritage Studies Center, 1973).

AMERICAN-CANADIAN SLOVAK CULTURAL INSTITUTE
7701 West Morrow Circle
Dearborn, Michigan 48126   (313) 582-7336
Principal officers: Joseph R. Kristofik, President
                  Rev. Rudolph Flachbarth, Vice President
                  Joseph Rimarcik, Secretary

Permanent staff: 5	Membership: NI
Date founded: 1969	Membership dues: none
Branches: 1 regional; 1 state; 1 local	Scope: regional

Special requirements for membership: Slovak ethnic background or interest

Nature of organization: social, cultural, educational, fraternal

Publications: *Newsletter*, 1969– (semiannual)

Comments: The major purpose of this organization is to help second-generation Slovak students in the United States and Canada attend the University of Bratislava or other Slovak universities, particularly for the annual international Slavic Studies Program. Exchange programs with European universities are also sponsored.

CATHOLIC SLOVAK BROTHERHOOD
342 Boulevard of the Allies
Pittsburgh, Pennsylvania 15222

Permanent staff: NI	Membership: NI
Date founded: 1912	Membership dues: NI
Branches: NI	Scope: national

Nature of organization: fraternal, religious

Publications: *Svornost* (Harmony), 1912– (bimonthly)

Comments: Major purpose is to provide life insurance benefits. The organization also attempts to preserve the Slovak religion and culture in the United States, and it is active in charitable projects involving aid to Slovaks.

FIRST CATHOLIC SLOVAK LADIES ASSOCIATION (FCSLA)
24950 Chagrin Boulevard
Beachwood, Ohio 44122   (216) 464-8015
Principal officers: Frances L. Mizenko, Executive Secretary

Permanent staff: 15	Membership: 96,000
Date founded: 1892	Membership dues: varies
Branches: 900	Scope: national

Special requirements for membership: Slovak descent

Nature of organization: fraternal

Publications: *Fraternally Yours* (monthly)

Affiliations: Slovak League of America

Major conventions/meetings: quadrennial

Comments: Major purpose of the organization is to provide life insurance benefits to members. It also operates a home for the aged. The original name of the organization was the First Catholic Slovak Ladies Union; in 1969 it absorbed the former Catholic Slovak Brotherhood.

FIRST CATHOLIC SLOVAK UNION OF THE UNITED STATES AND CANADA
3289 East 55th Street
Cleveland, Ohio 44127   (216) 341-3355
Principal officers: John A. Sabol, President
                  Michael J. Zahorsky, Vice President
                  Stephen F. Ungavarsky, Secretary

Permanent staff: 25	Membership: 96,800
Date founded: 1890	Membership dues: NI
Branches: 922 regional	Scope: national

FIRST CATHOLIC SLOVAK UNION OF THE UNITED STATES AND CANADA (cont'd)

Special requirements for membership: Catholic, Slavonic nationality

Nature of organization: fraternal

Publications: *Union* (Jednota), 1929– (weekly); *Almanac* (annual); also publishes a calendar

Major conventions/meetings: national convention (triennial)

Comments: Major purpose is to provide life insurance benefits to members. Other objectives are to unite Slovak Catholics in the U.S., to preserve the Slovak heritage and culture, and to provide social activities, camps, scholarship programs, and training programs. An archival collection is maintained.

JUNIOR SLOVAK CATHOLIC SOKOL

205 Madison Street
Passaic, New Jersey 07055

Permanent staff: NI	Membership: NI
Date founded: NI	Membership dues: NI
Branches: NI	Scope: national

Publications: *Priatel Dietok* (The Children's Friend), 1911– (monthly)

Affiliations: Slovak Catholic School

Comments: Provides activities that are social, recreational, athletic in nature as a junior division of the Slovak Catholic Sokol.

LADIES' PENNSYLVANIA SLOVAK CATHOLIC UNION

I.B.E. Building, Room 922
Wilkes-Barre, Pennsylvania 18701   (717) 823-3513

Principal officers: Irma A. Vrbancic, President
Cecilia Wysocki, Secretary
Cecilia Sarocky, Treasurer

Permanent staff: NI	Membership: 16,340
Date founded: 1900	Membership dues: vary
Branches: licensed in 9 states	Scope: national

Special requirements for membership: Slovak women

Affiliations: Slovak Catholic Federation

Comments: Major purpose is to provide life insurance benefits to members. The organization is also active in various charitable and relief projects—e.g., assisting the aged and handicapped, aiding the church and religious orders, supporting SS Cyril and Methodius Academy, contributing to Slovak Seminary in Rome.

THE NATIONAL SLOVAK SOCIETY OF THE U.S.A.

516 Court Place
Pittsburgh, Pennsylvania 15219   (412) 281-5728

Principal officers: John H. Pankuch, President
William W. Ciesar, Executive Vice President
Rudolph J. Pallan, Executive Secretary

Permanent staff: 15	Membership: 25,000
Date founded: 1890	Membership dues: on insurance basis
Branches: 21 state	Scope: national

Special requirements for membership: physical examination (age limitation: 16-65)

Nature of organization: cultural, recreational, sport, fraternal, scholarly, youth

Publications: *National News*, 1900– (biweekly)

Affiliations: Slovak World Congress; Fraternal Congress

Major conventions/meetings: quadrennial convention

Comments: The major purpose of this organization is to provide insurance benefits for members. It also provides social activities and grants scholarships. Until 1914 the organization was known as the National Slavonic Society. A library of 480 volumes and an archival collection are maintained.

PENNSYLVANIA SLOVAK CATHOLIC UNION (PSCU)
    173 North Main Street
    Wilkes-Barre, Pennsylvania 18701   (717) 822-7694

Principal officers: Stephen J. Kavulich, President
                    Leo Dusheck, Executive Vice President
                    Martin Podskoch, Executive Secretary

Permanent staff: 4   Membership: 18,000
Date founded: 1893   Membership dues: rated as of age at entry
Branches: 420 regional   Scope: national

Special requirements for membership: of Slovak descent and Catholic faith

Nature of organization: fraternal

Publications: *Brotherhood*, 1899– (monthly)

Affiliations: Pennsylvania Fraternal Congress; Slovak Catholic Federation of America; Slovak
    League of America

Major conventions/meetings: quadrennial convention

Comments: The organization's objectives are to promote the Catholic faith (particularly
    among those of Slovak descent); to preserve the Slovak language, culture and traditions;
    and to provide assistance to needy members. The organization was formerly known as
    the Pennsylvania Slovak Roman and Greek Catholic Union. It awards two $500.00
    scholarships to high school seniors.

PRESBYTERIAN BENEFICIAL UNION (PBU)
    1700 Walnut Street
    Philadelphia, Pennsylvania 19103   (301) 287-6497

Principal officers: Millan D. Stoller, President
                    Michael Vircsik, Executive Vice President
                    Andrew Brindzak, Executive Secretary

Permanent staff: 3   Membership: 1,500
Date founded: 1901   Membership dues: NI
Branches: 50   Scope: national

Special requirements for membership: Protestant; under the age of 60

Nature of organization: fraternal

Publications: *Calvin*, 1907– (monthly); also publishes books

Affiliations: Presbyterian Church

Major conventions/meetings: quadrennial convention

Comments: The major aim of the organization is to provide insurance benefits for its members.
    Until 1964 the name of the organization was the Slovak Calvinistic Presbyterian Union.
    It grants some scholarships to needy students.

SLOVAK-AMERICAN CULTURAL CENTER
    339 East 75th Street
    New York, New York 10021   (212) 744-1367

Principal officers: Rudolf Makel, President
                    Joseph Ihnat, Vice President
                    Stefan Palo, Secretary

Permanent staff: NI   Membership: 250
Date founded: 1967   Membership dues: $6.00 (annual)
Branches: NI   Scope: national

Special requirements for membership: Slovak descent

Nature of organization: educational, cultural

Publications: *Slobodna Tribuna* (Free Tribune), 1972– (quarterly); *Slova Press Digest*, 1968–
    (quarterly)

Affiliations: World Slovak Congress

SLOVAK-AMERICAN CULTURAL CENTER (cont'd)

Major conventions/meetings: annual

Comments: Conducts seminars and conferences, disseminates literature, and provides social activities that promote the Slovak heritage in the United States. The organization also sponsors athletic events and grants awards for cultural endeavors in various fields.

SLOVAK AMERICAN HERITAGE

471 Morgantown Street
Uniontown, Pennsylvania 15401   (412) 438-0697

Principal officers: John Bohunisky, President
Tom Hunchak, Vice President
Elizabeth Holly, Secretary
Albert Opest, Treasurer

Permanent staff: none   Membership: 15,000
Date founded: 1970   Membership dues: none
Branches: none   Scope: regional

Special requirements for membership: "To work for the promotion of Slovak culture in America."

Nature of organization: cultural, social

Publications: none

Comments: The organization's objectives are to establish and promote Slovak studies and cultural groups on the secondary and college level. It grants scholarships, sponsors Slovak activities (such as the Miss Slovak Heritage Pageants), and gives an annual Slovak Heritage Award.

SLOVAK CATHOLIC FEDERATION

2555 Wieneke Road
Saginaw, Michigan 48603   (517) 799-7910

Principal officers: Rev. Joseph V. Adamec, President
Rev. Msgr. Joseph A. Krispinsky, Vice President
Rev. George A. Jurica, Secretary

Permanent staff: none   Membership: unknown
Date founded: 1911   Membership dues: $1.00 individual;
Branches: NI $5.00 society; $10.00 parish
                                      Scope: international

Special requirements for membership: interest in Catholic activity among Slovak people

Nature of organization: religious

Publications: *Good Shepherd*, 1927– (bimonthly)

Affiliations: United States Catholic Conference

Major conventions/meetings: biennial

Comments: Members of the federation include parishes, Slovak-American organizations, and individuals endorsing Catholicism and aid to exiled or destitute Slovaks. It publishes Slovak literature, awards SS. Cyril and Methodius Awards for contributions to the advancement of the Slovak people, and sponsors Slovak refugee boys in training for the priesthood.

SLOVAK CATHOLIC SOKOL (SCS)

205 Madison Street
Passaic, New Jersey 07055   (201) 777-2605

Principal officers: Tiber T. Kovalovsky, Supreme Secretary

Permanent staff: 21   Membership: 51,000
Date founded: 1905   Membership dues: NI
Branches: 18   Scope: national

Special requirements for membership: of Slovak or Slav descent

Nature of organization: social, recreational, sport

SLOVAK CATHOLIC SOKOL (SCS) (cont'd)

Publications: *Katolicky Sokol*, 1915– (weekly); *Children's Friend*, 1911– (monthly); also publishes books

Major conventions/meetings: quadrennial convention; annual meeting

Comments: Major goal is to unite Catholic Slovak-Americans in social and recreational activities. The organization sponsors athletic events and provides scholarships. It also maintains a library collection.

SLOVAK EASTERN CATHOLIC SYNOD OF AMERICA
515 West Main
Monongahela, Pennsylvania 15063   (412) 258-6415
Principal officers: Ivan Dornic, President
                        Peter Haletsky, Executive Vice President
                        George Polak, Executive Secretary

Permanent staff: none   Membership: 5,611
Date founded: 1967   Membership dues: donations
Branches: none   Scope: national

Special requirements for membership: must be Catholic, of the Byzantine Slovak Rite

Nature of organization: educational, cultural, religious, recreational, youth

Publications: none

Affiliations: Slovak World Congress

Major conventions/meetings: annual conference

Comments: The major objectives of the organization are to preserve and promote the Byzantine Slovak religion in the United States, to preserve the Slovak-American heritage, to assist Slovak youth in finding employment or gaining admission to college, and to endorse political candidates who will most benefit the Slovak American while in office. The organization was known until 1971 as the Slovak G. C. Congress. It sponsors courses in history of St. Cyril and St. Methodius, a Slovak Institute, and a national newspaper, and it organizes missions in major cities. It sponsors a camping program and language and culture schools, and it grants scholarships to Slovak-American youth. It grants an annual SS. Cyril and Methodius Award. Maintains a library of 1,210 volumes.

SLOVAK FRANCISCAN FATHERS
232 South Home Avenue
Pittsburgh, Pennsylvania 15202

Permanent staff: NI   Membership: NI
Date founded: 1924   Membership dues: NI
Branches: NI   Scope: regional

Nature of organization: religious

Publications: *Listy Svateho Frantiska* (Leaflets of St. Francis), 1924– (monthly)

Comments: Publishes materials of a religious or spiritual nature. Also disseminates educational materials for members of Slovak Catholic parishes.

SLOVAK INSTITUTE
2900 East Boulevard
Cleveland, Ohio 14404

Principal officers: Jerome Koval, President
                        Andrew Pier, Director
                        Karol Strmen, Secretary

Permanent staff: none   Membership: NI
Date founded: 1952   Membership dues: NI
Branches: 1   Scope: national

Special requirements for membership: none

Nature of organization: cultural

Publications: *Bridge*, 1953– (quarterly)

SLOVAK INSTITUTE (cont'd)

Affiliations: none

Major conventions/meetings: none

Comments: The institute aims to preserve and promote Slovak culture in the United States. It publishes materials (history, literature, etc.) on Slovak studies and maintains a library of 10,000 volumes and an archival collection.

SLOVAK LEAGUE OF AMERICA (SLA)

313 Ridge Avenue
Middletown, Pennsylvania 17057   (717) 944-9933

Principal officers: Edward J. Behuncik, President
                      Milan V. Blazek, Executive Vice President
                      Joseph Pauco, Executive Secretary

Permanent staff: 1   Membership: NI
Date founded: 1907   Membership dues: NI
Branches: 14 regional; 10 state; 67 local   Scope: national

Special requirements for membership: must be of Slovak ancestry

Nature of organization: cultural, civic

Publications: *Slovakia*, 1951– (annual); also publishes books

Affiliations: none

Major conventions/meetings: annual conference; triennial convention

Comments: The organization aims to promote American-Slovak understanding and relations, to preserve Slovak traditions and culture in America, and to support freedom and independence for Slovakia. It grants scholarships through its member organizations. Maintains an archival collection.

SLOVAK NEWSPAPERS JOURNALIST'S ASSOCIATION

c/o Slovak League of America
313 Ridge Avenue
Middletown, Pennsylvania 17057

Permanent staff: NI   Membership: NI
Date founded: NI   Membership dues: NI
Branches: NI   Scope: national

Special requirements for membership: Slovak newspaper journalist

Nature of organization: professional

Affiliations: Slovak League of America

SLOVAK RELIEF FUND

c/o National Committee for Liberation of Slovakia
1065 National Press Building
Washington, D.C. 20004   (202) 347-7362

Principal officers: V. Stephen Krajcovic, President

Permanent staff: 2   Membership: NI
Date founded: 1953   Membership dues: NI
Branches: NI   Scope: national

Comments: Assists Slovaks in need, particularly those who are church members in communist Slovakia. It also helps Slovak refugees with economic and social problems of resettlement.

SLOVAK WRITERS' AND ARTISTS' ASSOCIATION

2900 East Boulevard
Cleveland, Ohio 44104   (216) 721-5300

Principal officers: Nicholas Sprinc, Secretary

SLOVAK WRITERS' AND ARTISTS' ASSOCIATION (cont'd)

Permanent staff: NI   Membership: 57
Date founded: 1954   Membership dues: NI
Branches: NI   Scope: national

Special requirements for membership: authors and artists of Slovak descent

Nature of organization: professional, cultural

Publications: *Most* (Bridge), 1954– (quarterly)

Major conventions/meetings: annual

Comments: Publishes and promotes works of Slovak authors and assists artists (including journalists, painters, editors, composers, musicians). A library on Slovak history and culture is housed in the Slovak Institute.

SOKOL GYMNASTIC UNION SOKOL OF THE U.S.A.
    276 Prospect Street,
    Box 189
    East Orange, New Jersey 07019   (201) 676-0280
Principal officers: Andrew Venglarchik, Jr., President
                John Bagel, Vice President
                John Spopci, Secretary

Permanent staff: 10   Membership: 23,000
Date founded: 1896   Membership dues: variable premium
Branches: 200   plus dues
                                    Scope: national

Nature of organization: educational, fraternal, recreational

Publications: *Sokol Times*, 1905– (biweekly)

Major conventions/meetings: quadrennial

Comments: The major goals of the organization are to provide insurance benefits to members and to promote Sokol ideals, history, literature, and physical culture. Social activities, lectures, and schools for youth instruction are maintained. It sponsors gymnastic schools and bowling tournaments, and it awards scholarships. An annual award is granted from the Milan Getting Scholarship Fund.

UNITED LUTHERAN SOCIETY
    223 East Main Street
    Ligonier, Pennsylvania 15658   (412) 238-9505
Principal officers: Daniel M. Zornan, President

Permanent staff: NI   Membership: 14,000
Date founded: 1962   Membership dues: NI
Branches: NI   Scope: national

Special requirements for membership: Lutherans of Slovak descent

Nature of organization: fraternal

Publications: *United Lutheran* (monthly)

Comments: Major purpose is to provide life insurance benefits to members. The organization was formed by merger of the Evangelical Slovak Women's Union and the Slovak Evangelical Union.

SLOVENIAN-AMERICAN ORGANIZATIONS

Additional information on Slovenian-American organizations may be obtained from the American Slovenian Catholic Union (351-53 North Chicago Street, Joliet, Illinois 60431). Regional and local information may be obtained from *Greater Cleveland Nationalities Directory 1974* (Cleveland: Sun Newspapers and the Nationalities Services Center, 1974) and *Ethnic Directory I* (Detroit: Southeastern Michigan Regional Ethnic Heritage Studies Center, 1973).

AMERICAN FRATERNAL UNION
111 South Fourth Avenue, East
Ely, Minnesota 55731   (218) 365-3110
Principal officers: F. J. Kress, President
                       Douglas L. Aldrich, Secretary

Permanent staff: NI   Membership: 22,441
Date founded: 1898   Membership dues: vary
Branches: in 17 states   Scope: national

Special requirements for membership: Slovenian descent

Nature of organization: fraternal, charitable

Publications: *Nova Doba* (New Era), 1925– (semimonthly)

Comments: Major objective is to provide life insurance benefits to members. The organization also assists the aged financially, supports various disaster relief projects and health projects. Maintains a financial aid program for Slovenian students in the form of grants and scholarships. It also maintains a recreational program for youth and other members.

AMERICAN MUTUAL LIFE ASSOCIATION (AMLA)
6401 St. Clair Avenue
Cleveland, Ohio 44103   (216) 361-2014
Principal officers: John A. Kodrich, Supreme Secretary

Permanent staff: NI   Membership: 21,300
Date founded: 1910   Membership dues: vary
Branches: 50 local groups   Scope: national

Special requirements for membership: Slovenian descent

Nature of organization: fraternal

Major conventions/meetings: quadrennial

Comments: The major purpose of the organization is to provide life insurance benefits to members. It also provides health and recreational facilities for members, as well as social and cultural activities designed to unite Slovene Americans and to preserve the Slovene heritage and tradition in the United States.

AMERICAN SLOVENE CLUB
c/o Mary Grlic
18220 Marcella
Cleveland, Ohio 44119   (216) 481-4436
Principal officers: Mary Grlic, President
                       Mrs. Charles Lausche, Secretary

Special requirements for membership: Slovenian descent

Nature of organization: cultural, social

Comments: The major purpose of the club is to promote the Slovenian culture and heritage in the United States.

AMERICAN SLOVENIAN CATHOLIC UNION (KSKJ)
351-53 North Chicago Street
Joliet, Illinois 60431
Principal officers: Joseph J. Nemanich, President
                       Edward J. Kucic, Executive Vice President
                       Robert L. Kosmerl, Executive Secretary

Permanent staff: 12   Membership: 44,421
Date founded: 1894   Membership dues: based on age, amount
Branches: 20 state; 154 local   of life insurance, etc.
                                        Scope: national, local

Special requirements for membership: must be Catholic in good standing, not more than 60 years of age, and of sound health

AMERICAN SLOVENIAN CATHOLIC UNION (KSKJ) (cont'd)

Nature of organization: fraternal

Publications: *Amerikanski Slovenec* (weekly; biweekly in July)

Affiliations: National Fraternal Congress; various state congresses

Major conventions/meetings: quadrennial convention

Comments: The major purpose of the organization is to provide insurance benefits to members and their families. It encourages adherence to the Catholic Church and preservation of the Slovenian language and culture. Until 1963 it was known as the Grand Carniolian Slovenian Catholic Union. It grants scholarships for religious vocations and college scholarships to members.

LEAGUE OF SLOVENE AMERICANS, INC.
P.O. Box 32
Brooklyn, New York 11227

Permanent staff: NI
Date founded: NI
Branches: NI

Membership: NI
Membership dues: NI
Scope: national

SLOVENE FRANCISCAN FATHERS
1400 Main Street
Lemont, Illinois 60439

Nature of organization: religious

Publications: *Ave Maria*, 1909– (monthly)

SLOVENE NATIONAL BENEFIT SOCIETY (SNPJ)
2657 South Lawndale Avenue
Chicago, Illinois 60623   (312) 762-4904

Principal officers: Joseph L. Culkar, President
               Frank Groser, Secretary

Permanent staff: 35
Date founded: 1904
Branches: 35 local groups

Membership: 21,300
Membership dues: varies
Scope: national

Special requirements for membership: Slovenian descent

Nature of organization: fraternal

Publications: *Prosveta*, 1906– (daily); *Voice of Youth*, 1922– (monthly)

Major conventions/meetings: quadrennial

Comments: Major objective is to provide life insurance benefits to members. Also sponsors a recreational center, assistance to members in need, and a scholarship program for students of Slovenian descent. Supports athletic programs and social, youth, and cultural activities. Pays Medicare for elderly members.

SLOVENIAN AMERICAN RADIO CLUB (SARC)
2032 West Cermak Road
Chicago, Illinois 60608   (312) 847-6679

Principal officers: Ludwig A. Leskovar, President
               Stanley Simrayh, Executive Vice President
               Mary Foys Lauretig, Executive Secretary

Permanent staff: 1
Date founded: 1950
Branches: none

Membership: 3,500
Membership dues: $2.00 (annual)
Scope: national

Special requirements for membership: none

Nature of organization: cultural

Publications: *New World Herald*, 1940– (irregular)

Affiliations: none

Major conventions/meetings: annual convention

SLOVENIAN AMERICAN RADIO CLUB (SARC) (cont'd)

Comments: The organization attempts to preserve the Slovenian culture and language in the United States by supporting Slovenian radio broadcasts and by sponsoring social and musical activities. It also supports political freedom for Slovenia, organizes annual Slovenian celebrations for the Midwest, and organizes chartered flights to the homeland for members. Until 1952 the organization was known as the American Friends of Slovenian Songs. It sponsors an annual Slovenian Award and maintains an archival collection.

SLOVENIAN FEDERATION OF SOCIALIST LABOR PARTY

14302 Schoolcraft Avenue
Detroit, Michigan 48227

Nature of organization: political

SLOVENIAN NATIONAL ART GUILD

c/o John J. Stuchal, President
20451 Naumann Avenue
Cleveland, Ohio 44123   (216) 481-1902

Principal officers: John J. Stuchal, President

Permanent staff: NI   Membership: NI
Date founded: NI   Membership dues: NI
Branches: NI   Scope: national

Nature of organization: cultural

SLOVENIAN RESEARCH CENTER OF AMERICA, INC. (SRCA)

29227 Eddy Road
Willoughby Hills, Ohio 44092   (216) 944-7237

Principal officers: Giles Edward Gobetz, Director
                       F. Kolednik, Associate Director
                       Milena Gobetz, Secretary

Permanent staff: 52 volunteers   Membership: NI
Date founded: 1951   Membership dues: none
Branches: NI   Scope: international

Special requirements for membership: "active involvement in at least one of the institute's projects"

Nature of organization: educational, scholarly, research, publication

Publications: publishes articles and reports

Affiliations: EURAM Books; United Slovenian Society, Inc.

Major conventions/meetings: annual conference

Comments: The goals of the center are to promote the best interests of and knowledge of the Slovenians in the United States. It conducts research on Slovenian immigrants, publishes books, articles, reports, and teaching aids about Slovenian history, education, and culture. It also sponsors lectures, classes, and conferences in Slovenian studies. A 3,000-volume library and an archival collection are maintained.

SLOVENIAN WOMEN'S UNION OF AMERICA (SWU)

1937 West Cermak Road
Chicago, Illinois 60608   (312) 247-2014

Principal officers: Antonia Turek, President
                       Marie A. Floryan, Executive Vice President
                       Fanika Humar, Executive Secretary

Permanent staff: 2   Membership: 10,140
Date founded: 1926   Membership dues: varies
Branches: 91   Scope: national

Nature of organization: fraternal

SLOVENIAN WOMEN'S UNION OF AMERICA (SWU) (cont'd)

Publications: *The Dawn*, 1928– (monthly, except combined issue in July-August)

Affiliations: Illinois Fraternal Congress

Major conventions/meetings: triennial convention

Comments: The objectives are to unite Slovenian women in the United States and to assist Slovenians in obtaining citizenship. It grants four or five annual $200.00 scholarships to Slovenian-American students and it assists with the funeral expenses of deceased members.

UNITED SLOVENIAN SOCIETIES
591 East 185th Street
Cleveland, Ohio 44119   (216) 481-7512

Principal officers: Tony Petkovsek, President
                      Cecelia Dolgan, Secretary

Special requirements for membership: Slovenian organization

Nature of organization: cultural, social, recreational, fraternal

Comments: Unites and coordinates the activities of various Slovenian societies in the Cleveland area.

THE WESTERN SLAVONIC ASSOCIATION (WSA)
5809 West 38th Avenue
Denver, Colorado 80212   (303) 421-3320

Principal officers: Anthony Jersin, President
                      Matthew E. Volk, Executive Vice President
                      Mary F. Johns, Executive Secretary

Permanent staff: 5   Membership: 10,511
Date founded: 1908   Membership dues: NI
Branches: 25 national; 15 state; 3 local Scope: national

Nature of organization: fraternal

Publications: *Fraternal Voice* (monthly)

Affiliations: National Fraternal Congress

Major conventions/meetings: quadrennial national convention

Comments: The major purpose of the organization is to provide life insurance benefits to its members. It also sponsors social activities and grants scholarships to high school seniors.

SPANISH-AMERICAN ORGANIZATIONS

*See also Costa Rican-American, Cuban-American,
Mexican-American, and Puerto Rican-American Organizations*

Additional information on Spanish-American organizations in the United States may be obtained from *Directory of Spanish Speaking Community Organizations* (Washington, D.C.: Cabinet Committee on Opportunity for the Spanish Speaking, 1970). Local organizations are listed in *Greater Cleveland Nationalities Directory 1974* (Cleveland: Sun Newspapers and the Nationalities Services Center, 1973).

ADVISORY COMMITTEE ON EDUCATION OF SPANISH AND MEXICAN AMERICANS
400 Maryland Avenue, S.W.
Washington, D.C. 20202   (202) 962-8566

ADVISORY COMMITTEE ON EDUCATION OF SPANISH AND MEXICAN AMERICANS (cont'd)

Permanent staff: 1
Date founded: 1967
Branches: NI

Membership: NI
Membership dues: NI
Scope: national

Affiliations: U.S. Office of Education

Major conventions/meetings: quarterly

Comments: An advisory group to the U.S. Office of Education with respect to policies and programs for the education of Mexican-Americans, Cubans, and Puerto Ricans. Sponsors nationwide conferences and publishes information on programs for the Spanish-speaking community.

AMERICAN SPANISH COMMITTEE

P.O. Box 119, Canal Street Station
New York, New York 10013   (212) 568-1191

Principal officers: Anthony F. Gonzalez, Chairman

Permanent staff: NI
Date founded: 1962
Branches: NI

Membership: NI
Membership dues: NI
Scope: national

Special requirements for membership: Spanish descent

Nature of organization: patriotic

Comments: This patriotic, anti-communist, pro-Christian organization attempts to assist and protect the civil rights of the Spanish-American community in the United States.

CENTRO HISPANO CATOLICO

130 Northeast Second Street
Miami, Florida 33132   (305) 371-5657

Principal officers: V. Rev. Orlando Fernandez, Executive Director

Permanent staff: 30
Date founded: 1959
Branches: NI

Membership: NI
Membership dues: NI
Scope: national

Nature of organization: religious, welfare, social

Comments: Also known as the Catholic-Spanish Center, this organization assists Cuban and other refugees as well as Spanish-speaking immigrants with respect to language, health and welfare, and employment opportunity.

CONFEDERATED SPANISH SOCIETIES

231 West 18th Street
New York, New York 10011   (212) 924-7177

Principal officers: Augustin Carcagente, Secretary General

Permanent staff: NI
Date founded: 1936
Branches: NI

Membership: 2,500
Membership dues: NI
Scope: national

Comments: The goal of the organization is to work for democracy in Spain and to aid political and other refugees. Also known as Sociedades Hispanos Confederadas.

COUNCIL OF SPANISH SPEAKING ORGANIZATIONS, INC.

2023 North Front Street
Philadelphia, Pennsylvania 19122   (215) 426-7985

Principal officers: Jenis M. Sierra, President
                      Serafin Mora, Executive Vice President
                      Nicky Lopez, Executive Secretary

Permanent staff: 15
Date founded: 1962
Branches: none

Membership: 3,000
Membership dues: none
Scope: regional

COUNCIL OF SPANISH SPEAKING ORGANIZATIONS, INC. (cont'd)

Special requirements for membership: none

Nature of organization: multi-purpose

Publications: *The Voice of Concilio*, 1968– (quarterly); *Puerto Rican Week Festival Journal*, 1965– (annual)

Affiliations: none

Major conventions/meetings: none

Comments: The council serves as a liaison between the Spanish-speaking community and society at large, also coordinating and advising the activities and officers of member organizations. It sponsors programs in employment placement and training, various social services, youth activities, health and family planning, etc.

DIVISION FOR THE SPANISH SPEAKING (United States Catholic Conference)
1312 Massachusetts Avenue, N.W.
Washington, D.C. 20005   (202) 659-6876

Principal officers: Paul Sedillo, Jr., National Director

Permanent staff: NI   Membership: 190
Date founded: 1945   Membership dues: NI
Branches: NI   Scope: national

Nature of organization: religious, welfare

Affiliations: U. S. Catholic Conference

Comments: Diocesan directors operate a consultation service for Spanish-speaking parishes of the Catholic Church. Sponsors religious, health and welfare, housing, employment, and educational programs and services. The organization was known as the Bishops' Committee for the Spanish-Speaking and also absorbed the Bishops' Committee for Migrant Workers. Acts as a liaison to religious, educational, and federal institutions and the Spanish-speaking community. A small library is maintained.

HISPANO YOUTH CONGRESS
431 West Colfax Avenue
Denver, Colorado 80219   (303) 292-5190

Principal officers: Mitch Ulibarri

Permanent staff: NI   Membership: NI
Date founded: 1968   Membership dues: NI
Branches: NI   Scope: regional

Special requirements for membership: Spanish-speaking

Nature of organization: cultural, educational

Comments: Purpose of the organization is to promote the Spanish tradition and heritage in the United States and to help Spanish-speaking Americans of the Southwest improve educational and employment opportunities.

MOVIMIENTO FAMILIAR CRISTIANO
1655 West Jackson Boulevard
Chicago, Illinois 60612   (312) 829-6102

Principal officers: Herman Machicado (Joint Presidents)
Marila Machicado

Permanent staff: 1   Membership: 2,000
Date founded: 1969   Membership dues: NI
Branches: NI   Scope: national

Publications: *MFC-USA Bulletin* (monthly)

Affiliations: Christian Family Movement

Comments: A family service agency in the Spanish community sponsoring training and dialogue sessions for husband and wife teams. Its literature is published in English and Spanish.

NATIONAL LATIN AMERICAN FEDERATION
P.O. Box 342
Cheyenne, Wyoming 82001   (307) 634-6293
Principal officers: Dolores Arenas, President

Permanent staff: NI   Membership: NI
Date founded: 1956   Membership dues: NI
Branches: NI   Scope: national

Nature of organization: educational, civil rights

Major conventions/meetings: monthly

Comments: The federation is made up primarily of Mexican-Americans, Puerto Ricans, and
    Cubans interested in seeking equality in educational and employment opportunity
    and social and political justice for the Spanish-speaking community.

PACIFIC LATIN AMERICAN DISTRICT COUNCIL OF THE ASSEMBLIES
OF GOD
850 East La Habra Boulevard
La Habra, California 90631   (213) 649-3783
Principal officers: Jose Girón, President
                       Victor De León, Vice President
                       José Ibarra, Secretary

Permanent staff: 7   Membership: 6,860
Date founded: 1972   Membership dues: none
Branches: none   Scope: regional

Special requirements for membership: none

Nature of organization: religious

Publications: *The Newsletter*, 1973– (bimonthly)

Affiliations: General Council of the Assemblies of God

Major conventions/meetings: biennial convention

Comments: A religious organization devoted to promoting public worship of God and
    evangelizing the Latin American community. It sponsors institutes for ministers,
    youth camps, seminars, departmental seminars, Sunday Schools, youth meetings,
    women's meetings, etc.

SPANISH AMERICAN ASSOCIATION
221 Swan Street
Buffalo, New York 14204   (716) 852-7459
Principal officers: Augustine Olivencia, President

Permanent staff: NI   Membership: 13 affiliates
Date founded: 1959   Membership dues: NI
Branches: NI   Scope: regional

Special requirements for membership: Spanish speaking and Spanish descent

Nature of organization: welfare, civil rights

Affiliations: Association for Mutual Help; Minority Coalition; Spanish Welfare Association;
    Puerto Rican Training Association; Mexican Club

Major conventions/meetings: monthly

Comments: Attempts to assist the Spanish community with financial or social problems and to
    preserve the Spanish identity in the United States.

SPANISH BENEVOLENT SOCIETY "LA NACIONAL"
239 West 14th Street
New York, New York 10011   (201) 929-7873
Principal officers: Juan Alvarez, Secretary

Permanent staff: NI   Membership: 3,500
Date founded: NI   Membership dues: NI
Branches: NI   Scope: national

SPANISH BENEVOLENT SOCIETY "LA NACIONAL" (cont'd)

Special requirements for membership: Spanish descent

Nature of organization: fraternal

Publications: *Plus Ultra* (annual)

Comments: Major purpose is to provide life insurance benefits to members. The organization also promotes the Spanish culture and heritage in the United States. It conducts Spanish language institute programs and maintains a 1,200-volume library.

SPANISH INSTITUTE
684 Park Avenue
New York, New York 10021   (212) 628-0420

Principal officers: Silvia F. Fernandez, Executive Secretary

Permanent staff' 7   Membership: 600
Date founded: 1954   Membership dues: NI
Branches: NI   Scope: national

Nature of organization: cultural, educational, scholarly

Publications: *Annual*

Comments: The organization conducts courses, art exhibits, concerts, and lectures on the language and culture of Spain. It sponsors a Research Fund of Art and Archaeology, awards graduate fellowships, and sponsors ophthalmologists from Spain on internships in American clinics. A library of 5,000 volumes is maintained.

SPANISH REFUGEE AID
80 East 11th Street
New York, New York 10003   (212) 674-7451

Principal officers: Nancy Macdonald, Secretary

Permanent staff: 7   Membership: NI
Date founded: 1953   Membership dues: NI
Branches: NI   Scope: national

Special requirements for membership: must be at least 21 years of age

Nature of organization: relief

Comments: The organization sponsors fund-raising activities to benefit refugees. It also operates a center for the aged.

UNION ESPAÑOLA BENEFICA DE CALIFORNIA
827 Broadway
San Francisco, California 94115   (415) 781-9147

Principal officers: Al Usoz, Secretary

Permanent staff: NI   Membership: NI
Date founded: NI   Membership dues: NI
Branches: NI   Scope: national

Nature of organization: fraternal

Comments: Major purpose is to provide life insurance benefits to members.

UNITED COUNCIL OF SPANISH SPEAKING ORGANIZATIONS, INC. (UCSSO)
829 Main Street
Martinez, California 94553   (415) 229-2210

Principal officers: Joe Ray Ramirez, President
Ernie Quintana, Vice President
Adelina Tafoya, Secretary

Permanent staff: 24   Membership: 32 organizations; 800
Date founded: 1966   individuals
Branches: 3   Membership dues: none
Scope: regional

UNITED COUNCIL OF SPANISH SPEAKING ORGANIZATIONS, INC. (UCSSO) (cont'd)

Special requirements for membership: "Any Spanish speaking organization based in Contra Costa, established at least one year prior to request of membership, and having a minimum of 15 members."

Nature of organization: social, educational, cultural, economic, youth

Publications: *The Enterado*, 1967– (monthly)

Affiliations: G. I. Forum, LULAC, Guadalupanas, Cursillistas

Major conventions/meetings: none

Comments: Attempts to better the education, employment, health, housing, and civil rights of the Spanish-speaking community. The organization has a Project Office funded by O.E.O. for community service; the Transportation Office provides transportation to county clinics and hospitals.

U.S. SPANISH MERCHANTS' ASSOCIATION
88 Clinton Street
New York, New York 10002 (212) 677-7110
Principal officers: Eduardo Roques, Executive Officer

Permanent staff: NI
Date founded: 1963
Branches: NI

Membership: 425
Membership dues: NI
Scope: national

Nature of organization: economic

Comments: Purpose of the organization is to assist small businessmen of Spanish descent in the New York area. It is also known as the Union de Comerceantes.

SWEDISH-AMERICAN ORGANIZATIONS

See also Scandinavian-American Organizations

Additional information on Swedish-American organizations in the United States may be obtained from the Office of the Swedish Embassy (600 New Hampshire Avenue, Suite 1200, Washington, D.C. 20037) and from *American-Swedish Handbook, Vol. VIII* (Rock Island, Illinois: Augustana Swedish Institute, 1973). Regional and local organizations are listed in *Greater Cleveland Nationalities Directory 1974* (Cleveland: Sun Newspapers and the Nationalities Services Center, 1974) and *Ethnic Directory I* (Detroit: Southeastern Michigan Regional Ethnic Heritage Studies Center, 1973).

AMERICAN DAUGHTERS OF SWEDEN
c/o Miss Ione M. Gustafson
5049 North Winchester Avenue
Chicago, Illinois 60640
Principal officers: Ione M. Gustafson, Recording Secretary

Permanent staff: NI
Date founded: 1926
Branches: NI

Membership: NI
Membership dues: $4.50 plus tax
Scope: national

Special requirements for membership: women of Swedish descent

Nature of organization: cultural

Affiliations: Federation of Women's Clubs

AMERICAN DAUGHTERS OF SWEDEN (cont'd)

Comments: Purpose is to unite Swedish women in the United States in social and cultural activities that preserve the Swedish heritage and tradition. The organization also supports civic and educational programs and participates in an annual Holiday Folk Fair, and an annual bazaar. A scholarship program for young women of Swedish descent who wish to study Swedish language and literature is maintained at the University of Chicago, Augustana College, and North Park College.

AMERICAN SOCIETY OF SWEDISH ENGINEERS (ASSE)

250 Park Avenue, Suite 727
New York, New York 10017   (217) 687-4020

Principal officers: Erik G. M. Tornqvist, President
Kjell Lagerström, Vice President
Leif G. Wikstrom, Secretary

Permanent staff: NI   Membership: 300
Date founded: 1888   Membership dues: NI
Branches: NI   Scope: national

Special requirements for membership: by vote of the Board of Directors

Nature of organization: professional

Publications: *Bulletin* (annual)

Major conventions/meetings: annual

Comments: Attempts to unite Swedish-American professionals in the field of engineering. Awards annual John Ericsson Medal to a Swedish subject or Swedish-American for outstanding contributions in technology or science, and the ASSE Award to the outstanding graduate in the field. Supports Scandinavian academic institutions and various relief and welfare programs.

AMERICAN SWEDISH HISTORICAL FOUNDATION

1900 Pattison Avenue
Philadelphia, Pennsylvania 19145   (215) 389-1776

Principal officers: Nils Y. Wessell, President
Esther C. Meixner, Executive Secretary

Permanent staff: 6   Membership: 1,000
Date founded: 1926   Membership dues: $10.00 (annual)
Branches: none   Scope: national

Special requirements for membership: none

Nature of organization: cultural, educational, historical

Publications: *American Swedish Historical Foundation Yearbook*, 1945– (annual); *American Swedish Historical Foundation Museum Newsletter*, 1930s– (irregular)

Affiliations: American Association of Museums; Philadelphia Museum Council; Philadelphia Cultural Alliance

Major conventions/meetings: annual convention

Comments: The foundation attempts to recognize contributions to the United States by Swedish Americans with respect to cultural, economic, sociological, and technological development. It strives to promote the Swedish culture in the United States and sponsors an exchange program for youth in various professional training programs. Maintains a museum on the history of Swedish-Americans, a 12,500-volume library, and an archival collection.

AMERICAN SWEDISH INSTITUTE (ASI)

2600 Park Avenue
Minneapolis, Minnesota 55407   (612) 339-0621

Principal officers: Gustave F. Johnson, President
O. Harold Swanson, Executive Vice President
David A. LaVine, Executive Secretary

AMERICAN SWEDISH INSTITUTE (ASI) (cont'd)

Permanent staff: 10

Date founded: 1929

Branches: none

Membership: 5,600

Membership dues: $10.00 single (annual);
$15.00 couple (annual)

Scope: NI

Special requirements for membership: none

Nature of organization: cultural

Publications: *Happenings* (9 issues per year)

Affiliations: none

Major conventions/meetings: none

Comments: Aims to "increase awareness of the Swedish cultural heritage" through Swedish language classes, films, lectures, cultural activities (music and dance) and genealogical research. The institute is housed in a historic landmark building. It sponsors charter flights to Scandinavia and cash scholarships for Swedish language study. A library of 3,000 volumes and an archival collection are maintained.

AMERICAN UNION OF SWEDISH SINGERS (AUSS)

6132 North Winchester Avenue

Chicago, Illinois 60626   (312) 238-9500

Principal officers: Henry Granat, President

C. E. Anderson, Executive Vice President

C. Anton Lindstrom, Executive Secretary

Permanent staff: 7

Date founded: 1892

Branches: 3 regional; 26 local

Membership: 730

Membership dues: $5.00 (annual)

Scope: national

Special requirements for membership: none

Nature of organization: cultural

Publications: *Musiktidning: A Musical Journal in English and Swedish*, 1905– (monthly except July and August)

Affiliations: none

Major conventions/meetings: quadrennial convention

Comments: This union of 32 singing groups attempts to preserve the Swedish culture through music. It also sponsors singing concert tours to Scandinavian countries.

AUGUSTANA HISTORICAL SOCIETY

Augustana College

Rock Island, Illinois 61201

Principal officers: Dorothy Liljegren, President

Betsey Brodahl, Vice President and Secretary

Permanent staff: NI

Date founded: 1930

Branches: 1

Membership: 150

Membership dues: $5.00 (annual)

Scope: national

Nature of organization: cultural, educational, religious

Publications: *Augustana Historical Society Publications* (irregular)

Affiliations: Augustana Evangelical Lutheran Church

Major conventions/meetings: annual

Comments: Sponsors Scandinavian research in the United States, particularly in historical and religious studies. The society absorbed the former Augustana Swedish Institute.

DELAWARE SWEDISH COLONIAL SOCIETY

The Hendrickson House

606 Church Street

Wilmington, Delaware 19801

DELAWARE SWEDISH COLONIAL SOCIETY (cont'd)

Permanent staff: NI	Membership: NI
Date founded: 1938	Membership dues: $2.00 (annual);
Branches: NI	$100.00 life membership
	Scope: state

Nature of organization: cultural, historical

Comments: Provides annual commemoration of the anniversary of the first landing of Swedes in the Delaware Colony on March 29. The organization also collects and preserves sources, records, etc., documenting Swedish immigration and colonial life in the Delaware River Valley settlements. It supported financially the restoration of Hendrickson House, a Swedish stone house built in 1690. Maintains a library collection.

THE FOLKE BERNADOTTE MEMORIAL FOUNDATION
Gustavus Adolphus College
St. Peter, Minnesota 56082

Permanent staff: NI	Membership: NI
Date founded: 1950	Membership dues: NI
Branches: NI	Scope: national

Comments: Commemorates the memory of the Swedish humanitarian Folke Bernadotte. Supports Gustavus Adolphus College and maintains the Folke Bernadotte Library on its campus.

INTERNATIONAL ORDER OF GOOD TEMPLARS
Utica, New York 13501

Permanent staff: NI	Membership: NI
Date founded: 1851	Membership dues: NI
Branches: NI	Scope: international, national

Nature of organization: fraternal

Comments: Founded as a total abstinence organization by Swedish immigrants.

SEAMEN OF SWEDEN, INC.
825 Third Avenue
New York, New York 10022

Principal officers: G. Westlin, Secretary-Treasurer

Permanent staff: NI	Membership: NI
Date founded: 1948	Membership dues: NI
Branches: NI	Scope: national

Special requirements for membership: seamen of Swedish descent

Nature of organization: recreational, welfare

Major conventions/meetings: annual

Comments: The organization operates the Swedish Seamen's Center in Brooklyn where boarding and recreational facilities are available for Swedish seamen.

SVEABORG SWEDISH-AMERICAN SOCIETY
3524 Milford Mill Road
Baltimore, Maryland 21207   (301) 922-4274

Principal officers: Herman E. Westerberg, President
                      Kent Johnson, Vice President
                      Birgitta Moylan, Secretary

Permanent staff: none	Membership: 95
Date founded: 1942	Membership dues: $3.00 (annual)
Branches: none	Scope: NI

Special requirements for membership: must be of Swedish ancestry or married to someone of Swedish ancestry

Nature of organization: social, cultural

Publications: *Sveaborg Newsletter* (monthly)

SVEABORG SWEDISH-AMERICAN SOCIETY (cont'd)

Affiliations: none

Major conventions/meetings: none

Comments: The organization attempts to preserve the Swedish culture in the United States and to promote Swedish contributions to American society. It sponsors social and cultural activities.

SWEDISH-AMERICAN CHAMBER OF COMMERCE

250 Park Avenue
New York, New York 10017   (212) 687-4020

Principal officers: Claes Ankarcrona, President
                    William Werner, Vice President and Secretary

Permanent staff: NI	Membership: 700
Date founded: 1906	Membership dues: NI
Branches: 1	Scope: national

Special requirements for membership: firms or individuals must be elected to membership by the Board of Directors

Nature of organization: economic

Publications: *Newsletter* (weekly); *Trade Opportunity Bulletin*

Major conventions/meetings: annual

Comments: Promotes, facilitates, and protects trade between the United States and Sweden. Helps members deal with tariffs and other regulations, legal problems, credit information, etc.

THE SWEDISH CLUB

1920 Dexter Avenue North   (206) 283-1077 or
Seattle, Washington 98109   (206) 283-1078 or
                               (206) 283-1090

Principal officers: Josef Oscarsson, President
                    Norm Jacox, Vice President
                    Bert Holm, Secretary

Permanent staff: 44	Membership: 7,600
Date founded: 1892	Membership dues: $20.00
Branches: none	Scope: regional

Special requirements for membership: Scandinavian descent (active membership); interest and willingness to support club (associate membership)

Nature of organization: social, educational, recreational

Publications: *Swedish Club Bulletin* (monthly)

Affiliations: none

Major conventions/meetings: monthly meetings

Comments: The organization provides social, cultural, and recreational facilities designed to promote the Swedish heritage for its members. It sponsors lectures and instruction in Swedish language and folk arts. It gives financial assistance to Swedes in need and grants scholarships and loans to University of Washington students. A library of 2,000 volumes is maintained.

SWEDISH COLONIAL SOCIETY

Hall of the Historical Society of Pennsylvania
1300 Locust Street
Philadelphia, Pennsylvania 19107

Principal officers: Sandra S. Pfaff, Secretary

Permanent staff: NI	Membership: NI
Date founded: 1908	Membership dues: NI
Branches: NI	Scope: national

Special requirements for membership: persons of Swedish descent

SWEDISH COLONIAL SOCIETY (cont'd)

Nature of organization: historical, scholarly

Publications: *Charter* (quinquennial); *Bylaws* (quinquennial); *Directory* (quinquennial); also publishes books

Major conventions/meetings: annual

Comments: This historical society is interested in preserving landmarks in the Swedish-American experience, and also in erecting monuments to early and prominent Swedes. It publishes various monographs on Swedish history and immigration. Originally the majority of the members were descendants of the Swedish immigrants who settled the Colony of New Sweden on the Delaware in 1638.

SWEDISH CULTURAL SOCIETY IN AMERICA
    1123 South Courtland Avenue
    Park Ridge, Illinois 60068

Permanent staff: NI	Membership: NI
Date founded: 1910	Membership dues: NI
Branches: 9	Scope: national

Nature of organization: cultural, social

Affiliations: Riksforeningen For Svenskhetens Bevarande it Utlandet (Sweden)

Comments: Attempts to preserve the Swedish language and culture in the United States. Provides lectures, films, and music, and sponsors chartered field trips for studying Swedish immigration and Swedish-American contributions to society. Collects historical documents, photos, and other materials. Disseminates Swedish books, journals, and newspapers.

SWEDISH HISTORICAL SOCIETY OF ROCKFORD
    404 South Third Street
    Rockford, Illinois 61108   (815) 965-5984

Principal officers: Arthur G. Larson, President
                    Adolf Miller, Vice President
                    Holger Pearson, Secretary

Permanent staff: none	Membership: 160
Date founded: 1937	Membership dues: $1.00 (annual)
Branches: none	Scope: regional

Special requirements for membership: none

Nature of organization: historical

Publications: none

Affiliations: none

Major conventions/meetings: none

Comments: Preserves and promotes the Swedish heritage in the United States by operating the Erlander Home Museum, which houses valuable exhibits from Sweden. The organization sponsors an annual Swedish folk festival, grants scholarships to Swedish students, participates in community affairs, and hosts visitors from Sweden. Its Women's Auxiliary sponsors fund-raising activities.

SWEDISH PIONEER HISTORICAL SOCIETY, INC.
    5125 North Spaulding Avenue
    Chicago, Illinois 60625   (312) 583-5722

Principal officers: Paul A. Varg, President
                    Nils William Olsson, Executive Vice President
                    P. Raymond Nelson, Executive Secretary

Permanent staff: 1	Membership: 1,500
Date founded: 1950	Membership dues: $7.00 (annual);
Branches: none	$15.00 (sustaining); $250.00 (life)
	Scope: international, national

Special requirements for membership: none

SWEDISH PIONEER HISTORICAL SOCIETY, INC. (cont'd)

Nature of organization: historical

Publications: *The Swedish Pioneer Historical Quarterly*, 1950– (quarterly); also publishes books

Affiliations: will be associated with the Swedish Council of America, now organizing

Major conventions/meetings: annual meeting

Comments: The organization attempts to preserve the Swedish culture and heritage in the United States. It promotes contributions of Swedish-American pioneers, conducts research into Swedish historical studies, provides genealogical research, translates Swedish works, and publishes biographies and other materials about Swedish Americans. It sponsors tours to Sweden, seminars, travel, and academic scholarships. A 2,000-volume library is maintained.

TEXAS SWEDISH CULTURAL FOUNDATION, INC.
3400 Montrose Boulevard
P.O. Box 66327
Houston, Texas 77006

Principal officers: S. N. Ekdahl, President
Bengt Rosio, Secretary

Permanent staff: NI	Membership: NI
Date founded: 1951	Membership dues: NI
Branches: NI	Scope: state

Nature of organization: educational, cultural

Comments: Establishes scholarship programs for Swedish students to study in Texas and for Texas students and faculty to study in Sweden–in all fields of science, industry, and art.

TEXAS SWEDISH PIONEERS ASSOCIATION, INC. (TSPA)
305 West 18th Street
Austin, Texas 78701   (512) 476-0833

Principal officers: Carl T. Widén, President
T. W. Holmstrom, Vice President
Russell Chalberg, Secretary

Permanent staff: none	Membership: 3,000
Date founded: 1938	Membership dues: $1.00 (voluntary)
Branches: NI	Scope: state

Special requirements for membership: Swedish pioneer ancestry

Nature of organization: social, cultural

Affiliations: Texas Wesleyan Foundation; Svea Mutual Fire Ins. Co.; Goetha Mutual Fire Ins. Assn.; Skandia Mutual Life Ins. Co.

Major conventions/meetings: annual meeting in Zilker Park, Austin, Texas

Comments: The purpose of the organization is to unite Swedish-Americans in the Texas area, to preserve the Swedish culture and heritage in America, and to commemorate the pioneer immigrants who settled in the United States.

UNITED SWEDISH SOCIETIES
420 East 23rd Street
New York, New York 10010

Principal officers: Gerhard T. Rooth

Permanent staff: NI	Membership: 7,500
Date founded: 1903	Membership dues: NI
Branches: NI	Scope: national

Nature of organization: religious, cultural, social, educational

Comments: The organization is a federation of 60 Swedish-American religious, cultural, historical, educational, and other associations.

VASA ORDER OF AMERICA
37 Temple Place
Boston, Massachusetts 02111 (617) 426-1075
Principal officers: Bertil Winstrom, Grand Master
Karl O. Kristenson, Grand Secretary

Permanent staff: 10 Membership: 36,000
Date founded: 1896 Membership dues: NI
Branches: 20 state; 400 local Scope: national

Special requirements for membership: must be of Swedish descent or married to someone of Swedish descent

Nature of organization: fraternal

Publications: *Vasa Star* (monthly)

Major conventions/meetings: quadrennial

Comments: The major purpose of the organization is to provide life insurance benefits to members. Maintains scholarship and loan funds. Also sponsors cultural exchanges between Sweden and the United States.

SWISS-AMERICAN ORGANIZATIONS

Additional information on Swiss-American organizations in the United States may be obtained from the Office of the Swiss Embassy (2900 Cathedral Avenue, Washington, D.C. 20008). Regional and local organizations are listed in *Greater Cleveland Nationalities Directory 1974* (Cleveland: Sun Newspapers and the Nationalities Services Center, 1974) and *Ethnic Directory I* (Detroit: Southeastern Michigan Regional Ethnic Heritage Studies Center, 1973).

AMERICAN-SWISS ASSOCIATION
60 East 42nd Street
New York, New York 10017 (212) 986-5442
Principal officers: Howard Browning, Executive Secretary

Permanent staff: 3 Membership: 500
Date founded: 1945 Membership dues: NI
Branches: NI Scope: national

Nature of organization: cultural

Major conventions/meetings: annual meeting (in May); annual dinner (in November in New York City)

Comments: The organization consists of individuals and businesses establishing a relationship or exchange with the Swiss. Films and cultural programs are provided for members and for use in American school classrooms.

AMERICAN SWISS FOUNDATION FOR SCIENTIFIC EXCHANGE (ASFSE)
Hoffman-LaRoche, Inc.
Nutley, New Jersey 07110
Principal officers: Dr. A. I. Rachlin, Secretary

Permanent staff: NI Membership: NI
Date founded: NI Membership dues: NI
Branches: NI Scope: national

Nature of organization: scholarly

Comments: Sponsors an advanced studies exchange program between American and Swiss post-doctoral researchers in science and medicine.

DETROIT SWISS SOCIETY
14338 Harper Avenue
Detroit, Michigan 48213   (313) 824-9818
Principal officers: Hans Hefel, President
                       Thomas Giger, Executive Vice President
                       Paul Widmer, Executive Secretary

Permanent staff: 4   Membership: 100
Date founded: 1868   Membership dues: $10.00 (annual)
Branches: none   Scope: NI

Special requirements for membership: none

Nature of organization: social, economic, fraternal

Publications: *Newsletter*, 1956– (monthly)

Affiliations: North American Swiss Alliance

Major conventions/meetings: none

Comments: Major purpose is to provide life insurance to members. The organization also
    sponsors tours and social activities for members, presents slide and movie presentations
    on Switzerland, and sponsors folk dancing and other cultural programs. An archival
    collection is maintained.

NORTH AMERICAN SWISS ALLIANCE (NASA)
33 Public Square
Cleveland, Ohio 44113   (216) 771-2414
Principal officers: Raymond F. Strasser, Secretary-Treasurer

Permanent staff: 4   Membership: 4,200
Date founded: 1865   Membership dues: vary
Branches: in 3 states   Scope: national

Special requirements for membership: Swiss descent

Nature of organization: fraternal

Publications: *Swiss-American*, 1869– (monthly)

Major conventions/meetings: quadrennial; Board of Directors meet annually (in May, in
    Cleveland, Ohio)

Comments: Major goal is to provide members with life insurance benefits. Until 1940 the
    organization was known as the North American Schweizer Bund.

SAN DIEGO COUNTY SWISS CLUB, INC.
2001 Main Street
Chula Vista, California 92011   (714) 423-9954
Principal officers: George Reber, President
                       Max Sommerhalder, Executive Vice President
                       Marilyn Pluss, Executive Secretary

Permanent staff: none   Membership: 275
Date founded: 1939   Membership dues: $5.00 individual
Branches: none   (annual); $10.00 family (annual)
                                           Scope: regional

Special requirements for membership: active members must be of Swiss descent; associate
    members must be recommended by active members

Nature of organization: social, cultural

Publications: *Swiss Club Newsletter*, 1969– (monthly); *Schwingfest Program Book*, 1950–
    (annual)

Affiliations: United Swiss Societies of Southern California; Swiss Ladies Society of San Diego

Major conventions/meetings: annual general meeting

SWISS AMERICAN HISTORICAL SOCIETY (SAHS)
Old Dominion University
Norfolk, Virginia 23508

Principal officers: Dr. Heinz K. Meier, President
Dr. Rolf Kieser, First Vice President
Philip Gelzer, Second Vice President
Dr. Leo Schelbert, Secretary

Permanent staff: none   Membership: 250
Date founded: 1927   Membership dues: $7.00
Branches: none   Scope: international

Special requirements for membership: none

Nature of organization: social, educational, scholarly, cultural

Publications: *SAHS Newsletter*, 1965– (3 times per year); also publishes books

Affiliations: none

Major conventions/meetings: annual conference

Comments: Conducts and encourages historical research on the achievements of Swiss-Americans and their influence on American industry, science, government, and education. Also analyzes U.S.-Swiss relations and publishes and distributes publications on Swiss-American programs.

SWISS AMERICAN SOCIETY OF PITTSBURGH
207 Churchill Road
Turtle Creek, Pennsylvania 15145

Principal officers: John Fankhauser, Jr., President
Robert Leuenberger, Vice President
Trudi Kuenzi, Secretary

Permanent staff: none   Membership: 250
Date founded: 1961   Membership dues: $2.00 (annual)
Branches: none   Scope: local

Special requirements for membership: of Swiss origin or friend of Swiss

Nature of organization: social

Publications: none

Affiliations: none

Major conventions/meetings: none

Comments: Major purpose is to unite Swiss-Americans in the United States and to promote the Swiss heritage and tradition. Plans cultural and social field trips and activities.

SWISS BENEVOLENT SOCIETY OF NEW YORK (SBS)
37 West 67th Street
New York, New York 10023   (212) 873-3761

Principal officers: Ernest Hollmuller, Executive Officer

Permanent staff: 19   Membership: 1,000
Date founded: 1851   Membership dues: NI
Branches: NI   Scope: national

Nature of organization: fraternal

Comments: The major purpose is to provide life insurance benefits to members. The organization also sponsors a home for the elderly and a home for girls, and it provides various community and family services.

SWISS SOCIETY OF BOSTON
535 Boylston Street
Boston, Massachusetts 02116   (617) 266-2038

Principal officers: Konrad Biber, President
Trudy Powell, Secretary
Agnes Montilio, Agent

SWISS SOCIETY OF BOSTON (cont'd)

Permanent staff: none	Membership: 700
Date founded: 1865	Membership dues: $2.00
Branches: none	Scope: regional

Special requirements for membership: interest in Switzerland and Swiss activities

Nature of organization: cultural, educational, recreational

Major conventions/meetings: annual meeting in January

Comments: The major objectives of the organization are to provide social and cultural activities for members and to provide scholarships and other charitable assistance.

SWISS SOCIETY OF NEW YORK
444 Madison Avenue
New York, New York 10022   (212) 758-2560

Principal officers: Georges L. Lagnaz, Secretary

Permanent staff: NI	Membership: 475
Date founded: 1930	Membership dues: NI
Branches: NI	Scope: national

Special requirements for membership: none

Nature of organization: cultural, social

Major conventions/meetings: annual (always in January)

Comments: The major objective of the organization is to preserve the Swiss heritage and culture in the United States and to maintain a cultural exchange and friendship with the Swiss. The organization was formed as a result of a merger of the New York Swiss Club (founded in 1882) and the Swiss Scientific Society.

UNITED SWISS SOCIETIES OF SOUTHERN CALIFORNIA, INC.
4002 Verdugo Road
Los Angeles, California 90065   (213) 256-2226

Principal officers: André L. Monney, President
Luc Benoît, Executive Vice President
Renée Kaderli, Executive Secretary

Permanent staff: 4	Membership: 10 organizations
Date founded: 1961	Membership dues: none
Branches: 10 regional	Scope: regional

Special requirements for membership: open to Swiss organizations located in Southern California

Nature of organization: cultural, recreational

Publications: *Newsletter*, 1972– (quarterly)

Affiliations: New Helvetian Society in Bern (Switzerland)

Major conventions/meetings: none

Comments: Coordinates social, educational, and charitable activities of the various Swiss societies of Southern California.

SYRIAN-AMERICAN ORGANIZATIONS

See Arab-American Organizations

THAI-AMERICAN ORGANIZATIONS

Additional information on Thai-American organizations in the United States may be obtained from the Office of the Thailand Embassy (2300 Kalorama Road, Washington, D.C. 20008).

AMERICAN SIAM SOCIETY
633 24th Street
Santa Monica, California 90402

Principal officers: H. Carroll Parish, President

Permanent staff: NI
Date founded: 1956
Branches: NI

Membership: 180
Membership dues: NI
Scope: national

Nature of organization: cultural

Affiliations: Siam Society in Bangkok, Thailand

Major conventions/meetings: biennial

Comments: Members of the organization study the arts and sciences of Thailand, entertain guests from Thailand, and maintain a library of Thai publications including periodicals and newspapers.

THE THAI ALLIANCE IN AMERICA
1906 23rd Street, N.W.
Washington, D.C. 20008

THE THAI PEN CLUB OF AMERICA
1475 Townsend Avenue, B. 51
Bronx, New York 10452

TURKESTAN-AMERICAN ORGANIZATIONS

Additional information on Turkestan-American organizations in the United States may be obtained from the Turkestan-American Association in U.S.A. (P.O. Box 1148, Grand Central Station, New York, New York 10017).

TURKESTAN-AMERICAN ASSOCIATION IN U.S.A.
P.O. Box 1148, Grand Central Station
New York, New York 10017   (212) 645-3236

Principal officers: Shouraf Alibek, President
Enver Bek, Vice President
Abdurrahman Donuk, Treasurer
Timur Kocaoglu, Secretary

Permanent staff: 7
Date founded: 1960
Branches: none

Membership: 120
Membership dues: $24.00
Scope: national

Special requirements for membership: any Turkestanian who lives in the U.S.A.

Nature of organization: social

Publications: *Turkestan*, 1973– (once every two months)

Affiliations: none

TURKISH-AMERICAN ORGANIZATIONS

Additional information on Turkish-American organizations in the United States may be obtained from the Office of the Turkish Embassy (1606 23rd Street, Washington, D.C. 20008) and from the Federation of Turkish American Societies (104 East 40th Street, Suite 100/118, New York, New York 10016). Regional and local information may be obtained from *Ethnic Directory I* (Detroit: Southeastern Michigan Regional Ethnic Heritage Studies Center, 1973).

AMERICAN RESEARCH INSTITUTE IN TURKEY (ARIT)

1155 East 58th Street
Chicago, Illinois 60637   (312) 753-2470

Principal officers: Hans G. Guterbock, President

Permanent staff: NI	Membership: 20
Date founded: 1964	Membership dues: NI
Branches: NI	Scope: national

Special requirements for membership: institutions of higher learning in the United States and Canada

Nature of organization: educational

Publications: *Newsletter* (irregular)

Major conventions/meetings: annual

Comments: Promotes and conducts research in Turkish studies in the fields of anthropology, art and archaeology, history, linguistics, and culture. The institute assists researchers in publishing their works, and it grants fellowships.

AMERICAN TURKISH SOCIETY, INC.

331 Madison Avenue
New York, New York 11563   (212) 582-0999

Principal officers: Osman Olcay, President
                     Parker T. Hart, President
                     W. C. Jerige, Executive Vice President
                     Feridun Demokaw, Secretary

Permanent staff: 1	Membership: 250
Date founded: 1949	Membership dues: $200 corporation;
Branches: NI	$10.00 individual; $25.00 sustaining

Special requirements for membership: none

Nature of organization: cultural, economic, social, educational

Publications: none

Affiliations: none

Major conventions/meetings: none

Comments: The society's aim is "to promote friendship, cultural understanding and business relations between the people of the United States and Turkey." An annual poetry prize to Robert College is awarded. Presents lectures and films and maintains a small library and archival collection.

FEDERATION OF TURKISH AMERICAN SOCIETIES (FTAS)

104 East 40th Street, Suite 100/118
New York, New York 10016   (212) 682-7688

Principal officers: Yuksel Oktay, President
                     Serafettin Tombuloglu, Executive Vice President
                     Hediye Akpinar, Executive Secretary

Permanent staff: none	Membership: 11 societies each with
Date founded: 1956	100-300 members
Branches: none	Membership dues: $100.00 (annual)
	Scope: national

FEDERATION OF TURKISH AMERICAN SOCIETIES (FTAS) (cont'd)

Special requirements for membership: Turkish-American organizations whose members
  are of Turkish descent

Nature of organization: social, cultural, scholarly

Publications: *Echo 2*, 1973– (monthly)

Affiliations: none

Major conventions/meetings: annual general meeting

Comments: Purpose is to unite persons of Turkish descent in social and cultural activities
  that preserve the Turkish heritage in the United States. The federation is comprised
  of 11 Turkish-American organizations, which are social, cultural, educational, professional, or relief societies. A 300-volume library is maintained.

FLORIDA TURKISH-AMERICAN ASSOCIATION, INC.
  2217 N.E. 2nd Street
  Pompano Beach, Florida 33062   (305) 943-6626
Principal officers: Kaya Kocaman, President
                       Mazlum Aras, Vice President
                       Musa Acar, Secretary
Permanent staff: 5   Membership: 50
Date founded: 1969   Membership dues: $5.00 (annual)
Branches: NI   Scope: state
Special requirements for membership: sponsored by two members

Nature of organization: cultural, social, scholarly, recreational

Publications: *News* (Haberler), 1969– (irregular)

Affiliations: Federation of Turkish-American Associations, New York

Major conventions/meetings: annual general assembly

Comments: The objectives of the organization are to aid Turkish-Americans in Florida, to provide opportunities for social and cultural exchange within the community, and to help
  Turkish people suffering from natural disasters. Sponsors a Turkish-American friendship program and a scholarship fund for students of Turkish background.

NEW YORK TURKISH STUDENTS' ASSOCIATION
  P.O. Box 6, Loeb Student Center
  566 LaGuardia Place
  New York, New York 10003   (212) 524-0150
Principal officers: Halil Can, President
Permanent staff: NI   Membership: 150
Date founded: 1959   Membership dues: NI
Branches: NI   Scope: NI
Special requirements for membership: Turkish students in the New York metropolitan area

Nature of organization: scholarly, educational, cultural, social

Publications: *News Bulletin* (bimonthly); *Ortam* (annual)

Major conventions/meetings: annual

Comments: The purpose of the association is to unite and assist Turkish students in the United
  States. The organization sponsors films, folklore presentations, lectures, and various
  social and cultural activities for members.

**SOCIETY OF TURKISH ARCHITECTS, ENGINEERS, AND SCIENTISTS
IN AMERICA**
  104 East 40th Street
  New York, New York 10016   (212) 682-7688
Principal officers: Dr. Deger Tunc, President

SOCIETY OF TURKISH ARCHITECTS, ENGINEERS AND SCIENTISTS IN AMERICA (cont'd)

Permanent staff: NI

Membership: 110

Date founded: 1970

Membership dues: NI

Branches: NI

Scope: national

Special requirements for membership: Turkish architects, engineers, and scientists in America

Nature of organization: professional

Publications: *Bulletin* (bimonthly)

Affiliations: Federation of Turkish American Societies

Major conventions/meetings: annual (always in November, in New York City)

Comments: The purpose of the organization is to unite and assist Turkish professionals in social and scholarly programs. The society grants an award for service to the Turkish community, and it conducts conferences and seminars.

TURKISH AID SOCIETY OF NEW YORK
1157 Theriot Avenue
Bronx, New York 10472

TURKISH-AMERICAN ASSOCIATION FOR CULTURAL EXCHANGE (TAA)
1472 Broadway
New York, New York 10036   (212) 524-3447

Principal officers: Omer Faruk Fenik, President
Inci Fenik, Executive Vice President
Mualla Peker, Executive Secretary

Permanent staff: 4

Membership: 10,000

Date founded: 1965

Membership dues: $5.00 (annual)

Branches: none

Scope: NI

Special requirements for membership: none

Nature of organization: cultural

Publications: *News from Turkey*, 1965– (semimonthly)

Affiliations: none

Major conventions/meetings: none

Comments: The organization sponsors social and cultural activities such as lectures, conferences, educational activities, films, theater, etc. Also sponsors tours and group flights to Turkey and a semiweekly Turkish radio program. Publishes documentary materials on Turkey.

TURKISH AMERICAN CLUB
P.O. Box 67134
Los Angeles, California 90067

Permanent staff: NI

Membership: NI

Date founded: NI

Membership dues: NI

Branches: NI

Scope: regional

Nature of organization: cultural

TURKISH-AMERICAN CULTURAL ASSOCIATION OF ATLANTA (TACAA)
1063 Clifton Road, N.E.
Atlanta, Georgia 30307

Permanent staff: none

Membership: varies between 20 and 60

Date founded: 1957

Membership dues: $10.00

Branches: none

Scope: local, state, regional

Special requirements for membership: Turkish nationality and/or interest in Turkish culture

Nature of organization: cultural, social

Publications: none

TURKISH-AMERICAN CULTURAL ASSOCIATION OF ATLANTA (TACAA) (cont'd)

Comments: Purpose is to unite Turkish-Americans in social and cultural activities and to provide opportunities for Americans to become acquainted with Turkish culture and tradition. The association entertains visiting Turkish dignitaries, and it assists Turkish students
with financial and other problems.

TURKISH AMERICAN CULTURAL CENTER OF MICHIGAN
29729 Foxgrove
Farmington, Michigan 48024   (313) 851-6024

Principal officers: Nedret Tavlan, President
                   Yildiz Hazneci, Vice President
                   Ayse Colak, Secretary

Permanent staff: NI   Membership: 190
Date founded: 1972   Membership dues: $50.00 (annual)
Branches: none   Scope: state

Special requirements for membership: none

Nature of organization: cultural, social

Publications: none

Comments: The center sponsors various charitable and cultural activities within the Turkish-
American community of Michigan. It also attempts to promote Turkish-American
friendship and advancement of the Muslim religion.

THE TURKISH-AMERICAN CULTURAL SOCIETY, INC. (TACS)
70 Austin Street   (617) 491-7734 or
Cambridge, Massachusetts 02139   (617) 354-2630

Principal officers: Erdogan Sunar, President
                   Bulent Platin, Vice President
                   Mevlut Koymen, Secretary

Permanent staff: none   Membership: 500
Date founded: 1964   Membership dues: $10.00
Branches: none   Scope: regional

Special requirements for membership: open

Nature of organization: social, educational, cultural

Publications: none

Affiliations: none

Major conventions/meetings: annual meeting in April

Comments: The purpose of the organization is to promote and preserve the Turkish heritage
and tradition in the United States. It sponsors concerts, exhibits, etc., and assists
Turkish immigrants and Turkish students in the United States. It promotes tourism in
Turkey and sponsors a scholarship program for Turkish students.

TURKISH AMERICAN FRIENDSHIP SOCIETY OF THE UNITED STATES
P.O. Box 17164
Philadelphia, Pennsylvania 19105

Principal officers: Muzaffer Bingol, President

Permanent staff: NI   Membership: 700
Date founded: 1960   Membership dues: NI
Branches: NI   Scope: national

Nature of organization: cultural, educational

Publications: *TAFSUS* (monthly)

Major conventions/meetings: semiannual

Comments: Purpose of the organization is to unite Turkish-Americans for cultural and social
activities and for exchange of information and educational programs between Turkey
and America—e.g., archaeological discoveries, dances, music, poetry, and other folk art.
Also sponsors various charitable activities and provides chartered flights to Turkey.

TURKISH AMERICAN PHYSICIANS ASSOCIATION
149 Main Street
South River, New Jersey 08882   (201) 254-1030
Principal officers: Dr. Ilhan Nuraltay, President

Permanent staff: NI   Membership: 1,260
Date founded: 1969   Membership dues: NI
Branches: 4 regional groups   Scope: NI

Special requirements for membership: physicians of Turkish descent

Nature of organization: professional

Major conventions/meetings: annual (always second Saturday in March, in New York City)

Comments: The association unites physicians of Turkish background in the United States and
provides opportunities for cultural, social, and professional exchange and interaction.
It also promotes Turkish-American relations and an exchange of medical knowledge.

TURKISH CULTURAL ALLIANCE, INC.
154-29 65th Avenue
Flushing, New York 11356   (212) 384-5669
Principal officers: Kamil Akbas, President
                       Saim G. Düzgüner, Secretary
                       Ali N. Ardakoc, Vice President

Permanent staff: 11   Membership: 80 families
Date founded: 1933   Membership dues: $24.00
Branches: 1 state   Scope: national

Special requirements for membership: Turkish-Moslem faith, or married to spouse of that
faith.

Nature of organization: educational, cultural, religious, fraternal

Affiliations: Federation of Turkish-American Societies

Major conventions/meetings: annual convention

Comments: Major goal is to preserve the Turkish culture and heritage in the United States.
Sponsors a Turkish cemetery, Turkish-language Sunday school, religious services, folk
dancing group, annual dinner dance, annual picnic and other cultural and social
activities. Maintains a multimedia library and an archival collection.

TURKISH EDUCATIONAL FOUNDATION, INC. (TEF)
P.O. Box 4487
Berkeley, California 94704
Principal officers: Duygu Demirlioglu, President
                       Dwight Larrabee, Vice President
                       Valerie Heatlie, Secretary

Permanent staff: 4   Membership: 80
Date founded: 1969   Membership dues: $15.00
Branches: 1 state   Scope: national

Special requirements for membership: open

Nature of organization: educational

Publications: newsletter (quarterly)

Major conventions/meetings: annual meeting

Comments: The purpose of this non-profit corporation is to educate needy village children
in Turkey. It sponsors three-year scholarships for Turkish secondary school children and
proposes purchasing dormitories and other school facilities.

TURKISH SOCIETY OF PITTSBURGH (TURKSOP)
    P.O. Box 7546
    Pittsburgh, Pennsylvania 15213
    Principal officers: Erdoğan Altuğlu, President
                     Mahmut Isildar, Executive Secretary
                     Nurettin Bilgin, Treasurer

Permanent staff: none   Membership: 50
Date founded: 1970   Membership dues: $6.00 (annual)
Branches: none   Scope: NI

Special requirements for membership: none

Nature of organization: social, cultural, scholarly

Publications: *Turkish Review*, 1970– (quarterly)

Affiliations: none

Major conventions/meetings: annual conference

Comments: The major purpose of the organization is to unite Turkish-Americans in social and
    cultural activities and to acquaint other Americans with Turkish history and culture.
    It sponsors exhibits, conferences, etc., and it also supports charitable activities that
    benefit the poor in Turkey.

TURKISH SPORTS CLUB (TSC)
    104 East 40th Street, Room 118
    New York, New York 10016   (212) 682-7688
    Principal officers: Faruk Terpis, President
                     Akif Görkey, Vice President
                     Samim S. Özant, Secretary

Permanent staff: 9   Membership: 98
Date founded: 1973   Membership dues: $10.00 (annual)
Branches: none   Scope: NI

Special requirements for membership: none

Nature of organization: social, educational, sport

Publications: *Turkish Home*

Affiliations: Federation of Turkish American Societies

Major conventions/meetings: annual convention; bimonthly Board of Directors meeting

Comments: Attempts to stimulate and promote unity among Turkish Americans through
    recreational sports activities. It also sponsors exhibits for the American public on
    Turkish sports, and sponsors trips and tours for members.

TURKISH WOMEN'S LEAGUE OF AMERICA
    P.O. Box 2143, Grand Central Station
    New York, New York 10017

Permanent staff: NI   Membership: NI
Date founded: NI   Membership dues: NI
Branches: NI   Scope: national

Nature of organization: cultural

UKRAINIAN-AMERICAN ORGANIZATIONS

Additional information on Ukrainian-American organizations in the United States may be obtained from the Ukrainian Congress Committee of America (302 West 13th Street, New York, New York 10014). Outdated, but useful for historical information about Ukrainian-American organizations, is *Guide to Ukrainian-American Institutions, Professionals and Business*, compiled and edited by Wasyl Weresh (New York: Carpathian Star Publishing Co., 1955).

Regional and local organizations are listed in *Greater Cleveland Nationalities Directory 1974* (Cleveland: Sun Newspapers and the Nationalities Services Center, 1974) and *Ethnic Directory I* (Detroit: Southeastern Michigan Regional Ethnic Heritage Studies Center, 1973), and *Directory of Ukrainian Professionals and Businessmen in Philadelphia, Pennsylvania, 1972* (Philadelphia: Ukrainian Savings and Loan Association, 1972).

ASSOCIATION FOR THE LIBERATION OF UKRAINE
P.O. Box 38, Greenpoint Station
Brooklyn, New York 11222   (212) 383-5019
Principal officers: Valentyn Koval, President
                      Ivan Marchenko, Vice President
                      Theodore Tarakhiwsky, Secretary

Permanent staff: 24   Membership: 2,500
Date founded: 1952   Membership dues: $25.00 (annual)
Branches: 15 regional   Scope: national

Special requirements for membership: of Ukrainian origin, anti-communist and anti-fascist, and in favor of a free Ukraine

Nature of organization: political

Publications: *Misia Ukrainy* (Mission of Ukraine), 1957– (quarterly); *Bulletin of Information*, 1957– (quarterly); *Illustrative Bulletin of Americans to Free Captive Nations*, 1966– (annual); also publishes books

Affiliations: Ukrainian American Congress Committee; Americans to Free Captive Nations; World Council of the Association for the Liberation of Ukraine

Major conventions/meetings: annual conference; quadrennial convention

Comments: The main objectives of the organization are "To bring all kinds of voluntary help to Ukrainian people in their struggle for liberation from the Communist occupation of Ukraine"; to cooperate with the anti-communist forces in the world, and to "defend the American way of life as against Communist oppression" (Certificate of Incorporation). Maintains an archival collection.

ASSOCIATION OF AMERICAN YOUTH OF UKRAINIAN DESCENT, INC.
221 Edridge Way
Catonsville, Maryland 21228
Principal officers: George Krywolap, President

Permanent staff: none   Membership: 1,200
Date founded: 1950   Membership dues: $6.00 (annual)
Branches: 9 local   Scope: national

Special requirements for membership: must be of Ukrainian descent

Nature of organization: social, educational, cultural, recreational, sport, fraternal, youth

Publications: *Young Ukraine*, 1951– (monthly); *ODUM Chronicle*, 1960– (quarterly) (supplement to Ukrainian daily *Svoboda*); *ODUM Chronicle*, 1962– (monthly) (supplement to Ukrainian weekly *Ukrainian News*); also publishes handbooks, almanacs, proceedings

ASSOCIATION OF AMERICAN YOUTH OF UKRAINIAN DESCENT, INC. (cont'd)

Affiliations: Ukrainian Democratic Youth Association in Canada, West Germany, and Great Britain; Friends of ODUM

Major conventions/meetings: annual conference

Comments: A non-profit organization based on Christian morals and ethics and democratic ideals. Objectives include the preservation of Ukrainian cultural heritage. Disseminates knowledge on Ukrainian history, politics, religion, customs, etc. Holds weekly meetings for various age groups. Sponsors summer camps devoted to the study of Ukrainian history, culture, art, literature, etc., as well as the Ukrainian contribution to American life. Also sponsors trips, instrumental and singing ensembles, dancing groups, concerts, sports, debates, lectures, and panels. Maintains a library of over 5,000 volumes as well as archives.

ASSOCIATION OF UKRAINIAN THEATER ARTISTS

1309 West Ruscomb Street
Philadelphia, Pennsylvania 19141   (215) 445-2946

Principal officers: Jurij Kononiw, President
Eugene Kurylo, Vice President
Wolodymyr Shasharowsky, Secretary

Permanent staff: NI   Membership: 109
Date founded: 1946 (reactivated in 1971)   Membership dues: $6.00 (annual)
Branches: none   Scope: national

Special requirements for membership: none

Nature of organization: cultural

Publications: *Actor's Voice*, 1971– (published irregularly in Ukrainian daily papers *Svoboda* and *America*)

Affiliations: none

Major conventions/meetings: biennial convention

Comments: Promotes Ukrainian theatrical productions in Ukrainian communities. Works for the preservation of various aspects of Ukrainian performing arts. Maintains a library and an archival collection. Presents a special award to the best Ukrainian theatre group.

"BOYKIWSHCHYNA" ASSOCIATION

2222 Brandywine Street
Philadelphia, Pennsylvania 19130   (215) 567-3186

Principal officers: S. Dasho, President
Olexander Tatomyr, Executive Vice President
Myron T. Utrysko, General Secretary

Permanent staff: none   Membership: 500
Date founded: 1967   Membership dues: $3.00 (annual)
Branches: 4 regional   Scope: national

Special requirements for membership: none

Nature of organization: cultural

Publications: *Litopys Bojkiwshchyny*, 1969– (quarterly); bulletins, circulars; *Obiznyk*, 1968– (quarterly); also publishes books

Affiliations: none

Major conventions/meetings: triennial convention

Comments: The main objective of the organization is to study and preserve the culture, history, art, literature, and customs of "Boyky"–a Ukrainian ethnic and regional group. Maintains a library of over 200 volumes and also archives.

BROTHERHOOD "BRODY-LEW," INC.
c/o Ukrainian National Home
140-42 2nd Avenue
New York, New York 10003

Principal officers: Roman Drazniowsky, President
Kyrylo Hryhorovych, Executive Vice President
Myron Zalipsky, Executive Secretary

Permanent staff: none   Membership: 560
Date founded: 1952   Membership dues: none
Branches: none   Scope: national

Special requirements for membership: must be Ukrainian or of Ukrainian descent

Nature of organization: social

Publications: *V Dni Zelenykh Sviat*, 1955 – (annual)

Affiliations: Brotherhood of the First Division Ukrainian National Army

Major conventions/meetings: annual convention

Comments: Major objectives are to provide assistance to disabled former Ukrainian soldiers, to aid in the record and location of missing Ukrainian soldiers, and to care for individual graves and monuments.

CENTRAL ASSOCIATION OF THE BUKOVINIAN UKRAINIANS IN U.S.A.
35 Montgomery Street
New York, New York 10002   (212) 233-4090

Principal officers: Ivan E. Zukovskyj, President
Ivan Novosivskyj, Vice President
Mykola Shpetko, Secretary

Permanent staff: 6   Membership: 120
Date founded: 1956   Membership dues: $3.00 (annual)
Branches: 3 regional, 1 local   Scope: U.S. and Canada

Special requirements for membership: of Ukrainian descent from Bukovyna

Nature of organization: social, cultural, fraternal

Publications: publishes books

Affiliations: none

Major conventions/meetings: annual and biennial

Comments: Union of Ukrainians from the region of Bukovyna. Provides material assistance to members. Maintains an archival collection.

CENTRAL COMMITTEE OF UKRAINIAN ORGANIZATIONS
3595 N.W. 35th Street
Miami, Florida 33142   (305) 864-4465

Principal officers: Nicholas Rakush, President
Bohdan Nahaniv, Executive Vice President
Nadia Mudreyko, Executive Secretary

Permanent staff: none   Membership: 22 delegates representing
Date founded: 1949   Ukrainian organizations
Branches: NI   Membership dues: $2.00 per
                             organization
                             Scope: state

Special requirements for membership: "Elected delegate from Ukrainian organization"

Nature of organization: educational, cultural

Publications: none

Affiliations: none

Major conventions/meetings: monthly meetings

Comments: This is an umbrella organization over all Florida Ukrainian associations. Organizes celebrations of Ukrainian national holidays, concerts, and lectures. Provides financial support to Ukrainian causes.

CONFERENCE OF HUTSUL ASSOCIATION

2453 West Chicago Avenue
Chicago, Illinois 60622 (312) 276-3918
Principal officers: Iwan Hawryluk, President
Iwan Andrusiak, Executive Vice President
Nicholas Donashevsky, Executive Secretary

Permanent staff: NI   Membership: 350
Date founded: 1971   Membership dues: NI
Branches: 8 regional   Scope: national

Special requirements for membership: Ukrainians from Hutsul region

Nature of organization: social, cultural

Publications: *Hutsuliya*, 1967– (quarterly)

Affiliations: none

Major conventions/meetings: annual meeting

Comments: The aim of the association is to unite the Ukrainian Hutsul ethnic group in the
United States for the purpose of preserving the Hutsul subculture.

THE DEMOCRATIC ORGANIZATION OF UKRAINIANS FORMERLY PERSECUTED BY THE SOVIET REGIME (DOBRUS)

P.O. Box 95, Cooper Station
New York, New York 10003 (212) 335-0753
Principal officers: Anatole N. Gudzowsky, President
Iwan M. Neseniuk, Vice President
V. Andrijewsky, Secretary

Permanent staff: 5   Membership: 60
Date founded: 1950   Membership dues: $6.00
Branches: 5   Scope: national

Special requirements for membership: none

Nature of organization: social, political

Publications: *DOBRUS*, 1952– (irregular)

Affiliations: World Congress of Free Ukrainians

Major conventions/meetings: biennial convention

Comments: Collects and preserves documentary evidence dealing with acts of terror and
repression occurring in the Ukraine under Soviet occupation. Works to preserve the
memory of the six million Ukrainian victims of genocide. Maintains an archival
collection consisting of documents, letters, etc.

FEDERATION OF UKRAINIAN STUDENT ORGANIZATIONS OF AMERICA (SUSTA)

P.O. Box 40121, Palisades Station
Washington, D.C. 20016 (301) 439-1573
Principal officers: Eugene M. Iwanciw, President
Andrij Michniak, Vice President

Permanent staff: NI   Membership: 2,500
Date founded: 1953   Membership dues: NI
Branches: 30   Scope: national

Nature of organization: student

Publications: *Prism*, 1974– (monthly)

Affiliations: Central Federation of Ukrainian Students

Major conventions/meetings: biennial

Comments: Promotes the study of Ukrainian culture; helps Ukrainian-American students obtain
scholarships; sponsors lectures, congresses, tours, and other activities that unite those of
Ukrainian background in social, cultural, sport, religious, or recreational activities. Also
an active voice in demanding the release of political prisoners in the Ukraine, and in
initiating a Committee for the Defense of Valentyn Moroz.

LEAGUE OF AMERICANS OF UKRAINIAN DESCENT

841 North Western Avenue
Chicago, Illinois 60622   (312) 489-4450

Principal officers: John Duzansky, President

Permanent staff: NI   Membership: 52 organizations; 8,000
Date founded: 1940   individuals
Branches: NI   Membership dues: NI
                                            Scope: national

Nature of organization: civic, religious, welfare

Affiliations: Ukrainian Congress Committee of America

Comments: Coordinates the activities of the civic, religious, and relief organizations in the area.
    Major emphasis is on aiding Ukrainians in need, particularly immigrants. Also sponsors
    English language classes and conducts and participates in cultural activities.

LEAGUE OF UKRAINIAN CATHOLICS OF AMERICA (LUC)

P.O. Box C
McAdoo, Pennsylvania 18237   (717) 668-4960

Principal officers: Joseph Lukiw, President
                       Anna Kupczak, Vice President
                       Marion Hrubec, Secretary

Permanent staff: 1   Membership: 3,000
Date founded: 1932   Membership dues: $2.00
Branches: 13 regional; 38 local   Scope: national

Special requirements for membership: member of Ukrainian Catholic Church, or
    recommended by a Ukrainian member; application must be signed by a Ukrainian
    Catholic priest

Nature of organization: religious, social, educational, cultural, youth

Publications: *Action*, 1960– (quarterly)

Affiliations: Ukrainian Congress Committee of America; World Congress for Free
    Ukrainians

Major conventions/meetings: annual National Convention; annual national sports rally

Comments: This is a national lay organization within the framework of the Ukrainian
    Catholic Church. It is youth oriented and upholds the cultural traditions of the
    Ukrainian people. Its overall objective is to become the congress of lay organizations
    recognized by the hierarchy of the Ukrainian Catholic Church.

ORGANIZATION FOR DEFENSE OF FOUR FREEDOMS FOR UKRAINE (ODFFU)

315 East Tenth Street
New York, New York 10009   (212) 982-1170

Principal officers: Ignatius M. Bilynsky, President
                       Andrew Sokolyk, Secretary

Permanent staff: 2   Membership: NI
Date founded: 1946   Membership dues: NI
Branches: 50   Scope: national

Nature of organization: political

Publications: *Visnyk* (Herald), 1947– (monthly); also publishes books

Affiliations: Ukrainian Congress Committee of America

Major conventions/meetings: biennial

Comments: This is one of the major Ukrainian political organizations supporting the ideology
    of the Ukrainian Nationalist Organization. Its aim is to preserve Ukrainian culture and
    language in the United States and to uphold the ideals of a free and independent
    Ukraine. Maintains archives.

ORGANIZATION FOR DEFENSE OF LEMKIVSHCHYNA (ODL)
P.O. Box 202
Camillus, New York 13031
Principal officers: Ivan Hvozda, President
                  N. Duplak, Secretary

Permanent staff: none	Membership: 500
Date founded: 1936	Membership dues: $3.00 (annual)
Branches: 20 regional and state	Scope: international, national

Special requirements for membership: Ukrainian background

Nature of organization: cultural, educational, relief

Publications: *Lemko News*, 1957 – (monthly); *Lemko Almanac*, 1957 – (annual)

Affiliations: Ukrainian Congress Committee of America; World Congress of Free Ukrainians; World Lemko Federation

Major conventions/meetings: biennial

Comments: Purpose is to unite Ukrainians from the Lemko regions of Ukraine and to provide financial assistance to various Ukrainian institutions, organizations, and individuals. Organizes lectures, held at the various branches, on Ukrainian culture, history, and traditions. Maintains archives and a museum of the Lemko subculture.

ORGANIZATION FOR REBIRTH OF UKRAINE, INC.
7012 Michigan Avenue
Detroit, Michigan 48210
Principal officers: Dr. D. Kwitkowsky, President
                  Dr. Roman Klufas, Secretary

Permanent staff: NI	Membership: NI
Date founded: 1930	Membership dues: NI
Branches: 32	Scope: national

Nature of organization: political

Publications: *Independent Ukraine*, 1948 – (quarterly); also publishes books

Major conventions/meetings: annual

Comments: One of the major Ukrainian political organizations in the United States. Promotes the ideology of Ukrainian nationalism and supports Ukrainian political and cultural life in America. Upholds the ideals and aspirations of a free and independent Ukraine.

PLAST FOUNDATION, INC.
144 Second Avenue
New York, New York 10003   (212) 982-4530
Principal officers: Wiacheslaw Wyshnewsky, President
                  P. Darmohraj, Vice President
                  M. Juzeniw, Secretary

Permanent staff: 1	Membership: NI
Date founded: 1963	Membership dues: $10.00 (annual)
Branches: none	Scope: national

Special requirements for membership: those of Ukrainian descent who agree with the principles of the Plast movement

Nature of organization: educational, charitable

Publications: *Bulletin*, 1968 – (irregular)

Major conventions/meetings: annual

Comments: Supports the activities of the Plast Ukrainian Youth Association. Objectives are to promote and preserve the Ukrainian heritage and traditions in the United States.

PLAST UKRAINIAN YOUTH ORGANIZATION, INC.
144 Second Avenue
New York, New York 10003   (212) 982-4530
Principal officers: Andrew Mycio, President
                       Eustachia Hoydysh, Secretary

Permanent staff: 1   Membership: 4,000+
Date founded: 1950   Membership dues: donation
Branches: 1 regional; 13 state; 33 local   Scope: national

Nature of organization: youth

Publications: *Hotujs'*, 1958– (monthly); *Plastovyilystok*, 1949– (quarterly)

Affiliations: Ukrainian Congress Committee of America

Major conventions/meetings: biennial

Comments: The main objective of the organization is to develop the physical and mental
      health of American youth of Ukrainian descent. Maintains summer camps for youth.
      Aims at preservation of Ukrainian cultural heritage in the United States. Plast is the
      Ukrainian Scouting organization and follows the Scouting code. Maintains an archival
      collection.

PROVIDENCE ASSOCIATION OF UKRAINIAN CATHOLICS IN AMERICA
817 North Franklin Street
Philadelphia, Pennsylvania 19123   (215) 627-4993
Principal officers: Very Rev. Myroslaw Charyna, Supreme President
                       Jaroslav Bernadyn, Supreme Organizer

Permanent staff: NI   Membership: 18,573
Date founded: 1912   Membership dues: NI
Branches: 215   Scope: national

Nature of organization: fraternal, charitable, cultural

Publications: *America*, 1912– (daily); also publishes books

Affiliations: Ukrainian Congress Committee of America

Major conventions/meetings: annual

Comments: Major objectives of the organization are to provide life insurance benefits to mem-
      bers and to aid Ukrainians in financial need. It also supports religious schools and
      grants scholarships to Ukrainian-American students. Sponsors various cultural activities
      and attempts to preserve the Ukrainian language in the United States. Maintains an
      archival collection.

REPRESENTATION OF THE UKRAINIAN NATIONAL COUNCIL IN THE U.S.
13 East 7th Street
New York, New York 10003

Permanent staff: NI   Membership: NI
Date founded: 1951   Membership dues: NI
Branches: NI   Scope: national

Nature of organization: political

Comments: Supports the activities of the Ukrainian National Council, which functions as the
      Ukrainian government in exile. Provides financial support for the council.

SELF RELIANCE ASSOCIATION OF AMERICAN UKRAINIANS
98 Second Avenue
New York, New York 10003   (212) 777-1336
Principal officers: Wasyl Palidwor, Executive Secretary

Permanent staff: 1   Membership: 13,000
Date founded: 1947   Membership dues: NI
Branches: 21   Scope: national

Special requirements for membership: Ukrainian-Americans

SELF RELIANCE ASSOCIATION OF AMERICAN UKRAINIANS (cont'd)
Nature of organization: cultural, relief
Publications: *Our World* (bimonthly)
Major conventions/meetings: biennial
Comments: Emphasis is on maintaining the Ukrainian culture in the United States. Encourages studies and offers courses in Ukrainian history and other subjects. Also assists Ukrainian immigrants.

SHEVCHENKO SCIENTIFIC SOCIETY, INC.
302-304 West 13th Street
New York, New York 10014
Principal officers: Osyp Andrushkiv, President
                      M. Chyrovskyi, Secretary

Permanent staff: NI   Membership: NI
Date founded: 1948   Membership dues: NI
Branches: NI   Scope: national
Nature of organization: scholarly
Publications: *Memoirs* (irregular); *Papers* (irregular)
Comments: One of the major Ukrainian scholarly institutions. Originally founded in 1892 in Lviv (West Ukraine) and chartered in 1948 in the United States. Promotes scholarly and cultural activities. Arranges conferences and cooperates with American scholarly institutions. Maintains a library and archives.

TERNOPILSCHYNA ASSOCIATION
6610 North 13th Street
Philadelphia, Pennsylvania 19126   (215) 424-2418
Principal officers: Bohdan Filinsky, President
                      Wolodymyr Mackiw, Executive Secretary

Permanent staff: 1   Membership: 60
Date founded: 1957   Membership dues: donation
Branches: none   Scope: national
Special requirements for membership: none
Nature of organization: fraternal
Publications: publishes books
Comments: Unites people from the region of Ternopil for the purpose of studying the historical past of the city of Ternopil.

UKRAINIAN ACADEMY OF ARTS AND SCIENCES IN THE UNITED STATES, INC.
206 West 100th Street
New York, New York 10025   (212) 222-1866
Principal officers: Olexander Ohloblyn, President
                      Vasyl Omelchenko, Learned Secretary

Permanent staff: 3   Membership: 55 full members (member-
Date founded: 1950   ship in other categories not indicated)
Branches: 2   Membership dues: NI
                                          Scope: national
Nature of organization: scholarly
Publications: *The Annals of the Ukrainian Academy*, 1951– (irregular)
Major conventions/meetings: annual meetings; special conferences
Comments: The major Ukrainian scholarly organization in the United States. Promotes Ukrainian research and studies, participates in scholarly conferences and congresses. Membership of the academy consists of full members and corresponding members. Maintains Museum-Archives, which contains many valuable manuscripts and printed materials on Ukraine and Eastern Europe.

UKRAINIAN AMERICAN ASSOCIATION

133 Lafayette Avenue
Trenton, New Jersey 08610   (609) 392-4213

Principal officers: Dmytro Kuzyk, President
                     Roman Baranowskyi, Chairman
                     Roman Borkowsky, Secretary

Permanent staff: 38   Membership: 500
Date founded: 1966   Membership dues: $10.00 (annual)
Branches: regional   Scope: national

Special requirements for membership: none

Nature of organization: social

Publications: *Our Voice*, 1972– (monthly)

Affiliations: none

Major conventions/meetings: quadrennial

Comments: Works toward improving the status of Ukrainian social and political organizations in the United States. Supports cultural activity of Ukrainians in America. The organization was formed in opposition to the Ukrainian Congress Committee.

UKRAINIAN AMERICAN ASSOCIATION OF UNIVERSITY PROFESSORS (UAAUP)

c/o Dr. Ihor Kamenetsky
Department of Political Science
Anspach Hall
Central Michigan University
Mt. Pleasant, Michigan 48859

Principal officers: M. Stepanenko, President
                     Ihor Kamenetsky, Secretary-Treasurer

Permanent staff: 5   Membership: 165
Date founded: 1961   Membership dues: $6.00 (annual)
Branches: 3   Scope: U.S. and Canada

Special requirements for membership: "Any Ukrainian American or Ukrainian Canadian who has rank of instructor or higher in accredited college or university in USA or Canada."

Nature of organization: professional

Publications: *Professors' News*, 1972– (quarterly)

Affiliations: Ukrainian Congress Committee of America

Major conventions/meetings: biennial

Comments: Promotes professional interests of the members through scholarly conferences, workshops, and meetings. Aims at collecting information about research projects and professional activities of Ukrainian professors in the United States and Canada. Supports educational activity of the Ukrainian community in the United States.

UKRAINIAN AMERICAN LEAGUE (ULA)

85 East Fourth Street
New York, New York 10003   (212) 473-1762

Principal officers: M. Hanusiak, President
                     M. Torchenko, Secretary

Permanent staff: NI   Membership: NI
Date founded: 1924   Membership dues: NI
Branches: 13   Scope: national

Nature of organization: political, cultural

Publications: *Ukrainski Visti* (Ukrainian News), 1920– (weekly); *The Ukrainian American*, 1940– (monthly)

Comments: This pro-communist organization promotes close ties with the Soviet Union. Encourages political and cultural activities.

UKRAINIAN AMERICAN SPORT CENTER (USO "TRYZUB")
4930-32 North Broad Street
Philadelphia, Pennsylvania 19141   (215) 324-9700
Principal officers: Stefan Brenzey, President
                        Wolodymyr Bilajiw, First Vice President
                        Michael Kiczula, Secretary

Permanent staff: 5 members of Executive   Membership: 350 active; 250 social
  Committee and 6 Directors   Membership dues: $5.00 active (annual);
Date founded: 1950 $3.00 social (annual)
Branches: none   Scope: regional

Special requirements for membership: none

Nature of organization: sport

Publications: publishes bulletins

Affiliations: Philadelphia Ukrainian Nationals (semi-pro soccer team)

Major conventions/meetings: none

Comments: Promotes various sport activities among Ukrainian Americans.

UKRAINIAN AMERICAN VETERANS
5 Birchwood Terrace
Clifton, New Jersey 07012
Principal officers: Vasyl Luchkiw, National Commander

Permanent staff: NI   Membership: NI
Date founded: 1950 (?)   Membership dues: NI
Branches: NI   Scope: national

Special requirements for membership: American veterans of Ukrainian ancestry

Nature of organization: veterans

Affiliations: Ukrainian Congress Committee

Comments: This association consists of American veterans of Ukrainian ancestry who have
    served in the wars of the United States. Participates in Ukrainian community life in the
    United States.

UKRAINIAN ARTISTS ASSOCIATION IN U.S.A.
149 Second Avenue
New York, New York 10003
Principal officers: Mykhaylo Chereshniowsky, President
                        Petro Andrusiw, First Vice President
                        Volodymyr Lasovsky, Executive Secretary

Permanent staff: 9   Membership: 110
Date founded: 1950   Membership dues: $12.00 (annual)
Branches: NI   Scope: national

Special requirements for membership: none

Nature of organization: cultural

Publications: *One Man Show Catalogues*, 1952– (6 to 8 annually); *Ukrainian Art Digest*,
    1963– (annual)

Affiliations: none

Major conventions/meetings: annual convention

Comments: Purpose of the organization is to promote the professional activities of
    Ukrainian-American artists—to help them exhibit their work and advance their
    studies. Maintains an archival collection.

UKRAINIAN CONGRESS COMMITTEE OF AMERICA (UCCA)
302 West 13th Street
New York, New York 10014   (212) 924-5617
Principal officers: Lev. E. Dobriansky, President
                       Ivan Bazarko, Executive Director

Permanent staff: 6   Membership: 10,000
Date founded: 1940   Membership dues: $15.00 (annual)
Branches: 94   and up
                                             Scope: national

Special requirements for membership: none

Nature of organization: cultural, social, political, educational

Publications: *The Ukrainian Quarterly*, 1944– (quarterly)

Affiliations: National Captive Nations Committee; American Council for World Freedom;
    All-American Conference to Combat Communism; Conference of Americans of Central
    and Eastern European Descent; many national, regional, state, and local organizations

Major conventions/meetings: biennial conventions until 1972; quadrennial after 1972

Comments: This is the major Ukrainian umbrella organization in the United States. Its
    objectives include maintaining the Ukrainian national and cultural heritage by support-
    ing the Ukrainian cultural and political development in this country. It promotes
    re-establishment of a free and independent Ukraine. Publishes brochures, journals, and
    books on Ukraine. Participates in national and international events; provides testimonies
    before U.S. government committees. Has a special UCCA Educational Council, which
    has jurisdiction over 75 Ukrainian schools, 495 classes, and 392 teachers. Presently more
    than 29,000 pupils receive instruction in the Ukrainian language, history, etc. Publishes
    handbooks; organizes major concerts and events. Serves as an information clearing-
    house. Maintains a large reference library and an archival collection which includes
    materials pertaining to the Ukrainian-American way of life and the history of UCCA.

UKRAINIAN COSSACK BROTHERHOOD
2100 West Chicago Avenue
Chicago, Illinois 60622   (312) 276-5171

Permanent staff: 8   Membership: 532
Date founded: 1917   Membership dues: NI
Branches: 29 regional   Scope: national

Publications: *Ukrainske Kozatstvo*, 1947– (quarterly)

Comments: Promotes the independence of Ukraine. Aims at preservation of the Ukrainian
    culture and the military traditions of Ukrainian Cossacks.

UKRAINIAN ECONOMIC ADVISORY ASSOCIATION, INC.
2351 West Chicago Avenue
Chicago, Illinois 60622   (312) 489-0520
Principal officers: Omelan Pleszkewycz, President
                       Bohdan Stefanowycz, Executive Secretary

Permanent staff: 7   Membership: 26 credit unions; 25,000
Date founded: 1957   individuals
Branches: none   Membership dues: varies according to
                                                 assets of credit union
                                             Scope: national

Special requirements for membership: must be Ukrainian credit union or cooperative

Nature of organization: economic

Publications: none

Affiliations: Credit Union National Association; National Credit Union Association

Major conventions/meetings: biennial convention

UKRAINIAN ECONOMIC ADVISORY ASSOCIATION, INC. (cont'd)

Comments: The purpose of the organization is to "centralize the Ukrainian cooperative movement in the U.S." Combined member organizations have approximately $50 million in assets. This organization issues instructions for credit union and co-op management. Conferences are held at the local organizations; the main association collaborates with the Credit Union National Association (CUNA) and the National Credit Union Association (NCUA). Annual records and statements are maintained in an archival collection.

UKRAINIAN ENGINEERS' SOCIETY OF AMERICA, INC.
2 East 79th Street
New York, New York 10021   (212) 535-7676

Principal officers: Eugene Ivashkiv, President
                        Iwan Mokriwskyj, Executive Vice President
                        Aleksander Leskiw, Executive Secretary

Permanent staff: none   Membership: 790
Date founded: 1948   Membership dues: $20.00 (annual)
Branches: 13 regional   Scope: national

Special requirements for membership: must be of Ukrainian descent, age 21 or over, a college graduate in engineering, mathematics, chemistry, or economics, of U.S. citizenship or with legal residence in the United States

Nature of organization: professional

Publications: *Ukrainian Engineering News*, 1950– (quarterly); *Bulletin of Ukrainian Engineers' Society of America*, 1969– (quarterly)

Affiliations: none

Major conventions/meetings: none

Comments: Organizes engineers of Ukrainian descent in order to further their professional knowledge, and to promote technical development of the Ukraine. The organization also provides social and cultural activities, provides lectures and discussions of scientific papers and publications, and publishes scholarly research and studies by Ukrainian-American engineers.

UKRAINIAN EVANGELICAL ALLIANCE OF NORTH AMERICA (UEA of NA)
5610 Trowbridge Drive
Dunwoody, Georgia 30338   (404) 394-2233

Principal officers: William Bahrey, President
                        M. Kozak, Executive Vice President
                        W. Borowsky, Executive Secretary

Permanent staff: 1   Membership: NI
Date founded: 1922   Membership dues: $3.00 minimum
Branches: none   (annual)
                                         Scope: U.S. and Canada

Special requirements for membership: none

Nature of organization: religious

Publications: *Evangelical Morning*, 1905– (quarterly); also publishes books

Affiliations: Reverend B. Kuziw Memorial Publishing Fund

Major conventions/meetings: triennial convention

Comments: The organization is a coordinating center for Protestants (primarily Reformed Presbyterians) of Ukrainian descent in the United States and Canada. Its emphasis is on publishing and distributing Christian literature as an evangelistic effort; the organization also aids refugees.

UKRAINIAN GOLD CROSS IN THE U.S. (UGC)
4435 Parkinson Avenue
Detroit, Michigan 48210   (313) 841-7186
Principal officers: Maria Kwitkowsky, President
                       Mrs. P. Riznyk, Executive Vice President
                       Mrs. V. Mushynsky, Executive Secretary

Permanent staff: none   Membership: NI
Date founded: 1931   Membership dues: $2.00 (annual)
Branches: 27 local   Scope: national

Special requirements for membership: "American women of Ukrainian descent"

Nature of organization: educational, cultural, charitable

Publications: publishes bulletins and books

Affiliations: Ukrainian Congress Committee

Major conventions/meetings: annual convention

Comments: Provides assistance to the sick, widowed, orphaned, crippled, needy, and to war
    veterans. Also offers its services and aid to Ukrainian churches and schools, the
    American Red Cross, and the March of Dimes. Organizes financial drives. Conducts
    cultural activities and sponsors summer camps for children.

UKRAINIAN HETMAN ORGANIZATION OF USA
11342 Hubbel Avenue
Detroit, Michigan 48227

Principal officers: M. H. Boyar

Permanent staff: NI   Membership: NI
Date founded: ca. 1929   Membership dues: NI
Branches: NI   Scope: national

Nature of organization: political

Affiliations: Ukrainian Congress Committee of America

Comments: Ukrainian political organization promoting monarchist ideology. Its aim is to
    preserve Ukrainian culture and the political ideals of Ukrainian Hetman State.

UKRAINIAN HISTORICAL ASSOCIATION, INC.
P.O. Box 312
Kent, Ohio 44240   (216) 673-6571
Principal officers: Olexander Ohloblyn, President
                       Lubomyr R. Wynar, Executive Secretary

Permanent staff: NI   Membership: 300
Date founded: 1965   Membership dues: $15.00
Branches: 6   Scope: national

Special requirements for membership: interest in East European history

Nature of organization: scholarly

Publications: *Ukrainian Historian*, 1965– (quarterly)

Affiliations: American Historical Association

Major conventions/meetings: quadrennial

Comments: Objectives are to promote studies on East European history, especially the history
    of the Ukraine, to bring together people interested in East European history, to collect
    materials concerning Ukrainian history, and to publish an historical journal and histori-
    cal monographs. Cooperates with various scholarly organizations. Sponsors scholarly
    conferences, congresses, etc. Maintains archives.

UKRAINIAN INSTITUTE OF AMERICA (UIA)
2 East 79th Street
New York, New York 10021   (212) 288-8660

Principal officers: John O. Flis, Secretary

Permanent staff: 8   Membership: 1,660
Date founded: 1948   Membership dues: NI
Branches: NI   Scope: national

Special requirements for membership: none

Nature of organization: charitable, cultural, educational

Major conventions/meetings: monthly

Comments: The major purpose is to preserve the Ukrainian culture in the United States and to conduct and promote research into Ukrainian history and other studies. Sponsors exhibits of folk arts, conferences, lectures, etc.

THE UKRAINIAN LAWYER'S ASSOCIATION IN USA
536 East 14th Street
New York, New York 10009   (212) 677-5965

Principal officers: Bohdan Dzerovych, President
                   Jaroslaw Padoch, First Vice President
                   Taras Kernyckyj, Secretary

Permanent staff: none   Membership: 237
Date founded: 1949   Membership dues: $5.00 (annual)
Branches: 6 regional   Scope: national

Special requirements for membership: college degree in law

Nature of organization: social, professional

Publications: *Law Journal*, 1955– (irregular)

Affiliations: Ukrainian Congress Committee of America; Conference of Ukrainian American Academic Professional Associations

Major conventions/meetings: biennial conventions

Comments: This professional, non-political association organizes lawyers of Ukrainian background in order to widen the professional knowledge of members, to aid Ukrainian-American lawyers and their families, to promote social and cultural activities that will provide fellowship and will help preserve the Ukrainian culture, and to edit professional literature and journals that give legal advise to Ukrainians in the United States. The organization also supports efforts to re-establish a free Ukraine.

UKRAINIAN LIBRARIANS' ASSOCIATION OF AMERICA (ULAA)
P.O. Box 3295, Country Fair Station
Champaign, Illinois 61820

Principal officers: Dmytro M. Shtohryn, President
                   Vasyl Luchkiw, Vice President
                   Oleg Kudryk, Vice President
                   Emil Basiuk, Secretary

Permanent staff: NI   Membership: 156
Date founded: NI   Membership dues: $6.00
Branches: 3   Scope: national

Special requirements for membership: professional librarian or adequate experience in library or archives work.

Nature of organization: professional

Publications: *Bulletin of Ukrainian Librarians' Association of America*, 1962– (irregular); *Newsletter of Ukrainian Librarians' Association* (irregular); *The Ukrainian Book*, 1971– (quarterly)

Affiliations: American Library Association; Ukrainian Congress Committee

Major conventions/meetings: biennial convention

UKRAINIAN LIBRARIANS' ASSOCIATION OF AMERICA (ULAA) (cont'd)

Comments: Objectives are to promote and coordinate professional and scholarly activities among Ukrainian-American librarians, to conduct research on Ukrainian materials, and to compile bibliographies and indexes of materials published in Ukrainian and other languages. It also serves scholars and students with bibliographical and reference data on Ukrainian subjects. Maintains a 1,000-volume library and a bibliographical-reference archive.

UKRAINIAN MEDICAL ASSOCIATION OF NORTH AMERICA (UMANA)
2 East 79th Street
New York, New York 10021   (212) 288-8660
Principal officers: Dr. Achil Chreptowsky, President
                       Dr. M. Kolensky, Secretary

Permanent staff: 1   Membership: 900
Date founded: 1950   Membership dues: $50.00 (annual)
Branches: 14 state and provincal   Scope: U.S. and Canada

Special requirements for membership: must be M.D., D.O., D.D.S., or Pharmacist

Nature of organization: professional

Publications: *Journal of the Ukrainian Medical Association of North America*, 1954– (quarterly)

Affiliations: Ukrainian Congress Committee

Major conventions/meetings: scientific conference

Comments: Purpose is to organize physicians and related professionals of Ukrainian descent in the United States and Canada for professional, social, and cultural activities. The organization also assists needy physicians of Ukrainian background and their families, publishes medical dictionaries and literature in the Ukrainian language, and grants scholarships to Ukrainian medical students or students of dentistry or pharmacy. An archival collection is maintained.

UKRAINIAN NATIONAL AID ASSOCIATION OF AMERICA (UNAAA)
527 Second Avenue
Pittsburgh, Pennsylvania 15219   (412) 261-2807
Principal officers: Wolodymyr Masur, President
                       Lew Futala, Executive Vice President
                       Rosalia Sykuta, Executive Vice President
                       Ananey Nykonchuk, Executive Secretary

Permanent staff: 5   Membership: ca. 9,550
Date founded: 1914   Membership dues: based on amount and
Branches: 174   class of insurance policy
                                            Scope: national

Special requirements for membership: must be of Ukrainian nationality or Ukrainian descent, or of any Slavic nationality; age requirement: from birth to age 65

Nature of organization: fraternal

Publications: *Ukrainian National Word*, 1914– (biweekly)

Affiliations: Ukrainian Congress Committee of America

Major conventions/meetings: quadrennial convention

Comments: In addition to financial assistance to members, UNAAA supports various Ukrainian social and cultural activities. Offers scholarships to members. Maintains a library of 500 volumes and archives.

UKRAINIAN NATIONAL ASSOCIATION (UNA)
30 Montgomery Street
Jersey City, New Jersey 07303   (201) 435-8740
Principal officers: Joseph Lesawyer, President
                       Walter Sochan, Supreme Secretary

UKRAINIAN NATIONAL ASSOCIATION (UNA) (cont'd)

Permanent staff: 60
Date founded: 1894
Branches: 464 local

Membership: 89,000
Membership dues: NI
Scope: U.S. and Canada

Special requirements for membership: of Ukrainian or Slavic origin

Nature of organization: fraternal

Publications: *Svoboda*, 1893– (daily except Saturday and Sunday); *Veselka* (The Rainbow), 1953– (monthly); *The Ukrainian Weekly* (supplement to *Svoboda*), 1933– (weekly); also publishes books

Affiliations: National Fraternal Congress; Ukrainian Congress Committee of America; United Ukrainian American Relief Committee

Major conventions/meetings: quadrennial convention

Comments: The largest and oldest Ukrainian fraternal association in the United States. In addition to providing various forms of insurance, it maintains schools, libraries, and other educational facilities; publishes and circulates various publications; maintains an old-age home for members. It also maintains a recreational estate which provides sports and other vacation activities, and it provides a fund for destitute members, etc. Sponsors children's camps and summer courses in Ukrainian culture. Awards scholarships. Maintains an 8,000-volume library and an archival collection.

UKRAINIAN NATIONAL WOMEN'S LEAGUE OF AMERICA, INC. (UNWLA)

108 Second Avenue
New York, New York 10003   (212) 533-4646

Principal officers: Mrs. I. Rozankovsky, President
                      Maria Sawchak, Executive Secretary

Permanent staff: 5
Date founded: 1925
Branches: 8 regional; 111 local

Membership: 5,000
Membership dues: NI
Scope: national

Special requirements for membership: must be a woman over 18, residing in the United States, of Ukrainian descent or an active member of the Ukrainian community

Nature of organization: educational, cultural, charitable

Publications: *Our Life*, 1954– (monthly); also publishes books

Affiliations: General Federation of Women's Clubs; National Council of Women of the U.S.; Ukrainian Congress Committee

Major conventions/meetings: triennial convention

Comments: The major aims of the organization are to preserve and promote the Ukrainian traditions, language, and art in the United States, and to provide humanitarian assistance to Ukrainians in America and abroad. Conducts conferences and seminars, arranges exhibits, organizes social welfare bureaus. The organization also supports 24 prekindergarten classes in the United States, maintains a folk art museum, and has a scholarship program.

UKRAINIAN ORTHODOX LEAGUE (UOL)

296 Deyo Hill Road
Johnson City, New York 13790

Principal officers: Paul Chebiniak, President
                      Alice Seska, Secretary

Permanent staff: NI
Date founded: 1947
Branches: NI

Membership: NI
Membership dues: NI
Scope: national

Special requirements for membership: Ukrainian Orthodox religion

Nature of organization: religious, social

Publications: the league has a regular page in *Ukrainian Orthodox World* (monthly)

Affiliations: Ukrainian Orthodox Church of U.S.A.

UKRAINIAN ORTHODOX LEAGUE (UOL) (cont'd)

Comments: The major purpose of the organization is to support the Ukrainian Orthodox Church in the United States and to promote the Orthodox faith. It also provides various social and recreational activities by which it unites members. Exhibits of folk arts and other cultural activities are also sponsored.

UKRAINIAN RESEARCH FOUNDATION, INC.
6931 South Yosemite
Englewood, Colorado 80110   (303) 770-1220
Principal officers: Bohdan S. Wynar, President

Permanent staff: 1   Membership: NI
Date founded: 1974   Membership dues: NI
Branches: none   Scope: international

Special requirements for membership: approval by the Board of Directors

Nature of organization: research, educational

Publications: newsletter

Affiliations: none

Major conventions/meetings: annual (in December)

Comments: The foundation's purposes are 1) to provide and encourage scholarly research and writing relating to Ukraine and Eastern Europe; 2) to establish and maintain a research library; 3) to offer grants, subsidies, and other financial support to accomplish these goals.

UKRAINIAN RESISTANCE VETERANS' ASSOCIATION
P.O. Box 303
48 Lincoln Terrace
Yonkers, New York 10702   (914) 476-9363
Principal officers: Ilarion Polishchuk, President
                       Wasyl Stanislaviv, Vice President
                       Dmytro Furmanec, Secretary

Permanent staff: 7   Membership: 500
Date founded: 1965   Membership dues: $10.00 (annual)
Branches: none   Scope: international, national

Special requirements for membership: veterans of the Ukrainian resistance against Germany and Russia during World War II

Nature of organization: veterans, military

Publications: none

Affiliations: none

Major conventions/meetings: none

Comments: Aims to unite the Ukrainian veterans in the United States who fought in the World War II resistance against the Germans and Russians.

UKRAINIAN WORKINGMEN'S ASSOCIATION (UWA)
440 Wyoming Avenue
Scranton, Pennsylvania 18503   (717) 342-0937

Principal officers: Ivan Oleksyn, President
                       Edward Popil, Secretary-Treasurer

Permanent staff: NI   Membership: 25,000
Date founded: 1910   Membership dues: vary
Branches: operates in 7 states and Canada   Scope: U.S. and Canada

Special requirements for membership: Ukrainian descent

Nature of organization: fraternal, cultural, charitable

Publications: *Narodna Volya*, 1911– (weekly); *Forum*, 1967– (quarterly)

Major conventions/meetings: quadrennial

Comments: A major Ukrainian fraternal organization, the UWA's objective is to provide life
    insurance benefits to members. It also sponsors summer camps and tries to preserve
    the Ukrainian cultural heritage. It provides financial aid to victims of disasters, awards
    scholarships to Ukrainian students, and maintains a library and archives.

UKRAINIAN YOUTH LEAGUE OF NORTH AMERICA (UYLNA)
602 Fanshawe Street
Philadelphia, Pennsylvania 19111   (215) 722-4738

Principal officers: Ray Karbiwnyk, President

Permanent staff: NI   Membership: 800 individuals (70
Date founded: 1933   organizations)
Branches: NI   Membership dues: NI
                                       Scope: national

Special requirements for membership: Ukrainian descent

Nature of organization: youth

Publications: *Trendette* (monthly); *Trend* (quarterly)

Major conventions/meetings: annual

Comments: Umbrella organization for 70 youth organizations that provide educational,
    cultural, recreational, and sport activities for youth of Ukrainian descent. Seeks also
    to preserve Ukrainian language and culture.

UKRAINIAN YOUTH ORGANIZATION OF AMERICA, INC. (SUMA)
P.O. Box 211
Cooper Drive
New York, New York 10003

Principal officers: M. Shmigel, President

Permanent staff: NI   Membership: NI
Date founded: 1950   Membership dues: NI
Branches: 35   Scope: national

Nature of organization: educational, youth

Publications: *Krylati*, 1963– (monthly)

Affiliations: Ukrainian Congress Committee of America

Comments: This is one of the major Ukrainian youth organizations. It promotes Ukrainian
    culture, sponsors summer camps, conducts schools, sponsors dancing groups, drama
    clubs, and choruses, etc. Supports the ideology of Ukrainian nationalism.

UNION OF UKRAINIANS OF REVOLUTIONARY DEMOCRATIC CONVICTIONS IN THE U.S.
1421 Easton
Somerset, New Jersey 08873

Principal officers: W. Hryhorenko

UNION OF UKRAINIANS OF REVOLUTIONARY DEMOCRATIC CONVICTIONS IN THE U.S. (cont'd)

Permanent staff: NI
Date founded: NI
Branches: NI

Membership: NI
Membership dues: NI
Scope: national

Nature of organization: political

Comments: Major purposes are to promote the ideals of democracy and to strive for the establishment of an independent Ukrainian Democratic Republic.

UNITED UKRAINIAN AMERICAN RELIEF COMMITTEE (UUARC)
1321 West Lindley Avenue
Philadelphia, Pennsylvania 19141   (215) 455-3774

Principal officers: Ostap E. M. Tarnawsky, Executive Director

Permanent staff: 3
Date founded: 1944
Branches: 9

Membership: over 500 organizations
Membership dues: NI
Scope: national

Special requirements for membership: a state or local relief organization aiding Ukrainians

Nature of organization: relief

Publications: pamphlets and books

Affiliations: Ukrainian Congress Committee

Major conventions/meetings: biennial

Comments: Main objective of the organization is to provide aid to homeless and helpless victims of the war and other disasters. Also aids Ukrainian immigrants in the United States and other countries.

UNITED UKRAINIAN ORTHODOX SISTERHOOD OF THE USA
P.O. Box 300
South Bound Brook
New Jersey, 08880   (201) 469-3379

Principal officers: Alexandra Selepyna, President
Lydia Makarenko, Vice President
Valentine Pacholuk, Secretary

Permanent staff: NI
Date founded: 1961
Branches: 50

Membership: 50 sisterhoods
Membership dues: $25.00
Scope: national

Special requirements for membership: none

Nature of organization: religious

Affiliations: Ukrainian Orthodox Church of USA; World Federation of Ukrainian Women's Organizations

Major conventions/meetings: triennial convention

Comments: Though its major objectives are of a religious nature, this organization also supports preservation of the Ukrainian language and culture as well as preservation of the Ukrainian Orthodox Faith. It maintains a scholarship fund and a welfare department for care of the elderly, orphans, and invalids.

UNITED UKRAINIAN WAR VETERANS OF AMERICA
1321 West Lindley Avenue
Philadelphia, Pennsylvania 19141   (313) 893-0528

Permanent staff: NI
Date founded: 1950
Branches: NI

Membership: NI
Membership dues: $3.00 (annual)
Scope: national

Special requirements for membership: Ukrainian war veteran

Nature of organization: military

Publications: *Veterans' News* (irregular)

UNITED UKRAINIAN WAR VETERANS OF AMERICA (cont'd)
Major conventions/meetings: none
Comments: Promotes military traditions of the Ukraine, assists Ukrainian war invalids, participates in special meetings and academies commemorating Ukrainian historical events.

VETERANS OF THE FIRST UKRAINIAN DIVISION UNA
140-42 Second Avenue
New York, New York 10003
Principal officers: Roman Drazniowskyj, President
                      Roman Hajecky, Secretary

Permanent staff: NI   Membership: NI
Date founded: NI   Membership dues: NI
Branches: NI   Scope: national
Nature of organization: military
Affiliations: Ukrainian Congress Committee of America
Comments: This association of World War II veterans of the Ukrainian National Army was organized to promote the ideals and traditions of their military division. Members are also interested in fostering the development of the Ukrainian heritage, tradition, and culture in the United States.

WORLD CONGRESS OF FREE UKRAINIANS
2200 Yonge Street, Suite 1701
Toronto, Ontario, Canada M4S 2C6
Principal officers: M. Rev. Vasyl' Kushnir, President
                      Mykola Plaviuk, Vice President
                      Yuri Shymko, Secretary

Permanent staff: 3   Membership: 220 organizations
Date founded: 1967   Membership dues: NI
Branches: in United States and other countries   Scope: international
Special requirements for membership: Ukrainian organization adhering to principles of the Congress
Nature of organization: political, cultural, social
Publications: *Bulletin of the SCFU*, 1974– (irregular)
Affiliations: Ukrainian Congress Committee of America; Ukrainian Canadian Committee
Major conventions/meetings: every 5 years
Comments: Supports efforts to restore independence and freedom in the Ukrainian government and provides financial aid to Ukrainians. Assists Ukrainians in achieving civil and human rights and attempts to promote and preserve the Ukrainian tradition, culture, language, and identity. The congress coordinates the activities of member organizations.

WORLD FEDERATION OF UKRAINIAN STUDENT ORGANIZATIONS OF MICHNOWSKY (TUSM)
P.O. Box 141
Riverton, New York 08077
Principal officers: Bohdan Futala, President
Permanent staff: NI   Membership: 600
Date founded: 1949   Membership dues: NI
Branches: 17   Scope: national
Publications: *Feniks*, 1951– (irregular)
Major conventions/meetings: biennial
Comments: An active voice in demanding humane treatment and release of political prisoners in Ukraine. Also active in preserving Ukrainian culture in the United States; sponsors cultural exhibits, meetings, and conferences on Ukrainian history and language.

WORLD LEMKOS FEDERATION (WLF)
P.O. Box 202
Camillus, New York 13031
Principal officers: Dr. John Hvosda, President
                       Myron Mycio, Vice President
                       Michael Fedak, Vice President
                       Nickolas Duplak, Secretary

Permanent staff: none	Membership: NI
Date founded: 1973	Membership dues: NI
Branches: 2 national	Scope: international

Special requirements for membership: Ukrainian ancestry

Nature of organization: cultural

Publications: *Annals of the World Lemkos' Federation*, 1974– (annual); *Lemko News*, 1959– (monthly)

Affiliations: Organization for Defense of Lemkivshchyna (US); Canadian Lemko Association

Major conventions/meetings: triennial convention

Comments: The purpose of the federation is to help the Ukrainian Lemkos in Poland, to preserve interest in the Lemko affairs and their culture, and to help Lemkivshchyna.

VIETNAMESE-AMERICAN ORGANIZATIONS

Additional information on Vietnamese-American organizations may be obtained from Vietnam Christian Service (c/o Church World Service, 475 Riverside Drive, New York, New York 10027). At present the South Vietnam Embassy is not functioning in Washington, D.C. Organizations listed include some of the American relief organizations concerned with Vietnamese refugees.

AMERICAN FRIENDS OF VIETNAM (AFV)
342 Madison Avenue
New York, New York 10017   (212) 749-4200
Principal officers: William F. Ward, National Chairman

Permanent staff: NI	Membership: NI
Date founded: 1955	Membership dues: NI
Branches: NI	Scope: national

Nature of organization: educational, cultural

Publications: *Southeast Asian Perspectives* (quarterly)

Comments: The major purposes of the organization are to promote cultural understanding between the Vietnamese and Americans, and to disseminate information about Vietnam to the American public. It sponsors lectures, seminars, and conferences, and it publishes informational materials.

FRIENDS OF CHILDREN OF VIETNAM (FCVN)
600 Gilpin
Denver, Colorado 80218   (303) 321-8251
Principal officers: Cheryl Markson, Executive Director

Permanent staff: 3	Membership: NI
Date founded: 1967	Membership dues: NI
Branches: 29 local groups	Scope: national

Nature of organization: adoption agency

Publications: publishes pamphlets

FRIENDS OF CHILDREN OF VIETNAM (FCVN) (cont'd)

Comments: This adoption agency attempts to help people in the United States adopt orphaned Vietnamese children. It also provides medical and financial relief for abandoned and orphaned children in Vietnam. Sponsors various fund-raising activities.

INTERNATIONAL COMMITTEE OF CONSCIENCE ON VIETNAM
P.O. Box 271
Nyack, New York 10960 (914) 358-4601

Principal officers: Alfred Hassler, Executive Secretary

Permanent staff: NI
Date founded: 1965
Branches: 37 local groups

Membership: 7,000
Membership dues: NI
Scope: international, national

Nature of organization: political, relief

Comments: The organization consists of clergymen united to seek the release of political prisoners in South Vietnam and to urge humane treatment of the same. It also aids refugees and immigrants from Vietnam. Until 1965 the committee was known as the Clergyman's Emergency Committee for Vietnam.

VIETNAM CHRISTIAN SERVICE (VNCS)
c/o Church World Service
475 Riverside Drive
New York, New York 10027 (212) 870-2074

Principal officers: Boyd B. Lowry, Operations Director

Permanent staff: 100
Date founded: 1966
Branches: NI

Membership: 2 agencies
Membership dues: NI
Scope: national

Special requirements for membership: must be a member of Church World Service or Lutheran World Relief

Nature of organization: relief, religious

Comments: Major purposes of the organization are to assist refugees from Vietnam and to provide medical, financial, and other social services to war victims.

VIETNAMESE-AMERICAN CHILDREN'S FUND (VACF)
P.O. Box 14543
Houston, Texas 77021 (713) 749-2155

Principal officers: Ben J. Cunningham, Director

Permanent staff: 25
Date founded: 1972
Branches: 15 local groups

Membership: NI
Membership dues: NI
Scope: national

Publications: *Newsletter* (monthly)

Affiliations: Welcome House; Welcome House Adoptive Parents Group

Major conventions/meetings: monthly

Comments: The organization seeks to protect war victims and Vietnamese children orphaned or abandoned as a result of war. Sponsors Hope I and Hope II homes for children where food, shelter, and medical care are provided. Also assists Vietnamese students.

WELSH-AMERICAN ORGANIZATIONS

Additional information on Welsh-American organizations in the United States may be obtained from the Office of the Great Britain Embassy (3100 Massachusetts Avenue, Washington, D.C. 20008) and from *Americans from Wales*, by Edward George Hartmann (Boston: Christopher Publishing House, 1967). Regional and local information may be obtained from *Greater Cleveland Nationalities Directory 1974* (Cleveland: Sun Newspapers and the Nationalities Services Center, 1974) and *Ethnic Directory I* (Detroit: Southeastern Michigan Regional Ethnic Heritage Studies Center, 1973).

ST. DAVID'S SOCEITY OF THE STATE OF NEW YORK
71 West 23rd Street
New York, New York 10010   (212) 924-8415
Principal officers: W. C. James, President
                       J. Yorweth, Vice President
                       Norman Morris, Secretary

Permanent staff: 1   Membership: 250
Date founded: 1801   Membership dues: $5.00
Branches: NI   Scope: state

Special requirements for membership: of Welsh descent or related by marriage

Nature of organization: cultural, charitable

Publications: *Yearly Report* (annual)

Major conventions/meetings: annual (always March 1, St. David Day, the anniversary of the patron saint of Wales, New York City)

Comments: Major objectives of the organization are to collect, promote, and preserve information on the Welsh traditions in the United States, particularly in the fields of history, language, and literature. The group sponsors charitable projects aiding those of Welsh descent. A 500-volume library is maintained. Until 1835 it was known as St. David's Benevolent Society, then it became St. David's Benefit and Benevolent Society of the City of New York, and until 1841, St. David's Benevolent Society of the Cities of New York and Brooklyn.

WELSH MEN'S SOCIETY OF NORTH AMERICA
16588 Manfred
Detroit, Michigan   (313) 837-3077
Principal officers: Robert Williams

Permanent staff: NI   Membership: NI
Date founded: NI   Membership dues: NI
Branches: NI   Scope: national

Nature of organization: cultural

Comments: The purpose of the club is to unite Americans of Welsh descent and to sponsor activities that promote and preserve the Welsh culture—e.g., concerts and folk music festivals. It also supports the Welsh church with financial contributions. Tours to Wales are sponsored for members.

THE WELSH NATIONAL GYMANFA GANU ASSOCIATION
4034 Southern Blvd.
Youngstown, Ohio 44512   (216) 782-0739
Principal officers: Jack Meadows, Secretary

Permanent staff: NI   Membership: 2,500
Date founded: 1929   Membership dues: $5.00 (annual);
Branches: NI $25-$50.00 life memberships
                                             Scope: national

THE WELSH NATIONAL GYMANFA GANU ASSOCIATION (cont'd)

Nature of organization: social, religious

Publications: *Y Drych* (The Mirror), 1850– (monthly)

Major conventions/meetings: annual

Comments: The organization is a federation of Welsh churches in America and Canada. One of its major purposes is the promotion and preservation of Welsh hymns and music. Until 1971 the organization was known as the National Gymanfa Ganu Association. Sponsors musical concerts.

WELSH SOCIETY
    109 Gladstone Road
    Lansdowne, Pennsylvania 19050   (215) 626-5302

Principal officers: R. Charles Davies, President

Permanent staff: NI   Membership: 320
Date founded: 1729   Membership dues: NI
Branches: NI   Scope: national

Special requirements for membership: men of Welsh descent

Nature of organization: cultural

Major conventions/meetings: semiannual

Comments: The purpose of the organization is to unite Welsh-Americans in social and cultural activities in order to preserve the Welsh tradition and heritage in the United States. It also sponsors charitable programs, assists Welsh immigrants, and provides lectures and historical programs. An archival collection is maintained.

WOMEN'S WELSH CLUB OF NEW YORK
    2300 Sedgwick Avenue
    Bronx, New York 10468   (212) 733-2375

Principal officers: Mrs. E. R. Edwards, Corresponding Secretary

Permanent staff: NI   Membership: NI
Date founded: NI   Membership dues: NI
Branches: NI   Scope: state

Special requirements for membership: women of Welsh descent

Nature of organization: cultural

WOMEN'S WELSH CLUBS OF AMERICA
    c/o Mrs. L. S. Hutton
    20120 Lorain Road
    Cleveland, Ohio 44126   (216) 333-7524

Principal officers: Mrs. L. S. Hutton, National President
                 Mrs. David M. Edwards, National Financial Secretary

Permanent staff: NI   Membership: NI
Date founded: 1911   Membership dues: NI
Branches: 46   Scope: national

Special requirements for membership: women of Welsh descent

Nature of organization: cultural, charitable

Publications: *Druid*

Comments: Major purpose is to support national homes for the Welsh aged. The organization now sponsors three such homes in the Cleveland area.

YUGOSLAV-AMERICAN ORGANIZATIONS

See Croatian-American, Serbian-American, and
Slovenian-American Organizations

APPENDIX

MULTI-ETHNIC AND RESEARCH ORGANIZATIONS

This section includes a selective listing of major multi-ethnic organizations, as well as professional and research organizations dealing with ethnicity. These organizations should not be regarded as typical "ethnic organizations" organized by individual ethnic groups; rather, they are organizations, associations, and centers whose aim is to coordinate activities of ethnic groups or to research ethnic topics.

Additional multi-ethnic or research organizations are listed in *Ethnic Studies in Higher Education*, edited by Winnie Bengelsdorf (Washington, D.C.: American Association of State Colleges and Universities, 1972). Current ethnic research projects funded by the U.S. Office of Education are listed in *The Ethnic Heritage Studies Program in Fiscal Year 1974, Facts and Figures* (Washington, D.C.: Department of Health, Education, and Welfare, Office of Education, 1974).

AMERICAN COUNCIL FOR NATIONALITIES SERVICE
20 West 40th Street
New York, New York 10018   (212) 279-2715
Principal officers: Wells C. Klein, Executive Director
                        Ivan Veit, President

Permanent staff: NI	Membership: 29 affiliate agencies
Dat e founded: 1924	Membership dues: NI
Branches: 29 affiliate agencies	Scope: national

Nature of organization: social service, educational

Publications: *Interpreter Releases*, 1924– (weekly)

Comments: Coordinates the activities of the affiliate agencies and cooperates with government agencies dealing with ethnic groups. Conducts surveys of foreign language radio broadcasts, and the ethnic press. Assists immigrants in the naturalization procedure; provides English language classes, and publishes and distributes informational pamphlets. Member agencies are as follows: International Institutes in Akron, Boston, Bridgeport, Buffalo, Cincinnati (Travelers Aid), Milwaukee, Oakland, Providence, St. Louis, St. Paul, San Francisco, Toledo, and Youngstown. Maintains a Nationalities Service Center in Cleveland and Philadelphia; Immigrants' Service League of Travelers Aid in Chicago; American Civic Association in Binghamton, Manchester (New Hampshire); Minneapolis, and Toronto.

AMERICAN ETHNIC RESEARCH INSTITUTE (AERI)
6931 South Yosemite
Englewood, Colorado 80110   (303) 770-1220
Principal officers: A. T. Kuzmych, Executive Secretary

Permanent staff: 2	Membership: NI
Date founded: 1975	Membership dues: NI
Branches: NI	Scope: national

Nature of organization: scholarly, educational

Publications: publishes books and other materials

Comments: Promotes historical, sociological, bibliographical, and other research dealing with ethnic groups in the United States and Canada. Conducts various comprehensive surveys of ethnic publications, organizations, and other topics relevant to ethnicity. Sponsors conferences and meetings on ethnicity. Maintains a library on ethnicity.

ASIA FOUNDATION

P.O. Box 3223
San Francisco, California 94119   (415) 982-4640

Principal officers: Haydn Williams, President

Permanent staff: 225   Membership: NI
Date founded: 1954   Membership dues: NI
Branches: NI   Scope: national

Nature of organization: educational, cultural, professional

Publications: *The Asian Student* (weekly); *Asian Foundation Program Quarterly* (quarterly); *The Asian Student Orientation Handbook* (annual); *President's Review* (annual)

Major conventions/meetings: quarterly

Comments: The foundation provides assistance to Asian educational and other institutions involved with national development or cultural exchange. It is concerned primarily with the development of human resources in Asia and funded by private and government monies. It has donated 13 million publications to Asian schools and institutions.

ASIA SOCIETY

112 East 64th Street
New York, New York 10021   (212) 751-4210

Principal officers: Phillips Talbot, President

Permanent staff: 60   Membership: NI
Date founded: 1956   Membership dues: NI
Branches: NI   Scope: national

Nature of organization: cultural, educational

Publications: *Asia Society Calendar*, 1961– (9/year); *Asia Journal*; *Annual Report* (annual)

Major conventions/meetings: annual

Comments: The purpose of the society is to promote cultural and educational exchanges between the United States and Asia. It also serves as a consultant for curriculum materials on Asian studies. Sponsors student tours to the library, art gallery, formal gardens and programs at Asia House. Maintains a council on 15 different Asian countries. Sponsors various cultural programs and activities open to the public. The society absorbed the former Conference on Asian Affairs. A 2,000-volume library is maintained.

ASSEMBLY OF CAPTIVE EUROPEAN NATIONS (ACEN)

29 West 57th Street
New York, New York 10019   (212) 751-3850

Principal officers: Stefan Korbonski, President
Feliks Gadomski, Secretary

Permanent staff: 3   Membership: 9 national committees
Date founded: 1954   Membership dues: contributions
Branches: 6 overseas   Scope: international

Special requirements for membership: unanimous decision of all the members

Nature of organization: political, educational

Publications: publishes books and pamphlets

Major conventions/meetings: annual Plenary Assembly meeting

Comments: Works for the implementation of human rights and self-determination in the nations of Albania, Bulgaria, Czechoslovakia, Estonia, Hungary, Latvia, Lithuania, Poland, and Rumania.

THE BALCH INSTITUTE
123 South Broad Street
Philadelphia, Pennsylvania 19109   (215) 985-8137

Permanent staff: NI   Membership: NI
Date founded: 1971   Membership dues: NI
Branches: NI   Scope: national

Nature of organization: research

Affiliations: North American Immigration Research Center

Comments: Stimulates and facilitates research on American political history; North American immigration; ethnic, racial, and minority group history; and American folklore. Publishes bibliographies, proceedings, and guides, and sponsors conferences, symposia, exhibitions, educational programs, and lectures open to the public. Maintains a major research library of books, periodicals, and microform publications. The projected building (1976) will house four exhibition galleries, an auditorium, a seminar room, and administrative offices. Coordinates research on ethnicity and serves as a planning agency for ethnic scholars.

CENTER FOR MIGRATION STUDIES
209 Flagg Place
Staten Island, New York 10304   (212) 351-8800

Principal officers: Rev. S. M. Tomasi, President
                       Rev. L. F. Tomasi, Associate Director

Permanent staff: 5   Membership: NI
Date founded: 1965   Membership dues: NI
Branches: NI   Scope: national

Nature of organization: educational, cultural, religious, scholarly

Publications: *International Migration Review*, 1965– (quarterly); *Migration Today*, 1973– (bimonthly)

Major conventions/meetings: irregular conferences

Comments: Promotes "the study of sociological, demographic, historical, legislative and pastoral aspects of human migration movements and ethnic group relations everywhere." Maintains a library of nearly 6,000 volumes, and an archival collection of newspapers, manuscripts, and correspondence.

CENTER FOR THE STUDY OF AMERICAN PLURALISM
National Opinion Research Center
6030 South Ellis Avenue
Chicago, Illinois 60637   (312) 684-5600
       or

817 Broadway
New York, New York 10003

Principal officers: Andrew M. Greeley, Director

Permanent staff: NI   Membership: NI
Date founded: NI   Membership dues: NI
Branches: 1 East Coast office   Scope: national

Nature of organization: scholarly, research

Publications: reference and other materials

Affiliations: National Opinion Research Center (University of Chicago)

Comments: Conducts studies on ethnicity, acculturation, racial problems, poverty, and other social problems. A part of the National Opinion Research Center, the Center for the Study of American Pluralism shares its library resources for research and participates in its research methodology of public opinion polling.

CENTER FOR THE STUDY OF ETHNIC PUBLICATIONS
Kent State University
Room 318, Library
Kent, Ohio 44242   (216) 672-2784

Principal officers: Dr. Lubomyr Wynar, Director

Permanent staff: NI   Membership: NI
Date founded: 1971   Membership dues: NI
Branches: none   Scope: national

Nature of organization: research

Affiliations: Kent State University

Comments: Promotes bibliographical, historical, and other research of ethnic publications and
   on other aspects of ethnicity. The program's objectives are to develop a plan for
   effective bibliographical control of non-English ethnic publications in the United
   States and to provide a special curriculum for library science students focusing on
   library services to ethnic groups. It also cooperates with scholarly, professional, and
   ethnic organizations in the study of ethnicity.

CENTER ON INTERNATIONAL RACE RELATIONS
Graduate School of International Studies
University of Denver
Denver, Colorado 80210   (303) 753-3506

Principal officers: D. John Grove, Director
                      Charlene M. Forbes, Secretary

Permanent staff: 2   Membership: NI
Date founded: 1969   Membership dues: NI
Branches: NI   Scope: international

Nature of organization: research

Publications: *Studies in Race and Nations*, 1969– (quarterly)

Comments: Studies variations in race and ethnic relations in different political and socioeconomic systems. The center, as a part of the Graduate School of International
   Studies at the University of Denver, sponsors a three-quarter core seminar on "Comparative Ethnic and Racial Factors in International Relations." It is in the process of
   developing a data bank on 70 racial/ethnic groups in 25 multi-racial/ethnic societies.

EMPAC (ETHNIC MILLIONS POLITICAL ACTION COMMITTEE) *see* p. 390.

THE ETHNIC FOUNDATION, INC.
562 Davis Building
Washington, D.C. 20006   (202) 338-8900

Principal officers: Walter Carey, National Chairman
                      Paul M. Deac, Vice Chairman
                      Joseph Snider, Secretary

Permanent staff: 6   Membership: NI
Date founded: 1959   Membership dues: NI
Branches: 10 regional   Scope: national

Nature of organization: educational, cultural, scholarly

Publications: none

Major conventions/meetings: biennial

Comments: The organization is non-profit and non-political, with an emphasis on education,
   research, and social service. It assists immigrants and ethnic youth in areas of vocational guidance and scholarships. The foundation studies trends on the domestic and
   foreign levels that affect ethnic groups in the United States, and it publishes information for these groups. Sponsors activities designed to improve the social and economic
   conditions of the needy and disadvantaged. Maintains a 2,500-volume library and an
   archival collection.

ETHNIC HERITAGE STUDIES BRANCH, DIVISION OF
INTERNATIONAL EDUCATION

Office of Education
U.S. Department of Health, Education, and Welfare
Washington, D.C. 20202   (202) 245-2561

Comments: Coordinates and administers the funds appropriated for the Ethnic Heritage
Studies Program. Publishes bibliographies and reports generated by the research
completed under this program.

IMMIGRATION HISTORY RESEARCH CENTER (IHRC)

826 Berry Street
St. Paul, Minnesota 55114   (612) 373-5581

Principal officers: Rudolph J. Vecoli, Director
                       Joseph D. Dwyer, Curator

Permanent staff: 8 full-time; 8 part-time   Membership: NI
Date founded: 1964   Membership dues: NI
Branches: NI   Scope: national

Nature of organization: educational

Publications: *Spectrum*, 1975– (3/year); also publishes books

Affiliations: University of Minnesota

Comments: Facilitates and encourages research on immigration and the ethnic communities
in the United States that originated from those immigrations. Primary goal of the
center is to establish a research collection on the history of all ethnic groups. At
present, the center's library and archives hold 23,000 monographs and bound serials,
1,700 serial titles, and 130 current newspapers, in addition to microfilmed and
manuscript materials. Maintains a committee for grants-in-aid and research
assistantships.

IMMIGRATION HISTORY SOCIETY

c/o Minnesota Historical Society
690 Cedar Street
St. Paul, Minnesota 55101   (612) 296-5662

Principal officers: Theodore Saloutos, President
                       Moses Rischin, President
                       A. W. Hoglund, Secretary
                       Carlton C. Qualey, Editor-Treasurer

Permanent staff: 1   Membership: 555
Date founded: 1965   Membership dues: $3.00 (annual)
Branches: NI   Scope: national

Special requirements for membership: none

Nature of organization: educational, professional, scholarly

Publications: *The Immigration History Newsletter*, 1969– (semiannual)

Affiliations: American Historical Association

Major conventions/meetings: annual

Comments: Promotes the study of the history of immigration to the United States and
Canada and the background of emigration from the countries of the immigrants' origin.
Also promotes the study of ethnic groups in the United States, including Native
Americans. Immigrant acculturation and immigrant problems are studied. The society
publishes information about ethnic research, organizations, meetings, and publications
on immigration history. It sponsors special programs on immigration for other professional and research organizations. Sponsors grants-in-aid and research assistantships for graduate students in studies related to American immigration and ethnic
history.

INSTITUTE ON PLURALISM AND GROUP IDENTITY, AN AMERICAN JEWISH COMMITTEE PROJECT ON GROUP LIFE AND ETHNIC AMERICA
165 East 56th Street
New York, New York 10022

Principal officers: Irving M. Levine, Director

Permanent staff: NI
Date founded: 1968
Branches: NI

Membership: NI
Membership dues: NI
Scope: national

Nature of organization: educational, research, civil rights

Publications: publishes books, pamphlets, bibliographies, etc.

Affiliations: American Jewish Committee

Comments: Promotes the idea of ethnic pluralism, the preservation of individual ethnic group traditions, and protection of the civil rights of each group. The activities of the organization are designed to acquaint scholars of ethnicity, government officials, and the public with group identity, group differences, and programs and policies that will facilitate better understanding among groups. Materials published by the Institute cover the fields of education, health, labor, community, and bilingualism, and they emphasize the appreciation of group differences.

THE INTERNATIONAL INSTITUTE OF MINNESOTA
1694 Como Avenue
St. Paul, Minnesota 55108   (612) 647-0191

Principal officers: Gertrude A. Esteros, President
Eldon Morrison, First Vice President
Antoinette Sargent, Secretary

Permanent staff: 10
Date founded: 1919
Branches: none

Membership: 2,000
Membership dues: $3.00 individual; $4.00 family; $1.50 junior; $10.00 associate; $25.00 sustaining; $150.00 life
Scope: national

Nature of organization: cultural, social, scholarly, educational, recreational, youth

Publications: *International Institute of Minnesota Newsletter* (monthly)

Affiliations: American Council of Nationalities Service; United Way of St. Paul area

Comments: Provides family services in case of illness, personal and family tragedies, etc. Also sponsors Intercultural Program for Youth. Sponsors classes in foreign languages, English, citizenship, and folk crafts, as well as cultural programs and activities.

THE NATIONAL CENTER FOR URBAN ETHNIC AFFAIRS
4408 Eighth Street, N.E.
Washington, D.C. 20017   (202) 529-5400

Principal officers: Msgr. Geno Baroni, President

Permanent staff: NI
Date founded: 1970
Branches: NI

Membership: NI
Membership dues: NI
Scope: national

Nature of organization: educational, service

Publications: *Newsletter, The National Center for Urban Ethnic Affairs*, 1973– (quarterly)

Affiliations: U. S. Catholic Conference

Comments: Provides assistance to urban ethnic and working-class groups in meeting community development needs. Disseminates information on the need to understand the ethnic factor in American cities. Develops models on the community level that demonstrate the kinds of organizations and programs needed for improvement of cooperative ethnic group efforts in the local neighborhoods.

NATIONAL CONFEDERATION OF AMERICAN ETHNIC GROUPS
1629 K Street, N.W.
Washington, D.C. 20006   (202) 338-8900
Principal officers: Judge Albert A. Fiok, President
                        Paul M. Deac, Vice President

Permanent staff: 7	Membership: 75 affiliate groups
Date founded: 1956	Membership dues: $100.00
Branches: 10 regional	Scope: national

Nature of organization: educational, cultural, economic, civil rights

Publications: *Ethnic Newsletter*, 1958– (monthly)

Major conventions/meetings: biennial

Comments: Major umbrella organization uniting ethnic organizations concerned with civil rights, welfare, economics, community service, and educational and cultural activities and programs. Promotes the American democratic government and strives to protect ethnic minorities from discrimination and to improve their general welfare. Sponsors Leadership Development Training Programs in regional branches, maintains a committee to assist immigrants in citizenship and other areas, and advises ethnic minorities on job opportunities. Maintains a 3,000-volume research library and archival collection.

NATIONAL ETHNIC STUDIES ASSEMBLY
P.O. Box 1335, Cardinal Center
Washington, D.C. 20036

Principal officers: Dr. Richard Kolm, President

Permanent staff: NI	Membership: NI
Date founded: 1971	Membership dues: NI
Branches: NI	Scope: national

Nature of organization: educational, social

Publications: *The National Ethnic Studies Assembly Newsletter*, 1973– (every 6 weeks)

Major conventions/meetings: annual

Comments: The organization is concerned with the funding, development, and implementation of Ethnic Studies Programs. It provides information on resources and research grants-in-aid available, including procedures for applying for them. Also provides information for scholars of ethnicity on available research assistantships. Sponsors national conferences on ethnicity.

NATIONAL OPINION RESEARCH CENTER. *See* Center for the Study of American Pluralism, p. 385.

SOUTH EAST MICHIGAN REGIONAL ETHNIC HERITAGE STUDIES CENTER
71 East Ferry
Detroit, Michigan 48202   (313) 872-2225

Principal officers: Dr. Otto Feinstein, Director

Permanent staff: NI	Membership: NI
Date founded: 1969	Membership dues: NI
Branches: NI	Scope: regional

Nature of organization: research, educational

Publications: *Heritage Exchange*, 1974– (bimonthly)

Major conventions/meetings: annual

Comments: Sponsors activities and programs dealing with and studying ethnicity. Publishes materials on ethnic studies and an ethnic directory. Maintains a program of TV broadcasts on ethnic studies. Received a federal grant for an Ethnic Heritage Studies Development Program.

EMPAC (ETHNIC MILLIONS POLITICAL ACTION COMMITTEE)
P.O. Box 48
Bayville, New York 11709   (516) 628-8825
Principal officers: Michael Novak, Executive Director

Permanent staff: 2   Membership: 200
Date founded: 1974   Membership dues: $20.00; $5.00
Branches: NI   (student)
                                            Scope: national

Special requirements for membership: dues

Nature of organization: political, educational, scholarly

Publications: *A New America*, 1975– (bimonthly)

Major conventions/meetings: biennial

Comments: The purpose of this consulting firm is to gain full equality and justice for white
    ethnic Americans in government, education, mass media, and corporations. Its inten-
    tion is to study these and other institutions and to publish its findings, hold press
    conferences, sponsor journal and newspaper articles or other publications that will give
    the American public insight into social problems. Also sponsors fund-raising drives,
    research, and counseling to ethnic organizations.

INDEX